THE SEX OFFENDER

ISSUES IN ASSESSMENT, TREATMENT, AND SUPERVISION OF ADULT AND JUVENILE POPULATIONS

VOLUME V

Edited by
Barbara K. Schwartz, Ph.D.

 **Civic Research Institute**

4478 U.S. Route 27 • P.O. Box 585 • Kingston, NJ 08528

This book is printed on acid free paper.

Printed in the United States of America

Library of Congress Cataloging in Publication Data
The sex offender: Volume V: Issues in assessment, treatment, and supervision
of adult and juvenile populations/Barbara K. Schwartz

ISBN 1-887554-49-1

Library of Congress Control Number 2005926716

This volume is dedicated to those survivors who have transformed their personal tragedies into proactive efforts to heal the victims, offenders, and communities. These include Andrea Casanova, Steve Stiles, Ida Balliasotes, Dick Nethercutt, and Ellen Halbert.

Preface

In 1990 Honey Faye Knopp gave a moving plenary address to the ATSA (Association for the Treatment of Sexual Abusers) conference in San Francisco when she praised the audience as being "bio-phils"—lovers of life, dedicated to helping the most despised among us. Few people in that auditorium had a vested, much less a financial, interest in discrediting sex offender therapy in general, specific treatment programs, or their fellow professionals. Unfortunately, civil commitment has changed that. The model of the profession has moved in many places from one of restorative justice, of which Honey was an early advocate, to one of adversarial criminal justice. While the Center for Sex Offender Treatment continues to advocate for a collaborative model in which all involved parties cooperate, those jurisdictions with involuntary commitment have seen professions and programs pitted against each other as lawyers on both sides of commitment hearings seek to impeach each others' witnesses or discredit the programs referenced by each side.

Poor Honey would weep to see the field she so gently nurtured as undergoing, at best, a conflict-ridden adolescence. Ideally, it will regain its healing vision as it matures. This volume, like its series predecessors, seeks to offer the current and innovative approaches to dealing with the complex issues facing the field of sex offender management. Although many of the chapters present hard-core, empirical evidence to substantiate their approaches, others do not even quote references. These latter chapters address practical issues of little interest to researchers but of great relevance to the front-line clinician (e.g., how to select and train inmate peer counselors, or how to conduct experiential treatment sessions).

Were the field to wait for empirical validation of its every move, there would be no new programs to study. Therefore, *The Sex Offender* series will continue to seek out and present innovative theories and approaches. Some will fall by the wayside. Others will set the standard for the future.

In preparing this volume, as in the past, I wish to thank my very patient publisher, Deborah Launer, with able assistance from editorial assistant Leslie Gwyn and copy editor Lori Jacobs. They have demonstrated inordinate patience, as my professional life has gone in numerous demanding directions. Again, I wish to thank my colleagues at Justice Resource Institute for their support, including Greg Canfield, M.S.W., Susan Wayne, M.S.W., and Robert Prinke, Ph.D. I wish to thank my colleagues at New England Forensic Associates, especially Dr. Carol Ball. Of course, I am only able to do this work with the support of my ever-patient husband Ed, the moral support of my children, Betsy and Ben, and the emotional support of the four-legged members of my family, including especially my ever-present professional and personal companion, Thomas, my service dog trained by Canine Companions for Independence.

Barbara Schwartz
March 31, 2005

About the Authors

Anmarie Aylward, M.A.

Anmarie Aylward received her master's degree from Northern Illinois University in sociology/criminal justice. She has been the director of the Washington State Sex Offender Treatment Program for five years. She has worked with sexual offenders and their families for more than fifteen years.

Debra K. Baker, M.A., L.H.M.C.

Debra Baker received her master's degree in counseling from Rider College. She has been treating sex offenders since 1985 and has supervised the treatment of sex offenders for the Departments of Correction in New Jersey, Washington, and Massachusetts. She is a clinical member of the Association for the Treatment of Sexual Abusers, a founding board member of the Massachusetts Association of Sexual Abusers and a member of the Massachusetts Coalition for Sex Offender Management. She has consulted with several states on the implementation of prison-based therapeutic communities treating sex offenders. She is currently in private practice treating sex offenders through a cognitive-behavioral relapse prevention model using a containment approach.

Geral Blanchard, M.A., N.C.P., L.P.C.

Geral Blanchard received his master's degree from Norwich University. He is the director of The Center for Peace Research in Sheridan, Wyoming, which provides counseling services for victims and perpetrators of sexual abuse, and develops innovative methods to prevent interpersonal violence. He is the author of three books on sexual abuse, including *The Difficult Connection.*

Guy Bourgon, Ph.D.

Guy Bourgon received his doctorate in clinical psychology from the University of Ottawa (Ontario) in 1994. As a registered psychologist, he provided assessment and treatment services to offenders for the Ontario Ministry of Community Safety and Correctional Services. In 1999, as the principle investigator, he initiated a long-term national multisite investigation of specialized services for sexually abusive youth and is the main force behind an annual Canadian conference on sexually abusive youth. He has been a researcher with Public Safety and Emergency Preparedness Canada, since 2001.

Kevin Creeden, M.A., L.M.H.C.

Kevin Creeden received his master's degree in counseling psychology from New York University in 1983. He is currently a doctoral candidate in counseling psychology at Boston College. Mr. Creeden is the director of assessment and research at the Whitney Academy in East Freetown, Massachusetts. He has more than twenty-five years of clinical experience working with adult sexual offenders and sexually and physically aggressive youth. Mr. Creeden trains and consults nationally to youth service, community, and mental health service agencies.

Maxine Daniels, B.Sc.(Hons.)

Maxine Daniels received her bachelor of science degree with honors in psychology and sociology from the Open University, Milton Keynes, England, her certificate of education in drama and English from The Birmingham School of Speech Training & Dramatic Art (England), and her postgraduate clinical qualification of psychodrama/psychotherapy from The London Centre of Psychodrama & Group Psychotherapy.

She has been working with HM Prison Service England for ten years developing the role-play components of treatment programs. To date she has been involved in the development and training for SOTP (Sex Offender Treatment Programme) Core, Adapted (for offenders with learning difficulties), Focus (a program for substance abuse users), and CSCP (for violent offenders). She also works with special hospitals and the probation service. She is a qualified psychodramatist/psychotherapist and works in private practice in London.

David L. Delmonico. Ph.D.

David Delmonico is a graduate of Kent State University with degrees in psychology, community counseling, and counseling and human development services. He is currently an associate professor in the Department of Counseling, Psychology, and Special Education at Duquesne University in Pittsburgh, Pennsylvania. Dr. Delmonico is a nationally recognized writer and speaker in the area of psychology and the Internet, including online sexual behaviors. He is the coauthor of *In the Shadows of the Net* and *Cybersex Unhooked*. Dr. Delmonico conducts trainings for a variety of audiences including helping professionals, parents, schools, clergy, and law enforcement on issues related to compulsive cybersex and cybersexual offense behavior. He is the director of the Online Behavior Research and Education Center and editor-in-chief of the *Sexual Addiction and Compulsivity Journal*.

Gregory Doucette, B.A.

Gregory Doucette received his bachelor's degree in mathematics from Merrimack College, Andover, Massachusetts, in 1967. He is a Massachusetts state parole officer and a certified postconviction sex offender testing (PCSOT) polygraphist. He has worked with and tested sex offenders for the Massachusetts Parole Board, including supervision of sex offenders using the IPSO (Intensive Parole for Sex Offenders) containment model. He has also provided polygraph examinations of offenders on state and federal probation. Mr. Doucette is a member of the American Polygraph Association and National Association of Polygraph Specialists.

William C. Ford, C.S.W.-R.

William Ford earned a bachelor of arts in psychology from Hofstra University and his master's degree in social work from Yeshiva University. He has previously served as associate director at CAP Behavior Associates and as a probation officer for the New York City Department of Probation. He has presented seminars on sex offenders and treatment before the Association for the Treatment of Sexual Abusers (ATSA). In October 2002, he presented "Supervision of Sex Offenders: The Relapse Prevention Model"; in October 2003 he presented "Steps to More Effective Program Development and Treatment Planning for African-American and Latino Sex Offenders." Mr. Ford is an ATSA member and was on the planning committee for the

2002 conference. He has also presented seminars to the New York City Department of Probation, Long Island College Hospital, correctional/residential facilities and youth-oriented groups in New York City. His publications include "Steps to More Effective Program Development and Treatment Planning for African-American and Latino Sex Offenders," a paper developed and presented at the 22nd annual ATSA conference (St. Louis, Missouri, October 2003) and "Utilizing Cognitive Behavioral Group Work with Mandated Clients," a paper presented before the Long Island chapter of the Association for the Advancement of Social Work with Groups (February 2004).

Elizabeth J. Griffin, M.A.

Elizabeth Griffin received her master's degree in marriage, family, and child counseling from the California Family Studies Center in Los Angeles in 1985. She is a licensed marriage and family therapist with more than twenty years of experience treating sexual offenders and those with sexually compulsive behaviors. She has worked in outpatient, inpatient, military, and prison settings. Ms. Griffin lectures nationally on the assessment and treatment of sexual offenders and those with sexually compulsive behavior, as well as issues related to cybersex. She has written numerous professional articles on these topics and is coauthor of *In the Shadows of the Net* and *Cybersex Unhooked*. Ms. Griffin is a director of Internet Behavior Consulting (*www.internetbehavior.com*), a company whose focus is on issues related to problematic online behavior.

Drew A. Kingston, B.A.(Hons.)

Drew Kingston completed his bachelor's degree with honors at Carleton University in Ottawa, Canada, in 2003 and is currently a doctoral candidate in clinical psychology at the University of Ottawa, Canada. He works as a program assistant for Correctional Service of Canada's Sex Offender Programs, where he manages the national sex offender assessment database. In addition, Mr. Kingston has participated in the organization of training sessions offered to facilitators across Canada. His primary research interests include pathways to sexual offending, risk assessment, and effective treatment with sexual offenders.

Elizabeth J. Letourneau, Ph.D.

Elizabeth Letourneau received her doctorate in clinical psychology from Northern Illinois University in 1995. She completed an internship at the Medical University of South Carolina in 1993 and a two-year postdoctoral fellowship at the National Crime Victims Research and Treatment Center from 1994–1996. She has conducted research with adult and juvenile sex offenders for the past fifteen years. She has numerous publications in this field and is active in the ATSA. Since 2000, Dr. Letourneau has conducted research at the Family Services Research Center in the Medical University of South Carolina. This center conducts research primarily on juvenile delinquency treatment effectiveness and Dr. Letourneau's research has focused on treatment effectiveness with juvenile sex offenders.

Gary Levitt

Gary Levitt is a parole officer for the Massachusetts Parole Board. Mr. Levitt's training and experience has included specialized supervision of sex offenders in the

IPSO containment model since 1996. He was instrumental in developing and implementing IPSO in Massachusetts. Mr. Levitt has also trained parole and probation officers in the supervision of sex offenders.

Ruth Lewis, Ph.D.

Ruth Lewis is a licensed psychologist who completed her doctoral psychology internship training and a research and clinical psychology fellowship at McLean Hospital, a Harvard University-affiliated psychiatric hospital in Belmont, Massachusetts. She is the assistant clinical director at New England Forensic Associates (NEFA). Since 1994, Dr. Lewis has provided specialized individual and group treatment at NEFA to sex offenders and clients with other sexual interest or behavior problems. Dr. Lewis is a member of ATSA and a board member of the Massachusetts Chapter of the Association for the Treatment of Sex Abusers (MATSA). She is included in the Massachusetts Coalition for Sex Offender Management (MCSOM) Treatment Providers Network. She has presented at MATSA conferences and provided consultation and training to treatment teams and other clinicians providing treatment to chronic mentally ill clients with sexual interest or behavior problems. In addition to her work with sex offenders, Dr. Lewis maintains a general private psychology practice in Arlington, Massachusetts.

Herman Lindeman, Ph.D.

Herman Lindeman earned his master's degree at Louisiana State University and his doctorate at Arizona State University, where he completed a 2,000-hour Veterans Administration Hospital internship. He is an Arizona-licensed psychologist with over twenty-six years' experience in private practice. His clinical practice incorporates direct patient services and community consultation. Dr. Lindeman specializes in evaluations and assessments. He has developed more than thirty proprietary assessment instruments or tests for court, probation, corrections, counseling, and treatment settings. He is the founder and president of Behavior Data Systems, Ltd., and Risk & Needs Assessment, Inc.

He is a member of several professional associations, including the Arizona Coalition Against Domestic Violence; Academy of Domestic Violence Counselors; American Association of Marriage and Family Therapy; National Association of Pretrial Service Agencies; California Probation, Parole and Correctional Research and the Western Correctional Association; American Society of Clinical Hypnotism; American Association of Hypnotherapists, American Probation and Parole Association; National Association of Drug Court Professionals; and California Coalition on Sexual Offending. Dr. Lindeman is also listed in the National Register of Health Service Providers in Psychology.

Gina Madrigano, Ph.D.

Gina Madrigrano is a registered clinical psychologist who received her doctorate from the University of Montreal (Quebec, Canada) in 2000. She has provided assessment and treatment services to young offenders for the Ontario Ministry of Community Safety and Correctional Services and for adult sex offenders for the Correctional Service of Canada and has conducted assessments for the National Parole Board of Canada. She is currently providing clinical services for adolescent and adult sex offenders both in the community and with the Royal Ottawa Hospital, in

Ontario, and is the principal investigator and co-applicant on grants involving the assessment of sex offenders.

Kelly E. Morton-Bourgon, M.A.

Kelly E. Morton-Bourgon received her master's degree in psychology from Carleton University (Ottawa, Ontario) in 2003. Her thesis evaluated the predictive accuracy of four risk assessments instruments on a sample of adolescent sexual offenders. She has been involved with the national multisite investigation of specialized services for sexually abusive youth as a research associate and conference director. She is currently working at the Department of Justice, Research and Statistics Division, as a research officer.

Christine O'Connor, B.A.

Christine O'Connor is a graduate of Saint Anselm College, where she received her bachelor of arts degree in criminal justice. She has been employed as a victim advocate for the Massachusetts Parole Board since 1997. In 2003, Ms. O'Connor had the opportunity to become part of IPSO. As the victim advocate, she raised victim awareness, provided notification of release, and addressed numerous victim's issues in an effort to help ensure an offender's safe transition into the community.

Janice E. Picheca, M.A.

Janice Picheca received her master's degree in psychology from Carlton University and is currently a doctoral candidate in clinical psychology at the University of Toronto. She is presently employed as a counselor in the Central Ontario Parole District of the Correctional Service of Canada, where she offers a variety of clinical services to offenders on conditional release. Her research interests include community-based risk management of sexual offenders, batterers, and intravenous drug abusers.

David Prescott, M.A., L.I.C.S.W.

David Prescott received a master's degree in clinical social work from Boston College in 1987. He has worked in and around inpatient settings for sexual abusers since 1987. Originally from the northeastern United States, he is the treatment assessment director at Sand Ridge Secure Treatment Center in Mauston, Wisconsin. Mr. Prescott has given lectures and workshops on the assessment and treatment of adolescents across North America and in Europe. He currently serves on the executive board of directors of ATSA and edits that organization's newsletter. Mr. Prescott is also on the expert panel of Stop It Now!, an organization dedicated to preventing sexual abuse, and a charter member of the International Association for the Treatment of Sexual Offenders.

Wilson Prunier, B.S.

Mr. Prunier earned a bachelor of communication studies degree from New York University. He has foster care, COBRA case management, administrative, operations, business development, public speaking, and public relations experience. He is currently involved with the New York City Alliance against Sexual Assault and is a member of the New York City Planning Collaborative for Generation Five, an organization whose mission is to end child sexual abuse within five generations. He has presented seminars on sex offenders and treatment before the Association for the Treatment of Sexual Abusers (ATSA). In October 2002, he presented "Supervision of Sex Offenders: The Relapse Prevention Model"; in October 2003 he presented "Steps to More Effective Program Development and Treatment Planning for African-American and Latino Sex Offenders"). In February 2004, Mr. Prunier presented a paper, "Utilizing Cognitive Behavioral Group Work with Mandated Clients," before the Long Island chapter of the Association for the Advancement of Social Work with Groups.

Deloris Tyler Roys, Ph.D.

Deloris Roys holds a master's degree in social work and a doctorate in criminal psychology and is licensed in Georgia as a clinical social worker. Dr. Roys, founder and director of Highland Institute for Behavioral Change, Inc., and executive director of Highland Foundation, Inc., has provided evaluation and therapeutic intervention for over sixteen years to children, adolescents, and adults who have been engaged in both legal and illegal sexual behaviors. She has lectured widely and conducted many training seminars across the country, including training for worldwide U.S. Navy psychiatrists and psychologists. She is coauthor of *Protocol for Phallometric Assessment: A Clinician's Guide*. She also is the author of manuals for the Sex Offender Psychoeducational Program offered to incarcerated adult male sex offenders in Georgia prisons and in community-based Georgia Department of Corrections Probation Detention Centers. She also authored a manual to use in psychoeducation programs for female sex offenders. Her peer-reviewed journal publications as author or coauthor address suitability of clients for program completion, effect of molestation by maternal caregivers, empathy in sex offenders, treatment outcome, and denial by sex offenders. In national professional symposiums, she has also presented her research in problem solving by child and adolescent sex offenders, child/caregiver disruptions, adolescent male sexual arousal patterns, and female sex offenders.

Joel Skolnick, M.S.W., L.I.C.S.W.

Mr. Skolnick received his master's degree in clinical social work from the University of Wisconsin. He has worked with sex offenders in community settings and in inpatient settings since 1991. He is a clinical member of the ATSA. He has conducted outcome studies in the treatment of psychiatric sex offenders and given numerous presentations on the application of relapse prevention modalities with both psychiatric and forensic offenders as well as the application of the containment model in the community for the Department of Mental Health. Mr. Skolnick currently is the chief operating officer of Westborough State Hospital and is a sex offender therapist in private practice.

Nancy M. Steele, Ph.D.

Nancy Steele received her doctorate in clinical psychology from Ohio University in Athens, Ohio. She has worked in the field treating sex offenders since 1972 in the prison systems in Colorado, Minnesota, Indiana and Ohio. She has served as a consultant for the National Institute of Corrections (NIC), teaching seminars in Longmont, Colorado, for three years to administrators from fifteen states on the development and management of programs for sex offenders. She has also served as a technical consultant from NIC to another eight states on the development of programs for sex offenders in prisons and in the community. Dr. Steele has appeared numerous times on local television shows and three times on national news shows on issues dealing with sex offenders, including NBC's *Dateline*. She has taught numerous seminars and workshops around the country to correctional staff and probation/parole staff and has served as an expert witness in court in several states. She has written two other chapters for books edited by Dr. Barbara Schwartz and has published many articles.

Cynthia Cupit Swenson, Ph.D.

Cynthia Cupit Swenson received her doctorate in clinical psychology with a subspecialty in school psychology from Florida State University. Currently she is associate professor and associate director at the Family Services Research Center in the Department of Psychiatry and Behavioral Sciences of the Medical University of South Carolina. She is Principal Investigator on an NIMH-funded randomized clinical trial comparing parent training and multisystemic therapy with physically abused adolescents and their families.

Dr. Swenson has worked extensively with children and families over the last twenty-five years. Her research is community based and focuses on community violence, child maltreatment, youth aggression, and substance abuse. She has published more than thirty journal articles and book chapters and a recent book on treating community violence and troubled neighborhoods. Dr. Swenson is currently on the board of the American Professional Society on the Abuse of Children.

Jerry M. Thomas, M.Ed.

Jerry Thomas received her master's degree in education from the University of Memphis. She is a recognized expert in the field of youthful sexual aggression, specializing in family treatment, and safety in out-of-home settings. She has developed six different programs for sexually abusive youth, conducted program evaluations for residential treatment centers, juvenile correctional systems, boarding schools, and foster care. She has also conducted a wide range of professional and staff training, provided consultation and expert witness services to legal professionals, and presented seminars and workshops across the United States, Canada and Great Britain.

In 1986 she was invited to join The National Task Force on Juvenile Sexual Offending sponsored by the National Council of Juvenile and Family Court Judges, and participated in writing *The National Task Force Report*. She was appointed a member of the 1995 National Mental Health Institute Special Committee on Female Sexual Offending and in 2002 was appointed by the Center on Sex Offender Management to the 2nd National Summit on Sex Offender Management. In 1999, as a founding member of the National Task Force on Offense Specific Residential Programs, she participated in writing the *Residential Standards for Sex Offense Specific Programs*.

C. Wilson Viar III, B.S., B.A., B.F.A.

Wilson Viar received his degrees from the University of Montana. He is an independent research and writing consultant focusing primarily upon problematic social issues and creative efforts to resolve them. For the last fifteen years he has enjoyed a close working relationship with Jerry Thomas, focusing on the most complex, difficult, socially disturbing, and professionally promising developments in the treatment of sexually aggressive and abusive juveniles, juvenile sexual victims, and their families. Since 1996, he has coauthored a wide variety of articles, chapters, handbooks, seminars, and training materials with Ms. Thomas on topics spanning the field.

Since 1995 Mr. Viar has also served as senior research consultant on teams working on projects ranging from efforts to expand educational opportunities in Nicaragua, the extension of Internet technology onto the Navajo-Hopi reservation in Arizona, and the building of low-income housing in Nanjing, China.

Robin J. Wilson, Ph.D.

Robin J. Wilson received his doctorate from the University of Toronto and has worked with sexual offenders in various settings for over twenty years. He is presently the chief psychologist for the Ontario Region (Community) of the Correctional Service of Canada and maintains a small private clinical and consulting practice. Dr. Wilson has published and presented widely on the assessment and treatment of sexual and other offenders and his current interests concern collaborative risk management and restoration in community settings. Dr. Wilson was the recipient of the 1996 ATSA Graduate Research Award and is currently the elected Canadian Regional Representative on ATSA's board of directors. He makes his home in Toronto, Canada, with his wife, three children, and several pets.

James R. Worling, Ph.D., C.Psych.

James Worling obtained his doctorate from the Ontario Institute for Studies in Education at the University of Toronto. Dr. Worling is a consulting and clinical psychologist who has worked extensively with adolescents who sexually offend and their families since 1988. During this time, he has presented many workshops and written a number of professional articles and book chapters regarding the etiology, assessment, and treatment of adolescent sexual aggression. In addition to his consulting and clinical practice, he is presently an associate faculty member at the University of Toronto and he serves on the editorial board for the ATSA journal, *Sexual Abuse: A Journal of Research and Treatment*. Dr. Worling values holistic, comprehensive, and empirically supported approaches to the assessment and treatment of sexual aggression and sexual victimization.

Pamela M. Yates, Ph.D., R.D.Psych.

Pamela Yates earned her master's degree and her doctorate in psychology from Carleton University in Ottawa, Ontario, Canada. Dr. Yates has worked in various capacities in the assessment, treatment, and management of sexual offenders. She has published and presented research on the assessment and treatment of sexual offenders, including risk, recidivism, treatment models, treatment effectiveness, sexual sadism, phallometric assessment and intervention, and the pathways model of intervention with sexual offenders. She has been involved in the development of treatment programs for sexual and violent offenders. She has been a member of various working groups and task forces on treatment of sexual offenders and program evaluation methodology and has worked within various correctional jurisdictions as a trainer in sex offender treatment delivery, psychologist and clinical director in the community with victims of familial and sexual violence, and in the areas of violence prevention, substance abuse, young offenders, and program evaluation.

Introduction

Our world has experienced many significant changes since the preparation of *The Sex Offender: Current Treatment Modalities and Systems Issues* (Volume 4). The public's pervasive fear of sex offenders has been compounded by fears of terrorism. When people operate out of fear and anger, they risk making poor decisions. Certainly clinicians see this operating in the deviant cycles of their sexually abusive patients, and it is equally true for the average citizen. Fear-driven decisions have had a direct impact on the world of sex offender treatment by draining resources and creating a harsher social climate. Programs have experienced staff cuts, as well as decreases in training budgets. National funding for research has been diverted from critical studies on the origin and prevention of sexual violence to a focus on terrorism. Loss of jobs, particularly in manufacturing, which would have provided low-risk occupations for sex offenders in the community, have deprived offenders of the ability to support themselves; and this, along with the continuing crisis in health care, has deprived many of these individuals of the funds to pay for treatment. All these issues challenge clinicians and supervisors to make do with fewer and fewer resources.

The field is also challenged by ongoing controversies. The public notification and sexually violent predator statutes passed in the 1990s continue to present numerous problems, with little evidence that they are accomplishing their intended goals. How many citizens are really safer because they can access information on sex offenders in their neighborhoods? Contrast this with the number of high-risk offenders who are now more dangerous because they cannot find employment or are repeatedly evicted from their residences. One state recently passed a law requiring high-risk sex offenders to wear bulky tracking devices to facilitate Global Position Monitoring, ensuring that these individuals will be immediately identifiable, and thus probably rendered unemployable and subsequently unable to pay for their treatment or offense-related fees. The number of individuals in sexually violent predator (SVP) programs continues to grow. Because few of these individuals are ever released (e.g., California has released one individual of the several hundreds on that state's rolls), the populations of these programs continue to swell, and while the cost of maintaining and treating these individuals is significant (ranging from $75,000 to $125,000 a year per person for care and treatment), the legal expenses of committing, recommitting, and defending related lawsuits can be staggering. These programs have spurred the development of actuarials which, although better than unaided clinical estimates of risk, leave much to be desired given the seriousness of the decisions they impact. Controversy continues to swirl around their statistical stability, with different cross validations producing radically different risk estimates. Furthermore, although the heterogeneity of sex offenders is one of the most salient characteristics of the group, the actuarials lump all types of sex offenders together, ignoring the dynamic differences between the violent, criminally oriented rapist and the pedophile priest.

However, rather than pooling their scientific expertise to improve risk assessment tools, we now witness the war of the experts (of which I admit I am one) over ROC (receiver operating curve analysis) and AUC (area under the curve) values, base rates, and survival curves.

In addition, the efficacy of treatment is widely debated in these arenas. In some states this amounts to public officials undermining the proven effectiveness of their own treatment programs in order to support state attorneys and SVP hearings of individuals who have completed those programs.

Other related controversies involve diagnoses related to involuntarily committed sex offenders under the SVP status. Is rape a paraphilia or is it criminal behavior. Do "psychopaths" actually exist, and if so, is this actually a condition reflecting some type of underlying pathology—such as attachment disorder, a neurologically based impairment of executive cognitive functioning, or a combination of the two.

The controversy over the diagnosis of psychopathy has largely revolved around challenges of the most popular assessment tool, the Psychopathy Checklist—Revised (PCL-R; Hare, 1991). Another diagnosis related to SVP commitments involves a diagnosis of paraphilia nonconsent. During the past two revisions of the *Diagnostic and Statistical Manual of Mental Disorders* (DSM-IV; American Psychiatric Association, 1994; DSM-IV-TR; 2000), the proposal was brought forward to include arousal to resistance on the part of the person with whom one is having sex and whether this represents a paraphilia. The advocates argued that, just as in pedophilia or exhibitionism, some individuals have preferential arousal to sex with nonconsenting individuals. They may prefer this to mutually consenting sexuality and may experience intrusive fantasies associated with this behavior. These fantasies and this conduct may even be distressing to the individual but he is unable to control these urges.

The opposition argued that, given the prevalence of this behavior in the male population as derived from self-reports of college males, forced sex cannot be considered an unusual behavior. Individuals representing feminist perspectives argued before the American Psychiatric Association that this conduct reflects the way our society socializes males, not a mental illness afflicting a few unfortunate individuals. It was also felt that labeling rape as the by-product of an illness would alleviate the offender's responsibility for his behavior.

It can certainly be argued that there are some people who show preferential deviant arousal directed specifically toward resistance and nonconsent. This would not include just any rapist capable of sustaining an erection despite his victim's distress. This can be attributed to many motives, including being oblivious to the suffering of others. Whatever the arguments on either side, the authors of DSM-III (American Psychiatric Association, 1980), DSM-IV, and the DSM-IV-TR have specifically rejected labeling any kind of rape behavior, other than sadism, as a paraphilia. Ironically, this is now an argument against the commitment of some individuals as SVPs, a result probably not intended by the parties in this debate.

In discussing the controversy swirling around psychopathy, it is recognized that anyone exposed to a large number of antisocial individuals recognizes that there exists a subset of individuals who present as glib, entitled, arrogant, and insensitive and whose behavior reflects a total indifference to the welfare of others.

The problem is in a specific evaluator using a particular instrument to diagnose a specific individual. Someone may appear to be "glib" to one evaluator but not to another. Indeed they may deliberately present as "glib" to one evaluator but not to another. In addition, there are a number of reasons for people to present with the Factor 1 personality dynamics. Victims of posttraumatic stress disorder may present as emotionally flat and lacking in empathy or remorse because they have completely repressed all their emotions.

Another problem with the PCL-R is the context in which a certain symptom is judged. If an offender, for example, violated another human being and at that time showed little or no empathy toward that person but now does express sincere remorse and understanding of her pain and, moreover, has shown empathy for scores of other people in his life, must he then get at least some points in the PCL-R for not being empathetic? The answer is not clear.

In making a diagnosis of psychopathy, we need research on the neurological and neuropsychological characteristics that clearly meet the criteria. Studies are now being conducted that will eventually lead us to an understanding of the actual nature of this condition, which can then lead to ways to measure these underlying processes. Until we have a better understanding of this condition, we as professionals should be cautious in applying what has become a damning label, suggesting that this person is highly dangerous and his condition is intractable.

Controversy continues to swirl around the efficacy of treatment. Despite the mounting evidence that treatment of sex offenders does reduce the offense rate (A. Aylworth, 2004, personal communication), some experts continue to argue that until strictly controlled studies are conducted with either matched samples or random assignment, the efficacy of treatment will remain unknown. Certainly from a purely empirical view, this cannot be disputed. However, as with all research on psychotherapy, the practical problems are immense. The subjects of this experiment would not be laboratory rats but real individuals who have actually sexually assaulted other people. The sponsoring institution would not be a university or research institute but a criminal justice agency or treatment program.

Even more alarming, the result would not be a test score or a self-report index but a real human victim. What the advocates of highly controlled studies are suggesting is that certain sex offenders who are highly motivated for treatment be denied that opportunity by agencies designed to protect the public. Furthermore, the measure of the success of this experiment would be the number of new victims of sexual assault. In addition, in sixteen states, this offender who is denied treatment and now has recidivated would probably be a candidate for civil commitment. Moreover, must any treatment guarantee long-term abstinence from certain conditions in order to be considered effective? If a substance abuser undergoes treatment followed by five years of abstinence before relapsing, was the treatment ineffective? If a medication alleviates depression for a substantial period of time but the depression recurs, was the drug ineffective? If an individual stops practicing the techniques he has learned in any kind of treatment, does this condemn the therapy or the therapist? Perhaps this is only true in the field of sex offender treatment where there is zero tolerance for reoffense. This places an unprecedented burden on the profession. Assuming that long-term abstinence is a goal of effective treatment, then how long should the follow-up period be—three years? five years? ten years?

The problems with extended follow-ups are multiple. The longer the period of time elapsed, the more difficult the follow-up. One may choose to rely on national crime data base such as National Crime Information Center (NCIC). However, if a name does not show up as a recidivist, should this person be considered a treatment success? Or might he be dead or physically incapacitated?

Another very significant issue is the changing field of sex offender treatment itself. This is a problem endemic to evaluating any long-term intervention. By the time the follow-up program is completed, will the treatment be obsolete? Hanson faces this difficulty in his recent twelve-year follow-up of an outpatient treatment program in Canada (Hanson et al., 2002). By the time his study was completed, the treatment standards had changed substantially.

In this Volume 5, the authors have attempted to wrestle with a number of issues that are current in the field today. For example, the new phenomenon of interstate pornography is addressed in Chapter 4, by David Delmonico, on cyber sex offenders. It has become a growing problem, and it is basically unknown whether these people are actually pedophiles or whether their behavior is more the by-product of aspects of the media.

The field of sex offender treatment continues to be involved in the vagaries of politics more than other forms of treatment. Politicians are quick to establish themselves as "tough on crime" by jumping on any bandwagon that claims to "get sex offenders." Unfortunately these policies are rarely based on reason, much less research. In addition, and unfortunately, sex offender treatment programs have often been the victim of intra-agency feuds and controversies over privatization. If public officials are serious about eliminating the tragedy of sexual abuse, they will quit making this issue the object of their personal ambitions and unite with all legitimate stakeholders seeking to reduce this problem.

Barbara Schwartz
March 31, 2005

References

American Psychiatric Association. (1980). *Diagnostic and statistical manual of mental disorders* (3rd ed.). Washington, DC: Author.

American Psychiatric Association. (1994). *Diagnostic and statistical manual of mental disorders* (4th ed.). Washington, DC: Author.

American Psychiatric Association. (2000). *Diagnostic and statistical manual of mental disorders* (4th ed., text rev.). Washington, DC: Author.

Hanson, R. K., Gordon, A., Harris, A. J. R., Marques, J. K., Murphy, W., Quinsey, V, et al. (2002). First report of the Collaborative Outcome Data Project of the effectiveness of psychological treatment for sex offenders. *Sexual Abuse: A Journal of Treatment and Research, 14*, 169–194.

Hare, R. D. (1991). *The Hare Psychopathy Checklist—Revised.* Toronto, Ontario, Canada: Multi-Health Systems.

Table of Contents

PART 1: THEORIES

Chapter 1: Trauma, Attachment, and Neurodevelopment—Implications for Treating Sexual Behavior Problems

Kevin Creeden, M.A., L.M.H.C.

Chapter 2: The Emotional World of the Sexual Offender—Does It Matter?

Deloris Tyler Roys, Ph.D.

Chapter 3: Pathways to Sexual Offending

Pamela M. Yates, Ph.D., R.D.Psych. and Drew A. Kingston, B.A.(Hons.)

PART 2: ADULT SPECIAL POPULATIONS

Chapter 4: Sex Offenders Online—What Clinicians Need to Know

David L. Delmonico, Ph.D. and Elizabeth J. Griffin, Ph.D.

Chapter 5: Working With African-American and Latino Sex Offenders

William C. Ford, C.S.W.-R. amd Wilson Prunier, B.S.

Chapter 6: Outpatient Treatment Considerations for Mentally Ill Clients With Problem Sexual Interests or Behavior

Ruth E. Lewis, Ph.D.

PART 3: ADULT TREATMENT

Chapter 7: Sex Offender Tests—SAI and SAI-Juvenile
Herman Lindeman, Ph.D.

Chapter 8: The Use of Role-Play to Develop Victim Empathy and Relapse Prevention

Maxine Daniels, B.Sc.(Hons.)

Chapter 9: Choosing, Training, and Using Offenders as Therapeutic Aides

Nancy M. Steele, Ph.D.

Chapter 10: Spirituality in Male Sex Abuser Treatment

Geral Blanchard, M.A.N.C.P., L.P.C.

PART 4: ADULT COMMUNITY SUPERVISION

Chapter 11: Intensive Parole Supervision of the Sex Offender—Putting the Containment Approach Into Practice

Debra K. Baker, M.A., L.M.H.C., Joel Skolnick, M.S.W., L.I.C.S.W.,
Gregory Doucette, B.A., Gary Levitt and Christine O'Connor, B.A.

Chapter 12: From Institution to Community—Successful Transitions Support in Washington State Sex Offender Treatment Program
Anmarie Aylward, M.A.

Chapter 13: Circles of Support and Accountability—Engaging the Community in Sexual Offender Management
Robin J. Wilson, Ph.D. and Janice E. Picheca, M.A.

PART 5: JUVENILE TREATMENT

Chapter 14: Multisystemic Therapy With Juvenile Sex Offenders

Cynthia Cupit Swenson, Ph.D. and Elizabeth J. Letourneau, Ph.D.

Chapter 15: Multisite Investigation of Treatment for Sexually Abusive Juveniles

Guy Bourgon, Ph.D., Kelly E. Morton-Bourgon, M.A. and Gina Madrigano, Ph.D.

Chapter 16: To Touch or Not to Touch—Issues for Therapists
Jerry M. Thomas, M.Ed. and C. Wilson Viar III, B.S., B.A., B.F.A.

Chapter 17: The Current State of Adolescent Risk Assessment
David S. Prescott, M.A., L.I.C.S.W.

Chapter 18: Assessing Sexual Offense Risk for Adolescents Who Have Offended Sexually
James R. Worling, Ph.D., C.Psych.

Part 1
Theories

If the treatment of sex offenders is to continue to grow and become more effective and efficient, our theories of the origin and modification of sexually inappropriate behavior must evolve as well. One could argue that the last great frontier of exploration is the human brain, which is, after all, the real origin of all human behavior. Current research promises to provide us with a much more sophisticated understanding of the biological basis of all types of human behavior. In addition, for a number of years, prominent researchers in the sex offender treatment field have argued that behavior is the outcome of thoughts or perhaps of thoughts that lead to emotions which then produce responses. However, is there really any hard evidence that thoughts lead to emotions rather than, in many cases, that emotions lead to thoughts? Certainly individuals suffering from depression may be experiencing biochemical responses which they then ascribe to some condition in their environment. For example, an individual may be experiencing a problem in the reuptake of neurotransmitters but may attribute his emotional state to his marriage or job. Place such an individual on the correct medication and his marriage or job becomes much more tolerable, and the thoughts associated with these situations change. Finally, sex offender therapists have for too long taken as gospel that relapse is the product of stress and of failed attempts to cope appropriately with high-risk situations. The field is being challenged to reconceptualize this assumption.

In Chapter 1, Kevin Creeden has written about the fascinating relationship between attachment theory and brain development. It has always made intuitive sense that abused children are harmed by their abusive experiences. However, only recently, with the introduction of the study of the neurological consequences, have we begun to understand how early disruption of the caretaker bond by either inconsistency or actual neglect or abuse can directly change the structure of various parts of the brain. This then becomes a vicious cycle as the more impaired bond produces physical changes which are correlated with behavioral changes which may further impair the bond or result in caretaker changes such as multiple foster placements. These behavioral changes may include sexually inappropriate behavior that may be the outcome of impaired empathy coupled with enhanced impulsivity. Can we then have an impact on this physiologically based problem? That will be an important area of exploration in the years to come. Moreover, it raises interesting legal issues as far as responsibility for one's behavior. If indeed one is suffering from a condition that is directly attributable to a physical condition (in this case changes to the structure of the brain), is one to be held legally responsible for one's behavior? This is an issue that has yet to be tested but will probably be brought before the courts in the near future.

In Chapter 2, Deloris Roys explores the world of the sex offender from the perspective of Erickson and Maslow, both of whom were concerned with emotional development as well as cognitive development. For the past several decades sex offender therapy has concentrated on the cognitions of sex offenders, grounding their assumptions on cognitive-behavioral therapy and insisting that this is the empirically verified approach. However, in actuality there has never been a study that contrasted a cognitive-behavioral program with another sex offender-specific program based on another model and controlled for relevant issues such as time in treatment, skill of therapists, and allocation of resources. Furthermore, it is unlikely that such a study can be conducted given that it is unlikely that a Department of Correction would establish two contrasting programs, just to measure the efficacy of one over the other. After all, it is not the role of prisons to do basic research in psychotherapy. In addition, it is unlikely that an outpatient therapy program would wish to conduct two contrasting programs for the sake of research. Perhaps some day another program such as the one conducted at Atascadero State Hospital in the late 1980s and early 1990s, established and funded specifically for the sake of research, can explore this question. In the meantime, therapists should not be content to believe that they have found the definitive answer to the question of how to treat sex offenders, and they should continue to explore new paradigms, especially with those offenders who do not respond to traditional models.

Finally, another sacred cow that is being challenged is "relapse prevention" (RP) as it has traditionally been defined. In Chapter 3, Pamela Yates discusses how Canada has taken to heart the criticisms by Laws and Ward and Hudson of traditional RP assumptions and has developed a new paradigm based on the self-regulation model. In making the assumption that all sex offenders wish to control their inappropriate behavior but lack effective coping skills and may be disinhibited by negative emotional states, we may overlook large numbers of offenders whose pattern of behavior simply does not follow this model. Yates presents four different pathways which may lead to the initial offense and subsequent relapse, all of which demand appropriate diagnoses and different treatment approaches.

In the past decade the field of sex offender treatment has been preoccupied with trying to develop assessment methods that can effectively predict reoffense. However, this has largely been an actuarial search that does not lead to a deeper understanding of the dynamics of the sexually deviant individual and has not addressed improvements in treatment. Indeed, arguments still rage over whether these individuals can be effectively treated as if they should be regarded as members of an alien species whose behaviors do not follow the same laws as those of the rest of us. It behooves researchers and clinicians to continue to refine their diagnostic tools to clearly identify individual problems and then devise helpful strategies, be they social, psychological, or physiologically based, to respond to these problems. Continuing to remain open to advances in theory will advance the pursuit of these goals.

Chapter 1

Trauma, Attachment, and Neurodevelopment— Implications for Treating Sexual Behavior Problems

by Kevin Creeden, M.A., L.M.H.C.

OVERVIEW

This chapter examines some of the recent research exploring the experience of early trauma and disrupted attachment on the neurodevelopment of children, with a focus on the perspective this research may offer in our understanding of the etiology of sexually abusive behavior and the characteristics exhibited by many of the clients we treat. Following this review, the chapter explores the implications this research might have in developing assessment protocols and treatment interventions for individuals who exhibit sexual behavior problems.

INTRODUCTION

Recent advances in brain imaging technologies have led to a more refined and broadly accessible level of neurological research and spurred greater opportunities for actively examining the connections between structural and functional neurodevelopmental processes and particular emotional states, cognitive processes, and behaviors. Currently, magnetic resonance imaging (MRI), including functional magnetic resonance imaging (fMRI), and emission tomography, which includes positron emission tomography (PET) and single photon emission tomography (SPECT), are the main technologies in use (Anand & Shekhar, 2003). These tools have allowed researchers to examine differences in brain structure, areas of increased brain activation, dynamic changes in neurotransmitter release, and synaptic concentration in a manner that was previously unavailable.

One aspect of this research has focused on the neurological consequences of trauma, with studies indicating that the experience of early childhood trauma has a significant structural and functional impact on neurodevelopment (Teicher, Andersen, Polcari, Andersen, & Navalta, 2002; Perry, 2001; Bremner et al., 1997). Intertwined with the research examining the neurodevelopmental effects of childhood trauma are the writings of Alan Schore, Daniel Siegel, and others, which argue that children's emotional experiences in relation to their primary caretakers are the central organizing feature in early brain development (Balbernie, 2001; Trevarthen & Aitken, 2001; Siegel, 1999; Schore, 1994). From this perspective, a child's attachment relationship with his or her primary caretakers will be an essential factor in mitigating or exacerbating the negative aspects of experiencing stress and trauma. It would also suggest that seriously impaired attachment relationships in early childhood may be traumatic in and of themselves.

The changes that occur in the brain as a consequence of trauma and disrupted attachment offer a way of understanding many of the behaviors we see in children and adults with significant behavioral and emotional difficulties (Bremner, 2002; Streeck-Fischer & van der Kolk, 2000). Understanding the brain's response to both trauma and disorganized attachment experiences can also direct us to interventions that are developmental, holistic, and strength based. As our understanding increases and brain-focused research technologies continue to improve, it seems conceivable that we

Figure 1.1
Hierarchical Organization of the Brain

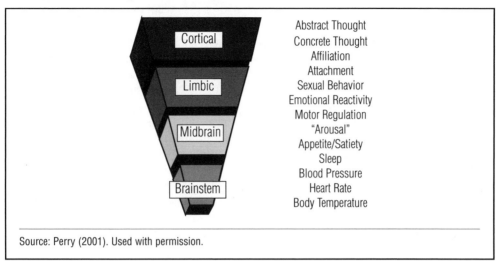

Source: Perry (2001). Used with permission.

might eventually be able to identify certain risk factors or measure aspects of treatment progress through identifying patterns and changes in functional and/or structural neurology.

BRAIN ORGANIZATION AND DEVELOPMENT

Perry (1997) writes that the human brain has evolved a functional hierarchical organization starting from the "lower simple portions to the more complex cortical regions" (p. 128) which acts to perceive, process, store, and act on both internal and external information all solely to promote survival (see Figure 1.1).

Perry (2001) explains that as the brain develops, the more complex limbic, subcortical, and cortical areas organize and begin to "modulate, moderate, and 'control' the more primitive and 'reactive' lower portions of the brain" (p. 4). This integration of stimulus input from the brainstem, midbrain, and limbic areas with cortical modulation and control is exactly that process which appears to be most affected by the young child's experience of trauma and persistent stressors.

PROCESSING AND LEARNING

The brain does not treat all information equally. Rather, there are *hard-wired* preferences for the rapid processing of information that is relevant to danger and reproduction (Le Doux, 1995; Gallistel, Brown, Carey, Gelman, & Keil, 1991). Mammalian brains have evolved to understand both *when* and *where* danger might occur. They identify and organize sensory information and coordinate motor behavior learned from the outcomes of previous behaviors (Crittenden, 1997; Ornstein & Thompson, 1984). This information tells the organism when to expect danger and enables the organism to engage in both the inhibition of danger-eliciting behaviors and the display of protective behaviors. It is important to understand that this processing is largely occurring in the lower brain, so that the causal or protective factors are identified through their temporal proximity to the learning stimulus. Therefore, although the protective or causal attributions may not always be accurate, the behaviors may nonetheless persist.

Human brains also transform certain privileged information into affect largely through processes centered in the limbic system (and the sensory cortices). This affective learning indicates context in which there are greater than usual probabilities for experiencing danger and generating anxiety or for being safe and experiencing comfort (Le Doux, 1995; MacLean, 1990).

Anxiety-producing cues have been shown to consist of stimuli such as darkness, sudden loud noises, and being alone and being entrapped. These anxiety-producing cues are not necessarily associated with a specific threat but are experienced as free-floating or unfocused anxiety that nonetheless encourages individuals to either flee or prepare to defend themselves. Comforting stimuli include close bodily contact, stroking, and rocking motions, behaviors frequently associated with early infant/caretaker attachment. These behaviors promote a sense of safety and tend to encourage exploratory behavior (Lang, 1995; Le Doux, 1994; Bowlby, 1973; Seligman, 1971).

This affective or contextual learning also occurs with cues that elicit sexual arousal, which signals opportunities for reproduction. As with cues eliciting protective behaviors, the stimulus that gets associated with sexual arousal can prove either predictive or erroneous. We see this frequently in particular fetish types of behavior. Crittenden (1997) writes that "there is also a considerable overlap in the experiential features of anxiety and sexual arousal and of comfort and sexual satisfaction; these can lead to an overlap of the sexual and attachment behavioral systems" (p. 40). This point might prove to be of considerable importance in understanding the motivation of individuals who engage in sexually inappropriate or abusive behavior.

NEUROLOGICAL IMPACT OF TRAUMA

Physiological and Neurodevelopmental Responses to Stress

Bremner (2002) argues that the physiological response to stress results in common changes in neurological function that underlies the symptoms frequently seen in the aftermath of trauma. This viewpoint moves us away from being limited to examining specific responses to specific traumas such as sexual victimization and focuses attention on traumatic experiences in a broader context that includes factors such as the developmental stage at which the trauma occurred, frequency, context, and available supports, as well as the particular type of experience the individual endured.

Researchers have been involved in describing the physiological responses to stress and identifying the areas of the brain involved in these responses for a considerable period of time (Cannon, 1927; Papez, 1937; MacLean, 1949; Selye, 1956). There is also a considerable body of research that has linked the experience of childhood stressors to higher degrees of behavioral difficulties, particularly aggression (Pynoos, 1990). More recently, researchers have begun to identify the neurodevelopmental consequences of these childhood stress experiences (Perry & Pate, 1994; Perry, 1997;

DeBellis, 2001) and more clearly connect these developmental processes to a range of behavioral and emotional difficulties exhibited by children and adults (Lewis, 1992; Loeber et al., 1993; MacEwen, 1994; Perry, 1997).

Diminished Functional Capabilities

Deprivation of developmental experiences or atypical or abnormal patterns of neurochemical cues due to the extremes of experience can lead to disrupted/abnormal neuronal organization and diminished functional capabilities (Perry, 2001). These diminished capacities may exhibit themselves through a loss of cortical modulation of responses mediated through the lower and midbrain (e.g., arousal, impulsivity, and aggression) or a lack of integration between cortical and subcortical processing (e.g., learning difficulties). Also, because the brain is organized in a "use-dependent" manner, persistent stressful environmental cues, especially those experienced during critical developmental periods in early childhood, can lead to malorganization and compromised function in the brain. While this stress-induced organization and function might have been adaptive to the child growing up in a highly chaotic or abusive environment, these continued patterns of neural processing and responses prove detrimental and maladaptive when the environment changes (Green, Voeller, & Gaines, 1981; Pynoos, 1990; Perry, 1996).

The effects of this malorganization in persistent neural response patterns can be seen in a variety of symptoms and presentations. Hyperarousal to potentially threatening cues in the environment can create difficulties in attending to tasks leading to frequent diagnosis of attention deficit disorder (Haddad & Garralda, 1992; Kafka & Prentky, 1998; Streeck-Fischer & van der Kolk, 2000; Fago, 2003). Pynoos (1990) and Perry (1997) would argue that the diagnosis of attention deficit hyperactivity disorder (ADHD) for many of these individuals is misleading. They suggest that these individuals do not have a core abnormality in their capacity to attend but, rather, that their lower- and midbrain responses have organized around experiencing persistent, low- level states of fear and anxiety resulting in a consistent focus on nonverbal, threat- related cues. Because these individuals are hypervigilant to threat-related cues there is a tendency to overinterpret neutral environmental input as traumatic. Conversely, if sensory input is not viewed as threat related, it is frequently interpreted as unimportant and therefore ignored (van der Kolk & Ducey, 1989; McFarlane, Weber, & Clark, 1993).

Studies have indicated that many traumatized children have difficulties with complex auditory and visuospatial processing tasks (Saigh, Mroueh, & Bremner, 1997; Bremner & Narayan, 1998; Teicher et al., 2002). Increasingly, research has found that the activation of fear and anxiety responses stemming from the amygdala and differentially from other subcortical stress response pathways can cause hippocampal atrophy and other effects on hippocampal functioning. This appears to affect functions such as verbal memory, spatial memory, contextual learning, and associative learning and memory (McHugh, Deacon, Rawlins, & Bannerman, 2004; Teicher et al., 2002; Bremner & Narayan, 1998). As a consequence, the neurodevelopmental organization of the brain in response to threat can create ongoing difficulties with the processing of new information and generates obstacles for the individual learning from experience and developing new coping and problem-solving approaches.

Neurobiological Impact of Stress and Trauma

Teicher et al. (2002) have reviewed the research related to the neurobiological impact of stress and trauma and have identified a variety of findings. They report significant alterations in the amygdala and increased limbic irritability. These changes generate a "kindling effect," leading to hypervigiliance, a greater tendency to interpret social/environmental cues and interactions as being threatening, and a stronger tendency to engage in fight/flight responses in reaction to these cues. Their research also identifies changes in the hippocampus increasing the possibility for the dissociative, amnestic, and disinhibitory aspects of posttraumatic stress disorder (PTSD), as well as deficits in verbal memory and processing. According to Teicher, trauma victims also evidence diminished left-hemisphere maturation, diminished corpus callosum size, decreased left–right hemisphere integration, and diminished capacities in the cerebellar vermis. Teicher suggests that there is a close fit between the symptoms observed in abused clients and the effects of early trauma on brain development. He points to depressive symptoms, PTSD, ADHD, borderline personality disorder, dissociative disorders, and substance abuse as having correlations in the neurodevelopmental responses to stress. Of specific importance to sexual behavior difficulties and sexual offenses, Teicher postulates that hippocampal alterations, reduced corpus collosum size, and diminished left–right hemisphere integration may augment the individual's capacity to shift into angry/aggressives states when threatened with danger or loss (Teicher et al., 2002, p. 414). He also notes that early stress can produce lifelong changes in the hormones vasopressin and oxytocin. Research has suggested that oxytocin is a critical factor in affiliative love and normal nonsexual social interactions (Carter, 1998; Uvnas-Moberg, 1998). "Theoretically, early neglect or abuse by altering levels of vasopressin and oxytocin could predispose mammals to suffer from enhanced sexual arousal, diminished capacity at sexual fulfillment, and deficient commitment to a single partner" (Teicher et al., 2002, p. 415).

Trauma and stress can affect the adaptive developmental path along which the brain organizes itself. The timing and persistence of the trauma in terms of when it occurs in the child's life combined with the environmental response to the child during times of stress, most notably by the child's primary caretakers, will greatly influence the structural and functional nature of those pathways. As a consequence, the degree of symptomatology, the level of impairment, and the pervasiveness of maladaptive behaviors are likely to be varied and complex.

ATTACHMENT THEORY

In his early formulation of attachment theory, Bowlby (1969) initially described an evolved behavioral process by which the attached person sought out a potentially protective attachment figure during periods of danger or threat. The primary goal of attachment was seen as being protection and safety. In infancy, these protective figures are identified as being the child's primary caretakers, most frequently the parents and in most attachment research specifically the child's mother. Further still, Bowlby integrates information processing with attachment theory, focusing on patterns of perceiving, representing, and using information, especially when that information is tied to danger (Bowlby, 1980; Crittenden, 1997). Bowlby expanded and refined attachment theory to include developmental processes that culminate in adaptive or mal-adaptive functioning. Bowlby believes that the child's experience of these early care-taking relationships results in the individual developing an "internal working model" or a framework for experiencing oneself in relation to others and that this "working model" is largely sustained throughout the individual's life.

Observing toddlers and their mothers in a laboratory experience described as "the Strange Situation," Ainsworth, Blehar, Waters, and Wall (1978) began to identify distinct attachment patterns, generally defined as secure, avoidant, ambivalent, and disorganized. Secure behavior was associated with a history of responsive and nurturing caretaking by the parent. The child experiences the parent as consistently and predictably available to meet both physical and emotional needs. Behaviorally, these children are emotionally and cognitively engaged, using their parent as a secure base from which to explore their environment. *Avoidant* behavior was associated with a history of rejection, neglect, or emotional distance by the caretaker. The child experiences the parent as emotionally unavailable or rigid. Behaviorally, these children frequently present with a blunted or flattened affect or are rigidly responsive to the specific expectations and demands of the environment. *Ambivalent* behavior was associated with a history of inconsistency by the parent. Behaviorally, these children frequently present as clingy, tense, and angry and with greater difficulties around impulse control. Main and Solomon (1990) later described a fourth category of attachment as disorganized. *Disorganized* behavior was associated with a parent's history of loss or severe trauma and has been found to predominate in children with a history of abuse, neglect, and family chaos. Behaviorally, these children present with contradictory approach/avoidance behavior associated with frightening or frightened behavior by the parent (Alexander & Anderson, 1997).

ATTACHMENT AND NEURODEVELOPMENT

Attachment Patterns

Patricia Crittenden (1997) argues that the infant attachment patterns identified by Ainsworth et al. (1978) are reflected in identifiable patterns of mental processing. Crittenden proposes a model for understanding attachment that incorporates neuro-processing with observations of affect and behavior. She would define secure attachment as the ability to effectively integrate the subcortical (limbic and lower brain) emotional responses to environmental stimuli with accurate cognitive transformation and discrimination of those emotions regarding their meaning. Secure attachment styles of processing information are likely to yield greater specificity in terms of responses to complex situations as well as greater flexibility in the individual's capacity to adapt behavioral responses to changing environmental cues.

Avoidant attachment styles are likely to have developed cortical pathways that may "overmodulate" limbic and lower brain input, creating a limited and often rigid cognitive transformation of emotional stimuli. Cognitive representations of emotions are less specific, less flexible, and less responsive to context. Ambivalent attachment styles correspond to the development of cortical pathways that "undermodulate" affect-related behavior. These pathways may respond more quickly and with greater intensity to a broad range of fear-eliciting stimuli. These responses bypass the cortex, leading to less discriminatory inhibition of behavioral responses and, as with the avoidant style, less specificity and flexibility in response to context. Initially for the child, these processing and behavioral patterns may have led to the development of successful strategies for effectively identifying and avoiding/decreasing/resolving dangerous conditions. However, as noted in the previous section, cognitive attributions that may have been accurate and responses that may have been protective in the context in which they were first learned may prove to be erroneous, maladaptive, and even dangerous when applied in a different context. Attachment patterns that cannot effectively integrate affective responses from the limbic system and lower brain with appropriate levels of modulation and adaptation from the cortex create obstacles for individuals in recognizing and/or adapting to those changes in context. Crittenden's proposal is especially important when viewed in the context of Teicher et al.'s (2002) findings that trauma experiences have a significant impact on the level of neural integration in the brain. One of the ramifications of trauma may be the development of neurological obstacles to developing secure attachment relationships.

Ability to Regulate Emotional Responses

Studies have shown that the ability to regulate emotional responses is an important aspect of effective peer interactions; successful cognitive performance in tasks involving delay, inhibition, or pursuit of long-term goals; and the management of stress at home (Galderisi & Mucci, 2000; Cummings, Vogel, & Cummings, 1989; Rubin & Rose-Krasnor, 1986; Mischel & Mischel, 1983). Rather than simply being a manifestation of the child's innate temperament, more recent studies suggest that emotional reactivity (what clinicians might typically see described as impulsive, explosive, tantruming, or intensely avoidant behaviors) results from an interaction of genetic and environmental influences. Primary among these environmental influences are the quality and nature of parental care (Galderisi & Mucci, 2000). Seigel (1999) argues that emotion is a central organizing process within the brain and that from the infant's perspective the most important aspect of the environment is the infant's emotional connection with caregiver.

Developmental Variables

Given that the period of helplessness and dependency is far longer for humans than for other species, developing a process for engaging the attention and responsiveness of a caregiver is an essential factor in childhood survival. This capacity to engage and maintain the involvement of a caregiver is the fundamental dynamic of attachment and defines in large part the experience-dependent environment in which neural stimulation, growth, and connectedness will occur. Because brain development is geared to progress from lower to higher degrees of complexity and organization, the activity-dependent shaping of brain circuitry through changes in synaptic connections is more prominent during different developmental periods and is different for different circuits and areas of the brain (Greenough, Black, & Wallace, 1987; Gottlieb, 1992; Galderisi & Mucci, 2000). This reinforces our view that it is not simply the presence or absence of severe stressors or trauma in an individual's history that might affect emotional or behavioral control but also the developmental stage when the trauma occurs, the persistence of the stressors, and a variety of other variables that define the environmental context in which the trauma occurs that will affect outcome. Again, from an attachment perspective, the most notable of these variables in the individual's early life will be the nature and quality of his or her attachment relationships.

The orbitofrontal cortex is seen as essential for regulating primary sensory and motor responses and critical periods for its development appear to occur at the end of the first and second years (Schore, 2000; Todd et al., 1995; Huttenlocher, 1979). Schore (2002) writes that the orbitofrontal cortex is highly involved in homeostatic regulation and attachment functions, playing an essential role in processing the interpersonal signals necessary for the initiation of social interaction between individuals. It is a part of the neural network that mediates empathic and emotional relatedness (Balbernie, 2001). When neurodevelopmental researchers and writers discuss the individual's capacity for transforming or regulating subcortical stimuli for the purpose of a more specified or flexible cognitive-behavioral response or when we later discuss the individual's *executive functioning* skills, it is largely functions centered in the orbitofrontal or prefrontal cortex to which they are referring.

The limbic system (containing the hypothalamus, hippocampus, and amygdala along with the temporal lobes) is primarily responsible for controlling emotions, appraising the value of stimuli, and processessing new information in the service of survival. Through its connection with the limbic system the orbitofrontal cortex monitors the state of the body, evaluates meaning, and translates sensations into recognizable emotions (Balbernie, 2001). Seigel describes *attunement* between the infant and caretaker as a way in which the caretaker initially serves as an affect regulator, an "auxiliary cortex" for the infant's still underdeveloped brain (Lott, 2003). Schore (1997) identifies these attunement experiences as being essential for the synaptic development of the orbitofrontal cortex and suggests that they serve as a template for processing emotional information. He also contends that abuse, neglect, and chronic states of misattunement lead to an overpruning of synapses in the orbitofrontal cortex, leaving individuals with an impaired capacity to modulate and regulate emotion in response to threat (Lott, 2003).

The brain is setting up synaptic connections in an activity-dependent manner. If specific brain structures are being regularly activated by abuse and other forms of trauma, then those circuits are the ones which are more firmly programmed and easily activated. The amygdala, which sends projections to all areas of the cortex, establishes an emotional bias to cognitive functions. That is, higher-intensity environmental stimuli identified as indicative of reduced safety (or increased sexual arousal) are given privileged attention (Le Doux, 1995; Crittenden, 1997). If threat and trauma persist, the brainstem and midbrain become undermodulated and the neurobiological responses to trauma (fear/flight, freeze) become established with little influence from cortical control (Balbernie, 2001).

Appropriately integrated levels of cortical control, primarily centered in the frontal cortex, can therefore be seen as essential for establishing arousal and impulse control, attunement, empathy, and a recognition of the impact and consequences of one's behavior. One might argue that these are exactly those issues that we attempt to address in our treatment of sexual behavior problems.

TRAUMA, ATTACHMENT, AND SEXUAL BEHAVIOR PROBLEMS

A variety of factors have been suggested as being contributory or causal in explaining the origins of sexually abusive behavior (Schwartz, 1995). Although a number of these factors have changed in focus or importance over time, certain variables appear to persist as being essential to our understanding of the etiology of sexual offending. I would contend that these persistent variables are (1) the presence, in childhood, of some type of trauma—if we define trauma to include not only incidents of physical and sexual abuse but also neglect, abandonment, witnessing domestic violence, and other experiences that the child may view as life threatening (McMackin, Leisen, Cusack, LaFratta, & Litwin, 2002; Leguizamo, 2002; Prentky et al., 1989); and (2) the deficits abusers appear to experience in intimacy, social competency, and empathy which from our perspective are best understood as problems offenders experience in their attachment relationships (Lisak & Ivan, 1995; Hudson & Ward, 2000; Marshall & Marshall, 2000; Burk & Burkhart, 2003).

Much of the research on the trauma histories of offenders appears to be either explicitly or implicitly driven by a social learning theory of sexual offending (Ryan, 1989; Garland & Dougher, 1990; Burton, Miller, & Shill, 2002). While this research provides evidence for a correlation between histories of sexual victimization and later sexual offending behaviors, these studies do not account for the majority of sexual abuse victims who do not go on to sexually offend, or for those offenders who experience trauma other than sexual abuse but go on to be sexually abusive. In addition, these studies frequently identify individuals who engage in sexually abusive behavior but have no reported history of prior trauma, though in these cases one might examine how broadly or narrowly the researchers and/or subjects are defining the terms abuse and trauma.

Marshall and Marshall (2000) suggest that the origins of sexual offending behavior are found in the poor attachment relationships offenders experience with their parents. They postulate that these poor relationships increased the risk of the offenders being sexually abused and led to offenders being more sexually preoccupied, less self-confident in relationships, and more likely to use sexualized behaviors as a preferred coping mechanism to manage stress in their lives. Marshall and Marshall highlight the importance of attachment in their model, with disrupted attachment providing the framework for the social learning process which ensues after victimization. While providing safety to the child is a fundamental function of early attachment relationships, the impact of poor attachment as described by Marshall and Marshall appears to identify only one of the pathways to sexual offending behavior in which disrupted or insecure attachment may play a part.

Along with maintaining proximity to a secure and trusted figure during periods of perceived danger and stress, developing and sustaining secure attachment relationships has been noted as increasing feelings of security, mastery, self-esteem, and social competence. In contrast, the loss, inconsistency, or unavailability of secure attachment can lead to sorrow, anxiety, anger, and confusion (Bowlby, 1969; Bowlby, 1980). Without specifically defining it as attachment, Baumeister and Leary (1995) write that the need for intimacy and connection is as fundamental a human need as food and sex. As noted earlier, one could argue that the need to develop attachment relationships is a biological imperative for humans, because the failure of a human infant to engage a caretaker, on at least a minimal level, would threaten the infant's existence. It is important to note that experiences that are perceived as a threat to one's life or sense of personal integrity are the very definition of trauma. This leads to our belief that sexually abusive behavior arises in large part from a fundamental need for attachment (safety, attunement, nurturance, acceptance, care) and that it is the process that some individuals follow to meet this need that can become distorted and abusive. To understand abusive behavior we need to view it in the context of attachment and relationship and to appreciate the anxiety that gets elicited when attachment is lacking or lost. To understand how the process becomes distorted we need to at least begin with an understanding of the neurological impact of trauma and disrupted attachment.

Hudson and Ward (2000) contend that the difficulties offenders experience in intimacy, empathy, social skills, and cognitive distortions can be understood as the consequences of their poor attachment relationships. This view is consistent with research by Webster and Beech (2000) and Fernandez and Marshall (2003) which has suggested that what was previously defined as a lack of empathy in offenders might more accurately be viewed as a lack of integration between affective and cognitive responses in the offender (cognitive distortions) rather than a broader inability to be emotionally responsive to others. Marsa et al. (2004) found that 93 percent of the sexual offenders in their study evidenced an insecure attachment style and that secure attachment was less common in the sex offender group than in any of the other three groups studied (violent, non-sex offenders; nonviolent, non-sex offenders, and community controls). Wahlberg, Kennedy, and Simpson (2003) in studying adolescent sexual offenders suggested that impairment in sensory-emotional integration contributed to a greater likelihood of violent behavior in their sample. This lack of integration is also what Crittenden (1997) described in her discussion of neuroprocessing patterns associated with insecure attachment styles. Galski et al. (1990) linked both violent and nonviolent manifestations of disordered sexuality to a wide range of deficits in brain functioning. When comparing the quantitative electroencephalograms (QEEG) of non-sex-offending and sex-offending subjects, Corely et al. (1994) specifically identified EEG abnormalities in the left hemisphere of the sex offender sample. These findings are consistent with Teicher et al.'s (2002) findings of a lack of differentiation and development in the left hemisphere of his trauma victims. Raine and Buchsbaum (1996) reviewed fourteen brain imaging studies indicating that frontal to temporal lobe dysfunction appears to be related to violence and sexual offending behavior, with frontal lobe dysfunction more closely related to violence while temporal lobe dysfunction was more aligned with sexual offending behavior. Gillespie and McKenzie (2000) found evidence suggesting left frontotemporal dysfunction in their mentally disorder sex offender sample when compared to a mentally disordered, non-sex offender sample. Environmental stimuli associated with threat and/or sexuality may be processed by the cortex in an overmodulated or undermodulated manner creating either distorted and rigid cognitive representations or more impulsive, subcortical responses with little (if any) cortical control. If the experiential features of the stimuli associated with threat and sexuality have considerable overlap, it would appear to create even greater possibilities for misrepresentation, distortion, and faulty learning.

VERBAL DEFICITS, EXECUTIVE FUNCTIONING, AND BEHAVIORAL PROBLEMS

Research has for some time indicated the impact of abuse and neglect on cognitive functioning (Martin, Beezley, & Conway, 1974; Hoffman-Plotkin & Twentyman, 1984; Cahill, Kaminer, & Johnson, 1999). Frequently, language delays and language processing difficulties have been specifically identified as an important aspect of the cognitive sequelae of child maltreatment (Fox, Long, & Langlois, 1988; Rogeness et al., 1986; Culp, Watkins, & Lawrence, 1991). These cognitive difficulties have also been correlated with increased behavioral problems in school (Hoffman-Plotkin & Twentyman, 1984; Wodarski, Kurtz, & Gaudin, 1990; Kendall-Tackett & Eckenrode, 1996), and in behavioral terms differences begin to appear in the behavioral problems exhibited by children who suffer physical/sexual abuse and those who are more generally neglected (Hoffman-Plotkin & Twentyman, 1984; Wodarski et al., 1990).

Neuropsychological deficits have also been identified in a number of studies involving delinquent youth (Morgan & Lilienfield, 2000; Teichner & Golden, 2000; Aguilar, Sroufe, Egeland, & Carlson, 2000; Moffitt, 1993, 1997). Particularly, verbal abilities appear to be affected in adolescents identified as antisocial or delinquent, with delinquent youth frequently showing significantly lower Verbal IQs than Performance IQs on standardized tests of cognitive abilities (Hirischi & Hindelang, 1977; Bleker, 1983; Grace & Sweeney, 1986; Lynam, Moffitt, & Stouthamer-Loeber, 1993; Teichner & Golden, 2000; Teichner et al., 2000). Murray et al. (2001) found that lower Verbal IQ scores distinguished sex offenders with learning disabilities from non-sex offenders with learning disabilities. These studies are consistent with the findings of Teicher et al. (2002), noted earlier, indicating a lack of right/left hemisphere integration as well as changes in the hippocampus of trauma victims which produce difficulties in verbal learning and verbal memory.

In addition to verbal deficits, delinquent youth are frequently identified as having difficulties in executive functioning. Executive functioning relates to a variety of brain functions that support effective learning and problem solving. These functions include attention; concentration; anticipation; planning; abstract reasoning and concept formation; cognitive flexibility; and the ability to control impulsive, unsuccessful, and inappropriate behavior. A recent review of the literature by Morgan and Lilienfield (2000) indicates that antisocial groups performed significantly lower than comparison groups on tests of executive functioning. Stone and Thompson (2001) specifically identified executive functioning difficulties in their testing of sixty-three sexual offenders, though they were quick to note that the type of executive functioning difficulty was individualized rather than specific to all the sex offenders. Most frequently, children with conduct disorders and adults with antisocial personality disorder have been identified as having prominent difficulties with attention and impulse control (Newman, 1987; Henry & Moffit, 1997; Teichner et al., 2000). Again, these findings parallel the neurological consequences that can result from early trauma, neglect, and attachment difficulties. As we discussed earlier, the lack of cortical and subcortical integration is likely to produce difficulties in modulating responses to environmental stimuli creating specific problems for individuals in attention and impulse control.

Conversely, overmodulation from the cortex, proposed by Crittenden (1997) as occurring in individuals with more avoidant attachment styles, is likely to limit cognitive flexibility and experience-based learning, and contribute to identified difficulties in performing complex auditory and visuospatial tasks.

ATTENTION DIFFICULTIES, PROCESSING, AND BEHAVIOR

Perhaps the neurological issue that has received the most attention from researchers in this area has been examining the correlation of ADHD and adolescent and adult antisocial behavior (Biederman, Newcorn, & Sprich, 1991; Klein & Manuzza, 1991; Lynam, 1996; Kafka & Prentky, 1998; Fago, 2003). Earlier in this chapter we noted the argument of Perry (1997) and Pynoos (1990) that the symptoms in these individuals which are frequently identified as indicative of ADHD are instead attentional problems generated by the trauma victims' hypervigilant scanning of the environment for threat cues or their ignoring of other stimulus as "unimportant" when it is not associated with threat. An additional or contributing factor for some individuals may be their difficulties with auditory and visuospatial processing. In particular environments, most notably school settings, where the demands for processing language and visual input are especially high, individuals who process language slowly or inaccurately, and individuals who have difficulties with visuospatial organization, may find themselves quickly overwhelmed and/or frustrated by these demands. For many of these individuals, the manifestations of ADHD symptoms are likely to appear (e.g. inattentive, disorganized, cannot finish tasks, loses things, and fidgety). Along with the obvious problems these difficulties create in academic and job performance, the additional consequences with regard to self-esteem, social acceptance, and impulsive behaviors generate a significant number of risk factors for engaging in delinquent or antisocial behavior. In addition to distinguishing between delinquent and nondelinquent groups, Vermeiren, De Clippele, Schwab-Stone, Ruchkin, and Deboutte (2002) have presented data to suggest that comparing overall IQ, verbal abilities, and executive functioning skills may also help distinguish different levels of recidivism risk among delinquent populations. Deckel, Hesselbrock, and Bauer (1996) found evidence suggesting that disturbances in executive functioning are associated with a diagnosis of antisocial personality disorder and a history of childhood behavior problems in young adults.

Despite the research indicating that language skills and executive functioning should be important considerations in deciding on treatment placement, treatment priorities, treatment style, and the evaluation of ongoing risk, attention to auditory processing, expressive/receptive language difficulties, and executive functioning deficits is rarely evident in the assessment protocols, treatment planning, or risk assessment discussions for adults, adolescents, or children. Of equal concern is the apparent lack of focus on presenting or developing treatment interventions that might effectively teach clients how to address, manage, or contain these issues even when some productive interventions might already be available through collaboration with speech and language educators, occupational therapists, developmental psychologists, and neuropsychologists.

IMPLICATIONS FOR ASSESSMENT AND TREATMENT

There appears to be sufficient research to indicate that our clinical perspective with regard to sexually inappropriate and abusive behavior needs to be significantly broadened to include developmental and neurological factors as primary components in our assessment and treatment (Fago, 2003; Ryan, 1999; Raine & Buchsbaum, 1996). If we accept the fact that the vast majority of our clients come into treatment with significant trauma histories and/or attachment difficulties, then an assessment protocol and treatment model that does not address these issues and their neurological consequences seems inadequate for meeting the needs of this population. There is reason to believe that the current focus on a cognitive-behavioral, relapse prevention model that is primarily presented in a language-based modality largely ignores the type of neuroprocessing obstacles that might make it difficult for many of our clients to learn, remember, and retrieve useful information and skills necessary to avoid or prevent further abusive behavior. With these concerns in mind it would seem imperative that we evaluate our current assessment and treatment protocols to ensure that they are keeping pace with current neurodevelopmental research.

Need for Multimodal Assessment

Cognitive Functioning. While current standards of care indicate the need to take into account the client's cognitive functioning, the actual assessment of cognitive skills in most adult evaluations for outpatient treatment either is limited to a standard IQ test or in many cases is based on the clinician's perception of how articulate or "bright" the client may be. Frequently, unless the client presents with a clear history of being developmentally disabled or with recent IQ testing that places him or her within (or very close to) the diagnostic range for mental retardation (Full Scale IQ below 70), significant changes or adaptations in treatment expectations, treatment modality, and assessment/treatment materials are not made. While knowing a client's Full Scale IQ is useful, it does not offer an adequate assessment of the client's cognitive functioning for the purpose of making specific recommendations for forensic settings or for future treatment planning. At the very least, attention should be paid to significant differences in Verbal and Performance abilities on cognitive testing. Ideally, further information should be gathered on the client's abilities in verbal memory, auditory processing, and visual organization/processing skills, and executive functioning. Specific inquiry into past diagnosis of learning disabilities, especially in the area of receptive/expressive language disorders, would also be pertinent to the client's capacity to participate in court-related matters as well as any future treatment.

While this information may already be available for many of the school-age children and adolescents we treat, it is frequently seen as being relevant only to the client's academic performance rather than being an indication of persistent obstacles the client experiences with regard to daily behavioral control, compliance, social relationships, and the learning of everyday life skills. For adults, information regarding cognitive functioning is less readily available; therefore, unless we include these areas as part of our assessment protocols, it is unlikely that we will garner specific information from other sources. As part of our assessment of the client's cognitive abilities, the research would suggest the utility of, at least, a broad assessment of the client's executive functioning skills. Executive functioning skills might be seen as including areas such as concentration, planning, impulse control, attention, working memory, and cognitive flexibility. Without these skills the client's capacity to effectively learn and use information presented in a treatment setting, especially in group treatment, may be severely hampered. There is also some research which suggests that differences in executive functioning skills and autonomic arousal levels might distinguish different types of sociopathy and different styles of attachment (Crittenden, 1997; Lynam,1996; Deckel et al., 1996; Raine & Buchsbaum, 1996).

Current Trauma Symptomatology. Given the ongoing impact that trauma can have on overall physiological arousal, cognitive functioning, and social functioning, some assessment of a client's current trauma symptomatology would appear to be an important aspect of a broadly based multimodal evaluation. At present, the assessment of trauma symptoms does not appear to be a regular aspect of the assessment process for most evaluators or treatment providers. Trauma symptom assessment is currently not suggested or even mentioned in the *Practice Standards and Guidelines* of the Association for the Treatment of Sexual Abusers (2003). A variety of self-report measures of current trauma symptoms exist that could be easily included into current assessment protocols.

Attachment Style. Assessment of attachment style creates a greater dilemma for the evaluator. Current measures of attachment style are either quite broad (Bartholomew & Horowitz, 1991) or, like the Adult Attachment Interview (Main & Goldwyn, 1994), not readily transferable to more typical clinical settings. Nonetheless, a broader knowledge of attachment theory and styles might be useful in examining offender dynamics, treatment issues, and ongoing risk (Ward, Hudson, & McCormack, 1997; Smallbone & Dadds, 2000).

Assessment Instruments

There are a variety of assessment instruments that might be used for each of the aforementioned assessment areas. Decisions regarding the purpose of the evaluation, clinical setting, age of the client, administration time, scoring, and expense will all be important factors in determining what a particular assessment protocol might contain. However, I believe that information regarding a client's current experience of trauma symptoms, a broad assessment of attachment style, and at least a screening for information processing and executive functioning strengths and deficits should become a standard part of every assessment. In some cases, initial screening for neurological and processing difficulties indicates the need for a full neuropsychological battery, but it is unreasonable and unnecessary that a full neuropsychological battery be completed as a matter of course. Several possible assessment tools might be easily incorporated into a regular assessment protocol:

- *Cognitive functioning.* Wechsler Intelligence Scale for Children (WISC-III; Wechsler, 1991b); Wechsler Adult Intelligence Scale (WAIS; Wechsler,

1981); Wide Range Assessment of Memory and Learning, 2nd Edition (WRAML2; Sheslow, & Adams, 1990); Test of Memory and Learning (TOMAL; Reynolds & Bigler, 1998).

- *Trauma symptoms.* Trauma Symptom Checklist for Children (TSCC; Briere, 1996); Trauma Symptom Inventory (TSI; Briere, 1995).

- *Executive functioning.* Wisconsin Card Sort-64 (Kongs, Thompson, Iverson & Heaton, 2000); Behavior Rating Inventory of Executive Functioning (BRIEF; Goia, Isquith, Guy, & Kenworthy, 2000).

- *Visual processing and organization.* Bender-Gestalt Test (Bender, 1938); Rey Complex Figure Test (RCFT; Meyers & Meyers, 1995).

- *Auditory processing.* SCAN-A (Keith, 1994).

- *Attachment style.* Relationship Style Questionnaire (RSQ; Griffith & Bartholomew, 1994).

The inclusion of assessment instruments that examine trauma symptoms, executive functioning, information processing, and attachment are not meant to replace current assessment measures that examine personality, cognitive distortions, sexual interests, or risk. Rather, this additional information should create a context in which to examine, analyze, and interpret the information that is already collected.

There do appear to be questions raised by the neurological research which specifically pertain to assessment instruments such as the plethysmograph, the Abel Screen, and the polygraph. The neurological research appears to indicate a broad level of subcortical arousal both in the amygdala and in the sympathetic nervous system as a consequence of early trauma and attachment experiences and that these individuals are likely to overinterpret a wide range of environmental cues as being threatening or trauma related (Teicher et al., 2002; Perry, 1997). When arousal is measured through penile erection, heart rate, galvanic skin response, or other physiological measures, the interpretation we make of what that arousal means and the conclusions we draw from those interpretations must account for what we have learned from the current state of trauma-related neurological research. It is not clear to me from reading the findings on either plethysmography or polygraphy that the role of trauma and the neurological/physiological impact of trauma are regularly accounted for or considered in interpreting these assessments. In addition, it is not clear whether the subcortical "freeze" response as a reaction to threatening or trauma-related cues has been considered a factor in determining increased viewing time on the Abel Screen. Research and protocols that take into account current neurological findings on the impact of trauma would appear to be an important area for inquiry and discussion when using these assessment instruments.

Treatment Considerations

Trauma-Focused Treatment. While there appears to be research indicating that the experience of early trauma and/or attachment difficulties contributes significantly to the etiology of sexually abusive behavior (Prentky, Knight, & Sims-Knight, 1989), frequently our treatment models fail to address either of these issues as treatment priorities. Many clinicians continue to believe that allowing clients to address their trauma history before completely addressing their abusive behavior somehow enables them to avoid responsibility for the harm they have caused others. This view would suggest that a client's trauma history and his or her abusive behavior are somehow distinct and separate issues. Clinicians who regularly treat trauma survivors would suggest that the experience of trauma and neglect, especially when that experience occurs early and frequently throughout life, can have a significant impact on important aspects of an individual's cognitive, emotional, and social functioning throughout his or her life (Allen, 2001; Dutton & Holtzworth-Monroe, 1997; van der Kolk, McFarlane, & Weisaeth, 1996).

Phased Treatment. The literature that addresses the treatment of trauma has currently reached a consensus regarding the need for a phase-oriented treatment approach (Allen, 2001; Chu, 1992; Herman, 1992; van der Hart, van der Kolk, & Bion, 1998; van der Kolk, McFarlane, & van der Hart, 1996). Allen (2001) notes that "we must foster our client's capacity to work on the trauma before tackling traumatic memories" (p. 292), and this would generally suggest that supportive interventions precede expressive interventions. The term "phase-oriented treatment" does not suggest a rigid, cookbook-like, step-by-step approach. Rather it suggests a shift of focus over time based on client needs, support, tolerance, control, and motivation.

Van der Kolk et al. (1996) write that phase-oriented treatment should include the following:

• Stabilization, including (1) education and (2) identification of feelings through verbalizing somatic states;

• Deconditioning of traumatic memories and responses;

• Restructuring of traumatic personal schemes;

• Reestablishment of secure social connections and interpersonal efficacy; and

• Accumulation of restitutive emotional experiences.

These authors suggest that while some clients may be able to move quickly from one phase to the next, many others will require that the stabilization phase be repeated frequently.

The Importance of Containment. Allen (2001) takes the notion of stabilization and broadens this phase through the use of the term "containment." He proposes that containment be given priority in treating trauma and writes of how containment is gained through increasing the client's level of self-regulation, developing a structure for treatment, and developing and sustaining supportive relationships.

A focus on self-regulation appears especially important and problematic in light of the neurological impact of trauma which may lead to either increased levels of hyperarousal or more frequent triggering of dissociative states. Both of these responses lead to diminished capacities for self-regulation as both occur at a subcortical level and are not immediately accessible to more conscious coping responses. While treatment for sexual behavior problems has often focused on how to modulate sexual arousal to "deviant" or "risky" triggers or stimulus there seems to have been far less focus on helping clients regulate the full range of emotional/physiological responses or to understand how sexual arousal fits into the client's broader experiences of over-all physiological arousal or dysregulation. It would appear that the teaching and prac-tice of skills to increase overall self-regulation might be considered a regular aspect of treating sexual behavior problems. A range of techniques, including but not limited to neurofeedback, yoga, tai-chi, music therapies, and more traditional deep breathing and progressive muscle relaxation techniques, might be effectively adapted for use in both an individual and group treatment approach.

While previously treatment for trauma victims had a more exploratory and expres-sive focus that either implicitly or explicitly encouraged clients to "dredge up" their previous traumatic experiences and "get it all out," a shift has occurred over the past decade that recognizes that an emphasis on exploration and expressiveness without adequate support, structure, and containment not only can be unproductive but can actually lead to deterioration in the client. The abuser field, with a focus on taking responsibility and holding the abuser accountable, has typically required abusers to provide detailed and repeated accounts of their offenses. When abusers avoided reporting particular offenses, fantasies, or details, these individuals were viewed as being avoidant, deceptive, and resistant to treatment. An alternative explanation could be that some clients' sexually abusive behavior is closely intertwined with their trau-ma histories and that discussing their offenses triggers both traumatic memories and intense affect that they have difficulty regulating or that the impact which trauma has on memory may make memory retrieval (especially for traumatic events) particularly difficult for some clients.

Understanding the Processing of Trauma. Foa (1997) identified three essential components for processing traumatic experiences: (1) engaging emotionally with the traumatic memories, (2) organizing a coherent narrative of the trauma, and (3) modi-fying core beliefs about the self and the world. In treating sexual behavior problems, we feel that this process is essential in addressing the client's own traumatic experi-ences and in addressing the client's abusive behavior toward others. While this process may appear obvious when addressing the individual's own trauma history, it may not be as clear when addressing abusive behavior. In treating abusers, clinicians are regu-larly confronted with individuals who engage in denial, avoidance, and cognitive dis-tortions or thinking errors in relation to the specifics of their abusive behavior. All these cognitive processes can be broadly thought of as avoidant coping responses. Generally, these cognitive processes are confronted by the therapist and/or the treat-ment group, often on a repeated basis, until the individual stops his or her expression of these cognitions. Quite frequently, we experience clients in treatment groups who learn to say the right thing but never integrate these cognitive lessons into their rela-tional behavior or belief systems.

Allen (2001) points out that avoidance is problematic in that it blocks more effec-tive coping responses but that avoidance of distress is generally adaptive. Our clients frequently have a great deal of embarrassment, shame, and negative self-beliefs con-nected to their abusive behaviors. In turn, their abusive behaviors often are connected to their own trauma histories through anxiety, fear, abandonment, anger, and other difficult (frequently overwhelming) affective states. In the same way that clients can develop a new narrative for how they think and feel about their own trauma, we want them to develop a new narrative about their abusive behavior. This new narrative seeks to emphasize taking responsibility for the abusive behavior, not as a means of blaming but as a foundation for new, nonabusive coping responses. The narrative seeks to include empathy for the victim as well as compassion for the self. The client may, in fact, experience a great deal of guilt while going through the process of developing this new narrative, and that is appropriate and generally productive. As treatment providers, we should be seeking to diminish or eliminate feelings of shame, which typically block adaptive change and are therefore unproductive. The goal is that clients will actively engage in changing how they participate in current relationships and also consider the possibilities for active restitution for past abusive behaviors.

As a prelude to this phase of treatment or perhaps as a bridge between deconditioning traumatic responses and restructuring the narrative, specific treatment techniques such as eye movement densensitization and reprocessing (EMDR) (Shapiro, 1995) and sensorimotor psychotherapy (Ogden & Minton, 2000) may prove to be useful in bringing physiological and affective states into conscious awareness where they can be identified and more effectively regulated.

Integration. It is during this restructuring phase of treatment that the more widely used cognitive-behavioral and cognitive restructuring techniques (Resick & Schnicke, 1992; Meichenbaum, 1994; Pithers, 1990) may prove to be more effective. However, even at this phase of treatment, the neurological research suggests that these techniques should be adapted so that multimodal treatment interventions (music, movement, art, psychodrama, etc.) are used. Given the language processing and verbal memory deficits in this population, the need for multimodal assessment and treatment interventions that are less loaded to receptive and expressive learning is perhaps the most obvious change we can make in our treatment with these clients. The greater the variety of ways in which we can help individuals learn and integrate new information and experiences, the greater the possibility that they can access and use this information when triggered by traumatic cues.

Given the broad range of trauma experiences in our clients' backgrounds, we may be able to learn from the neurological research and trauma-focused treatment approaches to adapt our treatment model and interventions to the particular presenting issues and treatment needs of our population.

CONCLUSION

The current level of research on neurological development and neurological functioning indicates that our understanding of brain structure and function will continue to grow at a steady rate over the coming years. The findings from this research are already beginning to have an impact on our understanding of issues such as criminal culpability for adolescents, the etiology of aggressive behavior, and the differences individuals evidence in how they perceive and learn. While specific research on populations with sexual offending issues is still relatively new, the increased understanding about the neurological impact of trauma on development, learning, and behavior certainly addresses many of the issues our clients present in treatment. In fact, it is the neurological research's capacity for explaining some of our most difficult treatment problems such as cognitive distortions, persistent negative behavior despite ever increasing negative consequences, the inability to accurately read and respond to social cues, and difficulties in effectively regulating affective responses that make it so compelling. The result is not to supplant our current level of understanding and intervention but to enhance, augment, and complement our theoretical models and treatment interventions.

The concern is that for years we have had research that has suggested language and other learning difficulties in some portion of the sexual offender population and yet we have done little to adapt our assessment protocols or treatment interventions. We have also had a wide range of research and clinical interventions available from the trauma field and other clinical populations, to which we have paid relatively little attention despite the obvious overlap in our client populations. An unwillingness to examine and use the information gained from present and future brain-based research would be a disservice not only to our clients but to the community at large. Recently, there appears to be a move toward considering a more "developmental" or "holistic" approach to understanding and treating sexual behavior problems. Increasing our understanding of neurodevelopment and neurological processing and incorporating this understanding into our theory and treatment of sexually abusive behavior would appear to be an important and necessary step toward that goal.

References

Aguilar, B., Sroufe, L. A., Egeland, B., & Carlson, E. (2000). Distinguishing the early onset/persistent and adolescence-onset antisocial behavior types: From birth to 16 years. *Development and Psychopathology, 12,* 109–132.

Ainsworth, M. D. S., Blehar, M. C., Waters, E., & Wall, S. (1978). *Patterns of attachment: A psychological study of the strange situation.* Hillsdale, NJ: Erlbaum.

Alexander, P. C., & Anderson, C. L. (1997). Incest, attachment, and developmental psychopathology. In D. Cicchetti & S. Toth (Eds.), *Rochester Symposium on Developmental Psychopathology* (Vol. 8, pp. 343–377). Rochester, NY: University of Rochester Press.

Allen, J. G. (2001). *Traumatic relationships and serious mental disorders.* New York: Wiley.

Anand, A. & Shekhar, A. (2003). Brain imaging studies in mood and anxiety disorders. *Annals of the New York Academy of Sciences, 985,* 370–388.

Association for the Treatment of Sexual Abusers. (2003). *Practice standards and guidelines.* Beaverton, OR: Author.

Balbernie, R. (2001). Circuits and circumstances: The neurobiological consequences of early relationship experiences and how they shape later behaviour. *Journal of Child Psychotherapy, 27*(3), 237–255.

Bartholomew, K., & Horowitz, L. (1991). Attachment styles among adults: A test of a four category model. *Journal of Personality and Social Psychology, 61,* 226–244.

Baumeister, R. F., & Leary, M. R. (1995). The need to belong: Desire for interpersonal attachments as a fundamental human motivation. *Psychological Bulletin, 117,* 497–529.

Bender, L. (1938). *A visual motor test and its clinical use.* New York: American Orthopsychiatric Association.

Biederman, J., Newcorn, J., & Sprich, S. (1991). Comorbidity of attention deficit hyperactivity with conduct, depressive, anxiety, and other disorders. *American Journal of Psychiatry, 148,* 564–577.

Bleker, E. G. (1983). Cognitive defense style and WISC-R P>V sign in juvenile recidivists. *Journal of Clinical Psychology, 39,* 1030–1032.

Bowlby, J. (1969). *Attachment and loss. Volume I: Attachment.* New York: Basic Books.

Bowlby, J. (1973). *Attachment and loss. Volume II: Separation: Anxiety and anger.* New York: Basic Books.

Bowlby, J. (1980). *Attachment and loss. Volume III.* New York: Basic Books

Bremner, J. D. (2002). *Does stress damage the brain?* New York: Norton

Bremner, J. D., & Narayan, M. (1998). The effects of stress on memory and the hippocampus throughout the life cycle: Implication for childhood development and aging, *Development and Psychopathology, 10,* 871–888.

Bremner, J. D., Randall, P., Vermetten, E., Staib, L., Bronen, R., Capelli, S., et al. (1997). MRI based measurement of hippocampal volume in posttraumatic stress disorder related to childhood physical and sexual abuse: A preliminary report. *Biological Psychiatry, 41,* 23–32.

Briere, J. (1995). *Trauma Symptom Inventory.* Odessa, FL: Psychological Assessment Resources.

Briere, J. (1996). *Trauma Symptom Checklist for Children.* Odessa, FL: Psychological Assessment Resources.

Burk, L., & Burkhart, B. (2003). Disorganized attachment as a diathesis for sexual deviance: Developmental experience and the motivation for sexual offending. *Aggression and Violent Behavior, 8*(5), 487–511.

Burton, D., Miller, D., & Shill, C. (2002). A social learning theory comparison of the sexual victimization of adolescent sexual offenders and nonsexual offending male delinquents. *Child Abuse and Neglect, 26,* 893–907.

Cahill, L., Kaminer, R., & Johnson, P. (1999). Developmental, cognitive, and behavioral sequelae of child abuse. *Child and Adolescent Psychiatric Clinics of North America, 8*(4), 827–843.

Cannon, W. B. (1927). The James-Lange theory of emotions: A critical reappraisal and an alternative theory. *American Journal of Psychology, 39,* 106–124.

Carter, C. S. (1998). Neuroendocrine perspectives on social attachment and love. *Psychoneuroendocrinology, 23,* 779–818.

Chu, J. A. (1992). The therapeutic roller coaster: Dilemmas in the treatment of childhood abuse survivors. *Journal of Psychotherapy: Practice and Research, 1,* 351–370.

Corley, A., Corley, M. D., Walker, J., & Walker, S. (1994). The possibility of organic left posterior hemisphere dysfunction as a contributing factor in sex offending behavior. *Sexual Addiction and Compulsivity, 1,* 337–346.

Crittenden, P. M. (1997). Toward an Integrative Theory of Trauma: A Dynamic-Maturation Approach. In D. Cicchetti & S. Toth (Eds.), *Rochester Symposium on Developmental Psychopathology* (Vol. 8, pp. 33–84). Rochester, NY: University of Rochester Press.

Culp, R., Watkins, R., & Lawrence, H. (1991). Maltreated children's language and speech development: Abused, neglected and abused and neglected. *First Language, 11,* 377.

Cummings, E. M., Vogel, D., & Cummings, J. S. (1989). Children's responses to different forms of expression of anger between adults. *Child Development, 60,* 1392–1404.

DeBellis, M. D. (2001). Developmental traumatology: The psychobiological development of maltreated children and its implications for research, treatment, and policy. *Development and Psychopathology, 13,* 539–564.

Deckel, W., Hesselbrock, V., & Bauer, L. (1996). Antisocial personality disorder, childhood delinquency, and frontal brain functioning: EEG and neuropsychological findings. *Journal of Clinical Psychology, 52*(6), 639–650.

Dutton, D. & Holtzworth-Munroe, A. (1997). The role of early trauma in males who assault their wives. In D. Cicchetti & S. Toth (Eds.), *Rochester Symposium on Developmental Psychopathy* (Vol. 8, pp. 379–403). Rochester, NY: University of Rochester Press.

Fago, D. P. (2003). Evaluation and treatment of neurodevelopmental deficits in sexually aggressive children and adolescents. *Professional Psychology: Research and Practice, 34*(3), 248–257.

Fernandez, Y. M., & Marshall, W. L. (2003). Victim empathy, self-esteem, and psychopathy in rapists. *Sexual Abuse: A Journal of Research and Treatment, 15*(1), 11–26.

Foa, E. B. (1997). Psychological processes related to recovery from trauma and effective treatment of PTSD. In R. Yehuda & A. C. McFarlane (Eds.), *Psychobiology of posttraumatic stress disorder* (Vol. 823, pp. 410–424). New York: New York Academy of Sciences.

Fox, L., Long, S., & Langlois, A. (1988). Patterns of language comprehension deficit in abused and neglected children. *Journal of Speech and Hearing Disorders, 53*, 239.

Galderisi, S., & Mucci, A. (2000). Emotions, brain development, and psychopathology vulnerability. *CNS Spectrums, 5*(8), 44–48.

Gallistel, C., Brown, A., Carey, S., Gelman, R., & Keil, F. (1991). Lessons from animal learning for the study of cognitive development. In S. Carey & R. Gelman (Eds.), *The epigenesis of mind: Essays on biology and cognition* (pp. 3–36). Hillsdale, NJ: Erlbaum.

Galski, T., Thornton, K., & Shumsky, D. (1990). Brain dysfunction in sex offenders. *Journal of Offender Rehabilitation, 16*, 65–80.

Garland, R., & Dougher, M. (1990). The abused/abuser hypothesis of child sexual abuse: A critical review of theory and research, In J. Fierman (Ed.), *Pedophilia: Biosocial dimensions* (pp. 488–509). New York: Springer-Verlag.

Gillespie, N., & McKenzie, K. (2000). An examination of the role of neuropsychological deficits in mentally disordered sex offenders. *Journal of Sexual Aggression, 5*, 21–29.

Goia, G., Isquith, P., Guy, S., & Kenworthy, L. (2000). Behavior Rating Inventory of Executive Functioning. *Child Neuropsychology, 6*(3), 235–238.

Gottlieb, G. (1992). *Individual development and evolution: The genesis of novel behavior.* New York: Oxford University Press.

Grace, W. C., & Sweeney, M. E. (1986). Comparisons of P>V sign on the WISC-R and WAIS-R in delinquent males. *Journal of Clinical Psychology, 42*, 173–176.

Green, A., Voeller, K., & Gaines, R. (1981). Neurological impairment in maltreated children. *Child Abuse and Neglect, 5*, 129–134.

Greenough, W., Black, J., & Wallace, C. (1987). Experience and brain development. *Child Development, 64*, 1439–1450.

Griffith, D., & Bartholomew, K. (1994). Models of the self and other: Fundamental dimensions underlying measures of adult attachment. *Journal of Personality and Social Psychology, 67*(3), 430–445.

Haddad, P., & Garralda, M. (1992). Hyperkinetic syndrome and disruptive early experiences. *British Journal of Psychiatry, 161*, 700–703.

Henry, B, & Moffitt, T. E. (1997). Neuropsychological and neuroimaging studies of juvenile delinquency and adult criminal behavior. In D. Stoff, J. Breiling, & J. D. Maser (Eds.), *Handbook of antisocial behavior* (pp. 280–288). New York: Wiley.

Herman, J. (1992). *Trauma and recovery.* New York, Basic Books.

Hirischi, T., & Hindelang, M. (1977). Intelligence and delinquency: A revisionist review. *American Sociological Review, 42*, 571–587.

Hoffman-Plotkin, D., & Twentyman, C. (1984). A multimodal assessment of behavioral and cognitive deficits in abused and neglected pre-schoolers. *Child Development, 55*, 794.

Hudson, S. M., & Ward, T. (2000). Interpersonal competency in sex offenders. *Behavior Modification, 24*(4), 494–527.

Huttenlocher, P. (1979). Synaptic density in human frontal cortex: Developmental changes and the effects of aging. *Brain Research, 163*, 195–205.

Kafka, M. P., & Prentky, R. A. (1998). Attention deficit/hyperactivity disorder in males with paraphilias and paraphilia-related disorders: A comorbidity study. *Journal of Clinical Psychiatry, 59*, 388–396.

Keith, R. W. (1994). *SCAN-A: A test for auditory processing disorders in adolescents and adults.* San Antonio, TX: Psychological Corporation.

Kendall-Tackett, K. A., & Eckenrode, J. (1996). The effects of neglect on academic achievement and disciplinary problems: A developmental perspective. *Child Abuse and Neglect, 20*, 161.

Klein, S., & Manuzza, S. (1991). Long term outcome of hyperactive children: A review. *Journal of the American Academy of Child and Adolescent Psychiatry, 30*, 1120–1134.

Kongs, S., Thompson, L., Iverson, G., & Heaton, R. (2000). *Wisconsin Card Sorting Test–64 Card Version: Professional manual.* Odessa, FL: Psychological Assessment Resources.

Lang, P. (1995). The emotion probe: Studies in motivation and attention. *American Psychologist, 50,* 372–385.

Le Doux, J. E. (1994, June). Emotion, memory, and the brain: Neural routes underlying the formation of memories about primitive emotional experiences, such as fear, have been traced. *Scientific American,* pp. 50–57.

Le Doux, J. E. (1995). In search of an emotional system in the brain: Leaping from fear to emotion and consciousness. In M. Gazzaniga (Ed.), *The cognitive neurosciences* (pp. 1049–1061). Boston: MIT Press.

Leguizamo, A. (2002). The object relations and victimization histories of juvenile sex offenders. In B. K. Schwartz (Ed.), *The sex offender: Current treatment modalities and systems issues* (Vol. IV, pp. 4-1–4-40). Kingston, NJ: Civic Research Institute.

Lewis, D. O. (1992). From abuse to violence: psychophysiological consequences of maltreatment. *Journal of the American Academy of Child and Adolescent Psychiatry, 31,* 383–391.

Lisak, D., & Ivan, C. (1995). Deficits in intimacy and empathy in sexually aggressive men. *Journal of Interpersonal Violence, 10*(3), 296–308.

Loeber, R., Wung, P., Keenan, K., Giroux, B., Stouthamer-Loeber, M., Van Kammen, W., et al. (1993). Developmental pathways in disruptive child behavior. *Development and Psychopathology, 5,* 103–133.

Lott, D. (2003). Brain development, attachment and impact on psychic vulnerability. *Psychiatric Times, 15*(5), 1–5.

Lynam, D. (1996). Early identification of chronic offenders: Who is the fledgling psychopath? *Psychological Bulletin, 120,* 209–234.

Lynam, D., Moffitt, T., & Stouthamer-Loeber, M. (1993). Explaining the relation between IQ and delinquency: Class, race, test motivation, school failure or self-control? *Journal of Abnormal Psychology, 102,* 187–196.

MacEwen, K. (1994). Refining the intergenerational transmission hypothesis. *Journal of Interpersonal Violence, 9*(3), 350–365.

MacLean, P. D. (1949). Psychosomatic disease and the visceral brain. Recent developments bearing on the Papez Theory of Emotion. *Psychosomatic Medicine, 11,* 338–353.

MacLean, P. D. (1990). *The triune brain in evolution: Role in paleocerebral functions.* New York: Plenum Press.

Main, M., & Goldwyn, R. (1994). *Adult attachment scoring and classification systems.* Unpublished scoring manual. Berkeley: Department of Psychology, University of California, Berkeley.

Main, M., & Solomon, J. (1990). Procedures for identifying infants as disorganized/disoriented during the Ainsworth Strange Situation. In M. Greenberg, D. Cicchetti, & M. Cummings (Eds.), *Attachment in the preschool years: Theory, research, and intervention* (pp. 121–160). Chicago: University of Chicago Press.

Marsa, F., O'Reilly, G., Carr, A., Murphy, P., O'Sullivan, M., Cotter, A., et al. (2004). Attachment styles and psychological profiles of child sex offenders in Ireland. *Journal of Interpersonal Violence, 19,* 228–251.

Marshall, L. E., & Marshall, W. L. (2002). The role of attachment in sexual offending: An examination of pre-occupied attachment style offending behavior. In B. K. Schwartz (Ed.), *The sex offender: Current treatment modalities and systems issues* (Vol. IV, pp. 3-1–3-8). Kingston, NJ: Civic Research Institute.

Marshall, W. L., & Marshall, L. E. (2000). The origins of sexual offending. *Trauma, Violence, and Abuse, 1*(3), 250–263.

Martin, H.P., Beezley, P., Conway, E. (1974). The development of abused children: A review of the literature. *Advanced Pediatrics, 21,* 25.

McEwen, B.S. (2000). The neurobiology of stress: From serendipity to clinical relevance. *Brain Research. 886,* 172–179.

McFarlane, A., Weber, D., & Clark, C. (1993). Abnormal stimulus processing in posttraumatic stress disorder. *Biological Psychiatry*, 34, 311–320.

McHugh, S., Deacon, R., Rawlins, J., & Bannerman, D. (2004). Amygdala and ventral hippocampus contribute differentially to mechanisms of fear and anxiety. *Behavioral Neuroscience, 118*, 63–78.

McMackin, R. A., Leisen, M., Cusack, J. F., LaFratta, J., & Litwin, P. (2002). The relationship of trauma exposure to sex offending behavior among male juvenile offenders. *Journal of Child Sexual Abuse, 11*(2), 25–40.

Meichenbaum, D. (1994). *A clinical handbook/practical therapist manual for assessing and treating adults with posttraumatic stress disorder.* Waterloo, Ontario, Canada: Institute Press.

Meyers, J., & Meyers, K. (1995). *Rey Complex Figure Test and Recognition Trial: Professional manual.* Odessa, FL: Psychological Assessment Resources.

Mischel, H., & Mischel, W. (1983). The development of children's knowledge of self-control strategies. *Child Development, 54*, 603–619.

Moffitt, T. E. (1993). The neuropsychology of conduct disorder. *Development and Psychopathology, 5*(1–2), 135–151.

Moffitt, T. E. (1997). Neuropsychology, antisocial behavior, and neighborhood context. In J. McCord (Ed.), *Violence and childhood in the inner city* (pp. 116–170). Cambridge, UK: Cambridge Criminology Series.

Morgan, A., & Lilienfield, S. (2000). A meta-analytic review of the relation between anti-social behavior and neuropsychological measures of executive function. *Clinical Psychology Review, 20*, 113–136.

Murray, G., McKenzie, K., Quigley, A., Matheson, E., Michie, A., & Lindsay, W. (2001). A comparison of the neuropsychological profiles of adult male sex offenders and non-offenders with a learning disability. *Journal of Sexual Aggression, 7*, 57–64.

Newman, J. P. (1987). Reaction to punishment in extraverts and psychopaths: Implications for the impulsive behavior of disinhibited individuals. *Journal of Research in Personality, 21*, 464–480.

Ogden, P., & Minton, K. (2000). Sensorimotor Psychotherapy: One method for processing traumatic memory. *Traumatology*, 6 (3).

Ornstein, R., & Thompson, R. E. (1984). *The amazing brain.* New York: Houghton-Mifflin.

Papez, J. W. (1937). A proposed mechanism for emotion. *American Medical Association Archives of Neurology and Psychiatry, 38*, 725–743.

Perry, B. (1996). *Maltreated children: Experience, brain development, and the next generation.* New York: Norton.

Perry, B. (1997). Incubated in terror: Neurodevelopmental factors in the "cycle of violence." In J. Osofsky (Ed.), *Children, youth, and violence: The search for solutions* (pp. 124–148). New York: Guilford Press.

Perry, B. (2001). The neurodevelopmental impact of violence in childhood. In D. Schetky & E. Benedek (Eds.), *Textbook of child and adolescent forensic psychiatry* (pp. 231–238). Washington, DC: American Psychiatric Press.

Perry, B., & Pate, J. E. (1994). Neurodevelopment and the psychobiological roots of post-traumatic stress disorders. In L. Kozoil & C. Stout (Eds.), *The neuropsychology of mental disorders: A practical guide* (pp. 81–98). Springfield, IL: Charles C. Thomas.

Pithers, W. D. (1990) Relapse prevention with sexual aggressors: A method for maintaining therapeutic gain and enhancing external supervision. In W. L. Marshall, D. R. Laws, & H. E. Barbaree (Eds.), *Handbook of sexual assault: Issues, theories, and treatment of the offender* (pp. 343–361). New York: Plenum Press.

Prentky, R. A., Knight, R. A., Sims-Knight, J. E., Straus, H., Rokous, F., & Cerce, D. (1989). Developmental antecedents of sexual aggression. *Development and Psychopathology, 1*, 153–169.

Pynoos, R. (1990). Post-traumatic stress disorder in children and adolescents. In B. Garfinkel, G. Carlson, & E. Weller (Eds.), *Psychiatric disorders in children and adolescents* (pp. 48–63). Philadelphia: Saunders.

Raine, A., & Buchsbaum, M. S. (1996). Violence, brain imaging, and neuropsychology. In D. Stoff

& R. Cairns (Eds.), *Aggression and violence: Genetic, neurobiological, and biosocial perspectives* (pp. 195–217). Mahwah, NJ: Erlbaum.

Resick, P. A., & Schnicke, M. K. (1992). Cognitive processing therapy for sexual assault victims. *Journal of Consulting and Clinical Psychology, 60*, 748–756.

Reynolds, C., & Bigler, E. (1998). *Test of Memory and Learning.* Austin, TX: Pro-Ed.

Rogeness, G., Amrung, S., & Maced, C. (1986). Psychopathology in abused or neglected children. *Journal of the American Academy of Child Psychiatry, 25*, 659.

Rubin, K. H., & Rose-Krasnor, L. (1986). Social-cognitive and social behavioral perspectives on problem solving. In M. Perlmutter (Ed.), *Minnesota Symposium on Child Psychology: Cognitive perspectives on children's social and behavioral development* (Vol. 18, pp. 1–68). Hillsdale, NJ: Erlbaum.

Ryan, G. (1989). Victim to victimizer: Rethinking victim treatment. *Journal of Interpersonal Violence, 4*, 325–341.

Ryan, G. (1999). Treatment of sexually abusive youth: The evolving consensus. *Journal of Interpersonal Violence, 14*, 422–436.

Saigh, P. A., Mroueh, M., & Bremner, J. D. (1997). Scholastic impairments among traumatized adolescents. *Behavior Research and Therapy, 35*, 429–436.

Schore, A. N. (1994). *Affect regulation and the origins of the self.* Hillsdale, NJ: Erlbaum.

Schore, A. N. (2000). Attachment and the regulation of the right brain. *Attachment and Human Development, 2*, 23–47.

Schore, A. N. (2002). Dysregulation of the right brain: A fundamental mechanism of traumatic attachment and the psychopathogenesis of posttraumatic stress disorder. *Australian and New Zealand Journal of Psychiatry, 36*, 9–30.

Schwartz, B. K. (1995). Theories of sex offenses. In B. K. Schwartz & H. R. Cellini (Eds.), *The sex offender: Corrections, treatment and legal practice* (Vol. I, pp. 2-1–2-32). Kingston, NJ: Civic Research Institute.

Seligman, M. P. (1971). Preparedness and phobias. *Behavior Therapy, 2*, 307–320.

Selye, H. (1956). *The stress of life.* New York: McGraw-Hill.

Shapiro, F. (1995). Eye movement desensitization and reprocessing: Basic principals, *protocols, and procedures.* New York: Guilford Press.

Sheslow, D., & Adams, W. (1990). *Wide Range Assessment of Memory and Learning.* San Antonio, TX: Psychological Corporation.

Siegel, D. (1999). *The developing mind: Toward a neurobiology of interpersonal experience.* New York: Guilford Press.

Smallbone, S., & Dadds, M.R. (2000). Attachment and coercive sexual behavior. *Sexual Abuse, 12*(1), 3–15.

Stone, M., & Thompson, E. (2001). Executive function impairment in sexual offenders. *Journal of Individual Psychology, 57*, 51–59.

Streeck-Fischer, A., & van der Kolk, B. (2000). Down will come baby cradle and all: Diagnostic and therapeutic implications of chronic trauma on child development. *Australian and New Zealand Journal of Psychiatry, 34*, 903–918.

Teicher, M., Andersen, S., Polcari, A., Andersen, C., & Navalta, C. (2002). Developmental neurobiology of childhood stress and trauma. *Psychiatric Clinics of North America, 25*, 397–426.

Teichner, G., & Golden, C. (2000). The relationship of neuropsychological impairment to conduct disorder in adolescence: A conceptual review. *Aggression and Violent Behavior, 5*, 509–528.

Teichner, G., Golden, C., Crum, T., Azrin, N., Donohue, B., & Van Hasselt, V. (2000). Identification of neurological subtypes in a sample of delinquent adolescents. *Journal of Psychiatric Research, 34*, 129–132.

Todd, R., Swarzenski, B., & Rossi, P. (1995). Structural and functional development of the human brain. In D. Cicchetti & D. Cohen (Eds.), *Developmental psychopathology* (pp. 161–194). New York: Wiley.

Trevarthen, C., & Aitken, K. (2001). Infant intersubjectivity: Research, theory, and clinical applications. *Journal of Child Psychology and Psychiatry, 42*(1), 3–48.

Uvnas-Moberg, K. (1998). Oxytocin may mediate the benefits of positive social interaction and emotions. *Psychoneuroendocrinology, 23*, 819–835.

van der Kolk, B. A., & Ducey, C. P. (1989). The psychological processing of traumatic stress. Rorschach patterns in PTSD. *Journal of Traumatic Stress, 2*, 259–265.

van derKolk, B., McFarlane, A., & Weisaeth, L. (1996). *Traumatic stress. The effects of overwhelming experience on mind, body, and society.* New York: Guilford Press.

van der Kolk, B. A., McFarlane, A. C., & van der Hart, O. (1996). A general approach to the treatment of posttraumatic stress disorder. In B. van der Kolk, A. C. Mac Farlane, & L. Weisaeth (Eds.), *Traumatic stress: The effects of overwhelming experience on mind, body, and society* (pp. 417–440). New York: Guilford Press.

van der Hart, O., van der Kolk, B. A., & Boon, S. (1998). Treatment of dissociative disorders. In J. D. Bremner & C. R. Marmar (Eds.), *Trauma, memory, and dissociation* (pp. 253–283). Washington, DC: American Psychiatric Press.

Vermeiren, R., De Clippele, A., Schwab-Stone, M., Ruchkin, V., & Deboutte, D. (2002). Neuropsychological characteristics of three subgroups of Flemish delinquent adolescents. *Neuropsychology, 16*(1), 49–55.

Wahlberg, L., Kennedy, J., & Simpson, J. (2003). Impaired sensory-emotional integration in a violent adolescent sex offender. *Journal of Child Sexual Abuse, 12*(1), 1–15.

Ward, T., Hudson, S., & McCormack, J. (1997). Attachment style, intimacy deficits, and sexual offending. In B. K. Schwartz & H. Cellini (Eds.), *The sex offender: New insights, treatment innovations and legal developments* (Vol. II, pp. 2-1–2-14). Kingston, NJ: Civic Research Institute.

Webster, S. D., & Beech, A. R. (2000). The nature of offenders' affective empathy: A grounded theory analysis. *Sexual Abuse: A Journal of Research and Treatment, 12*(4), 249–262.

Wechsler, D. (1981). *Wechsler Adult Intelligence Scale—Revised.* San Antonio, TX: Psychological Corporation.

Wechsler, D. (1991). *Wechsler Intelligence Scale for Children: Third edition: Manual.* San Antonio, TX: Psychological Corporation.

Wodarski, J., Kurtz, P., & Gaudin, J. M. Jr. (1990). Maltreatment and the school age child: Major academic socioemotional, and adaptive outcomes. *Social Work, 35*(6), 506–513.

Chapter 2

The Emotional World of the Sexual Offender— Does It Matter?

by Deloris Tyler Roys, Ph.D.

OVERVIEW

Sexual offenders are individuals who are reviled and maligned and thought to be incapable of change. However, if we look closely at this population we find that there are as many different aspects of the sexual offender as there are offensive behaviors. The hard-core pedophilic member of the North American Man Boy Love Association (NAMBLA) is as different from the sexually reactive adolescent as wolves are from rat terriers. The media loves a villain and exploits parents' fear for their children by blowing the horn of nonrepentance and impossibility of redemption. Yet the fact is that there have been thousands of sex offenders who have been repentant, have worked hard to gain control of their arousal, and have struggled to rebuild their lives in some meaningful way. Because of the overwhelming contempt levied against sex offenders, there has been very little effort to examine how a sex offender is created and what might be done to ascertain whether he learns to think and behave differently. The criminal justice system has attacked this problem from a punishment perspective—if we can make the pain great enough, these folks will learn not to do it again. For hundreds of years we have seen that pain and punishment seldom have the "learning" effect we hope for. Nevertheless, we continue on, hoping to change the outcome by practicing the same response. A much more novel approach to the problem of sex offenders among us is to examine their emotional world, plug into their affective resonance (or lack thereof) with others, and use that knowledge to bring about recognition by the offender of the need for change. It has been said by numerous treatment professionals that if the sexual offender ever "really" appreciated the damage he has done, he would literally vomit from this understanding (although we recognize that females as well as males can perpetrate sexual assaults, the pronoun "he" is used for expedience). Assuming this to be true, time and money would be better spent moving the offender along an emotional pathway that would allow him to recognize the harm he has done and open his mind to the need to change. To accomplish this task, a developmental approach to how the sex offender experiences his emotional world has been formulated. This approach opens the door to treatment options that effectively enhance the probability that a sex offender will reestablish an emotional connection with others, whereby his desire not to harm overrides his desire for self-gratification.

INTRODUCTION

Sexual offenders live in a world that views them as the underbelly of human society. They are seen as disgusting, disposable, and decidedly without potential for rehabilitation. Not only are they viewed this way by others, by and large they view themselves in the same negative terms. Is it any wonder then that they have become steeped in shame and humiliation—shame that they are so depraved, so vile, so without redemptive qualities that their neighbors, even their loved ones, would wish them dead.

The emotional world of the sexual offender is perplexing to people who cannot understand how an individual could possibly find pleasure in being sexual with a child; exposing himself to women; raping men, women, or children; or a multiplicity of other sexual behaviors. A number of well-known books (e.g., Brownmiller, 1975; Russell, 1984) and the media state that rape is not a sex act but, rather, the acting out of hatred or rage, a power act toward another. Seldom is it recognized as a complex dissociation of mind, body, and emotions, a coping style with a colossal cost to others. Sex crimes in general are a messy mix of avoidance of emotional connection, fear, distorted thinking, and perverted arousal which has been shaped into a parody of love.

All of us who have worked with sex offenders have listened to this litany of so-called love: "I wanted her to have her first sexual experience with someone who loved and cared for her"; "I love my son. I would never hurt him. I simply wanted to teach him to masturbate properly"; "I figured if she was gonna put it out there for anybody, I ought to be the one doing it for her 'cause at least I love her." It could all be perceived as a weird sort of auditory hallucination if we were not confronted daily with the emotional wreckage of this perverted "love."

Emotions have been studied by psychology, theology, political science, biology, and virtually every field that addresses why people feel the way they do and what that means in terms of their interaction with others. Psychology laid claim to the study of emotions when William James (1850/1950) decided in the 1800s that emotion was a reaction in viscera. But even before that, Aristotle had noted that emotions seemed connected to cognition, the things that people cared about and valued. Aristotle argued that even though emotion comes upon us unbidden, we can train "our passions" to act in moderation, possibly the first formula for controlling sexual offending (Gottlieb, 2000). Silvan Tomkins (1962) in the middle of the twentieth century began to stress emotional responding as a psychological function based on a "blueprint" (a pattern laid down during emotional development) to enjoy positive affect and dislike negative affect. Studies illuminate that individuals develop schemas (patterns or maps) about self and others on the basis of five psychological needs: safety, trust, esteem, control, and intimacy (Cunningham, 2003), and they operate in their environment from their needs.

The sexual offender is no different from any other human being in that he comes into the world a complex learning organism ready to learn and adapt. The capacity to experience each and every emotion of which all other individuals are capable is part of the biological/psychological makeup of each individual. Somehow, somewhere this capacity to experience the full gamut of emotions begins to be shut down in the sexual offender with the likely culprit being trauma, either large or small.

PATTERNS OF CHILDHOOD DEVELOPMENT

In contemplating the beginning of emotional connection and affective responding, the developmental patterns of infancy and childhood set the stage for lifetime patterns of behavior. The infant both absorbs information from its environment and gives feedback to its environment. It is this feedback loop of response and responding that begins to solidify the response style of the child not only physiologically but emotionally. A child who is well tended, whose cries and signals are appropriately responded to, begins to develop a sense that it is cherished and has value. A child whose cries and signals are ignored or unheard begins to develop a sense that nothing changes despite the intensity of the outcry. Childhood developmental patterns are fairly predictable and have demonstrated stability over the course of modern research. Ainsworth (1973) noted that strong emotional bonds between parent and child, such as love, grief, security, anxiety, and anger, predisposed the child to develop one of three types of attachment with the caregiver: secure, avoidant, or resistant. Both Ainsworth (1978) and Bowlby (1973) viewed attachment as specific developmental tasks of particular life phases.

Six patterns of childhood development are now commonly looked on as a standard guidepost for age-related transition from one developmental stage to another. These predictable and age-normative schedules are part of the standard growth and development of childhood, and it is noted that disruption of these stages of development by disturbing factors creates complex and sometimes destructive emotional upheaval for the developing child.

Dependence vs. Independence

The first stage to be negotiated is that of dependence to independence, or self-direction. This means that the child will move from depending on its mother, father, caregivers, and so on for direction, understanding, and the simple acts of feeding, clothing, and health care to relying on his own resources. He will gain a growing ability to perform these acts for himself and consequently develop a sense of personal identity in regard to what he wants to eat, wear, play, and so forth. Consider one of our sex offender clients, Diane.

Diane is a grandmother, in her 50s; she has bleached blond hair and is lean and angular. She has always answered to others. She has never made a decision on her own—not in childhood when her mother told her not to think about her father after he left the family and not when her 20-year-old neighbor told her to skip school so that he could have intercourse with her. He told her she would marry him after she graduated and she did, never thinking that she could make a decision for herself. Her life was proscribed by what others told her to do, eventually leading to her being told to be a good Christian and take in needy children. She did, and she continued to shun her independence right up until her 15-year-old foster son said, "Let's have sex," and she did. She continued willingly for a time, and when she became unwilling the foster son beat her, quashing any independent thought. Only when she was arrested, did she ever question herself, and still her cognitive distortions were so profound all she could say was, "I tried so hard to be what he wanted me to be."

Emotional self-worth, self-esteem, and belief in one's autonomy cannot be attained unless the child masters the dependence–independence state.

Pleasure Seeking vs. Delayed Gratification

The second stage to be negotiated is pleasure seeking to delayed gratification, which is critical to the child's being able to tolerate the frustrations of daily living. The baby has one goal—to satisfy his every wish. The baby is egocentric. He is isolated in his tiny little universe and eventually learns that his cries, whimpers, smiles, and coos operate on his environment in such a way that his needs for food, warmth, and nurturance are met. As the child grows, he must transition from the egocentric to the global reality of a less forgiving environment, one that does not respond instantly to his needs, and one where he will be expected to wait for his rewards.

Jerry obtained employment with a highly desirable company; in essence, he had achieved his dream. At about the same time he achieved his dream job, he discovered Internet pornography. He began spending more and more time involved in online chat and exchanging photos with others. He became so obsessed with the sexual excitement of the Internet that he could not wait to get home, and he began accessing these sites during his lunch hour. He began having longer and longer lunch periods, and, eventually, his employer checked his computer use logs. He lost his job and his financial security, and he was reported for having pornography involving underage girls.

Controlling impulses, emotions, and fears until gratification can be achieved is a major task of this developmental stage.

Ignorance vs. Information

The third stage, ignorance to information, redirects that "blank slate" of infancy to the acquiring of information in a coherent, logical format, thus creating a stable framework by which the child reflects on his world and deals with the emotional consequence of using new information.

Rebecca, age 10, was brought into a sexually reactive children's program for masturbating in public places where other children could see her. It was learned that she had been raped by her stepfather and at some point had been told by other girls that they knew of a 6-year-old girl who had given birth. Rebecca, who had no factual information about pregnancy or menstrual cycles, was terrified that she was now pregnant and would suddenly have a baby come out of her. Her experience of finally talking with someone who could put her experience into a logical format finally relieved her need to self-sooth with public masturbation.

Each new experience provides another building block to tie together emotions and cognitions to be used for further development.

Incompetence vs. Competence

The fourth stage, incompetence to competence, encompasses the years of development from infancy to adolescence whereby the child has learned to control emotions, problem-solve, pattern his sexual responses, and develop role performance and relationship capabilities.

Jack was born into a home where Dad was totally cold and controlling. Dad had pretty much allowed his own father to rear Jack next door while producing four more children (all girls), using the sofa in the family home to have sex with his wife. Jack was never sure where his loyalties lay. He could not

*figure out why his father didn't really want him in his home, and he never fig-
ured out his bond with his family or lack of bond with his sisters. His anger
and shame over his displacement coalesced into sexual harassment of his sisters and his attempted rape of two of them.*

Failure to complete the tasks of the fourth stage results in inadequate emotional
control, lack of ability to devise solutions to problems, and sexual responding devoid
of emotional connectedness and relationship enhancement.

Diffusion of Identity vs. Self-Identity

The fifth stage, diffusion of identity to self-identity, indicates the totality of learning that results in core identity being established. The individual has acquired a body
of information by which he has established and achieved internal consistency with
gender identity, life goals, relationship needs, and the ability to sort out the confusions
of multiple emotional responses to single events.

*Leroy, an African-American male in his mid-40s, entered our treatment pro-
gram after his adjudication for the anal sodomy of his 12-year-old nephew.
Leroy grew up in a traditional southern African-American family. Dad ruled
the home with an iron fist and all the children learned to never cross him.
Once one of Leroy's sisters tried it, and Dad took out a gun and fired it into
the wall over her head. Dad railed against homosexuality and let it be known
what he would do if he "caught one" in his territory. Unfortunately, Leroy was
homosexual. He hid his sexual identity from everyone, including himself. He
forced himself to walk straight, talk straight, be manly, date girls, and run
from anything that might lead someone to question his masculine presentation. He did all this so well that he even was able to convince those who knew
him that he raped his nephew in a "fit of craziness" because there was no possibility that he was gay. Only now, three years into treatment, is he able to say,
"I am a homosexual. I raped my nephew because I was sexually aroused. I
want to live in a relationship with a loving man and never again harm a
child." Only now is his presentation consistent with who he is internally.*

Amorality vs. Morality

The sixth stage, amorality to morality, reflects the child's growing awareness of
good and bad and right and wrong, and his increasing ability to appraise how this fits
within his cultural milieu, thereby providing him with the understanding of boundaries
and their potential violation.

*Jeffrey learned early to be sexual. He attended a one-room schoolhouse in the
country and found out quickly that the big boys could have their way sexually with the younger boys in the coat closet and that you better not tell. From
this early beginning, sex was an ongoing and pervasive part of his childhood
experience. He never talked about it and he never thought of it as right or
wrong—it just was sex and it felt good. He never forced anyone to have sex
who didn't want to be sexual with him, and he believed that was what he was*

doing as he became an adult and continued to have sex with younger males (as well as those in his own age group). His sexual boundaries were essentially unformed, and it was only when he entered treatment that he became aware that sexual behavior does in fact have boundaries and that he was a violator of those boundaries.

To negotiate these stages effectively, the developing child needs consistent direction and leadership. For some children the tasks may be so formidable that the child never negotiates them properly. For others, some form of traumatic emotional injury or disruption may stunt development or disrupt the progression from one stage to another. With such injury the child may be unable to progress without relearning a stage or without having specialized aid in repairing a stage. This may be critical to the child who is becoming emotionally mature and capable of rational and moral thought, as well as developing into an adequate or appropriate decision maker.

DEVELOPMENTAL STEPS AND SEX OFFENDERS

After years of work with sexual offenders, most therapists in the field come to the realization that the offenders' developmental tasks of childhood appear to have been poorly negotiated and have astounding gaps. The sex offender often remains dependent, pleasure seeking, generally demonstrates limited reflective capacity (particularly self-reflective), and is self-centered. Emotionally, he is limited, often able to address only the primary emotions of mad, bad, sad, or glad. Sexual response and role performance are deeply enmeshed to the extent that he often views himself only in relation to his sexual performance. Self-identity remains a mystery, and he may still be struggling to "find himself" well into his 50s and 60s. Moral development rarely has progressed to understanding boundaries and limits that are contrary to his own emotional or sexual needs. Reworking these stages effectively becomes part of the complex treatment needs of this challenging population. Aiding the sexual offender in gaining control of his deviance is to reawaken (or awaken for the first time) emotional cognitions representative of these childhood developmental stages in the hope that he will be able to become fully connected to his emotional self and the emotional world of others.

INFLUENCE OF TRAUMA ON DEVELOPMENT

A growing body of literature (Briere & Runtz, 1990; van der Kolk, 1994; Brock & Perry, 1995) involves the study of traumatic reactions in victims, and undergirds the challenge that faces us in trying to understand how sex offenders choose to behave in the ways that they do and how to devise strategies sufficient to repair the damage to allow the restoration of the emotional world as a prophylactic for further sex crime. Trauma research by van der Kolk (1994) and others indicates that experience and emotion are not processed and integrated during a traumatic event, thereby leading to ongoing frightening visual imagery and physical sensation. Malamuth, Sockloskie, Koss, and Tanaka (1991) noted that physical and sexual abuse between parents or between parent and child likely influence developmental processes such as the ability to inhibit behaviors and the development of social skills. Whitfield, Anda, Dube, and Felitti (2003) found that among men who had been exposed to family aggression and violence there was a strong correlation between the number of these types of experiences and the risk of subsequently perpetrating interpersonal violence. It is also well documented that children who are victims of abuse demonstrate more emotional lability, dissociation, and attention deficits (Shields & Cicchetti, 1998).

Trauma is a subjective experience, and the event that may induce horror and revulsion in one individual may leave another totally unfazed. Trauma is truly in the eye of the beholder. Thus a mother passing out drunk and unconscious in front of one child may be relatively uneventful, whereas another child may experience such panic and helplessness that he never recovers his sense of equilibrium. The fear that his mother has died and he is now alone and abandoned may leave this latter child permanently disconnected from future emotional events in a self-protective effort to avoid reexperiencing such devastating helplessness.

> *Ronnie was just such a child. As an adult male he still relates the horror of that moment when he was 10 years old and he thought his mother had died. She was wandering around the kitchen as she often did, sipping liquor from a glass. Suddenly she fell to the floor, and Ronnie could not see her breathing. His father, who was in the military, was off to some distant port as he always was, and all Ronnie could think was, "Now I've got to raise my sister." He ran screaming to a neighbor, shouting, "Mom is dead. Mom is dead." Neighbors came to help, an ambulance was called, and his mother was taken away. The helplessness and panic he experienced at that moment has haunted Ronnie for 20 years.*

The terrorized child is always with us in these treatment settings, raging against the memory of paralyzing horror. A common event such as a father divorcing the mother may be seen by observers as ordinary in today's society, yet the child whose father leaves the home may experience a total extinguishing of his belief in his own lovabilty, and the shame inherent in that knowledge of being unlovable will convince him to never again attempt to attach to a love object, whether it be a friend, relative, or even his own child.

INTERNALIZATION OF SHAME

Kaufman's (1996) work in developing a psychology of shame noted that individuals internalize interpersonally based scenes of shame and later reproduce them. Internalized scenes of shame joined with other negative affects become the models that shape distinct patterns of inner relating. New experiences are reinterpreted in the light of prior experiences and self-identity is shaped by the resulting affect-imagery-language internal dialogue. The less vulnerable individual appears to be able to develop what Kaufman refers to as defending scripts—scenes developed to help escape from or avoid further shame. On the other hand, identity scripts are scripts that are directed internally and look backward as well as forward to reproduce shame. They are usually organized around self-blame, comparison making, and self-contempt, all these being characteristics recognized by the sex offender therapist as being commonly held by our treatment population.

It is also noted by others that shame is a painfully devastating experience that, at least temporarily, leads to a crippling of adaptive self-functionings (Tangney, Wagner,

& Gramzow, 1992) and can lead to severe narcissistic pathology (Morrison 1989) as well. Psychoanalyst S. Miller (1996) extended this notion to the idea that obsession as well as narcissism is built around scripts that define the nature of shaming and then defend against that shame. Even Moses-Hrushovski (1994) seems to speak to the sex offender's cognitive distortion, in which he lacks perspective in regard to time from the trauma viewpoint, when she says that the shame-bound patient seems to ignore time, attempting to turn back time to the point before the devastating damage to the self occurred. For example, one sees men who remain boys, emotionally irresponsible and unable to make a commitment or women who remain girlish forever seeking a caring "daddy." They seem to know that somehow they are not the same as others, that their relationships do not work out like others seem to do, but they cannot understand their contribution to the problem.

To understand, then, the twists and turns of the emotional pathway followed by the traumatized child to the ultimate betrayal of sexual offending against another person, a comparison of the offender with the healthier functioning individual, the one who attains healthy un-shame-bound development, must be investigated.

SELF-ACTUALIZATION VS. EMOTIONAL IMPOVERISHMENT

Maslow (1968, 1970) spent a lifetime developing a body of knowledge concerning the conditions under which individuals will develop to their maximum potential. This included looking at life stages and the transition process through the primary stages of obtaining all of one's survival needs. With this accomplished, the individual could focus on the emotional growth and development that leads to what Maslow termed the self-actualized person. Although his work is more than thirty years old, it is still the model psychologists point to as the standard for human needs and social change within the context of survival needs, comfort needs, and then personal effectiveness needs. Self-actualized individuals demonstrate what could be termed "healthy personalities," and it is this older, structured set of principles that provides a useful framework to help in assessing how the emotional maturity of sexual offenders differs from that of hypothetically self-actualized individuals. Delineating the impoverishment of the emotional abilities of many sexual offenders using the self-actualized model illustrates the extent of the therapeutic work that must be accomplished to create change in the offender.

Comfortable With Reality

Maslow stated that the healthy person is comfortable with reality; he is able to deal with unpleasant or uncomfortable realities rather than retreating to a fantasy world. He does not have to invent a pleasing middle-class childhood if he grew up in poverty, nor does he feel the need to tell grandiose tales of how he served in Vietnam when he was a payroll clerk in Kansas. Who he knows himself to be is okay with him.

Many sexual offenders, on the other hand spend, inordinate amounts of time involved in fantasy—enhancing their past accomplishments and embroidering their future potential. One measure of fantasy is masturbatory activity. Smallbone (2003) found in his study of incarcerated sexual offenders and masturbation that half of the offenders in his study reported having been sexually abused, and they had begun masturbating on average more than two years earlier than had those in the study who had not been sexually abused. Pithers (1990) stated that the offender's sexual fantasies were "tantamount to a planning session for refinement of future behaviors" (p. 344). Consumers of Internet porn in our treatment program self-report spending virtually all of their spare time online engaging in fantasy and masturbation.

These qualitative examples seem to be reinforced by the findings of Proulx, Perreault, and Ouimetl (1999) and Dandescu and Wolf (2003). Proulx et al. (1999) found that offenders who were not coercive in their offense engaged in more deviant fantasy than did those offenders who were coercive during the course of their offense. Dandescu and Wolf (2003) found that both child molesters and exhibitionists experienced significantly more fantasies after their first offense than prior to their first hands-on offense, again possibly indicating mental rehearsal and planning for the future experiences. Fantasies of power, whether masturbatory or not, are the lifeblood of the offender's inner world, and assessment of those fantasies opens the door to understanding the risk posed by each type of sexual offender from exhibitionist to rapist.

> *Frank remembers clearly his first rush of power. When he was 12 years old, he was watching television, and in the program he saw a woman struck from behind (a detective show). As she fell unconscious to the ground, her dark hair swept forward over her face. He says he felt at that moment a surge of sexual arousal and erection like nothing he had ever before experienced in his life. From that moment forward, every fantasy found him replaying the scene, building the anticipation of actually acting it out. Twenty-two years later the fantasy became his life—he did it. He left a full confession for the police and attempted suicide, which was unsuccessful. He served time in prison, and ultimately came to us for help in ridding himself of the fantasy.*

Acceptance of Self

Another factor that Maslow found in the person striving for self-actualization was acceptance of self. These individuals were not ashamed of themselves and were generally accepting of shortcomings in themselves or others. In contrast, the typical sexual offender's view of self revolves around shame. The sex offender spends inordinate amounts of time protecting himself from what Yochelson and Samenow (1982) term the "zero state." The zero state reflects that emotionally destructive sense that one is worthless or a complete zero. Nathanson (1992) studied shame and the "cognitive shock" (1996) experienced by individuals when they discovered themselves in any of the following eight situations: matters of personal size, strength, skill, ability; being helpless or dependent; losing in competition; defects in self-image; attractiveness; sexuality; seeing and being seen; and wishes and fear of closeness.

Nathanson (1992) proposed that individuals reacted to these eight situations within what he termed "a compass of shame." The four points of the compass are withdraw, avoid, attack others, and attack self. He postulated that shame interferes with neocortical cognition, accounting for the moment of confusion one experiences in a shame episode. Shame clearly interrupts affective communication, limiting (by its very nature) intimacy and empathy. Because many sexual offenders are bound by shame due to the secrets they carry, they seem to be living in extreme from one pole of Nathanson's compass to the other at any given time. One might hypothesize that the desperate narcissism manifested by many sexual offenders may, in fact, be a strategic deployment of energy to attempt to draw attention to some aspect of themselves that will negate the intense self-loathing and shame that result in their being trapped at one of the four points of the compass.

> *Eddie was told by his mother, during her endless drunken tirades, how useless he was and how disgusted she was to be his mother, On occasion she would point her handgun at him and say, "I should just put you out of your misery right now." It was only after two years of treatment that he was able to allow himself to feel close enough to the treatment team that he was able to tell what his mother had done to him. With that shame exposed, he no longer had to continue behaving criminally to validate his mother's assessment of him, and he began rapid growth and change in treatment.*

Spontaneity, Simplicity, and Naturalness

This characteristic indicates a flexible immediacy in thinking, emotions, and behaviors—an ability to be either playful, serious, or whatever emotion is appropriate based on accurate and perceptive assessment of where others and self are at that moment.

An individual who operates with guile or manipulation, such as many sexual offenders, tends to be inflexible in his thinking—always looking for the trick, the catch, the con. He holds rigidly to erroneous beliefs, and he seldom recognizes that most issues are not black and white but have multiple shades of gray. He attempts to control with manipulation to coerce others into his rigid inflexible belief system. The most recent studies of recidivism in sex offenders identify negative affect and negative emotions as a component of the multifaceted pathway to reoffense in this population (Bickley & Beech, 2003; Curry & Larose, 2000; Firestone et al., 2000; Hudson, Ward, & McCormick, 1999; Lund, 2000; Proulx et al., 1999.) Although it is noted that reoffense is multifaceted, being unwilling or unable to review a menu of possible alternative behaviors and select the most positive approach to avoiding risky situations is one of the major reoffense characteristics.

> *John "knew" he would not reoffend. Because he was so certain of this he did not carry his ammonia deterrent in his pocket and he did not practice avoidance of high-risk settings or situations. He decided to go to the movie theater despite his training to avoid such settings unless he went with someone who knew his history and was willing to help him with his control plan. Instead he went with a friend who had no idea of his history. The friend brought along his 7-year-old nephew and placed him in the seat between himself and John. John did not remove himself from the situation, he had no backup plan, he had no deterrent at hand, and he reoffended despite his "knowing" that he would not do it again.*

Focus on Problems Outside Himself

Maslow states that the healthy individual has the ability to focus on problems outside himself. He can be problem-centered without being overly self-conscious, and therefore he is able to devote time to a task, his duty, or whatever he sees as his mission. His concerns are not how he looks or how others will view his efforts. He can face any task, focusing his energy and attention effectively.

Many offenders, on the other hand, are exceedingly self-conscious. They have little faith in their personal worth and tend to define themselves by what they "do," not who they "are." Consequently, a sex offender often views his task or duty as directly reflecting his personal worthiness rather than simply the worth or value of the task. He can focus and put inordinate amounts of energy into a problem that generates kudos for himself, but even after doing so he discounts such a reward. He constantly assesses what those kudos will cost him, who he will have to pay off for the reward, even how he may be being manipulated by kudos given. His sense of perfection can never be met. Each task or mission must meet the highest of standards, and if it does not do so (which it cannot because it does not exist), it proves his underlying worthlessness.

When Harold, an exhibitionist, was in college, he felt that in a class he always had to receive an A—not a 90 percent A, or a 99 percent A, but a 100 percent A+—and if another student also got an A, Harold had to be perceived as the student with the best A *or it would confirm that he was not good enough. The same sense of perfectionism was displayed in his workplace as well. If Harold was not declared the most valuable employee, he felt he had to move on because everyone could see that he didn't have what it takes. He was always measuring himself, and that measure was always against some impossible standard. Resting on his laurels, so to speak, could not be tolerated because the specter of the "other" surpassing him and shaming him brought him to such fury that he had to "show them" he was not worthless. For Harold, relief from his self-imposed drive to be the best came as he was struggling with a particularly challenging essay. He had been struggling for hours and was tired and allowing his mind to drift. He remembered when he was a kid, and he stood in front of his bedroom window naked and shook his penis at the girl next door. She laughed and smiled and waved at him and he felt so manly. He began to stroke himself at this memory and he heard the giggling of two coeds passing his dorm room. He stood up and quickly jerked the curtain away from the window exposing his erection for the girls to see. The girls looked astonished for a moment and then smiled before they looked away and quickly moved on. Harold felt elated, warm and tingly, and totally in control. At that moment he felt perfect.*

Solitude

The healthy person enjoys solitude and is able to meditate or muse about a subject without a sense of boredom. The need for privacy is understood as a time to regroup and is experienced as emotional privacy, not secretive loneliness. A sense of privacy is one's understanding that each individual deserves his own thoughts and feelings and has the right to decide when, and whether, to share them. He does not feel empty in his own space. He does not feel that he has to seek action to know that he exists.

Many sexual offenders are unclear about the difference between privacy and secrecy. Most often privacy feels empty, and the offender may suffer from boredom due to his inability to feel any enjoyment in himself. He needs action to generate energy, energy to shove unwanted feelings out of consciousness. He is much like the child who has never had to depend on himself to fill his world with imagination and play. Such a child has never developed the capacity for creativity and expects that things or people will always be provided to amuse him. It is interesting to note that Unnever and Cornell (2003) find there are six traits common to criminals of all types: impulsiveness, self-centeredness, short-tempers, risk taking, looking for simple tasks rather than complex ones, and preference for physical activity over mental exertion. Why is it so for many sexual offenders? Thinking opens the door to feelings, and feelings bring pain. The sexual offender avoids this potential pain rigorously. He may fill his mind with simple distractions, those things that keep him physiologically "revved" up and emotionally disconnected, such as pornography, pursuit of prostitutes, promiscuous sex, and trolling or grooming for victims, all of which provide immediate energy release.

Jim related his early childhood experiences to his treatment team, stating, "I never read a book outside of schoolwork. I just could not understand what the other kids found so fascinating sitting for hours doing nothing but reading. I wanted to be outside playing ball or killing frogs or getting into fights. Just sitting around made me crazy. It was boring beyond belief. When I got old enough to drive, I hardly ever spent any time at home. I was out cruising, drag racing, doing whatever, especially with the girls. After I married I still couldn't settle down. The routine everyday stuff was just too boring. I went back to cruising the strip where the action was and that's what made me start using prostitutes. They didn't expect me to settle down. They were about the action, just like me."

Integrity and Self-Worth

Whenever the healthy person faces rejection or unpopularity, he is able to continue with his interests and maintain his integrity and self-worth. Such an individual exhibits a high degree of autonomy, relying on his own understanding of his needs and the needs of others. He makes decisions based on accurate perceptions and social cues.

Many sex offenders, however, tend to be unable to rely on themselves to meet their own emotional needs, and thus dependency, objectification, and manipulation of others develop. Other persons, sexual partners particularly, are seen as objects to be used as if they belonged to the offender. At the same time, many sex offenders depend on others to fulfill their emotional neediness, often fusing their neediness with orgasm, making it seem as if achieving climax is an emotional connection. The ability to handle rejection is also emotionally undeveloped in many sexual offenders and is exemplified in cases of stalking; Tjaden and Thoennes (1998) found that 31 percent of women stalked by former intimates were raped by those former partners. Once again, orgasm or sexual ownership have been confused with emotional connectedness.

Ralph stated during interview that he had never masturbated. When asked, "Why?" he replied, "I've never had to because I've always had me a female to do it for me." When asked if these were girlfriends or love relationships, he laughed and said, "Of course not. They're just chicks I'd get to do it. It's nasty to do it to yourself, so I get me a girl and she does it. That way I get what I need and so does she."

Sees the Unique

The person striving for self-actualization sees the unique in commonplace experiences. For instance, a flat tire on the way to work is a commonplace experience. It was not planned, but it is there and must be dealt with efficiently and with a relatively short disruption of the day. The healthy person sees the flat tire as a situation in which he can demonstrate his unique abilities as a mechanic or demonstrate his unique abilities to summon help fast and efficiently and then continue on to handle his day's chores with minimal impatience. He may even view it as a unique opportunity to rest and relax and allow others to come to his rescue.

However, a sex offender typically views the world from a concrete position. Everything is black or white. It either fits his world view of "good" or "bad," "right" or "wrong," or it does not fit at all. The flat tire is bad or wrong (there is no middle ground such as a flat "just is"; it is neither bad nor wrong). It is bad because it interrupted his rigid daily routine, and it is wrong because it is a personal affront to his control of his day. He will not relax; he sees it as a personal attack; it was meant to happen; it only happens to him, and he just can't do anything right. It is bad, it is wrong, and it is a personal insult.

This rigid tendency to see "either/or," "right or wrong" would appear to mitigate against sexual offenses given that sexual offending is wrong. Unfortunately, the emotionally impoverished sex offender may view the world without the ethical or moral boundaries that most of us develop by assessing and processing the multiple ambiguities inherent in making moral and ethical "right" decisions. Often what the offender knows as "right" or "wrong" has been behaviorally reinforced in some frightening or unpleasant way. In other words, he has learned to respond in a limited way based on stronger needs or demands. He subjugates his thinking and feeling to the understanding he has of why things occur, thus becoming locked into either/or patterns of reinforcement from his past rather than examining the world for the unique aspects of any situation or experience.

> *Tom, arrested for child cruelty and sexual battery, grew up in a home where masturbation was a forbidden and "sinful" act. He never asked about masturbation as he grew to adulthood and he never read about it. He assumed what he had been punished for as a child was appropriate. When he caught his son masturbating at age 12, he handled it just as his father did. He whipped his son with a belt, not only on his buttocks but also on his penis. When he entered treatment he was still angry at the "system" for what to him was its incomprehensible response to what he believed to be an appropriate response to his child's unacceptable behavior.*

Moral Development

Three major developmental theorists, Jean Piaget, Erik Erikson, and Lawrence Kohlberg, are credited with formulation of the concept of moral development as it applies to childhood strivings. Piaget (1963) postulated that the ability for formal, logical thought did not occur until after age 12, when a child has had ample experience relating to and learning from multiple dimensions of problem solving. At this point the child has a rudimentary moral code but is not yet fully versed in handling moral dilemma. Kohlberg (1964) viewed the experience of moral development as a transitioning through principles of thought until the child understands that certain acts transcend individual needs. This is a reflection of the third stage of the patterns of childhood development as previously discussed (Ainsworth, 1978; Bowlby, 1973). Erikson's (1963) theory elucidated that social-emotional development, particularly by adolescence, resolves identity issues culminating with the knowledge that one is an individual in a world of others with mutual and independent responsibilities.

Many sex offenders seem to have poorly transitioned through these child and adolescent developmental phases, or they have never accomplished the tasks at all. Their world view is undeniably egocentric, still interacting in the world from the childish emotional set of "I want what I want when I want it." For moral development to occur the individual must have multiple learning experiences of role taking and empathic connection with others' experiences. A child reared in emotional impoverishment, fear or terror, neglect or abuse will have a limited opportunity to formulate good role expectations or to assess the needs of others in his surroundings. Curwen (2003) stated that the ability to empathize is related to how we treat others (this is partially learned by role observation), and empathic connection is considered necessary for altruism (moral development) and the inhibition of aggression. Impoverished emotional development in oneself impedes understanding of others as emotional beings. Knowing that others feel and have needs is a condition foreign to the objectifying sexual abuser, and it may contribute to the ability to abuse others.

> *Lewis left his first marriage immediately after the birth of his baby girl. He did not see this child again until she was 16 years old. She contacted him, begging for a meeting and a chance to have a "real father-daughter relationship." Lewis invited her to come to visit him and spend several nights in his trailer home. As he explained it, "There was only one bed because we were in a one-bedroom trailer, so it seemed logical that we would sleep in the same bed. As we were getting to sleep she rolled over against me and it occurred to me to ask her about her sexual development. We talked about sex, and I asked her if she wanted me to show her how to please her boyfriend. It never occurred to me that I was committing a crime, and moral obligation to my family never even entered the picture. My thought was, "This is a grown woman. She is willing, and why not since we had never been father and daughter."*

Empathy

The person striving toward self-actualization often experiences a sense of brotherly love, *Gemeinsschaaftsgefuhl* (Maslow, 1968), an identification with situations of others in all cultural settings. The closest emotional state to *Gemeinsschaaftsgefuhl* is empathy, the capacity for one to resonate with the emotional state of another human being. The empathic person is fully connected to the emotional world of himself and others. He is able to say, "I know what I would feel if I were in the situation you are experiencing. Therefore, I am mirroring your emotions in this situation."

Many sex offenders lack the capacity for empathy (particularly for their victims) and are so rigid in their thinking that they do not accept the experiences of others as having meaning. Their view of the world is egocentric, again much like the unformed child's, and they do not identify the feelings of others because they have not learned to identify their own. They project, rather than mirror. They see what they want to see. While molesting a child, the child's grimace is interpreted as a grin of pleasure. They impose their cultural and environmental understanding on others. If sex in their family is their norm, they will project that norm onto their own child, expecting acceptance, not rejection.

> *Daniel grew up in a home where there were no sexual boundaries. He often saw his mother having intercourse on the living room sofa, and he began having sex with his sisters at around age 10. When he married and gained a stepdaughter, he assumed she would respond as willingly as his sisters. He was shocked when she reacted with outrage when he fondled her breast. Even during the course of the divorce action, he stated, "I don't know why she and her mother reacted so strongly. It wasn't like I put my penis in her."*

Loving Relationships

The healthy person has the ability to establish truly close and loving relationships with others. Close and loving relationships are particularly difficult for the egocentric sexual offender. As defined in our treatment program, a person who loves another has the capacity to help the loved one achieve his or her highest potential, no matter the cost to the first person.

Seidman, Marshall, Hudson, and Robertson (1994); Marshall, Christie, and Lanthier (1979); Marshall and Mazucco (1995); and Marshall, Champagne, Brown, and Miller (1997) report that sexual offenders lack intimacy in their lives, demonstrate social anxiety, lack assertiveness, are aggressive, are self-focused, and are lonely. These characteristics are not qualities that tend to endear one to others, and they drive away those with healthy self-respect. In addition, relationships are often compromised by alcohol or drug problems. Hall and Powell (2000) noted that alcohol and drugs mediate feelings or memories of the offender's own sexual abuse or trauma, thus serving as a pseudo-amnesiac as well as a tool to be used to detatch. Loving relationships must have connectedness, attachment, and concern for the mutual welfare of each other. Substance misuse is often used to escape from these very things.

> *George explained his offense as being partially his wife's fault. After all, she was the one who knew he was a drinker. She never complained about him being a "fun" guy. She never even complained about his "whoring" around at the bar, so he said, "How was I to know she'd get mad if I had sex with her niece. She never objected to anything else I did."*

Judging People on Their Individual Merits

The healthy person tends to judge people on their individual merits. Most sexual offenders tend to judge others on the basis of what they understand about the people who were closest to them (i.e., their caregivers) and on what they understand about themselves. The early experiences of sexual offenders tend to be biased in the direction of betrayal, abandonment, and emotional pain. In addition, they have come to know themselves as untrustworthy and selfish and, therefore, their expectation of others follows these scripts. Because of rigid thinking, emotional impoverishment, and basic distrust of others, it is not likely that judgements of others will be unbiased.

> *Bob explained in group that his father "always told us we were selfish brats, that all we cared about was what we could get out of him. I always hated that, but I started thinking the same way about my own kids. Pretty soon I figured out that if they asked me for something, I could get them to give up a little something to get it. Pretty soon I had a regular routine of sex for toys worked out with them. That is, until I refused to give my daughter a car. That's when she told."*

Sense of Ethics

The person striving for self-actualization has a highly developed sense of ethics by which behavior is judged and acted out. Ethical thought or behavior is commonly described as the system of standards or values we each consider before we make a decision to act.

Ethical behavior has inherent in its execution a continuous flow of judgement about the morality and "rightness" of any course of action, action unsullied by inappropriate thoughts of self-gratification or sexual reward. Poor judgment and poor decision making about ethical and moral behavior are crucial aspects of sex offender dynamics, particularly when impacted by unstable emotions.

> *David, an offender who was arrested for a sex act with a 15-year-old male, argued vociferously with his fellow group members that he had the right to attend his young granddaughter's baseball games (his probation officer agreed with him), and so he did, "forgetting" to tell the group that he had done this for the entire first season. It was in his second year of treatment that he came to realize that his judgment was faulty. It occurred to him that he was a registered sex offender and, as such, his picture was on the Internet. If someone at his granddaughter's ball games saw him and called the sheriff to remove a known sex offender from the ball field, he would create grave humiliation for his grandchild as he would be led away in handcuffs. With this epiphany his judgment about the "rightness" of his choices began to crystalize around ethical versus selfish decisions.*

Sense of Humor

A nondisparaging sense of humor may be considered characteristic of a healthy individual. Recognizing humor inherent in the foibles of human behavior (rather than laughing at people) is an example of one's recognition of the emotional quirks of others.

Anger, on the other hand, is often the chosen state of the sexual offender. He uses it to ward off feelings, particularly those that make him feel vulnerable. Whenever he feels insecure or unsure, when he feels that he is being attacked, whenever he feels unacceptable, out of control, or humiliated he will erupt in anger. A continuous and pervasive feeling of anger does not foster a sense of humor. In fact, the sexual offender may use humor in the same self-protective way that he uses anger. He often uses it to make himself feel superior, in control of another, or to project his own contempt onto others. His sense of humor is directed at cutting others down so that he feels superior and in control. His script is one of hostility that provides a means for him to reduce another to being laughable while exaggerating his own sense of superiority.

> *Leroy found that humor allowed him to expose his penis hundreds of times without a complaint from anyone. He chose parties, gatherings or situations where there was an expectation that people were "just having fun." He would utilize this expectation of people acting silly when they are having fun and cheerfully ask, "Hey, you want to see this" or some other similar greeting, and nine times out of ten he would receive a skeptical, "Oh, yeah, sure, like you're really gonna do that," and then he would. His anger was profound at the stupidity of people who never challenged him on his behavior, and he complained how their compliance "made him do it."*

Creativity

The healthy person uses creativity to enhance his life, to bring joie de vivre to his daily activities and to expand his emotional connection to the sublime.

Sexual offenders may use creativity in building a "shadow person" to appear normal to those around him. They may examine the world around them and adjust what they reveal of themselves to maximize their potential to be able to get their needs met. They seldom "stop to smell the roses" because they do not recognize that the roses are there.

> *William created a caricature of himself that he called "Little Bill." Little Bill became a purveyor of holistic health through massage and hands-on healing. Little Bill dressed flamboyantly, carried a flute, and was known as a "medicine man." William was, of course, not American Indian, nor did he have medical or massage training, but his shadow man, Little Bill, was able to feel, fondle, massage, and manipulate hundreds of women and girls before one made a sexual complaint.*

Critical Thinking

Finally, according to Maslow, the healthy person has the ability to use critical thinking in understanding and coping with his environment. As already noted, most sexual offenders are deficient in using critical thinking in regard to issues in their life or the life of others. The sex offender is steeped in rigid belief systems that reinforce his negative emotional view of the world. That view is one in which he is constantly being victimized by the imposition of others' needs over his own. He believes that his way is the right way and those opposed to his way are only interested in putting him down. He does not adapt easily to change and feels that what he learned through his development is the only way to handle similar situations. Traumatic injury leads to repetition of the familiar, which is known to hurt but is a lot less scary than the new, which might hurt more. Critical thinking would open the door to processing what he has already experienced in his life and might possibly force change, an emotionally uncomfortable state for the rigid and controlling sex offender. However, his rigid cognitive style interferes with his ability to cope with his deviancy.

Todd was arrested in a pornography sting operation. He stated that he had been unfairly set up because he had been contacted by an undercover officer posing as a 14-year-old. Not once did he bring up to his group that when his computer was confiscated, there were more than 1,000 pictures of children ranging in age from infancy through young teens. He claimed that was not the issue. To him the issue was that he wouldn't have been discovered if he were not the victim of the sting.

TREATMENT OF SEX OFFENDERS

Identifying Feelings

It has been the experience in our treatment program, which uses both behavioral and cognitive restructuring, that an intense focus on emotional issues from childhood interwoven with confrontation of the cognitive distortions of adulthood leads to enhanced emotional functioning and growth of the client. The structure of our treatment program includes assignment of specific tasks during the course of group therapy sessions, such as a written full and complete autobiography (including early childhood memories and traumas) and other cognitive work assignments plus a weekly assignment of written "feeling statements." Such an approach appears to create emotional growth and recognition of feeling states in the clients. Feeling statements consist of the offender's stating precisely an emotion he experienced (beyond mad, bad, sad, or glad) during the course of the just completed group session and *why* he experienced that emotion. At the start of their treatment program, the clients are given a list of over 400 words that describe feelings for them to use in the formulation of their feeling statements. These statements are responded to each week as a written feedback loop from the group therapist and available to the clients at the start of the next group session. By examining and responding to the weekly feeling statements, we have qualitatively been able to track the progress of the clients' growth in their ability to recognize feelings and to expand on their understanding of the source and choice of their feeling states.

Encouraging Healthy Functioning

Duration of group sessions is two hours per week, and, in addition, every client engages in one hour of individual treatment with a second therapist on the treatment team. This latter component allows the individual to focus on behavioral work such as masturbatory satiation and covert desensitization. After the intense focus on immediate control of his behaviors, the individual therapist can then aid the client in reorganizing his life schemas.

To attempt to encourage healthy functioning in the offender using only behavioral treatment methods, or only relapse prevention techniques, or only punishment and humiliation via incarceration is to ignore the broad context in which development occurs and reduces the likelihood that the sexual offender can become emotionally complete. Behavioral treatment methods that address only change in the behavior miss the complexity of why the offender does what he does. Behavioral control works well in the short term because it gives the offender a new way to respond to the immediate pressure of his urges. For instance, instead of hitting someone, count to ten, breathe deeply, speak slowly; instead of fantasizing a sex act cause oneself pain by popping one's wrist with a large rubber band or sniffing from a vial of ammonia. What behavioral techniques do not address is the emotional aspect of why the individual is wanting to hit someone or wanting to move into a fantasy in the first place. If the offender can understand and change how he misinterprets his emotions along with putting in place new behavior patterns, he will enhance his chance of maintaining behavioral control over the long term.

Relapse prevention models also suffer from the same short-term focus. Even though the offender learns to identify his high-risk situations and his seemingly unimportant decisions, he does not focus on the long-term cognitive change necessary to rework the emotional basis from which he responds to stress, loneliness, and anger. He learns how to handle the future, but he does not rework his self-identity at the same time. Unless one learns to value oneself along with learning how to develop new plans of responding, the old shame and disgust soon undermine the motivation to continue on the prevention path.

Incarceration provides containment. As long as an individual is removed from society he will not reoffend against those in the free world. However, in the traditional prison setting he will not build mastery over his impulses and he will not develop intimate connections. What he will do is strengthen his deviant sexual fantasies by masturbation, learn to better con and manipulate to get his way, and gain a more pervasive sense that he is a victim of people and things arrayed against him to prove that he is worthless.

CONCLUSION

The clinical aspects of the emotional world of the sexual offender loosely fall into eight categories that span his developmental schemas regarding safety, trust, esteem, control, and intimacy, as well as addressing his arousal scripts and the pathologies that reinforce his deviant behaviors, including self-identity, impulse control, anxiety, deficits in understanding affect of self and others, loneliness, intimacy and arousal, self-esteem, and, finally, narcissism and personal relationships.

We have examined self-identity from the aspect of shame, loneliness, and dependency, and we have noted how limited the offender is in his ability to escape from these early patterns of relating to himself. The offender has learned early in life to seek novelty and action to distract from painful thoughts. His anxiety may constantly impinge upon his thinking, distracting him with thoughts of his imperfection, his worthlessness, and his fear that others will realize how flawed he is. He does not understand the affect of others; he reads all the signals wrong. He finds the idea of helping others to achieve their highest potential directly opposed to his pattern of self-interest, and he may not believe anyone would really respond to others in such a manner. He is chronically lonely because he is so disconnected from others, and he does not understand what it means to be intimate because sharing too much with another might open the door to humiliation and shame. The offender may instead assume that sex acts with others is the definition of what intimacy is all about, and he constantly uses the energy of sexual involvement to feel connected to others. Each time he realizes that he is not connected and is still lonely and alone, his self-esteem may be further battered. He continues down his narcissistic path, trying to attract attention to some aspect of himself that he believes will impress others and thereby create the meaningful relationship that eludes him so completely.

However, if the therapist has the opportunity to addresses these categories of development and functioning within the totality of a behavioral and cognitive restructuring sex offender treatment program, as noted by Marshall, Anderson, and Fernandez (1999) and Marshall, Jones, Ward, Johnston, and Barbaree (1991), the prognosis for development of an independent, critically thinking, competent, moral, and other-oriented individual appears to be enhanced.

References

Ainsworth, M. D. S. (1973). The development of infant-mother attachment. In B. C. Caldwell & H. R. Riciuti (Eds.), *Review of child development and research* (Vol. 3, pp. 1–94). Chicago: University of Chicago Press.

Ainsworth, M. D. S. (1978). *Patterns of attachment*. Hillsdale, NJ: Erlbaum.

Bickley, J. A., & Beech, A. R. (2000). Implications for treatment of sexual offenders of the Ward and Hudson model of relapse. *Sexual Abuse: A Journal of Research and Treatment, 15*(2) 121–134.

Bowlby, J. (1973). *Attachment and loss. Volume II: Separation: Anxiety and anger.* New York: Basic Books.

Brownmiller, S. (1975). *Against our will: Men, women and rape.* New York: Bantam Books.

Cunningham, M. (2003). Impact of trauma work on social work clinicians: Empirical findings. *Social Work, 48*(4), 451–459.

Curwen, T. (2003). The importance of offense characteristics, victimization history, hostility and social desirability in assessing empathy of male adolescent sex offenders. *Sexual Abuse: A Journal of Research and Treatment, 15*(4), 347–364

Dandescu, A. & Wolfe, R. (2003). Considerations on fantasy use by child molesters and exhibitionists. *Sexual Abuse: A Journal of Research and Treatment, 15*(4), 297–305.

Erikson, E. H. (1963). *Childhood and society* (2nd ed.). New York: Norton

Firestone, P., Bradford, J. M., McCoy, M., Greenberg, D. M., Curry, S., & Larose, M. R. (2000). Prediction of recidivism in extrafamilial child molesters based on court-related assessments. *Sexual Abuse: A Journal of Research and Treatment, 12*(3), 203–221.

Gottlieb, A. (2000). *The dream of reason: A history of Western philosophy from the Greeks to the renaissance.* New York: Norton.

Hall, J. M., & Powell, J. (2000). Dissociative experiences described by women survivors of childhood abuse. *Journal of Interpersonal Violence, 15*(2), 184–204.

Hudson, S. M., Ward, T., & McCormick, J. C. (1999). Offense pathways in sexual offenders. *Journal of Interpersonal Violence, 14*, 779–798.

James, W. (1950). *The principles of psychology.* New York: Dover. (Original publication 1890).

Kaufman, G. (1996). *The psychology of shame: Theory and treatment of shame based syndromes* (2nd ed.). New York: Springer.

Kohlberg, L. (1964). Development of moral character and moral ideology. In M. L. Hoffman & L. W. Hoffman (Eds.), *Review of child development research* (Vol. I). New York: Russell Sage.

Lund, C. A. (2000). Predictors of sexual recidivism: Did meta-analysis clarify the role and relevance of denial? *Sexual Abuse: A Journal of Research and Treatment, 12*(4), 275–287.

Malamuth, N. M., Sockloskie, R. J., Koss, M. P., & Tanaka, J. S. (1991). Characteristics of aggressors against women: Testing a model using a national sample of college students. *Journal of Consulting and Clinical Psychology, 59*, 953–962.

Marshall, W. L., Anderson, D., & Fernandez, Y. M (1999). *Cognitive-behavioural treatment of sex offenders.* New York: Wiley.

Marshall, W. L., Champagne, F., Brown, C., & Miller, S. (1997). Empathy, intimacy, loneliness and self-esteem in nonfamilial child molesters. *Journal of Child Sexual Abuse, 6*, 87–97.

Marshall, W. L., Christie, M. M., & Lanthier, R. D. (1979). *A descriptive study of incarcerated rapists and pedophiles.* Ottawa: Solicitor General of Canada.

Marshall, W. L., Jones, R., Ward, T., Johnston, P., & Barbaree, H. E. (1991). Treatment outcome with sex offenders. *Clinical Psychology Review, 11*, 465–485.

Marshall, W. L. & Mazucco, A. (1995). Self-esteem and parental attachments in child molesters. *Sexual Abuse: A Journal of Research and Treatment, 7*, 279–285.

Maslow, A. (1968). *Toward a psychology of being* (2nd ed.). Princeton, NJ: Van Nostrand Reinhold.

Maslow, A. H. (1970). *Motivation and personality* (2nd ed.). New York: Harper & Row.

Miller, S. B. (1996). *Shame in context*. Hillsdale NJ: Analytic Press.

Morrison, A. P. (1989). *Shame: The underside of narcissism*. Hillsdale NJ: Analytic Press.

Moses-Hrushovski, R. (1994). *Deployment: Hiding behind power struggles as a character defense*. New York: Jason Aronson.

Nathanson, D. L. (1992). *Shame and pride: Affect, sex and the birth of the self*. New York: Norton.

Piaget, J. (1965). *The moral judgement of the child*. New York: Free Press.

Pithers, W. D. (1990) Relapse prevention with sexual aggressors: A method for maintaining therapeutic gain and enhancing external supervision. In W. L. Marshall, D. R. Laws, & H. E. Barbaree (Eds.), *Handbook of sexual assault: Issues, theories, and treatment of the offender* (pp. 343–361). New York: Plenum Press.

Proulx, J., Perreault, C., & Ouimet, M. (1999). Pathways in the offending process of extrafamilial sexual child molesters. *Sexual Abuse: A Journal of Research and Treatment, 11*, 117–129.

Russell, D. E. H. (1984). *Sexual exploitation: Rape, child sexual abuse and workplace harassment*. Thousand Oaks, CA: Sage.

Seidman, B. T., Marshall, W. L., Hudson, S. M., & Robertson, P. J. (1994). An examination of intimacy and loneliness in sex offenders. *Journal of Interpersonal Violence, 9*, 518–534.

Shields, A., & Cicchetti, D. (1998). Reactive aggression among maltreated children. The contributions of attention and emotional dysregulation. *Journal of Clinical Child Psychology, 27*, 381–395.

Smallbone, S. W., & Dadds, M. R. (1998). Childhood attachment and adult attachment in incarcerated adult male sex offenders. *Journal of Interpersonal Violence, 13*, 555–573.

Tangney, J. P., Wagner, P., & Gramzow, R. (1992) Proneness to shame, proneness to guilt and psychopathology. *Journal of Abnormal Psychology, 101*(3), 469–478.

Tjaden, P., & Thoennes, N. (1998). *Stalking in America: Findings from the national violence against women survey* (NCJ-1669592). Washington, DC: Bureau of Justice Statistics, U.S. Department of Justice.

Tomkins, S. S. (1962). *Affect, imagery, consciousness: The positive affects* (Vol. I). New York: Springer.

Unnever, J. D., & Cornell, D. G. (2003). Bullying, self-control, and ADHD. *Journal of Interpersonal Violence, 18*(2), 129–147.

van der Kolk, B. A. (1994). Childhood abuse and loss of self-regulation. *Bulletin of Menninger Clinic, 58*(2), 145–168.

Ward, T., & Hudson, S. M. (2000). Sexual offenders' implicit planning: A conceptual model. *Sexual Abuse: A Journal of Research and Treatment, 12*(3), 189–202.

Whitfield, C. L., Anda, F. F., Dube, S. R., & Felitti, V. J. (2003). Violent childhood experiences and the risk of intimate partner violence in adults. *Journal of Interpersonal Violence, 18*(2), 166–185.

Yochelson, S., & Samenow, S. (1982). *The criminal personality: A profile for change* (Vol. I). New York: Jason Aronson.

Chapter 3

Pathways to Sexual Offending

**by Pamela M. Yates, Ph.D., R.D.Psych. and
Drew A. Kingston, B.A.(Hons.)**

OVERVIEW

Thousands of sex offenders have been treated with the original relapse prevention model that assumed, first, that sexually inappropriate behavior is a response to specific stressors that can be identified and, second, that the offender can then be taught more effective ways of coping with these high-risk situations, thus reducing the possibility of resorting to sexual assault. However, this assumption has not been based on empirical research but simply on clinical intuition. This chapter presents a more complex model based on research that suggests that there are at least four different paths to offending.

INTRODUCTION

Sexual offenders continue to be a growing public concern. The harms caused to victims and society are such that effective methods of intervention, treatment, and management of sexual offenders are of paramount concern to clinicians, researchers, and individuals working with these offenders in penitentiaries and in the community. Sexual offenders are a heterogeneous group with varying motivations and dynamics for offending behavior. As such, they present with significant variability in risk to re-offend, treatment needs, and supervision requirements. This chapter focuses on the treatment of adult male sexual offenders; it reviews and analyzes the self-regulation (pathways) approach to understanding offending behavior and suggests a framework for addressing the diverse treatment needs of sexual offenders. The chapter begins with a brief overview of treatment for sexual offenders, followed by a description of the self-regulation model and accompanying pathways. Research to date pertaining to the application of this approach to sexual offenders is next reviewed. The chapter concludes with the implications of this model for the treatment of sexual offenders.

TREATMENT OF SEXUAL OFFENDERS

The ultimate goal of sex offender treatment is the protection of the community through the prevention of a recurrence of sexually abusive behavior. To achieve this, it is essential that treatment of sexual offenders adhere to established principles and best practices of effective intervention. The principles of risk, need, and responsivity have guided the treatment of offenders (Andrews & Bonta, 1998). These principles are briefly reviewed here.

Risk Principle

It is well established that offenders, including sexual offenders, vary in the risk they pose to reoffend and in their observed rates of recidivism (e.g., Andrews & Bonta, 1998; Nicholaichuk, Gordon, Gu, & Wong, 2000; Nicholaichuk & Yates, 2002; Yates, 2002). According to the risk principle, effective intervention with sexual offenders is that which varies in intensity based on the level of risk to reoffend. Higher-intensity interventions are offered to higher-risk offenders, while lower-risk offenders require less intensive or minimal intervention. In addition to ensuring that offenders receive the most appropriate level of treatment that is likely to be effective, matching offenders to treatment intensity is also the most cost-effective, given limited treatment resources (Nicholaichuk, 1996; Prentky & Burgess, 1990; Shanahan & Donato, 2001)

Need Principle

Effective correctional intervention entails targeting the criminogenic needs of offenders (Andrews & Bonta, 1998; Gendreau & Goggin, 1996, 1997; Gendreau, Little, & Goggin, 1996). That is, intervention that aims to eliminate or reduce the influence of dynamic (i.e., changeable) risk factors associated with offending is more likely to be effective and to be associated with changes in risk and recidivism (Andrews & Bonta, 1998). For sexual offenders, criminogenic needs include such factors as attitudes, cognitive distortions, general and sexual self-regulation, and deviant sexual arousal (e.g., Hanson & Harris, 2000).

Responsivity Principle

Finally, effective correctional intervention is that which is applied according to the responsivity principle. Treatment should be delivered in a manner consistent with an offender's learning styles and abilities so the offender may derive maximum benefit from treatment (Andrews & Bonta, 1998; Gendreau & Goggin, 1996, 1997; Gendreau et al., 1996). Among offenders, responsivity factors include language, culture, personality style, intelligence, anxiety levels, and cognitive abilities. Treatment should be tailored according to these learning styles to maximize the potential effectiveness of the intervention.

Applied to the treatment of sexual offenders, these principles suggest that treatment will be most effective in reducing the likelihood of reoffending when it is offered at varying levels of intensity matched to the risk level posed by the offender; when dynamic risk factors associated with sexual offending are targeted for change; and when treatment is offered in a dynamic, flexible manner to ensure maximum engagement with, and benefit from, the treatment process. In addition, treatment of sexual offenders is most likely to be effective when it is cognitive-behavioral in orientation (Hanson et al., 2002), and when attention is paid to the therapeutic process by which it is delivered (Fernandez, Marshall, Serran, Anderson, & Marshall, 2002; Yates, 2004). Specifically, attention has recently been paid to the importance of such process issues as the working relationship between the client and therapist, essential therapist characteristics, and the use of effective treatment techniques to reinforce and maintain behavior change and skill development (Fernandez et al., 2002; Marshall, Anderson, & Fernandez, 1999; Yates, 2004). While not yet specifically evaluated with respect to the treatment of sexual offenders, such treatment factors have been found to be associated with positive outcome in multiple other clinical interventions, such as treatment of addictions, depression, and phobias, and are considered essential to effective treatment of sexual offenders (Fernandez et al., 2002; Marshall et al., 1999; Yates, 2004).

MODELS OF SEXUAL OFFENDING AND THEIR APPLICATION TO TREATMENT

Given the obvious importance of flexibility, as indicated previously, it is important that the development of models of sexual offending and their application to treatment allow for variability in interventions. With respect to the treatment of sexual offenders, various conceptual models have been applied to meet the needs of these offenders. These include medical and psychopharmacological models (e.g., Bradford, 1985, 1990), psychodynamic models (e.g., Becker & Murphy, 1998), behavioral models (e.g., Abel et al., 1984), and, most recently, cognitive-behavioral models (Hanson et al., 2002). Although psychopharmacological interventions are typically used as an adjunct to other treatment methods (e.g., Bradford, 1990), surgical and psychodynamic models of treatment are no longer used as a result of the lack of demonstrated efficacy in reducing reoffending (e.g., Marshall, Jones, Ward, Johnson, & Barbaree, 1991; Quinsey, 1977). In addition, behavioral models are generally no longer used in isolation from cognitive approaches. The most effective model of treatment to date is the cognitive-behavioral model (Hanson et al., 2002).

Linking of Cognitive Processes and Behavior

Cognitive-behavioral interventions are based on the premise that cognitive processes and behavior are linked, and that cognitions influence behavior. Sexual offending is viewed as a pattern of behavior that is developed and maintained through the principles of learning and reinforcement and results from maladaptive or antisocial responses and ineffective coping mechanisms. Cognitive-behavioral interventions aim to replace maladaptive or deviant responses with adaptive, prosocial beliefs and behavior through targeting specific need areas. Cognitive-behavioral interventions involve skills acquisition and rehearsal, development of effective problem-solving and coping strategies, social and victim perspective taking, sexual and social relationships, and examination of the relationship between cognition, affect, and behavior (Yates et al., 2000). The cognitive-behavioral model of treatment for sexual offenders, therefore, aims to develop and reinforce skills in those personal and situational areas which are associated with previous offending behavior and with risk to reoffend in the future. Treatment based on this model targets such factors as attitudes and cognitive processes that support sexual offending; management of emotional states, such as anger, associated with offending; victim empathy; and reconditioning of deviant sexual arousal.

Relapse Prevention Model

Over the past two decades, virtually all cognitive-behavioral sex offender treatment programs have used the relapse prevention (RP) model as "the treatment of choice for sex offenders" (Laws et. al., 2000, p. 5). Relapse prevention is a posttreatment maintenance strategy designed to assist individuals to gain self-control and to maintain acquired behavior change. Although this model was originally designed specifically for addictive behaviors and as a follow-up program to maintain treatment change (Marlatt, 1982; Marlatt & Gordon, 1985), it has been reconceptualized numerous times and applied to sexual offenders as treatment proper, posttreatment maintenance, or both (Marques, Day, & Nelson, 1992; Pithers, Marques, Gibat, & Marlatt, 1983). The application of this model to sexual offending has been widely accepted, despite an absence of research attesting to its applicability, utility, validity, and efficacy with this population (Hanson, 1996; Laws, 2003; Marshall & Anderson, 1996).

A review of the criticisms of this model is beyond the scope of this chapter. The reader is referred to Laws (2003) and Ward and Hudson (1996) for more detailed information. With respect to models of sexual offending, the RP model is viewed as insufficient to account for the multiple possible motivations for sexual offending due to its reliance on predominantly negative affect as a motivation for offending behavior, failure to account adequately for variations in the degree of planning of the offense, and its emphasis on avoidance-based strategies of risk reduction, which are more difficult to achieve than are more active, approach-oriented strategies (Mann,

2000; Mann, Webster, Schofield, & Marshall, 2004; Yates, 2004). The self-regulation model of sexual offending, proposed as an alternative to the RP model by Ward and colleagues (e.g., Ward & Hudson, 1998, 2000; Ward, Hudson, & Keenan, 1998; Ward, Louden, Hudson, & Marshall, 1995), is described next.

The Self-Regulation Model of Sexual Offending

Ward and colleagues' reconceptualized model of sexual offending is based on self-regulation theory (Baumeister & Heatherton, 1996; Karoly, 1993). This nine-stage model of sexual offending is based on the manner in which behavior is regulated by the individual and it identifies three potential self-regulatory problems and four pathways to sexual offending. A brief review of this theory is described, followed by descriptions of the four pathways to sexual offending.

Self-regulation allows individuals to engage in goal-directed behavior. This includes both internal and external processes and situations that guide behavior, including choosing, monitoring, modifying, and evaluating one's actions (Ward & Hudson, 1998, 2000). Goals are regarded as desired states or circumstances and thus involve the development and activation of cognitive scripts that guide behavior. Goals may also be associated with the avoidance of undesirable states or circumstances. Thus, individuals may regulate their behavior to achieve desired ends or to avoid undesirable results. The former are *acquisitional goals*, as the cognitive script directs behavior in such a manner as to achieve a desired state, while the latter are *inhibitory goals* guiding behavior so as to avoid an undesired state or situation (Ward & Hudson, 1998, 2000). Goals and their associated cognitive scripts are influenced by individuals' own behavioral and learning history, as well as their perceptions and interpretations of events and situations, emotional states, evaluation of the effectiveness of actions in achieving goals, and reinforcement for behavior.

According to this model, there are three types of problems that suggest self-regulation may be dysfunctional (Ward & Hudson, 1998, 2000).

1. Individuals may fail to control their behavior or emotional states, leading to acting in a disinhibited manner. This problem is typically associated with negative emotional states.

2. Individuals may attempt to control their behavior using strategies that are not effective, leading to behaving in a misregulated manner.

3. Individuals may have intact self-regulatory abilities but may have inappropriate goals, such as antisocial objectives (Ward & Hudson, 1998, 2000).

In explaining sexual offending, Ward and Hudson (1998, 2000) applied self-regulation theory using a nine-stage model, which includes four pathways. The model analyzes the influence of situational determinants, perceptions, cognitive distortions, degree of offense planning, and evaluation of behavior following the commission of an offense to explain sexual offending and reoffending. Sexual offending behavior is explained in terms of the individual's goals (inhibitory vs. acquisitional) and behavioral strategies to achieve these goals. The combination of goals and strategies reflects four separate pathways to sexual offending in this model. These pathways are reviewed here, followed by research pertaining to their application to sexual offenders and their implications for effective treatment of these offenders.

PATHWAYS TO SEXUAL OFFENDING

The four self-regulatory pathways associated with offending behavior are *avoidant-passive*, *avoidant-active*, *approach-automatic*, and *approach-explicit*. These pathways vary between and within individual offenders at varying stages of the offense progression. The four pathways address both the individual's goals with respect to the offending behavior (approach vs. avoidance) and the manner in which the individual attempts to achieve this goal (passive vs. active; Ward & Hudson, 1998, 2000).

Avoidant-Passive Pathway

With respect to self-regulation, this pathway primarily represents underregulation or disinhibition of behavior. Specifically, the individual's goal or desire is to refrain from offending sexually. However, the individual is unable to control his behavior or desire to offend and is unable to implement effective coping strategies. The individual experiences negative emotional states, which may disinhibit behavior and lead to a loss of control. According to Ward and Hudson (2000), individuals following this pathway are likely to lack coping skills, to act impulsively, to have low self-efficacy expectations, and to experience anxiety. They are also more likely to plan their offenses in a covert, rather than overt, manner, and they are unaware that their behavior functions to bring them closer to offending. The individual may manage the desire to offend by simply denying its existence or by using strategies designed to distract from the desire but which are ineffective. These individuals are hypothesized to be anxious about dealing with threats to self-control, are unable to cope if they fail to deal with these threats, and are most likely to experience negative emotional states following offending, as they have failed in their goal of avoiding offending (Ward & Hudson, 1998, 2000). This pathway most closely resembles the traditional relapse process.

An example of this type of offender is the child molester who experiences sexual attraction to a child and, simultaneously, experiences anxiety regarding these urges. Initially, in the early stages of the offending process, the individual attempts to simply ignore the desire (a passive strategy). As the desire recurs, in later stages of the offending process, this ineffective strategy ultimately fails and the individual commits the offense. At the time of the offense, anxiety has been replaced with excitement. However, after the offense has been committed, the excitement dissipates and the individual again experiences anxiety. His evaluation of his behavior after the offense is negative, he experiences a sense of failure, and he resolves not to offend again. However, he has not learned to manage his anxiety, desire, and sexual excitement and, thus, is likely to offend again.

Avoidant-Active Pathway

The avoidant-active pathway is a misregulation pathway (Ward & Hudson, 1998, 2000). Specifically, similar to the avoidant-passive pathway, the individual's goal is to refrain from offending. However, unlike the avoidant-passive pathway, the individual makes active or explicit attempts to suppress or control arousal, fantasy, or emotional states that threaten a loss of control. Rather than simply ignoring these thoughts, fantasies or emotions, the individual following an avoidant-active pathway actively attempts to regulate his behavior and to institute control. However, in this pathway, the strategies selected to achieve this goal are ineffective in that they do not increase self-regulation. In some instances, these strategies are likely to increase, rather than decrease, the likelihood of offending. Individuals following this pathway expect that their strategies will be effective and are able to plan, monitor, and evaluate their behavior. What they lack is the understanding that the strategies they select are ineffective. Like the avoidant-passive pathway, the avoidant-active pathway encompasses negative emotional states that tend to be predominant in the offending progression. This pathway also approximates in some measure the traditional relapse process.

An example of an offender following an avoidant-active pathway is the offender who experiences anger or resentment associated with experiences of rejection in sexual contexts with women. To manage these emotional states, the individual uses substances (e.g., alcohol) with the expectation that this will eradicate the anger. Should he experience a resurgence of anger when in this state, he will be more likely to offend because he has not resolved the previous experiences of rejection and has not learned to effectively manage anger. If alcohol is involved, the individual is also likely to be disinhibited and, therefore, less likely to be able to control his behavior. Another common example of this type of offense pathway involves the use of pornography to manage deviant sexual arousal or interest. The offender believes he is redirecting his sexual urges from an inappropriate object (i.e., rape) to an appropriate object (i.e., sexually aggressive pornography rather than acting out) and using an appropriate solution (i.e., masturbating). However, this strategy is not only ineffective in eliminating the sexual desire, it is likely to increase risk by associating positive reinforcement (i.e., orgasm) with the deviant stimulus (i.e., depictions of sexual violence).

Approach-Automatic Pathway

While the aforementioned pathways are similar to the RP model in that avoidance goals are predominant in the progression to offending, the two other pathways differ, as they encompass approach-motivated (acquisitional) goals with respect to offending. The approach-automatic pathway can be conceptualized as an underregulation or disinhibition pathway in that the individual fails to control behavior (Ward & Hudson, 1998, 2000). However, this pathway is characterized by approach-motivated (acquisitional) goals with respect to offending. That is, the offender does not desire to avoid acting out sexually or aggressively but, rather, progresses through the stages of the offending process with an acquisitional or appetitive goal. This goal may be the commission of the offense itself or engaging behaviors ultimately associated with sexual offending. The individual's behavior is considered automatic because it tends to be impulsive and based on well-entrenched cognitive and behavioral scripts. The offense is planned in only a rudimentary and unsophisticated manner, with goals and strategies activated by situational factors of which the individual may not be cognizant. In the early stages of the offense progression, the individual may experience positive emotions, such as anticipation of sexual or other gratification. In addition, positive emotions are evident following the offense, as this is associated with success in achieving one's goal (Ward & Hudson, 1998, 2000).

An example of an offender following this pathway is one who holds hostile or stereotyped attitudes toward women or who holds a strong sense of sexual entitlement (i.e., the cognitive schema), as well as cognitive distortions which justify offending. This individual may offend sexually against a woman whom he encounters in a vulnerable position, such as a woman who is intoxicated or perhaps unconscious. This offender impulsively makes the decision to offend upon encountering the woman, which activates the cognitive script and distortions and leads to a rapid decision to offend. This individual experiences anticipation of sexual gratification and is likely to experience positive emotional states, such as gratification, following the offense. Similarly, a child molester following this pathway may approach offending with the anticipation of being "loved" and may feel gratified through the achievement of "intimacy" he experiences following the offense.

Approach-Explicit Pathway

The approach-explicit pathway is characterized by good self-regulation. That is, in this pathway, there are no deficits in the ability to self-regulate behavior. The individual does not lose control or suffer from an inability to control behavior. Rather, it is the individual's goals that are problematic. It is proposed that early learning experiences lead to the development of a belief system that supports sexual aggression (Ward & Hudson, 2000). The individual holds attitudes and beliefs that sexual aggression is an appropriate means by which to achieve one's goals, such as sexual gratification or emotional release. In this pathway, the individual intentionally plans the offense and implements explicit strategies to achieve the goal of acting out. These offenders may offend sexually to maintain positive mood states. They experience a positive reaction after committing the offense, as they have successfully achieved their goal (Ward & Hudson, 2000).

An example of an offender following this pathway includes one who plans the location of his offense in advance, has available all the "tools" necessary to commit the offense (e.g., a "rape kit"), or who grooms his victims over a period of time, gradually establishing a relationship with them, setting up situations to be with the victims, providing gifts, and so forth.

Summary

As can be seen from this review, sexual offenders may follow very different pathways in the commission of their offenses. Traditionally, it has been assumed that all sexual offenders suffer from deficits in coping strategies and/or lack of skills, and the RP model of treatment has focused on developing skills to eliminate these deficits. However, it is evident that not all sexual offenders suffer from deficits in self-regulation, and that where such deficits are evident, these may be different for individual offenders and thus warrant different approaches to treatment.

ADVANTAGES AND APPLICABILITY OF THE PATHWAYS APPROACH

Advantages

The advantage of the application of self-regulation theory to the analysis of sexual offending is that it can account for variability in the dynamics of sexual offending behavior, as well as its development and maintenance. As clinicians are aware, sexual offenders presenting for treatment describe a wide array of factors contributing to their offending behavior. In addition, research supports the existence of a variety of risk factors associated with sexual offending (e.g., Hanson, Morton, & Harris, 2003) and demonstrates variation in recidivism rates for different types of sexual offenders (e.g., Nicholaichuk et al., 2000). It is proposed that the pathways model is superior to the understanding of sexual offending behavior—in particular, variability in individual motivations for offending—and that the self-regulation model is useful in ensuring that treatment of sexual offenders is conducted in such a manner as to maximize gain. The pathways approach also eliminates the reliance on the single pathway model inherent in RP and its accompanying focus on negative affect and deficits. Finally, it is argued that the self-regulation model is superior in that intervention with sexual offenders under this model can more closely adhere to the principles of effective intervention than other approaches, including the RP approach.

Although the self-regulation model appears to have an advantage over the previous conceptualizations of relapse, there has, however, been limited empirical study on this model (Laws, 2003). In addition, as the application of the self-regulation model to sexual offending is relatively recent, this model has not been applied in many treatment programs. However, some research has been conducted pertaining to the applicability of this model in various contexts. This research is reviewed next.

Research on Applicability of the Model

In a qualitative analysis of the offense chain, Ward, Louden, Hudson, and Marshall (1995) examined the cognitions of twenty-six untreated incarcerated child molesters while they described their most recent sexual offenses. Using grounded theory (Strauss, 1987), the analysis resulted in the development of the nine-stage model of the offense cycle, which was then applied to the offense descriptions of an independent sample of twelve incarcerated child molesters. The resultant model was able to accommodate two distinct types of child molesters. Specifically, the first type of child molester ($N = 5$) fit the profile of a typical pedophile (i.e., preferential). For these offenders, the offense progression incorporated explicit planning, and the offenders experienced high levels of positive emotion during the offense cycle and expressed a desire to reoffend. These offenders were said to follow a positive affect (i.e., approach-type) pathway. The second group of child molesters ($N = 6$) was characterized by high levels of anxiety and negative affect, consistent with child molesters who are regarded as situational. The offense progression was dominated by implicit, rather than explicit, planning, and the offender expressed a desire to avoid future offending. These offenders followed a negative affect (i.e., avoidant-type) pathway.

To examine pathways in the offending process of extrafamilial child molesters specifically ($N = 44$), Proulx, Perreault, and Ouimet (1999) gathered information from official sources (i.e., police records) and from interviews with offenders. The information gathered consisted of preoffense factors (e.g., loneliness, hostility toward women, and sexual dissatisfaction), disinhibitors to offending (e.g., use of pornography, substance use, and deviant sexual fantasies), modus operandi characteristics of the offense (e.g., planning), and victim selection characteristics (e.g., gender and relationship). Results were compared to the two pathways described by Ward et al. (1995) and differed in that offenders following a negative affect pathway as indicated by preoffense factors did not differ from those offenders following a positive affective pathway at the preoffense phase. However, Proulx et al. (1999) noted that these findings may have been influenced by demand characteristics, as the offenders may have been motivated at the time of the assessment to conceal relevant offense details. Conversely, results from analyses of factors evident during the offense phase of the progression supported the existence of two pathways. Specifically Proulx et al. (1999) found that offenders with approach goals ($N = 14$) engaged in deviant sexual fantasies and incorporated explicit planning in the offense progression, while offenders with avoidance goals ($N = 30$) used substances prior to the offense and engaged in implicit planning. The finding that positive emotions, such as pleasure and sexual arousal, were the emotions most frequently reported during the offense phase supported Ward et al.'s (1995) positive affective pathway. Proulx et al., (1999) concluded that the RP model is insufficient to account for the diversity in the offense process.

Webster (2003) also examined the content validity of Ward and Hudson's (1998; 2000) self-regulation model. The study examined twenty-five sexual recidivists who had participated in the HM Prison Service's sex offender treatment program to establish the offenders' predominant pathway and the stability of pathways during treatment. Data were gathered using an interview process and were subjected to grounded theory analysis (Strauss, 1987). A semistructured topic guide assessed sociodemographic and offense-specific details. The data were then transcribed based on Ward and Hudson's (1998, 2000) nine-stage model, and offenders were allocated to an offense pathway at both pretreatment and posttreatment. Webster's (2003) results supported the model in that offenders with approach goals expressed a desire to offend sexually. Results also supported the model in that the coping and planning strategies were different for offenders following different pathways. Specifically, offenders following an avoidant-active pathway were characterized by use of substances and pornography to cope with deviant thoughts. Offenders following an approach-automatic pathway demonstrated a tendency to respond rapidly and to have offense-supportive cognitions activated upon meeting the victim. Finally, offenders following an approach-explicit pathway were characterized by deviant behavior that was carefully planned. Findings from this study also indicated that pathways were stable and did not change during treatment for the majority of offenders in the sample.

Bickley and Beech (2003) examined treatment performance in relation to self-regulation in a sample of intrafamilial and extrafamilial child molesters ($N = 59$) who had attended a residential assessment and treatment program for sexual offenders. Two independent therapists trained in the Ward and Hudson (1998, 2000) model classified offenders as belonging to an approach pathway ($N = 44$) or an avoidant pathway ($N = 15$), based on observations made during individual and group treatment sessions. Results indicated that these two groups different significantly on a number of offense characteristics. Specifically, as compared to offenders following an avoidant pathway, fewer offenders following an approach pathway were involved in a stable marital or long-term relationship and had their own children. Offenders following an approach pathway were more likely to have either extrafamilial or both intrafamilial and extrafamilial victims, while offenders following an avoidance pathway were more likely to have exclusively offended against intrafamilial victims. Finally, more offenders following an approach pathway had offended against boys or against both boys and girls. Although not statistically significant, these offenders were also more likely to have prior convictions for sexual offenses and to have previously participated in treatment. With respect to pre/posttreatment change, Bickley and Beech (2003) found significant improvements in levels of cognitive distortions among offenders following an approach pathway, but not for offenders following an avoidant pathway, who endorsed significantly fewer cognitive distortions at pretreatment. In addition, although significantly different at pretreatment, offenders following an approach pathway demonstrated significant improvements in victim empathy during treatment, while offenders following an avoidant pathway did not evidence such improvement. Findings from this study again supported differences among offenders following different pathways and also demonstrated different treatment effects for each of two global pathway types.

In a study designed to evaluate specifically the relationship between actuarially measured risk to reoffend sexually and offense pathways, Yates, Kingston, and Hall (2003) examined the offense pathways of treated incarcerated sexual offenders (N = 80), including extrafamilial child molesters (N = 19), rapists (N = 33), incest offenders (N = 24) and mixed offenders (offenders having multiple victim types; N = 4). With the exception of Webster (2003), this is the only study to date to evaluate the pathways model with offenders having adult victims. Offenders were allocated to the four offense pathways identified by Ward and Hudson (1998, 2000) using file review.

Results from this study indicated that offenders could be allocated to each of the four pathways identified in the model, and that there were significant differences between the pathways groups. Specifically, rapists were most likely to follow the approach-automatic (58 percent) or approach-explicit (36 percent) pathway rather than an avoidant pathway, while child molesters with male victims were most likely to following an approach-explicit pathway (83 percent). Child molesters with female victims were equally likely to follow either an approach-automatic or approach-explicit pathway (43 percent). Finally, while half of intrafamilial (incest) offenders followed an approach-explicit pathway, a considerable number of these offenders also followed an avoidant-passive pathway to offending (38 percent). Yates et al. (2003) also found significant differences in risk to reoffend as measured by the Static-99 (Hanson & Thornton, 1999), with offenders following an approach-automatic pathway demonstrating significantly higher risk to reoffend than offenders following any of the other pathways. This study found significant differences in both the pathways to sexual offending followed by various types of sexual offenders and in risk levels across pathways.

TREATMENT OF SEXUAL OFFENDERS WITHIN THE PATHWAYS MODEL

As seen in the foregoing review, there is some support for the application of the self-regulation model to sexual offenders in that there appears to exist distinct pathways to offending. Ward et al. (1995) found that some child molesters followed a pathway resembling the avoidant type, whereas others followed an approach-motivated pathway. The former were characterized by negative emotional states and the use of cognitive distortions to justify offending, while the latter were characterized by positive affect and cognitive distortions suggestive of an offending lifestyle based on entrenched attitudes and beliefs supporting sexual offending. These findings were supported by other research (Bickley & Beech, 2002, 2003; Proulx et al., 1995). Research has also found differences in level of offense planning by different pathway groups (Proulx et al., 1995) and variations in risk and in offense characteristics reflective of risk, such as offenses against boys and a history of sexual offending (Proulx et al. 1999; Yates et al., 2003).

These results taken together support the notion that sexual offenders follow different pathways to offending and require different treatment approaches, even within a specific treatment program or within programs of similar intensity (Yates et al., 2003). While treatment should target established dynamic risk factors for offending (Yates, 2004; Yates et al., 2000), consistent with the need principle of effective intervention, there may nonetheless be different mechanisms of action among individual sexual offenders for the same criminogenic need. For example, among child molesters, cognitive distortions may represent well-entrenched attitudes and beliefs associated with cognitive scripts indicative of a lifestyle supportive of offending and may be associated with positive affect in the offense process (Bickley & Beech, 2003; Ward et al., 1995), representing an approach pathway to offending. Alternatively, these cognitive distortions may serve as a self-protective mechanism among child molesters whose offending behavior is triggered by situational factors and who experience negative affect during the offending process (Bickley & Beech, 2003; Ward et al., 1995), representing an avoidant pathway to offending. Thus, treatment would be different for these different offenders. When cognitive distortions represent well-entrenched attitudes and beliefs supportive of offending, treatment should focus on changing these attitudes in conjunction with other factors evident in the offense progression for that offender (e.g., deviant sexual preference, managing sexual arousal, or deviant fantasy reconditioning). For the situational offender, on the other hand, the appropriate targets of treatment may include increased coping skills, self-esteem, intimacy, and management of negative emotional states, such as loneliness, with a focus on cognitive distortions only to the extent that these facilitate the offending process by allowing the offender to overcome inhibitions to offending.

In addition to targeting approach and avoidance goals differently, treatment should also be differently applied based on the type of strategies used by the offender in the offense progression. Offenders using passive strategies, such as ignoring or denying the problem, may benefit from awareness-raising surrounding the lack of utility of these strategies, and the identification and rehearsal of new strategies that are likely to be effective in reducing the risk of offending. However, given their negative reaction to threats to control, these offenders may also benefit from motivational enhancement strategies that also build self-efficacy. Similarly, offenders actively using ineffective strategies to refrain from offending may benefit from the development and rehearsal of new strategies but likely do not require motivational enhancement or enhancement of self-esteem or self-efficacy, as these individuals already possess high self-efficacy and outcome expectancies with respect to the effectiveness of their actions. Offenders with automatic scripts that guide their behavior are likely to benefit from treatment for impulsivity as well as entrenched attitudes and beliefs that support offending, while offenders who plan their offenses explicitly likely require more intensive intervention for entrenched deviance and antisociality.

CONCLUSION

The self-regulation/pathways model of sexual offending is a recent theoretical development that has not yet been widely applied to treatment with sexual offenders.

The few studies to date pertaining to the validity of this model have been supportive and suggest that the model shows promise in the assessment and treatment of sexual offenders. Given that sexual offenders are a heterogeneous group varying in their treatment and supervision needs (Alexander, 1999; Hanson & Bussière, 1998; Nicholaichuk, 1996; Nicholaichuk et al., 2000; Nicholaichuk & Yates, 2002; Thornton, 2002), it is suggested that this model is superior to the traditional RP model in that it accounts for greater variability in the offense progression and allows treatment providers to deliver a more individualized intervention that focuses on offenders' unique dynamic risk factors and motivations for offending behavior (Yates et al., 2000). In addition, it is argued that this model is more amenable to demonstrating a treatment effect due to its potential to focus on the acquisition of prosocial goals, which are more easily achieved than avoidance goals (Mann, 2000) that are typically the treatment strategy of choice within the RP model. This model may also be more amenable to demonstrating a treatment effect as a result of its congruence with the methods of effective therapy and its consistency with the principles of effective intervention with offenders (Andrews & Bonta, 1998; Fernandez et al., 2002; Yates et al., 2000).

References

Abel, G. G., Becker, J. V., Cunningham-Rathner, J., Rouleau, J., Kaplan, M., & Reich, J. (1984). *The treatment of child molesters*. Atlanta, GA: Behavioral Medicine Laboratory, Emory University.

Alexander, M. A. (1999). Sexual offender treatment efficacy revisited. *Sexual Abuse: A Journal of Research and Treatment, 11,* 101–116.

Andrews, D. A., & Bonta, J. (1998). *The psychology of criminal conduct*. Cincinnati, OH: Anderson.

Baumeister, R. F., & Heatherton, T. F. (1996). Self-regulation: An overview. *Psychological Inquiry, 7,* 1–15.

Becker, J. V., & Murphy, W. D. (1998). What we know and do not know about assessing and treating sex offenders. *Psychology, Public Policy, and Law 4*(1-2), 116–137.

Bickley, J. A., & Beech, R. (2002). An empirical investigation of the Ward and Hudson pathways model of offending in child sexual abusers. *Journal of Interpersonal Violence, 17,* 371–393.

Bickley, J. A., & Beech, R. (2003). Implications for treatment of sexual offenders of the Ward and Hudson model of relapse. *Sexual Abuse: A Journal of Research and Treatment, 15*(2), 121–134.

Bradford, J. M. W. (1985). Organic treatments for the male sexual offender. *Behavioral Sciences and the Law, 3*(4), 355–375.

Bradford, J. M. W. (1990). The antiandrogen and hormonal treatment of sex offenders. In W. L. Marshall & H. E. Barbaree (Eds.), *Handbook of sexual assault: Issues, theories, and treatment of the offenders* (pp. 297–310). New York: Plenum Press.

Fernandez, Y. M., Marshall, W. L., Serran, G., Anderson, D., & Marshall, L. (2002). *Group process in sexual offender treatment*. Ottawa, Ontario: Correctional Service of Canada.

Gendreau, P., & Goggin, C. (1996). Principles of effective correctional programming. *Forum on Corrections Research, 8,* 38–41.

Gendreau, P., & Goggin, C. (1997). Correctional treatment: Accomplishments and realities. In P. Van Voorhis, M. Braswell, & D. Lester (Eds.), *Correctional counseling and rehabilitation* (pp. 271–279). Cincinnati, OH: Anderson.

Gendreau, P., Little, T., & Goggin, C. (1996). A meta-analysis of the predictors of adult offender recidivism: What works! *Criminology, 34,* 575–607.

Hanson, R. K. (1996). Evaluating the contribution of relapse prevention theory to the treatment of sexual offenders. *Sexual Abuse: A Journal of Research and Treatment, 8,* 201–208.

Hanson, R. K., & Bussière, M. T. (1998). Predicting relapse: A meta-analysis of sexual offender recidivism studies. *Journal of Consulting and Clinical Psychology, 66,* 348–362.

Hanson, R. K., Gordon, A., Harris, A. J., Marques, J. K., Murphy, W., Quinsey, V. L., et al. (2002). First report of the Collaborative Outcome Data Project on the effectiveness of psychological treatment for sex offenders. *Sexual Abuse: A Journal of Research and Treatment, 14*(2), 169–194.

Hanson, R. K., & Harris, A. J. R. (2000). *The sex offender need assessment rating (SONAR): A method for measuring change in risk levels.* Ottawa, Ontario: Department of the Solicitor General of Canada.

Hanson, R. K., Morton, K. E., & Harris, A. J. R. (2003). Sexual offender recidivism risk: What we know and what we need to know. *Annals of the New York Academy of Sciences, 989,* 154–166.

Hanson, R. K., & Thornton, D. (1999). *Static 99: Improving actuarial risk assessment for sex offenders.* Ottawa, Ontario: Department of the Solicitor General of Canada.

Karoly, P. (2003). Mechanisms of self-regulation: A systems view. *Annual Review of Psychology, 44,* 23–52.

Laws, D. R. (2003). The rise and fall of relapse prevention. *Australian Psychologist, 38*(1), 22–30.

Laws, D. R., Hudson, S. M., & Ward, T. (2000). *Remaking relapse prevention with sex offenders: A sourcebook.* Thousand Oaks, CA: Sage.

Mann, R. E. (2000). Managing resistance and rebellion in relapse prevention intervention. In D. R. Laws, S. M. Hudson, & T. Ward (Eds.), *Remaking relapse prevention with sex offenders: A sourcebook* (pp. 197–200). Thousand Oaks, CA: Sage.

Mann, R. E., Webster, S. D., Schofield, C., & Marshall, W. L. (2004). Approach versus avoidance goals in relapse prevention with sexual offenders. *Sexual Abuse: A Journal of Research and Treatment, 16*(1), 65–75.

Marlatt, G. A. (1982). Relapse prevention: A self-control program for the treatment of addictive behaviors. In R. B. Stuart (Ed.), *Adherence, compliance and generalization in behavioral medicine* (pp. 329-378). New York: Brunner/Mazel.

Marlatt, G. A., & Gordon, J. R. (1985). *Relapse prevention: Maintenance strategies in the treatment of addictive behaviors.* New York: Guilford Press.

Marques, J. K., Day, D. M., & Nelson, C. (1992). *Findings and recommendations from California's experimental treatment program.* Unpublished manuscript, Sex Offender Treatment and Evaluation Project, Atascadero State Hospital, California.

Marshall, W. L., & Anderson, D. (1996). An evaluation of the benefits of relapse prevention programs with sexual offenders. *Sexual Abuse: A Journal of Research and Treatment, 8,* 209–229.

Marshall, W. L., Anderson, D., & Fernandez, Y. M (1999). *Cognitive-behavioural treatment of sex offenders.* New York: Wiley.

Marshall, W. L, Jones, R., Ward, T. Johnson, P., & Barbaree, H. E. (1991). Treatment outcome with sex offenders. *Clinical Psychology Review, 11,* 465–485.

Nicholaichuk, T. P. (1996). Sex offender treatment priority: An illustration of the risk/need principle. *Forum on Corrections Research, 8,* 30-32.

Nicholaichuk, T. P., Gordon, A., Gu, D., & Wong, S. (2000). Outcome of an institutional sexual offender treatment program: A comparison between treated and matched untreated offenders. *Sexual Abuse: A Journal of Research and Treatment, 12*(2), 139–153.

Nicholaichuk, T. P., & Yates, P. M. (2002). Treatment efficacy: Outcomes of the Clearwater sex offender program. In B. K. Schwartz (Ed.), *The sex offender: Current treatment modalities and systems issues* (Vol. IV, pp. 7-1–7-18.) Kingston, NJ: Civic Research Institute.

Pithers, W. D., Marques, J. K., Gibat, C. C., & Marlatt, G. A. (1983). Relapse prevention with sexual aggressives: A self-control model of treatment and maintenance of change. In J. G. Greer & I. R. Stuart (Eds.), *The sexual aggressor: Current perspectives on treatment* (pp. 214–239). New York: Van Nostrand Reinhold.

Prentky, R. A., & Burgess, A. W. (1990). Rehabilitation of child molesters: A cost-benefit analysis. *American Journal of Orthopsychiatry, 60,* 108–117.

Proulx, J., Perreault, C., & Ouimet, M. (1999). Pathways in the offending process of extrafamilial sexual child molesters. *Sexual Abuse: A Journal of Research and Treatment, 11,* 117–129.

Quinsey, V. L. (1977). The assessment and treatment of child molesters: A review. *Canadian Psychological Review, 18,* 204–220.

Shanahan, M., & Donato, R. (2001). Counting the cost: Estimating the economic benefit of pedophile treatment programs. *Child Abuse and Neglect, 25*, 541–555.

Strauss, A. (1987). *Qualitative analysis for social scientists.* New York: Cambridge University Press.

Thornton, D. (2002). Constructing and testing a framework for dynamic risk assessment. *Sexual Abuse: A Journal of Research and Treatment, 14*(2), 139–153.

Ward, T., & Hudson, S. M. (1996). Relapse prevention: A critical analysis. *Sexual Abuse: A Journal of Research and Treatment, 8,* 177–200.

Ward, T., & Hudson, S. M. (1998). A model of the relapse process in sexual offenders. *Journal of Interpersonal Violence, 13*(6), 700–725.

Ward, T., & Hudson, S. M. (2000). A self-regulation model of relapse prevention. In D. R. Laws, S. M. Hudson, & T. Ward. (Eds.), *Remaking relapse prevention with sex offenders: A sourcebook* (pp. 79–101). New York: Sage.

Ward, T., Hudson, S. M., & Keenan, T. (1998). A self regulation model of the sexual offense process. *Sexual Abuse: A Journal of Research and Treatment, 10,* 141–157.

Ward, T., Louden, K., Hudson, S. M., & Marshall, W. L. (1995). A descriptive model of the offense chain for child molesters. *Journal of Interpersonal Violence, 10,* 452–472.

Webster, S. D. (2003). *Pathways to sexual offence recidivism following treatment: An examination of the Ward & Hudson self-regulation model of relapse.* Unpublished manuscript.

Yates, P. M. (2002). What works: Effective intervention with sex offenders. In H. E. Allen (Ed.), *Risk reduction: Interventions for special needs offenders* (pp. 115–163). Lanham, MD: American Correctional Association.

Yates, P. M. (2004). *Treatment of adult sexual offenders: A therapeutic cognitive-behavioral model of intervention.* In R. Geffner, K. C. Franey, T. G. Arnold, & R. Falconer (Eds.), *Identifying and treating sex offenders: Current approaches, research, and techniques* (pp. 195–232). Binghamton, NY: Howarth Press Maltreatment and Trauma Press.

Yates, P. M., Goguen, B. C., Nicholaichuk, T. P., Williams, S. M., & Long, C. A. (2000). *National sex offender programs.* Ottawa, Ontario: Correctional Service of Canada.

Yates, P. M., Kingston, D. A., & Hall, K. (2003). *Pathways to sexual offending: Validity of Hudson and Ward's (1998) self-regulation model and relationship to static and dynamic risk among treated sexual offenders.* Paper presented at the 22nd annual Research and Treatment Conference for the Association for the Treatment of Sexual Abusers, St. Louis, MO.

Part 2

Adult Special Populations

Sex offender treatment initially dealt with individuals who had been civilly committed to programs for sexual psychopaths or sexually dangerous persons in institutions for the mentally ill, such as Western State Hospital in Washington State or the Massachusetts Treatment Center for Sexually Dangerous Persons. Eventually these programs were either closed or transferred to the jurisdiction of departments of corrections. Prison-based programs were the next focus in the field, with community-based programs springing up around the country to treat sex offenders on probation and parole. However, today there are specialized services for all ages and both sexes of offenders in a variety of sites.

With the development of this heterogeneous group of therapy programs, professionals have continued to learn about various subpopulations and in many cases have challenged assumptions based on the original programs which were developed for adult males. Adolescents and younger children certainly have very different needs and dynamics as is discussed in Part 5. Females who behave in a sexually inappropriate manner certainly have gender-specific concerns. Developmentally disabled offenders are rarely able to understand or integrate highly verbal and cognitively oriented therapies and require treatments aimed at their functional abilities.

This section covers three subgroups of sex offenders. Mentally ill offenders are being recognized by departments of mental health around the country as the difficulty in transferring these individuals into community-based programs may force the maintenance of larger state-supported institutions. If these individuals, who may never have been formally charged with sexual crimes due to competency issues, are to be safely transferred to group homes or returned to their families, hospitals must be provide offense-specific treatment to prepare these patients to recognize "high risk" situations as well as community-based programs knowledgeable in dealing with these challenging individuals. Programs must be able to address the specialized needs of persons with a variety of conditions that are comorbid with their inappropriate sexual conduct.

Another emerging subgroup is the Internet offender. This individual might be a patterned pedophile who targets and lures children over the Web, or he might be a curious surfer of the Internet who chances onto child pornography or into chat rooms. There is little research and less consensus among professionals about whether these offenders will potentially turn their computer-based activities into hands-on offenses, or whether they are simply curious or inept in screening their e-mail. In our practice we have had individuals sentenced to jail time for having two or three pictures of children out of tens of thousands of adult images on their computers. Therapists must become informed not only about the dynamics of these offenders but also about the workings of the technical aspects of cybersex, realizing that every sexually inappropriate individual regardless of age or orientation may find the Internet an outlet for his or her deviancy.

Cultural sensitivity is an issue which is often given lip service by therapists as something that should be done, but rarely are there specific recommendations which the conscientious professional can follow. After all, in order to adapt treatment to a patient's background, an individual must first understand the differences between values and customs of his or her own value system and those of other cultures. This often requires sophisticated knowledge about one's own assumptions as well as those of a variety of subcultures and may only be recognized when a mistake has been made. In addition, not only must one understand differences in major groups but in subgroups as well. For example, Latinos from Northern New Mexico differ profoundly from recent immigrants from the Dominican Republic. African Americans who trace their origins to slaves have little in common with Haitians as far as customs or even language usage. Much more information is needed which is directed at helping therapists to understand the cultural biases prevalent in today's therapeutic approaches.

David Delmonico and Elizabeth Griffin, in Chapter 4, provide valuable information on understanding the Internet offender. Especially valuable for the "nontechies" among us is their discussion of the actual workings of the Internet, including how to track the trails and traces of illegal online behavior. These authors present a typology of cybersex users which helps to clarify this highly heterogeneous group. A process of assessing these individuals is discussed and subsequent treatment approaches suggested. Another useful approach discussed in this chapter is the use of electronic accountability, which can automatically block or record activity on a computer with varying degrees of sophistication. We are only just beginning to confront the interface between "reality" and "virtual reality" in all its complex forms. This will become ever more challenging as new technologies are developed. However, currently every therapist and supervising agent who works with sex offenders needs to understand some basics about cybersex in order to adequately monitor every offender who has or will have access to a computer.

In Chapter 5 on working with African-American and Latino sex offenders, William Ford and Wilson Prunier provide valuable insight into how to adapt sex offender treatment to these populations. Initially they discuss the impact of cultural, religious, economic, environmental, societal, and historical factors on these groups and then discuss the ramifications of these dynamics on risk and needs factors. Socioeconomic issues for these groups (e.g., housing, employment, and access to medical care) may have a profound impact on their treatment. Comorbid conditions such as mental illness and substance abuse also are influenced by cultural factors. Ideally, by understanding some of the important differences among our clients, treatment will have a greater impact.

In addressing the issue of serious mental illness among sex offenders, Ruth Lewis in Chapter 6 offers insight into the issues that must be addressed with this population. Sex offender treatment is based on the assumption that first and foremost the individual is responsible for his behavior. However, what about incidents where the individual is neither legally nor psychologically considered responsible? When sexually inappropriate behavior is the direct outcome of major mental illness, the approach to the offender needs be quite different. In some cases it may difficult to differentiate behavior which is the direct outcome of, for example, command hallucinations from a comorbid antisocial personality. With this population thorough assessment is crucial. When a serious mental illness is present and directly contributes to the sexually inappropriate behavior, it becomes crucial to work with a team of professionals, including the psychiatrist, the social worker, and whatever residential staff may be involved in the case in order to recognize and respond to precursors of offense behavior. It may be particularly useful to identify a psychiatrist who is familiar with the use of medication to assist in the control of inappropriate sexual behavior and to integrate this into the control of the primary mental illness. Dr. Lewis also discusses the adaptation of relapse prevention for use with these patients.

To maximize the benefits of sex offender treatment, the field must continue to refine its approach to specific subpopulations. In doing so we may find that what we thought was a universal approach actually is effective with only certain types of clients. The debate about the effectiveness of treatment may well be redefined as a discussion about what type of sex offender treatment approaches work best with what type of sex offender.

Chapter 4

Sex Offenders Online— What Clinicians Need to Know

by David L. Delmonico, Ph.D. and Elizabeth J. Griffin, M.A.

OVERVIEW

This chapter provides basic information about what clinicians need to know when assessing and treating sexual offenders who use the Internet. The chapter reviews pertinent literature; presents known characteristics and statistics about problematic online sexual behavior, including sex offense behavior; and suggests assessment and treatment protocols. The authors provide operational definitions of various online sex-related concepts and set out several theoretical models that explain the motives and behaviors of the sex offender online. They discuss methods used to engage in online sexual activity and consider characteristics that make the Internet such a powerful sexual arena. The Cybersex User Categories model (Delmonico, Griffin, & Moriarity, 2001) is used throughout this chapter to help understand, assess, and develop treatment and management strategies for sex offenders who use the Internet. Finally, the chapter looks at limitations regarding what we know about online sex offenders and addresses implications for future research.

INTRODUCTION

Over the past ten years the interconnection of personal computers through data lines has grown at a dramatic pace. The introduction of the Internet to the general public in the early 1990s established a new method of communication that has enticed millions of users worldwide. This new online community became a microcosm of the larger society including both desirable and exploitive sides.

The benefits of the Internet remain unchallenged. Individuals transmit hundreds of millions of emails each day, and billions of home pages provide information on everything from aardvarks to zebras.

Sexuality also found its place on the Internet. Sex became more open, varied, and understood—but as with all technologies, there was a darker side. Issues such as stalking, harassment, exploitation, gambling, theft, and sexuality were easily translated into this new electronic arena. Criminals, once limited by geographic location, now have access to new potential victims. Even individuals never involved in criminal activity find themselves lured into possible ways to exploit others. This chapter explores issues related to a specific group of individuals found on the darker side of the Internet: online sex offenders.

DEMOGRAPHICS, RITUALS, AND BEHAVIORS OF ONLINE SEX OFFENDERS

Little is known about the demographics, rituals, and behaviors of online sex offenders. Many researchers and clinicians have failed to see the significant relationship between pornography, sexual offense behavior, and its ties to the Internet (Quayle, Holland, Linehan, & Taylor, 2000). One common assumption is that online sex offenders are identical to their offline counterparts, but this assumption is not necessarily true. Several theoretical models help differentiate the characteristics, behaviors, and clinical considerations of sex offenders who use the Internet and those who do not.

Therapeutic Models

Lanning (2001) proposed a typology of "computer offenders"—those who use computers to sexually exploit children. Lanning (2001) categorized these computer offenders into three broad groups: situational offenders, preferential offenders, and miscellaneous offenders. These groups are further subdivided based on the types of behaviors in which they engage, victim characteristics, and the motivation behind the offense behavior.

Carnes, Delmonico, Griffin, and Moriarity (2001) proposed five basic categories of online sexual users. These included appropriate recreational users, inappropriate recreational users, discovery, predisposed, and lifelong sexually compulsive users. The model has been modified and the inappropriate recreational user has been renamed the sexual harasser. Figure 4.1 visually depicts these categories. (This model is discussed in more detail later in the chapter.)

Internet sex offenders have been classified by legal investigators as either travelers or traders (Lanning, 2001). A traveler is a sex offender who uses the Internet to find, groom, and arrange for offline sexual offense behavior. A trader is an individual who trades child pornography but has not been caught in or charged with a "hands-on" offense behavior.

Common Methods and Characteristics

Other researchers have focused not so much on a model for conceptualizing sex offenders online but, rather, on common methods and characteristics of travelers and traders. Wolak, Mitchell, and Finkelhor (2003) researched Internet sex crimes against children and divided their sample into three categories: (1) Internet crimes against identifiable victims, (2) Internet solicitations to undercover law enforcement officers, and (3) possession, distribution, and/or trading of child pornography. These categories name specific online behaviors and may be useful in classifying online sex offenders.

Wolak, Mitchell, and Finkelhor (2003) analyzed 2,577 cases involving online offenders and reported that 99 percent were male, 92 percent were non-Hispanic whites, and the majority (86 percent) were over the age of 25. Other findings includ-

Figure 4.1
Cybersex User Categories

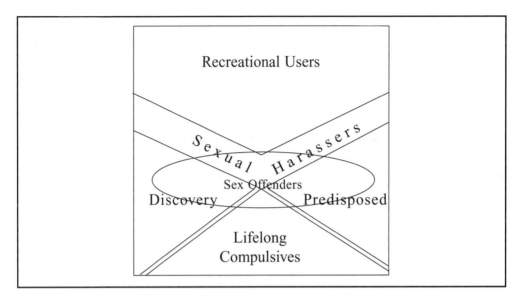

ed that 10 percent of the sample had prior arrests for sexual offenses against minors (offline) and 41 percent of individuals arrested during undercover solicitations possessed child pornography (in all forms). Of all child pornography found, 83 percent of the images included children between the ages of 6 and 12, while 80 percent of the pornography showed acts of sexual penetration of minors.

Malesky (2003) reported that sexually deviant Internet users had three times as many contact victims as those who did not use the Internet for sexually deviant behavior. The research also supported that sexually deviant Internet users tended to be Caucasian and more formally educated than other child sex offenders.

The foregoing paragraphs primarily focused on sex offenders who committed their offense behavior online. Even less is known about sex offenders who commit an offline sexual offense and use the Internet for other sexual purposes. Sex offenders are defined as individuals who have engaged in some form of illegal sexual behavior. Online sex offenders may fall into the following three groups, which are not mutually exclusive:

- Individuals who have committed a sexual offense online (e.g., downloading, distributing, or producing child pornography);

- Individuals who use the Internet as their primary method for grooming, planning, and meeting for an offline sexual offense; and

- Individuals who have committed an offline sexual offense, and currently use the Internet for sexually explicit purposes.

Figure 4.1 illustrates how, regardless of the sex offender group assignment, online sex offenders may fall into any of the five Cybersex User Categories (recreational, harassers, discovery, predisposed, or lifelong compulsive).

Cybersex Compulsivity

The overlap of sexual compulsivity and sexual offense behavior has been previously studied (Delmonico & Griffin, 2002). This issue can be taken one step further by examining cybersex compulsion and its overlap with sex offenders online.

Several large-scale studies have examined the characteristics and behaviors of online sexual users. Cooper, Delmonico, and Burg (2000) reported that 83.5 percent ($n = 7,736$) of online sexual users were not compulsive with their Internet sexual activities. However, 16.5 percent ($n = 1,529$) either were at risk for sexually compulsive online behavior or were currently sexually compulsive.

Cooper, Putnam, Planchon, and Boies (1999) conducted the first major survey research regarding online sex users and analyzed over 9,000 responses. They proposed a model based on three categories of online sex users: recreational users, at-risk users, and sexually compulsive. This model was based on the number of hours per week individuals spent in pursuit of online sexual activities, and the number of problems reported in their lives as a result of their online sexual use. Further analysis of the same data set demonstrated the importance of combining the frequency of use with the level of compulsion while engaged in the online sexual behavior (Cooper,et al., 2000).

The complexities of Internet sex use have yet to be fully captured by researchers. However, clinicians have been acutely aware of the role Internet sexuality plays in the lives of clients and the effect it can have on individuals, couples, and families.

CYBERSEX METHODS AND VENUES

To appropriately address the issue of cybersex, clinicians must have a basic working knowledge of technology and how it is used for Internet sexual activities. This basic knowledge will help clinicians ask the right questions, and appropriately interpret client responses. Quayle and Taylor (2002) interviewed nine practitioners regarding their knowledge of the Internet and technologies used for Internet sexual activity. All nine reported feeling a general lack of knowledge and understanding of the Internet as well as of how to manage a caseload of sexual offenders who may now have access to the Internet.

One common misconception is that the Internet and World Wide Web are synonymous. The World Wide Web is but one small part of the Internet. In fact, the most explicit and illicit materials are typically found in areas other than the World Wide Web. Figure 4.2 illustrates some of the various aspects of the Internet and the following paragraphs explain each area briefly.

World Wide Web

The most common method for accessing the Internet is through the World Wide Web (WWW). Internet browsers (e.g., Netscape, Internet Explorer, Opera, etc.) interpret and display text, graphics, and multimedia on a user's monitor. By pointing and

Figure 4.2
Parts of the Internet

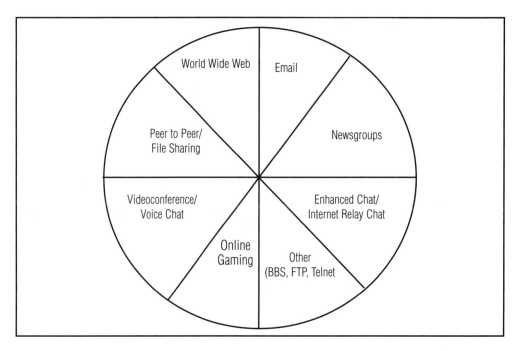

clicking, the user has the ability to explore the Internet in a user friendly environment. Web pages can display various forms of media (photos, videos, music, etc.) and facilitate the exchange of files between computers.

Newsgroups

This area serves as an electronic bulletin board system where individuals post and read text or multimedia (pictures, sounds, and video) messages. There are tens of thousands of newsgroups dedicated to specific topic areas, thousands of which are used to exchange messages with sexual content each day.

Email

Email is used for direct communication with other individuals or groups of individuals. In the case of cybersex, the message may be a sexual conversation, story, picture, sound, or video. Often individuals meet in other areas of the Internet and then begin communicating via email as a way to add more privacy and security to their sexual exchanges.

Enhanced Internet Chat

Casual users are familiar with chat programs such as Yahoo Messenger, ICQ, Excite SuperChat, or America Online's Instant Messenger (AIM). The evolution of standard text-based chatting was transformed by software programs that allow for the exchange of files (images, sounds, and programs), simultaneous web browsing, voice chat, and videoconferencing. These chat services might be termed an "Enhanced Internet Chat" area of the Internet.

Internet Relay Chat

Internet Relay Chat (IRC) is the largest and oldest chat area on the Internet. It is largely unfamiliar to most casual users and typically draws in the more tech savvy. In addition to standard text-based chatting, IRC includes a number of chat rooms that act as "file servers" to exchange various types of media including pornography. These file servers allow users to access one another's hard drives and trade images, music, videos, and so on. There are a host of file server rooms dedicated specifically to child pornography exchange.

Videoconferencing/Voice Chatting

Over the past five years technology enhancements and the widespread availability of high-speed Internet connections have increased the demand for voice and video-conferencing hardware and software. When combined with sexual behavior, a high-tech, interactive peep show results. These technologies have also been used to broadcast live sexual abuse of children and other exploitive behaviors.

Peer-to-Peer File Sharing

Software packages such as Kazaa® have made file sharing a popular hobby. Casual users of this software often exchange music files, but any file can be "shared" on the network. Many of the files on these networks are pornographic in nature. These pornographic files are numerous and easily found and can contain illegal child pornography. In fact, one study reported that 42 percent of all Kazaa requests were for pornography (Brown, 2003).

Online Gaming

Online destinations such as Multi-User Dungeons (MUDs) encourage participants to take on various characteristics and play out their roles in a game-like setting. A portion of these game areas are sexually charged and offer places for participants to engage in sexual conversations. Some individuals become compulsive with the fantasy, role-playing aspect of these games, whether sexualized or not. A new breed of online gaming has also taken over the market, in which individuals can play on teams against others on the Internet. Although not necessarily sexual, they can create compulsivity problems of their own.

Other Areas

Other methods used to engage in cybersex or offense behavior include Bulletin Board Systems (BBSs), file transfer protocol (FTP), and telnet. These represent some of the more archaic areas of the Internet and dialup technologies but remain problematic nonetheless. BBSs require a user to directly dial the phone number (or telnet address) of a specific computer that allows access to chat areas and file transfers. These BBSs can be dangerous because it is difficult for law enforcement to locate and monitor them. FTP is a method of transferring files over the Internet and makes a direct connection between two computers, again, making it difficult to monitor or infiltrate. Telnet is another method of directly connecting two computers, which can then exchange files, chat, or execute software programs over the Internet.

FORENSIC TRAILS AND TRACES

In addition to understanding how individuals access cybersex, it is important to understand the trail and traces left by the Internet. Although clinicians will not conduct forensic examinations of a computer, basic understanding of how law enforcement officials piece together cases of illegal online behavior is useful. In addition, clinicians, and probation/parole professionals need to have basic technical skills in order to manage sex offenders who now have access to the computer and Internet.

A list of some of the common trails and traces left by the Internet follows:

- *History.* Internet browsers keep track of the sites visited as a convenience to the site's users. However, this history can also be examined to see if an individual has visited off-limit sexual sites. Microsoft's Internet Explorer history can be viewed by hitting the CTL-H keys. Other browsers may differ in how you view their history.

- *Pull-down history.* The pull-down history is an abbreviated version of the history and shows the last few sites visited. You can view this by clicking on the arrow immediately next to the "address" or "location" text box where you input the uniform resource locator (http://...).

- *Cookies.* Cookies are small bits of data placed into a file known as the "cookie file." These data help track where an individual has gone and store unique information about an individual or a site. There are programs that allow you to view cookies easily, such as "Burnt Cookies." Cookies may also be viewed in a word processor or text editor. Simply type the term "cookies" into the Find or Search field on a Windows-based computer to find the exact location of the cookie file.

- *Cache.* To display text and graphics, an Internet browser must use temporary disk space to store files prior to displaying them on the screen. The area where these temporary files are stored is known as the cache. There may be hundreds or thousands of files in a cache area. Each file can be examined to look for illegal activity. You can search for "cache" or "temporary Internet files" to find the exact location of the cached files. Once the folder is located, turn on the "thumbnail" view in Windows XP to get a quick view of the contents of each file.

- *Downloads.* Individuals often take files from the Internet and store them on a hard drive or CD-ROM. These files may be photographs, videos, games, and so on. Because individuals who download files often have sophisticated organizational methods, take a close look at the folder names to help determine where illegal files may be stored. A program such as Windows Explorer can be useful in looking through directories for inappropriate folders and files, especially in the "thumbnail" view.

• *Recycle bin.* When files are initially deleted, they are placed in a holding area known as the "recycle bin" or "trash can." Files are stored here so accidentally deleted files can easily be recovered. This area is a good place to investigate, as the user may not have had an opportunity to delete incriminating files from the recycle bin. Even when files have been deleted from the recycle bin, they are not completely removed from the computer and may be restored by using specialized software applications known as "undelete" programs.

As easily as information is stored on a computer's hard drive, it can also be deleted. A deleted file can often easily be restored; however, a forensic expert may be needed if a sophisticated "shredding" or "wiping" program is used to delete information. Specific programs, often known as "Windows Cleaners," destroy the trail of an individual's Internet use with the single click of a button. These programs overwrite data on the hard drive and make data recovery extremely difficult and, in some cases, impossible. The primary reason for using such programs is to hide activity and information. The mere ownership of wiping and cleaning programs should be a red flag for clinicians and/or law enforcement professionals.

THE POWER OF THE INTERNET FOR SEX OFFENDERS

The Internet is an extremely powerful medium for any type of communication or electronic exchange, but when combined with sexuality, it becomes a positive reinforcement few can resist. There are certain characteristics of the Internet that contribute to its power. Cybersex theorists such as Cooper (1998) and Delmonico et al. (2001) have developed models to help explain this unique attraction to the Internet. Cooper (1998) explained this attraction through what was termed the "Triple A Engine." The three As refer to *A*nonymity, *A*ccessibility, and *A*ffordability. Delmonico et al. (2001) developed a model known as the "Cyberhex." The Cyberhex is a six-sided figure where each side represents a different facet of the Internet that, when combined, created an almost "hex-like" or trance state. These facets are Interactive, Intoxicating, Isolating, Integral, Inexpensive, and Imposing.

Regardless of the model one chooses to understand the power of the Internet, it is clear there is something unique about this medium that has not previously existed. Each of these models explains how the Internet can fulfill individual fantasies to a wide range of people. The sexually idiosyncratic needs of an individual are satisfied by the Internet through the false belief that the Internet was somehow specifically designed for his or her sexual desires. For example, some individuals prefer forming relationships and may meet in a chat room to form a virtual society that becomes a healthy way to meet and socialize with others. Some use these forums to "court" others and develop long-term healthy relationships. Others prefer to remain isolated and individualized on the Internet. They may prefer to view web pages or download media, far from the reaches of social relationships. Even in this dichotomy, the Internet can deliver.

Specific to sexual offenders, the Internet can feed into many of the already existing thinking errors and belief systems that allow an offense to take place. The Internet is filled with moments of instant gratification, lack of accountability, acceptance, and support by others who have similar interests, pornography (pictures, stories, movies, etc.) to reinforce the fantasy or behavior, a sense of anonymity, and a wide array of venues for paraphilic and/or offense behavior. For many sex offenders, the Internet helps maintain the negative thinking and behaviors associated with offline offense behavior.

Regardless of the conceptual model, the Internet is a powerful medium in many ways. It satisfies our unique curiosities, creates excitement/risk in lieu of boredom (Rotunda, Kass, Sutton, & Leon, 2003) and acts as reinforcer for our thoughts, feelings, fantasies, urges, and behaviors.

MODEL FOR UNDERSTANDING INTERNET SEX USERS

Delmonico et al. (2001) proposed a model for conceptualizing cybersex users: Cybersex User Categories (CUCs). Figure 4.1 illustrates a slightly revised version of this model. The CUCs illustrate how a large number of Internet sex users report little difficulty or interference in their lives, yet others have tremendous consequences. This model helps explain who uses the Internet for sex and provides possible explanations as to why.

Appropriate Recreational Users

An appropriate recreational user accesses cybersex on the Internet and does not experience any obsession, compulsion, or consequence as a result of this use. In fact, some individuals report that they use cybersex as an enhancement to their current relationship (e.g., learn new sexual techniques or positions, etc.). Some use the Internet as an avenue to remain healthy as they recover from an addiction, sexual or otherwise (Putnam & Maheu, 2000). Others simply use cybersex as a form of entertainment and do not experience any difficulties as a result of its use. As Barak and King (2000) wrote, the Internet clearly has two faces, one which can be enhancing and one which leads away from health. Others discuss the importance of the Internet for helping disenfranchised groups connect and form intimate, personal relationships—an option that was not otherwise so publicly available (Burke, 2000; Tikkanen & Ross, 2000).

Sexual Harassers

Harassers often use Internet material inappropriately, such as telling or showing sexually explicit materials to other adults. They may use sexually explicit backgrounds on their computer screens or screensavers, and they often use the material they find online to ignore or cross sexual boundaries with others, usually in an attempt to be humorous. Individuals in this group often border on problematic behavior or sexual offense and warrant further assessment. Their behavior may represent only the surface of other problematic sexual thoughts, feelings, fantasies, urges, or behaviors.

Discovery Group

The discovery group includes those who have never had any problems with sexual fantasy or behavior until they discovered sex on the Internet. Sex on the Internet triggered a compulsive behavior they may not have otherwise developed. Although this group is rare, it does exist.

Predisposed Individuals

The discovery group consists of individuals who have had some history of problematic sexual fantasies but have kept their urges and behaviors under control. The Internet fosters the development of an already existing sexual fantasy or urge that may not have developed into behavior until the introduction of the cybersex.

Lifelong Sexually Compulsive Individuals

Some cybersex users have dealt with sexually compulsive behavior throughout their lives, and the Internet simply becomes an extension of their inappropriate sexual behaviors. These individuals often have well-established patterns of problematic sexual urges, fantasies, and behaviors and a history of ritualized sexually problematic behaviors. They may see the Internet as an additional way to act out their sexual behaviors that enhances their already addictive patterns. Others may see it as a "safer" way of acting out their problematic sexual behaviors because it may reduce their direct contact with others.

ASSESSMENT

This section addresses assessment techniques to help classify an individual into the CUCs described earlier. CUCs are an important aspect of the assessment process, and will be useful in the eventual planning of an effective treatment plan.

Professionals often develop a strong identity within their given discipline; as a result they establish commonly practiced methods of assessment and treatment. Although in some respects this specialization helps develop expert practitioners, it can also lead to the exclusion of other effective models. To treat the Internet sex user, clinicians need to assess from various theoretical perspectives and intervene in ways not always traditional to their respective disciplines. The purpose of the assessment is to determine the CUC in which the client best fits, and the most effective treatment plans.

Many times clinicians assess only the sex offenders whose presenting problems include a history of problematic online behavior. However, sex offenders' use of the Internet may be undetected, or they may use the Internet to fuel their fantasies and not necessarily act out online. All sex offenders should be screened for their use of the Internet and any role it may play in their sexual behaviors.

Testing and Screening

Cybersex is often a complex issue with myriad coexisting problems. Individuals who struggle to control their cybersex use often experience other forms of psychological distress. Young and Rogers (1998) made the connection between general Internet use and increased levels of clinical depression. Depression is often a comorbid factor in cybersex cases as well. Cybersex may also be a symptom of underlying psychiatric issues, or part of a larger pattern of an Axis II disorder. As such, the following areas of psychological health should be assessed:

- General psychological profiles (e.g., Minnesota Multiphasic Personality Inventory—2nd Edition; Hathaway, McKinley, & Butcher, 1990; and Millon-2; Millon, Antoni, Millon, Meagher, & Grossman, 2001);

- Depression screening (e.g., Beck Depression Inventory—2; Beck, Steer, & Brown, 1996);

- Anxiety screening (e.g., Beck Anxiety Inventory; Beck & Steer, 1993);

- Adult attention deficit issues (e.g., Test of Variable Attention; Greenberg, Corman, & Kindischi, 1996);

- Addictive disorder screening (e.g., Substance Abuse Subtle Screening Inventory—3; Miller, 1997; and Gambling-Maroondah Assessment Profile; Loughnan, Pierce, & Sargis, 1999);

- Measures of sexual addiction/compulsivity (e.g., Garos Sexual Behavior Index; Garos, in press; Kalichman Sexual Compulsivity Scale; Kalichman & Rompa, 2001; Sexual Dependency Inventory, or SDIR; Carnes & Delmonico, 1994; and Sexual Addiction Screening Test; Carnes, 1989);

- General Internet use/misuse inventories (e.g., Internet Use Survey; Rotunda, Kass, Sutton, & Leon, 1989); and

- Internet sexual use inventories (e.g., Internet Sex Screening Test, or ISST; Delmonico, 1997; Cybersexual Addiction Quiz; Young, 1998; and Cybersex Addiction Screening Test; Weiss, 1997).

An in-depth discussion of each of these assessment instruments is beyond the scope of this chapter. However, it is important that any assessment include information from the ISST, as it is the only empirically derived measure of cybersex use. Thus, we provide a basic description of it here.

Internet Sex Screening Test. There are a number of screening tools designed to assess whether an individual warrants further assessment and intervention with regard to his Internet sexual behavior. However, the ISST (Delmonico, 1997) is one of the few instruments empirically derived and psychometrically examined for reliability and validity. The ISST consists of twenty-five core items and nine critical items to assess for general sexual compulsivity. Delmonico and Miller (2003) reported that the ISST had adequate internal consistency reliability (.51 - .86), and through factor analysis they determined that the ISST has five factors: Online Sexual Compulsivity;

Online Sexual Behavior; Social, Online Sexual Behavior; Isolated, Online Sexual Spending; and Interest in Online Sexual Behavior. The ISST remains under development, but it can offer one piece of data in determining whether an individual exhibits problematic use of the Internet.

Testing and screening provide necessary data in the evaluation of individuals who present with Internet sex problems. Equally important, however, is another assessment tool, the general clinical interview.

General Clinical Interview. In conducting a clinical interview, a variety of areas related to problematic online use should be considered. A general clinical interview should include questions related to the following areas:

- Family-of-origin issues;

- Abuse/trauma history;

- Relationship history;

- Complete sexual history (including sexual offense behavior and sexual compulsivity);

- Addictive disorder history;

- Work/education history (sexual harassment, attention deficit hyperactivity disorder);

- Psychiatric/medication history (depression, anxiety, obsessive-compulsive features, impulse control); and

- Current family issues.

The combination of psychological testing and the clinical interview will take multiple sessions to complete. It is not unusual for a comprehensive evaluation to range from four to six hours long. Family genograms, collateral interviews of other individuals (partner, employer, etc.), and structured sexual history forms such as the SDIR (Carnes & Delmonico, 1994) are just a few tools helpful in a clinical interview. Data gathered must interpreted and analyzed to fully understand the scope of the problem.

Internet Assessment. In addition to the general areas covered during the clinical interview, it is critical to assess the client's technical knowledge and skill level, the frequency and methods of his online sexual behavior, and the sexual, social, and psychological impact of his Internet behavior. Clinicians should have working knowledge of the Internet in order to know what questions to ask, how to ask them, and what the answers may implicate.

Questions during the technology aspects of the clinical interview cover three areas: technical knowledge; Internet behavior; and associated sexual, social, and psychological factors. Often a single question can provide information about both the technical skills and online behavior of the client. Internet-related questions should be incorporated into the comprehensive Internet assessment. Questions regarding the sexual, social, and psychological impact of the Internet have been modified and adapted in the checklist that follows from Quayle and Taylor's (2002) four factors for Internet assessment.

☐ *Technical knowledge and Internet behavior questions:*

- Where is your computer located? (Isolated areas are more problematic.)

- Have you and your partner ever had separate Internet accounts? (Separate accounts allow for more secrecy.)

- Over the past six months, how many hours per week have you spent online? (More time online increases likelihood of finding sexual content or developing compulsive use.)

- Over the past six months, how many hours per week have you engaged in Internet sex? (Eleven+ hours of Internet sex increases life problems as a result; number of hours is not the only indicator of Internet sex problems; calculate time online to time online for sex ratio. Higher ratios are found to be more problematic.)

- What are all the screen names or nicknames you have used while online? (Pay attention to sexualized names or names designed to be attractive to children/teens, etc.)

- What are the names of your favorite chat/IRC channels or rooms, past and present? (Pay attention to room names for indicators of child/teen/sexual content; IRC requires increased technical skills and may be a place for pornography trading.)

- Have you ever downloaded music or other files from Kazaa® or other peer-to-peer networks? (These are high pornography areas, including child pornography.)

- Have you ever attempted to conceal files you have downloaded from the Internet? (Changing file names and hiding files/folders are ways to preserve sexual secrecy.)

- Have you ever visited newsgroups/bulletin boards? If so, what types of boards? (Use of such features requires higher level of technical knowledge to access; there is increased anonymity in these areas and illegal files are often traded here.)

- Have you ever used PalTalk or other video/audio conferencing software? (Sexual areas exists in these forums; if client uses these, find out how, and whether adult areas are accessed.)

- Have you ever used chat rooms while online? If so, what types of rooms did you visit? (Listen for sexualized, teen, or other problematic room types, etc.)

- Have you ever played Internet games? (Many games have sexualized content.)

- Have you owned a digital, video, or Internet camera that connects to your computer? (Such cameras can be used to produce pornography online or transmit sexual images live; ask if cameras have ever been used to take nude pictures of anyone, including self.)

- Have you ever used file server software—for example, FTP, DCC, etc.? (If the client knows these terms, it may indicate higher technical skills; find out what types of files are traded and with whom.)

- Have you ever had real-life contact with someone you met online? (Such contact may indicate a progression toward offline offense and increased danger/risk.)

☐ *Sexual, social, and psychological impact of the Internet:*

- Has your real-life sexual behavior/activity been affected by Internet sex use?

- What is the relationship between masturbation and your cybersex behavior?

- How much time do you spend organizing or viewing sexual materials you collected online?

- Is there a noted progression in your sexual risk taking (on- or offline) as a result of cybersex behavior?

- Have you noticed a "ritual" around your Internet sex use (e.g., planning and preparing the same way each time, cleaning/deleting files after each Internet sex session)?

- Are you sexually aroused when engaging in cybersex?

- Are children intentionally or unintentionally exposed to sexual material as a result of your Internet sex use?

- Have you ever lied about your age, sex, or other characteristics about yourself while online?

- Have you ever attempted to contact children online, or met face to face with children you met online?

- Have you experienced consequences, or jeopardized important life areas (e.g., work, family, and friends) as a result of your online sex use?

- Have you become more isolated (physically or emotionally) from family and friends?

- Has your preoccupation with Internet sex intensified and interfered with your life in some way?

- Have you had difficulty in focusing or concentrating on other tasks because you are thinking about Internet sex?

- Has Internet sex affected your mood, either positively or negatively?

Common Defenses or Excuses. In the course of interviewing a client's defenses will be raised and the individual may provide a rationale or explanations for his Internet sexual behavior. This is especially true if there are significant consequences pending as a result of these online behaviors (legal issues, divorce, etc.).

Denial and minimization often occur in Internet sex cases. While the arguments may be valid, it is important to work with investigators, forensic examiners, and probation/parole officers to help determine the viability such of the arguments. Orput (2003) proposed six defenses sex offenders online used to explain or justify their sexual behavior. These defenses are modified and adapted in the list that follows:

- *Blaming others.* This defense is based on the argument that another individual (family member, coworker, hacker, etc.) used the person's account to engage in illegal behavior without the person's permission or knowledge.

- *Surprised.* An individual making the "surprise" argument reports unknowingly receiving illegal material, or that the material was unsolicited and/or accidentally mixed in with legal material being downloaded.

- *Ignorance.* The individual in this case claims that he did not know the file received was child pornography. He may claim that he believed the child in the image was an adult or that he did not understand the laws around child pornography.

- *Professional.* In these cases, the individual claims he engaged in illegal behavior online as part of his research or in a professional capacity. He may state that he was researching sexuality online or assessing how far children will go in chat rooms.

- *Vigilante.* An individual using this defense will admit to going online and engaging in inappropriate behavior but will claim that he did it as a way of catching others and was planning to report the others to authorities.

- *Entrapment.* This individual will not deny that he engaged in illegal online behavior but may report that he would not have engaged in such behavior if he had not been enticed or entrapped by law enforcement officers.

Other Assessment Tools

Other assessment tools available include the therapeutic polygraph and sexual arousal screens. The therapeutic polygraph should be conducted by a certified polygraph examiner who is familiar with Internet sex issues. A separate polygraph should be conducted for cybersex-related issues, as mixing questions may contaminate the results. The polygraph should be clinically helpful and not used in punitive ways. The polygraph can help break through denial about general thoughts, feelings, and fantasies, as well as address specific incidents.

Arousal and attraction screening tools, such as penile plethysmograph and the Abel Assessment for Sexual Interests (Abel, 1998), are most useful for detecting individuals who are showing some attraction to children or who are downloading child pornography. However, users may be downloading pictures of clothed children or may just not have been caught with child pornography, and therefore these screening tools may be useful to uncover a variety of Internet sex users. Individuals whose results indicate arousal to both sexes and many age groups should be carefully evaluated for sexual compulsivity, because generalized arousal patterns are often present in sexually compulsive individuals. Given the cultural taboo of child attraction, these instruments can address issues related to denial and refute common defenses employed by those caught engaging in illegal online behavior.

Medication Evaluation. Early in the assessment, cybersex users should be evaluated for possible psychopharmacological intervention. Medications that are used to treat depression, anxiety, and obsessive thinking may be useful in the treatment of problematic Internet sex users. Clients should be referred to a medical professional (i.e., psychiatrist) familiar with the complexities of treating depression, anxiety, and obsessive-compulsive disorder combined with sexual disorders. Early intervention with appropriate medications can often be the key to successful completion of treatment.

Classifying Into User Categories. Figure 4.3 is a checklist of various assessment data gathered as part of a cybersex user's comprehensive evaluation. Based on multiple data sources, assignment into the primary cybersex user category should be made. This determination is important, because treatment plans will be based on this primary group assignment. Following are some of the things to consider from the assessment to help clarify which user category the client best fits.

Figure 4.3
Internet Sex User Assessment Checklist

☐ Testing to determine psychological profile

☐ Screen for depression and/or anxiety

☐ Screen for attention deficit disorder/attention deficit hyperactivity disorder

☐ Screen for other addictive disorders

☐ Screen for general sexual compulsivity

☐ General Internet use/misuse

☐ Screen for Internet sex use

☐ Conduct comprehensive clinical interview (including collateral data)

☐ Assess technical knowledge and Internet behavior

☐ Assess sexual, social, and psychological impacts of the Internet

☐ Therapeutic polygraph (if warranted) specifically around cybersex issues

☐ Sexual arousal assessment (if warranted) (Abel Screen, phallometrics, etc.)

☐ Medication evaluation

☐ Determine the best group in CUCs

Sexual Harassers. The sexual harassers are often the most difficult group to categorize, as the inappropriate online behaviors may be due to their lack of education or ignorance about the inappropriateness of their behavior, or can be an indicator of other underlying problems. In Figure 4.1, the sexual harassers fall between the recreational users and the three problematic users. This visual representation is accurate because some sexual harassers may be recreational users with ignorance or poor boundaries. Conversely, sexual harassers may engage in this behavior as a symptom of being in the discovery, predisposed, or lifelong sexually compulsive category.

A thorough evaluation of sexual harassers is warranted because on the surface they may appear to be recreational users when in fact the psychological testing and clinical interview may help to identify a more serious underlying sexual problem.

Discovery Users. Discovery users are the small group of individuals who would most likely not have sexual difficulties if it were not for the Internet. Psychological testing reveals few if any current psychological or emotional difficulties. There is typically no significant history of depression, anxiety, or attentional difficulties. The family history contains little family dysfunction and lack of any addictive disorders. There is typically no reported abuse history (e.g., sexual, physical, or emotional), no signs of addictive behaviors, and no history of sexual behavior problems. Discovery users do not typically exhibit arousal or attraction patterns toward children.

At the conclusion of the assessment, clinicians feel no closer to understanding the reasons behind the problematic online behavior than before the interview. For discovery users, the Internet was the primary trigger of the problematic sexual behavior. The frequency and intensity of the online sexual behavior tends to escalate very quickly, and while at the onset the user may not have a great deal of technology knowledge, he quickly develops new skills to keep up with escalating patterns of cybersex use.

Collateral informants are often surprised to learn of the discovery user's sexual problems. The behavior is often described as being "out of character," and is ego-dystonic to both the discovery user and collateral informants.

Predisposed Users. The predisposed user has an identifiable problematic history (including his sexual history) but maintains a set of internal or external controls that prevents acting out his fantasies or urges. In the past, he avoided or stopped rituals before engaging in problematic sexual behavior. However, the Internet is the trigger that weakens those controls and allows the acting-out behavior to surface.

Periods of major depression and anxiety can be found on psychological testing or through reported history. Psychological testing may also reveal features of various personality disorders, even though the individual does not meet criteria for the full disorder. The evaluator may also note attentional difficulties, moderate levels of family dysfunction, and the presence of other addictive disorders or traits. Predisposed users may or may not show arousal toward children, but should be screened for sexual offense risk, especially if the cybersex behaviors included child pornography or sexual activity with children.

At the conclusion of the evaluation, clinicians will feel as though they can create a plausible explanation for how the individual developed online sex difficulties, even though there still may be pieces missing.

Collateral informants will often report a history with minor problematic events and suspect that the user has some current, unidentified problem. The double life of the predisposed user is easy to conceal as many of his sexual problems are limited to fantasy or other socially acceptable expressions.

Lifelong Sexually Compulsive Users. The lifelong sexually compulsive user (LSC) has an extensive problematic sexual history, often dating back to adolescence. The problems are often related to an inability to manage internal conflicts associated with sexual decision making and control impulses around sexual behavior. Sexual acting out often becomes ritualized, with both a pre- and postritual around the actual behavior. There is also a clearly identifiable acting-out cycle that includes a buildup phase, sexual acting out, and a period of shame/guilt often leading to a repeat of the cycle. In LSCs, cybersex behavior is an extension of an already existing lifelong pattern of problematic sexual behavior.

Psychological testing typically reveals numerous comorbid, problematic issues, often confirmed by collateral informants or the LSC himself. Underlying personality disorders are common, along with other issues such as dysthymia, anxiety disorders, impulse control problems, attentional difficulties (attention deficit disorder/attention deficit hyperactivity disorder), and obsessive-compulsive disorder or features. Of the problem groups, LSCs are the most likely to have a psychiatric history and to have used medications for some of the comorbid issues mentioned.

LSCs often report a significant history of family dysfunction and patterns of familial addiction or psychiatric histories. In the sexual history, clinicians often find extensive use of various forms of pornography, often dating back to a very young age. Chaotic financial, work, and relationship histories are not uncommon. Although they do not necessarily like this part of themselves, LSCs identify this behavior as part of who they are for a long period of time and see their behaviors as very ego-syntonic.

If the online behaviors involved child pornography or sexual activity with children, an existing arousal or attraction pattern toward children may be present. Sexual offense risk behavior should be assessed and treated appropriately. However, it is common for LSCs to have random and high arousal to nearly all stimuli—an indication of their lifelong, generalized sexual arousal patterns.

Collateral informants can identify problematic legal, social, occupational, or financial difficulties; however, many are surprised to learn the extent of the history as the LSC has had years of practice in hiding his double life.

At the conclusion of the evaluation the clinician is often clear about the history and reasons for cybersex-related problems. The significant and complex history of LSCs makes them one of the easier groups to identify, yet one of the most difficult to treat.

TREATMENT ISSUES

Treatment plans will vary based on the CUC assignment. However, there are basic concepts included in any treatment plan for problematic cybersex users. Carnes et al. (2001) called these basic changes "first order." First-order changes benefit all problematic online sex users; however, the CUC should be considered as the duration and intensity of these basic interventions may vary depending on the individual's placement into the CUCs.

In general, treatment is longer and more in-depth for LSCs because they have been struggling with the problem for a longer period of time and often have more severe complicating factors in their history. Discovery users may not need the same duration or intensity of these basic interventions as the other groups, because they may not have the predisposing or lifelong issues. The response of predisposed users to basic treatment strategies should be closely monitored in order to help determine the duration and intensity of these first-order changes.

Basic and Immediate Changes

Changing the Environment. One of the debates about sex offenders online is whether they should even be permitted to access the Internet. Although the Internet can be dangerous territory for offenders, it may also be argued that it is better for sex offenders to learn how to cope and manage their Internet access while in treatment (or on probation or parole) rather than after treatment. Given the fact that the Internet is widely available at public libraries, Internet cafes, schools, the workplace, and so on, teaching healthy ways to manage Internet access may be more advisable than prohibiting access altogether. If sex offenders are permitted to use the Internet, some suggestions to assist in managing their online behavior follow.

Increase Visibility. Isolation and secrecy perpetuate problematic online behavior. Moving the computer to a higher traffic area or arranging the monitor (at home or work) so others can fully see what the user is doing helps dramatically decrease the feelings of isolation and the ability to keep content secret from others. In addition, establishing a written contract about when the Internet can be accessed may be useful because many individuals wait until they are alone, everyone has gone to bed, or everyone at work has gone to lunch. An example of a contract addressing this and other acceptable use rules may be found at the Internet Behavior Consulting website (*http://www.internetbehavior.com*).

Decrease Fantasy. Internet sex can extract an individual from reality and place him into a virtual/fantasy world. To avoid getting stuck in fantasy, users should explore ways to keep one foot grounded in reality during their Internet use. Suggestions include using background images or screensavers of family members, probation officers, or other significant people/places/things. Placing photos of important individuals around the computer or on a mouse pad helps remind users of the risk and consequences of their online behavior.

Maintain Resistance. Many problematic online users report being able to resist temptations of negative online behavior for short periods. Therefore, setting time limits for how long the user may be online can take advantage of this internal resistance. If only fifteen minutes is allotted to check emails and/or look for legitimate information online, individuals stay focused on the task and are not tempted to browse for Internet sex. Similarly, users should have a specific task or goal for their online behavior. Problematic sex users should not "surf the web," because it is easy to stray into problematic areas. Users may also wish to set limits around the use of search engines, because search engines can often turn up unexpected results. The acceptable use contract with the client should specifically address this issue as well. Finally, prior to logging on to the Internet, users should do a short assessment of their "daily resistance level." Users may journal about the day's events and their current state of mind. The journaling may help some users determine that their resistance is too low that day and Internet access should be delayed until they are in a more psychologically stable frame of mind.

Electronic Accountability. There are several ways to prevent access to specific areas of the Internet. These methods are not failsafe, nor do they guarantee that an individual will not engage in inappropriate online behavior; rather, they impede the user's ritualized pattern of problematic online behavior. The technologically savvy or determined Internet sex user can easily bypass many of these controls. Discovery and predisposed users benefit most from these electronic methods of control; however, LSCs are masters at overcoming obstacles to their sexual acting out and may see this as another challenge to circumvent. Bissette (2004) categorized the methods for controlling Internet content into four main areas: (1) Internet or blocking software, (2) an Internet service provider (ISP) that filters itself, (3) an ISP that is a closed community, and (4) monitoring software that emails reports. We have "collapsed" this list into three areas:

Filtering. The most common method of filtering inappropriate Internet content is through software installed on a personal computer and password protected. Examples include CyberPatrol, NetNanny, and CyberSitter. This method is the least effective because workarounds exist and the blocking software does not typically work in all areas of the Internet. Filtering and blocking software are primarily focused on the World Wide Web and, to some extent, newsgroups, chat rooms, and emails. As shown previously in Figure 4.2, numerous areas of the Internet should be blocked.

Other filtering methods include "family friendly" ISPs. These ISPs filter content *before* it arrives at the computer, making it more difficult to circumvent. Other options include "closed community" ISPs, which hand select the content available to their subscribers. The website requested must be on the ISP's list of approved sites or the user will be unable to access it.

Spyware and Email Reports. Spyware can be installed by the user or unbeknownst to the user. Spyware typically monitors each user keystroke and captures random screenshots for later review. Most Spyware programs can email periodic reports, or report when the user violates a preset rule or condition (types a sexual word, etc.). Services such as "Covenant Eyes," although not considered true Spyware, can monitor visited websites and email a report to accountability partners. This service is limited to the World Wide Web area of the Internet.

Increased Sophistication. Technological developments and the need for monitoring software are inspiring hardware and software manufacturers to develop more sophisticated methods of tracking computer use. For example, some products connect a second computer directly to the client's computer to store *every* activity, from surfing the Internet to downloading files to installing new software. At random times, or when questions arise about an individual's computer use, logs can be searched or the client can be monitored in real time.

Other Treatment Basics

Due to the complexity of problematic online sexual behavior, various modalities of treatment including individual, couples, family, group, support groups, and accountability partners (sponsors), are all useful. Discovery users may not need all these forms of treatment and, depending on the specifics of the case, may not need extended terms of group therapy and support groups. This user category will benefit from psychoeducational information regarding triggers, rituals, problematic cycles, and relapse prevention plans. Certain medications may be useful to discovery users, particularly early in treatment, because depression and anxiety are common adjustment problems associated with their behavior being revealed. In the short term, medications may reduce the depression and anxiety and increase other therapies' effectiveness. The majority of discovery users do not need long-term medication intervention.

Predisposed users should examine the reasons behind the breakdown in their internal/external controls and put relapse prevention strategies in place to prevent similar occurrences in the future. Predisposed users often need intense and immediate treatment to diffuse the crisis situation created by their behavior. Typically, once predisposed users increase their awareness and understanding and put effective relapse prevention plans in place they can often manage their impulses and not require lifelong interventions. While predisposed users may benefit from support groups and sponsors for a time, they may not be candidates for lifelong membership in such groups. Psychoeducational sessions can build on the predisposed user's historical ability to use self awareness to prevent repeating previous types of acting out. Predisposed users can combine new information regarding cycles, triggers, self monitoring, and so on, with their existing coping strategies to help prevent future relapse. A medication evaluation is strongly recommended for predisposed users. Their current affective state and historical predispositions may improve with appropriate medical intervention and therapy.

LSCs should receive multiple modes of therapy and should be involved in some form of treatment for an extended period of time, if not on a lifelong basis. LSCs may eventually leave ongoing treatment, but in order to remain relapse free they will find they need to periodically return to treatment and/or support groups throughout their lives. Psychoeducational materials are important for LSCs, but it often takes years before the intellectual knowledge is incorporated into behavioral changes. Medications are often useful in helping LSCs move from understanding concepts to behaviorally applying them to their own lives. Depression, anxiety, attentional issues, obsessive-compulsive disorders, and poor impulse control are areas that should be considered for medication treatment. LSCs may need medication throughout their lives to prevent future relapses and deal with the multiple underlying issues of their behavior.

LSCs require a great deal of accountability during treatment. Structured therapeutic settings will be the most beneficial, especially early in treatment, to increase accountability. Therapeutic polygraphs should be considered one method of helping LSCs stay honest with themselves during the therapy process. More than any other user category, relapse for LSCs is a natural part of the change process. Relapse should not be seen as an indicator of lack of motivation, or desire to change but, rather, a result of the many complex issues the LSCs face in their recovery.

UNDERLYING AND ONGOING TREATMENT ISSUES

Similar to clients dealing with offline sexual offenses, online sex offenders share underlying and ongoing issues that need to be addressed. These issues can include the following:

- Relational issues (intimacy, abandonment, social skills, etc.);
- Internal struggles (shame, grief, loss, depression, spirituality, etc.);
- Past issues (trauma/abuse, family of origin, etc.); and
- Sexual issues (sexual health—physical/relational, etc.);

Problematic online behaviors are complex issues and treatment not only should focus on stopping the behavior but also should address the associated underlying and ongoing psychological issues. Many clients will have difficulty in recognizing the relationship between the underlying issues, such as grief and loss, and current problematic online behaviors. However, clients willing to explore deeper issues may be less likely to relapse and may feel far more successful in treatment. LSC users are the most likely to have significant underlying and ongoing treatment issues and will find it difficult to maintain their sexual health without addressing these issues. Clients in other user categories may benefit from examining these underlying issues, but it may not be as critical to maintaining their recovery.

In the process of developing treatment plans, clinicians should take into consideration the many unique aspects of the client's situation. Delmonico, Griffin, and Carnes (2002) provide a lengthy case example and an associated treatment plan for the case. This treatment plan incorporates both the basic and ongoing changes necessary for the successful treatment of the particular client. Clinicians are encouraged to develop treatment plans on a case-by-case basis, much as the example treatment plan does.

CONCLUSION

This chapter presented basic information about what clinicians need to know when presented with an online sexual offender. Although the chapter provided only introductory information, the intent was to do the following:

• Review the pertinent literature regarding online sex offenders;

• Provide models for conceptualizing online sex offenders;

• Discuss basic venues for online sexual behavior;

• Hypothesize about the powerful attraction of the Internet;

• Present assessment concepts unique to problematic online sex users; and

• Provide basic information to develop effective treatment plans.

This chapter was based on hypotheses and speculation from clinical experiences, early survey research, and anecdotal information. Aside from survey research cited, little has been done to gather data specifically regarding this population. As research is conducted, speculation will turn to more quantitative and/or qualitative data. These data may support the current theses or guide us in an entirely different direction regarding these issues. Technology is developing at a rapid pace, and the Internet continues to grow. High-speed Internet connectivity will become commonplace in homes across the United States, and as processing speeds increase and video capabilities improve, the world has yet to see the full implications of sex on the Internet.

Future research will continue to gather survey data regarding cybersex activities and those who engage in online sexual behaviors, including online sex offenders. Researchers are in the early stages of exploring the impact of online sexuality on children and adolescents. Victims of sex offenders online have been a neglected area of research, and the effects of online sexual abuse should be explored. New instrumentation should be developed to accurately identify individuals with Internet sex problems, especially online sex offenders. Instruments that currently assess for sexual offense risk need to include considerations for problematic online sex users and online sex offenders. Future research may also wish to address the impact of online behaviors for those who commit offline sexual offenses rapists, child molesters, etc) but who use the Internet to validate their fantasies and illegal sexual behavior. Because much of the treatment theories are based on anecdotal experiences, outcome studies specifically addressing treatment methods most likely to benefit online sex users are necessary.

The understanding of sexual offending through the Internet is in its infancy. However, by acknowledging the connections between the Internet and sexual offense behavior, clinicians will be better able to serve online sex offenders. It is hoped that this chapter provides a starting context for such understanding and intervention.

References

Abel, G. G., Huffman, J., Warberg, B. W., & Holland, C. L. (1998). Visual reaction time and plethysmography as measures of sexual interest in child molesters. *Sexual Abuse, 10*(2), 81–95.

Barak, A., & King, S. A. (2000). Editorial: The two faces of the Internet: Introduction to the special issue on the Internet and sexuality. *CyberPsychology and Behavior, 3*(4), 517–520.

Beck, A. T., & Steer, R. A. (1993). *Beck Anxiety Inventory* (1993 ed.). San Antonio, TX: Psychological Corporation.

Beck, A. T., Steer, R. A., & Brown, G. K. (1993). *Beck Depression Inventory* (2nd ed.). San Antonio, TX: Psychological Corporation.

Bissette, D. (2004). *Choosing an Internet filter.* Retrieved April 29, 2004, from *http://www. healthymind.com/filters.pdf.*

Brown, S. (2003, March 20). *Executive Summary of Peer to Peer File Sharing.* Retrieved April 30, 2004, from *http://www.palisadesys.com/news&events/p2pstudy.pdf.*

Burke, S. K. (2000). In search of lesbian community in an electronic world. *CyberPsychology and Behavior, 3*(4), 591–604.

Carnes, P. J. (1989). *Contrary to love.* Center City, MN: Hazelden.

Carnes, P. J., & Delmonico, D. L. (1994). *Sexual Dependency Inventory—Revised.* Wickenburg, AZ: Gentle Path Press.

Carnes, P. J., Delmonico, D. L., Griffin, E., & Moriarty, J. (2001). *In the shadows of the Net: Breaking free of online compulsive sexual behavior.* Center City, MN: Hazelden.

Cooper, A. (1998). Sexuality and the internet: Surfing into a new millennium. *Cyberpsychology and Behavior, 1*(2), 187–193.

Cooper, A., Delmonico, D., & Burg, R. (2000). Cybersex users, abusers, and compulsives: New findings and implications. *Sexual Addiction and Compulsivity: Journal of Treatment and Prevention, 7*(1–2), 5–30.

Cooper, A., Putnam, D., Planchon, L. A., & Boies, S. C. (1999). Online sexual compulsivity: Getting tangled in the Net. *Sexual Addiction and Compulsivity: Journal of Treatment and Prevention, 6*(2), 79–104.

Delmonico, D. L. (1997). *Internet Sex Screening Test.* Retrieved December 14, 2004, from *www.sex help.com.*

Delmonico, D. L., & Griffin, E. J. (2002). Classifying problematic sexual behavior: A working model revisited. In K. Adams & P. Carnes (Eds.), *Clinical management of sex addiction.* New York: Brunner/Routledge.

Delmonico, D. L., Griffin, E., & Carnes, P. J. (2002). Treating online compulsive sexual behavior: When cybersex is the drug of choice. In A. Cooper (Ed.), *Sex and the Internet: A guidebook for clinicians.* New York: Brunner/Routledge.

Delmonico, D. L., Griffin, E. J., & Moriarity, J. (2001). *Cybersex unhooked: A workbook for breaking free of online compulsive sexual behavior.* Center City, MN: Hazelden Press.

Delmonico, D. L., & Miller, J. A. (2003). The Internet sex screening test: A comparison of sexual compulsives versus non-sexual compulsives. *Sexual and Relationship Therapy, 18*(3), 261–276.

Garos, S. (in press). *Garos Sexual Behavior Index.* Los Angeles, CA: Western Psychological Services.

Greenberg, L. M., Corman, C. L., & Kindischi, C. L. (1996). *Test of Variables of Attention* (version 703). Los Alamos, CA: Universal Attention Disorders.

Hathaway, S., McKinley, J. C., & Butcher, J. M. (1990). *Minnesota Multiphasic Personality Inventory* (2nd ed.). Minneapolis: University of Minnesota Press.

Kalichman, S., & Rompa, D. (2001). The Sexual Compulsivity Scale: Further development and use with HIV-positive persons. *Journal of Personality Assessment, 76,* 379–395.

Lanning, K. V. (2001). Child molesters and cyber pedophiles: A behavioral perspective. In R. R. Hazelwood & A. Wolbert Burgess (Eds.), *Practical aspects of rape investigation: A multidisciplinary approach* (3rd ed.). London: CRC Press.

Loughnan, T., Pierce, M., & Sagris, D. A. (1999). *The Maroondah Assessment Profile for Problem Gambling.* Victoria, Australia: Australian Council for Educational Research.

Malesky, L. A. (2003). Sexually deviant Internet usage by child sex offenders. *Dissertation Abstracts International.*

Miller, G. A. (1997). *The Substance Abuse Subtle Screening Inventory* (3rd ed.). Springville, IL: The SASSI Institute.

Millon, T., Antoni, M., Millon, C., Meagher, S., & Grossman, S. (2001). *Millon Behavioral Medicine Diagnostic.* Minnetonka, MN: NCS Assessments.

Orput, P. (2003). *Internet crimes against children.* Paper presented at the meeting of the Minnesota Internet Crimes Against Children Task Force training. Hennepin County, MN.

Putnam, D. E., & Maheu, M. M. (2000). Online sexual addiction and compulsivity: Integrating web resources and behavioral telehealth in treatment. *Sexual Addiction and Compulsivity: Journal of Treatment and Prevention, 7*(1–2), 91–112.

Quayle, E., Holland, G., Linehan, C., & Taylor, M. (2000). The Internet and offending behavior: A case study. *Journal of Sexual Aggression, 6*(1–2), 78–96.

Quayle, E., & Taylor, M. (2002). Paedophiles, pornography, and the Internet: Assessment issues. *British Journal of Social Work, 32,* 863–875.

Rotunda, R. J., Kass, S. J., Sutton, M. A., & Leon, D. T. (2003). Internet use and misuse. Preliminary findings from a new assessment instrument. *Behavior Modification, 27*(4), 484–504.

Tikkanen, R., & Ross, M. W. (2000). Looking for sexual compatibility: Experiences among Swedish men in visiting Internet gay chat rooms. *CyberPsychology and Behavior, 3*(4), 605–616.

Weiss, R. (1997). *Cybersex Addiction Screening Test.* Retrieved July 7, 2004, from *www.sexual recovery.com.*

Wolak, J., Mitchell, K., & Finkelhor, D. (2003). *Internet crimes against minors. The response of law enforcement.* Washington, DC: National Center for Missing and Exploited Children.

Young, K. S., & Rogers, R. C. (1998). *Cybersex Addiction Quiz.* Retrieved July 7, 2004, from *www.netaddiction.com.*

Young, K. S. (1998). The relationship between depression and Internet addiction. *CyberPsychology and Behavior, 1*(1), 25–28.

Chapter 5

Working With African-American and Latino Sex Offenders

by William C. Ford, C.S.W.-R. and Wilson Prunier, B.S.

OVERVIEW

Barriers to healthy communication, socialization, and intimacy have varying causes and effects within African-American and Latino populations. Cultural, religious, economic, environmental, societal, and historical factors influence African-American and Latino social and sexual development, contributing to antisocial, violent, and sexually abusive behavior (Ford, Johnson, & Peña, 2003; Ford & Prunier, 2002). Culture sensitivity and the therapeutic alliance are key to successfully engaging this population in treatment. Compliance with supervision and treatment will be based on the offender's ability and/or willingness to cooperate, which may be compromised by presenting issues such as housing, employment, serious medical/mental illness, defense mechanisms, substance abuse, and the therapist's ability to engage clients in culture-sensitive treatment.

INTRODUCTION

Working with African-American and Latino[1] sex offenders can provide unique challenges and opportunities to treatment providers and supervisory agencies. The availability of affordable treatment for the diverse population of sex offenders is scarce at best. There are 17,900 known sexual offenders in the state of New York alone (Mahoney, 2004). Together native and foreign-born populations comprise more than one-quarter of the American population but they represent two-thirds of the criminal justice system population. With immigration comes the added complexity of diverse culture, practice, and beliefs that often clash with American values. Those values contribute to a dynamic process that will require culture sensitivity on the part of the therapist who can facilitate effective cognitive-based multicultural treatment. The therapist and treatment setting that reflect a mixture of best practices, multicultural understanding, and social skills building will be poised to assess, engage, and prepare African-American and Latino clients for increased accountability and productivity during and after community supervision. Successful behavior modification, assertive communication, and disclosure can facilitate the offender's ability to question and challenge harmful and abusive behavior in his environment and to effect increased awareness and reduced victimization. Foreign-born African-American and Latinos who have benefited from treatment and face deportation due to immigration violations may play a key role in reducing recidivism in their native countries. There are concerns, however, for family members and dependents of sex offenders who are emotionally, financially, and otherwise affected by the offense, sentencing, incarceration and/or community supervision. Deportation may further destabilize families and support systems of African-American and Latino sex offenders. It is our hope that all foreign-born sex offenders will have the opportunity to attend and complete sex offender treatment before deportation is considered.

POPULATION AND DEMOGRAPHICS

African-Americans and Latinos account for more than one-quarter of the U.S. population. In 2002, African-Americans comprised 36 million, or 13 percent, and Latinos replaced them as the largest minority with 37.4 million (13.3 percent) of the noninstitutionalized population (U.S. Census Bureau, 2002b). While immigration slowed for other racial/ethnic groups, legalization of documented and illegal immigrants in the United States with the passing of the Immigration Reform Act of 1986 was the main reason for the Latino population growth. Two in five Latinos are foreign-born (15 million, or 40.2 percent); of the foreign-born Latino population in 2002, 52.1 percent entered the United States between 1990 and 2002, 25.6 percent came in the 1980s, and the remaining 22.3 percent came before 1980.

Geographic Distribution

Most African-Americans and Latinos are geographically and/or ethnically concentrated in metropolitan regions within the United States. In 2002, 55 percent of African Americans lived in the South; Latinos, too, were geographically concentrated, with ethnic background playing a role: 44.2 percent of Latinos lived in the West, compared with 34.8 percent in the South. Latinos of Mexican origin were more likely to live in the West (54.6 percent), Puerto Ricans (58 percent) in the Northeast; and Cubans in the South (75.1 percent). People of Central and South American background had nearly equal distribution in the Northeast (31.5 percent), the South (34 percent), and the West (29.9 percent).

Statistics show that most African Americans and Latinos live in metropolitan areas. In 2002, 51.5 percent of all African Americans lived in a central city within a metropolitan area compared with 45.6 percent of Latinos; 36 percent of African Americans lived outside a central city but within a metropolitan area, compared to 45.7 percent of Latinos.[2]

Criminal Justice System: Incarceration Rates/Statistics

African Americans and Latinos are underrepresented in indicators of economic and social growth (Council of Economic Advisers, 1998, p. iii) and overrepresented in the criminal justice system. U.S. Justice Department statistics show that 64 percent of prison inmates belonged to racial or ethnic minorities in 2001; nearly one-third of former prisoners were still under correctional supervision, including 731,000 on parole, 437,000 on probation, and 166,000 in local jails (U.S. Bureau of Justice Statistics, 2000). Almost 46 percent of all prison inmates were African American; 36 percent white; 16 percent, Latino. African-American inmates comprised 40 percent of inmates in federal facilities, followed by Latinos (30 percent) and whites (27 percent). Some 47 percent of inmates in state prisons were African American; 14 percent were Latino. In private facilities, the largest category was African American (42 percent), followed by white (32 percent) and Latino (22 percent). Men made up 93 percent and women made up 7 percent of the correctional population. Fortunately, the number of juveniles, 96 percent of whom where held in federal facilities, dropped by 23 percent, from 5,309 to 4,095. This may be partially attributable to the number of alternatives to incarceration and other community supervision programs for youth. The number of immigrant inmates rose between 1995 and 2001 by approximately two-thirds in both federal and states facilities; immigrants accounted for 25 percent of the federal, 5 percent of the state, and 12 percent of the private correctional populations. Approximately 7 percent of all state and federal prisoners were not U.S. citizens, up 2 percent from 1995. No information was available regarding the ethnicity/race of the immigrant population.

FACTORS INFLUENCING SOCIAL AND SEXUAL DEVELOPMENT

Although we are ultimately responsible for the choices we make, our choices are also the result of developmental influences that have helped shape who we are, what we like, and how we approach situations in life. Several influences contribute to how we interact with others.[3]

The supportive environment afforded in group treatment encourages discussion regarding secrecy exhibited by African-American and Latino sex offenders. Clients and staff alike learn about the positive and negative aspects of culture, religion, and tradition, especially in families of foreign origin. Many foreign-born clients cite experiences where they have been treated differently or ridiculed because of their race, native language, culture, and customs. Instead of becoming acclimated to U.S. culture and customs, many cling to their own customs and become further isolated. As a result, situations that arise in the home often stay within the home, even if these issues are ignored, inappropriately resolved, or not addressed at all.

Sexual abuse may also be ignored in African-American and/or Latino families if the culture, society, or religion condones or enables the behavior under patriarchal, caste, or other privilege. Protective ground rules for disclosure in the treatment group provide a secure environment in which African-American and Latino clients can address issues that may otherwise be considered uncivilized, taboo, abusive, violent, and/or criminal. It is here that these offenders begin to realize that while the country of origin, race, and culture may vary, many of the contributing factors to anger, violence, and abuse may be similar. The diverse treatment group also facilitates peer-oriented, face-saving exchange, healing, and empowerment that can set the stage for continual disclosure during various stages of treatment.

Leading up to the discussion of criminal justice involvement, clients begin to develop empathy toward one another, which is the foundation for the group support system based on the group-work principle of mutual aid. This bond is one tool that a group setting creates and can facilitate the challenging of cognitive distortions throughout treatment. It can also set the foundation for the development of more meaningful victim empathy. Exhibit 5.1, at the end of this chapter, lists some helpful tips that can help therapists to learn about the following influences and how to overcome them during treatment.

Historical Influences

Many African Americans and Latinos believe that, more often than not, government, policy, and public systems are misrepresentative of the ethnic and cultural diversity within these populations, thereby contributing to their disenfranchisement. This belief is at the heart of debates regarding access to adequate health care, housing, and employment. African Americans and Latinos continue to address the effects of institutional racism, poverty, and other societal ills on their ability to progress. Notwithstanding, African-American and Latino sex offenders may attempt to rationalize or otherwise attribute their sexual deviance to any number of these issues. Although there may be some validity to these claims, clients are taught that there are choices in every situation and subsequent consequences that they must face. African-American and Latino sex offenders are made to know that ignorance regarding sexually abusive and exploitive behavior is no defense inside or outside the court of law.

Family Influences

The family's beliefs about a wide array of issues, including academic achievement, sex/sexuality, spirituality/religion, and culture may influence antisocial and sexually deviant behavior. In particular, the family's ability to support academic achievement has profound effects on the socioeconomic status and overall progress of African-American and Latino populations. Parents' ability to read and write can have an impact on the children's ability to succeed in school. Children up to age 5 whose parents are not able to read to them have an increased risk of communication or literacy issues, which can be correlated with their underachievement or failure on standardized tests in elementary school and beyond. These students, primarily African Americans/Latinos from poor, illiterate, and/or immigrant families in public school systems primarily within metropolitan areas may be the victims of social promotion or will have to repeat the same grade.

We have found that African-American and Latino sex offenders who have completed at least a ninth-grade education, and even those who have graduated from high school, can barely read, write, or perform simple mathematics, as evidenced during verbal and written exercises in treatment. Educational level can have an adverse effect on an individual's self-esteem or ability to socialize age appropriately, potentially contributing to arrested development and age-inappropriate relationships or relationships that are not necessarily based on intellectual capacity.

Some first-generation Americans who are sex offenders identify with playing the role of language translator or escort for immigrant parents and relatives who, for various reasons, do not learn the English language and customs. Some of our clients eventually realize a connection between their acting out and any combination of high expectations and excessive responsibility placed on them by codependent parents, relatives, partners, or others in an authoritative/dominant role. We are seeing an increased lack of assertiveness leading to antisocial and/or sexually deviant behavior among our clients who have had to assume adult responsibilities at an early age. These clients are often more comfortable around persons who are substantially younger or older than they are, contributing to age-inappropriate socialization and pedophiliac, hebophilic, and other and sexually deviant interests.

The client's connection to immediate and extended family should be explored to determine levels of secrecy within the family that enable sexual and other abuse to flourish.

A majority of our clients point to their parents, peers, or a combination thereof as the source of their sexual beliefs. Culturally isolated African-American and Latino youth who do not view their parents as viable sources of information regarding sex may turn to their siblings, relatives, or peers in ways that can lead to incestuous and otherwise sexually abusive relationships. Some may turn to peers who may identify with the oppression of their native culture and who are not as likely to hold the same moral standards as their parents. Others within these populations may even reject their native culture in order to adapt American customs and avoid negative attention.

In the absence of educated, mature cultural influences, many African-American and Latino sex offenders rely on culturally biased, misinformed sources of information that can lead to misogynist, antisocial, violent, or abusive behavior. The physical or emotional absence of many father figures in African-American and Latino families may contribute to arrested, antisocial, and expedited sexual development for youth who may have to protect and/or help provide for their families. Hypermasculine displays and other compensatory behaviors are frequently seen among many of the African-American and Latino adolescents and young adults in treatment.

Cultural Influences

There are many subcultures within the African-American and Latino populations. Similarities between the two can be attributed to African influences in the family, community, religion, art, folklore, and entertainment. African-American and Latino cultures have many ties to the "African traditions of being communal and collectivistic . . . interactions are valued that focus on the good of the whole family and group and not just on the needs of an individual" (Sanchez-Hucles, 1999, p. 5). This tradition has provided alternative role models to children who have absent or deceased parent(s). Some of these traditions also contribute to the secrecy that places greater value on family name and the negative stigma of child protective or law enforcement involvement than on the needs of victims.

The number of absent fathers—by death, incarceration, or choice—contributes to the increased number of single-parent families where the mother is the head of household and there may be a shortage of positive male role models. These youth may strive to live like hip-hop icons and sports stars. In search of the status symbols they hear about on the radio, see in music videos, magazines, television, and on the streets, these youth may feed into the negative stereotypes of many African-American and native-born/assimilated Latinos. Many hebophiles have similar likes and dislikes that transcend age groups. For instance, within urban African-American and Latino environments, many teenage females and young adult males like fast cars, expensive clothes, and expensive jewelry. Their lifestyle reflects a "living for today" attitude because the harsh realities within these environments, where street mentality and hustle are promoted as a survival skills, lend to higher mortality rates and criminal justice involvement. There may be limited or no investment in healthy relationships, property, and things of appreciating value because the communities in which these populations live often witness deterioration and destruction.

In many underdeveloped nations where domestic violence, sexual abuse, and human rights are not equally observed, the head of household may dictate traditionally patriarchal rules of law. As a result, abuses that persist under such conditions may be summarily justified as cultural by these offenders. These rationalizations often come up in treatment among African-American and Latino sex offenders who have cognitive distortions regarding consensual sex, roles of women/wives, and sense of entitlement.

Some foreign-born clients reveal that they acted out of desperation, citing issues of cultural isolation. One client stated that he, the only person from his family in the United States, was unaccustomed to American "courting rituals," as marriages were still arranged by parents in his native country. He engaged in frotteurism by rubbing his penis against an unsuspecting woman during a parade, was subsequently arrested and charged, pled guilty, and was mandated to attend sex offender treatment. This first-time offender had difficulty participating in treatment, citing depression and shame resulting from his acting out on feelings of desperation, isolation, and sexual frustration. In treatment, he would have to overcome a lack of assertiveness in order to adapt to U.S. customs and culture. This client would later reveal that he looked forward to completing the probation term so he could return home to a prearranged wedding. He stated that it would be easier for him to return home and marry a woman he did not know rather than to take a chance with courting rituals that did not guarantee binding marriage. Treatment allowed him to learn about American culture, sexuality, and socialization within the controlled group confines. Assertiveness and self-determination seemed to be new concepts to him and other offenders who feel their best chance at a committed, monogamous relationship is an arranged situation. The advantage of an arranged marriage is that there is an expectation or near guarantee of loyalty and obedience by the groom and especially the bride. It can even benefit those who are unskilled or unaware of the concept and consequences of incompatibility. Arranged marriage can relieve both parties of the complexities of self-determination and courtship that take compatibility into consideration. Many men and women who come to the United States in search of a better life often return to their native countries and family support systems in search of familiar customs/traditions. Exposure to American culture can complicate an individual's thinking when faced with unfamiliar sexual and social customs.

Economic Influences

Historical lack of wealth can be correlated with increased poverty and crime among these populations, especially in centralized metropolitan areas. Foreign-born persons of color often distinguish themselves from African Americans and American-born Latinos because of many perceptions that the latter two groups do not make the most of the opportunities afforded them in the United States. Many foreign-born African Americans and Latinos come to the United States determined to create a better life and earn the American dream that has eluded many of their American-born counterparts (Sanchez-Hucles, 1999).

Experts agree that a solid economic base increases access to safe, secure housing, good nutrition/health, education, and wealth. African-American and Latino populations, however, earn less income, on average, than other populations and have traditionally been less likely to hold positions of leadership in corporate and other industries. They tend to hold more low-end blue-collar, service, and other labor-intensive positions (Council of Economic Advisers, 1998, p. 24) and still trail other racial/ethnic groups as reflected in employment statistics and socioeconomic status indicators.

Although racial discrimination is still an issue in the workplace, affirmative action has made inroads in securing employment for populations that have been traditionally disenfranchised (Council of Economic Advisers, 1998, p. 24). The reality is, however, that individuals who have either been involved in the criminal justice system or have little or no employment history or scarce mentoring, apprenticeship, or training opportunities are more likely to seek alternative ways of earning income. "Many blacks have found the forces of institutionalized oppression too overwhelming and consequently believe that success is only possible operating outside the mainstream culture" (Sanchez-Hucles, 1999, p. 3). The result is the development and glorification of deviant ethics, values, and lifestyles within subcultures that rationalize their pursuit. Irrational, deviant, or criminal pursuit of material wealth may contribute to sexual exploitation and abuse. Sex offenders who were unemployed or had issues with their employment attributed at least some part of their sexually deviant ideation to anxiety or stress resulting from employment woes. The economic realities facing African-American and Latino communities contribute to the entrance of larger numbers of women and children from these populations into the work force.

Environmental Influences

In metropolitan cities, there are more quality-of-life issues, especially in the poorest areas where African Americans/Latinos primarily reside. The following conditions are often present and contribute to a poorer quality of life: air, water, and other pollution that contribute to increased exposure to pests, rodents, and respiratory disease; overcrowding in substandard housing and schools that contribute to increased boundary issues and age-inappropriate influences; unequal education in public schools that yield socially promoted and other children who may not be prepared for success in postsecondary and employment settings; and rampant drugs, child exploitation/prostitution, violence, and other crimes that feed antisocial behavior and sexual deviance. The effect of poverty and lack of access to resources contribute to the lower numbers of African-American and Latino males enrolled in college versus incarceration (Council of Economic Advisers, 1998, pp. 13, 50; U.S. Bureau of Justice Statistics, 2000).

These quality-of-life issues contribute to a lack of pride, or a distorted sense of territorial pride, in many neighborhoods. For example, residents of urban ghettos proudly refer to their neighborhood or the name of their tenement as a source of strength in adversity or to illicit fear or respect from their contemporaries and potential enemies.

Religious/Spiritual Influences

A person's spiritual or religious views may have a great influence on how he or she chooses to approach the issue of socialization, sex, and marriage. The issue of age appropriateness in various cultures and religions is viewed differently as evidenced in marriages worldwide. Priests and parents who uphold marriages between persons deemed, by the standards of more developed industrial nations, to be minors and adults legitimize or facilitate the exploitation of children. This is a complicated situation in countries that have little or no technological and cultural advancement and adhere to ancient customs. What may become more apparent is the clash between what is religiously sanctioned and what is potentially abusive.

For centuries, families have believed that having many children would guarantee sufficient hands for agriculture and other needs. However, in countries stricken with disease and famine, parents who cannot afford to care for their children are more likely to permit their teenage daughters to marry older men. Other parents, as evidenced in Africa, even prostitute or sell their children in order to survive; the obvious result of this practice includes sexual abuse, violence, and the proliferation of diseases including HIV/AIDS (human immunodeficiency virus/acquired immunodeficiency syndrome). Given the gravity of the crisis facing the Roman Catholic Church and the ongoing reports of sexual abuse, the respect customarily given to clergy and other religious authority figures has diminished. A dearth of human rights privileges may contribute to an even greater shroud of secrecy in underdeveloped nations where the impact of sexual abuse cannot be fully measured unless victims and bystanders feel assured that the benefits of reporting the abuse outweigh the possible repercussions.

FACTORS AFFECTING OFFENDERS' RECEPTIVITY TO TREATMENT

Communication/Language Barriers

Communication barriers can seriously affect one's ability to interact with staff and peers, socialize outside treatment, and find appropriate employment and other services without a translator or escort. Clients whose communication barriers are a result of developmental delays or other mental health issues may require individual counseling with specialized staff. As stated earlier, many non-English-speaking immigrants, as well as other persons with literacy issues, may rely heavily on others to interpret and assist in daily activities or whenever interaction with outsiders is necessary. In cultures where the family may be mistrusting of people outside the immediate family, children may be expected to carry the responsibility of accompanying family members to medical, court, employment, and other appointments.

Some clients may have issues participating in treatment if they are unable to read, write, or speak the language(s) in which services are provided. There are few treatment programs for persons who speak languages other than English and Spanish. Consequently, these clients may find it difficult to complete written assignments. Non-English-speaking and/or illiterate clients may ask family members and friends for assistance in completing take-home assignments. This may complicate relationships between offenders who have not fully disclosed their offenses and persons they enlist to assist them. It can be difficult for family members to assist African-American and Latino sex offenders who have trust issues, especially if accountability and empathy are not apparent. By inadvertently involving outside assistants who may have been bystanders or secondary victims to the offense, these assistants may feel obliged to live, or relive, events that can be discomforting, at the very least. For that reason, all offenders are encouraged to enroll in literacy courses that increase self-sufficiency. In the meantime, it is hoped that these offenders will seek the assistance of persons who are aware of the offense and able to be supportive without shouldering the offender's burden of accountability.

Until these clients become familiar with American language and culture, it is critical that they find therapists who can provide services in their native language (see Exhibit 5.1). Otherwise, community supervision may not be a viable option, and incarceration or deportation may be required. The Department of Homeland Security's

(DHS) Immigration and Customs Enforcement (ICE) program, established in 2003 during the creation of DHS, investigates immigration violations, human smuggling, and sex offenses. Note: Although the bulk of sex offenders investigated are legal and illegal residents residing in the United States, DHS's Project Predator also targets "sex tourists," that is, U.S. citizens who travel abroad for sex with children (Garcia, 2004).

While various countries are collaborating with ICE to identify and bring to justice sex offenders around the world, it is still unclear how these offenders will receive treatment, especially if they are to be released into the community. As stated earlier, deported sex offenders who received treatment while residing in the United States may help facilitate changes in the way foreign countries view cultural norms that contribute to antisocial behavior, sexual deviance, domestic violence, and other human rights violations. These changes can be achieved if the country of origin has a realistic system for managing and treating sex offenders and adequate educational and support systems that address cultural and other issues that contribute to sexual deviance. Deported sex offenders who have not received treatment in the United States that addresses the wide range of antisocial and sexually deviant behaviors may only compound issues within the native country that contributed to their offenses. The situation may be even more dire for potential victims as well as sex abusers in countries in which culture, economics, and policy may not facilitate awareness, prevention, and/or treatment. As a result, the fate of victims and sex offenders, including those who have been deported, may vary based on the country of origin.

Cultural Mistrust of Therapists

Many persons of African-American and Latino descent traditionally keep personal and family information private, at the expense of personal safety, security, and physical and mental well-being. The operating mantras are: "Don't air your dirty laundry in public" and "what happens at home stays at home." As a result, there is a greater risk of antisocial conditioning, violence, and failure to seek assistance from outsiders for emotional, physical, and sexual abuse. African Americans and Latinos have a traditional mistrust of therapists, and especially white therapists. During therapy, some African-American sex offenders may be resistant to building a working relationship with the therapist. Some avoid discussing their guilt, shame, and innermost secrets, attempting to deny or minimize their offenses because they view the therapist as yet another authority figure. An insensitive therapist may forget that, for many African Americans, visions of slavery are but one generation removed. "Whites have often forgotten that it was only one generation ago that many Black individuals were legally restricted to 'Coloreds Only' entrances, bathrooms, water fountains, schools, and services that were consistently inferior to the resources available to White Americans" (Sanchez-Hucles, 1999, p. 2). Many offenders in treatment speak of their own experiences with racism in the public education, judicial, law enforcement, and corrections systems, as well as in politics and the job market. Although many clients try to divert attention to external factors behind their sexual acting out, it is important to help them identify internal factors and their ability to make choices that change circumstances.

The view of minority sex offenders in particular held by predominantly white therapists may reflect varying levels and histories of cultural ignorance, intolerance, and stereotyping until more recent pushes toward culturally sensitive treatment by educational institutions and professional organizations. African-American and Latino therapists may not address issues of race and culture in practice with their white counterparts for fear of negative repercussions, including ostracism and fewer advancement opportunities.

On the other hand, the therapist's race/ethnicity may not necessarily be indicative of ability to provide quality, effective treatment. Some African-American and Latino therapists may dissociate from offenders of the same race, nation of origin, or culture out of shame, which can have a negative impact on the treatment alliance. Even absent such "therapist bias," common race/ethnicity is also not necessarily indicative of a better chance of success with African-American and Latino sex offenders. Some African-American/Latino sex offenders may have difficulty relating to therapists of African-American and Latino descent. These offenders may feel more comfortable opening up to a white therapist if they view persons of similar color or background as being punitive or unsympathetic toward offenders who may, in their opinion, reflect poorly on their race or culture. Issues of transference can be an even greater obstacle in the treatment process with African-American and Latino sex offenders and can jeopardize the treatment process.

Due to the heightened mistrust and fear of reprisal by culturally insensitive therapists and supervision entities, and lack of understanding and/or support among family, friends, and colleagues, many offenders from these ethnic groups can be expected to minimize regarding their offending behavior. The lack of faith in the judicial and other public systems among African Americans and Latinos can be directly related to the general mistrust of the U.S. criminal justice system and social policy. Clients may become aware of the potential for deportation during sentencing, which may prohibit them from fully disclosing their deviant behavior for the duration of community supervision. Secrecy can also affect the client's quality of life, as he may have to balance lies told to family, friends, and employers in order to maintain supervision and treatment compliance. The offender's need to keep friends, family, employers, and the therapist from finding out or reporting the true nature of the sexual deviance may affect his ability to participate and progress in treatment, ultimately threatening his emotional and mental health.

Therapists must understand the need to engage and keep these offenders internally motivated to deal with their sexual deviance. Self-referred clients normally have little or no external motivation to disclose. Fear of violation and incarceration and resulting loss of job, family, and home are external motivators for all sex offenders to comply. Because nearly all the mandated clients we have seen in treatment are African American and Latino, it is our hope that their successes in treatment will pave the way for future self-reporting and increased initial compliance. That will also depend on the therapist's ability and/or willingness to provide an environment that is conducive to the development of victim empathy and other internal motivation for nonrecidivism.

ENGAGING THE AFRICAN-AMERICAN/LATINO SEX ABUSER: THE THERAPEUTIC ALLIANCE

The shortage of qualified, culturally sensitive sex offender therapists means that clients of Latino or African descent will be faced with the possibility of being treated by therapists of a different ethnicity. More than likely, there will be issues of trust and the therapist must be prepared to deal with the offender's initial reluctance to disclose. Therapists who appropriately facilitate disclosure around cultural and other issues that contribute to antisocial and sexually deviant behavior can effect positive changes with African-American and Latino sex offenders.

Therapists must avoid making assumptions and drawing conclusions that are solely based on race, ethnicity, or other factors in order to develop and maintain the therapeutic alliance. Clinical judgment should be based on an objective assessment of the client's instant offense(s), presenting issue(s), and background information that can reveal patterns of antisocial or sexually deviant behavior. It is the responsibility of the therapist to be honest with the client regarding his or her role in treatment outcomes, which are primarily reliant on compliance.

The gender of the therapist may also hinder the treatment of African-American and Latino sex offenders. Clients who have hypermasculine, misogynistic, or culturally patriarchal views of the role of women may not feel comfortable with female therapists at the onset of treatment. The presence of the culturally sensitive female therapist can assist these clients in viewing women more appropriately. The therapeutic environment should foster the client's ability to engage with the therapist regardless of gender. This can be achieved by reclarifying the purpose of the interview or treatment when issues of the therapist's gender arise. It is also helpful for therapists to consult their supervisors or other mental health professionals to help prevent the intrusion of the therapist's own personal issues into professional practice.

Therapists who are not trained to deal with the myriad viewpoints, values, and beliefs among their clientele and the impact of these on their cognitive distortions may apply a standard treatment paradigm that does not take into consideration the various influential factors discussed earlier in this chapter. Given the different views on what constitutes emotional, physical, and sexual abuse among sex offenders from different countries around the world, therapists will need relevant training to develop a more culturally sensitive approach working with African-American and Latino clients. Clients may feel as though their values and belief systems are under attack by culturally insensitive therapists. (See Exhibit 5.1 at the end of this chapter.)

Challenges for Therapists at the Onset of Treatment

Identifying the best method of engaging a client during the intake, assessment, and treatment processes can be difficult, depending on the client, the medium, the therapist, and process issues that have yet to reveal themselves. Historically African Americans and Latinos have had an aversion to traditional mental health institutions due to the stigma attached to "counseling" and "psychiatry" by the prevailing culture. Typically these ethnic groups are accustomed to handling family dysfunction within the confines of the family setting. Many of this population's fears of "the system" have been affirmed by the misdiagnosis of learning needs as mental health issues among African-American children, especially boys, in public education and other systems. Many of these children are still misdiagnosed and the resulting permanent blemishes on their school conduct and mental health records may be long-lasting and reinforce racial or cultural stereotypes.

Referral/Intake. Although there are numerous issues that can affect the gathering of information regarding the African-American and Latino sex offender during referral and intake, the two on which we focus here are the lack of referral documentation and denial/minimization.

It is hoped that there is sufficient information, similar to data provided in detailed physical/mental health records or a presentencing investigation (PSI), regarding the client that facilitates assessment of denial/minimization, prerequisite treatment needs, presenting issues, and influences that contribute to antisocial, violent, and abusive behavior. PSIs may not be available due to bureaucracy and/or protection of sensitive information about the sexual abuse victim(s). A compromise must be achieved to facilitate improved referral, intake, assessment, and treatment processes.

African-American and Latino clients may have varying reasons for denial/mini-mization of sexual deviance. Feelings of shame or guilt are likely among clients at various stages of treatment. In general, men are not expected to share their feelings and are uncomfortable speaking about private matters, especially family issues and sexual deviance. African-American/Latino men within these cultures are often viewed as weak if they do. Disclosure may take longer than expected from those whose cultures promote sexual exploitation and males who are victims rarely disclose the full extent of their own sexual victimization. The fear may be greater due to the fear these men may have of being labeled on admission of being victimized by a female or especially by another male in a society in which hypermasculinity and culturally sanctioned sexual objectification are the norm.

Clients may not want to share information they think will be "damning" and result in judgment, as may be the case for clients who have had bad experiences with public assistance and other public systems. Sex offenders do not typically volunteer for treatment, and ethnic populations may be even less likely to do so. Polygraphs alleviate some of the obstacles clinicians face during the assessment process and treatment plan development. Polygraph/plethysmograph specialists can be invaluable in determining denial/minimization, especially at the onset of treatment. Therapists need to remove doubt concerning the severity of the offending behavior in order to accurately assess the client's instant offense, history of deviant behavior, and risk for reoffense. The client's ability to feel comfortable and speak truthfully about his offending behavior and subsequent urges can be enhanced in an open and engaging treatment environment.

Assessment. Effective treatment addresses multiple needs of the individual, not only sexual behavior. An effective assessment, including a mental status review, using psychosocial, psychosexual, polygraph/plethysmograph, and suitable psychometric tools can assist in identifying issues that feed deviant sexual behavior. An individual's ability to engage appropriately in social settings may reveal precursors for deviant behavior. Poor social skills and/or lack of assertiveness are often present among sexual offenders. An effective biopsychosocial assessment should identify life experiences that contribute to the client's existing cognitive distortions and their impact on his sexual-offending behavior. As stated earlier, the more information that can be compiled, the better the understanding of the specific clinical needs and potential risk factors.

One common theme we have seen among many African-American and Latino sex offenders, especially those who are foreign-born, is the relative lack of education in comparison to other populations. Also prevalent among many of our foreign-born clients is poverty that contributes to a shortened childhood and early adulthood. Children whose parents cannot afford to care for them may allow their young daughters to marry older men or may be less likely to prevent the exploitation of their children. Some of the clients identify with being abused or witnessing the abuse of others who lived within the extended family.

Because many clients' countries of origin may not be as industrialized as the United States, it will be helpful to find out about the offender's knowledge of sexuality, sex, utilization of safer-sex precautionary devices, and HIV/AIDS. Especially useful is the assessment of domestic violence and his exposure to other physical, sexual, and emotional abuse within the culture and society and in the home. One major concern in the assessment process is that many African-American and Latino sex offenders who have not had access to adequate health care may not have accurate diagnoses of physical/mental illness during their lives. As a result, the treatment process can simulate, at times, the effect of a retroactive-to-present-day/ongoing assessment. Many clients have issues dealing with their past as well as that of their family (neglect, abuse, violence, physical/mental illness, death, etc.). Once the therapeutic alliance has been developed, clients will care more about moving the process along smoothly and will increasingly share issues in a supportive environment that may not exist outside treatment. Continual development of the assessment and dynamic treatment plan is necessary. Changes in deviant responses may also be measured by changes in the offender's lifestyle which should be reviewed periodically. The client's involvement in the assessment process and development of the treatment plan can be empowering, redirecting time and energy from deviant exploits to more productive pursuits.

When developing an effective treatment plan, the therapist must be aware of the client's mental health issues and how his or her native culture and other factors may contribute to the condition. Overlooking mental health issues and cultural influences could be harmful to treatment staff and other clients. The culturally sensitive therapist will be better prepared to assess verbal/nonverbal cues, posture, interpersonal communication styles, social deficiency, aggressive/passive behavior, and/or lack of assertiveness among these offenders.

Presenting Issues

Lack of appropriate housing and employment, mental or physical illness, and substance abuse are, perhaps, the most important presenting issues that can affect the client's ability to enroll in and benefit from treatment. Supervision and treatment entities are encouraged to assess the client's presenting issues to determine whether any are prerequisite to their enrollment in treatment. Failure to do so can result in the development of unrealistic treatment plans and supervision conditions that may result in noncompliance, violation, and incarceration.

Housing. Securing appropriate housing is a condition for community supervision and can be especially difficult for child abusers. In the New York State, for example, there are very few resources for sex offender housing, and those who do not have financial resources have an even more difficult time finding affordable housing that is not near schools, playgrounds, and other locations that potential victims may frequent. Tenants and landlords often find out about sex offenders through local precincts and the Internet and during background checks, while applying for housing, or parole/probation field visits. Consequently, African-American and Latino sex offenders may rely on family members whose lives may become compromised by invasion of privacy by parole/probation officers. Sex offenders face the risk of being "found out" in the workplace and at home.

Employment. Employment options for African-American and Latino ex-offenders, especially sex offenders, are relatively scarce given the high unemployment rates and competition in metropolitan settings. Clients who have jobs are encouraged to take them more seriously, improve and learn new skills, enroll in school if and when possible, and update their resumes. Since the September 11 attacks on the United States, more employers are conducting background and credit checks which increasingly disqualify the poor, irresponsible, and those who have involved with the criminal justice system. Even minor infractions can justify the disqualification of even the most qualified candidate. African-American and Latino sex offenders may consequently resort to applying for jobs that do not conduct background checks, pay less, and offer fewer benefits and opportunities to advance. For these jobs, African-American and Latino sex offenders will compete against other parolees, probationers, ex-felons, youth, the elderly, and immigrants. Many African-American and Latino sex offenders will not disclose to employers for fear that they might lose irreplaceable jobs and benefits. Those who previously held good-paying, higher-status jobs find themselves unemployed and fighting for menial jobs.

Seeking gainful employment may be more complicated for those with a criminal history, but it is still possible provided that the offender is able to prove he has the right skills or attitude to impress a potential employer. On the other hand, there are young Americans who are not employed, in school, or supported by a parent, spouse, or family member. African-American and Latino sex offenders under community supervision who fall into this category may seek alternative ways to pay for treatment. "Off-the-books" employment, however, does not afford the employee health, retirement, or other benefits and are unacceptable to agents of the court.

Clients may even depend on a spouse, family member, or others to assist with the cost of treatment. This financial dependence shifts the responsibility from the offender and may be a sign of other codependent or manipulative behaviors. Some clients risk violation of community supervision conditions by resorting to criminal behavior as a means of generating income to support their lifestyles and dependents and pay for treatment. Some employers are more likely to keep employees who have committed sex offenses if they have valuable skills and high productivity and/or if they are deemed to pose a low risk to others in the workplace. Most of our clients, however, choose not to disclose the nature of their offenses and would rather deal with the consequences if and when their criminal history is found out.

Physical Health. African-American and Latino sex offenders may pose a significant health risk while in the community or incarcerated if they have HIV/AIDS, sexually transmitted diseases (STDs), tuberculosis (TB), and other communicable illnesses. The risk of transmission of active TB is higher in overcrowded and poorly ventilated environments. There may be a higher potential risk of transmission of HIV and other STDs to child victims of sex abuse as well as to spouses and other sex partners, especially among sex offenders who have traditionally had lower access to health care. Upon reflecting on the promiscuity that is often associated with hypermasculinity and misogyny, clients exhibit heightened fear surrounding HIV/AIDS issues, awareness, and testing. While the fear of being tested "positive" is a major cause for many individuals not getting tested, all clients should be encouraged to practice safe sex in age-appropriate, mutually beneficial relationships that reduce the transmission of sex-related illness among these highest-risk populations.

Many of our clients who depend on low-income employment or off-the-books employment, as well as those who may sacrifice health benefits to meet other living costs, have inadequate or no health care. As a result, many first become aware of health issues during untimely medical crises. Qualified offenders should be encouraged to take advantage of low-income medical health benefits that can help address a variety of medical and mental health issues that are more costly when paid out-of-pocket. "Poor health can lead to high expenditures on medical care at the expense of other goods" (Council of Economic Advisers, 1998, p. 42). Clients are encouraged to take advantage of available health benefits and take medications that can improve the quality of their lives and reduce the risk of certain sexual illness.

Mental Health. Clients who have not had adequate medical coverage, which would have facilitated appropriate physical/mental health diagnoses, may not be able to participate in treatment to the satisfaction of the therapist. Mental health issues may be obvious in some clients but not necessarily in others. Clients may be unaware of mental health issues until personality disorders and other mental health issues are discussed in treatment. Clients in treatment have the opportunity to recognize how personality disorders may contribute to their antisocial and/or sexually deviant behavior and dysfunctional relationships. Clients can then begin to identify ways to control their mental health issues, which can make treatment more meaningful and increase quality of life.

Studies indicate that African Americans are more likely than any other racial or ethnic group to be hospitalized and to be diagnosed as schizophrenic (Sanchez-Hucles, 1999, p. 11). The history surrounding this diagnosis has attached an inaccurate stigma to African Americans conveying an incorrect perception that this ethnic group is somehow more disturbed than others. This perception can lead African Americans to underuse mental health services or seek services only in times of crisis. The perception then becomes that treatment can do more harm than good. Consequently, the diagnosis often results in a prescription for medication rather than a hands-on approach to these clients' treatment.

Substance Abuse. Clients who have substance abuse issues need to learn new coping strategies in order to deal with the rigors of treatment. Clients with serious substance abuse issues should be encouraged to enroll in drug rehabilitation programs prior to sex offender treatment enrollment; otherwise the pressure that accompanies accountability and compliance may lead to recidivism. In the 1980s and 1990s, the crack cocaine epidemic destroyed thousands of African-American families. Some of our African-American and Latino clients who have habitually abused substances confirm that children and adults are often neglected, abused and/or exploited by self-destructive addicts in search of drugs. Some of our clients were the children of such substance abusers who were subsequently placed into kinship or other foster homes and group homes where the housing issues may be resolved by the neglect or abuse may be overlooked, misdiagnosed, or untreated.

All dually diagnosed—sex-offending substance abusers—clients must learn to be accountable for their substance abuse before they can be accountable for their sexual deviance. The stress of being dually accountable warrants extra supervision and treatment for substance-abusing sex offenders. This stress can also trigger substance use or sexual deviance relapse. Unfortunately, it is extremely difficult to find inpatient facilities that treat substance abusers who are mandated to attend sex offender treatment.

DEALING WITH RISK FACTORS

Many African-American and Latino sex offenders first become aware of the concept of risk factors while in treatment. Upon learning how risk factors play into the behavior they initially thought was "normal," they can begin to make connections to antisocial, violent and/or abusive behavior conditioning during childhood and adulthood. Many of these factors are often taken for granted because they may be inherent in domestic subcultures, foreign countries of origin, or changing circumstances.

Some clients in treatment may deny or minimize these factors until they become comfortable disclosing the issues of anger, stress, depression, and low self-esteem that are related to cultural isolation or ignorance. Risk factors may be overlooked due to lack of awareness in the culture or family, low access to adequate health care during childhood and/or adulthood, fear of disclosure, or mistrust of medical/mental health professionals. Risk factors therefore should be assessed numerous times during treatment due to our clients' varying levels of self-awareness, denial, and minimization, which may also delay identification and disclosure. Issues of loss, family dysfunction, isolation, social anxiety, and peer pressure that are disclosed during the autobiography exercise normally lead to eventual disclosure of their effect on lack of intimacy, sexual anxiety/dysfunction, abusive ideation, and other high-risk situations.

Unfortunately, many clients underestimate their risk factors, stating that they are in control of thoughts, behaviors, and actions they have not fully examined and that "it"—a reoffense—"will never happen again." A client who initially believes that his offense was a one-time event often comes to realize that the deviant fantasy was more graphic than the actual offense and the client was unable to carry out the entire fantasy. In cases in which a lot of thought went into the offense, the potential for a reoffense is more likely if the offender has gotten away with previous attempts or the desire is now increased due to the victim's silent, nonphysical resistance.

Many of these clients are only able or willing to look at the offense in a hands-on sense; these offenders do not see fantasy as offending or leading up to an offense. African-American and Latino sex offenders in treatment begin to learn about the power of ideation and the realization that a series of deviant thoughts can precede a single hands-on offense. Too often clients either deny the existence of a plan or simply refuse to see the two as being connected to the offense, which can easily lead to a reoffense. A client's lack of awareness regarding his personal risk factors and triggers can contribute to the opinion that the culturally insensitive therapist may aggravate or misdiagnose conditions that contribute to sexual and other recidivism. Sex offender-specific polygraphy can help identify risk factors and other issues that can either help or hinder the offender's progress. Unfortunately, polygraphs are too expensive for sex offenders, who may be struggling to support themselves, a family, and/or dependents while under community supervision. This can make it difficult to track progress or recidivism via maintenance polygraphs.

TREATMENT METHOD AND MODALITY

Cognitive-Behavioral Therapy

Cognitive-behavioral therapy (CBT) is widely accepted as the best method of treating sex offenders (Jennings & Sawyer, 2003). CBT can address the impact of the influential factors discussed earlier on the cognitive distortions exhibited by African-American and Latino clients. Components of psychoeducational, psychodrama ("role playing"), trauma therapy, and other treatment methods may effectively be used to increase comprehension and retention of treatment themes, and complement CBT. The diversity in clientele, thought processes, and opinions encountered in therapy may help clients as well as therapists "think outside the box" when applying these methods.

CBT is designed to foster independence and management of one's own behavior during a finite supervision term but should be incorporated into an offender's lifelong modus operandi. Therapists must be prepared to augment their assessment processes in order to capture issues faced by African-American and Latino sex offenders—especially those who are foreign-born. The more information that can be compiled regarding these offenders' background and contributors for antisocial and deviant behavior, the better the potential for sound treatment and successful cognitive restructuring.

CBT in a diverse group setting can effectively function as a peer-oriented multicultural mutual support and accountability system. African-American and Latino clients who are introverted or culturally isolated are more apt to overcome skepticism about therapy and disclose where there are others whose experiences they can appreciate or identify with. The group format is essential to increasing awareness, facilitating clients' ability to identify the influential factors that contribute to sexual and other deviance within their respective relationships, households, cultures, communities, and nations of origin.

Group Therapy

Group therapy allows sex offenders to discuss their sexual deviance and other issues in a supportive yet accountable setting among peers who are less likely to be judgmental and more likely to empathize. Jennings and Sawyer (2003) refer to the group treatment approach's "therapeutic potency from the interactions and relationships that emerge during the group process" (p. 254) (see also Rutan & Stone, 1993; Yalom, 1995). At first, it can be very difficult for clients to open up and overcome their shame, guilt, and/or fear of judgment. The fear may be even more intense for clients who feel their belief systems are under attack. One of our more socially inept clients disclosed to his group that he had planned a vacation during which he was going to get married in his native country. The group shared in his happiness until they learned that he was going home to marry his first cousin. The group members did not agree with the choice of wife but agreed to respect their peer's decision to follow his native custom.

To Develop Mutual Support System. The mutual support system that develops within the group is vital in helping clients overcome denial, minimization, and other thinking errors and contributes to clients' desire to seek similar kinds of support in outside relationships. As clients continue to progress in treatment, they can begin to rely on each other's accomplishments to inspire their own. Treatment may be the first medium in which many African-American and Latino sex offenders can practice and report on the real-time application of healthy social and sexual skills in everyday living. For that reason, it is important to review exercises that introduce new concepts including the identification of risk factors, the offense chain, feelings, thinking errors, assertive communication, and empathy. These exercises may introduce ways of thinking and being that are new or underused by African-American and Latino sex offenders.

To Illustrate Various Concepts. Treatment material may illustrate various concepts using fictitious people and circumstances. These concepts can be more easily comprehended and retained when the fictitious people and circumstances are substituted by persons in the offenders' respective realities. For example, clients who lack consideration toward nonrelated victims may have a better understanding of victim empathy if they imagine the victim was their mother, wife, or daughter. Many African-American and Latino men are often conditioned and expected to be more emotional when a mother, sister, or other beloved person's namesake is used jokingly or to antagonize them into responding with verbal or physical aggression. Clients who have poor views of women outside their immediate family may be able to better empathize with strangers only after being asked to consider how they might feel if a woman they valued was the victim in a violent, misogynistic, or sexually abusive scenario.

The information gathered during the initial intake, assessment, and various stages of treatment facilitates ongoing accountability for clients by the therapist and eventually by others in the group. It is important to follow up on issues that clients bring up during treatment sessions and tie them into the client's respective realities (see Exhibit 5.1). Because many of the cognitive distortions may be the result of unresolved family, cultural, or environmental issues that are shared by many of these offenders, tying these issues into relevant treatment themes or stages will be helpful. It is best that treatment reflect the individual and collective realities of African-American and Latino sex offenders. Many African-American males continue to address the issues they face while living in American society which expects less from them and then punishes them for being uninformed. All clients, especially those who are not working full time, are encouraged to enroll in GED (general education degree), vocational training, college, and other programs to increase their ability to meet or exceed societal expectations.

Group Process. Treatment duration may vary based on the client's issues or group process issues. Assignment to the appropriate setting may depend on the client's ability to interact with others. Individual therapy may be appropriate for clients who present issues that have a negative impact on the group process. Clients who have serious mental health and collateral issues (substance abuse, anger management, suicidal ideation, etc.) may be better suited for individual therapy until they are emotionally capable of group interaction.

The group process is more effective when members start and finish together. It is a valuable tool for socialization, support, and accountability within a familiar setting that can translate to relationship building outside treatment. New clients are generally required to attend once weekly for the intensive phase of treatment and, upon successful completion, graduate to monthly relapse prevention meetings that address the client's ongoing ability to manage in life with the tools that he has learned in treatment. It is also hoped that clients develop support systems outside treatment, especially as community supervision normally has a finite term. The outside support systems (family, friends, spouses/partners, etc.) may see the offender through after treatment.

It is important to follow up with offenders regarding the significant people in their lives. The increased awareness regarding the influential factors that contribute to sexual and other abuse should encourage clients to discuss their relationships as they develop (see Exhibit 5.1). Once they have developed trust within the group, these clients are more likely to identify potential issues within their relationship(s) and consult the group "think tank." This process can encourage African Americans and Latinos to begin to overcome their mistrust of outside help, especially from therapists, and address fears that lead to power or control dynamics in their relationships.

Some clients may begin to identify the need for couples or family counseling after realizing the benefits of sex offender therapy. The benefits of disclosure include increased accountability, empathy, and cognitive restructuring that may lead the offender to seek continued growth as he begins to separate from toxic relationships or reunify with his family. The offender's partner(s) and family members should be encouraged to see an outside therapist if and when necessary in order for the offender to maintain the therapeutic alliance within his own treatment setting.

The CBT group has many benefits. One of the most important features is its impact on sex offenders' ability to develop and maintain healthy social, family, and intimate relationships. The purpose of the treatment group is to facilitate successful behavioral modification among peers who should strive individually and collectively toward improved social and other functioning. Individuals assigned to the group may leave once they have completed their community supervision terms, or after being found noncompliant, in violation, and at risk of being incarcerated. It is preferable that the group progress and graduate together, but that may vary depending on various factors. Some clients may have issues that require individual therapy instead of or in conjunction with group therapy. Since the ultimate goal for persons under community supervision is to improve social functioning, some sex offenders may temporarily be transferred to an individual or smaller, specialized group settings to disclose and address issues that may be difficult to initially discuss with the larger group. It may, however, be advantageous to prepare them for return to the group setting so they can continue to improve their social functioning.

Sex offenders may not have a choice in deciding who enters the treatment group, as that is usually decided by intake and other treatment personnel. Those who desire to progress may, however, contribute to the determination of who stays and who goes based on issues that affect the overall progress of the group. African-American and Latino sex offenders' progress in treatment, especially within the treatment circle, illustrates their ability to weed out negative and high-risk influences with one exception: Outside treatment, offenders can also choose who they want to let in their circle. Treatment provided to these populations must be culturally sensitive so African Americans and Latinos can learn to apply these tools to developing more assertive social, family, and intimate relationships outside treatment.

CONCLUSION

American civilization has modernized faster than that of many African-American and Latino sex offenders' countries of origin. The same distinction can be made between general American culture and the varying African-American and Latino sub-cultures within the United States. Outside some obvious cultural, historical, and socioeconomic differences between African-American and Latino sex offenders and those of other ethnic/racial groups, the underlying causes behind deviance may be the same. Many of the differences lie in some racial and cultural influences that shape the socioeconomic parameters in which antisocial and sexually deviant behavior may thrive.

Sex offender treatment provides African-American and Latino clients and their therapists the opportunity to learn about influences that contribute to the different forms of neglect, abuse, and violence and the thinking errors behind each. By providing culturally sensitive treatment, we not only modify the African-American and Latino sexual offenders' cognitive distortions, we improve their understanding of sexual deviance in the context of their family, social, and sexual development and its varying effects (global, national, and local) on the victim/victim's family and the offender's family. We also encourage the offenders to differentiate between what is and is not acceptable behavior, which may conflict with the offender's upbringing, sense of entitlement, and/or culture. This will ultimately have an impact on societal, cultural, and other "norms" around the world and may be viewed by some as cultural imperialism. Global intervention can help countless women and children who appear to represented in greater proportion among sexual abuse victims.

Treatment professionals and others who understand the range of influences contributing to the various antisocial and deviant behavior may begin to understand the push to recognize sexual abuse as a public health issue instead of a criminal justice issue. These behaviors are rooted in ideation that may be realized under adverse conditions that persist in many homes, cultures, communities, and nations.

African-American and Latino clients can eventually become the strongest defense in the fight against sexual abuse in their homes and communities here in the United States and abroad if they should be deported under Operation Predator. Many of our clients report that they have become more outspoken at home or with friends about sexual abuse and the effects on the victims and offenders with the hope that their loved ones and friends can avoid a similar fate. There is a plethora of information regarding how culture, socioeconomic status, and family violence facilitate the development of maladaptive patterns. By focusing on preventing abuse before it is perpetrated, using science to understand the problem and identify solutions, changing social norms, and making programs available in our communities, "we can assure African-American, Latino and all children the future they deserve" (Henry & Rosenberg, 2004, p. A19).

Footnotes

[1] Census Bureau and other government statistical information, including President Clinton's *Changing America: Indicators of Social and Economic Well-Being by Race and Hispanic Origin* (Council of Economic Advisers, 1998) refers to African Americans as blacks and Latinos as Hispanics. "African American" is used in this chapter to refer to persons of color who were American- or foreign-born not including Hispanics/Latinos.

[2] Information in this paragraph is based on statistics from U.S. Census Bureau (2002a, 2002c).

[3] African-American and Latino clients have the opportunity to explore these influences in treatment during the autobiographical exercise. This exercise can be thought provoking and emotional; especially for those who either do not have close family ties or are separated from family by immigration, migration, death, or other causes. Many of these clients find it difficult to complete this exercise because it forces them to revisit uncomfortable life experiences or share personal information with strangers. Some, however, realize their strength in adversity, having survived neglect, abuse, trauma, death in the family, and societal and sexual biases. Not all African-American and Latino sex offenders speak of mostly negative childhood and/or adulthood experiences. Many clients describe similar experiences and yet have varying outlooks on life. Nonetheless, this exercise illustrates diversity within African-American and Latino populations, cultures, and each group member's unique life experience. The autobiography exercise is often more powerful in the group setting because it facilitates multicultural exchange and appreciation, as well as a reflective personal, family, and social inventory that may usually be shared only between immediate and, possibly, extended family members. The exercise facilitates the development of trust outside the offender's preferred circle and the identification of similar lifestyle, behavioral, social, and sexual patterns that are often rationalized by culture or environment.

References

Council of Economic Advisers. (1998). *Changing America: Indicators of social and economic well-being by race and Hispanic origin.* Washington, DC: The White House.

Ford, W., Johnson, S., & Peña, J. (2003). S*teps to more effective program development and treatment planning for African-American and Latino sex offenders.* Paper presented at the 22nd annual Research and Treatment Conference of the Association for the Treatment of Sexual Abusers, St. Louis, MO.

Ford, W., & Prunier, W. (2002). *Supervision of sex offenders: The relapse prevention model.* Paper presented at the 21st annual Research and Treatment Conference of the Association for the Treatment of Sexual Abusers, Montreal, Quebec Canada.

Garcia, M. (2004). *U.S. "Operation Predator" protecting children around the world.* Washington, DC: U.S. House of Representatives Subcommittee on Immigration, Border Security and Claims.

Henry, F., & Rosenberg, M. (2004, March 23). Stop abuse before it starts. *Washington Post*, p. A19.

Jennings, J., & Sawyer, S. (2003). Principles and techniques for maximizing the effectiveness of group therapy with sex offenders. *Sexual Abuse: A Journal of Research and Treatment, 15,* 251–267.

Mahoney, J. (2004, March 9). Sex fiends AWOL: 2000 cons defying state's registry. *New York Daily News,* p. 12

Rutan, J. S., & Stone, W. N. (1993). *Psychodynamic group psychotherapy* (2nd ed.). New York: Guilford Press.

Sanchez-Hucles, J. (1999). *The first session with African Americans.* New York: Wiley.

U.S. Bureau of Justice Statistics. (2000). *Census of state and federal correctional facilities.* Washington, DC: U.S. Department of Justice.

U.S. Census Bureau. (2002a). *The black population in the United States.* Washington, DC: U.S. Department of Commerce.

U.S. Census Bureau. (2002b, March). *Current population survey* (annual demographic supp.) Washington, DC: U.S. Department of Commerce.

U.S. Census Bureau. (2002c). *The Hispanic population in the United States.* Washington, DC: U.S. Department of Commerce.

Exhibit 5.1
Seven Steps Toward Improved Outcomes With
African-American and Latino Sex Offenders

1. Get to know your clients and their family structure, origin, and dynamics; find out how their culture, customs, environment, and other factors contribute to antisocial and sexually deviant behavior.

2. Review the treatment exercises and make sure they can be translated in terms with which all offenders can identify.

3. Hire multilingual staff and/or interns to assist in providing culturally sensitive treatment that bridges language and other communication barriers.

4. Test the clients' understanding of treatment themes and concepts.

5. Have clients update the group regarding the application of these concepts in their respective realities.

6. Follow up on clients' progress, or lack thereof, in overcoming the influential factors that contribute to their antisocial and deviant behavior.

7. Have clients maintain a journal so they can learn to measure their own growth.

Chapter 6

Outpatient Treatment Considerations for Mentally Ill Clients With Problem Sexual Interests or Behavior

by Ruth E. Lewis, Ph.D.

OVERVIEW

In the context of government budget cuts and deinstitutionalization, the mental health system and local communities are faced with the challenge of managing mentally ill clients with problem sexual interests or behavior on an outpatient basis. If problem sexual interests and behavior are not identified and addressed during inpatient hospitalizations, then it is unrealistic to believe that clients will not relapse upon release to less restrictive levels of care. And, if such problems are identified, not treated, and then used as a rationale for "warehousing" clients in psychiatric hospitals, their legal rights to receive treatment are marginalized. Balancing the legal rights of these clients to receive treatment and to work toward less restrictive levels of care while protecting communities' safety can be a daunting task.

Much of the research to date does not consider the impact of psychotic disorders on the treatment of sexual interest and behavior problems. In particular, practical issues require consideration when providing treatment to this client population. This chapter addresses outpatient treatment considerations for mentally ill clients with problem sexual interests or behavior. In so doing, it is hoped that the chapter will provide a template of issues to consider as well as specific practical interventions and approaches when planning and providing treatment. By discussing issues to address with the treatment team, a unified strategy can be developed to engage the client, increase or maintain motivation for and compliance with treatment, and ensure the client understands, learns, and generalizes the treatment material. Ultimately, effective treatment helps prepare clients for discharge from inpatient hospitalizations to community-based treatment while keeping both the community and the client safe.

INTRODUCTION

Why is it necessary to explore treatment considerations for clients with problem sexual interests or behavior and a co-occurring Axis I psychotic disorder according to the fourth edition of *Diagnostic and Statistical Manual of Mental Disorders* (DSM-IV; American Psychiatric Association, 1994)? One reality is that in the context of deinstitutionalization, managed care, and government budget cuts, one major focus of treatment for mentally ill clients is moving them to the least restrictive level of care that is clinically appropriate. On the surface, this is a noble endeavor. It respects that mentally ill clients ought not be warehoused in psychiatric hospitals. They deserve treatment that prepares them for fuller and less restrictive lives. However, this goal is complicated for mentally ill clients with problem sexual interests or behavior.

Sex offenders are a heterogeneous group with no single pathway to problem sexual interests or behavior (Seghorn & Ball, 2000; Blasingame, 2001). Research has already focused on hypothesizing that there is a subgroup of sex offenders who are psychotic and empirically identifying that subgroup of offenders (Craissati & Hodes, 1992; Henderson & Kalichman, 1990). The existence of this subgroup is not in dispute. In addition, although a small sample ($n = 11$), Craissanti and Hodes (1992) note a complex relationship between sex offending and mental illness. And, unlike the tendency of nonpsychotic sex offenders, the psychotic offenders in their sample tended not to look sociopathic. Jones, Huckle and Tahaghow (1992), describing schizophrenic sex offenders ($n = 4$), found that their psychotic disorder contributed to their sex-offending behavior. Smith and Taylor (1999), with a larger sample ($n = 80$), also explore the relationship between sex offending and psychosis. They conclude that psychosis can play a role in the sex offense. Phillips, Heads, Taylor, and Hill (1999) found that psychosis was not always driving the sex-offending behavior ($n = 15$). This suggests that some offenders are paraphilic independent of their mental illness, while others' sex-offending behavior occurs in relation to their mental illness. As such, treatment considerations ought to take into account the special needs of particular subgroups (for the purpose of this chapter, psychotic offenders) even though there can be some overlap between psychotic and nonpsychotic sex offenders regarding the psychology of offending and their treatment needs.

Given the differences between psychotic and nonpsychotic offenders and the complex relationship between mental illness and sex offending, this chapter identifies and explores the practical treatment considerations for clients with problem sexual interests or behavior and a co-occurring major mental illness. Mentally ill (MI) sex offenders can be divided into several subgroups. However, for the purpose of this chapter, I address treatment considerations for clients with problem sexual interests or behavior and any of the following DSM-IV Axis I disorders: schizophrenia, schizoaffective disorder, major depression with psychotic features, and bipolar disorder. For each of these diagnostic groups, a dual diagnosis of substance abuse or posttraumatic stress disorder (PTSD) may also be present.

INTEGRATING TREATMENT FOR SEXUAL OFFENDING AND MENTAL ILLNESS

MI sex offenders have special treatment considerations, compared to sex offenders without a psychotic disorder, which need to be taken into account when planning and implementing treatment. These clients must be helped not only to understand their deviant cycle but also to understand their mental illness cycle and how the two relate to each other. For clients who also have a substance abuse disorder or PTSD, the interrelationship of these disorders, as well, must be understood as potential factors in the client's deviant cycle. Treatment is further complicated by symptoms of mental illness that can affect a client's understanding, acceptance, and sense of responsibility regarding his sexual interest or behavior problem, as well as his motivation and capacity for treatment. Such symptoms may include auditory or command hallucinations, paranoia, ideas of reference, lack of motivation secondary to mental illness (as compared to resistance in non-mentally ill clients), faulty reality testing, impaired affect regulation, and skills deficits such as social and independent living skills deficits, impaired judgment, and isolation. Depending on other factors, such as cognitive ability and intelligence, learning style, limits in empathy, and degree of institutionalization, the client's capacity for understanding and using treatment may be compromised. Thus, as treatment focuses on managing and decreasing a client's risk of re-offending sexually, it must also address relapse prevention around the client's mental illness, while taking into account each client's special needs and capacity for treatment.

USE OF TREATMENT TEAM TO PROVIDE A COMPREHENSIVE PROGRAM

During both the individual and group phases of treatment, clients learn about the concept of deviant cycles in general and specifically as it relates to their own relapse cycles: deviant sexual behavior, mental illness, and, if present, substance abuse or PTSD. Clients with a co-occurring mental illness require access to psychiatric support services, not merely specialized sexual offender treatment. In addition to the sex offender psychotherapist, multidisciplinary treatment teams often include a department of mental health (DMH) case manager to advocate for the client and to maintain communication among the various team members; a psychopharmacologist to address medication issues; a psychotherapist to provide psychotherapy regarding issues related to past trauma, interpersonal issues, and other psychotherapy issues; community residential or other supervised living situation staff to support all aspects of the client's treatment and to focus on independent living and social and relationship issues; day program or rehabilitation program staff to address therapy issues and to develop cognitive behavioral, social, and vocational skills in a community and group format; and a rehabilitation counselor to advocate for the client regarding vocational issues.

Some MI clients attend day or rehabilitation programs; others have volunteer or paid employment that can accommodate their mental illness. Dialectical behavior therapy (DBT) groups can be a useful resource to help clients acquire mindfulness, affect tolerance, interpersonal effectiveness, and affect regulation skills (Gann, 2000; Quigley, 2001; Lewis, 2001; Guidry, 2004a, 2004b). DBT and other cognitive-behavioral skills help clients learn to identify, tolerate, and appropriately express their feelings (intense or painful emotions or sexual urges) without acting out.

Other considerations may need to be addressed by treatment team members. MI sex offender clients may have criminal records for their offenses, which complicates whether they can obtain and retain their jobs. Their criminal records may also interfere with access to subsidized housing. MI clients are eligible for government-funded medical insurance, such as Medicare and Medicaid, and social security disability insurance. In some instances, MI clients are committed, under guardianship, or on probation and the treatment is ordered rather than voluntary. The guardian or probation officer would then play a role (although limited) on the treatment team. Consideration of how a client's status in treatment can affect motivation, engagement in treatment, and confidentiality can be useful.

TIMING OF TREATMENT COMPONENTS

Pretreatment Considerations

Certain pretreatment considerations must be addressed in order to ensure that the client is psychiatrically stable enough and contained to begin treatment. The pretreatment phase is an integral part of treatment that focuses on developing the therapeutic alliance, a sense of trust, and a sense of safety to address this problem area which, for many clients, feels shameful and potentially ostracizing and stigmatizing. The pretreatment phase begins with stabilizing the client psychiatrically because impaired judgment, psychosis (commonly auditory hallucinations, ideas of reference, paranoia, and other delusions), or disturbances in mood accompany the disorders addressed in this chapter. Often, psychiatric medication and securing an adequate and structured "holding environment" (such as an inpatient or community residential placement) are required. Such living situations provide safety, containment, adequate monitoring by staff, medication supervision, and emotional support, all of which are necessary preconditions to treatment.

Medications

Medication is a part of stabilization as well as the maintenance of stability. The MI population of clients requires medication that addresses not only sexual compulsivity, impulsivity, and sex drive but also the psychotic mental illness. Psychopharmacology ought to be provided by or in consultation with a psychiatrist who has specialized knowledge of psychiatric medication for the treatment of MI clients with problem sexual interests or behavior. There is a body of research which addresses comorbidity and psychopharmacology for sex offenders (American Psychiatric Association, 1999; Land, 1995; Sherak, 2000; Kafka, 2001; Kafka & Hennen, 2002; Kafka & Prentky, 1994). Selective serotonin reuptake inhibitor (SSRI) antidepressants and neuroleptics have been found to be effective in treating mentally ill sex offenders. In extreme cases, an antiandrogen (e.g., Depo-Provera or Lupron) may be prescribed as a means of dampening a client's libido and controlling his compulsive or impulsive sexual behavior.

Evaluation

Once the client is clinically stable, a comprehensive evaluation at the start of treatment ensures accurate diagnosis and formulation of a treatment plan that takes into account the relationship between the sexual interests, behavior, and mental illness. Similarly, the evaluation assesses the mental illness, the nature of the problem sexual interest or behavior, and the relationship between the two. It is important to distinguish sexual behavior which is offensive, such as lewd or inappropriate sexual comments, from sexual deviance or sex-offending behavior, such as rape, exhibitionism, frotteurism, voyeurism, or pedophilia (Blasingame, 2001). For some clients, psychotic symptoms can be disinhibiting or create problems in reality testing resulting in an increased risk of sexual deviancy. Other clients become more self-conscious and inhibited, preoccupied by nonsexual psychotic delusions, or catatonic and not at all focused on sex. Mania, depression, and substance abuse increase risk of sex offending for some clients but not for others. Evaluation helps to ascertain the interrelationship between clients' mental illness, substance abuse, trauma history, and problem sexual interests or behavior. And, certain warning signs of the sex-offending cycle or lapses may occur at different stages of decompensation around mental illness or substance abuse.

Evaluation also provides baseline testing, from which follow-up testing can be compared, in order to assess treatment progress and effectiveness. Testing allows for a client's sexual interests and risk to be evaluated despite how forthcoming and self-aware the client is. It is beyond the scope of this chapter to address, in depth, considerations in evaluation of MI sex offenders, except to say that assessments ought to be conducted by evaluators who follow the Association for the Treatment of Sexual Abusers (ATSA; 1997) guidelines for sex offender evaluations and should include physiological testing (such as the Penile Plethysmograph (PPG) and the Abel Assessment of Sexual Interests (AASI)) as well as other standard tests. Active psychosis, cognitive impairment, mood disturbances, and ability to communicate accurately can have an impact on the evaluation process and the accuracy of testing. Also, impotence or dampened libido can be side effects of some psychiatric medication. As such, results of some tests routinely used in evaluations (e.g., AASI and PPG) may be skewed. These considerations help inform the timing of when testing is appropriate, and if so, which tests will be given and to what degree they are likely to be valid. (For a complete discussion of considerations for the evaluation of MI clients with sexual interest or behavior problems, consult Guidry, 2004a, 2004b.)

Therapeutic Alliance

Developing a therapeutic alliance is the cornerstone to the effective treatment of any client population. This is especially true, and at times challenging, with MI clients. The alliance begins to develop in the pretreatment phase and must be nurtured throughout treatment. The therapy relationship is an aspect of a necessary holding environment in which to develop trust and to adequately contain the MI client. The development of an adequate therapy relationship is based on a foundation of respect. It involves developing a sense of trust and safety; fostering and rewarding honesty, compassion, and accountability through constructive and respectful confrontation; and being available for support, encouragement, and tutoring. Therapists introduce the idea of approximating goals rather than perfectionism. In this way, clients can work toward treatment goals, breaking down the goals into manageable, understandable tasks and developing skills to handle the tasks. Privileges can be adjusted according to the client's capacity for internal control. For instance, privileges are decreased as the client requires external controls and increased, in a stepwise fashion, only as the client exhibits and generalizes adequate internal controls. Clients can begin to take pride in their accomplishments along the way, thus fostering a sense of motivation and efficacy rather than a sense of discouragement, failure, or powerlessness. Ideally, therapists begin to help clients feel that they are decent people who have the potential to act out indecently under certain circumstances. Thus their mental illness becomes a condition or set of symptoms that can be understood and managed rather than an identity or excuse for irresponsible, offensive, or offending behavior.

The therapeutic alliance is broadened once the client enters a specialized therapy group for MI clients with sexual interest or behavior problems. In individual treatment, the therapeutic alliance is between the client and therapist. In group treatment, the alliance also includes the other group members. Thus, group therapists must tend to their relationships not only with each client but also with all the group members. Issues regarding confidentiality, safety, therapeutic goals, and treatment format need to be revisited and agreed to by the group. The alliance among group members needs to be encouraged, supported, and protected by the group therapist. Ideally, a strong treatment alliance continues even when the client leaves specialized treatment, which increases the likelihood that the client can return to treatment, at some point in the future, if necessary.

THE COGNITIVE-BEHAVIORAL MODEL

MI sex offender treatment follows a cognitive-behavioral relapse prevention model set forth by ATSA. The ultimate goal of treatment is the same for psychotic and nonpsychotic clients: to develop a client's capacity to not act out inappropriate sexual interests or behavior. The initial phase of treatment is the same for both populations and includes the development of a therapeutic alliance and trust, establishing treatment foci and goals, addressing issues of shame and fear of others' reactions "if they find out," and the development of basic cognitive-behavioral therapy (CBT) skills or DBT skills (including mindfulness and radical acceptance, affect tolerance, interpersonal effectiveness, and emotion identification). Ideally, clients gain a basic understanding of cycle theory and relapse prevention concepts in general and as they relate to the client specifically. At the start of treatment, an impulse control plan (ICP) is developed and the therapist assesses whether aversive reconditioning treatment is indicated. How these areas are addressed varies and will be determined by the MI client's mental status, intelligence, capacity for abstract versus concrete or rigid thinking, fixed delusions related to the offending behavior, use of psychological defenses (e.g., denial, minimization, and justification), and effectiveness of medication.

Treatment for any client is a vehicle for exploring and identifying under what circumstances the client increases his risk for relapse; identifying and understanding the client's sexual deviancy cycle; and developing adequate impulse control, sexual behavior reconditioning, and relapse prevention skills. Mental illness complicates this process. MI clients have symptoms and biological factors that can affect motivation, consistency, judgment, internal controls, and capacity to maintain treatment relationships. These clients also may be emotionally fragile, frightened of retaliation, or paranoid. As treatment progresses, clients work on maintaining stabilization of their sexual behavior problems. They broaden and practice their ICPs, a set of steps clients can take to stop themselves from acting out problem behaviors. They revise their deviant cycles, written descriptions of how they move from not offending to acting out problem behaviors and justifying that behavior. They complete relapse prevention plans and learn relapse prevention interventions, coping skills, and tools that can be used to prevent or interrupt a relapse. At best, clients gain insight about triggers, the conditions under which a cycle is started. They identify self-cons that fuel their deviant cycles, the cognitions used by clients to "fool" themselves into moving deeper into their deviant cycles. They develop cognitive restructuring skills in order to challenge or argue against the cognitive distortions that fuel their problem sexual interests or behavior. In addition, they develop coping and self-soothing strategies that can be relied on as healthy alternatives to sexually deviant behavior. Constructive treatment fosters self-esteem, a greater sense of belonging, ability to function in the community, and social skill development, symptom management (which must include symptoms related to the problem sexual behavior as well as to the major mental illness), and sex education.

ISSUES FOR TREATMENT PROVIDERS

Countertransference and Therapist Biases

No matter how well intentioned, therapists' countertransference issues and biases affect the treatment they provide and the therapy relationship they develop with any client population. Clients with sexual interest and behavior problems pose unique challenges. Professional and personal attitudes toward any sex offender and client with other sexual behavior or interest problems play a role in whether the therapist exhibits a therapeutic versus a punitive or retaliatory stance. When treating clients with a co-occurring mental illness, biases toward mental illness must also be addressed. A therapeutic stance has the potential to foster growth and change whereas a punitive or retaliatory stance provides punishment without facilitating a means for clients to develop coping strategies to replace inappropriate sexual behavior or interests. Openness to exploring one's countertransference or bias can help to minimize its being acted out countertherapeutically on the client. Countertransference is also a challenge to other treatment providers and treatment settings, especially if treatment providers are not adequately trained to work with sex offenders, or if there is no support available to front-line staff. Therapists and other treatment providers must also be cognizant of the potential impact of their own experiences of having treated sexual abuse survivors or having survived sexual abuse themselves. Outpatient treatment providers and settings must protect clients and staff in the residential settings and day programs without jeopardizing the MI offender's treatment and safety (Lewis, 2001, 2002).

Coordinating Sex Offender and Psychiatric Treatment

In most cases, sex offender treatment occurs in an outpatient sex offender group or individual sex offender therapy while clients' mental illness-related treatment occurs at their community or hospital-grounds residences, day or vocational programs, or dual recovery or self-help groups. None of these programs are sex offender specific. The plus side of this configuration is that clients may feel as if they can be more forthcoming about their sexual interests and behavior because the therapy occurs in a location away from their psychiatric treatment programs and consequently they may feel more private and safe. They may also feel relieved to meet other men who are dealing with similar issues, less alone, and more open to sharing all of themselves (rather than hiding the sex offender self). While these two "arms" of treatment are separate and distinct, they must also be integrated.

Although residential and day program involvement is often necessary, the strengths and weaknesses of each system need to be assessed as well as whether or not the weaknesses can be compensated for or rectified. The community residential and treatment program milieu provides a rich opportunity for treatment. Relationship and interpersonal issues can be addressed there. Emotional support can be provided during treatment to help clients cope with issues regarding motivation, fear, and shame. Staff members should be part of the client's support system. They are aware of clients' relapse prevention plans and treatment goals and are able to monitor whether clients are completing homework assignments and know their triggers and early warning signs of relapse. They also serve as an external monitor of clients' mental status and problem sexual interests and behavior.

On the other hand, because treatment teams for MI clients are typically larger than those for non-MI offenders, this configuration can result in fragmented treatment. Communication can be unwieldy at times. Thus, identification of each team member's role and how they all interface with each other is essential. A review at the start of treatment not only assists in creating a collaborative treatment plan but also serves as a way to bring together the various team members and programs involved in the client's treatment. Thereafter, adequate communication can be maintained through regularly scheduled team meetings, check-ins by phone between meetings and as needed, written behavioral plans, staff attendance at a portion of the client's session if there are special concerns or as a way that client and therapist can keep the halfway house staff apprised of the client's focus and progress in treatment, and monthly progress letters sent to halfway house staff. Multidisciplinary treatment team communication and collaboration must be established at the start of treatment and maintained throughout the course of treatment in order to integrate team members' contributions and minimize the risk of fragmentation. The sex offender therapist also serves as a resource and coach to the treatment team via articles or other suggested reading, treatment reviews, phone calls, or in-service training.

Level of Functioning as a Factor in Treatment

MI clients have a wide range of cognitive and intellectual abilities or deficits. Thus, the therapist needs to make treatment material understandable and relevant to clients of varying levels of functioning. The material will need to be adapted for the MI population as existing treatment workbooks do not include units on major mental illness (with the exception of trauma histories and substance abuse). Treatment workbooks can be a way to organize and make consistent sex offender treatment concepts (consider Bays and Freeman-Longo's (1989, 1999; Bays, Freeman-Longo, & Montgomery-Logan, 1999; Longo, 2001) sex offender treatment workbook series, Schwartz and Canfield's (1996) *Facing the Shadow*, Blasingame's (2001) *Developmentally Disabled Sexual Offender Rehabilitative Treatment*, and Morin and Levenson's (2002) *The Road to Freedom*). Clients can review concepts or read ahead for homework. Some workbooks target higher intellectual functioning, while others target impaired cognitive and intellectual functioning. In any case, creative presentation of the material and attention to clients' unique learning styles and cognitive and intellectual abilities make the therapy interesting and relevant. Adapting treatment workbooks serves as a resource for group discussions, handouts, exercises, role play, and games. Clients can take notes during individual and group therapy, as needed.

Individual "tutoring" or slowing down the pace of group treatment may be necessary for some clients. The pace of treatment often depends on the client's ability to understand and remember concepts, concrete versus abstract thinking capabilities, degree of motivation (which can be influenced by mental illness), whether or not the client is delusional about having committed the sexual offense in question, or whether the client admits to the problem sexual interest or behavior. The therapist must deter-

mine a client's need for tutoring versus being capable of completing homework independently. Also, the therapist must assess the degree to which the MI client has the
same treatment goals for himself as the sex offender treatment program, therapist, or
group has for him. The therapist must consider the client's capacity to hold and manage the intensity of emotions or problematic sexual urges. Does the client have adequate self-awareness and insight regarding his sexuality and sexual interest or behavior problem? Or, does he escape into psychosis, mania, substance abuse, dissociation,
or denial as a means of trying to cope with emotional discomfort or stress? Does the
client have a capacity to self-contain and to maintain motivation versus intentional
acting out?

Individual vs. Group Treatment

It often saves time later to begin treatment in individual cognitive-behavioral sex
offender treatment in order to establish an initial sense of trust and to first teach basic
relapse prevention principles and deviant cycle theory, have an initial map of the
client's cycle, create individualized ICPs, and complete aversive reconditioning treatment (if indicated) before having the client enter group therapy.

Aversive reconditioning treatment is ATSA-recommended individual behavior
therapy to change the client's deviant sexual interest and arousal pattern. It involves
reading deviant sexual scenarios for homework; at the point the client begins to feel
aroused (or at the end of the scenario if not aroused), the client stops and inhales an
ammonia capsule. Often, community residence support is necessary to assist the client
(Lewis, 2001, 2002). Practical considerations need to be addressed regarding ensuring privacy for the client to do aversive reconditioning homework. During this phase
of treatment, therapy also focuses on the client's increasing appropriate sexual interests and arousal via masturbation to appropriate fantasy. This initial treatment phase
gives the therapist a chance to gain a better sense of the client and the client a chance
to develop a therapeutic alliance and to learn basic cycle theory and relapse prevention principles so he will have the "vocabulary" to join a sex offender group therapy
program specifically for MI offenders. When clinically indicated, a client may be in
group and individual therapy concurrently or attend individual tutoring sessions, as
needed.

While comprehensive relapse prevention plans are part of treatment for all sex
offender populations, MI offenders can take longer to complete their plans, include
multiple cycles, and may need more individualized help. Relapse prevention plans
need to be presented in understandable terms and in an accessible format so they can
be reviewed easily by a client and members of his treatment team. Typical relapse prevention files are individualized for each client and include low-, medium-, and high-
risk situations; a description of each phase of the client's cycle (pretend normal; triggers; buildup phase; groom and control; acting-out phase; justification phase; promises to stop); and interventions at each step in the cycle and for each potential risk situation that work best for the client. ICPs are a set of steps a client can take to control
his problematic sexual thoughts/fantasies, impulses, or urges. By thinking about problematic impulses and their triggers when *not* experiencing them, ways to stop acting
out can be developed for when a client *does* experience them. In addition to an ICP,
relapse prevention files include a "toolbox" of interventions: cognitive interventions

such as self-talk and cognitive restructuring, meditation and relaxation exercises, physical interventions, medication, imagery, relapse rehearsal, escape and avoidance strategies, guidelines for living relapse free, support system names and telephone numbers, a crisis plan, and a listing of self-help groups. If the client has a capacity for empathy (or a capacity to develop empathy), then some focus on empathy can be an effective tool for relapse prevention and impulse control. Theoretically, it is more difficult to offend if one is aware of the impact of his behavior on others. However, it is also imperative to monitor levels of depression and suicidality, which may be exacerbated as clients become increasingly aware of the impact of their sexual acting-out behavior on others. A sense of remorse or guilt is useful as a source of motivation to be dedicated to treatment and relapse prevention. It is a danger and countertherapeutic if remorse or guilt is used as a trigger for self-berating, self-destructive, or suicidal behavior.

MONITORING TREATMENT PROGRESS

Throughout treatment, progress is monitored via PPG (baseline and follow-up), AASI, and psychosexual inventory (a self-report monitor of clients' sexual thoughts, urges, and behaviors which can be reviewed on a weekly basis in treatment). Other potential indicators of progress include the client's attitude and use of cognitive distortions; ability and motivation to use an ICP; presence and awareness of warning signs; response to warning signs; understanding of the relapse prevention plan and concepts; ability to make responsible decisions (identifies seemingly unimportant decisions); willingness to report difficulties, lapses, and early warning signs and to ask for help; and ability to generalize to less supervised, more stressful, or riskier situations. A client's willingness and degree of consistency in living by guidelines to decrease or control relapse risk is a noteworthy sign of progress, whereas signs of disinhibition and impulsivity secondary to psychiatric symptoms (e.g., psychosis or mania) are cause for concern. Adequate psychiatric medication and medication compliance are essential to maintaining progress. Polygraphs have not yet been validated for use with the MI population and are not routinely used in the treatment of MI offenders (this is especially true for clients who are actively psychotic).

OTHER TREATMENT CONSIDERATIONS

Life and Social Skills

Several other issues are salient to the treatment of MI sex offenders. Resistance and denial (or another defense such as minimizing or justifying) must be discriminated from delusional thinking, cognitive or memory impairment, and poor social judgment. Treatment also addresses developing friendships, intimacy, and connections in order to replace deviancy with appropriate relationships and to decrease a need to use deviant sexual interests or behavior as an alternative to real relationships. This is a particular challenge with MI offenders as social anxiety and skills deficits often accompany mental illness. Social skill building and maintaining adequate hygiene are major treatment foci to increase a client's ability to relate to others, to have the skills to promote a sense of belonging, and to be able to navigate in the community.

Sex education and healthy sexuality are addressed to help clients direct their sexuality positively, to reinforce healthy safe sexual expression that does not hurt the client or create victims, to decrease a need for secrecy and open the channels of communication, and to answer questions clients may have, especially those who are institutionalized and have not had the opportunity and privacy for healthy sexual development.

Vocational rehabilitation helps clients work toward meaningful daily activities or paid employment which gives meaning and purpose to life, decreases boredom, increases self-esteem, and provides an opportunity to make money.

Developing hobbies and a sense of fun in life establishes nondeviant ways to spend leisure time which can be rewarding and enjoyable, decreases boredom, replaces time spent on deviancy, contributes to a more positive sense of self, supports establishing and maintaining relationships, and serves as a stress reducer. Problems with motivation and anxiety, which often accompany mental illness, complicate this goal for MI offenders. Treatment, then, must facilitate clients' gaining a sense of how managing their sexual interest or behavior problems ultimately is in their best interest. As treatment facilitates clients' identifying their hopes and dreams in life, a link can be made between clients' own personal goals and their sexual interest or behavior problem treatment plans.

Length of Treatment

There is no set length of treatment. Level of risk to reoffend may decrease and problem sexual interests and behavior may be in "remission" for prolonged periods of time. However, as is the case with major mental illness, problem sexual interests or behaviors are not "cured." Under certain circumstances, the problem can be triggered and can reemerge. Treatment is an effort to understand the client's sexual deviancy cycle and to identify the circumstances under which the cycle operates. The goal is to manage the problem sexual interests or behavior and to be prepared for times of increased risk in order to prevent relapse. Once the pretreatment and active treatment phases are completed, the client enters a maintenance treatment phase to remain relapse free. In collaboration, the treatment team and the client review criteria for identifying whether the client has completed the active treatment phase and identify the client's treatment needs, set new treatment goals, and decide where those goals would be best addressed. Some clients remain in a group for MI clients with sexual interest or behavior problems on a weekly or monthly basis, while others use other modes of treatment focusing on new treatment goals (e.g., individual psychotherapy, dual-diagnosis groups, and day programs).

Family Involvement in Treatment

The potential role of family needs to be clarified. For instance, is family a resource to the client? If so, is family therapy indicated? If family members are at all involved in the client's life, they need to be to be aware of any behavioral guidelines or contracts regarding the client's problem sexual interests or behavior, especially during visits home or outings in the community. Family biases, fears, denial, or minimization regarding this problem may need to be addressed.

Client Advocacy

Finally, MI sex offenders require advocacy in dealing with the communities in which they live. Often, even on an inpatient unit, if the "community" is not familiar with or specially trained in the treatment of sexual behavior/offending problems, then the therapist will need to play a more active role in advocating for the client and communicating the treatment plan, its rationale, and the necessary role of staff (and, in some cases, the role of the milieu) in the implementation of the treatment plan. In some instances a hospital, halfway house, or DMH may hire specialized staff and provide training for specialized multidisciplinary treatment teams (consider the Massachusetts DMH which has been developing such a statewide program and staff training; Guidry, 2004a, 2004b). Once living in a halfway house or in an independent apartment, MI offenders are not only dealing with the stress of living independently with a mental illness but are also managing their problem sexual interests or behavior. Community attitudes about mental illness and sex offending affect how secure and comfortable clients feel. While sex offender registry boards vary from state to state, MI offenders who have gone through the legal system are leveled. If an offender receives a high-risk level, his picture, name, and address are disseminated to the community. Although arguments can be made for and against the usefulness and necessity of state sex offender registry board level of risk ratings of convicted sex offenders, MI offenders deemed to be at high risk to reoffend can be particularly vulnerable as community notification makes public clients' identities and whereabouts. Treatment teams need to be a resource to their clients regarding managing the stress and sense of vulnerability of community notification and actively advocate for clients if necessary (Lewis, 2001, 2002).

CONCLUSION

Government budget cuts, managed mental health care, and deinstitutionalization have created a context in which MI clients with problem sexual interests or behavior are either identified as sex offenders and then "warehoused" in state psychiatric hospitals because they receive no specialized treatment and remain at a high risk to reoffend or discharged to less restrictive levels of care after having received no specialized treatment because their sexual interest or behavior problems have not been identified and evaluated. Neither scenario constructively addresses MI clients' sexuality. In so doing, either clients' right to treatment or community safety is ignored. Providing specialized treatment for these MI clients is imperative to protect clients' right to treatment while ensuring community safety. This chapter has outlined specific treatment considerations in an effort to provide a template for comprehensive and effective treatment by mental health professionals who are faced with the task of treating MI clients with problem sexual interests or behavior. It is hoped that both clients and their treatment providers will be empowered in this shared endeavor.

References

American Psychiatric Association. (1994). *Diagnostic and statistical manual of mental disorders* (4th ed.). Washington, DC: Author.

American Psychiatric Association. (1999). Pharmacological treatment of sex offenders. In APA

(Eds.) *Dangerous sex offenders: A Task Force report of the American Psychiatric Association* (pp. 103–128). Washington, DC: Author.

Association for the Treatment of Sexual Abusers. (1997). *The ATSA practitioners handbook.* Beaverton, OR: Author.

Bays, L., & Freeman-Longo, R. (1989). *Why did I do it again?: Understanding my cycle of problem behaviors.* Brandon, VT: Safer Society Press.

Bays, L., & Freeman-Longo, R. (1999). *Empathy and compassionate action: Issues and exercises* (4th printing). Brandon, VT: Safer Society Press. (Copyright 1996)

Bays, L., Freeman-Longo, R., & Montgomery-Logan, D. (1990). *How can I stop?: Breaking my deviant cycle.* Brandon, VT: Safer Society Press.

Blasingame, G. (2001). *Developmentally disabled persons with sexual behavior problems: Treatment management, supervision.* Oklahoma City, OK: Wood 'N' Barnes.

Craissati, J., & Hodes, P. (1992). Mentally ill sex offenders: The experience of a regional secure care unit. *British Journal of Psychiatry, 161,* 846–849.

English, K. (1998). The containment approach: An aggressive strategy for the community management of adult sex offenders. *Psychology, Public Policy and Law, 4*(1/2), 218–235.

Gann, M. K. (2000, November 1) *Dialectical behavior therapy with personality disordered sexual abusers.* Paper presented at the 19th annual ATSA Research and Treatment Conference, San Diego, CA.

Guidry, L. (2004a, April 7 & 8). *Assessing, treating & managing mentally ill sex offenders.* Paper presented at the MASOC/MATSA conference, Marlborough, MA.

Guidry, L. (2004b, April 7 & 8). *Managing mentally ill sex offenders in the community.* Paper presented at the MASOC/MATSA conference, Marlborough, MA.

Henderson, M. C., & Kalichman, S. C. (1990). Sexually deviant behavior and schizotypy: A theoretical perspective with supportive data. *Psychiatric Quarterly, 61*(4), 273–284.

Jones, B., Huckle, P., & Tanaghow, A. (1992). Command auditory hallucinations, schizophrenia and sexual assaults. *Irish Journal of Psychological Medicine, 9,* 47–49.

Kafka, M. P. (2001, June 28 & 29). *The diagnosis and medical management of sex offenders with major mental illness.* Paper presented at the first annual MI/SBD Training Conference: The treatment of MI/SBD inpatients. Medfield: Massachusetts Department of Mental Health and University of Massachusetts Medical School, Medfield State Hospital.

Kafka, M. P., & Hennen, J. (2002). A DSM-IV Axis I comorbidity study of males (*n* = 120) with paraphilias and paraphilia-related disorders. *Sexual Abuse: A Journal of Research and Treatment, 14*(4), 349–366.

Kafka, M. P., & Prentky, R. A. (1994). Preliminary observations of DSM-III-R Axis I comorbidity in men with paraphilias and paraphilia-related disorders. *Journal of Clinical Psychiatry, 55,* 481–487.

Land, W. (1995). Psychopharmacological options for sex offenders. In B. Schwartz & H. Cellini (Eds.), *The sex offender: Corrections, treatment and legal practice* (Vol. I, pp. 18-1–18-7). Kingston, NJ: Civic Research Institute.

Lewis, R. E. (2001, June 28 & 29). *Comprehensive treatment for mentally ill clients with sexual behavior disorder.* Paper presented at the first annual MI/SBD Training Conference: The treatment of MI/SBD inpatients, Medfield, MA.

Lewis, R. E. (2002, December 19). *Comprehensive treatment for mentally ill clients with problem sexual behavior.* Baldwinville: Massachusetts Department of Mental Health, Baldwinville Community Residence.

Longo, R., with Bays, L. (2001). *Who am I and Why am I in treatment* (13th printing). Brandon, VT: Safer Society Press. (Copyright 1998)

Morin, J. W., & Levenson, J. S. (2002). *The road to freedom.* Oklahoma City, Oklahoma: Wood 'N' Barnes.

Phillips, S. L., Heads, T. C., Taylor, P. J., & Hill, G. M. (1999). Sexual offending and antisocial behavior among patients with schizophrenia. *Journal of Clinical Psychiatry, 60*(3), 170–175.

Quigley, S. (2001, June 28 and 29). *Integrating dialectical behavior therapy into sex offender treatment for mentally ill patients.* Paper presented at the first annual MI/SBD Training Conference: The treatment of MI/SBD inpatients. Medfield: Massachusetts Department of Mental Health and University of Massachusetts Medical School, Medfield State Hospital.

Schwartz, B. K., & Canfield, G. M. S. (1996). *Facing the shadow.* Kingston, NJ: Civic Research Institute.

Seghorn, T., & Ball, C. (2000). Assessment of sexual deviance in adults with developmental disabilities. *Mental Health Aspects of Developmental Disabilities, 3*(2), 47–53.

Sherak, D. (2000). Pharmacological treatment of sexually offending behavior in people with mental retardation/developmental disabilities. *Mental Health Aspects of Developmental Disabilities, 3*(2).

Smith, A. D., & Taylor, P. J. (1999) Serious sex offending against women by men with schizophrenia. *British Journal of Psychiatry, 174,* 233–237.

Part 3
Adult Treatment

Research on the treatment of adult sex offenders uniformly states that cognitive-behavioral treatment is the method of choice, as if there was any agreement whatsoever as to what that means. The Safer Society for a number of years produced a survey of treatment providers who reported on the methods they used. Cognitive-behavioral therapy and relapse prevention were always listed as separate methods. Yet, in sex offender treatment circles, to say that one's treatment is cognitive-behavioral is to assume that it is obvious that one's patients routinely develop relapse prevention plans. Consistent with the basic cognitive-behavioral approach, one would also assume that patients are taught that thoughts produce feelings, which produce behaviors. However, psychopharmacological therapy is also considered an effective treatment approach. Consequently, one may have a basic conflict between the basic assumptions of these two approaches. If biochemicals produce feelings, these feelings may also produce thoughts to explain them. On one hand, a person may have low self-esteem and continually tell himself that he is "no good" or "a loser." Naturally, these thoughts may cause feelings of depression and may lead to the behavior of isolating. The cognitive-behavioral therapist would challenge the thoughts that lead to the maladaptive behavior. However, what if the feelings of depression are really related to an imbalance in neurotransmitters? The person may search for reasons to explain why he is feeling badly and conclude that it is because he is an inadequate person. Attempting to challenge these thoughts will do little to correct the biochemical dysfunction. Therefore, strict adherence to one therapeutic model can be counterproductive.

Many cognitive-behavioral programs have also interpreted this term to identify two different models—cognitive and behavioral—and may include behavioral techniques such as covert sensitization, aversive techniques, and satiation techniques. In addition, psychoeducational classes are routinely included in comprehensive programs, particularly those in institutions. Following the advice of adult educators, these classes often focus on experiential learning and address differing learning styles. This has led to the inclusion of drama therapy, art therapy, music therapy, and dance therapy.

When recommendations are offered or testimony is given in courtrooms regarding the efficacy of cognitive-behavioral sex offender treatment programs, one should acknowledge that this by no means refers to a uniform approach. The model depends on where it is offered, how long the program is, the staff-participant ratio, and the individual interests of the therapists. In this section, we explore a variety of different approaches, including drama therapy, therapeutic communities, and the use of spirituality. All of these techniques can complement the basic "cognitive-behavioral" approach—whatever that may be.

Finding useful psychometric tools for evaluating sex offenders is often a challenge. Many of the tools developed for this population are questionnaires that have never been standardized or normed. They have face validity but little more. Herman Lindeman has developed the Sexual Adjustment Inventory, which assesses sex offenders on a variety of scales, including two truthfulness scales. The test measures different types of sexual deviance along with substance abuse scales and measures of aggression, judgment, and antisocial attitudes. He discusses the use of these scales in Chapter 7.

Whether or not to attempt to "teach" or sensitize sex offenders to the plight of their victims by offering therapies that evoke empathy is a topic of intense controversy. Research supporting cognitive-behavioral treatment is quoted to suggest that only cognitive, not affective, approaches are efficacious. However, many of the more comprehensive treatment programs have used experiential therapies to help sex offenders identify with the pain that their victims have endured. Drama therapy is one of the more commonly used techniques. In Chapter 8, Maxine Daniels presents specific role-playing approaches used in Her Majesty's Prison Service in England.

The treatment of incarcerated sex offenders often results in the emergence of a group of inmates who have completed treatment and who, with the right guidance, may be a valuable resource for the prison-based sex offender treatment program. In Chapter 9, Nancy Steele, who has decades of experience identifying and training inmates to be therapeutic aides, offers specific suggestions on selecting, training, and monitoring program participants.

In Chapter 10, Geral Blanchard advocates for the role of spirituality in the treatment of sex offenders. Incorporating this facet into a comprehensive therapy program allows the therapist to deal directly with issues including morals and morality as these concepts relate to sexual abuse. In addition, spiritual practices throughout history have offered healing practices that can be incorporated into the recovery process.

Chapter 7

Sex Offender Tests— SAI and SAI-Juvenile

by Herman Lindeman, Ph.D.

OVERVIEW

Increased public awareness of sexual abuse as a growing problem in our society has led to an increased need for sex offender screening and, as warranted, intervention and treatment. Public awareness and concern have led to escalating demands for accountability, which have placed new professional responsibilities on professionals working with sex offenders.

One aspect of this responsibility is evaluation (screening, assessments, or testing). Assessment—perhaps better stated as "problem identification" with measured "problem severity"—is a necessary prerequisite for effective sex offender treatment. The evidence demonstrates that matching offenders to appropriate treatment programs and incorporating cognitive and behavioral techniques reduces the risk of recidivism by 15 percent (Andrews & Bonta, 1994; Andrews et al., 1989; Carey, 1997). Thus any measure that enhances the appropriate pairing of treatment to the particular needs of the offender will enhance the effectiveness of the process. This chapter discusses two assessment devices that facilitate crucial treatment and supervision decisions: the Sexual Adjustment Inventory (SAI) and the SAI-Juvenile.

INTRODUCTION

There are different approaches to sex offender evaluation (screening, assessment, testing), and the role of these assessments must not be taken for granted. After all, referral and treatment decisions are largely based on these test findings, and risk assessment results can improve decision making (Hudson, Wales, & Ward, 2002). Indeed, many health care professionals now espouse the virtues of "assessment driven treatment" (Davignon, 2003a; Gendreau, Little, & Goggin, 1996; Hanson, 2000) and "evidence-based practices" (Drake et al., 2001).

Concurrently, courts, assessors, counselors, therapists, and treatment staff (along with other health care professionals) are now asked to document or otherwise verify their actions. Intuition, hunches, interviews, and poorly constructed questionnaires are now considered unacceptable sex offender evaluations. Moreover, the justice system and other professionals insist on valid, reliable, and accurate sex offender tests. The purpose of screening is to identify people with problems serious enough to warrant counseling or treatment referral. And when problems are present, it is important to measure their severity. Contingent upon these test results, clients (offenders, patients) are referred to appropriate types and levels of treatment. The assumption is that, as with emergency room triage, patients with serious problems are referred to intensive treatment programs. Or are they?

Andrews, Bonta, and Hoge (1990) pointed out that placing offenders (patients) in the wrong "treatment intensity" programs is detrimental to both the offenders (patients) and society. Placing low-risk offenders in high-risk intensity treatment programs contributes to an unusually high relapse rate. In contrast, low-risk offenders were better served in low-intensity treatment programs, and similar results were demonstrated with high-risk offenders. These findings emphasize the importance of identifying problems accurately and correctly measuring problem severity. Researchers have investigated sexual recidivism risk factors (Beech, Friendship, Erikson, & Hanson, 2002; Dempster & Hart, 2002; Hudson et al., 2002; Thornton, 2002) such as antisocial attitudes, violence potential, and substance abuse. As noted previously, matching treatment to an offender's specific needs in a cognitive-behavioral treatment program greatly reduces the risk of recidivism, by 15 percent, to 50 percent (Andrews & Bonta, 1994; Andrews et al., 1989; Carey, 1997). Thus it is incumbent upon treatment professionals and program administrators to accurately assess these risks and needs.

Most evaluators know that the interview is still widely used for assessment despite its paradoxical lack of reliability and validity. Several literature reviews have pointed out the poor performance of the interview, when used alone, for problem identification (i.e., diagnosis) or the prediction of recidivism (Avery & Cannon, 1992; Zimmerman, 1994), and most experienced evaluators agree that the interview is not a defensible technique for making diagnostic or treatment decisions. Reasons for this impaired reliability are many and include different interviewer personalities, equivocal motivation, and dissimilar training. Moreover, interviewers must repeat, paraphrase, and probe for answers, a process that introduces even more subjectivity into the process. In contrast, there are objective and standardized tests. Unfortunately, all tests are not equal.

Ward and Stewart (2003) discuss the importance of assessing the "primary constructs" (e.g., sexual adjustment), while concurrently assessing criminogenic needs. Particular criminogenic needs, such as substance abuse (alcohol and other drugs), antisocial attitudes, violence potential, perceived distress, and poor judgment, are relevant to sex offender assessment and are amenable to change (Hanson, 2002; Peugh & Belenko, 2001; Ward & Stewart, 2003). Such cognitive and behavioral changes are often necessary for rehabilitation success and recidivism reduction (Aytes, Olsen, Zakrajsek, Murray, & Ireson, 2001). This approach provides the evaluator with the information needed to make informed referral and treatment decisions.

Multiple scaled tests designed for specific offender (patient) groups and standardized (normed) on that client population sets standards for scale inclusion, in that each scale must contribute to better understanding of the person (offender, patient, client) being evaluated.

This chapter describes an adult and a juvenile sex offender test that can help practitioners answer some of these critical assessment questions. Selected tests include the Sexual Adjustment Inventory (SAI) and the SAI-Juvenile.

THE SEXUAL ADJUSTMENT INVENTORY SCALES

The SAI is an automated (computer-scored with reports printed onsite in two and a half minutes) assessment instrument or test that identifies sexually deviate and paraphiliac behavior in people accused or convicted of sexual offenses. It has 214 items and takes forty-five minutes to an hour to complete.

The SAI contains thirteen scales (measures), six sex-related scales and seven non-sex-related scales commonly associated with sex offenders' problematic attitudes and behavior.

Sex-Related Scales

Sex Item Truthfulness Scale. The Sex Item Truthfulness Scale measures how truthful the client was while answering sex-related questions. The SAI presents a very open and candid approach to sex-related items and makes no attempt to trick or deceive the client; consequently, sex-related items are easily recognized. Sometimes sex offenders who want to minimize sex-related problems answer non-sex-related questions honestly but minimize problems or even lie when answering sex-related questions. In these cases (denial, attempts to minimize problems, or "fake good") this scale detects the client's attempts to deceive, lie, or deny because it has been correlated with all the SAI sex-related scales, enabling scale scores to be "truth-corrected." Each sex-related scale's proprietary conversion equation transforms the scale's raw scores into truth-corrected scores, which are more accurate than raw scores.

Sex Item Truthfulness Scale scores in the 70th–89th percentile range reflect problem minimizing, whereas scores in the 90th–100th percentile range are so severe they invalidate the test and negate all other sex-related scale scores. Scores at or below the 89th percentile suggest that all sex-related scale scores are accurate.

Sexual Adjustment Scale. The Sexual Adjustment Scale measures the client's self-reported sexual adjustment. High scores reveal sexual dissatisfaction in a person who has an unsatisfying sex life (i.e., high scorers do not like their sexual adjustment). The Sexual Adjustment Scale includes sex-related items with which most people in our society would agree or disagree. Norming the scale on both normals and deviates allows comparison scoring. The higher the score, the greater the impairment.

Child (Pedophile) Molest Scale. The Child (Pedophile) Molest Scale measures a person's sexual interests, urges, and fantasies involving prepubescent children. Pedophilia is a pathological sexual interest in children, and the child molester is often unable to comprehend the reasons for his or her actions. Isolated sexual acts with a child do not necessarily warrant the classification of pedophilia. These circumstances often make accurate classification difficult.

Problem risk range (70th–89th percentile) scorers have a greater than average interest in young boys and/or girls. Severe problem (90th–100th percentile) risk scorers have an abnormal interest in children (young boys and/or girls). Consequences associated with severe problem (90th–100th percentile) scores on this scale vary according to the evaluation's purpose (e.g., pedophile classification, referrals to a licensed mental health professional for a diagnosis and treatment plan, probation or incarceration decision making, and selection of treatment alternatives).

Sexual (Rape) Assault Scale. The Sexual (Rape) Assault Scale measures sexual assault proneness. Rape refers to sexual assault or sexual intercourse against the will and over the objections of the partner. It is often accompanied by force or the threat of force. Problem risk range (70th–89th percentile) scorers on this scale have more than an average interest in aggressive sex and often fantasize about forceful sex against the will of their partner. They are capable of sexual assault. Severe problem (90th–100th percentile) risk scorers have a high probability of sexual assault.

Exhibitionism Scale. The Exhibitionism Scale measures a person's need to expose his or her sex organs to unsuspecting individuals. Exhibitionists are often identified by the repetitive, compulsive, and patterned nature of their acts. An elevated (70th percentile or higher) Exhibitionism Scale score identifies people with exhibitionistic tendencies. Severe problem (90th–100th percentile) scorers have a high probability of being exhibitionists.

Incest Scale. The Incest Scale measures incestuous behavior (i.e., coitus between persons related by blood or marriage—e.g., parents, siblings, or children); noncoitus forms of sexual intercourse do not constitute incest. Problem risk range (70th–89th percentile) scorers on this scale are interested in incest. Severe problem (90th–100th percentile) scorers have a high probability of incestuous behavior. Note: It is important when treating a person engaging in incest to determine if the client is the aggressor or the victim.

Non-Sex-Related Scales

Test Item Truthfulness Scale. As with the similar scale for sex-related items, the Test Item Truthfulness Scale measures how truthful the client was while answering non-sex-related items. Clients can distinguish between sex-related and non-sex-related items, and some clients might only minimize or lie in responding to non-sex-related items. The Test Item Truthfulness Scale is correlated with all non-sex-related scales. Each scale's proprietary conversion equation transforms its raw scores to truth-corrected scores. Thus, raw scores reflect what the client wants the examiner to know; truth-corrected scores are more accurate than raw scores. Test Item Truthfulness Scale scores at or below the 89th percentile mean that all non-sex-related scales are accurate because they have been truth-corrected. Scores in the severe problem range (90th–100th percentile), however, indicate that all non-sex-related scale scores are inaccurate and invalid.

Comparison of the Test Item Truthfulness Scale score with the Sex Item Truthfulness Scale score can provide considerable insight regarding the client's test-taking motivation. The higher of these two scores usually represents the client's greatest area of concern.

Alcohol Scale. The Alcohol Scale measures alcohol (beer, wine, and other liquors) use and the severity of abuse. An elevated (70th–89th percentile) Alcohol Scale score is indicative of an emerging drinking problem; a score in the severe problem range (90th–100th percentile) identifies serious drinking problems.

In intervention and treatment settings, the Alcohol Scale score helps staff work through client denial. Most clients accept the objective and standardized Alcohol Scale score as accurate and relevant. This is particularly true when it is explained that elevated scores do not occur by chance. Clients must show a definite pattern of alcohol-related admissions for an elevated score to occur.

Drugs Scale. The Drugs Scale measures drug use and the severity of abuse. Drugs refer to illicit substances—marijuana, crack, cocaine, ice, amphetamines, barbiturates, ecstasy, and heroin. An elevated (70th–89th percentile) Drugs Scale score is indicative of an emerging drug problem; a score in the severe problem range (90th–100th percentile) identifies serious illicit drug abusers.

Violence (Lethality) Scale. The Violence (Lethality) Scale measures the client's use of physical force to injure, damage, or destroy and identifies people who are dangerous to themselves and others. An ever-present concern when evaluating sex offenders is their violence and lethality potential. An elevated (70th–89th percentile) Violence Scale score is indicative of emerging violent behavior in a potentially dangerous person; a score in the severe problem range (90th–100th percentile) identifies very dangerous individuals. As with the two truthfulness scales, Violence Scale findings are of interest when reviewing both sex-related scales and non-sex-related scale scores. This wide applicability emphasizes the important role of the Violence Scale in the SAI.

Antisocial Scale. The Antisocial Scale measures the attitudes and behaviors of selfish, ungrateful, callous, and egocentric people who seem to be devoid of responsibility and fail to learn from experience. From a social perspective, their conduct often appears hostile with little guilt or remorse. Extreme cases are called sociopaths or psychopaths. An elevated (70th–89th percentile) Antisocial Scale score identifies people in an early antisocial stage of development; a score in the Severe Problem range (90th–100th percentile) identifies people with severe antisocial attitudes.

Distress Scale. The Distress Scale measures two symptom clusters (anxiety and depression) which, taken together, represent distress. The blending of these symptom clusters is clear in the definition of dysphoria (i.e., a generalized feeling of anxiety, resentment, and depression). Anxiety is an unpleasant emotional state characterized by apprehension, stress, nervousness, and tension. Depression refers to a dejected emotional state that includes melancholy, dysphoric moods, and despair. Added together, these symptoms lead to a very uncomfortable person who may be overwhelmed and, in extreme cases, on the verge of giving up. An elevated (70th–89th percentile) Distress Scale score identifies hurting individuals who need help; a score in the severe problem range (90th–100th percentile) identifies people who are on the verge of being emotionally overwhelmed. These individuals are often desperate. Consideration might be given to referring such individuals to a certified or licensed mental health professional for a diagnosis, prognosis, and treatment plan.

Judgment Scale. The Judgment Scale measures a person's ability to compare facts or ideas, to understand relationships, and to draw conclusions. As judgment decreases, client risk increases. Judgment is necessary for a person to understand the consequences of his or her actions. An elevated (70th–89th percentile) Judgment Scale score identifies people who are relatively unaware and easily manipulated or exploited and who, in turn, can act without thinking things through or fully considering consequences. A Judgment Scale score in the severe problem range (90th–100th percentile) reflects a person with very poor judgment who can be easily confused and can often act without full regard to future consequences.

CRITICAL SAI FEATURES

In addition to its comprehensiveness, which allows measurement of many non-sexual attitudes and behaviors important in understanding sex offenders, the SAI has several features of special interest.

The Truthfulness Scales

One of the most distinctive features of the SAI is its two truthfulness scales, described earlier. These two proprietary scales are very important when evaluating sex offenders because many of the people accused of sex offenses are aware of the severe penalties associated with admissions of guilt, let alone sex offender convictions. When evaluated, these individuals often attempt to minimize, rationalize, and deny their sexual interests and behavior. This is one of the many reasons why sex offender interviews are so lacking and unproductive. The SAI's two truthfulness scales enable evaluators to account for an offender's denial, problem minimization, and attempts to "fake good." These two truthfulness scales have been shown to be reliable, valid, and accurate (Davignon, 2003b).

Truth-corrected scores are important for sex offender assessment accuracy. These proprietary truth-correction programs are comparable to the Minnesota Multiphasic Personality Inventory (MMPI) K-scale correction.

Ease of Administration

The SAI can be administered in several different ways (Behavior Data Systems, n.d.-a):

1. Paper-pencil test booklets in English or Spanish, administered individually or in groups.

2. Administered directly on the computer screen in English or Spanish.

3. "Human voice audio" in English and Spanish. This SAI presentation requires a computer, a headset, and simple up-down arrow key instructions. As the client goes from questions to answers, the questions or answers are highlighted on the screen (monitor) and simultaneously read to the client. The SAI can also be be administered over the Internet (see *www.online-testing.com*).

Each mode of administration has potential advantages and disadvantages, depending on the particular client and situation. For example, more than 20 percent of tested sex offenders are reading impaired. Clients' passive vocabularies (what they hear and understand) are usually greater than their active vocabularies (what they speak). Hearing items read out loud in their native language (English or Spanish) helps reduce both cultural and communication problems.

To verify the accuracy of data input, test data taken from client answer sheets are input twice, and any inconsistencies are highlighted until corrected. Only when the first and the second data entry match or are the same can the staff person continue. It is an understatement to note that it is important to ensure accurate data input for scoring, interpreting, and printing SAI reports.

Note: To meet confidentiality and HIPAA requirements (Health Insurance Portability and Accountability Act, 45 C.F.R. § 164.50 (1996)), test users delete client names from diskettes before they are returned for scoring. Once client names are deleted they are gone and cannot be retrieved. Deleting client names does not delete demographics or test data which are downloaded into the SAI database for subsequent analysis.

The final SAI report is presented in a readable narrative format (see Exhibit 7.1 at the end of this chapter for a sample report).

SAI-JUVENILE

Over the last fifteen years many evaluators, sex offender therapists, and other professionals have asked for a juvenile version of the SAI. To meet this need the SAI was modified for juvenile sex offender assessment. Its reading level was lowered while concurrently maintaining the integrity of the SAI's thirteen measures or scales. Some of the sexual deviancy language is rather unique and could not be changed. However, wherever possible the language was simplified for juveniles ranging in age from 14 to 18. It should be noted that the SAI-Juvenile is a separate test that was normed and standardized on the juvenile sex offender population. (For a discussion of the SAI-Juvenile, including normative and standardization research and a sample report on the web, see the website *www.sex-offender-tests.com* (Risk & Needs Assessment, n.d.-a, n.d.-b).)

Two procedures for measuring sexual interest and/or arousal are the penile plethysmograph and the Abel Assessment for Sexual Interest (Abel, 1998) procedure. However, neither of these procedures is appropriate for use in court settings during the guilt-finding phase of juvenile sex offender assessment (California Coalition on Sexual Offending, 2002). Experienced juvenile sex offender evaluators are very aware of juveniles' reluctance to respond to test items, vignettes, sexual fantasies, nude pictures, and inquiries (interview questions) having a sexual connotation. Their reasons for not responding include not wanting to incriminate themselves, apprehensions about direct admissions and further disclosure, and plethysmograph concerns. Regardless of the reason, this reluctance to answer sexually related questions is a formidable hurdle that must be overcome in juvenile sex offender assessment.

The SAI-Juvenile has two truthfulness scales that help overcome this problem. The Test Item Truthfulness Scale and the Sex Item Truthfulness Scale were discussed earlier in relation to the SAI. In brief, these scales are also used to measure denial, problem minimization, and attempts to "fake good" while completing the SAI-Juvenile. One of these scales determines if the youth was truthful while answering sex-related items and the other measures the youth's truthfulness while answering non-sex-related items. These two scales (measures) provide important motivation, attitude, and mind-set information in addition to juvenile truthfulness data. These SAI-Juvenile truthfulness scales correlated highly significantly with the MMPI-2, 16PF (Cattell, Cattell, & Cattell, 1993), ACDI-Corrections Version II (Lindeman, n.d.-a),

Juvenile Substance Abuse Profile (Lindeman, n.d.-b), and so on. Much of this research is summarized by Davignon (2000a).

The SAI-Juvenile identifies sexually deviate and paraphiliac behavior in juveniles accused or convicted of sexual offenses. The SAI-Juvenile has 195 items and takes forty-five minutes to an hour to complete. It has the same thirteen scales (measures) as the adult SAI: the Sex Item Truthfulness Scale, Sexual Adjustment Scale, Child (Pedophile) Molest Scale, Sexual (Rape) Assault Scale, Exhibitionism Scale, Incest Scale, Test Item truthfulness Scale, Violence (Lethality) Scale, Alcohol Scale, Drugs Scale, Antisocial Scale, Distress Scale, and Judgment Scale. These scales were defined earlier for the SAI, and the same definitions apply to the SAI-Juvenile. SAI-Juvenile research has demonstrated that it is an objective, reliable, valid, and accurate test. Similarly, the discussion of SAI "Unique Features" is also descriptive of the SAI-Juvenile. For a sample SAI-Juvenile report, see website: *www.sex-offender-tests.com* (Risk & Needs Assessment, n.d.-a, n.d.-b). SAI and SAI-Juvenile research is discussed separately in the following sections.[1] However, the "Scale Interpretation" discussion near the end of this chapter applies to both instruments.

SAI RESEARCH

Population Studied

The validity of the SAI was investigated in a sample of 3,616 adult sex offenders who were administered the SAI as part of their standard intake procedure in court and community service programs (Davignon, 2000b). There were 3,480 males (96.2 percent) and 136 females (3.8 percent). Participant age ranged from 18 to 49 years; the average age of males was 35.0 (SD = 12.49) and the average age of females was 30.7 (SD = 8.23).

The demographic composition of participants was as follows:

- Race: Caucasian (78.5 percent), black (14.1 percent), Hispanic (5.4 percent), and other (2.0 percent).

- Education: eighth grade or less (7.6 percent), some high school (29.6 percent), high school graduate/GED (41.4 percent), some college (15.3 percent), and college graduates (6.0 percent).

- Marital status: married (29.9 percent), single (43.1 percent), divorced (18.8 percent), separated (7.6 percent), and widowed (0.7 percent).

Criminal histories were obtained from SAI answer sheets, which were completed by the offenders. Participants reported this information and it was verified by staff. Over 87 percent of the participants, or 3,055 offenders, reported having one (present offense) sex-related arrest. Of these 3,055 offenders, 2,940 were males (96.2 percent) and 115 were females (3.8 percent). These offenders were designated Group 1.

Ten percent of the participants had two sex-related arrests, 2 percent had three arrests, and 1 percent had four or more sex-related arrests. Offenders with two or more sex-related arrests were designated Group 2. There were 436 offenders (12.5 percent) in Group 2; 423 of these participants were male and 13 were female.

One-fourth of the offenders (participants) had one or more alcohol arrests. Fourteen percent had one or more drug arrests. Just over 60 percent of these offenders had been placed on probation one or more times. Forty percent had been sentenced to jail and 30 percent of the offenders were sentenced to prison one or more times.

Participants completed the SAI as part of the normal intake procedure for court-related services and community service programs. Probation departments also used the SAI to select appropriate levels of supervision and treatment for their sex offenders.

SAI Reliability and Validity

Table 7.1 presents interitem reliability (alpha) coefficients for the thirteen SAI scales. The professionally accepted standard for acceptable reliability is an alpha coefficient of .80.

All the SAI scales were highly reliable. All scales' alpha reliability coefficients were significant at the $p < .001$ level of significance. These results demonstrate that the SAI is a reliable sex offender test: All SAI scales have alpha coefficients well above the professionally accepted standard of .80 and are highly reliable.

First Offender vs. Multiple Offender Comparisons. In this study ($N = 3,616$), discriminant validity was demonstrated between Group 1 (first offenders) and Group 2 (multiple offenders). Multiple offenders scored significantly higher than first offenders on all SAI scales, with the exception of the Incest and Truthfulness Scales. Truthfulness Scale findings suggest that all, or most, sex offenders are very defensive and evasive and

Table 7.1
SAI Reliability ($N = 3,616$)

SAI Scales	Coefficient Alpha	Significance Level
Test Item Truthfulness	.88	$p < .001$
Sex Item Truthfulness	.85	$p < .001$
Sexual Adjustment	.88	$p < .001$
Child Molest	.85	$p < .001$
Sexual Assault	.86	$p < .001$
Incest	.91	$p < .001$
Exhibitionism	.89	$p < .001$
Alcohol	.93	$p < .001$
Drugs	.92	$p < .001$
Violence	.85	$p < .001$
Antisocial	.89	$p < .001$
Distress	.88	$p < .001$
Judgment	.86	$p < .001$

Table 7.2
Mean SAI Scale Difference, First vs. Multiple Offenders (*N* = 3,616)

SAI Scales	Mean	SD	Max	Mean	SD	Max	*t*-value
Test Item Truthfulness	7.76	5.37	21	6.87	5.39	21	*t* = 3.22*
Sex Item Truthfulness	8.60	4.62	19	7.32	4.72	19	*t* = 5.34*
Sexual Adjustment	13.62	11.09	51	19.65	12.55	52	*t* = 9.39*
Child Molest	8.79	8.17	37	10.73	9.30	34	*t* = 4.07*
Sexual Assault	5.29	5.32	33	6.61	6.15	34	*t* = 4.19*
Incest	1.01	1/97	7	1.09	2.0	7	N.S.
Exhibitionism	1.29	2.47	18	3.41	4.99	18	*t* = 8.59*
Alcohol	6.62	8.99	38	21.03	12.94	38	*t* = 21.95*
Drugs	5.65	7.67	34	16.86	9.96	33	*t* = 13.75*
Violence	3.90	5.33	33	4.55	6.06	33	*t* = 2.08***
Antisocial	1.97	2.80	18	2.36	3.10	19	*t* = 2.49**
Distress	'6.22	7.20	29	7.45	7.74	29	*t* = 3.06*
Judgment	3.12	2.71	17	3.49	3.01	16	*t* = 2.42**

*Significant at *p* < .001; **Significant at *p* < .01; ***Significant at *p* < .05.

attempt to "minimize their problems" or "fake good." This defensiveness was apparent in both "first" and "multiple" offenders, with the exception of the Incest Scale.

Table 7.2 sets forth the "first offender" versus "multiple offender" comparisons. It consists of *t*-test comparisons between "first offenders" and "multiple offenders." Comparison of "first offenders" and "multiple offenders" demonstrates impressive discriminant validity. As noted earlier, multiple offenders scored significantly higher than first offenders on most SAI scales. The nonsignificant Incest scale difference may be due to the publicly abhorrent and offensive nature of incest in our society.

Problem Identification. SAI validity was also demonstrated by the correct identification of problems. The Distress, Alcohol, and Drugs scales were examined in terms of offenders having participated in prior treatment. The Sexual Adjustment, Exhibitionism, Incest, Antisocial and Judgment scales were studied in terms of offender self-admissions. The Child (Pedophile) Molest, Sexual (Rape) Assault, and Violence (Lethality) scales were analyzed in terms of the offender's court records (priors). Table 7.3 presents these results. All SAI scales demonstrated impressive accuracy in identifying offender problems, as indicated by the percentage of offenders who had or admitted to having problems and who scored in the problem risk range (70th percentile) or higher. Similarly, offenders scoring in the low risk range did not admit to problems and their records did not reflect prior treatment, arrests, or self-admissions. These results support the validity of the SAI scales.

Admittedly, prior treatment, self-admissions, and court records are not the most

Table 7.3
SAI Scale Problem Identification (N = 3,616)

SAI Scales	Correct Percentage	SAI Scales	Correct Percentage
Sexual Adjustment	99.6	Alcohol	100
Child Molest	97.6	Drugs	100
Sexual Assault	100	Violence	100
Incest	100	Antisocial	100
Exhibitionism	100	Distress	100
		Judgment	100

ideal comparison criteria, yet after a test has been normed and standardized, utilization of comparison tests for concurrent validity becomes impractical, primarily because of time, cost, and inconvenience. Yet, this database analysis does support the validity of the SAI: The lowest correct identification percentage is 97.6 percent, and most scales have a 100 percent correct identification percentage.

Accuracy. Accuracy was demonstrated by comparing predicted scale score distributions for the study sample with attained scale scores. Predicted distributions are divided into four risk ranges: low risk (0–39th percentile), medium risk (40th–69th percentile), problem risk (70th–89th percentile), and severe problem risk (90th–100th percentile). As shown in Table 7.4, attained percentages in each risk range were very close to their predicted risk range percentages. These results further support SAI validity, and they demonstrate that risk range percentile scores are accurate.

Risk range percentile scores were derived by adding test item points, truth-correction points, and criminal history points when applicable. These raw scores were converted to percentile scores. Predicted risk range percentages are presented in each column heading next to the risk range label. The percentage of attained scores in each risk range is shown for all SAI scales (to the right of SAI scale names). The observed percentages (to the right of scales names) of offender attained scores in each risk range were compared to the predicted percentages (at the top of each risk range column) and the difference is presented in bold parentheses to the right of the observed or attained percentage (between predicted and attained scores). For example, looking at the Sexual Adjustment Scale and going across the table (from left to right), you have an attained low risk score of 40.0, an attained medium risk score of 30.3, an attained problem risk score of 18.7, and an attained severe problem score of 11.0. To the right of each attained percentage in bold parentheses is the difference between the predicted and attained percentages. Again with regard to the Sexual Adjustment Scale and reading from left to right, the following differences between predicted and attained percentages are as follows: low risk (1.0), medium risk (0.3), problem risk (1.3), and severe problem (0.0).

All attained percentages are within 3.6 percent of the predicted percentages. A majority of the attained percentages, thirty-one of the possible fifty-two comparisons, fall within one percentage point of the predicted percentage.

Table 7.4
SAI Scale Accuracy (N = 3,616)

SAI Scale	Low Risk (39%)	Medium Risk (30%)	Problem Risk (20%)	Severe Problem (11%)
Test-item Truthfulness	40.8 **(1.8)**	28.1 **(1.9)**	20.6 **(0.6)**	10.5 **(0.5)**
Sex-item Truthfulness	37.5 **(1.5)**	33.4 **(3.4)**	18.1 **(1.9)**	11.0 **(0.0)**
Sexual Adjustment	40.0 **(1.0)**	30.3 **(0.3)**	18.7 **(1.3)**	11.0 **(0.0)**
Child Molest Scale	39.4 **(0.4)**	28.9 **(1.1)**	20.3 **(0.3)**	11.4 **(0.4)**
Rape Scale	38.3 **(1.7)**	29.2 **(0.8)**	20.8 **(0.8)**	11.7 **(0.7)**
Incest Scale	37.6 **(1.3)**	33.6 **(3.6)**	18.0 **(2.0)**	10.8 **(0.2)**
Exhibitionism Scale	37.1 **(1.9)**	32.1 **(2.1)**	20.6 **(0.6)**	10.2 **(0.8)**
Alcohol Scale	41.3 **(2.3)**	27.1 **(2.9)**	20.7 **(0.7)**	10.9 **(0.1)**
Drugs Scale	38.1 **(1.9)**	32.5 **(2.5)**	18.2 **(1.8)**	11.2 **(0.2)**
Violence Scale	39.9 **(0.9)**	29.6 **(0.4)**	19.8 **(0.2)**	10.7 **(0.3)**
Antisocial Scale	39.3 **(0.3)**	27.7 **(2.3)**	23.3 **(3.3)**	9.7 **(1.3)**
Distress Scale	39.6 **(0.6)**	30.7 **(0.7)**	19.2 **(0.8)**	10.5 **(0.5)**
Judgment Scale	39.5 **(0.5)**	31.4 **(1.4)**	18.9 **(1.1)**	10.2 **(0.8)**

Summary. This research demonstrates that the SAI is a reliable, valid, and accurate sex offender instrument or test. Discriminant validity analysis showed that multiple offenders typically scored significantly higher than first offenders. Validity analysis also demonstrated that SAI identified offenders with elevated scale scores had corresponding or related problems. Furthermore, attained risk range percentages on all SAI scales closely approximated predicted percentages. These results further support SAI validity and accuracy.

SAI-JUVENILE RESEARCH

SAI-Juvenile research began in 1985. Several studies have been conducted on thousands of juvenile sex offenders using several validation methods. Early studies involved concurrent validity (MMPI, Adolescent Chemical Dependency Inventory, ACDI-Corrections Version II, 16PF, Domestic Violence Inventory-Juvenile, Juvenile Substance Abuse Profile, etc.). Much of this research is reported by Davignon (2000a, 2000b, 2002, 2003a, 2003b). Subsequent database research continues to support SAI-Juvenile validity, reliability, and accuracy.

Recent Study Sample Demographics

The validity, reliability and accuracy of the SAI-Juvenile was investigated in a study of 766 juvenile sex offenders tested with the SAI-Juvenile (Davignon, 2002). Data for this study were provided by court evaluators, juvenile probation departments and community service agencies. The demographic composition of this sample was:

- Race: Caucasian (70.7 percent), black (21.3 percent), Hispanic (4.3 percent), and other (2.4 percent).

- Education: sixth grade or less (13.1 percent), seventh grade (16.1 percent), eighth grade (19.8 percent), ninth grade (24.4 percent), tenth grade (15.6 percent), eleventh grade (7.3 percent), high school graduate (2.7 percent), and some college (1.0 percent).

Just over 7 percent of these juvenile sex offenders had one or more alcohol arrests; over 12 percent had one or more drug arrests. Just over 63 percent of the juveniles had been placed on probation one or more times; 53 percent of the sample had been placed in juvenile confinement.

Participants completed the SAI-Juvenile as part of the intake procedure in court service, community service, and sex offender treatment programs. Probation departments used the SAI-Juvenile to determine appropriate levels of supervision and treatment.

Reliability

Table 7.5 presents interitem reliability (alpha) coefficients for the thirteen SAI-Juvenile scales. All alpha reliability coefficients for all SAI-Juvenile scales are at or above .83, well above the professionally accepted standard of .80 and are reliable, and all coefficient alphas are significant at the $p < .001$ level, demonstrating that the SAI-Juvenile is a reliable test for juvenile sex offender assessment.

Discriminant Validity Results

Table 7.6 presents discriminant validity results. Comparison of SAI-Juvenile scale scores between Group 1 (first offenders) and Group 2 (multiple offenders) shows that Group 2 scored significantly higher than Group 1 on nearly all SAI-Juvenile scales. Child (Pedophile) Molest scores are nearly identical for both Groups 1 and 2. In this case both groups may have been equally concerned about the consequences associated

Table 7.5
Reliability of the SAI-Juvenile ($N = 766$, 2002)

SAI-Juvenile Scales	Coefficient Alpha	SAI-Juvenile Scales	Coefficient Alpha
Test Item Truthfulness	.86	Alcohol Scale	.92
Sex Item Truthfulness	.85	Drugs Scale	.92
Sexual Adjustment Scale	.83	Violence Scale	.86
Child Molest Scale	.83	Antisocial Scale	.83
Sexual Assault Scale	.86	Distress Scale	.83
Incest Scale	.83	Judgment Scale	.83
Exhibitionism Scale	.89		

Table 7.6
Comparison Between First and Multiple Offenders (N = 766, 2002)

SAI-Juvenile Scale	Mean	Group 1 SD	Max	Mean	Group 2 SD	Max	t-Value
Test Item Truthfulness	5.59	4.49	21	4.41	4.27	21	t = 3.61*
Sex Item Truthfulness	9.48	4.39	19	7.76	4.57	19	t = 5.22*
Sexual Adjustment Scale	19.97	15.49	51	23.31	14.29	52	t = 2.99*
Child Molest Scale	6.84	6.48	34	6.74	7.03	34	t = 4.18*
Sexual Assault Scale	5.93	6.47	33	8.37	8.64	34	t = 3.11*
Incest Scale	1.01	1.97	7	1.09	2.0	7	t = 8.21*
Exhibitionism Scale	1.43	2.32	18	2.04	2.83	18	t = 8.96*
Alcohol Scale	4.41	9.36	38	25.07	7.72	38	t = 8.70*
Drugs Scale	6.06	10.39	34	23.27	8.23	33	t = 8.37*
Violence Scale	12.26	11.23	33	19.00	9.03	33	t = 1.91***
Antisocial Scale	6.70	5.22	18	10.25	6.01	18	N.S.
Distress Scale	10.66	10.39	29	11.97	6.98	29	t = 1.91***
Judgment Scale.	5.00	8.58	17	4.44	2.58	16	N.S.

*Significant at p < .001 level, *** significant at p < .05. Alcohol and Drugs Scale offender status based on alcohol-related arrests for the Alcohol Scale and drug-related arrests for the Drugs Scale.

with Child (Pedophile) Molest. Incest Scale scores were low for both offender groups, which may reflect the small number of offenders who admitted to incestuous behavior. Incest presents as an all-or-none distribution in that the client (offender, patient) either admits to it or does not. The abhorrence of incestuous behavior in urban settings may be overwhelming. In other words, members of both Group 1 and Group 2 may have found incestuous behavior repugnant. With regard to the Judgment Scale, both groups (first and multiple sex offenders) seem to have equally impaired judgment.

These discriminant validity results support the validity of the SAI-Juvenile. Multiple offenders believed to have severe problems scored significantly higher on most scales than first offenders. Distress Scale results indicate that multiple arrest offenders have impaired stress coping abilities when compared to first offenders. In other words, multiple arrest offenders do not handle stress as well as first offenders.

Predictive Validity

Table 7.7 presents predictive validity results for the correct identification of problems (sex-related and non-sex-related). The table shows the percentage of offenders who admitted problems and who also scored in the problem risk range.

The Sexual Adjustment Scale correctly identified 97.4 percent (75 of 79 offenders) who admitted to serious sexual adjustment problems; the Child (Pedophile) Molest Scale correctly identified all 175 offenders who had been arrested for child

Table 7.7
SAI-Juvenile Correct Identification of Problems (N = 766, 2002)

SAI-Juvenile Scales	Correct Identification of Problems	SAI-Juvenile Scales	Correct Identification of Problems
Sexual Adjustment	97.4%	Alcohol Scale	100%
Child (Pedophile) Molest	100%	Drugs Scale	100%
Sexual (Rape) Assault	100%	Violence Scale	98.4%
Incest Scale	100%	Antisocial Scale	93.0%
Exhibitionism Scale	100%	Distress Scale	92.5%
		Judgment Scale	89.7%

molestation; the Sexual (Rape) Assault Scale identified all 11 offenders who had forced someone to have sex; the Incest Scale correctly identified all 155 offenders who had sex with a close family member; the Exhibitionism Scale correctly identified all 150 offenders who were arrested for exhibitionism. These results support the validity and accuracy of the SAI-Juvenile sex-related scales.

As for the non-sex-related scales, the Violence (Lethality) Scale correctly identified 98.4 percent (123 of the 125 offenders) who admitted to being violent; the Antisocial Scale correctly identified 93 percent (119 of 128) who admitted to antisocial behavior; the Alcohol Scale correctly identified all 59 offenders who admitted having drinking problems; the Drugs Scale correctly identified all 130 offenders who admitted to having a drug problem; the Distress Scale correctly identified 92.5 percent (136 of 147) of offenders who admitted being in counseling/treatment for anxiety and depression; the Judgment Scale correctly identified 89.7 percent (61 of 68) who admitted they did not know right from wrong.

These results provide support for the validity and accuracy of the SAI-Juvenile non-sex-related scales. Taken together these results strongly support the validity and accuracy of the SAI-Juvenile.

SAI-Juvenile scale scores are divided into four risk ranges: low risk (0th–39th percentile), medium risk (40th–69th percentile), problem risk (70th–89th percentile), and severe problem risk (90th–100th percentile). By definition the expected percentage of offenders scoring in each scales risk range is: low risk (39 percent), medium risk (30 percent), problem risk (20 percent), and severe problem risk (11 percent).

Accuracy

Table 7.8 compares attained risk range percentiles with predicted risk range percentiles. Predicted percentages are set forth at the top of the table under the risk range—that is, low (39 percent), medium (30 percent), problem (20 percent), and severe problem (11 percent). SAI-Juvenile scales are listed on the left side of the table. Then under each risk range are listed the attained percentage next to each scale's name. Numbers on bold parentheses are the percentage difference between the attained scale score and the predicted scale score.

Table 7.8
Accuracy of SAI-Juvenile Risk Range Percentile Scores

SAI-Juvenile Scales	Low Risk (39%)	Medium Risk (30%)	Problem Risk (20%)	Severe Problem (11%)
Test Item Truthfulness	36.8 (2.2)	29.3 (0.7)	22.3 (2.3)	11.6 (0.6)
Sex Item Truthfulness	39.8 ((0.3)	30.5 (0.5)	20.0 (0.0)	10.8 (0.2)
Sexual Adjustment	38.7 (0.3)	30.5 (0.5)	20.0 (0.0)	10.8 (0.2)
Child Molest Scale	38.3 (0.7)	28.8 (1.2)	21.6 (1.6)	11.3 (0.3)
Rape Scale	39.3 (0.3)	30.2 (0.2)	19.8 (0.2)	10.7 (0.3)
Incest Scale	41.4 (2.4)	28.6 (1.4)	17.4 (2.6)	12.6 (1.6)
Exhibitionism Scale	40.5 (1.5)	29.6 (0.4)	18.9 (1.1)	11.0 (0.0)
Alcohol Scale	37.5 (1.5)	31.6 (1.6)	19.3 (0.7)	11.6 (0.6)
Drugs Scale	37.1 (1.9)	32.7 (2.7)	19.8 (0.2)	10.4 (0.6)
Violence Scale	39.0 (0.0)	30.0 (0.0)	20.4 (0.4)	10.6 (0.4)
Antisocial Scale	38.9 (0.1)	28.6 (1.4)	21.9 (1.9)	10.6 (0.4)
Distress Scale	38.1 (0.9)	31.5 (1.5)	20.1 (0.1)	10.3 (0.7)
Judgment Scale	38.5 (0.5)	29.8 (0.2)	20.9 (0.0)	11.7 (0.7)

Table 7.8 shows that the attained percentage of offenders falling in each risk range very closely approximates the predicted percentage for each risk category. All the attained risk range percentages were within 2.7 percentage points; thirty-five of fifty-two possible comparisons were within one percentage point of the predicted percentages.

The 70th percentile cutoff for problem identification (70th–89th percentile) correctly classified 90 percent or more of problem offenders. The 39th percentile cutoff (0–39th percentile) for low risk is so accurate that only 3 percent of offenders who even admitted to a problem were included. The low risk (zero to 39th percentile) level representing 39 percent of the offenders avoids erroneously putting a large percentage of offenders into the "moderate" range. Analysis of Table 7.8 strongly supports the accuracy of the SAI-Juvenile.

SCALE INTERPRETATION

The SAI and the SAI-Juvenile assess attitudes and behaviors that contribute to meaningful sex offender profiles. The thirteen scales collect a vast amount of information that is important in sex offender evaluation. Each SAI and SAI-Juvenile scale measures the severity of assessed problems. Space limitation precludes a complete discussion of "scale interpretation." Consequently, this section focuses on independent scale interpretation and simplifying the concept of scale interrelationships.

Sex Offender Screening

Screening or assessment instruments filter out individuals with serious problems who may require adjusted supervision levels or referral for further evaluation and, where warranted, treatment. This filtering system works on both the SAI and SAI-Juvenile. As shown in Table 7.9, a "problem" is not identified until a scale score is at the 70th percentile or higher. These risk range percentiles are based on a test's normative (standardization) sample, database research, psychometric literature, and experience. This procedure avoids extremes such as overidentification and underidentification of problems. An "elevated" score is indicative of a problem. It is a problematic (indicative of emerging problems) score at or above the 70th percentile. A "severe problem" scale score is at or above the 90th percentile.

There are several levels of SAI scale interpretation ranging from viewing the SAI as a self-report to interpreting scale elevations and scale interaction between sexual deviate/paraphiliac scales and non-sex-related item scales. These interrelationships are often influenced by myriad offender characteristics (attitude, personality, and behavior) and situations or specific factors that brought the sex offender to the court or assessor's attention. Sex offender assessment is particularly complex, involving clinical considerations (victim, family, and perpetrator), concern about harm to others (victims and society), and legal issues.

Interactions of SAI Scales

The SAI and SAI-Juvenile measure a wide variety of attitudes and behaviors that are important for sex offender understanding, in addition to identifying sexual deviates and paraphilias, as discussed earlier in this chapter. In addition to the sex-related scales, the assessor (evaluator or screener) should review all other SAI scale scores to identify codeterminants and stressors. For example, a client could have an elevated (70th percentile or higher) Sexual Adjustment Scale score along with other sexually deviate scores. The "other" elevated scale score(s) could add guilt, concern, or distress to the client's perceived sexual adjustment. Other elevated SAI scale scores could exacerbate existing problems or concerns and thereby contribute to a client's perceived sexual maladjustment. And concerns about one's sexual adjustment can be exacerbated by other elevated non-sex-related scale scores like the Alcohol Scale, Drugs Scale, Violence Scale, Antisocial Scale, Distress Scale, and Judgment Scale.

Table 7.9
SAI Risk Ranges

Risk Category	Risk Range (%)	Total (%)
Low risk	0–39%	39%
Medium risk	40–69%	30%
Problem risk	70–89%	20%
Severe problem	90–100%	11%

The impact of these non-sex-related scales on the Sexual Adjustment Scale can be rather direct (e.g., alcohol, drugs, and violence) or more cognitive (e.g., antisocial thinking or judgmental logic) and emotional (e.g., distress).

The role of non-sex-related SAI scale scores becomes apparent in court-related sexual assault evaluations. For example, substance (alcohol and other drugs) abuse, violence (lethality) potential, and a person's judgment are common areas of related inquiry. The thirteen SAI scales were selected because they provide important information on their own merits and in terms of their relationships with each other.

Other elevated (70th percentile and higher) SAI scale scores, in conjunction with an elevated Sexual Assault Scale score, can provide insight into the client's situation while identifying important areas for subsequent inquiry. For example, a severe problem score on the Violence Scale in conjunction with an elevated Sexual Assault Scale score would influence the direction of the assessment. Then add an elevated Alcohol Scale or Drugs Scale score and you can see how these scales interrelate. In this example, the client is violent in life as well as in his sexual relationships. All that is needed is a triggering mechanism such as opportunity, alcohol, or drugs. It should be noted that the Sexual (Rape) Assault Scale can also be interpreted in combination with other SAI scale scores.

Elevated Alcohol Scale and Drugs Scale scores indicate polysubstance abuse, and the higher score often reflects the client's substance of choice. Elevated Alcohol and Violence scale scores are a malignant sign. Alcohol abuse can magnify a person's violent tendencies. Similarly, alcohol abuse can serve as a release mechanism for antisocial thinking and acting-out behavior. Alcohol Scale scores in the severe problem range (90th–100th percentile) compound client risk even more. Judgment decreases as alcohol consumption increases. Elevated Alcohol Scale and Distress Scale scores may initially represent an attempt to self-medicate, while further intoxication may exacerbate suicidal ideation. The more of these scales that are elevated with the Alcohol Scale, the more problem prone the client's situation becomes. When alcohol abuse is problematic, it becomes an important part of the sex offender's treatment program. The Alcohol Scale can be interpreted independently or individually. However, when an elevated Alcohol Scale exists it is usually interpreted in combination with other SAI scales.

When both the Alcohol and Drugs scales are elevated, the higher score typically represents the client's substance of choice. When both the Alcohol and Drugs scale are in the severe problem range (90th–100th percentile), polysubstance abuse is likely.

Elevated Alcohol, Violence, Antisocial, and Distress scales with an elevated Drugs Scale score are malignant signs. Drug abuse can be part of polysubstance (drugs and alcohol) abuse, exacerbate violent tendencies, magnify antisocial beliefs (paranoia), and further impair judgment. Elevated Drug and Distress scale scores may represent self-medication attempts, whereas severe scores may be associated with suicidal thinking and acting out. The more of these scales that are elevated with the Drugs Scale, the more problem prone the client's situation becomes. When drug use is problematic, it becomes an important problem to be worked through in sex offender treatment.

Elevated Alcohol, Drugs, Antisocial, and Distress scales with an elevated Violence Scale are dangerous combinations because each of these scales represents a potential violence magnifier. When the elevated Distress Scale score is higher than the elevated

Violence Scale score, we can anticipate an emotionally overwhelmed person who is in great pain and manifesting suicidal ideation. Elevated Antisocial Scale and Violence scales scorers are problematic in that the client may externalize violent feelings to others, authority figures, institutions or federal agencies. Severe problem range (90th–100th percentile) scorers on the Violence Scale are very dangerous to themselves and others. These individuals warrant prompt intervention and treatment. The Violence Scale is of particular interest in sex offender cases in that high scorers tend to be associated with rape, whereas low scorers tend to be more associated with exhibitionism.

With regard to the non-sex-related scales, the relationship between the Violence Scale and all these scales (Alcohol, Drugs, Antisocial, Distress, and Judgment) is of importance. The relationship between the Violence Scale and the Antisocial Scale would be of particular interest to the courts, probation departments, and corrections. Elevated Alcohol and/or Drugs Scale scores with an elevated Violence Scale score could exacerbate violence. An elevated Violence Scale and Distress Scale would characterize a dangerous and potentially suicidal person. The more these scales are elevated the more dangerous the client becomes. In summary, the Violence Scale can be interpreted individually. However, the Violence Scale is best understood when it is studied in terms of its relationships with other SAI scale scores.

An elevated Antisocial Scale score in combination with an elevated Judgment Scale score is a malignant sign. Antisocial thinking becomes progressively more problematic as these scores increase. Elevated Alcohol Scale and Drugs Scale scores are often associated with antisocial thinking. And antisocial thinking becomes more extreme as these scale scores escalate into the severe problem range (90th–100th percentile).

An elevated Antisocial Scale score in combination with an elevated Distress Scale score can be problematic—particularly when scores are in the severe problem range (90th-100th percentile). These scale scores often identify people on the verge of being emotionally overwhelmed (anxiety, depression, and distress) with progressively antisocial thinking exacerbated. In these instances, the client feels progressively more and more isolated and desperate. Such people can be dangerous to themselves and others. The Antisocial Scale is best understood within the context of its relationship with other SAI scale scores. However, the Antisocial Scale score can be interpreted independently.

Sometimes, elevated (70th percentile and higher) Alcohol and Drugs scales scores, in conjunction with an elevated Distress Scale score identify hurting individuals who are attempting to self-medicate. Concurrently, elevated Violence and Distress scales scores are problematic. The highest severe problem range (90th–100th percentile) score can provide insight regarding internalization (suicide) or externalization (violence/homicide) of frustration and hostility. These would be malignant prognostic signs.

Severe problem (90th–100th percentile) Antisocial and Distress scales scores are descriptive of a dangerous person. Add an elevated (70th percentile and higher) Violence Scale score and such a person could engage in extremely violent terrorist-type activities. An elevated Distress Scale score with elevated sex-related scales could be interpreted directly in terms of dissatisfaction. A person with a severe problem Distress Scale score typically discusses his or her feelings with a sincerely interested staff member.

An elevated (70th percentile or higher) Judgment Scale in combination with an elevated Alcohol Scale or Drugs Scale score could identify even more extremely judgment impaired individuals. And if these scores are in the severe problem range the person's impaired judgment could be greatly exacerbated. It goes without saying that elevated (70th percentile and higher) Judgment Scale and Violence scales scores would be problematic. And severe problem (90th–100th percentile) scorers could be disastrous.

CONCLUSION

It is widely acknowledged that sex offenses are a significant problem in our society. Yet, there are few reliable and valid evaluation procedures designed for sex-offender assessment. The first step in understanding sex offenders and their problems, however, is sex offender assessment (evaluation, screening and testing).

There is consensus among evaluators (assessors, screeners, and testers), mental health professionals, and treatment staff that accurate sex offender problem identification is important for effective treatment. Similarly, it is also important to match problem severity with treatment intensity.

Most experienced evaluators, mental health practitioners, and treatment staff are familiar with clients' defensiveness, guardedness, and attempts to minimize their problems. Most assessment professionals agree that it is important to know if a client was truthful when tested. The two truthfulness scales in the SAI and SAI-Juvenile measure the amount of denial and problem minimization the client (offender, patient) manifested when tested.

Sex offender evaluations are among the most demanding evaluations conducted given the serious nature of the offense, human victimization, family suffering, the threat to society, legal consequences, severity of sentences, and so on. Psychometric standards like reliability, validity, and accuracy are especially important in sex offender tests.

The SAI and the SAI-Juvenile are sex offender tests that identify sex-related problems and related criminogenic needs. Criminogenic needs are offender traits, attitudes, and behaviors that contribute to inappropriate sexual behavior, negativistic attitudes, and recidivism (Andrews & Bonta, 1994). Criminogenic needs are risk factors that are capable of change. Because sex offender assessment involves predicting the likelihood that the offender will commit similar crimes in the future, and a critical goal of all sex offender treatment programs is to reduce sex offense recidivism, it is important to identify sex-related problems and related criminogenic needs. A major goal of sex offender assessment is to identify sex-related problems. Consequently, both the SAI and SAI-Juvenile identify and measure the severity of sex-related problems.

When problems are identified their severity is important. Only then can assessors (evaluators) appropriately match problem severity with treatment intensity. Scale interpretation was covered to illustrate how scale scores, their elevations, and their interrelationships can be understood.

In any evaluation or assessment the evaluator should review available records, other evaluation results, interviews with victims and their families, available medical records, and present evaluation results. In sex offender evaluations the assessor needs to put all evaluation and test results within the context of the client's life situation. Invariably the following question arises "Is he or she a danger to society? And if so, "to what degree?" the SAI and SAI-Juvenile help answer this question. In the beginning of this chapter it was stated, "The need for sex offender information has been expressed in a variety of ways. For example, 'Is this person a sex offender?' 'What contributes to this sex offenders problems?' And 'What sort of treatment is needed?'" This chapter discussed in detail the SAI and the SAI-Juvenile. Within reasonable limits, these tests help answer the questions set forth in this chapter.

Footnote

[1] Readers desiring more in-depth empirical research are referred to Behavior Data Systems website *www.bdsltd.com* (Behavior Data Systems, n.d.-b, n.d.-c). More inclusive research sources are the "SAI: An Inventory of Scientific Findings" and the "SAI-Juvenile: An Inventory of Scientific Findings" documents which are referenced at the end of this chapter (Davignon, 2000a).

References

Abel, G. G., Huffman, J., Warberg, B. W., & Holland, C. L. (1998). Visual reaction time and plethysmography as measures of sexual interest in child molesters. *Sexual Abuse, 10*(2), 81–95.

American Psychiatric Association. (1994). *Diagnostic and statistical manual of mental disorders* (4th ed.). Washington, DC: Author.

Andrews, D., & Bonta, J. (1994). *The psychology of criminal conduct.* Cincinnati, OH: Anderson Press.

Andrews, D. A., Bonta, J., & Hoge, R. D. (1990). Classification for effective rehabilitation: Rediscovering psychology. *Criminal Justice and Behavior, 17*, 19–52.

Andrews, D. A., Zinger, I., Hoge, R., Bonta, J. Gendreau, P., & Cullen, F. (1989). *Does correctional treatment work? A clinically relevant and psychologically informed meta-analysis.* Paper presented at the Research Seminar of National Associations Active in Criminal Justice, Ottawa, Canada.

Aytes, K. E., Olsen, S. S., Zakrajsek, T., Murray, P., & Ireson, R. (2001). Cognitive/behavioral treatment for sexual offenders: An examination of recidivism. *Sexual Abuse: A Journal of Research and Treatment, 13*, 223-231.

Beech, A., Friendship, C., Erikson, M., & Hanson, R. K. (2002). The relationship between static and dynamic risk factors and reconviction in a sample of U.K. child abusers. *Sexual Abuse: A Journal of Research and Treatment, 14*, 155-167.

Behavior Data Systems. (n.d.-a). *Sexual Adjustment Inventory (SAI): Orientation and training manual.* Retrieved January 2005, from *www.online-testing.com/documents/OTM-ONLINE-SAI.doc.*

Behavior Data Systems. (n.d.-b). *Juvenile sex offender evaluation.* Retrieved July 1, 2004, from *www.bdsltd.com/index2.htm.*

Behavior Data Systems. (n.d.-c). *Sexual Adjustment Inventory.* Retrieved July 1, 2004, from *www.bdsltd.com/index2.htm.*

California Coalition on Sexual Offending. (2002, June). *California coalition on sexual offending's 5th annual training conference.* Symposium conducted at the meeting of the California Coalition on Sexual Offending, Sacramento, CA.

Carey, M. (1997, Spring). Cog probation. *Perspectives*, pp. 27–42.

Cattell, R. B., Cattell, A. K. S., & Cattell, H. E. P. (1993). *The Sixteen Personality Factor Questionnaire (16PF).* Champaign: University of Illinois. (Original work published 1949)

Davignon, D. (2000a). *Sexual Adjustment Inventory—Juvenile: An inventory of scientific findings.* Unpublished manuscript.

Davignon, D. (2000b). *Sexual Adjustment Inventory: Sex offender assessment.* Unpublished manuscript.

Davignon, D. (2002). *Sexual Adjustment Inventory—Juvenile: Juvenile sex offender assessment.* Unpublished manuscript.

Davignon, D. (2003a, March/April). Assessment driven treatment. *Corrections Forum*, pp. 30, 32.

Davignon, D. (2003b). *Sexual Adjustment Inventory (SAI): An inventory of scientific findings.* Unpublished manuscript.

Dempster, R. J., & Hart, S. D. (2002). The relative utility of fixed and variable risk factors in discriminating sexual recidivists and nonrecidivists. *Sexual Abuse: A Journal of Research and Treatment, 14*, 121–138.

Drake, R. E., Goldman, H. H., Leff, H. S., Lehman, A. F., Dixon, L., Mueser, K. T., et al. (2001). Implementing evidence-based practices in routine mental health service settings. *Psychiatric Services, 52*, 179–182.

Gendreau, P., Little, T., & Goggin, C. (1996). A meta-analysis of the predictors of adult offender recidivism: What works! *Criminology, 34*, 575-607.

Greenfield, L. A. (1997). *Sex offenses and offenders: An analysis of data on rape and sexual assault* (NCJ-163392). Washington, DC: U.S. Department of Justice, Bureau of Justice Statistics.

Hanson, R. K. (2000). *Risk assessment.* Beaverton, OR: Association for the Treatment of Sexual Abusers.

Hanson, R. K. (2002). Introduction to the special section on dynamic risk assessment with sex offenders. *Sexual Abuse: A Journal of Research and Treatment, 14*, 99–101.

Hays, W. L. (1994). *Statistics.* Orlando, FL: Harcourt Brace.

Hudson, S. M., Wales, D. S., Bakker, L., & Ward, T. (2002). Dynamic risk factors: The Kia Marama evaluation. *Sexual Abuse: A Journal of Research and Treatment, 14*, 103–119.

Lindeman, H. (n.d.-a). *ACDI-Corrections Version II.* Retrieved August 1, 2004, from *www.bdsltd.com/bds_acdi_cv2.htm.*

Lindeman, H. (n.d.-b). *Juvenile Substance Abuse Profile.* Retrieved August 1, 2004, from *www.bdsltd.com/bds_JSAP.htm.*

McDonald, R. P. (1999). *Test theory: A unified treatment.* Hillsdale, NJ: Erlbaum.

Peugh, J., & Belenko, S. (2001). Examining the substance use patterns and treatment needs of incarcerated sex offenders. *Sexual Abuse: A Journal of Research and Treatment, 13*, 179–195.

Risk & Needs Assessment. (n.d.-a). *SAI-Juvenile report.* Retrieved July 13, 2004, from *www.sex-offender-tests.com/index_SAI-EXAMPLE-REPORT.htm.*

Risk & Needs Assessment. (n.d.-b). *Unique test features.* Retrieved October 2004, from *www.riskandneeds.com/rna_UNIQUE_FEATURES.htm.*

Thornton, D. (2002). Constructing and testing a framework for dynamic risk assessment. *Sexual Abuse: A Journal of Research and Treatment, 14*(2), 139–153.

Ward, T., & Stewart, C. (2003). The relationship between human needs and criminogenic needs. *Psychology, Crime and Law, 9*, 219–224.

Zimmerman, M. (1994). Diagnosing personality disorders: A review of issues and research models. *Archives of General Psychiatry, 51*, 225–245.

Exhibit 7.1
Example SAI Report

```
SEXUAL ADJUSTMENT INVENTORY
* * * * * * * * * * * * *
```

```
NAME          : Example Report
ID#           : 123abc55555
DATE SAI SCORED: 12/11/2007
AGE: 37    SEX: Male              CONFIDENTIAL REPORT
ETHNICITY/RACE : Caucasian
EDUCATION/GRADE: H.S. graduate
MARITAL STATUS : Separated
EMPLOYED      : Yes
```

Sexual Adjustment Inventory (SAI) results are confidential and should be considered working hypotheses. No diagnosis or decision should be based solely upon SAI results. The SAI is to be used in conjunction with experienced staff judgment and review of available records.

```
MEASURES        %ile                SAI PROFILE
--------        ----        +--------------+-------+-------------+

                            -LOW RISK  -MEDIUM  -PROBLEM     -MAX

                               -          -          -       -    -

TEST ITEM        19         **********........-.............-...-
TRUTHFULNESS                   -          -          -       -    -
SEX ITEM         20         **********........-.............-...-
TRUTHFULNESS                   -          -          -       -    -
                            ---------- PERCENTILE SCORES --------
```

```
ADDITIONAL INFORMATION PROVIDED BY CLIENT
-----------------------------------------
```

```
Total number of arrests.....  1   Number of times in jail.......0
Age at first conviction..... 17   Number of times in prison.....0
Misdemeanor convictions.....  1   Sex-related arrests...........1
Felony convictions.........   0   Sex-related convictions.......1
Times on probation.........   1   Alcohol-related arrests.......1
Times on parole.............  0   Drug-related arrests..........1
```

ADDITIONAL INFORMATION PROVIDED BY CLIENT

Total number of arrests.....	1	Number of times in jail.......0
Age at first conviction.....	17	Number of times in prison.....0
Misdemeanor convictions.....	1	Sex-related arrests...........1
Felony convictions..........	0	Sex-related convictions.......1
Times on probation..........	1	Alcohol-related arrests.......1
Times on parole.............	0	Drug-related arrests..........1

TRUTHFULNESS SCALE SCORES

TEST ITEM TRUTHFULNESS SCALE: LOW RISK RANGE   RISK PERCENTILE: 19

This person's response pattern on the Test Item Truthfulness Scale is in
the Low Risk (zero to 39th percentile) range. The client was generally
cooperative and nondefensive. This scale determines how open and truthful
the client was while completing the SAI. Responses to non-sex related SAI
test items are valid, accurate and truthful. Review the SAI Sex Item
Truthfulness Scale results. The Test Item Truthfulness Scale score reveals
this client was truthful when answering non-sex items on the SAI.

SEX ITEM TRUTHFULNESS SCALE: LOW RISK RANGE   RISK PERCENTILE: 20

This person's response pattern on the Sex Item Truthfulness Scale is in the
Low Risk (zero to 39th percentile) range. The client was truthful when
responding to test items having an obvious sexual connotation and
relationship. With regard to sexual areas of inquiry, sex-related scale
scores are likely accurate and valid.

```
NAME: Mr. Example                               SAI REPORT


MEASURES           %ile              SAI PROFILE
--------           ----     +------------+----------+-------+---+

                            -LOW RISK  -MEDIUM  -PROBLEM      -MAX

                            -            -           -         -   -

SEXUAL ADJUSTMENT  67       ************************.-.........-...-

                            -            -           -         -   -

CHILD MOLEST       20       *******.......-............-......-...-

                            -            -           -         -   -

SEXUAL ASSAULT     46       ****************.........-......-...-

                            -            -           -         -   -

INCEST             0        *............-.........-......-...-

                            -            -           -         -   -

EXHIBITIONISM      0        *............-.........-......-...-

                            +------------+----------+-------+---+
                            --------- PERCENTILE SCORES -----------
```

SEXUAL ADJUSTMENT SCALE: MEDIUM RISK RANGE   RISK PERCENTILE: 67

This person's score on the Sexual Adjustment Scale is in the Medium Risk
(40 to 69th percentile) range. Some caution and concern are evident
regarding this person's sexual adjustment responses. However, truth-
corrected scale scores should be accurate. This client's response pattern
is in the Medium risk range. Yet, some sexual adjustment worries or
concerns are becoming evident.

CHILD MOLEST SCALE: LOW RISK RANGE   RISK PERCENTILE: 20

This client's response pattern on the Child Molest Scale is in the Low Risk
(zero to 39th percentile) range. Few, if any, indicators of child molest
behavior (pedophilia) are present. This client does not present as a sexual
risk to children. However, review this client's court-related records
carefully for any prior sex-related convictions. Also review SAI
truthfulness scales to determine how open, cooperative and truthful this
client was at the time of testing.

SEXUAL ASSAULT SCALE: MEDIUM RISK RANGE   RISK PERCENTILE: 46

This person's score on the Sexual Assault (Rape) Scale is in the
Medium Risk (40 to 69th percentile) range. This client does not present a
high probability of sexual assault. A few indicators of sexual hostility
and/or aggressiveness are present. However, in all sex offender assessments
SAI truthfulness scale scores should be checked to determine how truthful
and cooperative the respondent was while completing the SAI. This scale
score does not reflect an established pattern of sexually assaultive
behavior.

INCEST SCALE: LOW RISK RANGE   RISK PERCENTILE: 0

This individual's score on the Incest Scale is in the Low Risk (zero to
39th percentile) range. Low risk scorers reveal few, if any, indicators of
incestuous behavior.

EXHIBITIONISM SCALE: LOW RISK RANGE   RISK PERCENTILE: 0

This person's response pattern on the Exhibitionism Scale is in the Low
Risk (zero to 39th percentile) range. Low risk range scorers typically do
not expose their sex organs to unsuspecting persons. This is a Low risk
exhibitionism profile.

```
NAME: Mr. Example                              SAI REPORT


MEASURES          %ile              SAI PROFILE
--------          ----       +-------------+-----------+-------+---+

                             -LOW RISK   -MEDIUM  -PROBLEM      -MAX

                                -          -          -        -   -

ALCOHOL            71        ***************************.......-...-

                                -          -          -        -   -

DRUGS              69        **************************-.......-...-

                                -          -          -        -   -

VIOLENCE           55        ********************.....-.......-...-

                                -          -          -        -   -

ANTISOCIAL         88        **********************************-...-

                                -          -          -        -   -

DISTRESS           72        **************************.......-...-

                                -          -          -        -   -

JUDGMENT           68        *************************-.......-...-

                             +-------------+-----------+-------+---+
                             --------- PERCENTILE SCORES -----------
```

ALCOHOL SCALE: PROBLEM RISK RANGE   RISK PERCENTILE: 71

This person's response pattern on the Alcohol Scale is in the Problem Risk
(70 to 89th percentile) range. Alcohol (beer, wine or other liquor) use or
abuse is indicated. An established pattern of alcohol abuse is indicated,
or this person is a recovering alcoholic. A drinking-related problem is
evident. Participating in counseling (individual or group), augmented with
regular Alcoholic's Anonymous meetings might be considered. If recovering,
relapse is possible.

DRUGS SCALE: MEDIUM RISK RANGE   RISK PERCENTILE: 69

This person's response pattern on the Drugs Scale is in the Medium Risk (40
to 69th percentile) range. Some indicators of drug use are present,
however, an established pattern of drug abuse is not evident. Yet, there
may be a "proneness." Important areas of inquiry include the client's
history and pattern of drug exposure, experimentation or involvement. Drug-
related problems do not present as "serious" at this time.

VIOLENCE SCALE: MEDIUM RISK RANGE   RISK PERCENTILE: 55

Violent tendencies are indicated, however, an established pattern of
violence is not evident. Medium risk individuals are neither brutal nor
passive. When provoked, frustrated or during periods of substance abuse,
they can become abusive and combative. However, their lifestyles are
usually free from violence. They are typically respectful of human rights.
Yet, stress or substance abuse could exacerbate violent behavior. With
regard to the Violence Scale, this is a medium risk score.

ANTISOCIAL SCALE: PROBLEM RISK RANGE   RISK PERCENTILE: 88

An established pattern of antisocial behavior is evident. Problem risk is
characterized by many antisocial behaviors and difficulty maintaining
responsible relationships and loyalties. These individuals are frequently
callous, irresponsible, and lack a foundation of mutual affection or trust.
Many are boastful, deceitful and given to tantrums or outbursts of rage.
Poor work histories, nonpayment of bills and difficulty conforming to
social norms are common. Problem risk score.

NAME: Mr. Example   SAI REPORT

DISTRESS SCALE: PROBLEM RISK RANGE   RISK PERCENTILE: 72

This person's score on the Distress Scale is in the Problem Risk   (70 to
89th percentile) range. Symptoms of distress include anxiety and
depression. This person has a problem with distress and may need help to
cope with anxiety or depression. In interview explore prescription drug
use. Continued counseling is the treatment of choice.

JUDGMENT SCALE: MEDIUM RISK RANGE   RISK PERCENTILE: 68

This individual's score on the Judgment Scale is in the Medium Risk (40 to
69th percentile) range. This client has low-average judgment abilities.
Understanding and comprehension are adequate under normal conditions.
However, this person's emotions can all too easily interfere with his or
her judgment.

                        * * * * *

OBSERVATIONS/RECOMMENDATIONS: _____

_____

_____

_____

_____

_____   _____   _____
STAFF MEMBER SIGNATURE   ID# OR BADGE#   DATE

                            SAI RESPONSES   (SAI TEST # 1)

                            --- ---------

   1- 50 TTFFTTFTTT TFFTFTTFTT FTTFFFFTFF FTTTFFFTTT FFTFTFTFFF
  51-100 TFTFTFFTTF FFFFFTFFTF FFFTFTFTTF TFTTFFFTTT FFTFFTFFTT
 101-150 FFTFFTFTTT FTFTFTTFFF TTFTFTTFFF TFTFFTTTFF FFTFTFTFTF
 151-200 FFTTTFFTFF FFTFFFTFTT FFFFTFFFF2 3333123334 3443441444
 201-214 4444234444 3444

NAME: Mr. Example   SAI REPORT

SIGNIFICANT ITEMS: These answers are the client's self-reported
responses. And, they represent direct admissions or unusual
responses, which may help in understanding the client's
situation.

CHILD MOLEST   SEXUAL ASSAULT
------------   --------------
123. Sexually molested a child   116. Forced a date to have sex

                                      126. Has used force to have sex

ALCOHOL   DISTRESS
-------   --------
59. Is concerned about drinking   39. Been very depressed past
                                           year
93. Drinking problem past year   84. Often feels depressed &
                                           alone
                                      117. Feels no one really cares
                                      167. Been very unhappy past
                                           year

DRUGS
-----
19. Admits uses marijuana (pot)

STRUCTURED INTERVIEW: These items report the client's opinions regarding self, sexual matters, substance abuse, counseling and treatment. This self-report incorporates the client's opinion with all its biases, introspection and defensiveness. Comparison of these subjective answers with objective SAI scores can sometimes be helpful.

189. Drinking a slight problem

190. Drug use not a problem

191. Sex adjustment slight problem

192. Not sexually abused as child

193. No physical force conviction

194. Alcohol treatment: not sure

195. Drug treatment: no need

196. Sex treatment: no need

197. Has forced sex once

198. No rape/sex assault convictn

199. Has never exposed sex organs

200. No arrest for child molest

201. Not a recovering abuser

202. Not suicidal or homicidal

203. No sexual treatment programs

204. No incestuous relationships

205. Sex adjustment: unusual

206. Fair sexual adjustment

207. No substance abuse treatment

208. No prior sex therapy

209. No emotional/mental hlth prob

210. Sexual counseling not needed

211. Mixed feelings about sex life

212. No prior sexual treatment

213. No time in sexual treatment

214. Not a registered sex offender and not on lifetime probation

Chapter 8

The Use of Role-Play to Develop Victim Empathy and Relapse Prevention

by Maxine Daniels, B.Sc.(Hons.)

OVERVIEW

This chapter focuses on the use of role-play techniques with sex offenders for both victim empathy components of treatment and skills practice in relapse prevention. "Role-play," a tool commonly used in treatment programs, is a generic term used for all kinds of games, exercises, and simulations in a variety of situations from educational, business, and therapeutic to entertainment. This chapter looks specifically at role-play techniques that have been conducted within a sex offender treatment program, currently delivered in Her Majesty's Prison Service–England (HMPS), for male sex offenders of medium to high risk. The chapter aims to present the theory and techniques in a practical way, through a case study of an offender in one of the programs.

INTRODUCTION

The Sex Offender Treatment Programme Core (SOTP Core; Mann & Thornton, 1994, 2000) first introduced role-play into the victim empathy module of the program in 1994 in order to "expose treatment clients to the cognitive, emotional and behavioural experiences of victims" (Webster, Bowers, Mann, & Marshall 2002, p. 3). This theory was based on methods used by Pithers (1994) in the Vermont Treatment Program for Sexual Aggressors (VTPSA). The difference between the program in Vermont and the one in England is that Pithers and his team worked with outside visiting dramatherapists who conducted the role-play sessions whereas in the HMPS SOTP model, all therapists are trained in role-play techniques to be delivered as part of treatment. A fundamental difference, in terms of victim empathy and role-play techniques, is that VTPSA required each offender to role-play the offense, first from his own role as perpetrator and then from that of the victim. In SOTP Core, we ask group members to assume the role of their victim(s) and not role-play themselves (Pithers 1997). This is important in terms of the type of role-play techniques we use. This chapter sets out how to structure role-play sessions to develop victim empathy and discusses how to access a client's empathy deficits about his victim(s)—deficits that are, by definition, cognitive distortions (Marshall, Anderson, & Fernandez 1999)—and then examines how the role-plays are victim specific to achieve the goals of the session. The distinction between the victim empathy role-plays, where the client only plays others (i.e., victims), and relapse prevention (RP) components of SOTP is that in RP, clients role-play themselves in a variety of situations to enhance their development of new skills. This is based on the "good lives" model (Ward & Stewart 2003) as well as ideas from Marques, Nelson, Alarcon, and Day (2000) and Haaven, Little, and Petre-Miller (1990) used in adapted SOTP for clients with learning difficulties. The relapse prevention model is about skills practice, using psychodrama techniques to access the internal triggers of the client (Moreno, 1953). This technique challenges the client when he is working toward a new behavior. Role-play techniques are easily transferable techniques within therapy, education, and business; however, it is how they are used that makes them effective. Planning, safety of the group, role of therapist, understanding treatment aims, and conducting the sessions within sex offender treatment work are more important than having a bag of techniques that can be pulled out to make a dramatic impact but actually have little treatment effect. The essence of this work is about structure, planning, and safety combined with the role-play techniques.

VICTIM EMPATHY ROLE-PLAYS

Objective and Outcomes of Role-Plays

The first question we need to ask ourselves as therapists is: Why do we want clients to role-play their victims? One of our responses is that in terms of therapeutic value, we are endeavoring to create a situation in which our clients will gain a deeper understanding of their victims' pain and powerlessness and insights into the consequences of the short- and long-term effects and disruption to lifestyle for victims.

All sex offenders in HMPS SOTP Core who have received treatment go through victim empathy role-plays. This means that up to 1,000 sex offenders a year go through this process. Does it work? Webster et al. (2002) conducted a study of role-play effectiveness of offense reenactment (first described by Pithers, 1994). Webster et al.'s results indicated that men who had completed offense reenactments and empathy deficit scenarios demonstrated that both types of intervention were effective in bringing about clinical change.

Guidelines and Planning for Victim Empathy Role-Plays

There are different variables to be considered when using role-play as a therapeutic tool; namely, therapist style (Rogers, 1961), group process (Yalom, 1975), clients' defense mechanisms (Pithers, 1997), and general empathy deficits (Anderson & Dodgson, 2002), along with individual risk assessments. The obvious challenge to the therapist in conducting these types of role-plays is the practical implications involved: How do we engage our clients in taking on these roles and what are we looking for? Pithers (1997) describes in detail the implications for abuse (by the therapists) in forcing these men to relive their experiences with little or no clear aims of the treatment goals.

In SOTP Core 2000 the following guidelines are used for planning these types of role-plays:

- The offender's distortions or empathy deficits about his victim—for example, "It's five years since I touched her; there's no harm now" (long-term effects), or "She seemed to enjoy it because she didn't tell me to stop" (at the time of offense).

- Think of the time scale: past, present, or future. We tend to use the present or future because we want the offender to understand the impact the offense has made on his victim's lifestyle.

- The client (offender) will be playing his primary victim or friends and family related to his victim. In the case where the victim is a relative, the offender would only take on the roles of people *in relation* to his victim. For example:

His Wife	becomes	*Mother*	to the victim
His Son	becomes	*Brother*	to the victim
His Mother	becomes	*Grandmother*	to the victim

The offender would take on the roles in italics—that is, roles in relation to his victim rather than to himself. We list the victim-specific empathy deficits to use in the role-play scenarios. These are based on work previously conducted in the group where the offender discussed his deficits.

Group Process

Because the role-plays are conducted within a group setting, it is important to have certain professional boundaries in place. The group is the holding process for the individual as described by Zinkin (1989). He describes the group as container and contained. "The therapist, in forming a group provides a relatively fixed structure with which the desired changes in the members of the group can take place" (p. 228).

Rules for Role-Play. For these structured role-plays, the rules for the group while conducting the sessions need to be observed. Therefore, a *no-touch* rule maintains client and therapist safety. The therapist assumes the role of *director* (Kellerman, 1992), which enables him or her to take an active part in the role-plays (not taking on roles but conducting the scenes and achieving the goals). There is also a *time-out* facility. If at any time either the director or a group member is not sure what needs to happen, he or she can have a "time out" to clarify the situation. In order to maintain safety, as we are working in high-security establishments, we avoid the use of props.

Role of Director. During the role-play sessions, the therapist takes on the role of director (Mann, Daniels, & Marshall, 2002). It is important that the relationship of therapist, individual, and group is maintained safely to conduct effective role-plays. Again, an empathic therapist is important for successful treatment (Fernandez & Serran, 2002); authenticity is needed (Corey, 1996) in this work. If group members suspect that the therapist is fearful of participating in role-plays and anxiety is high, it is likely there will be resistance. Therapists who can openly admit that they feel nervous about directing role-plays will stand a far better chance of a successful outcome than those who try to bluff through it. The therapist actively takes the role, standing up, directing the action, giving cues to each role-player to let him or her know when to speak and when to remain silent. The director needs to engage with the client when he is in role "as if" he is the victim, and "as if" the situation is real (Blatner & Blatner, 1988). This engagement is fundamental to conducting safe, focused victim empathy role-plays. The director needs to be prepared for the role-play session, having a plan, knowing which group members will take on roles, what the client is expected to do and how much time will be needed for the work. We recommend approximately thirty minutes for each role-play, including the deroling and debriefing.

Role-Play Techniques and Process

Because we are usually working in treatment rooms that do not represent environments conducive for the situations we wish to create, we need a lot of imagination and creativity and a period of time to "warm up" our client to the role he will be playing. Therefore, we spend time helping our client warm up to role and helping him think about the situation he is going to encounter as his victim. We call this technique Hot Seat. There are three stages: (1) set the scene, (2) ask for a physical description, and (3) get information about the situation being played out.

Therapist Training

All SOTP therapists with HMPS undertake at least three days of training on the victim empathy role-play module, with the opportunity for further re-training once they are delivering role-play. This method has been in operation for the last ten years and thus has gone through many changes. Although group members find the victim empathy role-plays very difficult during treatment, they find them very powerful and a part of the program that has a lasting effect.

CASE STUDY OF VICTIM EMPATHY ROLE-PLAY

Bill is 35 years old and is in prison for rape. He broke into a woman's apartment and raped her at knifepoint. His victim is called Mary and he knew that she was in a relationship at the time of the rape.

Role-Play Plan

Bill's *cognitive distortion* about Mary is that the rape happened five years ago and he says: "It was a long time ago, she'll get over it, she'll be okay now." He shows little understanding that Mary may still be affected by the rape. The *time scale* of the role-play will be five years after the offense. Bill will take on the role of Mary (victim, five years after the offense). The role-play will focus on empathy deficits. During the role-play, the therapist wants Bill to explore the effects of the rape on Mary that he doesn't see, so he can come to understand how Mary's life is affected five years after the rape. The therapist will address flashbacks; difficulty in relationships, particularly with men; not feeling safe at home by herself; and mistrust. The overall aim is to let Bill experience the longer-term consequences for Mary of having flashbacks, feeling mistrustful, and having difficulty in some relationships.

Therapists plan the scenarios out of the treatment room and even practice the role-plays beforehand. They are clear about the aims of the role-play and what they are going to be observing during the role-play. It is important to take the overall deficits and time scale to work out the role-play aim.

This is a structured role-play situation with Bill taking on the role of his victim, projected five years into the future. This form of structured role-plays is used in cognitive therapy (Beck, 1995; Padesky, 1994) and in schema-focused work and is about the ability to gain "action insight" (Kellerman, 1992) while perspective taking. Perspective taking and empathy are also used in relapse work (Pithers, 1997). Bill will take on the role of Mary (perspective take) in a situation five years in the future where she is having a dinner party with a male boyfriend and friends.

Role-Play in Action

THERAPIST: Okay, Bill, I'd like you to move to the front of the group to begin your role-play. Today you will be taking on the role of Mary, your victim, five years after the rape. Before we begin, let's just remind ourselves of the role-play rules; no touching, no props, time out if you want one at any time during this process, and after the role-play you will be deroled and debriefed. Any questions?

BILL: No, I've seen other role-plays, so I've got some idea how they go.

Set the Scene

THERAPIST: When I ask you to sit in this chair (*therapist places a chair in front of the group, facing them and assumes the director role*) I would like you take on the role of Mary in five years time after her rape. The situation is: you as Mary, are going to be having a meal with friends, work colleagues, and a guy with whom you are currently in a relationship.

BILL: (*sits down*)

DIRECTOR: (*speaks to Bill "as if" he is Mary and sets the scene*) Mary, it is now five years ago to the day that you were raped. (*Empathy deficit—flashback*) You are here at a friend's house, with a guy that you're in a relationship with and you're having a meal—there are different friends here. Tell me what can you see?

BILL (*in role as Mary*): We are sitting around a large table with some of my friends I've known for a long time and Mac, he's the guy I've been seeing for the last year, we are in the kitchen, it's warm and there are drinks on the table.

Physical Appearance

DIRECTOR: What are you wearing Mary?

BILL (*Bill, in role, will now be called Mary*): I have blue trousers, a blouse, earrings, and my hair is tied up. (*This is helping Bill connect with the role of Mary*)

DIRECTOR: (*director now needs to get information, keep role-play focused, and think of Bill's empathy deficits about his victim, namely, that she will not be affected five years after the offense*) Let's put the other people in their places. Tell us who they might be. (*Bill decides there are four others plus Mac. He places out five chairs and tells us they are two girlfriends back from school days and a colleague from her work place, plus her male partner. We give them names.*)

[We are working in "surplus reality" (Moreno, 1953), which is a psychodrama term.

This situation has probably not happened and is unlikely to happen, but we are creating it for the purposes of our role-play. It does not have to be real or factual, because we are working toward challenging Bill's empathy deficits, and the role-play is the structure that allows us to do this.]

DIRECTOR: (*to Bill*) "Mary, it's five years to the day that you were raped, what thoughts have you had about this?

[This technique, called Thought Track, freezes the action and gets Bill's private thoughts as Mary, which may not be shown in the scene.]

MARY: I've tried not to think about it.
DIRECTOR: Oh, that's interesting. Why not?
MARY: Because it's too painful.
DIRECTOR: Tell me about the pain.
MARY: I feel sick when I think about it, I can't believe it's five years ago—it only feels like yesterday. (*empathy deficit—flashback*) I go silent, still feel frightened, and sometimes won't stay at home by myself.

Get Information
DIRECTOR: Why won't you stay at home by yourself?
MARY: Because it happened in my apartment and I still feel nervous when I hear noises if I'm by myself. It's not comfortable and I don't like it.
DIRECTOR: You were in a relationship at the time, what happened?
MARY: We finished, I had difficulties with being able to talk about the rape.
DIRECTOR : Have you told Mac? (*empathy deficit—about relationships with men*)
MARY: Only some of it—I didn't tell him all the details.
DIRECTOR: Why is that?
MARY: I don't know how to. It's not something I want to talk about.
DIRECTOR: So if you haven't told him everything, what does this mean for your relationship?
MARY: That I keep things from him, I'm not sure I can trust how he will be with me if I tell him all the details. Also I had problems with my boyfriend at the time of the rape. So it's not easy for me being in a relationship.
DIRECTOR: How do you see yourself ever trusting in a relationship to be able to say everything? (*empathy deficit of mistrust*)
MARY: Not sure I will, nobody can really understand what I went through.
DIRECTOR: How many people around this table know that you were raped?
MARY: My two friends from school, but not my work colleague or her partner.
DIRECTOR: So what does this mean for you this evening, knowing some people are aware of what happened to you and others have no idea? (*empathy deficit—will affect her relationships*)
MARY: It makes me feel sad, because I feel different from them and know there will always be that barrier between us even with my old school friends.
DIRECTOR: How would you feel if Sue (*work colleague and one of the dinner guests*) found out you had been raped and was to tell her partner what had happened?
MARY: I would hate it. I have a problem even now with men; I'm beginning to

slowly trust Mac, but I don't tell him everything, so the thought of other men knowing makes me feel odd.

DIRECTOR: What do you mean by odd?

MARY: Not safe, I do see men differently, not trusting them. (*empathy deficit of feeling unsafe, even in a familiar environment*)

[Most of the work during the role-play centers around the Thought Track technique, with the director asking the questions and then directing the action. For example, after the Thought Track, the director will cue other role-players with trigger lines (these will have been worked through in the planning). For Bill (as Mary) to experience some of the feelings that have been described there needs to be a trigger. The fact that it is the same day that she was raped five years ago is a trigger, but we can also have the dinner guests asking questions to promote anxiety within Mary. For example, they might refer to Mary's previous partner.]

DIRECTOR: Can you say your line. (*to role-player who is school friend*)

SCHOOL FRIEND: You'll never guess who I saw last week. It was Steve coming out of the grocery store. (*Steve was Mary's partner at the time of the rape.*) He looked really well and we talked about you Mary.

DIRECTOR: (*to Mary*) How do you feel about what your old school friend, has just said? (*Thought Track*).

MARY: Really uncomfortable, especially in front of Sue and her guy.

DIRECTOR: Why is that?

MARY: Because Steve was my boyfriend when I was raped, and as I've said it was one of the reasons we split up.

DIRECTOR: (*signals to old school friend and other one to keep the action going and gives them cue lines if necessary*)

SCHOOL FRIEND: Yes, he was asking about you, wanted to know how you're doing now.

MARY: I can't forget the rape—there's always something to remind me of it. (*empathy deficit challenged—she'll get over it*)

[When we have group members taking on other roles in the role-play, they need clear directions. Bill had selected the role-players (we are working collaboratively) and they were given their roles. The director would explain in a sentence how they should play the roles. This can be said in front of Bill; the whole exercise needs to be transparent and collaborative with the director in control and guiding the whole process.]

Three-Stage Process of Deroling and Debriefing

This is a very important part of the role-play process and yet it is often lost in role-plays. It is really surprising how many conductors of role-play think it is finished when the action stops. It is imperative to stay with the moment, as this is the period of "processing," and for the therapists to ask questions to see if the goals (empathy deficits) of the role-play have been met.

First Stage

[The first part of this process is to keep client in the role but to hold the role-play and let other group members go back to the group.]

DIRECTOR: Right let's hold the role-play there. (*to Bill*) I'd like you to stay in the role of Mary, everyone else can return to the group, thank you. (*speaks to Bill, as Mary, about what has just happened*) So Mary, tell me what you just experienced in there?

MARY: That a lovely evening had a shadow over it for me.

DIRECTOR: Could you explain what you mean?

MARY: Well, I couldn't stop thinking that I was different from the others because I'd been raped.

DIRECTOR: Different in what way?

MARY: Couldn't forget what had happened, didn't feel honest, felt I had a secret, felt nervous that Sue and her partner would find out. Didn't want my school friends to mention it. I didn't want to be left by myself.

DIRECTOR: Why didn't you want to be left?

MARY: I felt scared again about being on my own, as that happened when I was raped.

[The questions continue until the therapists believe they have information about Bill's understanding of Mary's situation.]

Deroling: Bringing Bill Back to Himself

SECOND THERAPIST: (*It is a useful exercise as part of the deroling process to let the other therapist do the deroling; it gives the director a break.*) Let's derole you now. I want you to stand up and leave the chair where you will be leaving Mary behind and when you sit back in the group you will be Bill. (*Bill stands up and goes back to the group.*)

THERAPIST: Tell me who you really are?

BILL: I'm Bill, not Mary, I'm in the group room and it's morning, I'll be working this afternoon.

THERAPIST: (*to other role-players in the group*) Tell the group who you are. (*Group members introduce themselves back to the group.*)

Final Debrief With Bill

[For the final debrief as Bill, we are hoping to hear Bill pick up on the empathy deficits and say the opposite of his statements prior to role-play. Thus we repeat some of the questions we asked in the role-play but this time to Bill. It is necessary for Bill to separate Bill from the role of Mary, so that he talks about Mary and does not slip back into role.]

THERAPIST: Bill, how did Mary feel with all those people having a meal?

BILL: Nervous, not quite engaged and she kept thinking about the rape.

THERAPIST: What kind of thoughts did she have?

BILL: Hoping they wouldn't find out, couldn't forget what happened even though it was five years ago, and feelings of mistrust.

THERAPIST: What is the difference between your thoughts about Mary before the role-play and now after completing the role-play?

BILL: I really thought it wouldn't still affect her—not after five years. But I can see she won't forget easily and also it will affect how she is with other people—not feeling safe and not trusting.

[Once again to complete this process we would unpick more thoughts about Mary's situation in the future.]

Case Study Summary

This role-play is an example of an empathy deficit scenario that would be used in SOTP Core (Mann & Thornton, 2000). Other techniques are incorporated into the program and role-play scenarios for use at the time of offense (although not offense reenactments) and ripple effect role-plays where the client plays more than one victim, to help him understand the consequences of the offense for other people close to the victim All the role-plays are planned and structured around the clients' empathy deficits about their victims and therapists are trained in a variety of techniques to be able to use in the sessions. Each group member would have a total of two hours in the treatment room for victim empathy role-plays. These would be conducted in rotation (one hour per session). Each group member completes between three and five role-plays during the total two hours.

WHAT CAN GO WRONG IN A ROLE-PLAY

Four problems may arise in any role-play:

1. The client may not stay in the role.

2. The client may find it difficult to articulate his feelings.

3. The client may be resistant, saying "I don't want to do it," or "how do I know what she thinks?" or refusing to be involved in other group members' role-plays.

4. The client may still be in denial about aspects of his offense.

It is not possible to solve all these problems for specific cases and resistance will surface in the group at various times. However, from experience we have learned some ways to deal with the four common areas of difficulty.

Helping the Client Stay in Role

Help the client stay in role by using the victim's name and calling the client by the victim's name. For example:
DIRECTOR: Let's just remind ourselves who you are, Mary.
BILL: (*as Mary*) I'm Mary, I was raped five years ago.
DIRECTOR: How old are you Mary?
BILL: I'm 35 years old.
DIRECTOR: You are at at the dinner table, what's happening this evening?

[Use the victim's name consistently through the role-play to focus him into the role.]

Helping the Client Articulate Feelings

DIRECTOR: What feelings do you have about what's been said, Mary?
BILL: (*as Mary*) Dunno! Scared.
DIRECTOR: What does this mean?"
BILL: Frightened.

DIRECTOR: What does frightened mean?
BILL: Scared.
DIRECTOR: What color is scared to you?
BILL: Dark red, nearly black.
DIRECTOR: What shape is it?
BILL: Sharp, like broken stones.

[Then the therapist can comment on the shape and color as images as a way into Bill's feelings.]

Dealing With Resistance

DIRECTOR: (*to Bill*) How are you feeling, Mary?
BILL: How do I know how Mary feels?
DIRECTOR: It's okay; go with the flow, just make it up. We are not looking to create a realistic situation, we want you to imagine how Mary might feel, it's okay to improvise. (*Give Bill permission to get it wrong and calm any anxieties.*)
DIRECTOR: Just try to imagine yourself as Mary in this situation. (*Bill may need to share his anxieties with you before proceeding with the role-play.*)

These examples are a way of persevering and working with the client through his resistance rather than getting into confrontation. Hildebran and Pithers (1989) state: "It is not uncommon for a man to be able to respond throughout a 2 hour group in the person of either a male or female victim. The offender is often as surprised as anyone in the group to find himself identifying with victim feelings that he had previously refused to believe were present" (p. 242).

Dealing With Denial

If the client is denying certain aspects of his offense, it is pointless to try to get him to admit to this in the role-play. He will come out of role. For example:
BILL: I didn't use a knife.

[This statement needs to be challenged in other areas of treatment rather than victim empathy role-plays. The role-play component is to allow the client to try to gain an understanding of the offense from the victim's perspective, not to tick off a list of all the aspects of the offense so far denied.]

Role-Play Diaries

Group members record their feelings about the role-play in a diary. They are expected to complete it a few weeks after victim empathy role-plays to see if they are still in touch with their victim's feelings. The therapists can then carry this work forward into the relapse prevention model later in the program.

RELAPSE PREVENTION ROLE-PLAYS

The differences between relapse prevention (RP) and victim empathy role-plays was discussed earlier. The RP model is a cognitive-behavioral treatment approach originally designed for the treatment of addictive behaviors. However, it has also been incorporated into the treatment of sex offenders (Parks & Marlatt, 1999; Laws, 1989; Laws, Hudson, & Ward, 2000). SOTP Core (Mann & Thornton, 2000) works toward approach goals based on Ward's (2003) good lives model. In this relapse model therapists help the clients identify old behaviors and work toward new behaviors, rather than avoidance. The basis for group members' treatment is to help them understand the RP model, teach them coping skills, and work toward an approach-focused intervention (Mann, Webster, Schofield, & Marshall 2004).

Skills Practice

In various treatment approaches where skills practice is incorporated into relapse prevention, the client is expected to demonstrate and work through a new behavior. The client is expected to repeat and practice the new behavior in either an old situation or a new one. For example, in a sex offender group, the client may decide he wants to practice his social skills. The new behavior is being able to introduce himself to somebody new in an appropriate environment. The situation is set up and the client will practice being able to say his name, to ask the other person his or her name, and to speak a little about himself. This skill can be transferred to a variety of situations: calling a friend's house, meeting new people, meeting new neighbors, speaking to people when out shopping, and so on. The situation may change, but the *skill* does not. To maximize practice, we put the client into various new situations and ask him to keep repeating the technique (e.g., the broken record technique). The client will practice this skill (or new behavior) and it becomes the focus of his RP session. The repetition often requires the therapist to be creative in the treatment room to help the client try out the skill until he is ready to do it in the outside world.

Old Me vs. New Me

In SOTP Core we introduce the idea of "Old Me" and "New Me," a treatment intervention developed by Jim Haaven (Haaven et al., 1990) to produce an "internal" creation of a nonoffending persona. The group members develop these aspects of themselves and make collages, producing both an Old Me and a New Me collage. Eventually, as they work through this process, they are directed to think about role-plays they would like to practice. They are encouraged to think about how Old Me would react and how differently New Me would react. The therapists are conscious of how Old Me is interpreted and the new skills required to work toward a new behavior. When the role-play is conducted, therapists not only direct the client to practice a new behavior or skill but also bring Old Me to life to challenge the client's New Me cognitions in the situation. This method is a psychodramatic technique known as concretization, which gives us access to the internal world of the client (Moreno, 1953). This technique enables the therapist to work with the client on two levels (1) external—behavioral changes and (2) internal process—of both thoughts and feelings.

Process

The same rules for skills practice applies in terms of therapists' roles. The therapist who assumes the role of director is active in maintaining control of the role-play.

The director controls the pace, time, and content of the sessions. There are clear boundaries: time out, no props, when the director says stop, the action stops, and no touch. The aim of the rules is to create a safe, contained space in which to work and, again, all group members are expected to participate and play other roles in the session but not that of the perpetrator.

Treatment Goals for Relapse Prevention

The therapist must have clear ideas about individual treatment needs. Each group member will have a specific skill he wishes to practice and also individual Old Me thoughts and feelings that hinder him. Old Me is something like a core belief the client holds that drives his behavior. Christine Padesky (1994) discusses the use of psychodrama to work with schema change process, using an action method (role-play) to access the internal world of the client. The therapist works collaboratively with the client to find out the core beliefs. Some therapists find a plan as a basic structure very helpful until they become more spontaneous and are able to use the plan as a template to create short, quick scenarios.

CASE STUDY OF A RELAPSE PREVENTION ROLE-PLAY

Here is a typical RP scenario for Bill. One of the areas he has identified for himself is low self-esteem.

THERAPIST: So, Bill what have you decided that you would like to practice today?

BILL: I know I feel better about myself when I'm occupied.

THERAPIST: What do you mean occupied?

BILL: Busy, I've got things to do . . . working for instance and also being with other people.

THERAPIST: So, what would stop you from working or being with other people?

BILL: Not feeling confident. Wanting something but giving up because I don't feel good about myself.

THERAPIST: (*working out treatment goals—(1) behavior: being able to be in a situation where he wouldn't normally feel comfortable and staying with it; (2) internal process—the core belief of Old Me: I'm not good enough*) What situation can you identify that you wouldn't normally feel comfortable about and walk away from because you probably don't feel good enough.

[Approach goal: Bearing in mind we want Bill to practice a positive situation, so he's working toward an achievement.]

BILL: Well, the one that comes to mind is going for a job, an interview would be really difficult—I'd want to walk out at the first difficult question.

THERAPIST: Okay. Well let's look at that situation, what do you think is a difficult question?

BILL: Something like—tell me something about yourself.

[The therapist can write on a flipchart the following plan to help structure the scene:

Goal:	Find a job release
Old Me Behavior:	Unemployed, not confident
Role-Play Situation:	Office—job interview

Role-Play Trigger:	Interviewer says, "Can you tell me something about yourself that is relevant for this job?"
Overall Goal:	Sell himself as an employee
Skills to Practice:	• Confident body language
	• Voice tone/eye contact
	• Responding positively to questions
	• Talk about strength/skills as a person
New Behavior:	Be more positive and confident about self; stay in the interview room.

[Using this plan the therapist has clear ideas about the new behaviors Bill wants to practice that are approach goal focused.]

Practice of Relapse Prevention Role-Plays

The next stage is to bring Bill to the front of the group again and suggest to him that the interview situation needs to be set up. Let Bill set the scene. He can say where it is, who is in the scene, and so on. Again, the situation does not have to be real; Bill can be creating it.

THERAPIST AS DIRECTOR: Right Bill, let's see how we can help you to strengthen your New Me and practice your new goals. We need a role-player to be the Interviewer. (*group member volunteers*)

DIRECTOR: (*places two chairs opposite each other, with a table in between, if there is a table*) Bill, I want you to take a seat in the interview and we'll imagine the interview has started. You said, "It's at the point when the interviewer asks me something about myself, that I begin to doubt myself." Is this correct?

BILL: Yeah, that's right and I'd walk out feeling useless.

DIRECTOR: Okay, we'll we need to see this *and* hear what Old Me Thinking says to you in this situation so we can change it.

[We know the Old Me behavior but we need to hear the Old Me Thinking.]

DIRECTOR: (*to role-player*) Let's have the trigger line.

INTERVIEWER: Can you tell me something about yourself that's relevant for this job?

DIRECTOR: What does Old Me Thinking say to you? (*Bill's internal trigger*)

BILL: (*speaking Old Me Thinking aloud*) Oh no! He knows I'm not up to the job. I can't do this. I feel useless. I want out of here. Get out.

[As Bill speaks, the co-therapist records the Old Me Thinking on the flip chart.]

DIRECTOR: So what would Old Me do?

BILL: Get up and walk out feeling bad.

[During this exercise Bill demonstrated his Old Me behavior, did not make eye contact, slipped down in the chair, and listened to the internal voice of Old Me Thinking.]

DIRECTOR: Well, we came here to do something different. Let's remind ourselves about New Me.

BILL: (*talks about New Me positively, and the skills he wishes to practice*)

DIRECTOR: We need someone to take on the role of Old Me. (*group member vol-*

unteers) Can you come and sit next to Bill and speak as his Old Me thoughts during this role-play.

[The therapist must make sure Old Me has eye contact with Bill so they can see each other.]

DIRECTOR: We are going to rerun this scene bringing Old Me to life. We now have Bill's *external triggers*, the interviewer asking him questions, *and* his *internal triggers,* which is Old Me thinking telling him he's not good enough. We are working with both of these triggers, by focusing on behavior (external), thoughts, and feelings (internal).

Directing Old Me

The object of the session is to make Old Me thinking as provocative as possible, which taps into Bill's core belief that he is not good enough. We need to see this, so Bill can demonstrate his New Me thinking and then his New Me behavior.

DIRECTOR: (*to Old Me Thinking*) As we go through this scene, I will cue you to speak as Old Me Thinking. Try to sound like Bill's voice which sounded dejected, frightened and is desperate to get out of the room. Are you ready?

INTERVIEWER: Yes.

DIRECTOR: (*to Bill*) As Old Me Thinking speaks, you need to use your New Me Thinking to counteract him.

BILL: Well I'll try.

DIRECTOR: Let's start, let's go from the trigger. (*Trigger speaks the line.*)

OLD ME THINKING: He knows I'm not up to the job.

DIRECTOR: (*to Bill*) Let's hear your New Me Thinking—tell Old Me how you think as New Me.

BILL: (*as New Me Thinking to Old Me Thinking*) That's not true, I've worked in factories before, I can do it. (*internal processes*)

OLD ME THINKING: No, I can't do this.

BILL: (*as New Me Thinking*) Yes, I can, I've seen the job description and I stand as much chance as anyone of doing the job. I'm a good time-keeper, I work hard and it will be a great opportunity to meet people. (*approach focus*).

DIRECTOR: Now you've spoken to Old Me Thinking; what about your new behavior, we need to see this.

BILL: (*makes eye contact with interviewer and sits up straight in chair, keeping open body language—external*) (*to interviewer as New Me behavior*) I have done this type of work before, I'm familiar with working in factories, packing boxes.

OLD ME THINKING: I'm just about holding this together, underneath I feel really useless . . . useless.

BILL: (*as New Me Thinking to Old Me Thinking—internal*) No, I'm doing okay. I got here, I've been in the interview for about ten minutes. I might get the job and the money is quite good. I'll be able to save for a holiday. That makes me feel good.

DIRECTOR: (*to Interviewer*) Cue line.

INTERVIEWER: What experiences do you have for this job—why should I give it to you?

BILL: (*as New Me to interviewer—demonstrating New Me behavior and focusing on skills he wants to practice*) I'm a good time-keeper, I work hard and I have experience of factory work. Also I'm willing to learn and would appreciate any training you offer.

OLD ME THINKING: (*internal*) He doesn't believe me—this is useless, I want to get out of here.

BILL: (*as New Me Thinking*) No I don't! I'm staying, I'm doing well. (*internal*) (*to interviewer demonstrating New Me behavior*). I can start immediately, if that's any help.

INTERVIEWER: Well it could be, I need a person to start very soon.

DIRECTOR: Let's hold the scene there.

At this point it may be necessary to continue to practice some of the New Me thinking or New Me behavior with Bill. Once the director feels confident that Bill has worked through this challenge, Bill would repeat the scene without Old Me but just focusing on his New Me behavior and the skills. The Old Me Thinking adds a more challenging and realistic dimension to the work. Most clients want Old Me to either shut up or move away. The fact they have to try to minimize this dysfunctional part of self makes the relapse closer to the difficulties they will encounter in their lives. These exercises can also be relevant to their everyday lives, not just when they are released back into the community.

Role Reversal

Role reversal is a very useful technique during relapse prevention because it helps the clients to take perspective. For example in the scenario with Bill, it might have been useful to ask Bill to role reverse with the interviewer. This supports the empathy/perspective-taking skills previously learned during victim empathy. Role reversing with the interviewer and being Hot Seated in this role would give Bill the opportunity to see the situation from a management perspective.

DIRECTOR: (*to Bill*) Role reverse; you become the interviewer. How do you see this man Bill opposite you?

BILL: (*as Interviewer*) He seems very keen, open, confident and it's good he can start work immediately.

This process helps to strengthen Bill's New Me thinking and behavior. This technique can be used at any point during the RP role-plays.

Deroling and DeBriefing for Relapse Prevention Role-Plays

It is important to derole the client from the situation he has been playing to the "here and now" of the treatment room. A few simple questions will help to refocus him.

- Who are you?

- Where are you?

- Who else is in the group room?

The deroling and debriefing process is different for RP than for victim empathy role-plays as we are hoping to achieve different aims. The steps to debriefing are as follows:

1. Derole key client plus other group members.

2. Ask client what he believes he did well and then what he could do differently.

3. Open this question to the group members: What do they believe went well and what could be done differently?

4. Give feedback. It is important to keep feedback motivational yet honest about any further work.

5. Let the client have the right to reply and identify any other areas/skills he could work on. Always leave the session on a positive note—there may be lots of learning points and more work, but the therapist should help the clients feel they have managed to do something different, no matter how small.

CONCLUSION

Role-play with sex offenders as a therapeutic tool needs careful consideration and planning. It is important as a therapist to be clear about the aims and goals of the individual sessions. Victim empathy focuses on working with clients' empathy deficits about their victims and relapse prevention on core beliefs which drive behavior. The introduction of Old Me and New Me for relapse prevention helps to focus treatment goals at both the cognitive and affective levels and skills practice to demonstrate new behaviors. The role-play techniques described in this chapter are highly structured and contained within a framework of offending behavior treatment group work. As a word of caution, role-play is not to be regarded as a tool for treating clients' victimization issues. This type of personal therapy work needs to be contained in a different kind of treatment group. It is easy to blur boundaries when using role-play techniques where clients can feel exposed and vulnerable. Therefore, it is important for therapists to remain clear about treatment goals and to deliver the sessions with preplanning, clear aims, a warm therapeutic style, and confidence in the method. Ideally, the response from group members will be less resistance and more emphasis on a motivation to change.

References

Anderson, D., & Dodgson, P. G. (2002). Empathy deficits, self esteem, and cognitive distortions in sexual offenders. In Y. Fernandez (Ed.), *In their shoes* (pp. 73–90). Oklahoma City, OK: Wood 'N' Barnes.

Beck, J. (1995). *Cognitive therapy basics and beyond.* New York: Guilford Press.

Blatner, M. D., & Blatner A. (1988). *Foundations of psychodrama, history, theory & practice* (3rd ed.). New York: Springer.

Corey, G. (1996). *Theory & practice of counseling and psychotherapy* (5th ed.). Pacific Grove, CA: Brooks/Cole.

Fernandez Y. M., & Serran, G. (2002). Empathy training for therapists and clients. In Y. Fernandez (Ed.), *In their shoes* (pp. 110–131). Oklahoma City, OK: Wood 'N' Barnes.

Haaven, J., Little R., & Petre-Miller, D. (1990). *Treating intellectually disabled sex offenders: A model residential program.* Orwell, VT: Safer Society Press.

Hildebran, D., & Pithers, W. D. (1989). Enhancing offender empathy for sexual abuse victims. In D. R. Laws (Ed.), *Relapse prevention with sex offenders* (pp. 236–243). New York: Guilford Press.

Kellerman, P. F. (1992) *Focus on psychodrama: The therapeutic aspects of psychodrama.* London: Jessica Kingsley.

Laws, D. R. (Ed.). (1989). *Relapse prevention with sex offenders.* New York: Guilford Press.

Laws, D. R., Hudson, S. M., & Ward, T. (2000). *Remaking relapse prevention with sex offenders: A sourcebook.* Thousand Oaks, CA: Sage.

Mann, R. E., Daniels, M., & Marshall, W. L. (2002). The use of role-plays in developing victim empathy. In Y. Fernandez (Ed.), *In their shoes* (pp. 132–148). Oklahoma City, OK: Wood 'N' Barnes.

Mann, R. E., & Fernandez, Y. M. (2001). *HM Prison Service Sex Offender Treatment Manual: SOTP Rolling Programme: Treatment manual.* Unpublished manuscript.

Mann, R. E., & Thornton, D. (1994). *HM Prison Service Sex Offender Treatment Programme: SOTP core training manual.* Unpublished manuscript.

Mann, R. E., & Thornton, D. (2000). *HM Prison Service Sex Offender Treatment Programme: SOTP core training manual* (rev.). Unpublished manuscript.

Mann, R. E., Webster, S. D., Schofield, C., & Marshall, W. L. (2004). Approach versus avoidance goals in relapse prevention with sexual offenders. *Sexual Abuse: A Journal of Research and Treatment, 16*(1), 65–75.

Marlatt, G. A. (1985). Lifestyle modification. In G. A. Marlatt & J. R. Gordon (Eds.), *Relapse prevention* (pp. 280–348). New York: Guilford Press.

Marques, M. J. K., Nelson, C., Alarcon J. M., & Day, D. M. (2000). Preventing relapse in sex offenders:: What we Learned from SOTEP's experimental program. In D. R. Laws, S. M. Hudson, & T. Ward (Eds.), *Remaking relapse prevention with sex offenders* (pp. 321–340). Thousand Oaks, CA: Sage.

Marshall, W. L., Anderson, D., & Fernandez, Y. M (1999). *Cognitive-behavioural treatment of sex offenders.* New York: Wiley.

Moreno, J. L., (1953) *Who shall survive? Foundations of sociometry, group psychotherapy, and sociodrama.* New York: Beacon House.

Padesky, C. A. (1994). Schema change processes in cognitive therapy. *Clinical Psychology and Psychotherapy, 1,* 267–278).

Parks, G. A., & Marlatt, G. A. (1999) Relapse prevention therapy for substance-abusing offenders: A cognitive-behavioural approach. In E. Latessa (Ed.), *What works: Strategic solutions: The International Community Corrections Asociation examines substance abuse.* Lanham, MD: American Correctional Association.

Pithers, W. D. (1994). Process evaluation of a group therapy component designed to enhance sex offenders' empathy for sexual abuse survivors. *Behaviour, Research and Therapy, 32*(5), 565–570.

Pithers, W. D. (1997). Maintaining treatment integrity with sexual abusers. *Criminal Justice and Behavior, 24*(1), 34–51.

Rogers, C. (1961). *On becoming a person.* Boston: Houghton Mifflin.

Ward, T., & Stewart, C. A. (2003). Good lives and the rehabilitation of sexual offenders. In T. Ward, D. R. Laws, & S. M. Hudson (Eds.), *Sexual deviance: Issues and controversies* (pp. 21–44). Thousand Oaks, CA: Sage.

Webster, S. D., Bowers, L. E., Mann, R. E., & Marshall, W. L. (2005). Developing empathy in sex offenders: The value of offence re-enactments. *Sexual Abuse: A Journal of Research and Treatment, 17,* 63–77.

Yalom, I. D. (1975). *The theory and practice of group psychotherapy,* New York: Basic Books.

Zinkin, L. (1989) The group as container and contained. *Group Analysis, 22,* 227–234.

Chapter 9

Choosing, Training, and Using Offenders as Therapeutic Aides

by Nancy M. Steele, Ph.D.

OVERVIEW

Almost all programs and most effective groups rely on the help, support, and confrontation that comes from other offenders. There is both clinical- and research-based support for this idea. There are, however, pitfalls and potential problems and conflicts that arise when offenders work as therapeutic aides. The author of this chapter has developed and run programs in prisons for more than twenty years. Many of the ideas she presents were learned the hard way. Some of the approaches may be specific to the situations in which the programs were run. This chapter presents the theoretical rationale for this approach and some of the studies that support it. It addresses how to pick offenders for the role of aides and, most important, how to supervise, support, and train these aides. Finally, the author addresses the necessity of letting go and training new aides, so that there is continuous turnover in the program.

INTRODUCTION

Recent changes in the direction of treatment efforts with sex offenders have pointed out the importance of understanding the attachment style of sex offenders and the need for offenders to see some hope of leading improved lives once they finish treatment (Ward, 2002; Ward & Stewart, 2003). Increasingly, clinical research is demonstrating the role of loneliness, depression, and anger in the etiology of sexual offending behavior. It seems likely that for a variety of reasons, men who commit aggressive sexual acts have had very little opportunity to learn how to trust others and to relate to others in a supportive and understanding manner (Ward, Hudson, & McCormick, 1997). They are driven by loneliness and yet see no way ito correct this problem. Some researchers have concluded that sex offenders typically have great difficulty in relating to peers (Blaske, Borduin, Henggeler, & Mann, 1989; Tingle, Barnard, Robbin, Newman, & Hutchinson, 1986). If treatment is to be effective there must be an opportunity for offenders to experience a supportive and mutually rewarding relationship with staff and with other offenders in treatment. An important element in any treatment is to learn about and to experience supportive close relationships with others.

RATIONALE FOR USING OFFENDER AIDES

Most treatment programs, especially in prisons, struggle with an abundance of offenders and a small number of staff members who are busy, busy, and busier. There is a limit to how many offenders any one staff member can relate to in a given period. Staff become quickly drained if they alone try to form the therapeutic relationships necessary for change with more than a few offenders at a time. There is no clear answer to the question, "How many offenders at a time can a staff member relate to effectively?"—but it is probably not more than twenty in any one week.

Inevitably, especially in residential programs, certain offenders become leaders and have a great influence over the feelings, attitudes, beliefs, and behaviors of other offenders. This compression of the social system is especially powerful in prison, and there really is no way to escape it. The problem becomes one of how to mold this social pressure toward a therapeutic end rather than allowing the typical pro-criminal thinking and behavior that flourish in the normal prison living unit. Just as we have learned over and over that groups have a powerful effect on treatment with offenders, it is also an important strategy within treatment programs to pick and mold the offenders who will become leaders within the program milieu and/or living unit. Staff can and should shape these leaders to become positive forces for productive change for all offenders within the program. Picking and molding leaders within the peer culture is what Agee (2002) has referred to as forming a "seed group" in a therapeutic residential mileu.

WORKING WITH OFFENDER AIDES

When the first residential program in Minnesota was begun for treating offenders, we had a thirty-bed cottage with four treatment staff and nine custody staff assigned to the program full time to develop and implement the treatment. Even though there was a good ratio of staff to offenders and a very small unit, it was still beneficial to have a few selected offenders work as aides and/or clerks in the program. The "leaders" seemed to naturally emerge out of the group of offenders with whom we were working and in time they became an important adjunct in the program.

Fifteen years later, when I moved to Ohio and was given the job of starting a residential program there, the ratio of staff to offenders was quite different. The living units were large dormitories, double-bunked; each unit held 220 offenders. Initially, just one staff position was available to work full time in the sex offender program. Eventually three other staff members were assigned to work full time in the program, which had 150 active offenders at a time in classes or groups. The rest of the living unit was filled with offenders who had graduated or who were waiting to begin treatment.

In Ohio at that time approximately 9,000 sex offenders in the system were waiting for treatment in the hope that this would make a difference with the parole board. This meant that many sex offenders began to transfer to the prison and apply to be admitted to the program. As the number of applications mushroomed, an opportunity developed to select offenders most amenable to treatment. Offenders were screened fifteen to twenty at a time and eventually a waiting list was developed of offenders who had admitted to their sexual crime by writing a description of the crime on paper. In the description they were to list the age and gender of their victim or victims, the exact sexual acts they performed, and the method of coercion or threat they used to get cooperation from the victim. An offender's written descriptions had to substantially match the official version of the crimes in his presentence investigation (PSI) report. In the process of screening sex offenders we found some who had received treatment at other prisons and were much farther along in admitting to their crimes, understanding themselves, and changing their behavior. Many of them wanted to continue in treatment, either to get a completion certificate or because they recognized some ongoing benefit of staying involved. They were the natural ones to help us select and begin treatment with the hundreds of sex offenders who had not yet had even a beginning class. These treated offenders led primarily by example, being willing to discuss their own crimes in detail—what they did, and why and how they did it. Their input was powerful and could only be provided by another offender. Those in treatment could read about other offenders, see videotapes, and talk among themselves, but nothing was as effective as another offender owning up to his behavior face to face with them.

Eventually ten program aides were hired and assigned to work with the four staff members in implementing the program. Several ingredients, discussed next, were critical to using these offenders effectively.

Selection

With a number of offenders from whom to choose, we learned to look for five critical characteristics.

1. *Offenders who have done well in their own treatment.* They can talk specifically and in detail about their own crimes, with genuine remorse.

2. *Offenders who have a minimal criminal background.* Sex offenses should predominate in their history with a minimum of other types of offenses.

3. *Offenders who are liked and respected by other inmates in the system.*

4. *Those who represent different types of sex offenders.* Try to reflect the proportion of sex offender types in the treatment population: rapists, incest offenders, and extrafamilial offenders.

5. *Racial balance, to reflect the racial composition of the treatment group.* In Ohio, this meant that almost half the aides were black and we usually had at least one Hispanic aide if possible, preferably one who could speak Spanish when it was necessary.

Monitoring of and Support for Aides

Any force that is potentially good can be misapplied and become potentially negative. Probably the biggest mistake typically made with aides is to hire them and then leave them on their own and allow them to act independently of the staff. As with a garden, even when the best seeds have been planted, we have to cultivate and nurture the plot or we get a lot of weeds. The best aides cannot function effectively without continued contact and involvement with treatment staff. The purpose of program aides is not to let the clinical treatment staff slough off; rather, it is a way to enhance or multiply the effect of the work that professional treatment staff do.

In our program, essentially all four of the staff members supervised the ten aides. The aides were assigned three or four to a class. The curriculum for the classes was decided on by the staff and written up in a manual. Parts of the curriculum were changed from time to time, but the manual helped keep the process systematic. The manual listed the books, reading assignments, homework assignments, and videotapes used in each class. Typically the classes consisted of a lecture by the staff member, the showing of a videotape, and then smaller discussion groups led by the program aides with the staff member in the room circulating among the smaller groups.

Therapy groups for the higher-risk offenders were conducted in the second year and were always led by staff in the more traditional manner. The class discussions were not considered to be group therapy, but sometimes they became quite serious and intense. They were initially regarded as a training ground for therapy groups. The aides were to keep the discussion going on the topic, to work to get each offender to talk a bit in each group, and to teach the more talkative members to listen to and pay attention to others. The groups were mixed as to types of sex offenders.

After each class, staff members would meet with all the program aides involved to process the events in the discussion groups. Aides were available on the unit to help with homework assignments, answer questions, or continue discussion in an individual manner based on what had come up in the class discussions. The expectation instilled in the offenders and the aides by staff members was that they could discuss anything that came up with staff and/or with the other aides if necessary. By meeting daily with the aides in a group the expectation was enforced that the aides were to help each other when necessary and back each other up in the unit as problems developed.

Frequent meetings are necessary to keep things moving forward in a positive direction. At least once a week all the staff would meet with all the aides to review the overall direction of things in the unit and in the program itself. Also, at least once a week the staff met with each other and without the aides present. This much structure was necessary to keep splits and factions from developing. It is easy for a staff member and one or two aides to develop a relationship that is too close or excludes others. At times staff fight with each other by picking on aides whom they think are the favorites of other staff members. Splits can develop from the bottom up also. Inmates in the program can easily pit one aide against another or aides against staff. Staff and aides must model good communication and cooperation if they are to ever teach offenders to use these tools.

With this kind of a model we found that the staff actually spent as much time with five or six aides as they did with the rest of the inmates in treatment. Time spent with the aides was to train and support them so that they did not get burned out or overly involved with some of the most dependent clients. Each of the aides then had between ten and twenty offenders with whom they were working. Given this, it is important to keep the door open so that any inmate at any time can talk to any staff member. This gives clients protection from exploitation or misuse of power by a program aide.

The "Power" of Aides

Essentially the only power the aides have is that of persuasion and understanding. They have more ready access to the staff and sometimes they can influence the staff, but basically staff members make the major decisions. Staff essentially empower the selected inmates. In our prison it was also possible to send a complaint outside the unit to the superintendent and other administrators in the prison. Thus every staff member was also accountable to make reasonable decisions and to act in a respectful way with all the inmates. In practice, the most frequent complaints that went outside the unit concerned getting admitted to the program, as more and more inmates tried to get in sooner.

The program was one to two years long. Higher-risk offenders were usually placed in therapy groups for a year after they had finished their classes. Aides could begin working after they had completed their own treatment and could stay in the position no more than two to three years. If they stayed any longer than this they might have more seniority than some staff members for whom they were working. In practice, when a new staff member was hired the aides tended to change over of their own volition. Thus, greater seniority was not a major problem. The aides for the most part did not receive disciplinary tickets, but they knew if anyone committed a major infraction he would be out of the unit and out of his job. All the inmates in the program knew that they would be expelled for drug use or fighting or if they were caught in sexual behavior.

Assigning Tasks to Inmate Aides

Appropriate Tasks. Some important work in the therapeutic process can be effectively and safely carried out by inmate aides. For example:

- In the discussion groups aides can encourage every offender to talk some about himself. They can quiet the louder ones and teach them to listen to and pay attention to others. They can keep the discussion groups focused on the topic at hand.

- If an offender is too timid to talk much in group the aides can talk to him outside class and then gradually bring him into the discussion group.

- If an offender is so ashamed of his crime that he cannot discuss it at all, an aide can be found who has committed a similar or worse crime. Listening to someone else describe his feelings and behaviors makes it much easier eventually to talk about one's own behavior, first one on one and then in small groups. (This is probably most common with male child molesters.)

- Aides can involve the quieter and shyer offenders in social activities on the unit: card playing, walks, puzzles, cooking, or whatever is available.

- If a family or home crisis develops at night or on the weekend and an offender needs someone to talk to, one of several aides is usually available.

- Aides can type homework questions and worksheets. They can file and keep track of books, articles, videotapes, and class handouts.

- Aides can watch the TV schedule every week and recommend the taping of any TV show with potential program material in it. Similarly, they can suggest new books or videos that might be appropriate material for the program.

- They can keep a scrapbook of program activities and newspaper articles of interest to the program participants.

- Aides with special skills (e.g., in art, crafts, or music) can be recruited and used to enrich the program.

- They can set up rooms and move chairs, tables, video machines, and TVs around.

- They can clean offices and classrooms.

- They can read and translate for offenders who are illiterate, slow, or handicapped. They can write out answers that are dictated to them in assignments from inmates who have trouble writing or spelling.

- If aggressive inmates are preying on or taking advantage of more timid offenders, aides can often speak to them about the necessity of backing off.

- If racial tensions or arguments develop in the living unit often an aide of the appropriate race can intervene in a way that everyone will listen to.

- Offenders are encouraged to talk their conflicts out with each other, to seek the help of a program aide if necessary in discussing their differences, and to involve staff if and only if all other attempts to settle their problems have failed.

Inappropriate Tasks. That said, there are definitely tasks that should not be assigned to program aides. Among these are:

- In general, aides should not be encouraged to turn in their fellow inmates; rather, they should be encouraged to teach the men to settle their problems among themselves appropriately and without violence.

- They should not grade tests or homework or take attendance in class.

- They should not score psychological tests. (Stories were rampant in the prison population about the going price of certain Minnesota Multiphasic Personality Inventory profiles, which were thought to sway the parole board.)

- They should not recommend who is expelled from the program, or who stays in it. That is a staff responsibility.

- They should not become snitches for the security department in prison.

- They should not be put in charge of managing the waiting list for the program or have influence in moving inmates into or out of the unit.

- They should not write or suggest the content of clinical or therapy reports.

- They should not be left alone to run a class. A staff member should be in the class or close at hand.

WHAT MAKES A DIFFERENCE TO OFFENDERS IN A PROGRAM?

After eight years, 616 sex offenders had completed our Ohio program. Questionnaires about the various components of the program were administered anonymously to eighty-six of them in the last two graduating classes. We were looking for information on which parts of the program the offenders thought were most important or helpful. Sometimes they were not sure or they left an answer blank, in which case it was scored as "NA." To the question "Who or what helped you the most in the Magellan Program?" they rated the program aides almost as highly as the staff (see Figure 9.1).

Although a great deal of staff time is spent on lessons and learning materials it is important to note that it really is the human relationships that make a difference in a program as far as the participants are concerned. Only 9 percent of survey respondents thought the lessons were the most important thing. Fortunately, 24 percent saw the

Figure 9.1
Who or What in the Program Was Most Helpful to You?

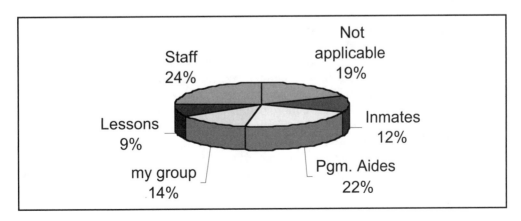

staff as the most important thing, but the next largest group, 22 percent, believed the program aides were the most important in terms of helping them in the program. "My group" referred to respondents' assigned discussion or therapy group, and this proved less important than we expected. Apparently another 12 percent had found help from some other inmate in the unit, a friend, bunkmate, or someone. It is not surprising that, altogether, almost half of the respondents, 48 percent, found other inmates in the unit the most helpful influence in terms of their progressing in the program. This is very similar to research conducted by Yalom (1995) on the effectiveness of group therapy. When he asked group participants who or what influenced them the most in group they generally reported that it was another group member. We as staff members are not nearly as important as we like to think. We are important only inasmuch as we create the climate or culture that allows the therapeutic force of groups and individuals to work in a productive way. Staff are the catalyst for change.

The same "who or what" question was asked in each of the specific classes. The class on victim empathy was probably the hardest; it was the first class program participants took. During these ten weeks they had to verbally admit to their crimes in detail and discuss them with appropriate affect in order to pass on to other classes. Twenty-eight percent of respondents said that the program aides were the most helpful in this class. In writing their autobiographies, they often had to relive some painful and unhappy moments in their lives, Twenty-one percent said that the aides were the most helpful in this part of the program and 31 percent indicated that the aides were the most important help they had in writing their relapse plans.

Of course, there is always some danger that the aides will do the work for the offender, which is not helpful. The best check on this problem is to have offenders discuss and explain their relapse plans in group or class without notes. They can do this several times and answer questions from group members about how they should react in given situations. This is just one more example of how everything that the aides do is to some extent checked and, if necessary, modified by staff. Generally staff can see if an aide is having a beneficial effect on the inmates. They see it by how aides and inmates react to each other inside and outside class and groups. They get it in reports from other staff around the prison. In our experience, staff would also often hear it in spontaneous comments from the inmates, especially when the inmates were beginning treatment. It was not uncommon that inmates would be very distrustful of staff in the beginning, and they trusted the aides before they trusted the staff.

THE BENEFIT TO THE AIDES

As well as benefiting the clients in the program, the aides themselves benefited from and seemed to like their jobs very much. We usually had many more applicants than we could hire. Some of them waited years to get a job. Their own self-esteem flourished. They had to learn to have more patience, to listen better, to cooperate more, and to work with all sorts of inmates whom they might not otherwise have gotten to know. Nothing really restores one's confidence in oneself as much as knowing that he has made a positive difference for someone else.

One aide in particular is worth mentioning. He had been in prison for over thirty years for the murder and rape of a girl when he was a very young man. While in prison he had learned to read and write; he was fairly bright and he gradually changed from a vicious, bitter young man to a savvy and hardened inmate. He did well in the program, went to the board, and received a ten-year setback. He accepted that there was little hope that he would ever get out of prison, but by this time he was caught up in the program and found that he had a knack for helping others. He was quite good with the paperwork, but he also got along well with all kinds of inmates, and he was respected in part because he had done so much time and in part because he earned it. Finally he found in working with the other men some redemption for his life. It gave meaning to him in what otherwise had been a pretty unhappy life. He was attached to many of the inmates with whom he worked and when they got through the program and were released he followed their progress and lives. After he left the program he became ill and did in fact die shortly thereafter, still in prison.

Fortunately, most of the other aides had a better outcome. Three or four were fired because of drug usage while they were aides, and one was fired when it was discovered that he was corresponding inappropriately with a young man in another prison. The vast majority, however, did well as aides, while in prison, and upon their release. It was hard at times to let them go after two or three years of working with them, but most of them reached the point where they wanted to move on to other prisons or other jobs or to school. Usually staff could see that this was what we were working for.

CONCLUSION

When there are too many offenders and not enough staff there is always something we can do. Each problem is also an opportunity. Using clients to help one another in the treatment process is not a new concept. It has been around in various forms for years. It is the heart of the Alcoholics Anonymous model and numerous other 12-Step programs. It was key to the ideas that Jones (1953) used in developing therapeutic communities in England during World War II. It was also important in the theories of psychodrama developed by Moreno (as reported by Yablonski, 1989). What might be new or different at this point is the effort to systematize how this approach is best applied to the treatment of sex offenders. It is likely to be to some degree or another a part of most residential programs. There are pitfalls in using offenders in this manner, but there are many benefits as well. Most of the ideas for this chapter have been learned from experience, and some have been learned the hard way.

References

Agee, V. M. (2002). Creating a positive milieu in residential treatment for adolescent sexual abusers. In B. K. Schwartz (Ed.), *The sex offender: Current treatment modalities and systems issues* (Vol. IV, pp. 29-1–29-22). Kingston, NJ: Civic Research Institute.

Blaske, D. M., Borduin, C. M., Henggeler, S. W., & Mann, B. J. (1989). Individual, family, and peer characteristics of adolescent sex offenders and assaultive offenders. *Developmental Psychology, 25*(5), 846–855.

Jones, M. (1953). *The therapeutic community*. New York: Basic Books.

Tingle, D., Barnard, G. W., Robbin, L., Newman., G., & Hutchinson, D. (1986). Childhood and adolescent characteristics of pedophiles and rapists. *International Journal of Law and Psychiatry, 9*, 103–116.

Ward, T. (2002). Good lives and the rehabilitation of offenders: Promises and problems. *Aggression and Violent Behavior, 7*(5), 513–528.

Ward, T., Hudson, S., & McCormick, J. (1997). Attachment style, intimacy deficits, and sexual offending. In B. K. Schwartz & H. R. Cellini (Eds.), *The sex offender: New insights, treatment innovations and legal developments* (Vol. II, pp. 2-1–2-14). Kingston, NJ: Civic Research Institute.

Ward, T., & Stewart, C. A. (2003). Good lives and the rehabilitation of sexual offenders. In T. Ward, D. R. Laws, & S. M. Hudson (Eds.), *Sexual deviance: Issues and controversies* (pp. 21–44). Thousand Oaks, CA: Sage.

Yablonski, L. (1989). *The therapeutic community*. New York: Gardner Press

Yalom, I. (1995). *The theory and practice of group psychotherapy* (4th ed.). New York: Basic Books.

Chapter 10

Spirituality in Male Sex Abuser Treatment

by Geral Blanchard, M.A., N.C.P., L.P.C.

OVERVIEW

University training in the fields of psychology, psychiatry, social work, and related professions has rarely addressed the integral role of spirituality in the resolution of behavioral and emotional problems. Spirituality is difficult to quantify, can be controversial, and consequently has never received respected standing in the counseling arena. However, although it would be theologically irresponsible for counselors to ignore scientific findings, it would be scientifically suicidal to disregard the deep impulses of the human spirit.

INTRODUCTION

Mental health professionals have shared an almost universal discomfort broaching matters of spirituality and religion. There has been a hesitancy to address spiritual issues with clients, because of treatment providers' fear that in doing so they might be perceived as being on the perimeter of their profession and thus might invite challenges to their legitimacy or be accused of imposing their personal belief system on vulnerable patients. Clinical psychologists are four times as likely to be atheists as average Americans (Shoto, 1999), which may, in part, help to explain some of the discomfort with religious and spiritual issues. Spirit-sensitive, transpersonal, and depth psychologists, although not considered mainstream, routinely recognize matters of the soul.

As forensic psychology and sex abuser treatment specializations rapidly developed over the last two decades, criminal issues entered the counseling profession's purview. As a result, legal and moral questions increasingly became counseling topics. While moralizing over client behavior leaves many counselors feeling ill at ease, it remains a requisite duty to alert every abuser to society's stance toward sexual crimes. Authors such as Doherty (1995) have reintroduced therapists to the important duty of developing client morality while being careful not to be shaming.

Spiritually based healing posits that sexual assaults are symptomatic of something greater, namely, a profound spiritual malaise or bankruptcy. As such, counselors must respect the symptom (Bettelheim, 1985). For some men, sexual abuse may have been the only perceived solution to a seemingly unmanageable and painful existence. However heinous or egodystonic the symptom, an abuser would likely not have risked engaging in the act unless it was thought to be desperately needed. To respect a symptom, then, means to recognize its urgent function. It further implies a need to respect the person creating the symptom.

SPIRITUALITY VS. RELIGION

Religion has been closely linked to and confused with spirituality. Separating the two concepts is useful, especially when attempting to increase the comfort level of counselors in approaching matters of morality and the soul. For the purposes of this treatise, religion will be regarded as the study of a set of commonly shared and practiced beliefs which are usually linked to a deity. Religion usually entails collective worship under a common set of beliefs, often with a priest figure serving as a middleman, go-between, and interpreter of externally sourced doctrines, duties, and prohibitions. Believers may tend to rely on an external locus of control and a vertical relationship with a deity.

Spirituality can be defined as *purposeful belongingness*. This suggests a connect-edness to other people along with an understanding of the meaning of human exis-tence. Spiritual practices are much more individually tailored than are religious prac-tices. Spirituality relies on the individual to look without and within, to develop and choose deeply personal creeds that positively guide his life. An inner locus of control is central to developing one's spirituality, yet it is nourished within a humble context of interrelatedness and interdependence. Spiritually based thinking purports that exis-tential crises are best seen as opportunities for developing spiritual beliefs that provide an inner refuge of hope, giving rise to personal agency, gratitude, joy, and courage (Sams, 1999; Griffith, 2003).

Spirituality has a relational focus. While emphasizing individual truths, it also focuses on interpersonal obligations. Native American/Canadian cultures recognize man's connection to all life forces and the attendant responsibilities to each of them. Aboriginal spirituality links all sources of energy—whether the power of the wind or the abstruse energy of a rock—as equally important partners in the Great Mystery. Unlike religion, which is hierarchical in nature, with man being subservient to a god, Native spirituality emphasizes equality.

Religion, with its shared beliefs and central deity, is celebrated in ceremonial and ritualized ways. In *Religion Explained*, Boyer (2001) wrote anthropologically of reli-gion's attempt to explain puzzling natural and mental phenomena: the origins of things, evil, suffering, causal powers of nonobservable entities, as well as salvation and deliverance of the soul. Religions are born of fears and feelings of helplessness; their parent-like gods and associated beliefs provide comfort and social order. They offer certitude and security, especially in difficult times.

Religions have evolutionary stages of development from fundamentalist unifor-mity (one size fits all) to manifesting uniquely mystical characteristics (Peck, 1987). Gods and institutions provide outside strength—an exoskeleton. When an external locus of control is central to a set of incipient religious beliefs, the god is often regard-ed as a despotic judge of human behavior, a celestial accountant who keeps a running tab of good and bad behaviors, a cosmic bellhop or heavenly vending machine that doles out gifts and favors, or simply a prayer depository where wishes are directed. At rudimentary levels of religious development, communication with a god is often a monologue, typically empty of fresh ideas, which supports old habits rather than inno-vation. It is likely that monological conversations sustain problems rather than resolve them (Griffith, 2003).

While religions often rely on rigid dogma with fateful consequences, spiritual practices tend to be "soft," emphasizing personal choice in their formation. As in Buddhist philosophy, Quaker faith, Sufism, or Native American world views, a fun-damental spiritual tenet holds that in looking inward one can find answers to almost any searing dilemma. These perspectives emphasize connections between all people and life forms. It follows that all life is a sacred interwoven network. No answer lays outside a person. Truths are carried within each individual because humans are con-nected to a giant universe inherently holding the answers to all matters of existence and survival. Using Thomas Edison's words, there is a "Supreme Intelligence" that flows through all of us with vast creative potential. As part of a universal intelligence or consciousness, humans can access solutions by drawing from that part of the whole residing within.

Religion and spirituality are ancient, abiding quests to connect with something greater and more trustworthy than our egos (Wolman, 2001). Recognizing that individuals are affiliated with a god, a system, or a humanity much larger and more powerful than themselves can be empowering. Tapping that connection is thought to provide a psychological immunity to many potentially pathological conditions. The key is not to lose one's individual integrity while living in relation to a system.

SPIRITUAL ISSUES IN THERAPY

The Sex Abuser's Soul

The wording of this subheading may seem sacrilegious to some individuals. To suggest that sex abusers have a preexisting spirit life, before therapists or priests get their hands on them and "fix" them, unnerves many people. Others may vindictively wish that an abuser's soul be left to languish eternally in some horrible, hellish place.

Despite contentious ideas about the possible soul life of men who have abused, the majority of people seem to struggle when defining the concept. Comparing definitions, the range of meanings is wide. Before helping professionals tamper with the souls of others, it is essential to identify what they are and where they can be found. Are they located in the brain, the heart, or in one's aura? Or are they more ethereal, with their whereabouts even more difficult to pinpoint?

The soul can be regarded as a nonmaterial essence of the universe embodied in humans. Generally it is thought to have moral and emotional facets—described by many as a force. Some envision this unseen force as connecting humans to creative and sustaining energies far bigger than themselves—something Native Americans term "the Creator" or "Great Mystery." Or, the soul may be entirely a mental construct. It has been described as spiritual principles and inner feelings that set one's countenance. It is different from a conscience, which is a faculty or power, that guides behavior along paths of right and wrong.

To better understand the soul, imagine it as a spirit life emanating from two sources: external and internal experiences. The external realm of development comes from the culture in which a person is embedded. Religion may be such an influential factor. The internal realm is more amorphous and can be experienced through feelings, imagination, dreams, meditations, hallucinations, rituals, ceremonies, spirit worlds, or magic. When people speak of soul work, they are usually referring to going within, exploring holy inner landscapes, and developing themselves along sacred paths. From this perspective, going within usually requires a person to leave behind culturally instilled messages of wrongdoing and rightdoing (Breton & Largent, 1998). Soul searching has to do with unearthing who a person is and what he or she stands for. Staying awake and attuned to the soul is central to spiritual development—where it has been, where it is now, and in what direction it yearns to move.

Morality and Moralizing

Over the first seven or more decades of psychotherapy's history, patients routinely came to therapy with clear, but often rigid, ideas of personal responsibility for a wide array of problems. Therapists attempted to liberate people from oppressive guilt, inhibitions, and strict rules of conventional religious morality. They catered to the self-interest of patients. Therapists may unwittingly have promoted an ethic called expressive individualism, by which social responsibilities were ultimately satisfied by attending to personal interests (Bellah, 1985). Hillman and Ventura (1992) contend that the most accepted models of psychotherapy have contributed to the breakdown of community by ignoring societal needs while championing personal concerns. Morality, however, must be a personal as well as a communal matter.

While psychotherapy has helped individuals grow while attending to their narcissistic needs, rarely has it addressed community well-being (May, 1992). Doherty (1995) expanded the recrimination, writing, "Psychological language tends to be long on explanation and short on responsibility" (p. 27). In today's sex abuser treatment field a decidedly different posture must be assumed, one that takes into account selfish and harmful choices made by exploitive individuals and holds them accountable.

It has often been deemed politically incorrect to discuss morality in the psychotherapeutic domain. Many professionals express fear that by injecting moral considerations into therapeutic dialogues, some counselors may cave into a conservative agenda of the political right. It must be noted that the counseling profession has already been prevailed upon by powerful public pressure to retributively respond to abusers. Often therapists capitulate to society's longing for vengeance and, while desiring to retain community status and financial viability, they assume parallel postures. This can come at the expense of jettisoning the professional principle of providing respectful, humanistic care to all clients. Abusive men are routinely objectified by both the public and their counselors, being reduced to denigrating labels (perverts, chi-mos, etc.), with antagonists refusing to acknowledge our clients' individual humanity. Similar references would never be tolerated from abusers when speaking of victims (Blanchard, 1998).

Moral discourse is a legitimate and integral component of sex abuser treatment. Like pastoral counselors, sex abuser therapists are also moral consultants. Not moral judges or moral dictators but facilitators of ethical and moral dialogues. Therapists accompany clients on the "Healing Path" as they explore, formulate, reject, revise, and better apply their revered beliefs. A therapist's first charge is to create a fertile, safe, reverent, and inviting climate for this work to be done. In an attempt to ennoble men on this sacred journey, a therapeutic task is to validate and reinforce individual values that approximate societal mores.

Feminist therapy has made many contributions to our field. A vigorous moral undergirding has always been an integral facet of feminist theory. It compels counselors to be explicitly clear about their stance on issues of sexual aggression and other injustices. Unlike the sex abuser treatment field and its oversight organizations, feminist therapists have been unafraid to challenge existing political and societal paradigms. With uneasiness the counseling profession has been challenged to rethink its way of doing business, being cajoled instead in the direction of doing justice. After all, sex abuser-specific therapy is a corrective intervention applied in response to oppression and abuse arising out of power differentials, privilege, prejudice, and injustice.

Understandably, therapists occasionally experience anger toward clients. It is even more comprehensible to expect abusers to engender strong countertransference reactions when recounting their crimes. At such times it is not uncommon to hear moralistic comments being directed toward clients, often with a shaming tone. Shame alienates clients from their therapists and hampers recovery. Moralizing, however, can be delivered in a fashion that is devoid of harmful shame and, in fact, enhances self-esteem. It functions best when appealing to virtues held closest to the abuser's heart—as therapists acknowledge and affirm the client's moral sensibilities and language. When clients sense a therapist is endeavoring to unearth the best in them, they are more likely to fully engage in treatment.

Healing vs. Retributive Models

A collective frustration in containing the epidemic of sexual abuse has caused some healers to reexamine historical spiritual practices that offer solutions to contemporary problems. One very inspirational challenge to the retributive approach of sexual abuse treatment was undertaken by the Hollow Water Ojibway Nation of Manitoba (Ross, 1996). A tribal mover and shaker, Burma Bushie—after years of frustration dealing with the powerful male-dominated administration of her tribe, the federal courts, and psychologists—returned to the sacred teachings of tribal elders and resurrected ancient, spiritual healing ceremonies. At the core of Hollow Water's treatment program is the community's responsibility for eradicating sexual abuse. It collectively teaches interpersonal obligations rather than merely the prohibition of sexual abuse. A healing shift occurred from expounding "Thou shalt nots," to teaching interpersonal duties expressed as "Thou shalts." Another shift was to not think of sexual abuse as broken laws but as fractured relationships.

Duality has a divine purpose, Sams (1999) wrote; it teaches through opposites. By comparing retributive legal systems to Hollow Water's healing model, spiritually based treatment gains clarity. Central to this model are several dichotomies:

- Healing is more humane and effective than punishing.

- People can be taught more effectively by storytelling than by lecturing or shaming.

- Therapists do not represent the primary change agent; support circles and communities do.

- Sexual abusers are not the only persons on the Healing Path; all people heal in the supportive company of each other.

- *Nouning* abusers ("nounsense") with pathologizing diagnostic labels freezes them in unhealthy identities and prohibits growth. *Verbing* them (referring to them as growing, evolving, unfolding, etc.) creates attitudes of hopefulness, fostering change.

- Healing abusers is more likely to occur in the company of victims, while the abuser is being reintegrated into the community, rather than when the abuser is banished to penitentiaries. If isolation is symptomatic of sexual abuse, community involvement will encourage healing.

Canadian Crown Prosecutor Rupert Ross (1996) asserted, "Aboriginal healing processes constantly stress values like respect, sharing, humility, and so forth. It has to do with an understanding that the Healing Path is not something that 'sick' people need, totally 'healthy' people supervise and the rest of us ignore." He concluded, "It is a path we must all walk on" (p. 189).

Spiritually based intervention projects, such as Hollow Water's Community Holistic Circle Healing Program, have certainly had their skeptics, not least of which was the Canadian government. The Solicitor General of Canada (Buller, 2000) researched the purported effectiveness of this project and discovered that not only did restorative justice dramatically reduce recidivism, it saved millions of tax dollars too. Ellerby (2003) applied similar spiritual components to an urban (Winnipeg) sex abuser program. The wellness programming at Native Clan diminished recidivism far more effectively than conventional methods of treatment, and it encouraged more participants to stay engaged in the healing program postdischarge.

PSYCHOEDUCATIONAL AND SPIRITUAL ISSUES AND TECHNIQUES IN SEX OFFENDER PROGRAMMING

Fifteen years ago, Blanchard (1989) identified many psychoeducational issues integral to sex abuser programming, among them anger, control, conflict resolution, amends, self-esteem, victim empathy, narcissism, cognitive distortions, personal victimization, addictions, and humor. Almost as an afterthought, and with trepidation over collegial rebuff, Blanchard referenced spiritual development as part and parcel of all recovery plans. Upon later examination of spiritually oriented literature, it became clear that most spiritual traditions focused on similar developmental issues as sex abuser treatment, simply using different language. What follows are examples of how some of these issues are addressed in groups.

Meditation

Daily reflection is a disciplined way to continuously examine spiritual matters. It is called meditation by some clients, prayerfulness by others. The purpose is to create a reverent attentiveness and inner silence that allows self-knowledge to unfold. The quiet, still time can be imagined as a way to exercise spiritual muscles, building their strength. The Monks of New Skete (1999), in their book on happiness, used the term "spiritual athletes" to describe persons who regularly practice contemplative regimens. What characterizes such individuals are the questions that consume them, as opposed to the clear answers they once professed to have. Slowing down the wheels of the mind through meditation tends to diminish impulsivity, which is a frequent catalyst to sexual assaultiveness. A meaningful spiritual journey requires seekers to abandon notions of "what we can get out of it." Instead, it entails a process of stripping the bond to selfishness through quiet self-examination.

Narcissism, Personal Awareness, and Self-Control

When Buddhist scholars reference *egolessness*, *selflessness*, *dying to self*, or *ego death*, they are addressing a movement away from narcissism and self-absorption. The *false self* falls away as seekers discover who they really are. Buddhist philosophy emphasizes altruism by offering service to others. Abusers are more receptive to hearing a message that invites (rather than dictates) change and may be more inclined to "sign on" when ideas originates from outside the field of psychology and are delivered in reverent language. Many therapists have found that Buddhist psychology provides a more palatable approach than conventional modalities (Welwood, 2000; Epstein, 1998).

People tend to control things primarily because they fear them. The Eastern concept of *mindfulness* provides a way to reclaim control over emotions. It is also challenges distorted and airtight thought processes. Mindfulness resembles the cognitive therapy technique of *thought stopping*. It can be taught as a form of self-monitoring when individuals learn how to hone skills of self-observation to razor sharpness, as they search for raw truths about themselves and the world.

From a Buddhist perspective, an ordinary state of consciousness can be likened to a form of sleep. Mindfulness entails a total commitment to awakening (or remaining awake) to all thoughts and feelings, and to ride out painful emotions like a surfboarder atop a powerful wave. This viewpoint does not suggest the immediate eradication of pain but, rather, a willingness to stay with it and come to know it.

Buddhist psychology sees unconsciousness (or unawareness) as an adversary residing within, having little to do with other persons or outside threats. Clients are encouraged to note how often they hijack their own thoughts, holding themselves captive in jails of their own minds—prisons of their own construction.

The bottom line is: Men can't be allowed to cognitively play dirty with themselves. And if they tend to envision the mind as a computer, they must realize who is sitting at the keyboard. At the same time, they are encouraged to realize how certain forms of control are healthy—like mental and emotional control.

Cognitive Distortions

Exploring mental schemas is described in the spiritual text, *Emotional Alchemy* (Bennett-Goleman, 2001). The author offers a way of reexamining ingrained prejudices, fears, judgments, and erroneous mind-sets. Using Eastern spiritual philosophies for guidance, men can be encouraged to continuously reexamine childhood ideas from a more mature adult viewpoint. Because many abusers have not developed a discerning mind, their schemas serve as screening systems generating fear and rage when anything reminiscent of past, painful experiences unfolds. Men are encouraged to patiently investigate feelings rather than immediately repress them. This mindful walking challenges unconscious habits. It appeals to some clients as a way to unshackle themselves from chronic attachments to unhealthy thought processes.

Vision Quests as Therapy

By applying Native spiritual concepts of the vision quest, men are again invited to look inward during periods of solitude to find answers to perplexing issues. I have personally observed how one of Sweden's maximum security prisons has used this ancient practice by allowing sexual murderers to go on escorted vision quests in the forested north country. There they endeavor to find answers to hurtful patterns that have enveloped them.

Therapists may find success by appealing to masculine concepts of bravery or courage as an abuser is exhorted to become a *spiritual warrior* on his quest. While men frequently regard psychotherapy as a "waste of time," or "something women do," the vision quest is a repackaged form of self-examination that works for many.

Anger, Victimization, and Conflict Resolution

To formulate an ethical center, men are presented with a menu of belief systems designed to provoke thinking and growth. Quaker philosophy, for example, speaks of the *light within*—a divine internal truth that can be discovered in a circle of individual silent, inward reflection while in the reverent company of Friends. Quaker beliefs profess taking social action against injustice, oppression, victimization, and suffering. There is an emphasis on equality and service to others (vs. exploitation) that diminishes narcissistic thinking and promotes altruism, offering an escape from selfish habits. In service, men also honor themselves by discovering their own gifts and recognizing them as being worthy of sharing.

Nonviolence, another Quaker tenet, is professed to require great courage. When attacked in volatile interpersonal encounters, men have the opportunity to do more than just emotionally react. They can elect to take a measured, strong, yet peaceful response to resolving heated conflicts, one that affords them personal dignity. Viewing the movie *Gandhi* in group therapy, for example, has served as a springboard for discussing the bravery implicit in choosing a nonviolent posture when confronted with hostility or violence.

The Alternatives to Violence anger management program, developed by the Friends General Conference, uses a spiritual approach to manage men's anger (Apsey, Bristol, & Eppler, 1991). Numerous prisons now use this method, which emphasizes nonviolent conflict resolution techniques from a Gandhian perspective.

Addictions and Spirituality

Addiction can be defined as the excessive use of pleasure and excitement to obliterate emotional pain. It reflects spiritual starvation. Addictions are often described in spiritual language as a clinging or an attachment. Kasl (1999) wrote, "When we don't find meaning in life, we seek stimulation instead" (p. 123). She further contends that a person cannot be spiritual and addictive at the same time; they are mutually exclusive.

Without spiritual anchoring, abusers are left bereft and discontented. Eastern spiritual philosophies have traditionally suggested embracing one's addiction for its lessons, quite a contrast to the eviction remedy espoused by most counselors and religions. German psychoanalyst Fritz Perls warned, "What we resist, persists." Pushing the problem aside without examining it, guarantees its return. Similarly, in *Saints and Madmen* (Shorto, 1999), Papineau is quoted as saying, "god is in the beer" (p. 232) a provocative way of suggesting addictions hold many spiritual clues to recovery. Sexual abuse, a pain-relieving, addictive activity begs the questions, "What pain and suffering is being sedated?" Spiritual angst perhaps?

Childhood Maltreatment

Lifelong suffering can result from unresolved childhood abuse that ultimately is acted out in exploitive ways. Confronting an abuser's histories of maltreatment allows them to be reframed as opportunities for insight and growth afforded through suffering. Black clients frequently look to the words of Martin Luther King, Jr., for spiritual guidance in making sense of suffering. King spoke of the redemptive power of suffering; a potential fuel for change, not just an albatross weighing a person down, hindering his enjoyment of life.

From a Buddhist perspective, present-day attachment to pain creates resentment and suffering. Relief comes from focusing on the fact that the trauma is over—that it is best regarded as history. And instead of retaliating, the *Tao Te Ching* of Chinese Taoism suggests, "Repay resentment with integrity" (Lao Tzu, 1990, p. 33).

Using Native American language, therapists can encourage men to bravely approach and confront painful histories and, in doing so, envision themselves as *counting coup*. Like an Indian warrior, they boldly approach disturbing memories on their terms, at their chosen time. In doing so, intrusive memories and flashbacks are less inclined to erupt. In addition, an animal totem may be sought on vision quest that emboldens them in times of distress. A strong and symbolic animal—perhaps a bear, a wolf, or an eagle—can be used as a guide that imbues the men with their unique survival powers.

Clinicians are frequently irritated by the abuser's victim language. Many clients with abuse histories are quite comfortable posturing themselves as victims. This can reflect irresponsibility, helplessness, and fear. It may indicate an underdeveloped ability to empower themselves and take responsibility for their emotional condition. Abusers can eventually come to the realization that nobody has ever abused them more than they themselves have. Overcoming a victim mentality requires clinicians to encourage men to become explorers, adventurers, and risk takers who must leap into the fire of spiritual growth and take charge of their thinking, their lives, and ultimately their happiness. The men can conceptualize themselves as warriors who are fighting to shed a parasitic influence on their minds. The counselor's task is to help them examine child-like, fear-based, and self-limiting thinking while throwing logs on their spiritual fire. This is done by carefully speaking of the need to wisely let go of timidity, to claim hidden inner strengths, and to be courageous—all ways of appealing to culturally sanctioned masculine values.

Abandoning Negativity

Cynicism and negativity can be presented as handicaps to be defeated. Again, abusers are often victims of themselves, creating unhappiness by electing to continuously replay depressing thoughts. The enemy they are searching for is usually not lurking outside of themselves, but hides in the locked recesses of their minds. The Monks of New Skete (2002) suggest that happiness is created through spiritual growth, and they provide a "softer" version of Orthodox Catholicism that emphasizes personal choice. They recommend taking a verbal inventory of personal blessings when disheartened, something they call "attitudes of gratitude." In doing so, negativity is quickly neutralized.

Friedrich Nietzsche (1886) alluded to a vital link between lightheartedness and spirituality when he wrote, "I can only believe in a God who dances" (p. 191). Humor can be used to help clients drop their guard, laugh at themselves and their foibles, and be less overcontrolled. It is often easier to expose touchy issues, or to swallow difficult information, when laughter or teasing is present. As said in the old adage, "A spoon full of sugar helps the medicine go down."

SPIRITUAL RECOVERY IN ACTION

Practicing mindfulness and examining old schemas is important to recovery. They are essentially cognitive therapy techniques that are insight-oriented. Action, however, is even more important than altered thinking. Borrowing from Alcoholics Anonymous slogans, abusers are invited to "Act as if," to "Fake it 'til you make it," or to "Act your way into a new way of feeling." Moving from thoughts to action takes men to another level of recovery, helping them realize they are accomplishing something tangible in the counseling process. Men who have abused must dramatically alter their entire way of *being* in the world. Dramatic changes in behaviors must permeate their everyday activities and generate an entirely new lifestyle. The behavioral alterations serve as constant reminders of the abusive lifestyle they are leaving behind.

Believing—as most spiritual teachers and humanistic psychologists do—that every person has inherent goodness inside them, clinicians must find ways to bring out that positive essence. Men often require demonstrable evidence of their worthiness—especially after committing a sex crime. Cheerleading is not enough. Positive behavioral changes offer tangible proof of self-worth and must be spotlighted whenever possible. To this end, some clinicians are moving away from a strict and exclusive emphasis on assault cycles and, instead, are inviting men to develop wellness cycles. What sets wellness cycles apart is an emphasis on what is strong rather than what is broken. These clinicians require clients to identify behavioral choices that are linked to positive experiences. As *Reality Therapy* (Glasser, 1965) suggests, clients are to be asked, "What are you doing?" and "Does it seem to be helping?" By making healthy choices along with personal judgments of their effectiveness, men are inclined to ascertain the necessary components of a wellness plan. In doing this work, group facilitators ask men to "defend" their successes, explaining what is responsible for their happiness—an exercise that is entirely new to most of them.

Amends Through Community Service

Without relinquishing significant personal disdain for the commission of their crimes and coming to an acceptance of their good side, men can languish in unproductive shame (vs. healthy guilt). And shame has been linked to explosive rage (Fossum & Mason, 1986). Making amends and providing community service not only demonstrate responsibility but bolster self-esteem and commence self-forgiveness.

Direct and indirect amends may take many forms. Examples include the following: a man who molested children delivered "Meals on Wheels" to senior citizens; men incarcerated for rape tamed wild horses, readying them for adoption; an abusive counselor provided musical worship at his church; a client who engaged in fetishistic burglaries anonymously shoveled sidewalks for the elderly; a parolee convicted of rape visited prisons, inspiring inmates toward growth; a doctor convicted of patient rape spoke to other physicians about the abuse of power. The focus on community service resembles *communitarian* philosophy, which strongly encourages heeding social responsibilities and moral commitments (Etzioni, 1993).

Restorative Justice

Restorative justice approaches to healing relationships can be powerfully therapeutic for victims and abusers. Perpetrators of sex crimes (and, often more effectively, surrogate abusers) can sit in peacemaking circles with victims of sexual assault and learn of the aggrieved person's confusion, suffering, and traumatization (Pranis, Stuart, & Wedge, 2003). It is astonishing to witness the healing that occurs within both persons when careful planning has gone into this type of *carefrontation*. Even when a surrogate sits in for an absent or uncooperative abuser, the restoration to health for both parties can be phenomenal.

Enhancing Social Skills

Most sexual abusers have deficits in their social skills. Until they learn how to relate to all parts of themselves, they cannot take the next step of practicing how to relate to others. This necessitates carefully chosen and monitored social encounters that provide opportunities to practice assertiveness, small talk, setting boundaries, breaking the ice, or developing healthy intimacy through judicious self-disclosure. Men's groups—whether service or therapy oriented—can provide settings to enhance social skills. One man found that Toastmasters, a public speaking club, bolstered his self-confidence. Other men have chosen Bible study groups as a place for growth. Recreational opportunities can be helpful too; men have joined softball, bowling, and hockey teams. A secondary benefit of socializing is to assist the successful reintegration of these men into their communities so they no longer feel alienated or estranged. Community acceptance is a powerful antidote to offending.

When it comes to satisfying dating and marital relationships, two frequently recommended relationship guides are *If the Buddha Dated* (Kasl, 1999) and *If the Buddha Married* (Kasl, 2001). The value-based books provide methods to effectively overcome relationship hurdles by addressing topics such as defenselessness, face-saving apologies, compromise, assertiveness, time-outs, constructive use of anger, "I" statements, self-soothing (particularly important for sexually addicted sex abusers and anger rapists), brainstorming, and forgiveness. Almost universally, men report pride and deepened intimacy after implementing relationship-enhancing techniques.

Forgiveness

Struggling to forgive others, many abusers cannot "bury the hatchet," or understand the concept of "letting go." Generally, they cannot forgive another person until they have forgiven themselves. One definition of forgiveness that offers a desirable degree of personal control, while putting anger and resentment behind, states: "I no longer hold you responsible for how I am feeling today." In assuming this position the past is not forgotten, nor its seriousness or consequences, but they cast aside some animosity by choosing to take responsibility for their current emotional state. Again, the strong need to control their own thoughts and emotions can initiate a willingness to forgive.

Often men fear that forgiveness will open them up to be hurt again. Fear sets in. When they realize, however, that they can choose any emotional state in the moment and are not merely reactors, the process of letting go can diminish their fears. Similarly, resentment is a choice to remember and to refeel the original hurt and anger. Forgiveness is a way of putting those unpleasant emotions in the past as well. It is a way to feel good in the moment.

Building a Personal Identity

Creating or retooling a personal identity starts with an examination of disowned parts of the self. Men are asked to develop a personal creed and commit themselves to it. By telling personally sacred stories of justice or injustice, suffering and pain, or even politics, the memorable narratives highlight individual values. The clinician underscores the strength of character displayed in the stories, culling out noble truths.

For example, one man described a 70-year-old storekeeper who was being robbed when he came upon the scene. He frightened the youthful thieves upon entering the store and pursued them as they fled, pinning one against a fence until the police arrived. Then he personally returned a stolen item that had been retrieved to the storekeeper. Upon the man's recounting the story in group, a facilitator was able to call attention to several values upheld in the story: a distaste for exploitation of vulnerable individuals, respect for elders, and a desire to undo similar behavior committed during the man's adolescence. The story served as a springboard for updating his personal identity.

Similarly, men are asked to bring inspirational videos to "movie night" and play selected portions that are of importance to them. By witnessing their heroes (vs. celebrities) in action—from John Wayne to Jesus—other group members see what each man wants to stand for, and the facilitators seize every opportunity for the personal enactment of those beliefs. On other occasions men read books about spiritual mentors or display photos of role models in different places. Always, the intent is to accelerate them in the direction of purposeful choices that are grounded in values rather than being thoughtless and impulsive. Ultimately, each man is encouraged to become his own hero by bringing his whole person to consciousness.

Sweatlodge

Having Apache and Northern Cheyenne spiritual advisers on staff has provided novel therapeutic experiences in the Sheridan clinic. The sweatlodge is a place where men are introduced to reverent, prayerful ways. After work hours, or on weekends, clients periodically sit partially clothed on Mother Earth giving thanks for their many blessings, while sending good wishes upward on behalf of friends and antagonists alike. Meditations of gratitude are essential components of a spiritually based recovery program. The sweatlodge affords an excellent environment to nurture attitudes of thankfulness that can supplant vengeful emotions. Again, Jamie Sam's poignant words from *Dancing the Dream*:

Every time we show gratitude for the millions of ways we are blessed daily, we send our energy into the unseen world of the Dream Weave, and those threads of gratitude strengthen our spiritual connections. The resulting fabric of trust and faith is the safety net that catches us when we go through a Dark Night of the Soul, protecting us against the internal enemy of victim thinking. (p. 22)

Inspirational Readings

Meditation is an activity that begins and ends satisfying days. Men in recovery may post inspiring words at key work or home locations that are remindful mantras. Just as they realize that unhealthy sexual fantasies lead to harmful choices, analogously, uplifting thoughts can stimulate random acts of kindness. Surrounded by photos, quotes, and slogans, their values remain in the forefront and become integrated into daily decision-making processes.

For instance, one man struggled with his anger toward a prosecutor (a man with a history of being sexually abusive himself) who had a penchant for arbitrarily recommending unreasonably long jail sentences for sex criminals. This client, wanting to take the high road, taped a note to his dashboard that cited Booker T. Washington's quote: "Let no man pull you so low as to hate another." It was his way of reminding himself to rise above resentment and vengefulness.

Spiritually oriented groups customarily begin and end with an uplifting reading, a "thought for the day." Group members volunteer to select inspirational readings that set the tone for the onset and closing of meetings. Facilitators have noted how men banter with each other over the chance to be a lector, wanting to disclose messages dear to them. From the readings, they often leave each other with a challenge to carry the thought into daily life.

USING RITUALS, CEREMONY, AND GRADUATIONS

When spirituality becomes central to sex offender-specific groups, a sense of family rapidly develops. Instead of revulsion and a resistance to being in an abuser group, the reverent tone of the meetings fosters feelings of belonging. Identities and positive bonds are fashioned around sacred activities, and routinely men express the desire to return to group following graduation

Roose-Evans (1995), distinguished between ritual and ceremony. Rituals, he explained, mark a conceived transition from one way of being to another, often accomplished in the company of others. They work on two levels, the psychological and the spiritual, and sometimes they merge. Rituals reach beneath consciousness to a deeper intelligence. They heighten the intensity of shared activity by establishing a profound experience: bringing order to people's lives, helping them cope in an uncertain world, and creating feelings of belonging. Ancient rituals bring timeless and sanctified power to groups. When clients are given opportunities to devise their own rituals, the results can be uniquely poignant.

Ceremonies are different than rituals in subtle ways. Ceremonies are the elements of rituals. Examples could include smudging, music, readings, periods of silence, lighting a candle, and so on. Collectively, they comprise a ritual.

Rites of passage mark transformations and change. They are commonly associated with moving from childhood to adulthood. One of their primary functions is to facilitate a change in personal identity. Clients who have sexually abused must reconcile the fact that they are what society has defined as "sex offenders." It is important, late in the healing process, to discard pathological identities, moving men from being sex offenders to seeing themselves as recovering abusers. As healing progresses, clinicians must outwardly note how unhealthy facets of men's personalities are being discarded in favor of more prosocial beliefs and behaviors. Graduation from the group is a rite of passage and as much a sine qua non of treatment, if not more so, as any other therapeutic technique.

Graduation rituals and ceremonies are important. Adding pomp and circumstance to graduations cements client lifestyle changes in place and graduations are most effective when great reverence and significance are attached to the transition. The process also locks new identities more firmly in place—old criminal identities being abandoned. How the men experience themselves thereafter will be dramatically altered. Graduates are in essence *verbed*, meaning they are formally being reminded of their change. They have moved to new developmental levels. And with the transition comes the realistic hope that the risk of recidivism has been diminished.

QUALITIES OF A SPIRITUALLY BASED CLINICIAN

The field of psychology, through its ethical guidelines and licensing agents, has attempted to ensure quality client care. In this effort, a rule-bound approach has been instituted with only a modicum of success. While rules set limits to therapist's conduct, restrictions do not address the desired character of spiritually oriented healers, nor the tone of therapeutic relationships.

Psychology has been much more comfortable with the language of ethics and techniques than with language of caring and morality. Yet, caring almost always surpasses technique in its curative value. And spontaneous natural care goes much further in effectuating change than does constrained ethical care. Effective sex abuser clinicians generally exhibit a dignified, respectful, and sensitive regard toward their often difficult clients (Blanchard, 1998). Being empathically present with clients is significantly more important than figuring them out. When injecting a spiritual component in counseling, even more careful consideration of the therapist's characteristics and "way of being" is essential.

Many clinicians, much like aboriginal shamans, enter the healing arts as a result of traumatic life experiences (Sander & Wong, 1997). This is not necessarily a drawback. It can be a legitimate initiation experience upon entering the profession. Knowing suffering—and, more important, knowing how to overcome the effects of suffering—can be valuable assets for counselors who carry their own wounds while accompanying clients on the Healing Path. Unacknowledged or unresolved pain, however, can threaten client safety. This is especially true when dealing with sexual issues, circumstances under which boundary problems easily arise.

It is incumbent upon therapists to manifest a solid base of spirituality when guiding spiritually based healing. This approach requires healers to be grounded in the similarity—the common humanity—between therapists and clients (Frattaroli, 2001). Client struggles are resonant with clinician struggles. As clients grow, counselors must simultaneously journey in the same honest fashion. In addition, clinicians must recognize that they do not cure their clients; they stand witness, which is an honor by itself. *Every* traveler on the path is a messenger offering gifts for mutual change. As psychiatrist Jonas Robitscher (1980) aptly wrote: "Good psychotherapy is an engagement of two people that leaves both changed. If only one changes, therapy has been a failure" (p. 488).

CONCLUSION

We are more than human beings on a spiritual journey. We are spiritual beings on a human journey. No exceptions. All of us are growing and transforming—together on the Healing Path. The journey requires an ongoing creation and recreation of a personal spirituality and belief system, which is more important than a static adherence to a set of fixed beliefs. The process of spiritually unfolding is an essential factor to happiness. And happy men are not inclined to assault.

Psychologists can be likened to fisherman, throwing lines into an unexplored lake. The fish caught depends on the kind of hook and bait used. Alert to their own limitations, wise healers bring to the healing situation a wide array of fishing tackle. Among the tackle available is the power of spirituality. Native clients have repeatedly and emphatically avowed that spirituality is the most crucial and engaging factor at the core of any recovery program. Because their languages tend to be heavily reliant on verbs over nouns, change is expected, is assumed, and occurs.

Decisions to abuse, along with the damaging consequences, are frequently the catalysts for spiritual transformations—facilitating major breakthroughs rather than breakdowns. To assist the recovery process, healers must be careful not to freeze clients in the Dark Nights of the Soul with a penchant for labeling or pathologizing, or with an unfounded pessimism about the potential for recovery. Every person holds the potential to walk into a stiff wind and be blown over by it or, like an airplane, to be uplifted. It is about personal choice. An informed, positive choice can be made most easily in a spiritually alive environment.

> If we treat people as they are, they are going to remain the same. If we treat them as they can be, then there is all that potential for health, healing, change, and hope.

> —Ojibway elder

References

Apsey, L. S., Bristol, J., & Eppler, K. (1991). *Transforming power for peace.* New York: Alternatives to Violence Project.

Bellah, R. (1985). *Habits of the heart: Individualism and commitment in American life.* Berkeley: University of California Press.

Bennett-Goleman, T. (2001). *Emotional alchemy.* New York: Three Rivers.

Bettelheim, B. (1985). *A home for the heart.* Chicago: University of Chicago Press.

Blanchard, G. (1989). *Sex offender treatment: A psychoeducational model.* Minneapolis, MN: Institute for Behavioral Medicine.

Blanchard, G. (1998). *The difficult connection.* Brandon, VT: Safer Society Press.

Boyer, P. (2001). *Religion explained.* New York: Basic Books.

Breton, D., & Largent, C. (1998). *Love, soul & freedom.* Center City, MN: Hazelden.

Buller, E. (2000). *A cost benefit analysis of Hollow Water's community holistic circle healing process.* Ottawa, Ontario: Solicitor General Canada.

Doherty, W. (1995). *Soul searching.* New York: Basic Books.

Ellerby, L. (2003, October 10). *Entering the gateway of indigenous knowledge.* Paper presented at Research and Treatment Conference of the Association for Treatment of Sex Abusers, St. Louis, MO.

Epstein, M. (1998). *Going to pieces without falling apart.* New York: Broadway Books.

Etzioni, A. (1993). *The spirit of community.* New York: Simon & Schuster.

Fossum, M., & Mason, M. (1986). *Facing shame.* New York: Norton.

Frattaroli, E. (2001). *Healing the soul in the age of the brain.* New York: Penguin Putnam.

Glasser, W. (1965). *Reality therapy.* New York: Harper & Row.

Griffith, J. (2003). *Encountering the sacred in psychotherapy.* New York: Guilford Press.

Hillman, J., & Ventura, M. (1992). *We've had a hundred years of psychotherapy—And the world's getting worse.* San Francisco: Harper.

Kasl, C. (1999). *If the Buddha dated.* New York: Penguin.

Kasl, C. (2001). *If the Buddha married.* New York: Penguin Compass.

Lao Tzu. (1990). *Tao Te Ching.* New York: Bantam.

May, R. (1992). Foreword. In K. Freedheim (Ed.), *History of psychotherapy* (p. xxv). Washington, DC: American Psychological Association.

Monks of New Skete. (1999). *The Monks of New Skete.* Boston: Little, Brown.

Nietszche, F. (1989). *Beyond good and evil.* New York: Vintage Books. (Original work published 1886)

Peck, S. (1987). *The different drummer.* New York: Simon & Schuster.

Pranis, K., Stuart, B., & Wedge, M. (2003). *Peacemaking circles.* St. Paul, MN: Living Justice Press.

Robitscher, J. (1980). *The powers of psychiatry.* Boston: Houghton Mifflin.

Roose-Evans, J. (1995). *Passages of the soul.* Rockport, MA: Element Books.

Ross, R. (1996). *Returning to the teachings.* Toronto, Ontario, Canada: Penguin.

Sams, J. (1999). *Dancing the dream.* San Francisco: Harper.

Sander, D., & Wong, S. (1997). *The sacred heritage.* New York: Routledge.

Shorto, R. (1999). *Saints and madmen.* New York: Holt.

Welwood, J. (2002). *Toward a psychology of awakening.* Boston: Shambala.

Part 4

Adult Community Supervision

This section presents three descriptions of programs that attempt to aid in the transition of sex offenders back into their communities, thus enhancing the readjustment process and not only benefiting the individual offender but increasing community safety as well. The models range from a prison-based approach in Washington State, to educating family and friends regarding the offender's treatment, to an example of the containment model that is operating in the Commonwealth of Massachusetts to enhance parole supervision for sex offenders, to a Canadian-based implementation of a restorative justice program.

As good as a residential program may be, regardless of whether it is based in a prison or in a commitment facility or is a juvenile residential treatment center, transition is a crucial time. The changes an offender experiences as he moves from a highly structured environment into the freedom of the community can be overwhelming. Not only must one overcome the subtle and not so subtle effects of institutionalization but today the sex offender must also cope with the effects of public notification and its implications.

In an ideal world, the released sex offender would be on some type of mandated community supervision using a model with a specialized sex offender treatment provider working closely with a probation/parole or other type of community supervisor with expertise in this population, and with both having access to a specifically trained polygrapher. The U.S. Department of Justice's Center for Sex Offender Management has endorsed the containment approach as the most effective model for supervision of sex offenders in the community. In Chapter 11, Debra Baker, who serves as the therapist representative on the team, describes this paradigm, which involves the close networking of the supervising officer who may be a parole or probation officer, the sex offender therapist, and a polygrapher. The close cooperation and communication of these professionals provides a way to supervise the offender using a variety of approaches as well as the latest technology (e.g., global positioning monitoring). Massachusetts has implemented the Intensive Parole Supervision for Sex Offenders program at their Framington office, which provides supervision for individuals in many of the surrounding communities. The parole officers have a caseload of twenty-five offenders rather than the usual fifty. More recently, victim advocates have been added to the team with the role of representing the victim in the decision-making process and, if desired, keeping these individuals informed of relevant information. Intensive Parole for Sex Offenders (IPSO) has had outstanding success in improving community safety.

In dealing with the problem of reintegrating sex offenders back into knowledgeable support systems, the Washington State Department of Corrections Sex Offender Treatment Program, located at Twin Rivers Correctional Center, instituted a series of family support seminars. In Chapter 12, Anmarie Aylward discusses how family and friends of incarcerated sex offenders participating in the program are invited to the facility to meet with the staff and become familiar with the treatment program and the staff providing it. Helping the support system members understand concepts such as relapse prevention will ideally make these individuals better able to provide the offender with informed assistance when the offender returns to the community.

Today sex offenders must contend with public notification that can often impede their ability to gain housing and/or employment. If the goal is to lower the risk of reoffense, wouldn't it be much more efficacious if the community were willing to offer support rather than enmity to returning offenders? Robin Wilson and Janice Picheca in Chapter 13 offer a Canadian-based model grounded in the philosophy of restorative justice (known as Circles of Support and Accountability). According this approach, knowledgeable community volunteers are trained to provide support to the reintegrating sex offender. They have demonstrated an impressive level of success in helping these individuals become functioning members of the community.

Community safety is of utmost importance in dealing with sex offenders. However, what appears on the surface to enhance safety is not always an empirically sound approach. Legislators are all too ready to attach their names to policies that may appeal to the general public but may actually make the problem worse. Only by carefully studying the efficacy of various approaches will public officials be able to implement programs that truly assist sex offenders in controlling their behavior after their release.

Chapter 11

Intensive Parole Supervision of the Sex Offender—Putting the Containment Approach Into Practice

by Debra K. Baker, M.A., L.M.H.C., Joel Skolnick, M.S.W., L.I.C.S.W., Gregory Doucette, B.A., Gary Levitt and Christine O'Connor, B.A.

OVERVIEW

It has long been realized by community supervision professionals that sexual offenders require different supervision and management standards than do non-sexual offenders. Over the past several years, researchers and practitioners have developed numerous concepts related to the successful management of sexual offenders in the community. Many locales have successfully implemented several of these ideas into winning strategies that have dramatically improved public safety. In Massachusetts a small group of professionals has developed a protocol implementing a hybrid containment model advocated by the Center for Sex Offender Management (CSOM; *www.csom.org*) in the mid-1990s. This is their story.

INTRODUCTION

In February 1996, the Massachusetts Parole Board initiated Intensive Parole for Sex Offenders (IPSO). This pilot program was established in Framingham, Massachusetts, and was staffed by two senior parole officers with numerous years of experience in the supervision of adult offenders. These officers were assigned a special caseload of paroled sex offenders living in the Framingham area. Stricter standards of supervision were developed and implemented. Sex offender-specific treatment was recognized as a key component of supervision, and the officers sought out and developed close working relationships with two of the local sex offender treatment providers. Over the next few years, they added the services of a specially trained polygraph examiner and, most recently, those of a victim advocate.

THE CONTAINMENT APPROACH

Triangle of Supervision

The IPSO team views its work as a collaborative approach to the management of sex offenders in the community. As Strate, Jones, Pullen, and English (1996) discuss in their observation of the jurisdictions visited during field research, "The team includes, at a minimum, the probation or parole officer, the treatment provider, and a polygraph examiner. . . . Working together the team forms a 'triangle' of supervision that requires accountability from the offender, who is in the center of the triangle. The goal is to closely monitor the offender's lifestyle and contain the offender inside the boundaries set by the team. Each member of the team contributes to the supervision of, and requires accountability from, the offender."

It is this "triangle of supervision" that is the strength of the IPSO program. The team consists of a specially trained parole officer, a treatment provider, a polygrapher, and a victim advocate. The common goal that unites the team is its work toward achieving public safety. All members of the team have great respect for one another and trust that information is shared on a weekly basis. The flow of information works across the board from the time the offender is released on parole until he completes his supervision.

Collaborative Approach

Collaboration between the team members has two distinct but related dimensions. The first is functional and the second is relational. For collaboration to be effective, both of these dimensions must be operating maximally.

On the functional side there are very clear agreements and procedures that must be adhered to. Communication must be frequent, relevant, substantive, and both in writing and oral. There must be agreement by the therapist to share the relapse prevention plan and risk areas that emerge in group. The parole officer (PO) must agree to share risk areas that come up in supervision and polygraph results. The offender must sign a release enabling the therapist to communicate freely with the PO.

There must be agreement regarding common goals that focus on community safety. There is room for discussion regarding the way to deal with lapses and progress, but all parties must recognize and respect one another's role. The PO is ultimately more liable for community safety and is in charge of the case from this perspective. The therapist may need the support of the PO to encourage the client to confront various issues or to engage family members in case conferences. The therapist will determine treatment strategies. When there is conflict on these issues, it is the role and challenge of the containment team to use the denominator of community safety as the ultimate guide. The therapist should also be a resource, bringing data and research to the table not as a means of pressure but, rather, as additional background to consider.

On the relational process side there must be explicit agreement not to allow the offender to split between the PO and the therapist, and there must be explicit acknowledgement that neither the PO nor the therapist will keep secrets. Issues in this area are most likely to emerge when the offender is in group or meeting one on one with the PO. It is most effective to state to the offender, in front of the group, that the therapist does not make deals or keep secrets from the PO. Maligning either the therapist or the PO leads to splitting and is not tolerated in groups or in one-on-one meetings. Prior to case conferences it is important to establish who will be leading the case conference and what the goals of the conference are. Similarly, prior to meetings with offenders and their support systems, the therapist and PO should get together to discuss the goal of the meeting and the process of the meeting, in order to prevent misunderstandings.

These agreements and process discussions foster trust between PO and therapist which allows for discussion, disagreement, negotiation, and ultimately more effective collaborative management. Mutual respect of one another's areas of expertise and experience enhances the collaboration and makes an effective containment approach possible. It is not only the frequency and content of the communication but also the mutual respect and trust that enable this collaborative relationship to function effectively.

THE ROLE OF THE SUPERVISING OFFICER: ESTABLISHING THE FRAMEWORK

The baseline of the triangle of supervision for sex offenders has to be the supervising officer. The officer from intake to termination establishes the framework for success or failure. For this reason, only seasoned and highly experienced officers should be selected for IPSO duty. Their caseloads should reflect the fact that they are expected to spend more time and effort in supervising each offender. In Massachusetts, an IPSO officer has a caseload not to exceed twenty-five parolees, as compared to the average of fifty or more cases that other officers may have. This allows the IPSO officer to conduct closer and more frequent supervision of his or her cases.

To illustrate how the containment model program functions, we review the step-by-step process beginning with the time the Parole Board grants a parole to an inmate convicted of a sex offense.

Prior to release on parole, an inmate convicted of a sex offense must be screened for civil commitment by the district attorney's office. Once an inmate is cleared for release, he submits a home plan to the institution PO, which in turn is sent to the field PO to be investigated.

The home investigation is vital. To properly supervise a paroled sex offender if he is living with others, it is desirable to recruit the adults who will be residing with the parolee as part of his support network. At a minimum the PO should ascertain whether household members will be enablers or positive support people. Prior to approving a home plan, the IPSO PO should not only interview all members of the home but also explain to them what IPSO and the parole conditions (see Exhibit 11.1 at the end of this chapter) are, and what the consequences will be if the parolee violates any of the conditions. It is imperative that every adult in the home be aware of the parolee's offense. This is accomplished by asking each one specifically why the offender was incarcerated.

The victim advocate should be present during the home investigation. This process familiarizes the advocate with the entire parole situation and allows him or her to speak with an absolute understanding of the case when conferring with the parolee's victim. It shows the prospective sponsors that due to the seriousness of the offense there is a mechanism in place to which they can reach out should they ever feel intimidated or victimized by the offender. Of course, it is also great to have an extra pair of eyes when doing a physical investigation of the house. In cases of pedophile offenders, it is critical when conducting a home investigation to check out the neighborhood to see where the schools and playgrounds are in proximity to the residence. In all cases, the PO should also be aware of the likelihood of the offender coming into contact with the victim by residing at the proposed home.

A PO needs to recognize and accept that to properly supervise a paroled sex offender, there will be some infringement upon the sponsor's personal privacy. It is important that sponsors understand the reasons for unannounced visits, observing common areas around the house, or asking some very direct questions. It is enough to make a lot of people uncomfortable, but by going through all the conditions, explaining the parole process, and assuring the sponsors that it is in everyone's interest that the parole be successful, sponsors become more cooperative.

The home investigation includes notification of the local police by the PO of the parolee's pending release. This is mainly done as a courtesy to the police.

Once the home plan is approved, the paroled inmate reports directly to the IPSO Parole Office on the day of release. All IPSO conditions are reviewed with the parolee. Photos are taken at this time, and the parolee is instructed to register with the Sex Offender Registry Board. He is given a diary and instructed in its use. A time is set to meet and be interviewed by the sex offender treatment provider and the parolee is also scheduled to be placed on electronic monitoring.

THE ROLE OF THE SPECIALIZED PAROLE OFFICER

The PO meets with the sex offender parolee at a minimum once a week. This is accomplished by home visits, worksite visits, contact at a places of business, counseling offices, surveillance, or having the parolee report directly to the parole office. Home visits are important and are conducted at least once a month. Unannounced home visits, done at random, are preferable. Drug testing is important and also is done on a random basis. The IPSO program has a zero tolerance for drugs and alcohol and the first indication of use will result in a return to custody.

The sex offender parolee is required to keep a daily diary, noting anywhere he goes, along with times, names of people with whom he goes, and the odometer reading if he is driving. The diary is checked regularly by the PO, allowing the PO to keep an "eye" on what is happening outside home-visit periods.

The IPSO PO visits the local police departments from time to time. Photos and other pertinent information about the parolee are provided. Keeping the police advised of parolees in their jurisdiction ensures their cooperation, which enhances the monitoring process. The goal of the IPSO team is to ensure public safety. Sex offenders are manipulative, secretive, and often treacherous, and thus they require intensive supervision. One person, no matter how expert in the field, cannot do this alone. A team of experts dedicated to a common goal can accomplish a more effective way of supervising sex offenders on parole. Until a better mousetrap is built, intensive parole for sex offenders using the containment model is the best there is.

THE ROLE OF THE SEX OFFENDER TREATMENT PROVIDER

Weekly Sessions

The sex offender parolee is mandated to attend weekly group sex offender counseling at his own expense. The parolee is allowed to choose a therapist from a list of treatment providers who have already been approved by the parole agency and who have also agreed to charge an affordable rate (currently not to exceed $35 a session). The treatment provider also provides the PO with monthly progress reports and keeps the PO advised should the parolee miss a scheduled session. What sets the IPSO program apart is that the PO works very closely with parolees' therapists and meets with them regularly to discuss each case on a weekly basis.

IPSO works with several specialized sex offender treatment providers throughout their region. In Framingham, IPSO refers to two private practice clinicians who have become critical components to the team. Both clinicians hold master's degrees and are licensed in their respective disciplines. Combined, they have more than thirty years of experience in the field of sex offender treatment.

Treatment Model

Sex offender treatment is provided from a cognitive-behavioral, relapse prevention model. Treatment is conducted in the form of group therapy, one time per week, for one-and-a-half-hour sessions, with no more than eight members per group. There is much focus on the development of relapse prevention plans, with specific focus on avoiding high-risk situations.

It is the role of the clinician to teach an offender internal controls over his thoughts, feelings, and behaviors while the rest of the team generally uses external controls, such as polygraph, close monitoring, and special conditions of parole. Ideally, an offender will gain self control and gradually demonstrate his ability to manage himself in the community. IPSO generally begins with a very structured format, and as an offender demonstrates his progress, supervision conditions are slowly decreased. Examples include removing electronic devices after a polygraph is passed after six months of supervisions or gradual reduction in curfew times, particularly around work schedules.

Issues of Confidentiality

An important part of the containment model is the issue of confidentiality. During the intake process, an offender is informed that the therapist works under a team approach and will be discussing his case with the IPSO team. Consent to release information is signed. There is often group discussion about what the men can and cannot say in group that will be held in confidence. This issue has been a balancing act over the years—providing offenders with a safe place to talk about their issues within the collaborative approach that demands open, trusting relationships between all members. The offenders are informed that the clinicians will not keep their secrets, and that they will be held accountable for their behavior. From the treatment provider's perspective, any violation of a condition of supervision, or any engagement of high-risk behavior, will be reported to the supervising PO. This has been handled in different ways, from informing an offender that disclosure will be made by the clinician to requesting that the offender report the behavior himself and then following up with the PO to accompanying the offender in meeting with the IPSO team to support him in his disclosure.

Collaboration With Team Members

A critical element of treatment is the monthly treatment status report that is provided to the PO and the offender. This report outlines how a man is doing in treatment and provides him with a treatment plan. The report includes the offender's attendance and payment record; whether he is an active group participant who is able to confront his distorted thinking, admits to the commission of his offense, and that admission corresponds with the official version of the crime; whether he is able to identify what motivated him to offend; and what disinhibitors were present. He is evaluated on how he is progressing in the development of a relapse prevention plan, whether he demonstrates using it and whether he has shared it with at least one support person in the presence of the therapist and possibly other members of the IPSO team. Does he know how to intervene on deviant fantasy? In addition, the report identifies the date and outcome of an offender's last polygraph. There is also documentation of any support visits that have been conducted during the month.

Another important aspect of treatment is to meet with the offender's support persons. If an offender is living with someone, that person has already met with the PO during the investigation of the home plan. In the initial part of treatment the family members will meet with the clinician. In addition, as the offenders get involved in other relationships, they are required to bring those people to meet the therapist. And, prior to an offender getting involved in a sexual relationship, he is expected to disclose to his partner, and often the partner is brought is to meet the therapist to ensure that a full disclosure has been made. Compliance with this issue is monitored through a polygraph exam.

Treatment in Practice

For years, Tuesdays have been IPSO treatment day. For the clinician, it begins with a short meeting with the PO for an exchange of information about any events that have occurred over the week. Then, the clinician makes a brief visit to the polygrapher's office to discuss any polygraphs that were conducted that week or to formulate any questions necessary for exams for the next week. A quick check-in with the victim advocate is made to share any necessary information. These meetings can be brief because, after the last group ends, another IPSO meeting begins. The entire team meets for an hour to do a case review of IPSO clients. After briefly checking in at the parole office, group begins. The day may involve an intake with a new client, a meeting with an offender and a support person, such as a new girlfriend, a spouse, a pastor, and so on.

If groups are the core of the treatment program. The men arrive, make payment, and do a brief check-in as to how their week has gone and to ask for group time as needed. The men are expected to disclose any lapses in recovery or supervision violations (remember, they are aware of an impending polygraph). Once the check-in is complete, time is allowed for specific issues for which the men have requested time. Typically these issues involve any urges, deviant fantasies, or masturbation in excess. These issues are addressed from a relapse prevention perspective. Other frequent topics include relationship and/or work problems. In Massachusetts, offenders often talk about civil commitment or concerns regarding public notification as a result of their classification by the Sex Offender Registry. Of course, it is with great joy that they can also celebrate group members' successes such as a job promotion, wedding, or even a passed polygraph.

Each group has its own personality; however, there are some common elements. A good group is one in which all members are active, feeling safe enough to both contribute and receive feedback around issues that can be difficult to discuss. Group is a place the men can feel safe enough to cry, grieve, and often laugh with each other. For many of them it is the only place they can be completely honest with others about the horrific crimes they have committed, without feeling judged.

As anyone who has witnessed a successful group knows, it can have amazing power. When a small group of people can come together, create a safe environment, and influence positive changes in behavior through both discussion and appropriate modeling, knowing that the IPSO team will support their success, they are all one step closer to living in a world with *no more victims.*

THE ROLE OF THE POLYGRAPHER

The examiner is a member of the containment team and as such he is included in the information flow and in the case conferences whenever possible. Members of the team are always learning from each other, educating each other on their respective roles and responsibilities, and forming reasonable expectations and respect for each other's roles. This includes how to use the polygraph most effectively. We have seen how a mutually supportive team environment and a reduction of overlapping responsibilities and misunderstandings enhance supervision and prevent the confusion that previously arose from the traditional isolated roles.

In the Massachusetts parole system, the polygraph examiners are POs on staff with the Massachusetts Parole Board. They are members of the American Polygraph Association (APA) and are certified in postconviction polygraph testing through an APA-approved school. All examinations are conducted using standardized procedures for testing and scoring and are subject to quality control.

Typically a parolee placed on IPSO supervision will be on electronic monitoring for at least the first six months. Electronic monitoring is important in ensuring that the parolee is keeping his curfew and in determining whether a parolee is in an inappropriate location.

After six months of parole supervision the parolee is required to take a polygraph exam. It is important that the PO work with the polygrapher and therapist in setting up the questions to be used on the test. If the parolee's first six months are without incident and he scores a "nondeceptive" on his polygraph exam, the electronic monitoring device is usually removed.

Importance of the Polygraph Examination

In 1996, when the Massachusetts Parole Board began the IPSO pilot program, it included postconviction sex offender testing (PCSOT). The success of this program led to the Parole Board's expanding the use of polygraph testing to the supervision of all sex offenders on parole in Massachusetts. Limitations and controversy about validity and reliability of the polygraph have been taken into consideration in departmental policy decisions. Findings of "deception" or "no deception" in polygraph examinations are used only in conjunction with other information when case management decisions are being made. Use of PCSOT has shown that it can uncover the secretive (unseen) behavior of the offender while he or she is under community supervision. The exam is used to encourage disclosure and to identify behavior where deception is indicated. The polygraph examination procedure often provides leverage to obtain more accurate and complete sexual histories. Polygraph examinations help to break down an offender's denial of specific offenses or deviant behavior where that denial may be stunting progress in treatment. As a supervision and treatment tool, in the interest of public safety, it provides admissions, confessions, and other useful information for supervising officers and therapists to act on. It functions as an external control, screening for offending and high-risk behavior. It also functions as an internal control in that offenders are aware that their behavior is always the subject of their next polygraph exam.

One PO, who was assigned to IPSO and worked as a member of the containment team, later became a polygraph examiner. Following is his firsthand account demonstrating the usefulness of a polygraph examination as an integral part of intensive supervision:

> My first IPSO parolee to be scheduled for a polygraph examination was a 46-year-old pedophile who was paroled after having been in treatment while

incarcerated. Six months later he reported to the regional parole office for his first maintenance polygraph examination to determine if he was in compliance with his conditions of treatment and supervision. Prior to the exam there were no indications of violations of parole or high-risk behavior. His progress in treatment revealed no lapses. He did not appear to be in denial about his sexual offenses or his history of pedophilia.

As a result of this polygraph examination, he admitted that he had been grooming and sexually fantasizing about two prepubescent boys in his neighborhood. He already knew where one of them lived and used binoculars to view this boy in his home. The boys were part of a group of children who congregated at the end of a dead-end street near the residence of the offender. His selection of the two children revealed that he was at a dangerously advanced stage of his deviant cycle. Using well-developed social skills, he was deliberately working toward winning the trust of a child and anyone who would have made it possible for him to have access to one of these children.

Following these admissions, the offender was immediately taken into custody and returned to prison. The parole board subsequently decided to keep him in custody.

At what point would we have discovered this dangerous behavior without the benefit of the polygraph? Would we have discovered it at all before, or even after, an offense had been committed? The IPSO team was made up of seasoned POs and an experienced sex offender therapist. Yet, until the polygraph examination, no one on the IPSO team observed any indicators of escalation of deviant behavior.

This is one example of many, in our experience, of the effectiveness of the polygraph as a supervision and treatment tool *to see what is usually unseen*. We know that many sex offenders have honed their ability to skillfully "fool" and manipulate victims, family, friends, coworkers, neighbors, and so on. They even seem to manipulate the criminal justice system, often avoiding jail or prison all together.

Types of Polygraph Exams

The polygraph instrument used is a computerized Axciton system which measures and stores certain cardiovascular, electrodermal, and respiratory responses. These responses are charted. The examiner evaluates the responses for deception. The finding by the examiner is presented as *deception indicated, no deception indicated, or no opinion* (inconclusive). The Axciton system also has Chart Analysis, an algorithm for computerized analysis which is used in conjunction with the traditional method of a visual analysis of the charts. For quality control, a second examiner reviews the charts.

In general, we use three types of examinations.

- The *maintenance examination*, which is conducted periodically, or at the discretion of the PO, to verify that the offender has not reoffended and to investigate compliance with parole/treatment conditions.

- *Disclosure examinations,* given to verify an offender's sexual history.

- *Instant offense examinations*, which can be given when an offender is in denial about the offense for which he or she was convicted.

The Maintenance Polygraph Examination. The maintenance polygraph examination is the primary examination for supervision and treatment. This exam is conducted after the first six months on parole and then on a periodic basis, usually every six months, or at the discretion of the PO when the offender's behavior has raised suspicions. The exam focuses on verifying that the offender is not engaging in criminal sexual behavior or high-risk activities and is not violating the conditions of his community supervision (IPSO conditions) or the relapse prevention plan. For example, violations may be "trigger behaviors," such as using intoxicants, masturbating to deviant fantasies, use of pornography, or being unsupervised around children. When deception is indicated and/or an admission to a violation is made, the team will confer to decide on the appropriate action to be taken. An investigation may be initiated or sanctions imposed such as restriction of travel, electronic monitoring, and increased drug testing, up to placement in custody. Any serious violation requires the PO to submit a parole violation report to the Parole Board.

The Sexual History Disclosure Examination. The sexual history disclosure examination is used to confirm completeness of the offender's disclosure of his or her history of sexual abuse. The disclosure includes all sex offenses with the pertinent details of each offense. It also includes specific forms of sexual behavior, masturbation, and fantasies in which the offender has engaged. In addition, the offender is asked to reveal any other victims of abuse (sexual and nonsexual) who may have not reported this abuse. It is believed that the best predictor of future behavior is past behavior.

This exam usually takes place after the offender has been in treatment at least three months and under community supervision. In some cases, such as with New Hampshire parolees under Massachusetts supervision, the offender has passed a disclosure examination prior to release on parole. If the offender is still in denial of the offense, or specific details of the offense, for which he or she was sentenced, an instant offense examination needs to be administered before pursuing a sexual history disclosure. The inherent limitations in polygraph testing would make it impracticable to test a full sexual history disclosure if the offender is lying about the offense for which he was convicted.

The Instant Offense Examination. The instant offense examination addresses the extent to which the offender abused the victim of the offense for which he was convicted. If the offender is in complete denial of the offense of conviction or any significant detail of the offense, this exam can be helpful in breaking down denial. A finding of deception may produce an admission of guilt. We have found that even if the offender remains in denial, he often admits to some part of the offense for which he had not previously taken responsibility. For example, an investigative report of an offender convicted of statutory rape described use of force by means of a knife. The offender denied use of any force even after several months in therapy. The therapist referred the offender to the examiner to try to get beyond this issue. Following the failure of the examination, the offender admitted holding the victim against her will while she kicked and screamed but maintained that he did not use a knife. By his admission, he established that this was a crime of violent rape. Some other offenders have admitted to their crimes just before taking the test.

Polygraph Examination Procedure

Typically there are three phases to any polygraph examination. The preparation for the exam begins as soon as the offender is made aware that the polygraph process is an important part of his treatment and he comprehends the significance of it. This awareness is often evidenced to therapists when an offender is approaching the scheduled time of a polygraph and then begins to open up and reveal new information.

In the maintenance examination the first phase is the pretest interview in which the offender completes a questionnaire addressing behavior, thoughts, fantasies, and feelings that are related to his compliance with standards of treatment and supervision. The time frame in which his behavior is examined is the period of parole since his last polygraph exam or any other appropriate time frame (e.g., since his or her release from prison). The offender's responses to this questionnaire combined with information acquired from the other members of the containment team produce the substance for interviewing and constructing questions for the examination. For example, a therapist may report to the examiner that an offender is not forthcoming about involvement in a romantic relationship. The examiner can subsequently explore that issue. It must be emphasized that our examination process is greatly enhanced by the healthy collaboration between the examiner and other team members. A good flow of information among the team is essential to keeping the containment concept working. It can prevent "splitting" behavior by the offender, as well as give the examiner more information to work with. Frequently, we have found that it is just before or during the pretest interview that the offender makes significant admissions.

The next phase is the in-test phase where the offender is tested on the polygraph instrument. Test questions are constructed by the examiner and reviewed with the examinee to be sure that the examinee knows and understands each question before the test is given. At the completion of the test the examiner evaluates the tracing of physiological responses to determine whether or not deception is indicated.

The last phase is posttest where the results are made known to the offender. If deception is indicated, the examiner confronts the offender with the finding. The examiner now interrogates the offender to find out as much as possible about the issue where deception is indicated. In addition, when deception is indicated and/or serious admissions are made, the examiner immediately notifies the supervising PO with the results and follows up with a written report. The examiner should also be included in a case conference to assist in determining the appropriate action to be taken.

A finding of deception without a confession or admission does not always result in a sanction on the parolee. And a parole revocation is never based solely on a finding of deception. However, it sets in motion an action policy that triggers an investigation, increased supervision, or other options (including sanctions). The Massachusetts Parole Board policy is that appropriate action must be taken whenever deception is indicated and/or serious admissions are made, requiring the PO and the regional supervisor to document the action taken.

From our experience, the polygraph has been a remarkably valuable tool, especially when cooperation and the flow of information among the containment team members are preserved. The results have demonstrated that the use of polygraph is a powerful practice that increases offender accountability and produces more honest and complete disclosure. To supervise and treat sex offenders without the benefit of poly-graph testing would seriously reduce the effectiveness of supervision and compromise public safety. Our own surveys of offenders' responses to questions about effective-ness of the polygraph reveal that 100 percent of those surveyed reported disliking to take the exam, but 90 percent reported that they felt it was effective in preventing them from engaging in high-risk behavior. Although it is essential to take notice of its lim-itations and potential for misuse, we proceed with cautious optimism. Based on our experience, continuing research, and the knowledge gained from other jurisdictions that apply the polygraph to supervision of sex offenders, we believe that PCSOT along with the collaborative approach to containment will continue to be at the core of supervision and treatment of sex offenders.

THE ROLE OF THE VICTIM ADVOCATE

The victim advocate position for the IPSO team was established in 2002, through a federal grant applied for by the Massachusetts Coalition for Sex Offender Management (MCSOM). MCSOM identified victim representation and input as an essential element in sex offender management. While the Massachusetts Parole Board already had a victim services unit, it was determined that there should be an additional victim advocate assigned specifically to the IPSO team who is specially trained in sex offender management. This advocate could focus on the specific needs of victims of sex offenders who are being intensely supervised while living in the community.

The duties of the victim advocate for the IPSO team include providing the parolees' victims with accurate information and notification regarding the offender's parole status and parole conditions, listening to the victims' concerns, offering refer-rals, and answering any other questions victims may have. By working directly with the PO, the advocate is able to obtain firsthand knowledge of how an offender is adjusting to community supervision. This allows the advocate to provide victims with thorough and accurate information that can aid them in safety planning and provides overall assurance that the offender is being closely monitored. Many victims have found comfort in knowing that there is an advocate on the team representing their con-cerns.

The victim's advocate assists the PO in making decisions regarding home and work plans and parole conditions. She also works with the sex offender's family mem-bers/support persons in an effort to help prevent any further victimization. By accom-panying the PO on home investigations and field visits, the advocate observes any danger that offenders may pose to past or potential victims. Because nearly 75 percent of victims know their offender well, it is important for the PO and advocate to get acquainted with the offender's family/support persons to be on guard for any potential victims. It is also important that the advocate goes on these visits so that family/sup-port persons become familiar with her, in hopes that they will be comfortable speak-ing with her if they have any concerns or problems. Often, family members are too intimidated to speak directly to the PO and the advocate is a good alternative for them to voice their concerns to so that the situation can be properly addressed.

The advocate's job involves participating in weekly case review meetings with the PO, polygrapher, and treatment providers. At these meetings, the IPSO team shares information, discusses concerns and potential problems, and makes any necessary decisions around action to be taken. While the PO's and treatment provider's main focus is on the offender and his behaviors, the advocate's role is to consider how the offender's behaviors may be affecting his victim(s) and the people around him. This allows the team to make more informed, well-balanced decisions.

The advocate also maintains an institutional caseload. She is responsible for notifying victims of upcoming parole hearings for inmates who are serving their sentences at the Massachusetts Treatment Center for sexual offenders. If the victims choose to attend, the advocate prepares and accompanies them to the victim access hearings and notifies them of the results of the hearings. Having the Massachusetts Treatment Center on the victim advocate's caseload is important because offenders there, if paroled, are likely to be in the IPSO program. This is helpful because the advocate is a consistent, informative instrument for the victims in this difficult time.

Another aspect of being a victim advocate for IPSO includes establishing and maintaining strong working relationships with other agencies and programs that are dealing with the same population of offenders. The advocate works closely with the Sex Offender Registry Board, the district attorney's offices for civil commitment proceedings, and police departments and participates in the monthly MCSOM meetings. The final aspect involves providing information and education to the community and other criminal justice agencies. The advocate has presented information on the IPSO collaborative approach to the state police, the district attorneys' offices, community roundtable meetings, and the Massachusetts Association for the Treatment of Sexual Abusers.

Both the CSOM and the Governor's Task Force on Sexual Assault and Abuse have expressed the need for victim advocacy in the management of sex offenders in the community. At the Massachusetts Parole Board, important steps have been taken to address this need. Because the IPSO advocate is a relatively new initiative, we are still looking to further define and expand the victim advocate's role in sex offender management. Ideally, the result will be to further serve victims and, ultimately, to enhance public safety.

CONCLUSION

If the success of any sex offender management program is demonstrated by the absence of sexual reoffenses attributed to its participants, the IPSO program is arguably extremely successful. While there have been the expected technical violations, most frequently for drug or alcohol usage, to date, not one IPSO-managed offender has reportedly re-offended sexually in the nine-year history of the program.

Despite this success, there is certainly room for improvement in the Massachusetts IPSO program. Currently funded for only one region in Massachusetts, IPSO could be expanded statewide. Over the past eight years, programs for transitioning newly released sex offenders have become less available. The loss of housing and employment opportunities has impacted offender stability and adversely effects supervision and support resources. It is hoped that newly initiated reentry programs from both the Department of Correction and the Parole Board will provide some relief.

The IPSO model provides an approach to the supervision and treatment of sex offenders in the community that is worthy of replication. This collaborative approach not only increases the opportunity to successfully transition back into the community, but also enhances public safety by providing multiple levels of monitoring an offender's behavior and activity. Offenders are treated fairly and with respect. They develop strong support networks. It is a win-win solution.

References

Strate, D., Jones, L., Pullen, S., & English, K. (1996). Criminal justice policies and sex offender denial. In K. English, S. Pullen, & L. Jones (Eds.), *Managing adult sex offenders: A containment approach* (p. 48). Lexington, KY: American Probation and Parole Association.

Exhibit 11.1
IPSO Conditions

1. You will agree to allow shared communication among Treatment, Polygraph Examiners, Probation/Parole, District Attorney's Office, and the Court; and disclosure to any others as deemed appropriate.

2. You will enroll and participate in a treatment program for sex offenders approved by the Parole Officer.

3. You will assume responsibility for paying counseling costs.

4. You will develop and abide by a Relapse Prevention Plan, which has been reviewed and signed off by an approved sex offender therapist.

5. You will not engage in use of pornography or frequent adult bookstores, sex shops, topless bars, massage parlors, or other such establishments, including those places that just serve alcohol. You will also not be involved with nudist organizations.

6. You will not engage in use of personal ads or Internet to contact or meet people.

7. You may not use videotapes; or watch television programs that act as a stimulus for your abusive cycle, or act as a stimulus to arouse you in an abusive fashion. In other words, a pedophile may not view programs whose primary character is a child.

8. You will be monitored electronically for the first six (6) months of supervision. You shall be electronically monitored thereafter if the Parole Officer determines that it is necessary for effective supervision.

9. You will be monitored by Polygraph Examination every six (6) months or more often, if required, at the discretion of the Parole Officer.

10. You will observe special curfew restrictions, as imposed by the Parole Officer.

11. You will keep a daily log of activities, as required by the Parole Officer.

12. You must keep a detailed driving log, including time, place, and miles driven, unless told otherwise, at discretion of Parole Officer. You will not drive without a destination.

13. You will not pick up strangers or hitchhikers regardless of whether you are the driver or passenger in vehicle.

14. You will not drive after dark except with approval for employment and treatment.

15. You will not travel out of state at any time unless approved by Parole Board.

16. You will not have contact of any kind with the victim(s) or their families.

17. You will not use the Internet without permission of your supervising officer and you must submit to an examination and search of your computer to verify that it is not used in violation of your supervision and treatment plans.

18. You will not possess a camera, camcorder, or videocassette recorder/player without the approval of your supervising officer.

19. You will not have sexual, intimate, or living arrangements with any individuals without the individual being informed of your Parole Status, sexual deviancy, and criminal history. You must reveal to Parole Officer names of anyone you are involved with as stated above.

20. You will not socialize or otherwise have contact with individuals under the age of 18 in work or social situations unless accompanied by an adult who has been made aware of your sexual deviant tendencies, as approved by the Parole Officer.

21. You will not frequent places where individuals under the age of 18 congregate, such as parks, playgrounds, and schools and not attend movies without permission.

22. Any home plan must be approved by Parole Officer before moving in to ensure minimum contact with individuals under the age of 18.

23. You will have no involvement with individuals who have children under the age of 18, without approval of the Parole Officer.

24. You will not possess any equipment or devices that are designed for the purpose of restraining or confining a person (handcuffs, restraint chains, leg irons, etc.)

Chapter 12

From Institution to Community—Successful Transitions Support in Washington State Sex Offender Treatment Program

by Anmarie Aylward, M.A.

OVERVIEW

One of the crucial features of the successful reintegration of the sex offender into the community is to build an informed and supportive network of individuals devoted to assisting the offender to remain in recovery. All too often programs have neither the motivation nor the resources to include the support system in the treatment process. However, the Washington Department of Corrections (DOC) Sex Offender Treatment Program (SOTP) has developed an efficient and effective method to educate and encourage support team members. By offering a one-day seminar conducted by the staff, family, and friends of the treatment program participants are made to feel that they are an important part of the rehabilitation of the offender. This chapter describes the program and the concrete difference it has made in the lives of these offenders.

INTRODUCTION

Treating sex offenders is one component of a comprehensive strategy to ensure safe communities. Informed members of the community acting as part of the treatment intervention can be a fruitful component of an overall strategy. This chapter focuses on the effort of Washington DOC's SOTP to educate the support systems of the participants regarding their relapse prevention plans. By familiarizing supportive citizens with the high-risk situations of their friends or family members who are in the program, it is hoped that they can assist with proactive interventions in times of crisis (Kazura, Temke, Toth, & Hunter, 2002).

SEX OFFENDER TREATMENT IN WASHINGTON STATE

Washington State has provided institutional treatment for convicted sex offenders since the early 1970s. In 1988, the DOC established the SOTP at Twin Rivers Correctional Center in the Monroe Correctional Complex in Monroe, Washington, as part of a comprehensive strategy to enhance community safety and hold offenders accountable for their behavior. It is one of the larger programs in the nation, providing treatment for up to 200 offenders institutionally and another 200 offenders in the community at any given time. All adult male sex offenders in the DOC may volunteer for the program. Because of the lengthy waiting list, most offenders enter treatment when they are within eighteen months of release. All offenders accepted into the program are expected to continue to receive services in the community. Community aftercare services are available upon release for up to three years as part of the Twin Rivers SOTP. Research indicates that treatment is an important and effective means of reducing risk for sexual reoffense (Hanson et al., 2002).

Cognitive-Behavioral Paradigm

The SOTP uses relapse prevention techniques within a cognitive-behavioral paradigm. Treatment focuses on teaching prosocial skills and attitudes and training offenders when to use these skills to avoid offending. Although treatment must address the unique needs of each offender, common treatment goals include increasing acceptance of responsibility, identifying offense precursors, and learning adaptive skills to manage stress, communicate effectively to resolve problems, manage sexual arousal, and avoid risky situations.

Because offenders who fail to complete treatment are at an increased risk to reoffend (Hanson & Bussiere, 1998), Twin River's staff persists in their efforts, even with very resistant offenders. In fact, fewer than 12 percent of offenders are terminated from or quit the program.

Although offenders must volunteer for treatment, the degree to which they take responsibility for their behaviors varies widely. In addition, offenders vary widely in their motivation to make the changes demanded by treatment and in their learning styles and abilities. The challenge to treatment providers is to present treatment in a way that makes sense to the offender and optimizes his learning. Thus, assignments are modified to meet the offender's needs, and an attempt is made to assign therapists whose treatment approach is consistent with the offender's learning style.

Many offenders minimize the extent or impact of their sexual offending or the need to change their behavior. In some cases the offender is simply lying. However, minimization often results from cognitive distortions and rationalizations that the offender truly believes. Considerable time is spent helping the offender change the thoughts, beliefs, and attitudes that help maintain sexually deviant behavior.

Because offenders vary widely in their motivation and commitment to change. Treatment is likely to be successful to the extent the offender is able to:

1. Recognize and understand the factors that contribute to his offense(s).

2. Monitor himself and his environment to detect changes indicating that his risk is increasing.

3. Develop the cognitive, emotional, and behavioral skills necessary to intervene, manage, and reduce increasing risk.

The offender must remain motivated and able to apply his monitoring and intervention skills in a timely and effective manner, including seeking outside assistance when necessary.

Group Treatment Plus Individual Counseling

A major part of sexual deviancy treatment is identifying each offender's crime cycle. Offenders identify the sequence of internal factors and external factors that lead to offending. Treatment helps the offender correct skill deficits while learning to control excesses.

Because each offender's crime cycle is unique, treatment is individualized to each offender's needs. The preferred treatment modality is group therapy because it is more efficient and allows for challenges, feedback, and problem solving from an offender's peers. Groups generally have twelve to fourteen members and meet from eight to ten hours per week. Additional classes and groups addressing sexual deviancy issues are also available. However, individual treatment is provided to resolve specific issues. In some case medications can be a useful supplement to behavioral treatment (e.g., by helping more obsessive-compulsive offenders focus on learning self-control skills).

Each SOTP participant completes comprehensive assessments, including psychological tests, actuarial risk evaluations, and clinical interviews to help define treatment goals and strategies and to help evaluate progress. Participants receive both intensive group therapy and individual counseling. The family support seminar is an innovative addition to the treatment program.

The SOTP recognizes that treatment is only one strategy that contributes to protecting the communities. Preliminary research indicates that relatively few men (fewer than 7 percent) who have completed the Twin Rivers program return to DOC prison with a new conviction. Moreover men who continue receiving treatment and supervision in the community do especially well.

TRANSITION GOALS FOR HIGH-RISK SEX OFFENDERS

In Washington State there is much energy and focus on the risk management of high-risk offenders to include sex offenders, specifically in regard to the supervision of offenders as they transition from institutions into communities. There has been an impetus to develop collaborative release planning based on the risk and needs of each offender. These plans are for offenders who present a high risk of harm to the community. It is believed that the safest reentry into the community by high-risk offenders requires the collaboration of many systems and individuals.

The goals of risk management transition in Washington State are to increase the collaboration between the institution and the field staff, to involve community stakeholders in release planning, to maximize community resources, and to release offenders closer to their earliest date possible in order to maximize supervision opportunities. In Washington State, the transition of high-risk sex offenders by policy is "team based" and is date driven as far as expectations and activities. The transition team develops a plan to maximize community resources and create specific intervention plans. The Twin Rivers SOTP's family support seminar is part of sex offender treatment and falls under the risk management and transition strategies for the state.

Transition and Treatment

Because many programs are confronted with time and resource limitations, it is important to identify adjunct treatment processes that provide useful support to traditional sex offender therapy and are effective. Support is an essential component of best-practice treatment and aftercare. Ultimately, support people need to be part of a network that the offender has developed and integrated into the treatment process. Reinforcing the importance of this group by including them in the therapeutic process is important (Carich & Mussack, 2001).

Many professionals contribute to effective sex offender treatment. The SOTP team includes institutional custody staff, classification counselors, supervisors, support staff, administrative staff, and assessment and treatment professionals. An active Advisory Committee ensures that our efforts are professionally and ethically sound, and that they meet the community's expectations. The SOTP works closely with key partners in the community, including DOC mental health counselors, community corrections officers, social service agencies, private sex offender treatment providers, and the offender's support network, to minimize future offenses. As much as possible, treatment staff work with community supports to help develop strategies to monitor and manage the offender's risk. Most offenders welcome this input as an important safeguard. Long-term success is greatly increased when all these partners contribute to our common goal: safe communities.

Building a Strong Support System

The chance of the offender remaining offense free over the long term is enhanced if the offender has an informed and vigilant support system (Gordon & Packard, 1998). Such support may include community corrections officers, family, friends, coworkers, or church members. The offender is expected to educate support system members about his crime cycle and observable indicators that would indicate he is in "cycle."

Research shows that family support for inmates during incarceration reduces the likelihood of recidivism (Paolucci, Violato, & Schofield, 1998). Inmate's needs focus on three themes: family support and education programs; the importance of improved visitation environments and opportunities; and the value of educating families about the rehabilitation process and facility policies. Popular belief suggests that family ties, employment, marriage, children, and holding other social bonds within the community mitigate criminal behavior by providing people with a social investment in conformity. In both community and institutional settings, it is recommended that mental health and correctional professionals endeavor to provide opportunities for regular, positive offender family interactions.

The public generally believes that the vast majority of sex offenders will reoffend and that treatment does not reduce recidivism. These beliefs have helped shape public and criminal justice policy toward these offenders. The support system of these offenders is impacted by the beliefs as well. But, as noted previously, an offender's support group, composed of people with whom he has regular and prosocial contact, is an integral component of treatment. In prison the segue from institution to community is often difficult. Effective support systems built in prison (in treatment) can be of great value during this transition. Toward this end, the Twin Rivers SOTP has developed family support seminars as a component of sex offender treatment. These seminars, described in the following section, in addition to individual contact with the offender and the primary therapist, offer a resource and support for families, friends, and others. Participation in the seminars, as in treatment, is voluntary.

FAMILY SUPPORT SEMINARS

Seminar Goals

The goals of the family support seminar are:

1. To educate participants toward risk management and safe communities;

2. To improve and educate participants on their ability to be positive support;

3. To increase collaboration between institution treatment, community, and other resources; and

4. To increase the number of collateral contacts, thereby increasing information about the offender.

The goals of the family support seminar are to assist in educating supportive individuals and family members to become an effective support/monitoring system for the offender with the end goal being to improve community safety and to assist families.

The support seminar is managed through treatment staff. It is conducted in the visiting room at Twin Rivers Correctional Center. Offenders are notified in their treatment groups of the scheduling of the seminars. The offenders then share information with support members. Each support member in turn calls the SOTP to respond for the event. If visitors are not already on the offender's visit list, SOTP staff must conduct security clearances to allow the visitors to participate in the seminar. Offenders themselves are not present for the seminar.

The Seminar Program

The seminar itself is three and a half hours (i.e., a half day). Participants receive focused presentations specific to treatment goals, community notification, transition issues, and victim advocacy. In addition to the presentations, participants meet face to face with staff. Resource lists are made available for the participants to take home. These lists include notification information, victim advocacy resources, and referred reading lists as well as organizational information and telephone lists for the program itself. The unstated goal is to encourage ongoing communication and understanding among an offender's support group members. In addition, program staff provide refreshments to enhance the collegial atmosphere of the meeting.

The staff participation in the seminars includes the superintendent of the institution, treatment staff, community treatment staff, classification/living unit staff, victim advocates, and risk management staff.[1] The support systems include mothers, wives, siblings, and friends; faith-based support people; and whole-family groupings.

Family involvement can be useful for sex offenders in two ways. In the more general context it is a modality that should be made available to every sex offender involved in a comprehensive program. The anger and resentment toward women characteristic of the rapist and the fear and immaturity associated with many pedophiles are often associated with dysfunctional family interactions which may be still occurring or may be replicated in other relationships. In dealing with families, it is not assumed that the family shares a deviation but that the unit may have become dysfunctional in response to the offender's deviation. Families are involved in therapy to include support systems. Working with issues of grief, anger, and forgiveness may assist in freeing the offender from his pattern of displacing rage onto innocent victims. Learning new communication techniques is vital, not only in improving existing relationships but also in building a support system that can be used to interrupt the offense cycle. In addition, the Twin Rivers SOTP used spouses, parents, and significant others to help the offender recognize the warning signs of his deviant pattern. Note: Family reunification is not part of the family support seminar.

HOW SUPPORT MAY AID TRANSITION

A preliminary review has been conducted to identify potential differences between offenders who have had support people participate in the family seminars and those for whom there was no involvement in the seminars. This review matched forty-seven offenders whose support teams participated in three separate family support seminars with forty-nine offenders who were active in treatment during the same time frames but did *not* participate in the support seminars. The offender groups (supported and not supported) were matched for age, early release date, offense type, and time in treatment. The *supported group* had outside support people actively participate in a scheduled support seminar. The *nonsupported group* did not have any active participants in the scheduled support seminar. We were interested to see, preliminarily, if the

Table 12.1
Participation in a Family Seminar an Indicator of Timely Release From the Institution

	Supported Offenders (Combined Seminars Attendance)	Offenders Not Supported
Not yet released	30% (14)	41% (20)*
Released to community	70% (33)	59% (29)
Average days past ERD	40 days	101 days*

* One offender died prior to release.

supported group showed any indicator of timely release from the institution. What was found indicated that offenders with active support people (as measured through their participation in the family support seminar) were not only more likely to be released and in the community but also more likely to be released closer to their early release date (Aylward & Sayer, 2002).

It is important to note that in Washington State in order to obtain release prior to a maximum expiration date an offender must have an "approved" plan. An "approved" plan consists of knowledgeable support persons, appropriate housing, and minimal resources that are not in conflict with any known risk factors for that offender. The hypothesis is, therefore, that if an offender has support people interested enough to come into the institution to learn about treatment, the likelihood of that offender developing an "approved" address is higher. Table 12.1 identifies the numbers reviewed in a preliminary look at supported group offenders at their early release date compared to matched nonsupported group offenders

CONCLUSION

Because many programs are confronted with time and resource limitations, it is important to identify adjunct treatment processes that provide useful support to traditional sex offender therapy and processes that are effective. Support is an essential component of best-practice treatment and aftercare. Ultimately, support people need to be part of a network the offender has developed and included in his therapy. Reinforcing the importance of the development of support by including support people in the therapeutic process is important (Carich & Mussack, 2001).

The vision of the family support seminar of the Washington DOC SOTP is to increase positive communications so those adults in the offender's life will be helpful and useful monitors to his transition and life in the community. Policies and practice require that the nonoffending parent or support person(s) be aware of the offender's sexually abusive behavior and participate as needed in the offender's supervision and treatment. Support persons must recognize the impact that the abuse has had on the victim and ensure that they are unequivocally willing to monitor the safety and well-being of the victim.

Collaboration among criminal justice agencies as well as stakeholders in the community must be extended to the support systems of the offender. The most comprehensive approaches to sex offender treatment and supervision involve the collaboration and coordination of efforts among all the agencies involved in the process for the purpose of preventing further sexual victimization.

It is hoped that by creating a safety net of concerned individuals around the sex offender, the chances of his recidivating may be mitigated.

Footnote

[1] The advocate's primary role is to explain her role in the supervisory collaboration as well as her role as liaison and advocate for victims and their families. Her position offers ongoing services, addresses victim concerns, and provides referrals to the community. The victim advocate is another role that assists the families and support persons to relate to the offenders, offering assistance to understand the dynamics of sex offending and the offender's manipulative behavior.

References

Aylward, A., & Sayer, M. (2002, October). *The Impact of Family Support Seminar on Release and Recidivism.* Paper presented at the annual Research and Treatment Conference of the Association for the Treatment of Sexual Abusers, Montreal, Quebec, Canada.

Gordon, A., & Packard, R. R. (1998). *The impact of community maintenance treatment on sex offender recidivism.* Paper presented to the annual meeting of the Association for the Treatment of Sexual Abusers, Vancouver, British Columbia, Canada.

Hanson, R. K., & Bussière, M. T. (1998). Predicting relapse: A meta-analysis of sexual offender recidivism studies. *Journal of Consulting and Clinical Psychology, 66,* 348–362.

Hanson, R. K., Gordon, A., Harris, A. J., Marques, J. K., Murphy, W., Quinsey, V. L., et al. (2002). First report of the Collaborative Outcome Data Project on the effectiveness of psychological treatment for sex offenders. *Sexual Abuse: A Journal of Research and Treatment, 14*(2), 169–194.

Kazura, K., Temke, M., Toth, K., & Hunter, B. (2002). Building partnerships to address challenging social problems. *Journal of Extension, 40*(1). Available: *www.joe.org/joe/2002february/iw7.html.*

Paolucci, E. O., Violato, C., & Schofield, M. A. (1998). Case need domain: Marital and family. *Correctional Services Canada Forum, 10*(3). Available: *www.csc-scc.gc.ca/text/pblct/forum/e103/103e_e.pdf.*

Chapter 13

Circles of Support and Accountability—Engaging the Community in Sexual Offender Management

by Robin J. Wilson, Ph.D. and Janice E. Picheca, M.A.

OVERVIEW

In an effort to protect citizens from sexual assault, many jurisdictions have instituted measures such as public notification, involuntary commitment, electronic tracking, and intensive supervision. Many of these measures are based on restricting offenders' activities or making the public aware of their whereabouts. Over thirty states in the United States currently require designated sex offenders to wear elaborate global tracking equipment that immediately identifies them to the general public and particularly to potential landlords or employers. But is preventing sex offenders from reestablishing themselves in their communities or obtaining housing or employment really the way to support their rehabilitation? Proponents of the current practices cannot point to any research that suggests that these approaches in and of themselves have increased public safety.

Yet there is a different possible paradigm. Restorative justice is based on a non-adversarial approach to criminal justice in which the community takes an active role in supporting not only the victim and his or her needs but the offender as well. One of the approaches taken with this model is use of Circles of Support; community volunteers are recruited and trained to form a network of support around the offender returning to his home.

In this chapter the authors describe a pilot project in which Canada's Solicitor General awarded a small grant to the Mennonite Central Committee of Ontario to establish Circles of Support and Accountability to aid in the community reintegration of sexual offenders. The results of this innovative approach are indeed encouraging and offer support for an alternative to the punitive models currently being proliferated.

INTRODUCTION

In the summer of 1988, Joseph Fredericks, a repeat child molester on conditional release, kidnapped 11-year-old Christopher Stephenson from a suburban shopping mall, sexually molested him, and ultimately killed him. Although other tragedies had occurred at or about the same time, this case was arguably the one that provided the greatest catalyst for sociopolitical change with respect to the management of sexual offenders in Canada. Surprisingly, and in spite of the undoubtedly long history of child abuse and molestation in our country, this incident was like a cold, hard slap in the face to a previously blissfully complacent populace ignorant about such things as pedophiles and child murderers. In the ensuing years, sexual offending has become arguably the most discussed of all social pathologies, particularly as the spotlight begins to settle on some of our culture's sports and entertainment icons. In their recent book, *Innocence Betrayed*, Silverman and Wilson (2002) have likened the public's abhorrence of and morbid fascination with child molesters to a "moral panic." Certainly, readers of major Canadian daily newspapers in the late 1980s would have been very unlikely to happen upon the word "pedophile" in print, whereas hardly a news day goes by now when there is not at least one such story.

OFFICIAL CONTROL OF SEX OFFENDERS IN CANADA

Sentence Release Policy

The recommendations of the Coroner's Jury in the Stephenson Inquest of 1993 had a dramatic impact on the Canadian judicial system. Indeed, the past ten years have been marked by numerous attempts to ensure greater official control of offenders. In Canada, these attempts generally fall into the following categories: (1) changes to sentencing practices; (2) orders of prohibition; (3) peace bond modifications; and (4) sex offender registries (SORs).

Canada has a long tradition of conditional release and parole; however, incidents such as the one previously noted have caused lawmakers to consider that there may be some offenders who should not be released at any point prior to sentence completion (referred to as warrant expiry date, or WED, in Canada). The following criteria must be met in order to "detain" an individual past his statutory release date (SRD), which comes at the two-thirds point in any Canadian custodial sentence:

1. The offender must be serving a sentence for an offense set out in Schedule 1 (essentially, crimes of violence or crimes against persons); and

2. The commission of the offense caused the death of or serious harm to another person and there are reasonable grounds to believe that the offender is likely to commit an offense causing death or serious harm to another person before the expiration of the offender's sentence; or

3. The offense was a sexual offense involving a child and there are reasonable grounds to believe that the offender is likely to commit a sexual offense involving a child before the expiration of the offender's sentence

One of the more unfortunate side effects of detaining offenders past their SRD is that those offenders most in need of a gradual, supervised reentry to the community are least likely to receive any assistance. Indeed, for many of these men, the term "reintegration" becomes something of a misnomer, as many of them were never "integrated" in the first place. Thus, while the practice of detention is intended to protect the public for as long as possible (by keeping the offender inside until the very last day of his sentence), it often sets up both the community and the offender for failure and further victimization.

Interestingly, in the realm of official control in Canada, it appears that some measures have been instituted as a means to accommodate the problems caused by earlier measures. For instance, the practice of detention has required the passage of at least two further pieces of legislation, both intended to manage the community risk of persons released at WED with no official supervision. In 1996, the Canadian federal government introduced changes to the peace bond section of the Criminal Code of Canada (§§ 810.1, 810.2):

Any person who fears on reasonable grounds that another person will commit an offense under certain sections of the Criminal Code of Canada, in respect of one or more persons who are under the age of fourteen years, may lay an information before a provincial court judge, whether or not the person or persons in respect of whom it is feared that the offense will be committed are named. (Criminal Code of Canada § 810.1)

In general, the police lay the information before the Court, acting as agents of the community. The result of a successful application is that the individual in question (who, actually, need not ever have offended) is placed on terms and conditions akin to being on probation or parole. Although civil libertarians have labeled Section 810 orders "proactive sentencing," the Ontario Court of Appeal has upheld the constitutionality of the community's right to safety in abridging individual (i.e., potential offenders) rights (*R. v Budreo* [2000], 142 C.C.C. [3d] 225 [ONT C.A.]; leave to appeal to Supreme Court of Canada dismissed [2000] S.C.C.A. #542).

The other legislative attempt to ensure longer accountability for offenders comes in the form of long-term supervision orders (LTSOs). LTSOs are a period of community supervision (up to ten years) to be served following completion of a sentence. These orders were instituted as a means to manage risk in the community for those offenders whose risk profile did not warrant an indeterminate sentence (i.e., designation as a dangerous offender) but where detention to WED was likely.

Sex Offender Registries

Although SORs have been in place in the United States for many decades (e.g., Jacob Wetterling Act, Megan's Law, and Pam Lyncher Sex Offender Identification and Tracking Act), Canada's first SOR, instituted in Ontario and named Christopher's Law, was only enacted in 2001.

Questionable Premises. When the Ontario SOR was launched, it was heralded as a "bold measure in community safety" (Ministry of Community Safety and Correctional Services, 2004); however, many have questioned whether the people of Ontario are really any safer now that Christopher's Law is in effect. SORs are based largely on three premises: (1) sex offenders are "predatory prowlers," (2) reoffense rates are high, and (3) nothing else will work (John Howard Society of Alberta, 2001).

- *Predatory prowlers?* Relatively few sexual crimes (23 percent—Canadian Centre for Justice Statistics, 1999) involve a stranger to the victim. In fact, it is generally known in the sex offense literature that over two-thirds of offenses occur in homes, specifically, the victim's home. It is also well-known that the mixed feelings held by child victims of a parent often prevent the child from reporting abuse by that parent. As a result, SORs are unlikely to protect people from victimization by a parent or other family member. The public's view of a sex offender as a sex-crazed, dirty old man with greasy fingers hanging out in parks and playgrounds is patently false. In fact, the vast majority of child molesters seen by these authors look and behave quite similarly to most men in our communities, save for the sexual offending.

- *Reoffense rates are high?* Essentially, the question to ask here is, "Will past criminal records tell us who the future sex offenders will be?" A 1991 national survey of sex offenders in federal penitentiaries found that only 25 percent currently serving a sentence for a sexual offense had been convicted in the past for sexual offenses (Porporino & Motiuk, 1991). The average reoffense rate noted by Hanson and Bussière (1998) in their seminal meta-analysis of predictor variables was only 13.4 percent, while other studies have noted rates slightly above or below that percentage. Taking the rough average of these two, the most likely scenario is that four of five sex offenders will not reoffend sexually. This means that a high proportion of currently active sex offenders will not appear on any SOR.

- *Nothing else will work?* One review of studies relating to the effectiveness of treatment found that far more studies reported positive results (treated group with significantly lower recidivist rates than untreated group) than inconclusive results (Federoff & Moran, 1997). The Association for the Treatment of Sexual Abusers (ATSA) Collaborative Data Project (Hanson et al., 2002) has recently demonstrated a significant treatment effect, in which the treated group reoffended at a rate 7 percent less than the untreated control group (10 percent vs. 17 percent, respectively).

Compliance Issues. In 1947, California was the first U.S. state to establish an SOR. There are now registries in each state, with the number of registered sex offenders reportedly reaching a U.S. national total of 250,000 by 1998. However, issues related to compliance abound, with state SOR compliance rates varying from less than 50 percent to better than 80 percent (Center for Sex Offender Management, 1999). With respect to the sole Canadian SOR, the Ontario government has stated (Ministry of Community Safety and Correctional Services, 2002) that the compliance rate for signing onto the Ontario SOR is 93 percent. However, that percentage drops when one looks at the compliance rate for maintenance of current addresses and yearly check-ins (offenders listed on the Ontario SOR are required to report changes of address within fifteen days and are to physically check in with police on an annual basis). One could reasonably argue that those offenders who diligently comply with the terms and conditions of any SOR are least likely to be a problem. It only makes sense that those who flout the law are those most likely to break it—in this case either by refusing to register or maintain current data or, ultimately, by reoffending.

Despite the possibly faulty or misleading premises on which SORs are based, and the obvious difficulties in regard to compliance, SORs continue to be particularly popular with law enforcement, politicians, and the general public. Clearly, the police require accurate data regarding dangerous offenders, and for that reason we believe that SORs do have some merit. However, we also strongly believe that the public has been misled as to the true value-added of SORs in ensuring community safety. No matter how good any individual police service may be, it is unlikely that there will ever be sufficient resources to hire enough officers to ensure the totality of public safety. Other means and measures must be introduced if we are to truly protect the vulnerable in our communities, and these initiatives must seek to involve the community in the process.

THE BIRTH OF CIRCLES OF SUPPORT AND ACCOUNTABILITY

In the summer of 1994, "Fred" (not his real name) was sitting in Warkworth Institution, a medium-security penitentiary managed by the Correctional Service of Canada (CSC), rapidly approaching the end of his sentence. This was Fred's fifth time in jail for sexually molesting young boys, and on this occasion the National Parole Board of Canada (NPB) had decided to deny him any form of release prior to his WED. The fact that Fred had reoffended following each of his four previous sex crime-related conditional releases provided the rationale for the NPB's detention order. A prerelease risk assessment (using the Sex Offender Appraisal Guide; Quinsey, Harris, Rice, & Cormier, 1998) completed in the institution put Fred's risk at 100 percent chance of recidivism in seven years.

Fred's institutional psychologist recognized that without a coordinated effort in the community, Fred was going to fail again. That would mean at least one child victim, and probably more. Calls to community-based corrections staff (unfortunately, including the first author of this chapter) were met with the following: "He'll be at the end of his sentence, so we'll have no jurisdiction." This response was, indeed, true— CSC has no mandate to provide treatment or other services to offenders who are no longer serving a sentence. Thus was the beginning of Fred's "Catch-22": He desperately needed assistance in the community, but there were no official means by which to get that assistance.

In discussing this predicament with Fred, the institutional psychologist learned that Fred had once been a member of a Mennonite congregation in Hamilton, Ontario, just outside Toronto. The Reverend Harry Nigh was the pastor of the Welcome Inn Church when he received the call from Warkworth Institution. Rev. Nigh barely recalled Fred, and, in fact, he only recalled enough about Fred to remember that he was not particularly fond of him. Nonetheless, when asked if there was anything that could be done about Fred's predicament, Rev. Nigh pledged to speak to his congregation and come up with a solution. That solution consisted of a handful of congregants offering to volunteer their time to assist Fred in making a smoother transition to the community.

Chaos erupted when Fred was released. While Rev. Nigh and his volunteers were pulling together a Circle of Support, the media in Hamilton were publishing daily warnings about the risk posed by Fred, including photographs and reports on his whereabouts. The Hamilton-Wentworth Police Service was also providing "around-the-clock" surveillance of Fred, at an eventual cost of tens of thousands of dollars. Essentially, as Rev. Nigh was doing everything in his power to bring Fred back to the community, the community was doing everything in its power to drive him out. This was the environment in which Circles of Support and Accountability (COSA) was born.

Over the ensuing weeks and months, Rev. Nigh met with various community agencies, including the police, and gradually convinced them to give Fred's fledgling Circle a chance to develop and to see if it would ultimately assist in keeping him out of trouble. With time, the police came to see that the Circle could act as several more sets of eyes and ears—a means by which to increase the accountability factor for Fred.

When the time came for the next sensational release, this time with "George," there was another option. Based on the experience of Rev. Nigh and his volunteers, the same process was used with George, and he was "Circled" by several volunteers from the faith community in Toronto. Like Fred, George had a lifelong history of sexually abusing young boys, and he too had been detained until the end of his sentence, effectively prohibiting him from getting the help he needed in the community (e.g., counseling by a community-based correctional psychologist, supervision by a parole officer).

In watching the successes of these first two Circles, CSC Chaplaincy and the Mennonite Central Committee of Ontario (MCCO) agreed to undertake a pilot project to see whether or not the Circles model could be expanded to assist other men in similar circumstances. In an extraordinary move, the Solicitor General of Canada approved the establishment of a small contract to provide funding for this initiative. This was extraordinary because the government had no legal responsibility; however, the Solicitor General acknowledged that the government had a "moral responsibility" to the community in assisting these men to remain offense-free. Given its long history of innovation in restorative justice in Canada, MCCO was a natural choice for stewardship of this fledgling initiative.

THE CIRCLES OF SUPPORT AND ACCOUNTABILITY MODEL

COSA Mission

The philosophy on which the COSA model was built is not a new one. Generally, it is understood in psychology and health that people with problems are more likely to succeed or recover when they have genuine care and assistance from others. Aboriginal groups have long used the circle as a mode of engagement, whether for religious, justice, or other restorative and community functions. Indeed, this can be easily seen in the current international restorative justice zeitgeist, specifically regarding family group conferencing, sentencing circles, and healing circles (see review by Cormier, 2002; also Wilson & Prinzo, 2001; Wilson, Huculak, & McWhinnie, 2002).

Specifically, we know that offenders are more likely to succeed when their reentry to society is facilitated by informed parole supervision and the application of appropriate human service (Wilson, Stewart, Stirpe, Barrett, & Cripps, 2000). Actually, this is the linchpin of conditional release. Two interesting studies have recently demonstrated the need for facilitated release in identifying significant drop-offs in offender motivation and treatment readiness following release from prison (Stirpe, Wilson, & Long, 2001; Barrett, Wilson, & Long, 2003). The process of maintaining dedication to proactive change is clearly one that requires ongoing attention (Cullen & Wilson, 2003). It is clear that simply because someone is no longer under correctional control does not mean that the benefits of support and accountability cannot be achieved by other means.

The COSA initiative seeks to assist those sex offenders who continue to present significant risk to the community but for whom the normal support and accountability framework is absent. The official COSA mission statement is:

> To substantially reduce the risk of future sexual victimization of community members by assisting and supporting released men in their task of integrating with the community and leading responsible, productive, and *accountable* lives. (Correctional Service of Canada, 2002)

Target Population. The COSA initiative was originally conceived as a means to fill a gap in service left by government policy. Essentially those at highest risk of reoffense were being released at the end of their sentences without a formal process of aftercare. As such, COSA projects have generally set their sights on men released after having completed their entire sentence (i.e., WED offenders), who have been judged to be at high risk to reoffend. In fact, the general rule of thumb has been to target individuals who seem most likely to fail, due to a lack of prosocial support in the community. Those who are likely to attract significant media attention have also been targeted.

Goal of the Project. The goal of COSA is "to promote successful integration of released men into the community by providing support, advocacy, and a way to be meaningfully accountable in exchange for living *safely* in the community" (Correctional Service of Canada, 2002). In doing so, safety is enhanced for the community, where the concern is to minimize any risk for women, children, or other vulnerable persons; victims (past or potential), where the concern is to address victims' need for healing, and to decrease feelings of future vulnerability for self or others; and the ex-offender, where the concern is to hold him accountable for behaving responsibly while ensuring that his rights as a citizen are protected and that reasonable liaison is achieved with the community, police, and the media.

Circle Mechanics

A Two-Ring Circle. A COSA is actually two circles: an inner circle consisting of community volunteers and the ex-offender (known as a Core Member) and an outer circle consisting of professionals who have volunteered their expertise to support the inner circle (see Figure 13.1). The inner circle manages the day-to-day aspects of the Core Member's community reentry, while more difficult or complicated issues (e.g., breach of conditions, treatment concerns, and reports to law enforcement or child protection) are addressed by the outer circle.

Although we originally conceived a COSA as being ideally comprised of one ex-offender and seven community volunteers, difficulties in volunteer recruitment forced us to revise this such that a realistic Circle size is now five volunteers.

A Relationship Scheme. Each COSA has at least one primary volunteer who, in the initial phase of Circle development (typically sixty to ninety days), will meet with the Core Member virtually daily. We expect that each other Circle Volunteer will be in contact with the Core Member on one or two occasions weekly during this initial phase. This enhanced degree of coverage during the beginning of the Core Member's time in the community provides him with support as he meets treatment, social, and other needs. In addition to these individual meetings, the full Circle meets on a weekly basis. A COSA is a relationship scheme based on friendship and accountability for behavior. As is expected in any friendly relationship, openness is key, and the motto "no secrets" is held close to the hearts of all involved as this is seen as the method by which accountability is most likely to be maintained.

From the inception of the project, we anticipated that a Circle's involvement in a Core Member's life would be necessarily long term, potentially continuing for years. We also expected that demands on members would decrease as the Core Member

Figure 13.1
Graphic Representation of a COSA

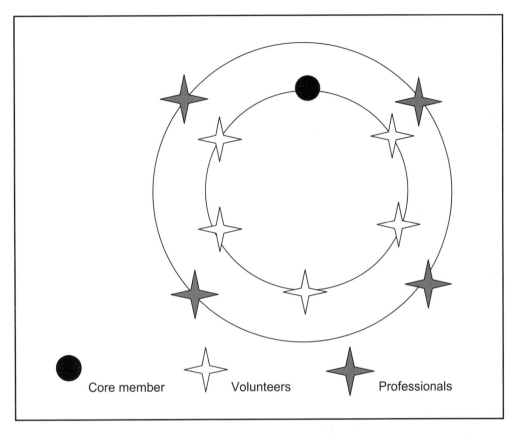

adjusted to his personal responsibilities in the community. However, it appears that we seriously misjudged what a COSA could (or would) become. Essentially, COSAs have become surrogate families for many of our Core Members. What was supposed to be a stopgap for a crack in the justice system's management of offenders has become a way of life.

Volunteer Recruitment and Training

Volunteer recruitment is by far the most rigorous aspect of Circle development and has certainly provided the greatest challenge to the various projects currently running in Canada and elsewhere. Generally, volunteers have been recruited from the faith community, but distaste for the target population is the overwhelming impediment to garnering positive interest in COSA. There is also a great need to ensure that potential volunteers are both knowledgeable about the project and honorable in their motives for wanting to be involved. The latter point requires that we select only those persons who:

• Are stable in the community;

- Are known in the community (references checked);

- Have demonstrated maturity;

- Possess healthy boundaries;

- Are available; and

- Have balance in lifestyle and viewpoint.

The knowledge-ability aspect is addressed through a rigorous training schedule, the core components of which are provided prior to volunteering in an actual COSA, with continuing education opportunities being available via the partnership with local professionals.

The first step in training, which actually provides an opportunity for screening of potential volunteers, is a half-day orientation session during which the basics of the project are outlined. This is available in two formats, one for potential volunteers and another for professionals willing to volunteer expertise to the project. Provided that volunteers are screened in following the orientation session, they progress through a four-phase training regime, consisting of an additional four days (or equivalent) and followed by placement in a Circle:

- Phase I: "The Core Workshop" (one full day);

- Phase II: Skill Building (two full days);

- Phase III: Forging a Circle (one full day); and

- Phase IV: Walking With a Core Member.

Topics of training over the four days or equivalent period include the following:

- Overview of the criminal justice system

- Restorative justice;

- Needs of survivors;

- The Circle model;

- Effects of institutionalization;

- Human sexuality and sexual deviance;

- Risk assessment;

- Boundaries and borders;

- Conflict resolution;

- Group dynamics;

- Building group cohesion;

- Circle functions;

- Crisis response and preparing for critical incident stress;

- Working with correctional officials, police, news media, and other community professionals;

- Needs assessment;

- Building a covenant;

- Court orders; and

- Closing a Circle.

EVALUATION: DO CIRCLES WORK?

The corrections literature, beginning in the 1990s, has been dominated by catchphrases such as "What Works?" and "evidence-based practice." Canadian correctional workers have been greatly influenced by the "risk, need, and responsivity" mantra of Andrews and Bonta (2003), which states that effective interventions are those that match treatment intensity to offender risk, while ensuring that criminogenic needs are precisely targeted in a manner that gives the offender ample opportunity and motivation to change in the desired direction.

One critical aspect of the evidence-based practice movement is the need to demonstrate empirically that an intervention is in fact achieving the desired goal. Project effectiveness has been traditionally gauged by relative rates of recidivism between treatment subjects and matched controls; however, given relatively low base rates in many offense categories (sex offenders, in particular—see Barbaree, 1997), *statistical* significance has often been difficult to achieve. Thus, other researchers (see Gendreau, Little, & Goggin, 1996) have suggested that we consider the *social* significance associated with an X percent decrease in recidivism that may not reach the traditional $p < .05$ level.

The evaluation of the COSA pilot project in South-Central Ontario was accomplished in two phases: (1) a quantitative examination in which traditional comparisons were made of offenders in a Circle with matched controls not in a Circle, and (2) a qualitative examination in which the experiences of various COSA stakeholders were sampled.

Quantitative Analyses—Recidivism Data

Data regarding the quantitative aspect of the evaluation of the COSA pilot project are summarized in Table 13.1, with a detailed explanation in the following paragraphs.

There are thirty WED offenders in each group included in this analysis. The groups were "matched" *a priori*, meaning that there was a conscious process involved in selecting the control sample, so that it would be a more comparable group for the COSA participants. The matching variables were "detained by NPB" (a de facto risk assessment as per the criteria outlined earlier) and "date of release." This is an admittedly crude matching protocol; however, we completed analyses after the fact to see if the groups are different in regard to prior treatment participation, completion, or otherwise. We found no significant differences between the two groups in that regard, or with respect to age or the percentage of members who have deviant phallometric test

Table 13.1
Circles of Support and Accountability: Demographic and Recidivism Data

	COSA (30)	Control (30)
M (SD) age	45.6 (11.65)	43.5 (11.13)
Deviant PHM	46.7%	46.7%
M (SD) STATIC-99	6.03 (2.17)	5.17 (1.95)
M (SD) STATIC 2002	7.17 (2.15)	6.47 (1.94)
M (SD) RRASOR*	3.17 (1.60)	2.20 (1.38)
Victims		
M number	2.63	1.60
Female only	53.3%	83.3%
Familial only	7.0%	13.0%
Children only	46.7%	46.7%
M (range) follow-up	65 (43–106)	51 (23–71)
Recidivism (N)		
Sexual‡	10.0% (3)	26.7% (8)
Expected sexual+	35.74% (10.7)	27.95% (8.4)
Violent	33.3% (10)	46.7% (14)
General	36.7% (11)	50.0% (15)
Dispositions	23	32

* $F (1,58) = 6.30$, $p < .05$; ‡ $\chi^2(1) = 2.783$, $p < .10$; +The difference between the observed and expected rates of sexual reoffending for the COSA group is significant: $\chi^2(1) = 6.667$, $p < .05$.

results. Thus, we are confident that the groups are sufficiently matched to support our findings.

Although not significantly different on the Static-99 (an actuarial risk assessment tool used with sex offenders; Hanson & Thornton, 1999), there is a somewhat higher average risk score for COSA participants. We also scored both groups on the STATIC-2002 pilot (Hanson & Thornton, 2003). Again, the COSA group is at higher relative risk. The RRASOR is a four-item actuarial risk scale (wholly contained in the STATIC-99; see Hanson, 1997). The COSA group is at significantly higher risk for sexual recidivism than is the control group, if we judge by this scale ($F (1,58) = 6.30$,

$p < .05$). However, the two groups should not differ on risk if the matching process was foolproof. In this case, it is clear that there is an overrepresentation of higher-risk sex offenders in the COSA group. Our interpretation of that finding is that the COSA project is appropriately recruiting higher-risk offenders for participation in a Circle. What this finding means, however, is that the COSA group should do more poorly on everything we measure because it comprises a higher-risk group.

In looking at the victim profiles for the two groups, the most important points to note are that the COSA group has a higher average number of victims and there are more offenders in the control group with "female only" victims and "familial only" victims. This likely explains why the two groups were different on actuarial prediction scores, as "number of previous sexual offenses," "male victim," and "unrelated victim" are points on each of the actuarial measures noted.

As one of the matching variables was "date of release," the groups should be identical in time at risk, if COSA has no effect. Also, if there was to be a difference, it should be the COSA members who are in the community for a shorter time. The opposite was found in our comparisons, with the COSA members being in the community for an average of more than a year longer.

In perusing the recidivism statistics in Table 13.1, we see that the COSA group is reoffending in all domains at a rate considerably lower than their matched counterparts, despite having a higher-risk profile. If we look at "sexual," the control group has more than double the number of reoffenses. This result approaches statistical significance ($\chi^2[1] = 2.783$, $p < .10$) and would certainly be seen as socially significant according to the aforementioned argument. In regard to actuarial projections, the control group is pretty much in line with Static-99 (8 observed vs. 8.4 expected), whereas the COSA group is reoffending sexually at a rate significantly below statistical projections (3 observed vs. 10.7 expected—$\chi^2[1] = 6.667$, $p < .05$). Overall, 36.7 percent of COSA participants have reoffended in any way in comparison to 50 percent of the controls.

We also examined the details of the sexual reoffenses in each group and, interestingly, there appears to be a harm reduction function (Marlatt, 1998) at work in the COSA group. In each instance in which a Core Member reoffended sexually, the reoffense was less invasive and violent than the offense for which he had most previously been incarcerated. For example, a Core Member who had previously committed a violent rape reoffended with an obscene phone call. No such reduction in harm was observed in the control sample.

In Table 13.1, "Dispositions" refers to the number of discrete reoffense occasions. It is more or less equivalent to "sentencing dates" on the STATIC-99. In the COSA group, eleven offenders were responsible for twenty-three events, while fifteen offenders were responsible for thirty-two events in the control. Although not statistically significant, the lesser number of offenses is clearly socially significant.

Qualitative Analyses—Experiences

The qualitative portion of the COSA pilot project evaluation was conducted to assess the impact of Circles on a variety of COSA stakeholders—Core Members, Circle Volunteers, volunteer professionals, and, equally important, the community-at-large. To achieve this aspect of the evaluation, specific surveys were developed for each of these four groups of individuals. The surveys were distributed to potential respondents through several means: following a general meeting of Circle Volunteers and Core Members, following administrative meetings of professional/agency members, or mailed electronically or through the Canadian postal service. Surveys were distributed to members of the community-at-large primarily through prearranged workshops/lectures and personal contact with faith communities and places of employment.

Survey Content. In addition to demographic information, the surveys for the Circle Volunteers, Core Members, and Professional/Agency members covered several different areas related to the experience of being involved in the COSA project, such as motivation levels, relationships with other Circle members, and organizational and professional support. The survey developed for the community-at-large was considerably shorter than that developed for the other groups, with items designed to address feelings regarding three areas: existence of the COSA project, knowledge that a high-risk offender was in the community, and knowledge that a high-risk offender was part of a Circle.

Table 13.2 outlines the demographic characteristics of each of the groups of respondents sampled in the qualitative phase.

Circle Volunteers' Perspective on Being Involved in COSA. To obtain a profile of the Circle Volunteers, various questions were asked regarding their volunteer experience, how they became involved in the COSA project, and the duration of their involvement. The majority of volunteers (63 percent) were first made aware of the COSA project through friends or family members who had either heard about the project or who were actually participating. Previous experience with corrections or contact with a Core Member provided 40 percent of the volunteers with knowledge of the COSA project. Twenty-eight percent of volunteers learned of this project through their participation in the faith community. The transition from first becoming aware of the project to actually becoming involved was motivated, for a large number of volunteers (72 percent), by wanting to work with this type of population. Approximately 30 percent of the volunteers were motivated by wanting to give back to their respective communities. Most of the volunteers (96 percent) had volunteer experience prior to their participation in the COSA project, and, overall, their dedication to volunteerism has been clear. Approximately one-third (31 percent) of the volunteers have been involved in two or more Circles and almost half (42 percent) have been involved for more than two years.

To understand Circle Volunteers' qualitative experience with COSA project, a series of questions were asked regarding personal interactions with the Core Member and with the organization (i.e., MCCO) itself. In terms of the Circle Volunteers' relationship with the Core Member, the vast majority of respondents (92 percent) felt they were at least somewhat positively received by the Core Member. Only 25 percent reported that they experienced some pressure to assist the Core Member in a way with which they did not feel comfortable. Almost all the volunteers (96 percent) reported that they believed the Core Member felt supported by the Circle, while 90 percent believed that the Core Member received a sense of acceptance by others and 82 percent believed the Core Member was able to establish friendships. As a by-product of their participation in a Circle, 84 percent of the volunteers reported that they felt the

Table 13.2
Demographic Information

	Volunteers (N = 57)	Core Members (N=12)	Professionals (N = 16)	Community (N = 77)*
Gender				
Male	63%	100%	75%	38%
Female	37%	0%	25%	62%
M (SD) Age	55 (14)	41 (14)	48 (9)	40 (15)
Marital status				
Married/C-L	57%	0%	94%	62%
Divorce/separated	25%	42%	6%	11%
Widowed	4%	0%	0%	1%
Never married	14%	58%	0%	25%
Education				
≤ 8 years	0%	17%	0%	0%
9–13 years	9%	58%	6%	8%
College	9%	17%	6%	43%
University	30%	0%	19%	33%
Graduate school	51%	0%	69%	16%
Other	2%	8%	0%	0%
Dependent children				
0	61%	83%	44%	41%
1	17%	0%	13%	14%
2+	23%	16%	43%	45%

* Note: Initially, there were 176 community respondents (65 men, 107 women, and 4 who did not specify gender). However, this sample was reduced to 77 when we excluded those respondents who indicated that they were employed in the area of criminal justice or who had prior volunteer experience in the correctional system. It was on this latter sample that analyses were conducted.

Core Member experienced an increase in self-worth, and 68 percent felt the Core Member experienced a sense of self-acceptance.

Although the vast majority of Circle Volunteers reported that they were at least moderately satisfied with their Circle (93 percent), only 35 percent reported that they would not change anything about their Circle if they had the opportunity: 23 percent reported they would make it larger, 19 percent reported they would include more social activities, and 14 percent reported they would like to see more younger volunteers.

In terms of experience with the organization 82 percent found the members of the organization to be generally helpful and 63 percent thought the organization provided support when needed. Almost 83 percent of the Circle Volunteers felt they were working as a team with the professionals involved in the Circle.

Core Members' Perspective. To obtain descriptive data documenting the Core Members' experiences with the COSA project, survey items addressed issues pertaining to their rationale for entering a Circle, as well as particular experiences at the onset of their joining a Circle ("initially") and at the time of completing the survey ("currently"). Unfortunately, only slightly less than half of those approached for information actually completed the questionnaire. Reasons for refusal ranged from literacy difficulties to mistrust of "the system." Regarding this latter point, although well-known within the COSA network, both authors are employed by the CSC, ostensibly the same organization that has meted out the justice system's punishment of all or most of the Core Members for many years.

Three-quarters of the Core Members responding reported that they decided to enter a Circle because they would have no other form of social support upon release. Fifty-eight percent reported that they were willing to try anything that would help them with their reentry to the community. Negative community reaction including increased police and media attention to their release was the motivation for half of the respondents entering into a Circle. As an aside, a good number of Core Members are initially referred to COSA by police, knowing that community risk management will be greatly assisted if the offender is involved in a Circle. So, in some cases, agreeing to enter COSA garners the offender considerable credibility with the local police service.

In terms of their initial feelings about being in a Circle, all responding Core Members expressed that they were anxious, yet thankful and relieved for having this type of help available. Half of them were proud of their involvement, and one-third felt confident that being supported by others would assist them in coping with difficult situations that might arise. There were substantial mixed feelings noted in the Core Member respondents. Just over half of the respondents reported initially experiencing negative feelings, such as concerns about confidentiality, skepticism that their involvement would actually make a difference, and a degree of pressure regarding their participation in a Circle. Over the course of involvement in the project, negative feelings dropped by approximately 25 percent and the feelings of confidence increased by approximately 25 percent.

When first released, two-thirds of the Core Member respondents reported that the Circle helped them cope with/adjust to the community by providing assistance with practical issues, such as finding a job or getting identification, in addition to providing emotional support. Fifty-eight percent reported that the Circle provided them with an opportunity to socialize. This percentage rose to 70 percent after having some experience with a Circle, indicating an increase in self-perceived social functioning. Despite expectations, only 50 percent reported that the Circle helped them with practical issues, indicating a possible area for further attention in future COSA endeavors.

Core Member respondents were asked to reflect on what they thought their experience in the community would have been like if the COSA project did not exist. All of the respondents reported that they would have felt lonely, isolated, and powerless. Eighty-two percent reported they would have had more difficulty adjusting to the community and almost two-thirds reported they would have had difficulty with relationships and would have returned to crime.

Professionals' Perspective. The COSA project in Toronto has been quite fortunate in having access to support from police, psychology, social work, corrections, psychiatry, and an advisory board. In a survey that was specifically designed for this group of respondents, the professionals were asked a series of questions regarding training provided to the Circle Volunteers, and what they liked most and least about the program. About half of the respondents reported they had been asked to provide training workshops or consultations to the Circle Volunteers. Of these respondents, 57 percent reported that they provided workshops on self-care, and 25 percent provided workshops on sex offenders (relapse prevention). Twenty-five percent reported providing the workshops or consultations on more than three occasions.

The professionals reported that they felt the COSA project increases offender responsibility and accountability (70 percent) and that attention is focused on community safety and support (63 percent). They expressed some concern in regard to Circle Volunteers' maintenance of healthy boundaries (33 percent) and that there was a lack of structure/formality (22 percent) to the program. This is to be expected given the usual safeguards most professionals maintain in regard to potential dual relationships; however, it is important to stress that COSA relationships are not professional relationships. They are intended to be much more intimate but with appropriate precautions. Otherwise, three-quarters of the respondents felt their agency was part of a "team" with the other professionals involved with the program.

Community's Perspective. Of the initial 176 community members who completed the survey, 72 percent had prior volunteer experience and 52 percent had prior experience with corrections. Forty-four percent of those with no prior corrections experience had heard of COSA prior to receiving the survey. The following results are reported on the respondents ($n = 77$) who were neither employed nor had any prior volunteer experience in the area of criminal justice. Survey items addressed feelings regarding knowledge of the existence of COSA, as well as regarding knowledge that a high-risk offender was released to the neighborhood. Knowing that the COSA project exists, 69 percent reported that they were glad that these offenders received extra support, and 62 percent reported relief that offenders were getting help. While 30 percent reported being positively surprised, approximately 14 percent reported being skeptical that the initiative would reduce crime. A few reported negative feelings, such as anger that these offenders are getting extra support (8 percent) and irritation that people would want to help these offenders (3 percent). That these sentiments were expressed by so few is interesting given the community's perspective on sex offenders in general.

If they knew that a high-risk offender had moved into their community/neighborhood, 33 percent of the respondents reported that they would feel unsafe, 30 percent would feel afraid for their safety, and 25 percent would feel shocked. About one-fifth reported that they would feel angry that this offender was in their neighborhood and

14 percent would feel angry that the offender had been let out of prison. These feelings, however, would change for 68 percent of the respondents if they knew that the offender belonged to a Circle. Participation in a Circle would indicate that the offender would be receiving additional support from others (48 percent), that he would be under some kind of supervision (53 percent), and that he was motivated not to reoffend (48 percent).

Discussion of Evaluation Information

We have been exceptionally pleased with the outcome data compiled in evaluating the COSA pilot project. Sexual reoffending by COSA Core Members is less than half that of the matched control sample, and less than one-third of that projected by Hanson and Thornton's (1999) STATIC-99 survival curves. While reoffending in any manner is tragic and regrettable, the harm reduction effect observed in those unfortunate instances in which a Core Member did reoffend sexually is also particularly encouraging.

Generally, reinvolvement in crime was also considerably less in the COSA group. An internal review conducted by Detective Wendy Leaver of the Toronto Police Service has shown that offenders according to Section 810.1 of the Criminal Code of Canada (i.e., the peace bond modification referred to earlier) are substantially less likely to reoffend when that order is paired with involvement in a COSA. In fact, Detective Leaver is a convert. After years of "putting these guys in jail," she is now a particularly active and vocal COSA adherent, having sat on several Circles as a volunteer and served as a critical liaison between the MCCO project and the Toronto Police Service.

In looking at the qualitative aspect of the COSA evaluation, we have also been struck by the positive elements of public education and engagement noted in the questionnaire responses of the community-at-large. In several recent instances in Canada where public outcry has followed the release of a "high-risk sex offender," the popular media has eventually focused on the COSA project as a bright light in an otherwise troubling state of affairs. With each piece of television or newspaper coverage, more citizens learn about the challenging work being undertaken by their counterparts. We hope that the eventual result will be that the community learns that risk management is something within their grasp.

Earlier, we noted that "Fred's" final institutional risk assessment put him at 100 percent chance of reoffending in seven years. We are pleased to announce that Fred has recently celebrated his tenth anniversary of offense-free life in the community. "George" has a similar risk rating and, despite having one of the largest collections of one-year Alcoholics Anonymous medallions (a reflection of his difficulties in remaining sober), he is also approaching his tenth year of community integration.

FUTURE DIRECTIONS

The future of COSA rests fully in the hands of the community. Recent fiscal restraint measures have demonstrated that governments are reticent to carry the full burden of financially supporting this endeavor. In many respects, sexual offending is a community-based problem that should, perhaps, be managed in a more intentional manner by the community itself. In this respect, we wholeheartedly agree with

Silverman and Wilson (2002), who suggest that a viable solution to community violence is found in community engagement of the criminal justice system. COSA is an excellent example of the community taking an active role in managing risk in its midst. However, the unpalatable nature of our target population continues to make solicitation of both volunteers and funding particularly difficult.

As the politicians and citizens of Canada call for the institution of a national sex offender registry, we would argue that support of initiatives such as COSA represents a far more credible means by which to manage offender risk in the community. Further, it is eminently likely that the financial burden of supporting such endeavors will be less than that required to establish and maintain an SOR. And, as COSAs are offered to only those offenders with demonstrated high potential for reoffending, the excessive cost of maintaining data on countless low-risk offenders would be all but eliminated.

GAINING MOMENTUM—THE INTERNATIONAL PROLIFERATION OF THE COSA MODEL

Based on the positive results achieved by the COSA pilot project in South-Central Ontario, COSA projects have been initiated in all Canadian provinces. As we write this chapter, we are aware of six COSA-type projects in development in the United States, including a relatively well-established endeavor in Minnesota and a very enthusiastic group in Denver, Colorado. In addition, projects based on the Canadian COSA model are also in progress or development in all the member nations of the United Kingdom (i.e., Northern Ireland, Scotland, Wales, England, and, interestingly, the Isle of Man), the Republic of Ireland, and the Netherlands. Interest has also been generated in South Africa, Bermuda, and Australia. Despite the oft-noted unpalatable character of sex offenders, there is clearly an international will to try other means by which to increase offender accountability and community safety. As it has always been, "No more victims" is our shared goal.

> They are my best friends. You can't share what we've shared and not become friends. If they weren't there, I'd be back inside by now.
>
> —"Kevin" in *No More Victims* (Correctional Service of Canada, 2001)

CONCLUSION

Understandably, citizens are concerned about protecting themselves and, particularly, their children against sexual predators. Consequently, legislatures have insituted public notification and involuntary commitment laws as responses to these fears. However, there was no research available at the time these laws were passed to suggest that the measures successfully protect citizens from sexual assault. In fact, surely it is counterintuitive to suggest that preventing individuals from being able to obtain employment or housing and publicly stigmatizing them would enhance their successful reintegration into the community. This chapter presents an alternative approach, grounded in the philosophy of restorative justice. In this model, citizen volunteers agree to provide support and assistance to recently released sex offenders. These volunteers are fully trained in spotting and responding to the potential for relapse. Their ability to provide practical as well as personal support to their charges has resulted in a significant lowering of the reoffense rate. Ideally, this approach will be replicated in other jurisdictions that wish to consturctively address the problem of sexual assault.

Authors' Note

The views represented in this paper do not necessarily reflect those of the Correctional Service of Canada or the Government of Canada. The authors wish to thank Michelle Prinzo and Ralph Serin for their statistical and methodological assistance, as well as Harry Nigh, Eileen Henderson, Hugh Kirkegaard, Wendy Leaver, Andrew McWhinnie, and the Mennonite Central Committee of Ontario for their unflinching dedication to trying and sticking with something a little different.

References

Andrews, D. A., & Bonta, J. (2003). *The psychology of criminal conduct* (3rd ed.). Cincinnati, OH: Anderson.

Barbaree, H. E. (1997). Evaluating treatment efficacy with sexual offenders: The insensitivity of recidivism studies to treatment effectiveness. *Sexual Abuse, 9*, 111–128.

Barrett, M., Wilson, R. J., & Long, C. (2003). Measuring motivation to change in sexual offenders from institutional intake to community treatment. *Sexual Abuse, 15*, 269–283.

Canadian Centre for Justice Statistics. (1999). Sex offenders. *Juristat, 19*.

Center for Sex Offender Management. (1999). *Sex offender registration: Policy overview and comprehensive practices* [Online]. Silver Spring, MD. Available: *www.csom.org/pubs/sexreg.html*.

Cormier, R. B. (2002). Restorative justice: Directions and principles—Developments in Canada (User Report 2002-02) [Online]. Ottawa, Ontario: Department of the Solicitor General of Canada. Available: *www.psepc-sppcc.gc.ca*.

Correctional Service of Canada. (2001). *No more victims.* Ottawa, Ontario: CSC and Red Herring Production [Eric Geringas, Director].

Correctional Service of Canada. (2002). *Circles of support and accountability: A guide to training potential volunteers, Training manual 2002* [Online]. Ottawa, Ontario: Author. Available: *www.csc-scc.gc.ca/text/prgrm/chap/Circle/cs_guide_final3_e.shtml*.

Cullen, M., & Wilson, R. J. (2003). *TRY—Treatment readiness for you: A workbook for sex offenders.* Lanham, MD: American Correctional Association.

Federoff, J. P., & Moran, B. (1997). Myths and misconceptions about sex offenders. *Canadian Journal of Human Sexuality, 6*, 263–276.

Gendreau, P., Little, T., & Goggin, C. (1996). A meta-analysis of adult offender recidivism: What works! *Criminology, 34*, 575–607.

Hanson, R. K. (1997). *The development of a brief actuarial scale for sexual offense recidivism* (User Report 1997-04) [Online]. Ottawa, Ontario: Department of the Solicitor General of Canada. Available: *www.psepc-sppcc.gc.ca*.

Hanson, R. K., & Bussière, M. T. (1998). Predicting relapse: A meta-analysis of sexual offender recidivism studies. *Journal of Consulting and Clinical Psychology, 66*, 348–362.

Hanson, R. K., Gordon, A., Harris, A. J., Marques, J. K., Murphy, W., Quinsey, V. L., et al. (2002). First report of the Collaborative Outcome Data Project on the effectiveness of psychological treatment for sex offenders. *Sexual Abuse: A Journal of Research and Treatment, 14*(2), 169–194.

Hanson, R. K., & Thornton, D. (1999). *Static-99: Improving actuarial risk assessments for sex offenders* (User Report 1999-02) [Online]. Ottawa, Ontario: Department of the Solicitor General of Canada. Available: *www.psepc-sppcc.gc.ca*.

Hanson, R. K., & Thornton, D. (2003). *Notes on the development of Static-2002* (User Report 2003-01). Ottawa, Ontario: Department of the Solicitor General of Canada. Available: *www.psepc-sppcc.gc.ca*.

John Howard Society of Alberta. (2001). *Offender registry* [Online]. Available: *www.johnhoward.ab.ca/PUB/offender.htm*.

Marlatt, G. A. (1998). *Harm reduction: Pragmatic strategies for managing high-risk behaviors.* New York: Guilford Press.

Ministry of Community Safety and Correctional Services. (2002). *First year of Ontario Sex Offender Registry a success* [Online]. Available: *www.ogov.newswire.ca/ontario/GPOE/2002/04/05/c1651.html?lmatch=&lang=_e.html.*

Ministry of Community Safety and Correctional Services. (2004). *Ontario Sex Offender Registry* [Online]. Available: *www.mpss.jus.gov.on.ca/english/police_serv./sor/sor.html.*

Porporino, F. J., & Motiuk, L. L. (1991). *Preliminary results of National Sex Offender Census* (User Report R-29). Ottawa, Ontario: Correctional Service of Canada. Available: *www.csc-scc.gc.ca.*

Quinsey, V. L., Harris, G. T., Rice, M. E., & Cormier, C. A. (1998). *Violent offenders: Appraising and managing risk.* Washington, DC: American Psychological Association.

Silverman, J., & Wilson, D. (2002). *Innocence betrayed: Paedophilia, the media and society.* Cambridge, UK: Polity Press.

Stirpe, T. S., Wilson, R. J., & Long, C. (2001). Goal attainment scaling with sexual offenders: A measure of clinical impact at post-treatment and at community follow-up. *Sexual Abuse: A Journal of Research and Treatment, 13,* 65–77.

Wilson, R. J., Huculak, B., & McWhinnie, A. (2002). Restorative justice innovations in Canada. *Behavioral Sciences and the Law, 20,* 1–18.

Wilson, R. J., & Prinzo, M. (2001). Circles of Support: A restorative justice initiative. *Journal of Psychology and Human Sexuality, 13,* 59–77.

Wilson, R. J., Stewart, L., Stirpe, T., Barrett, M., & Cripps, J. E. (2000). Community-based sex offender management: Combining parole supervision and treatment to reduce recidivism. *Canadian Journal of Criminology, 42,* 177–188.

Part 5

Juvenile Treatment

Although the field of juvenile sex offender treatment was initiated subsequent to that of the treatment of adults, it may be that this is the arena for the most creative progress in the field. Therapists working with children may be more open to looking at the holistic needs of their clients. Although prominent researchers may tell audiences that the treatment of an offender's own victimization is not indicated, as recently happened at an international conference, it can probably be assumed that what was being recommended was not that this issue be ignored in sexually reactive children. The recent advances in theory focusing on attachment disorders and the impact of trauma on brain development are most closely associated with therapy for juvenile offenders. Therapists working with adult offenders as well as those who work with juveniles should keep a close eye on development in this specialized field.

"It takes a village to raise a child," and it may take a whole community to treat juvenile sex offenders. According to Cynthia Swenson and Elizabeth Letourneau, in Chapter 14, multisystemic treatment (MST) has been shown to be a highly effective approach to the remediation of the juvenile sex offender. MST is based on the assumption that the youthful offender needs to be treated in his own environment, and it focuses on the strengths and needs of the child's family and his community. The treatment then addresses the multiple problems occurring in multiple domains. In MST, a family's lack of transportation may present as a major issue in providing the youth with the resources for changing his behavior. Thus, the therapist becomes involved in finding transportation resources for the family. Building appropriate peer and family relations may provide the most effective means to restructure a sexually inappropriate juvenile's behavior.

The controversy over the efficacy of treatment, particularly among juveniles, continues to rage. The difficulty in devising empirically based research methodology has limited our ability to draw valid conclusions on this question. In Chapter 15, Guy Bourgon, Kelly Morton-Bourgon, and Gina Madrigrano describe how fifteen different treatment programs in Canada participated in a research project designed to assess that issue. Information was gathered from the therapist, the juvenile sex offenders, and the parents of the juveniles at three points in each program. Conclusions from this study may help therapists design more effective approaches for this population.

Sex offenders in general and juvenile sex offenders in particular have often been deprived of appropriate experiences of touch. This may result in the sexualization of all tactile sensation. Thus, in dealing with this issue, touch would appear to be a natural therapeutic consideration. However, accusations against staff in residential programs have made any use of touch highly controversial, and most programs have opted for a "no touch" policy. Yet research has shown that therapeutic touch can be a highly effective modality if only it can be provided in a competent, professional manner. In Chapter 16, Jerry Thomas and C. Wilson Viar present a carefully thought out approach to dealing with touch in a residential program for juvenile sex offenders.

While researchers have rushed to develop risk assessments for adult sex offenders, tools for assessing risk among juveniles have lagged behind. David Prescott, in Chapter 17, first distinguishes between risks, needs, and responsivity as they relate to this population and then goes on to discuss types of risk factors for juveniles, including both static and dynamic factors. The key to evaluating adolescent offenders is to distinguish the child from the adult offenders so that the relevant factors are accurately identified, and so that the labeling of juveniles as high-risk sex offenders is based on scientific evidence rather than groundless assumptions.

Writing specifically about the development of a risk assessment tool for juveniles in Chapter 18, James Worling, developer of the ERASOR, discusses the development of his instrument and the specifics for conducting a juvenile sex offender risk assessment.

Ideally, focusing on the differences between adult and juvenile sex offenders will prevent misunderstandings that may have tragic consequences, either in underestimating or overestimating the risk that a juvenile may present.

Chapter 14

Multisystemic Therapy With Juvenile Sex Offenders

by Cynthia Cupit Swenson, Ph.D. and
Elizabeth J. Letourneau, Ph.D.

OVERVIEW

This chapter expounds on the issue of the provision to youthful offenders of services that have little empirical support with juvenile sex offenders. Despite a wealth of literature involving clinical description and uncontrolled studies, the case is made that we still know little about what works for this important population. A clear and scientifically based argument is made for changing both the content of interventions for juvenile sex offenders and the way treatment is currently provided.

INTRODUCTION

The majority of treatment models applied to juvenile sexual offenders (JSOs) use an individual or group modality to address specific characteristics of this population. While these models are commonplace in the United States and other countries, they have generally not been scientifically evaluated. Concerns exist that individual and group treatment models do not address the multiple factors (e.g., family, youth, and school) that relate to youth sexual offending (Chaffin, Letourneau, & Silovsky, 2002). Multisystemic therapy (MST) is a treatment model that addresses multiple factors within the youth's ecology for which efficacy has been supported by two randomized controlled trials (Borduin, Henggeler, Blaske, & Stein, 1990; Borduin & Schaeffer, 2002). This chapter (1) defines juvenile sexual offending; (2) examines the prevalence of juvenile sexual offending; (3) presents reasons to target JSOs; (4) discusses the etiology of youth sexual aggression; (5) briefly reviews the literature on youth sexual aggression; and (6) presents MST as a potential model for treating juvenile sexual offenders.

PREVALENCE OF YOUTH SEXUAL AGGRESSION

Juvenile sex offenders are minors who have committed sexual acts defined as crimes by law (Chaffin et al., 2002). Typically, they are teenagers, although the number of younger children adjudicated for sex crimes in departments of juvenile justice or prosecuted as adults in criminal courts has increased markedly during the past decade (Cauffman & Steinberg, 2001; Griffin, Torbet, & Szymanski, 1998).

The observed prevalence of juvenile sexual offending varies considerably with the method of measurement. At the low end, arrest records indicate that adolescents account for 17–20 percent of all sex crimes, excluding prostitution (Federal Bureau of Investigation, 1978–1988, as cited in Sipe, Jensen, & Everett, 1998; Maguire &

Pastore, 1998). These figures translate to a rate of approximately 150 arrests per 100,000 adolescents for rape and other sex crimes. Victim reports, however, indicate that approximately 40 percent of all sexual assaults were committed by offenders under the age of 18 (Finkelhor & Dzuiba-Leatherman, 1994; White & Koss, 1993). Similarly, self-report data from adolescent offenders (Ageton, 1983) suggest a relatively high rate for adolescents, with approximately 2,200 sexual assaults reported per 100,000 male adolescents. Finally, self-report data indicate that approximately 50 percent of male adult offenders began offending during adolescence (Abel, Mittelman, & Becker, 1985). Although each of these data sources has limitations, all suggest that juvenile sexual offending is a significant problem, especially when the psychosocial and financial costs are considered.

WHY TARGET JUVENILE SEX OFFENDERS FOR TREATMENT?

Given the prevalence rates of youth sexual aggression and the data indicating that adult offenders may start sexual offending in adolescence, providing treatment geared toward reducing recidivism is warranted. However, other factors related to costs also highlight the importance of stopping sexually aggressive behavior.

Affect on Victims

Victims of sexual assault are at increased risk for short- and long-term mental and physical health difficulties. Victims evidence relatively high rates of posttraumatic stress disorder, major depression, and substance abuse (Ageton, 1983; Boney-McCoy & Finkelhor, 1996; Browne & Finkelhor, 1986; Letourneau, Resnick, Kilpatrick, Saunders, & Best, 1996; Saunders, Villeponteaux, Lipovsky, Kilpatrick, & Veronen, 1992; Widom & Morris, 1997). Moreover, sexual assault victims are more likely than nonvictims to engage in high-risk sexual behaviors (Finkelhor, 1987; Letourneau et al., 1996). These problems often continue many years past the initial sexual assault (Saunders, Kilpatrick, Hanson, Resnick, & Walker, 1999) and increase the risk for sexually transmitted diseases and even suicide (Koss, Heise, & Russo, 1994).

Long-Term Trajectories of Sexual Offenders

Although offenders who commit sexual assault rarely engender compassion from community stakeholders, the long-term trajectories of such offenders are highly pertinent from a societal perspective. The legal consequences for JSOs include probation, incarceration, placement on offender registries (often for the remainder of their lives), public notification procedures, and indefinite civil commitment. Although community stakeholders agree that JSOs should be subject to juvenile justice processing to ensure appropriate supervision and control (Association for the Treatment of Sexual Abusers, 1997; Chaffin et al., 2002; National Task Force on Juvenile Sexual Offenders, 1993), no empirical data support the contention that more intrusive and expensive interventions are more effective at reducing recidivism than are less intrusive and costly interventions. Indeed, offenders who receive long-term juvenile justice or mental health placements are not afforded the opportunity to complete normal developmental tasks (e.g., develop same- and opposite-gender relationships with same-age prosocial peers, develop academic and social competencies in real-world academic settings, and develop the competency and independence needed to effectively emancipate from family). Consequently, it seems reasonable to hypothesize that institution-based services have the potential to decrease the probability that JSOs will mature into responsible adults (Caldwell, 2002; Chaffin et al., 2002).

Financial Costs

Sexual victimization presents a significant financial burden to both victims and society. Victims of sexual assault have annual medical expenditures two and a half times those of nonvictims (Kimerling & Calhoun, 1994; Koss et al., 1994; Koss, Koss, & Woodruff, 1991) and are more likely to obtain mental health and substance abuse treatment than are nonvictims (Saunders et al., 1999). Cohen, Miller, and Rossman (1994) concluded that mental health costs for rape victims (including lost productivity costs) were five to ten times those for robbery and assault victims, and that the aggregate costs of rape in the United States (combining monetary costs and estimates of pain and suffering as well as other nonfiscal costs to victims, society, and offenders) range between $8 billion and $9.6 billion.

Correctional and mental health costs for sexual offenders can be staggering. First, each felony conviction costs taxpayers approximately $30,014 prior to incarceration (Aos, Phipps, Barnoski, & Lieb, 1999). Incarceration (without treatment) of a single person costs between $19,000 and $30,000 per year, while civil commitment costs between $60,000 and $100,000 per year (DesLauriers & Gardner, 1999; Schwartz, 1999). Similarly, residential treatment programs are very expensive. For example, South Carolina Medicaid reimburses from $91,250 (at $250 a day per youth, minimum length of stay approximately twelve months) to $219,000 (twenty-four months at $300 a day per youth) for residential treatment of juvenile sex offenders. In contrast, community-based services are far less expensive. Regular probation is estimated to cost $625 per year (with an average of three years) and parole costs $740 per year (with an average of two years) for felony offenders (Cohen et al., 1994). Intensive probation for juvenile offenders costs $1,347 per juvenile per year (Aos et al., 1999). Outpatient treatment costs for juvenile sex offenders vary by provider and state. Personal communications with several treatment providers (see W. Murphy, January 5, 2001; multiple exchanges via ATSA listserve, retrieved January 16, 2001, from *www.atsa.org*) indicate that a twelve-month outpatient treatment program with weekly group sessions and bimonthly individual or family sessions costs between $3,000 and $4,000 a year per youth, with an average of one to two years in treatment.

In sum, the personal and financial costs of sexual offending indicate that this problem should be a high priority for treatment. Providing such treatment may prevent further victimization of others and may increase the likelihood that offenders can lead productive nonoffending lives. However, to reduce the costs to individuals and society treatments applied must be clinically effective and cost-effective. In designing such treatments, etiological factors can serve as an initial guide for treatment targets.

ETIOLOGY OF YOUTH SEXUAL AGGRESSION—CORRELATES OF SEXUAL AND NONSEXUAL AGGRESSION

Several methodological factors must be considered when examining the sparse literature that exists on the correlates of juvenile sexual offending. First, to assess unique correlates of sexual offending, a comparison group consisting of juvenile offenders who have not committed sexual offenses must be included. Otherwise, observed correlates might be associated with criminal offending in general, rather than sexual offending in particular. Second, research should include both incarcerated and non-incarcerated offenders. Research that relies only on incarcerated samples is subject to the biases associated with such samples (Reppucci & Clingempeel, 1978). Third, research should rely on measures that have demonstrated adequate reliability and validity. Fourth, analyses should be conducted separately for potentially meaningful subgroups of offenders (e.g., child molesters vs. peer rapists) to determine whether these groups differ on risk factors (Weinrott, 1996). The following review focuses on those studies that generally include such methodological strengths. Consistent with findings in the general delinquency literature (Loeber & Farrington, 1998), the correlates of juvenile sexual offending tap individual characteristics of the youths and the social contexts in which they are embedded (i.e., family, peer, and school).

Individual Characteristics

JSOs have long been assumed to have deviant sexual arousal patterns and cognitive distortions regarding their crimes. Recent research, however, has shown that JSOs demonstrate highly variable patterns of sexual arousal (Hunter, Goodwin, & Becker, 1994) that neither consistently differentiate them from other delinquents (Smith & Fischer, 1999) nor correlate with other important clinical characteristics (Becker, 1998). Nor has research demonstrated that JSOs endorse more deviant sexual fantasies than do delinquent and nondelinquent control groups (Daleiden, Kaufman, Hilliker, & O'Neil, 1998). Similarly, in contrast with their adult counterparts, research does not support the view that JSOs have more cognitive distortions regarding their crimes than do other delinquents (Ageton, 1983; Hastings, Anderson, & Hemphill, 1997).

On the other hand, several differences have been observed in the individual characteristics of JSOs versus other delinquents. JSOs are more likely to have been sexually assaulted than nonoffenders (Davis & Leitenberg, 1987), and studies indicate equal or greater rates of sexual assault for sex offenders compared with other delinquents (i.e., without sexual offenses) (Awad & Saunders, 1989; Milloy, 1994). Research has also supported the view that JSOs have higher rates of internalizing problems (e.g., anxiety and depression) than do other delinquents and nonoffending controls (Blaske, Borduin, Henggeler, & Mann, 1989; Kempton & Forehand, 1992). Finally, JSOs report similar or lower rates of alcohol and illicit substance use as compared with other delinquents (Ageton, 1983; Milloy, 1994).

Family Relations

Controlled studies have found that families of JSOs are characterized by less positive communication and warmth (Bischof, Stith, & Whitney, 1995) and more parental violence (Ford & Linney, 1995) than families of nonsexual juvenile offenders. Ageton (1983) found that JSOs reported more family disruptions (e.g., divorce) than did nonoffending controls. In a small study, Blaske et al. (1989) found that families of sexual offenders and other offenders had lower rates of positive communication than did families of nonoffenders. Currently, therefore, evidence suggests that family factors may play a role in sexual and nonsexual delinquency.

Peer Relations

The peer relations of JSOs show important differences from those of other juvenile offenders and nondelinquents. In general, JSOs tend to evidence peer deficits that are more characteristic of youths with internalizing problems, such as social isolation, low bonding with peers, low popularity, and low association with deviant peers (Blaske et al., 1989; Ford & Linney, 1995; Milloy, 1994). Moreover, juveniles who offend against young children tend to be immature relative to same-age peers (Graves, Openshaw, Ascione, & Ericksen, 1996), suggesting possible subgroup effects (i.e., child molesters vs. offenders against peers). Consistent with this perspective, JSOs who had assaulted a peer, versus those who had molested a younger child, reported significantly higher rates of association with deviant peers (Ageton, 1983).

School Functioning

Several uncontrolled studies indicate that JSOs tend to have academic deficits (Awad & Saunders, 1989; Fehrenbach, Smith, Monastersky, & Deisher, 1986), but controlled studies have not found intellectual or achievement differences between JSOs and other juvenile offenders (Ford & Linney, 1995; Jacobs, Kennedy, & Meyer, 1997). Although poor school functioning is a risk factor for delinquency in general, such problems do not seem to be related to sexual offending in particular.

In summary, with the exception of higher rates of internalizing symptoms and deficient relations with same-age peers, research suggests that JSOs may have more in common with other delinquents than is generally assumed. As discussed subsequently, these findings have important implications for the design of effective interventions.

IMPLICATIONS OF A MULTIDETERMINED ETIOLOGY FOR TREATMENT

Considering that multiple factors correlate with the risk for juvenile offending and juvenile sexual offending and that these factors range across multiple systems, several implications for treatment seem indicated. These include:

1. Intervention should occur at multiple levels in the youth's ecology;

2. Intervention should be tailored to the strengths and needs of a particular family;

3. Intervention should occur in the family's setting; and

4. Interventions should address multiple problems in multiple domains.

Next, we review what is known about the treatment of JSOs from the empirical literature. The reader is urged to keep the aforementioned implications for treatment in mind to critically evaluate how close the science regarding treatment is to the science regarding causes and correlates of youthful sexual aggression.

WHAT WE KNOW ABOUT TREATMENT FOR JUVENILE SEXUAL OFFENDERS

Although juvenile sexual offender treatment programs have proliferated during the past twenty-five years, only a few controlled research studies have examined the efficacy of the prevailing cognitive-behavioral treatment approaches with JSOs, and these studies (reviewed next) provide only modest support for this approach. Program evaluations (i.e., outcome studies with no comparison groups) have indicated that JSOs treated with cognitive-behavioral approaches have low recidivism rates (Barbaree & Cortoni, 1993; Bremer, 1992; Hagan, King, & Patros, 1994; Hunter & Santos, 1990; Schram, Milloy, & Rowe, 1991; Smets & Cebula, 1987). Nevertheless, the absence of control groups from these program evaluation studies makes it impossible to determine whether recidivism rates were influenced either positively or negatively by treatment.

Studies Examining Efficacy of Cognitive-Behavioral Juvenile Sex Offender Treatment

A recent meta-analysis on the treatment of adult and juvenile sexual offenders (Hanson et al., 2002) identified four studies of juvenile sex offender treatment that included the key criteria of comparison groups and measures of sexual recidivism. Of these four studies, only three (Borduin et al., 1990; Guarino-Ghezzi, & Kimball, 1998; Worling & Curwen, 1998) were used by Hanson and colleagues in determining the treatment odds ratio (OR). The fourth study (Lab, Shields, & Schondel, 1993) was excluded when determining the OR because assignment to groups was based on need, thus potentially confounding treatment outcome results.

Of these three studies used to generate the OR, one examined the efficacy of MST (Borduin, 1990) and two examined the efficacy of cognitive-behavioral, sex offender-specific treatment (Guarino-Ghezzi & Kimball, 1998; Worling & Curwen, 1998). Cognitive-behavioral treatment is generally considered state of the art and is the most common type of treatment provided to JSOs (McGrath, Cumming, & Burchard, 2003). At a one-year follow-up, Guarino-Ghezzi and Kimball (1998) found that none of thirty-three (0 percent) youth who received cognitive-behavioral treatment had sexually reoffended compared with one of twenty-five (4 percent) youth who received nonspecific treatment. Overall, 30.3 percent of the youth in the sex offender-specific group reoffended (sexually or nonsexually) versus 48 percent of youth in the comparison group. Guarino-Ghezzi and Kimball (1998) concluded that sex offender treatment works for adolescents. However, in the absence of random assignment, groups may have differed at pretreatment on important characteristics that were not assessed (e.g., noncriminal delinquent behavior, family composition, delinquent peer associations, and school achievement) and it is possible that such confounds may account for some portion of the between-groups variance in recidivism. In addition, the one-year follow-up of this study is quite brief and would not be considered sufficient by current standards (e.g., Hanson & Bussière, 1998, p. 358, suggest that five to ten years of follow-up is preferable). In summary, the results from this study are supportive of cognitive-behavioral treatment but lack the methodological rigor necessary for drawing firm conclusions about treatment effectiveness.

Worling and Curwen (1998; see also the published version of Worling & Curwen, 1998; Worling & Curwen, 2000) compared youth who completed cognitive-behavioral sex offender-specific treatment with youth who refused such treatment, youth who dropped out of treatment, and youth referred for assessment only. The results showed significant between-group differences in recidivism across an average follow-up period of 6.23 years ($SD = 2.02$). Youth receiving cognitive-behavioral treatment had a sexual reoffense rate of 5 percent (three of fifty-eight) and an overall reoffense rate of 35 percent (twenty of fifty-eight). Youth in the comparison groups (combined after analyses indicated no significant differences) had a sexual reoffense rate of 17.8 percent (sixteen of ninety) and a general reoffense rate of 54.4 percent (forty-nine of ninety). These results suggest a positive effect for treatment, relative to various no- or partial-treatment control groups. However, as with the study reviewed previously (Guarino-Ghezzi & Kimball, 1998), this study lacked random assignment. Another concern with the Worling and Curwen study is the inclusion of youth who refused or dropped out of treatment in the comparison group. These youth may have differed from those youth who completed treatment (or who were referred for assessment only) on factors related to recidivism risk. Consequently, in their meta-analysis, Hanson and colleagues (2002) reassigned treatment dropouts to the treatment group, and removed from consideration the treatment refuser group. After doing so, the results produced an OR of .87, the highest of the studies reviewed (ORs near or at 1.0 indicate no significant difference between groups). Consequently, these results, already limited by lack of random assignment, do not provide substantial evidence of a treatment effect. In combination, the evidence from the two studies (Guarino-Ghezzi & Kimball, 1998; Worling & Curwen, 2000) examining the effectiveness of cognitive-behavioral treatment may be considered promising but inconclusive.

Why Empirical Research on Adults May Not Reflect Treatment Efficacy in Youth

Based largely on its success in treating adult sexual offenders, cognitive-behavioral approaches have proliferated in the treatment of JSOs. While the two studies reviewed previously provide some support for cognitive-behavioral sex offender-specific treatment when compared to no treatment (Worling & Curwen, 1998) or non-specific treatment (Guarino-Ghezzi & Kimball, 1998), there are several good reasons why such treatment may not provide the most effective treatment for adolescent sexual offenders. First, little evidence suggests that JSOs possess the cognitive biases and deficits that are the foci of these treatments. Second, an extensive literature in the area of delinquency and adolescent substance abuse treatment (Arnold & Hughes, 1999; Dishion, McCord, & Poulin, 1999; Dishion, Patterson, Stoolmiller, & Skinner, 1991) suggests that group treatment of adolescents with antisocial behavior can be iatrogenic (i.e., the treatment itself can have unintended negative consequences). This is an important consideration in light of the aforementioned findings that JSOs may be more similar to other juvenile offenders than not. Third, the cognitive-behavioral model delivered in clinic and institutional settings provides little consideration of the real-world contexts in which adolescents develop. In fact, treatments that have been shown to be more effective in both the areas of delinquency (Elliott, 1998) and adolescent substance abuse (National Institute on Drug Abuse, 1999) focus interventions on risk factors across youths' natural ecologies (i.e., family, peers, and school). Likewise, and as described in greater detail later, there is evidence of a strong treatment effect for MST when employed to treat JSOs (Borduin et al., 1990; Borduin & Schaeffer, 2002).

NEW DIRECTIONS FOR TREATMENT OF JUVENILE SEXUAL OFFENDERS—MST

Although the scientific literature on causes and correlates of youth sexual aggression point out the multidetermined nature of sexual offending, in practice few treatments address these multiple factors. Instead, treatments continue to be implemented that address individual youth factors. As noted earlier, MST is one of the few treatments that addresses multiple determinants of delinquency and has scientific support for efficacy across two studies with trials of JSOs (Borduin et al., 1990; Borduin & Schaeffer, 2002). This section describes the MST model. Importantly, ongoing work is described regarding a project that is applying MST to adolescent sexual offending.

Historical Perspective

At the time that MST was developed in the late 1970s, the prevailing assumption in the fields of criminology and mental health was that "nothing works" in the treatment of juvenile offenders (i.e., nonsexual offenders). As research on the causes and correlates of adolescent antisocial behavior emerged, however, reasons for the failure of the predominant treatment at that time—individual therapy—started to become evident. Investigators were consistently finding that adolescent criminal behavior is multi-determined (Dishion et al., 1991; Loeber & Farrington, 1998). The causes were found not only in characteristics of the youth but also in family, school, peer, and neighborhood factors. Understanding the multiple determinants of antisocial behavior made it clear that treatment that focused on the individual or only one of the systems would yield little gain on the average. Rather, to be successful, treatment needed the capacity to address pertinent factors across the multiple systems in which youths are embedded. Recognition of the need for treatment to address multiple systems led to the development of MST (Henggeler & Borduin, 1990).

MST's Theoretical Foundation

The theoretical foundation of MST is rooted in systems theory and social ecological models of behavior. From these theories, behavior is understood to be multi-determined and driven largely by the relationships that children have with others in their natural environment. Based primarily on the work of Bronfenbrenner (1979), Haley (1976), and Minuchin (1974), the MST theoretical framework assumes that (1) children and adolescents are embedded in multiple systems that have direct and indi-

Figure 14.1
The Ecological Environment Showing Systems in Which a Youth Is Embedded

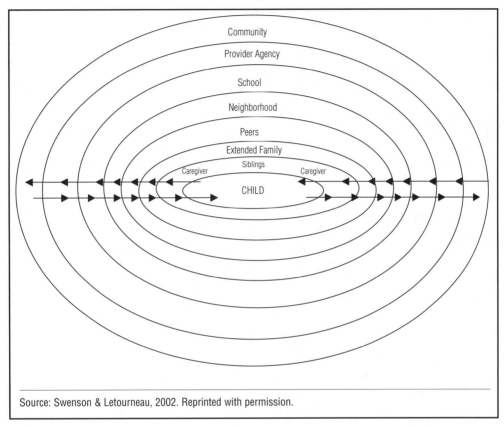

Source: Swenson & Letourneau, 2002. Reprinted with permission.

rect influences on their behavior, and (2) these influences are reciprocal and bidirectional.

Children and Adolescents Are Embedded in Multiple Systems. Based on Bronfenbrenner's (1979) formulations, Figure 14.1 shows the various systems in which youths are embedded, depicting these systems as a series of concentric circles. The child is in the center. Those systems that are closer to the child are assumed to have more relative power and influence over the child's behavior. For example, the family has influence over the child twenty-four hours per day, seven days per week; and family influence extends well into the child's adult life.

Though they are not as influential as the family, the child also has daily access to peers and other social systems. Furthermore, peer influence increases as the child ages. When that influence is with deviant peers, the likelihood is increased that the youth will exhibit antisocial behavior.

The school system's influence also can be strong, but school is typically not in session during the weekend, on evenings or holidays, or during summer vacation. Likewise, although neighborhood is an important predictor of the behavior of children, that influence is diffused among the multiple people who live within the neighborhood and by the general characteristics of the neighborhood. Finally, in the outer circle is the greater community with its laws and preferences. Children are certainly influenced by characteristics of the city in which they live and by the region of the country. Nevertheless, the influence of the family and peers remains the greatest.

Very distant from the child is the treatment provider. The relationship between the treatment provider and the child is the least influential relationship when compared with those that occur naturally. Given that service providers have the least influence of all the systems, the MST model assumes that the relationship between the therapist and child is neither necessary nor sufficient to obtain favorable clinical outcomes. This is not to say that the therapist should not have a good working relationship with the child. Rather, the primary relationship for the therapist is with the caregiver(s) who manage the child's ecology. Treatment aims to foster the development of a multilayered context in the natural ecology that supports and reinforces prosocial behavior in children and adolescents.

Influences Are Reciprocal and Bidirectional. As shown by the arrows in Figure 14.1, the interactions between each of the systems are reciprocal. That is, children are influenced by each of the systems but also exert some influence on these systems (e.g., children influence family, and family influences children). Similarly, the reciprocal and bidirectional influences extend to the other systems (e.g., treatment provider influences school, and school influences treatment provider).

MST's Research Foundation

MST has been cited as an effective treatment of adolescent antisocial behavior by the Surgeon General (U.S. Public Health Service, 1999, 2001), Elliott's (1998) Blueprints series, and leading reviewers (e.g., Farrington & Welsh, 1999; Kazdin & Weisz, 1998). These distinctions are based on the outcomes of several well-controlled and scientifically rigorous studies that examined the capacity of MST to reduce behavioral difficulties and rearrest in juvenile offenders.

The strongest evidence supporting MST in the treatment of adolescent antisocial behavior is provided by three randomized trials of MST with violent and chronic juvenile offenders conducted in the 1990s. In the Simpsonville, South Carolina Project, Henggeler, Melton, and Smith (1992) studied eighty-four juvenile offenders who were at imminent risk for out-of-home placement because of serious criminal activity. This study is one of the first in the field to demonstrate long-term reductions in criminal activity among serious juvenile offenders. Youth and their families were randomly assigned to receive either MST or the usual services provided by the Department of Juvenile Justice (DJJ). Youth receiving usual services received court orders that included a variety of stipulations (e.g., curfew, school attendance, and participation in treatment) and probation officers met with the youth to ensure that the orders were followed. Youth who did not follow probation received another chance or were placed in a DJJ facility. Youth committing additional offenses were typically placed in a DJJ facility. At posttreatment, youth who participated in MST reported less criminal activity than did their counterparts in the usual services group, and at a fifty-nine-week follow-up, MST had reduced rearrests by 43 percent. In addition, usual-services youth had an average of almost three times more weeks incarcerated (average = 16.2 weeks) than MST youth (average = 5.8 weeks). Moreover, treatment gains were maintained at long-term follow-up (Henggeler, Melton, Smith, Schoenwald, & Hanley, 1993). At 2.4 years postreferral, twice as many MST youth had not been rearrested (39 percent) as usual-services youth (20 percent).

In the second of the three randomized controlled trials, the Columbia, Missouri Project (Borduin et al., 1995), participants were 200 chronic juvenile offenders and their families that were referred by the local DJJ. Families were randomly assigned to receive either MST or individual therapy (IT). Four-year follow-up arrest data showed that youth who received MST were arrested less often and for less serious crimes than were their counterparts who received IT. While youth who completed a full course of MST had the lowest rearrest rate (22.1 percent), those who received MST but prematurely dropped out of treatment had better rates of rearrest (46.6 percent) than did IT completers (71.4 percent), IT dropouts (71.4 percent), or treatment refusers (87.5 percent).

In the third trial, the Multisite South Carolina Study, Henggeler, Melton, Brondino, Scherer, and Hanley (1997) examined the role of treatment fidelity in the successful transport of MST to community mental health clinics. In contrast with previous clinical trials in which the developers of MST provided ongoing clinical supervision and consultation (i.e., quality assurance was high), MST experts were not significantly involved in treatment implementation and quality assurance was low. Participants were 155 chronic or violent juvenile offenders who were at risk of out-of-home placement because of serious criminal involvement and their families. Youth and their families were randomly assigned to receive MST or the usual services offered by DJJ. The usual-services youth were placed on probation and participated in weekly or monthly visits with the probation officer. Youth were also referred for mental health or substance abuse treatment with community agencies. Youth with severe school problems could participate in alternative school programs. If there was no progress in the case after a six-month probation period, DJJ had the option of initiating an out-of-home placement. Not surprisingly, MST treatment effect sizes were smaller than in previous studies that had greater quality assurance. Over a 1.7-year follow-up, MST reduced rearrests by 25 percent, which was lower than reductions in rearrest in the previous MST studies with serious juvenile offenders. Days incarcerated, however, were reduced by 47 percent. Importantly, high therapist adherence to the MST treatment protocols, as assessed by caregiver reports on a standardized measure, predicted fewer rearrests and incarcerations. Thus, the relatively modest treatment effects for rearrest in this study might be attributed to considerable variance in therapist adherence to MST principles.

CLINICAL IMPLEMENTATION OF MST

Consistent with its theoretical foundation and the risk factors for youth antisocial behavior, MST is an ecological treatment model that takes into account key systems and their influences in the design of interventions. In involving each of the systems in treatment, MST takes a flexible approach where interventions are tailored to the specific strengths and needs of each individual family.

To facilitate replication studies and the transport of MST programs to community settings, MST implementation procedures have been operationalized and described extensively.

Table 14.1
The Nine Principles of MST

Principle 1: The primary purpose of assessment is to understand the fit between the identified problems and their broader systemic context.

Principle 2: Therapeutic contacts emphasize the positive and use systemic strengths as levers for change

Principle 3: Interventions are designed to promote responsible behavior and decrease irresponsible behavior among family members.

Principle 4: Interventions are present focused and action oriented, targeting specific and well-defined problems.

Principle 5: Interventions target sequences of behavior within and between multiple systems that maintain the identified problems.

Principle 6: Interventions are developmentally appropriate and fit the developmental needs of the youth.

Principle 7: Interventions are designed to require daily or weekly effort by family members.

Principle 8: Intervention effectiveness is evaluated continuously from multiple perspectives with providers assuming accountability for overcoming barriers to successful outcomes.

Principle 9: Interventions are designed to promote treatment generalization and long-term maintenance of therapeutic change by empowering caregivers to address family members' needs across multiple systemic contexts.

Nine Principles Guiding the Formulation of Clinical Interventions

The clinical practice of MST follows nine principles (see Table 14.1). As noted earlier, several studies have shown that youth outcomes are significantly associated with therapist adherence to these nine principles.

Understanding the Fit Between Identified Problems and Broader Systemic Context. MST assessment, a process that is ongoing throughout treatment, identifies specific factors within the child's social ecology that are associated with the identified behavior problems. Assessment of the strengths and needs in each of the systems (e.g., youth, family, school, peers, and neighborhood) is conducted as one of the first clinical steps, along with the development of hypotheses regarding the key factors that seem to be maintaining the problems.

Emphasis on Positive; Use of Systemic Strengths as Levers for Change. MST seeks to maintain a strength focus in treatment by identifying the strengths within each system that can be used to influence behavior change. For example, a parent may not be supervising a child adequately because the parent works at multiple jobs. Having full time employment is a strength, and in this case having a supportive grandparent is another strength that the family can draw on for assistance with supervision. A strength-focused approach extends to all other aspects of program functioning, including therapist behavior. For example, a negative view of parents will come across in supervision (e.g., comments such as "he did not do his therapy homework, he must not really want help") and in behavior toward the family (e.g., canceling appointments and not returning calls in a timely manner). Supervisors work with the therapists to have more of a strengths focus and entertain alternate explanations of parental behavior rather than the negative.

Promoting Responsible Behavior Among Family Members. MST focuses on increasing responsible behavior in the child while also influencing others in the ecology to take active and effective roles in managing the child's behavior and promoting his or her competencies. Increasing responsible behavior in caregivers is often accomplished by altering those behaviors that tend to support and sustain the problem behavior of the child, while increasing behaviors that are considered protective. For example, weak parental monitoring and supervision of a child might be changed by interventions that result in decreased depression and increased skill in parenting practices.

Present-Focused, Action-Oriented, Targeted Interventions. The fourth MST principle involves clearly defining the target behavior, determining how to measure the behavior and change in the behavior, and using well-defined interventions that specifically focus on the behavior. The advantage of such specification is that the therapist, family members, and others will know exactly whether the intervention is being implemented and whether it is working. If the intervention is not producing the desired outcomes, the therapist must be able to rapidly determine so and change the course. This principle keeps the key goals and targeted outcomes in the forefront of the case.

Targeting Sequences of Behavior Within and Between Multiple Systems That Maintain Identified Problems. Consistent with systems theory, by defining the sequence of behaviors and making key changes to that sequence, one can change the behavioral outcomes. Importantly, with JSOs, these sequences can pertain to behaviors that lead to grooming and victimizing children or peers or even to interactions between parent and child that affect family relations. This principle helps the therapist to remember that changes in relations are the keys to changing problem behavior.

Developmentally Appropriate Interventions. The implication of Principle 6 is that interventions should be geared to the developmental needs of the youth. Developmental appropriateness, however, not only refers to what an individual can handle cognitively but also to where a child or parent is developmentally in the treatment process. For example, assume the therapist is working with a youth who is trying to make friends but does not have the requisite experience to accomplish this task with same-age peers alone. Here, the therapist determines that the youth is at the early stages of developing social skills (i.e., existing skills might be lower than that of peers). Therefore, the therapist works with the youth to demonstrate basic skills for interacting with peers or joining in a group through role-play, with the parent present, before the behavior is tried out *in vivo*. Thus, MST gears interventions to the developmental needs of the youth with support from the parent by ensuring that intervention participants have the requisite knowledge, skills, and support to succeed.

Requiring Daily or Weekly Effort by Family Members. This seventh principle involves engagement of all participants in a series of tasks that produce incremental successes. By accomplishing these tasks on a daily basis, the likelihood is increased that goal-oriented behavior-change tasks will become a part of the family's repertoire. In addition, the assignment of frequent but clinically pertinent homework assignments provides valuable information to the therapist regarding family engagement in the treatment process.

Evaluating Intervention Effectiveness Continuously From Multiple Perspectives. Each intervention is designed to allow all participants to monitor progress and success. The therapist collaborates with the participants to design the interventions and teaches them to adapt the interventions based on an ongoing evaluation of effectiveness. The evaluation of the effectiveness comes from the observations and feedback of all the participants involved in the intervention. If the intervention is not producing the desired behavior change, the therapist is responsible for determining the barriers to success and working with the participants to design strategies to overcome those barriers.

Promoting Treatment Generalization and Long-Term Maintenance of Therapeutic Change by Empowering Caregivers. The generalization of outcomes means that the caregivers can continue to manage the behavior of the child in the natural ecology when the therapist is no longer present. Thus, through the treatment process, therapists must give caregivers the tools to solve the child and family's day-to-day difficulties. Parents are empowered with the knowledge and skills to take care of the clinical needs of their child. They must be empowered to carry out the interventions in the absence of the therapist both during treatment and after treatment is completed.

Family-Friendly Engagement Process

The MST therapist and clinical team are responsible for family engagement and outcomes (Cunningham & Henggeler, 1999). In the United States, the typical dropout rate is high for a clinic providing outpatient mental health services. Rather than waiting for a family to engage and closing a case due to lack of response when they do not engage in a timely fashion, with MST the therapist must discover how to engage the family and others in the ecology in treatment. In fact, this is the first step in treatment. Until the family is engaged, treatment can neither begin nor progress. At first, families may be hesitant to collaborate with the therapist (e.g., canceling appointments). There are, however, many valid and understandable reasons why a family might not be willing to engage in treatment. For example, family members might not trust the system providing the therapy, or they might have financial or other stressors that are a more important priority. One of the therapist's tasks is to address these reasons to the satisfaction of the family members.

Several aspects of the MST process are designed to promote family engagement in treatment. First, as suggested previously, the strengths focus of MST therapists contrasts favorably with the deficits focus that many families have experienced in their interactions with service systems. Second, as noted subsequently, the home-based model of service delivery used in MST helps engagement by overcoming barriers to service delivery. Third, treatment is a collaborative process and collaborative relations facilitate engagement. Fourth, rather than giving up on a family or labeling them "resistant" when they do not initially engage, the treatment team is responsible for assessing and understanding family barriers to engagement. Then, new engagement strategies are implemented to overcome these barriers. Finally, engagement is viewed as an ongoing process rather than a task that is completed and requires no further work. Thus, therapists continuously monitor the family's level of engagement and take corrective actions when engagement is waning.

Structured Analytical Process Used to Prioritize Interventions

The MST analytical process shown in Figure 14.2 is used to operationalize the nine treatment principles, as is further detailed below.

Referral Behavior. Starting with the identification of referral behaviors from multiple vantage points (i.e., caregivers, youth, child protective services, probation officer, other invested parties, and official records), the therapist consolidates the targets for change and measures the current level of these problem behaviors as a baseline.

Desired Outcomes of Family and Other Key Participants. Next, the key individuals in the child's natural ecology are identified and recruited as participants in treatment. All persons are interviewed to gain their perspective of the problem, to identify the strengths that they bring and their view of the child and family strengths, and to determine from their perspective what changes will be necessary to achieve success. Information from key participants is used to develop the overarching goals of treatment.

Overarching Goals. The overarching goals define the scope and the end point of MST treatment. When these goals are attained, treatment is complete. Overarching goals must be realistic for the treatment time frame and concrete and measurable so that any of the key participants can tell if the goal is met. To remain focused and on task, all subsequent interventions must serve at least one of the overarching goals.

MST Conceptualization of "Fit." After the overarching goals are set, the next step is to identify the "fit" of the problem behaviors within the context of the youth's natural ecology. For example, assume a case in which a male juvenile has touched his sister in a sexual way, which led to the referral, and assume that this behavior is the key behavior to stop. Considering input from each of the systems and knowledge of the family based on observations, the therapist records possible factors that are driving the sexual behavior on a "fit circle." She determines the following fit factors: (1) the youth has low skills for making friends and interacting with peers; (2) the youth has been left to baby-sit his sister, so parental monitoring is low; (3) the sequence of events that led up to the sexual abuse started with the parent "putting down" and yelling at the youth; and (4) the school frequently leaves messages for the parent concerning the youth's difficulties at school, and these messages precipitate conflict between the parent and youth that results in name calling.

Intermediary Goals. After the fit factors have been comprehensively identified, the therapist and clinical team determine which of the factors are the primary drivers of

Figure 14.2
The MST Analytical Process

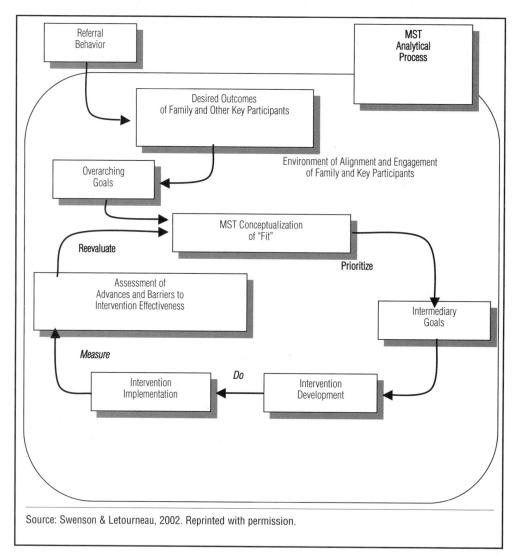

Source: Swenson & Letourneau, 2002. Reprinted with permission.

the behavior problems. Those factors are targeted initially for change, and those changes are defined as intermediary goals. For example, low parental monitoring might be viewed as the primary factor that gives the youth in the foregoing example access to his sister, and therapeutic attention (i.e., who will do what, when, where, and how) might initially focus on planning how the youth will be monitored and not left alone with any children. Changes in parental monitoring are viewed as intermediate outcomes—targets that lead to desired changes in the overarching goal.

Intervention Development and Implementation. The interventions are implemented with all participants monitoring the success and providing feedback to the therapist and caregivers. Throughout the intervention process, the therapist and caregivers compare the intended outcomes with the actual outcomes and measure the successes achieved. If sufficient success has not been obtained, the therapist and treatment participants identify the barriers to achieving the treatment goals. This new information is then compared with or added to the current understanding of how the behaviors "fit" within the natural ecology, and the process is reinitiated each week (i.e., fit → prioritization → interventions → evaluation). The structured analytic process continues until such time as the overarching goals have been completed. At the end of treatment, the therapist and family review each of the goals and the successes in achieving those goals. Throughout treatment, the therapist helps the family to address the problems as independently as possible and to build an indigenous support system that supports the interactional changes that have been achieved.

Evidence-Based Treatment Techniques Integrated Into MST Conceptual Framework. A core feature of the MST model is the integration of evidence-based treatment approaches. MST incorporates interventions that have empirical support, such as the cognitive-behavioral therapies, behavior therapies, pragmatic family therapies, and certain pharmacological interventions (e.g., for attention deficit hyperactivity disorder). There are several major differences between using these techniques within MST and using them alone, however. First, within MST, the ecology, rather than the individual child or the family alone, is the client. Whereas the aforementioned evidence-based treatments have historically focused on a limited aspect of the youth's social ecology (e.g., individual cognitive-behavioral social skills training), MST integrates those interventions into a broad-based ecological framework that addresses a range of pertinent factors across family, peer, school, and community contexts. Second, because caregivers are viewed as critical to achieving favorable long-term outcomes, interventions are delivered primarily by the caregivers whenever possible. For example, the therapist might teach the mother cognitive-behavioral therapy skills for improving the youth's social skills, and the mother would then teach these skills to her son.

Although evidence-based techniques are used and high value is placed on treatment fidelity, however, those techniques must sometimes be adapted to better fit the developmental level of a particular family. For example, in cases in which skills training is used, the therapist must understand what is feasible for the parent or youth. Cognitive or experience limitations might be a barrier to complicated interventions. Instead, the therapist (with support from the treatment team) might have to adapt the intervention to its simplest components and provide very concrete cues and instructions for implementing the intervention. Thus, treatment techniques might have to be modified to forms that can be implemented by parents of varying strengths and limitations.

Home-Based Delivery of Services

MST has been delivered via a home-based model of service delivery in all the MST research studies and across all the MST dissemination sites in the United States and internationally. The home-based model removes barriers to service access and promotes the capacity of interventions to alter the youth's ecology. The characteristics of MST service delivery include:

1. Clinicians carry low caseloads of three to six families, which allows intensive services to be provided to each family.

2. Therapists work within a team of three to four practitioners, though each clinician has his or her own caseload.

3. Treatment occurs daily to several times a week, with sessions decreasing in frequency as the family progresses (i.e., titrated to family need).

4. Treatment is time-limited and generally lasts four to seven months, depending on the seriousness of the problems and success of the interventions.

5. Treatment is delivered in the family's natural environment: in the home, community, or other places convenient to the family.

6. Treatment is delivered at times convenient to the family; thus therapists work a flexible schedule.

7. Therapists are available to clients twenty-four hours per day, seven days per week; generally, a shared on-call system is developed for use after hours.

The home-based service delivery system allows the provision of very intensive clinical services that are designed to keep children with their families and prevent out-of-home placements.

Highly Supportive Supervision Process

The purpose of MST clinical supervision is to help therapists achieve desired clinical outcomes with their families. MST clinical supervision explicitly provides therapists with an understanding of the MST model, facilitates adherence to the nine treatment principles, assists in determining ways to engage families and professionals from other systems, assists in learning and implementing evidence-based techniques, and helps identify barriers to the success of interventions. To fulfill these goals, MST provides a high level of weekly supervision (i.e., average two to four hours of face-to-face contact with each therapist) along with supervisor availability that matches the therapist schedule—twenty-four hours a day, seven days a week. The clinical supervisor is available to consult with the therapist when needed and even to visit the family with the therapist to address safety concerns or for clinical skill building. As specified in the MST supervisory manual (Henggeler & Schoenwald, 1998), the supervisor is responsible for building the therapists' capacity to be effective by determining the barriers to low adherence, when evident, and developing strategies to overcome those barriers (e.g., additional learning experiences, listening to tapes of sessions, or accompanying the therapist on a family session).

Weekly supervision sessions, held in a group format, are structured and goal oriented. Each therapist becomes familiar with every case. Such familiarity is important when a therapist responds to an after-hours crisis call for a family that is not on the therapist's primary caseload, as it increases both the family's and therapist's comfort in interacting.

Stringent Quality Assurance Process to Promote Treatment Fidelity

Several published studies (Henggeler et al., 1997; Henggeler, Pickrel, & Brondino, 1999; Huey, Henggeler, Brondino, & Pickrel, 2000; Schoenwald,

Henggeler, Brondino, & Rowland, 2000; Schoenwald, Sheidow, Letourneau, & Liao, 2003) have demonstrated significant associations between therapist fidelity to MST treatment principles and outcomes for youths (e.g., rearrest and incarceration) and families (e.g., improved functioning). In light of the importance of treatment adherence to MST outcomes, considerable attention is devoted to quality assurance mechanisms aimed at enhancing treatment fidelity. The quality assurance system includes an orientation training week; quarterly booster training; weekly on-site MST supervision; weekly consultation from an MST expert; feedback on adherence ratings from parents and therapists; and, in MST clinical trials, feedback via expert ratings of audiotaped therapy sessions.

With the exception of MST treatment that is provided within the context of research programs in clinical trials, all components of the quality assurance system are provided by MST Services, which has the exclusive license for the transport of MST technology and intellectual property through the Medical University of South Carolina.

Orientation Training Week. Prior to beginning an MST program, therapists, supervisors, and administrators participate in an initial five-day orientation. This training provides an overview of the MST treatment model and carefully reviews the treatment manual (Henggeler, Schoenwald, Borduin, Rowland, & Cunningham, 1998). The week includes some didactic instruction along with role-play techniques and group exercises to provide practice.

Booster Training. Clinical teams participate in quarterly booster trainings. The content of that training is specific to the needs of the clinical team. Examples of the types of booster training that occur include specific techniques for treating juvenile sexual offenders and their families and treatment for serious mental illness in caregivers.

Weekly On-Site Supervision. As noted previously, weekly supervision is intensive and geared toward helping therapists achieve the overarching goals for each family.

Weekly Consultation From an MST Expert. Following the MST consultation protocol (Schoenwald, 1998), an MST consultant who is distal to the program site provides weekly consultation to the team with the aim of promoting positive client outcomes through adherence to the MST treatment model. This consultation is over the phone and generally involves one hour per week. Similar to the supervisory process, the consultant receives faxed copies of the status of each case (i.e., goals, progress, and barriers) prior to the conference call for review. Feedback on adherence ratings from parents and therapists and standardized ratings measuring adherence to the nine principles are completed by the caregivers on a regular basis. The Therapist Adherence Measure (TAM; Henggeler & Borduin, 1992) is completed by the parent during the second week of MST, and once every four weeks thereafter. Feedback is given to the therapist regarding how closely the model is being followed, and corrective strategies are developed when treatment adherence is low. Similarly, the Supervisor Adherence Measure (SAM; Schoenwald, Henggeler, & Edwards, 1998) is completed by the therapists one month after the MST program begins and every two months thereafter. The SAM evaluates the supervisor's adherence to the MST model of supervision. The TAM and SAM and their scoring are available on the MST Institute website (*www.mstinstitute.org*).

Feedback Via Expert Ratings of Audiotaped Sessions. In MST clinical trials, where treatment fidelity is absolutely critical for the validity of the research, therapists audiotape every treatment session. On a weekly basis, a session tape is randomly selected and rated by an expert to measure adherence to the nine principles. Therapists are given feedback on the adherence ratings, and comments are provided on adherence to each principle.

RESEARCH EVIDENCE SUPPORTING MST WITH JUVENILE SEXUAL OFFENDERS

Completed Studies

Two randomized clinical trials have provided initial evidence of the efficacy of MST for reducing sexual crime among juveniles (Borduin et al., 1990; Borduin, Schaeffer, & Heilblum, 2000; Borduin & Schaeffer, 2002). In the first study, sixteen adolescents and their families were randomly assigned to home-based MST services provided by doctoral students in clinical psychology or to outpatient individual therapy provided by master's-level mental health professionals in the local community. Three-year recidivism data were collected from juvenile court records, adult court records, and state police records. None of the adolescents had moved out of the area at follow-up. Recidivism for sexual offenses was 12.5 percent for adolescents who received MST (with a mean of 0.12 sexual arrests per adolescent) and 75 percent for adolescents who received individual therapy (mean of 1.62 sexual arrests per adolescent). Recidivism for nonsexual offenses was 25 percent for MST adolescents (mean of 0.62 arrests per adolescent) and 50 percent for adolescents in the individual therapy condition (mean of 2.25 arrests).

Borduin and his colleagues recently completed a larger study with a longer follow-up (Borduin & Schaeffer, 2002). Forty-eight adolescents who had raped peers or adults ($N = 24$) or had molested younger children ($N = 24$) were randomly assigned to MST, delivered by doctoral students in clinical psychology, or usual services. Adolescents in the usual-services condition received court orders including one or more stipulations (e.g., individual or group therapy at local agencies, alternative schooling, or curfew), and adherence to these stipulations was monitored weekly by deputy juvenile officers. At posttreatment, adolescents in the MST condition had fewer behavior problems, less criminal offending (self-reported), more positive and less negative family relations (i.e., more warmth, less conflict) and improved peer relations (i.e., more emotional bonding with peers and less involvement with deviant peers), and better grades in school than did adolescents in the usual-services condition. Parents in the MST condition reported decreased symptomatology relative to their counterparts in the usual services condition. In addition, adolescents in the MST condition spent seventy-five fewer days in out-of-home placements during the first year following referral to treatment than did adolescents in the usual-services condition. Most important, an eight-year follow-up revealed that adolescents in the MST condition were less likely than their usual-services counterparts to be arrested for sexual (12.5 percent vs. 41.7 percent) or nonsexual (29.2 percent vs. 62.5 percent) crimes and spent one-third as many days incarcerated as adults. The two-year recidivism rate was 12.5 percent (i.e., all sexual reoffenses occurred within the first two years) for the

MST group and 37.5 percent for the usual services group (i.e., 96 percent of all sexual reoffenses occurred within the first two years (Borduin & Schaeffer, 2002). Importantly, offender type (peer/adult rapists vs. child molesters) did not moderate MST treatment effectiveness. For both offender types, recidivism was about three times greater for youth in the comparison group. These recent findings replicated and extended those of Borduin et al. (1990) and provide support for the efficacy of MST with juvenile sex offenders. It is now time to assess the effectiveness of MST with a more substantial sample and using practicing clinicians from a real-world community mental health setting.

Current Clinical Trial

At present, a five-year randomized clinical trial funded by the National Institute of Mental Health (NIMH) is under way, examining the effectiveness of MST with JSOs. This study expands on the two smaller efficacy studies by employing a larger sample size (sample goal = 160 youth and families); providing MST within a "real-world" provider setting (vs. the doctoral-level students who provided MST in the two efficacy trials); and comparing MST with an outpatient, community-based, cognitive-behavioral sex offender treatment program (Letourneau, 2004a; Swenson & Letourneau, 2002). For the purposes of treating JSOs and their families, MST has been adapted to address issues believed to occur more commonly among these families than among families of other juvenile delinquents). These adaptations focus on community safety, interrupting the offender's grooming process (i.e., those strategies used by some adolescents to gain access to sexual assault victims), and reducing denial, particularly in caregivers (e.g., see Swenson, Henggeler, Schoenwald, Kaufman, & Randall, 1998). At present, too few participants are enrolled to provide even preliminary information on results. The following case study illustrates some of the techniques used.

Case Study

Referral Behavior. The following case was drawn from our records. Names and some facts have been altered to protect the identity of the family. "Randall" was a 12-year-old boy referred following conviction in juvenile court for fondling his younger sister (age 10) on numerous occasions. He was also alleged to have inappropriately touched other girls at his school, though no formal charges resulted from these reports.

Desired Outcomes—Strengths and Needs. At the time of referral, numerous strengths were noted. Randall resided with both parents and his younger sister. He was doing well at school, liked sports, and was closely monitored within a close-knit neighborhood. The family had both formal and informal supports at their disposal and the father was working full time. Systemic weaknesses or needs were that Randall was impulsive, verbally aggressive to family members, and denied that he had touched his sister. His parents also denied the incidents and tended to blame their daughter for this "problem." Both parents had developmental delays and the father had serious physical problems. Randall was bullied at school and in his neighborhood and did not have many friends. Finally, although his father worked, the family was frequently late with bills.

The family's denial of Randall's sexual crime was further supported by his probation officer, who suggested to the MST therapist that the father may have actually done the touching. Despite this widespread denial of Randall's culpability, it seemed clear from the sister's statements to child protective workers, and from the additional allegations made by schoolmates, that Randall did indeed have a "touching problem" that needed to be specifically targeted in treatment. Furthermore, the probation officer was unable to provide a convincing rationale for why he believed the father may have molested Randall's sister.

Treatment goals were obtained from both parents, Randall, his sister, one close friend of the family who provided substantial support, the probation officer, a family therapist who was already working in the home, and the MST therapist. These goals tended to focus on (1) elimination of inappropriate touching (goals of MST therapist and sister); (2) improved behavior at home (goals of both parents); (3) improved peer relationships and social skills (goals of Randall and the probation officer); and (4) improved parenting (goals of MST and family therapists and family friend).

Safety First. Because of the widespread denial, safety was of immediate concern and increasing the sister's safety from further acts of touching or other inappropriate behaviors took priority. Despite their unwillingness to view Randall as the wrong-doer, both parents agreed to increased monitoring of Randall and they implemented new rules in the house that prohibited Randall from touching his sister and from being in the same room as his sister unless monitored by an adult. When the MST therapist dropped by unannounced to visit the family and found Randall and his sister playing video games in their parent's room without direct adult supervision (i.e., the mother was in another room in their trailer home), he convinced the parents to place an alarm on Randall's door that sounds whenever Randall leaves his room. Also, the family friend who stopped by nearly every day was asked to help implement the new household rules and agreed to do so.

Interventions for Fit Factors. Randall's father became ill shortly after MST began and was hospitalized for the first half of the treatment. Family tension and fighting decreased markedly during this time. However, the MST therapist also noticed poor boundaries between Randall and his mother and worked to correct these. For example, when seated next to one another on a couch during sessions, Randall would practically sit in his mother's lap and there was substantial physical contact between the two. Furthermore, it was clear that Randall's mother treated Randall more as an equal and as a friend than as a 12-year-old child. The MST therapist worked with the mother to solidify her role as caregiver and Randall's role as child. Household rules that supported nonsexual behavior were not in place, so additional household rules were implemented to reduce the level of family sexuality in the home (e.g., no sitting in laps and no nudity). When the father returned home after a lengthy hospitalization, the MST therapist worked on marital issues, specifically to improve the parents' low bond with one another.

While the safety plan and household rules were being implemented, the MST therapist worked with the caregivers and school personnel to help Randall increase his involvement in prosocial activities with prosocial peers. Unfortunately, because Randall attended special education classes, he was prohibited from participating in school-based sports. After several weeks of searching, a YMCA program was located, as was funding for both the program and transportation to/from the facility.

Frequent communication between parents and the school was facilitated by the MST therapist until the caregivers demonstrated the ability to contact the school on their own. Randall's behavior at school and at home improved markedly in response to the new rules in place at home and most of the attention eventually shifted to solidifying the marital relationship and the parents' ability to maintain safety for their daughter. Specifically, throughout the course of treatment, no new allegations about inappropriate sexual behaviors were made.

Intervening With Other Systems. Unbeknownst to the MST therapist, and prior to the start of MST, Child Protective Services (CPS) had recommended removal of both children from the home. This petition was heard by the courts about halfway through the MST process, when no new claims had been made regarding inappropriate touching or other behaviors and after significant progress had been made with Randall and his caregivers. The MST therapist presented evidence that though developmentally delayed, the caregivers were able to implement rules to improve the safety of both their children. In addition, both Randall and his sister continued to do well in school and Randall's social skills were improving with his increased exposure to prosocial peers. The MST therapist successfully argued for keeping the children with their parents for an additional two months, after which the case would be reevaluated by CPS.

Summary of the Case. Through MST, the major fit factors addressed were parental monitoring, poor parent-child boundaries, lack of rules that inhibited sexual behavior in the home, low husband-wife bond, and Randall's low involvement in age-appropriate activities with prosocial peers. In addition, the therapist had to intervene and communicate with CPS to prevent out-of-home placement, which appeared unwarranted. As a result of family changes, the risk to Randall's sister of further sexual behavior by Randall was reduced (though it would be impossible to verify, and imprudent to suggest, that such risk was eliminated altogether). Further, Randall improved his social skills with peers and prosocial activities. Finally, the increase in parenting and in the parental bond helped the parents establish themselves in a parental role and the children in a child role.

CONCLUSION

To decrease the risk for future victimization of children and to keep families together, effective treatments must be applied to the problem of juvenile sexual offending. At present, research indicating which treatments are effective for reducing sexual offending is in embryonic stages. Several studies have been published on treatment of sexual offending (Hanson et al., 2002). However, the majority of these studies do not use scientific methods that can actually determine whether they are effective (Letourneau, 2004b).

Additional research is badly needed in this field (see Letourneau, 2004b). In particular, there is a great need for scientifically rigorous research examining the most common treatment modalities used with JSOs (i.e., residential sex offender treatment, outpatient cognitive-behavioral sex offender-specific group treatment). At this juncture, we are working to meet this scientific standard with MST studies. Thus far, preliminary evidence supports the efficacy of MST as used with JSOs as well as the efficacy of cognitive-behavioral treatment. A current study is under way to compare these two types of treatment and to determine whether the positive results from the two smaller MST efficacy trials can be replicated in a real-world setting with a larger sample of JSOs and their families. We believe that any treatment that purports to reduce sexual recidivism rates should, at minimum, address factors across a youth's ecology and should not focus solely on changing individual characteristics as this strategy seems likely to be insufficient in the face of the multitude of factors associated with sexual offending. However, only good research that compares well-defined treatments is capable of addressing this belief answering this question.

With regard to the future, although expensive and complex, randomized clinical trials are the gold standard for examining treatment effectiveness. If we are to take seriously the problem of sexual abuse, we must take seriously the scientific evaluation of treatments and use the best methods to determine if we are truly protecting and helping our children.

Author's Note

Correspondence should be addressed to Cynthia Cupit Swenson, Family Services Research Center, Department of Psychiatry and Behavioral Sciences, Medical University of South Carolina, 67 President Street—Suite CPP, PO Box 250861, Charleston, SC 29425. Preparation of this manuscript was supported by grants MH60663-01 and MH06541401A1 from the National Institute of Mental Health.

References

Abel, G. G., Mittelman, M. S., & Becker, J. V. (1985). Sex offenders: Results of assessment and recommendations for treatment in clinical criminology. In M. H. Ben-Aron, S. J. Hucker, & C. D. Webster (Eds.), *The assessment and treatment of criminal behavior* (pp. 191–205). Toronto, Ontario, Canada: M & M Graphic.

Ageton, S. S. (1983). *Sexual assault among adolescents.* Lexington, MA: Lexington Books.

Aos, S., Phipps, P., Barnoski, R., & Lieb, R. (1999). *The comparative costs and benefits of programs to reduce crime: A review of national research findings with implications for Washington State* (Version 3.0). Olympia: Washington State Institute for Public Policy.

Arnold, M. E., & Hughes, J. N. (1999). First do no harm: Adverse effects of grouping deviant youth for skills training. *Journal of School Psychology, 37,* 99–115.

Association for the Treatment of Sexual Abusers. (1997). *Ethical standards and principles for the management of sexual abusers.* Beaverton, OR: Author.

Awad, G. A., & Saunders, E. B. (1989). Adolescent child molesters: Clinical observations. *Child Psychiatry and Human Development, 19,* 195–206.

Barbaree, H. E., & Cortoni, F. A. (1993). Treatment of the juvenile sex offender within the criminal justice and mental health systems. In H. E. Barbaree, W. L. Marshall, & S. M. Hudson (Eds.), *The juvenile sex offender* (pp. 243–263). New York: Guilford Press.

Becker, J. V. (1998). What we know about the characteristics and treatment of adolescents who have committed sexual offenses. *Child Maltreatment, 3,* 317–329.

Bischof, G. P., Stith, S. M., & Whitney, M. L. (1995). Family environments of adolescent sex offenders and other juvenile delinquents. *Adolescence, 30,* 157–170.

Blaske, D. M., Borduin, C. M., Henggeler, S. W., & Mann, B. J. (1989). Individual, family, and peer characteristics of adolescent sex offenders and assaultive offenders. *Developmental Psychology, 25*(5), 846–855.

Boney-McCoy, S., & Finkelhor, D. (1996). Is youth victimization related to trauma symptoms and depression after controlling for prior symptoms and family relationships? A longitudinal, prospective study. *Journal of Consulting and Clinical Psychology, 64,* 1406–1416.

Borduin, C. M., Henggeler, S. W., Blaske, D. M., & Stein, R. J. (1990). Multisystemic treatment of adolescent sexual offenders. *International Journal of Offender Therapy and Comparative Criminology, 34,* 105–113.

Borduin, C. M., Mann, B. J., Cone, L. T., Henggeler, S. W., Fucci, B. R., Blaske, D. M., et al. (1995). Multisystemic treatment of serious juvenile offenders: Long-term prevention of criminality and violence. *Journal of Consulting and Clinical Psychology, 63,* 569–578.

Borduin, C. M., & Schaeffer, C. M. (2002). Multisystemic treatment of juvenile sexual offenders: A progress report. *Journal of Psychology and Human Sexuality, 13,* 25–42.

Borduin, C. M., Schaeffer, C. M., & Heilblum, N. (2000, May). *Multisystemic treatment of juvenile sexual offenders: A progress report.* Paper presented at the sixth International Conference on the Treatment of Sexual Offenders, Toronto, Ontario, Canada.

Bremer, J. F. (1992). Serious juvenile sex offenders: Treatment and long-term follow-up. *Psychiatric Annals, 22,* 326–332.

Bronfenbrenner, U. (1979). *The ecology of human development: Experiments by design and nature.* Cambridge, MA: Harvard University Press.

Browne, A., & Finkelhor, D. (1986). Impact of child sexual abuse: A review of the research. *Psychological Bulletin, 99,* 555–584.

Caldwell, M. F. (2002). What we do not know about juvenile sex offender risk. *Child Maltreatment, 7,* 291–302

Cauffman, E., & Steinberg, L. (2001). Immaturity of judgment in adolescence: Why adolescents may be less culpable than adults. *Behavioral Sciences and the Law, 18,* 741–760.

Chaffin, M., Letourneau, E. J., & Silovsky, J. F. (2002). Adults, adolescents and children who sexually abuse children: A developmental perspective. In J. E. B. Myers, L. Berliner, J. Briere, C. T. Hendrix, C. Jenny, & T. A. Reid (Eds.), *The APSAC handbook on child maltreatment* (2nd ed., pp. 205–232). Thousand Oaks, CA: Sage.

Cohen, M. A., Miller, T. R., & Rossman, S. B. (1994). The costs and consequences of violent behavior in the United States. In A. J. Reiss, & J. A. Roth (Eds.), *Understanding and preventing violence: Consequences and control* (vol. 4, pp. 67–167). Washington, DC: National Academy Press.

Cunningham, P. B., & Henggeler, S. W. (1999). Engaging multiproblem families in treatment: Lessons learned throughout the development of multisystemic therapy. *Family Process, 38,* 265–281.

Daleiden, E. L., Kaufman, K. L., Hilliker, D. R., & O'Neil, J. N. (1998). The sexual histories and fantasies of youthful males: A comparison of sexual offending, nonsexual offending, and nonoffending groups. *Sexual Abuse: A Journal of Research and Treatment, 10,* 195–209.

Davis, G. E., & Leitenberg, H. (1987). Adolescent sex offenders. *Psychological Bulletin, 101,* 417–427.

DesLauriers, A. T. & Gardner, J. (1999). The sexual predator treatment program of Kansas. In A. Schlank & F. Cohen (Eds.), *The sexual predator: Law, policy, evaluation and treatment* (pp. 11-2–11-26). Kingston, NJ: Civic Research Institute.

Dishion, T. J., McCord, J., & Poulin, F. (1999). When interventions harm: Peer groups and problem behavior. *American Psychologist, 54,* 755–764.

Dishion, T. J., Patterson, G. R., Stoolmiller, M., & Skinner, M. L. (1991). Family, school and behavioral antecedents to early adolescent involvement with antisocial peers. *Developmental Psychology, 27,* 172–180.

Elliott, D. S. (Series Ed.). (1998). *Blueprints for violence prevention.* Boulder, CO: Blueprints Publications, University of Colorado, Center for the Study and Prevention of Violence.

Farrington, D. P., & Welsh, B. C. (1999). Delinquency prevention using family-based interventions. *Children and Society, 13,* 287–303.

Fehrenbach, P. A., Smith, W., Monastersky, C., & Deisher, R. W. (1986). Adolescent sexual offenders: Offender and offense characteristics. *American Journal of Orthopsychiatry, 56,* 225–233.

Finkelhor, D. (1987). The sexual abuse of children: Current research reviewed. *Psychiatric Annals, 17,* 233–241.

Finkelhor, D., & Dzuiba-Leatherman, J. (1994). Children as victims of violence: A national survey. *Pediatrics, 94,* 413–420.

Ford, M. E., & Linney, J. A. (1995). Comparative analysis of juvenile sexual offenders, violent non-sexual offenders, and status offenders. *Journal of Interpersonal Violence, 10,* 56–70.

Graves, R. B., Openshaw, D. K., Ascione, F. R., & Ericksen, S. L. (1996). Demographic and parental characteristics of youthful sexual offenders. *International Journal of Offender Therapy and Comparative Criminology, 40,* 300–317.

Griffin, P., Torbet, P., & Szymanski, L. (1998). *Trying juveniles as adults in criminal court: An analysis of state transfer provisions.* Washington, DC: U.S. Department of Justice, Office of Justice Programs, Office of Juvenile Justice and Delinquency Prevention.

Guarino-Ghezzi, S., & Kimball, L. M. (1998). Juvenile sex offenders in treatment. *Corrections Management Quarterly, 2,* 45–54.

Hagan, M. P., King, R. P., & Patros, R. L. (1994). Recidivism among adolescent perpetrators of sexual assault against children. *Journal of Offender Rehabilitation, 21,* 127 137.

Haley, J. (1976). *Problem solving therapy.* San Francisco: Jossey-Bass.

Hanson, R. K., & Bussière, M. T. (1998). Predicting relapse: A meta-analysis of sexual offender recidivism studies. *Journal of Consulting and Clinical Psychology, 66,* 348–362.

Hanson, R. K., Gordon, A., Harris, A. J., Marques, J. K., Murphy, W., Quinsey, V. L., et al. (2002). First report of the Collaborative Outcome Data Project on the effectiveness of psychological treatment for sex offenders. *Sexual Abuse: A Journal of Research and Treatment, 14*(2), 169–194.

Hastings, T., Anderson, S. J., & Hemphill, P. (1997). Comparisons of daily stress, coping, problem behavior, and cognitive distortions in adolescent sexual offenders and conduct-disordered youth. *Sexual Abuse: A Journal of Research and Treatment, 9,* 29–42.

Henggeler, S. W., & Borduin, C. M. (1990). *Family therapy and beyond: A multisystemic approach to treating the behavior problems of children and adolescents.* Pacific Grove, CA: Brooks/Cole.

Henggeler, S. W., & Borduin, C. M. (1992). *Multisystemic Therapy Adherence Scales.* Unpublished instrument, Department of Psychiatry and Behavioral Sciences, Medical University of South Carolina.

Henggeler, S. W., Melton, G. B., Brondino, M. J., Scherer, D. G., & Hanley, J. H. (1997). Multisystemic therapy with violent and chronic juvenile offenders and their families: The role of treatment fidelity in successful dissemination. *Journal of Consulting and Clinical Psychology, 65,* 821–833.

Henggeler, S. W., Melton, G. B., & Smith, L. A. (1992). Family preservation using multisystemic therapy: An effective alternative to incarcerating serious juvenile offenders. *Journal of Consulting and Clinical Psychology, 60,* 953–961.

Henggeler, S. W., Melton, G. B., Smith, L. A., Schoenwald, S. K., & Hanley, J. H. (1993). Family preservation using multisystemic treatment: Long-term follow-up to a clinical trial with serious juvenile offenders. *Journal of Child and Family Studies, 2,* 283–293.

Henggeler, S. W., Pickrel, S. G., & Brondino, M. J. (1999). Multisystemic treatment of substance abusing and dependent delinquents: Outcomes, treatment fidelity, and transportability. *Mental Health Services Research, 1,* 171–184.

Henggeler, S. W., & Schoenwald, S. K. (1998). *The MST supervisory manual: Promoting quality assurance at the clinical level.* Charleston, SC: MST Institute.

Henggeler, S. W., Schoenwald, S. K., Borduin, C. M., Rowland, M. D., & Cunningham, P. B. (1998). *Multisystemic treatment of antisocial behavior in children and adolescents.* New York: Guilford Press.

Huey, S. J., Henggeler, S. W., Brondino, M. J., & Pickrel, S. G. (2000). Mechanisms of change in multisystemic therapy: Reducing delinquent behavior through therapist adherence and improved family and peer functioning. *Journal of Consulting and Clinical Psychology, 68,* 451–467.

Hunter, J. A., Goodwin, D. W., & Becker, J. V. (1994). The relationship between phallometrically measured deviant sexual arousal and clinical characteristics in juvenile sexual offenders. *Behavioral Research and Therapy, 32*, 533–538.

Hunter, J. A., & Santos, D. (1990). The use of specialized cognitive-behavioral therapies in the treatment of juvenile sexual offenders. *International Journal of Offender Therapy and Comparative Criminology, 34*, 239–248.

Jacobs, W. L., Kennedy, W. A., & Meyer, J. B. (1997). Juvenile delinquents: A between-group comparison study of sexual and nonsexual offenders. *Sexual Abuse: A Journal of Research and Treatment, 9*, 201–217.

Kazdin, A. E., & Weisz, J. R. (1998). Identifying and developing empirically supported child and adolescent treatments. *Journal of Consulting and Clinical Psychology, 66*, 19–36.

Kempton, T., & Forehand, R. L. (1992). Suicide attempts among juvenile delinquents: The contribution of mental health factors. *Behaviour Research and Therapy, 30*, 537–541

Kimerling, R., & Calhoun, K. S. (1994). Somatic symptoms, social support, and treatment seeking among sexual assault victims. *Journal of Consulting and Clinical Psychology, 62*, 333–340.

Koss, M. P., Heise, L., & Russo, N. F. (1994). The global health burden of rape. *Psychology of Women Quarterly, 18*, 509–537.

Koss, M. P., Koss, P. G., & Woodruff, W. J. (1991). Deleterious effects of criminal victimization on women's health and medical utilization. *Archives of Internal Medicine, 151*, 342–357.

Lab, S. P., Shields, G., & Schondel, C. (1993). Research note: An evaluation of juvenile sexual offender treatment. *Crime and Delinquency, 39*, 543–553.

Letourneau, E. J. (2004a). *Treatment of juvenile sex offenders with multisytemic therapy*. Workshop presented at the seventh annual conference of the California Coalition of Sexual Offenders, San Francisco.

Letourneau, E. J. (2004b). A comment on the first report: Letter to the editor. *Sexual Abuse: A Journal of Research and Treatment, 16*, 77–81.

Letourneau, E. J., Resnick, H. S., Kilpatrick, D. G., Saunders, B. E., & Best, C. L. (1996). Comorbidity of sexual problems and posttraumatic stress disorder in female crime victims. *Behavior Therapy, 27*, 321–336.

Loeber, R., & Farrington, D. P. (Eds.). (1998). *Serious and violent juvenile offenders: Risk factors and successful interventions*. Thousand Oaks, CA: Sage.

Maguire, K., & Pastore, A. L. (1998). *Sourcebook of criminal justice statistics 1998* (p. 337). Washington, DC: U. S. Department of Justice, Bureau of Justice Statistics.

McGrath, R. J., Cumming, G. F., & Burchard, B. L. (2003). *Current practices and trends in sexual abuser management: The Safer Society 2002 nationwide study*. Brandon, VT: Safer Society Press.

Milloy, C. D. (1994). Specialized treatment for juvenile sex offenders: A closer look. *Journal of Interpersonal Violence, 13*, 653–656.

Minuchin, S. (1974). *Families and family therapy*. Cambridge, MA: Harvard University Press.

National Institute on Drug Abuse. (1999). *Principles of drug addiction treatment: A research-based guide* (NIH Publication No. 99-4180). Washington, DC: National Institutes of Health.

National Task Force on Juvenile Sexual Offending. (1993). The revised report. *Juvenile and Family Court Journal, 44*, 1–120.

Reppucci, N. D., & Clingempeel, W. G. (1978). Methodological issues in research with correctional populations. *Journal of Consulting and Clinical Psychology, 46*, 727–746.

Saunders, B. E., Kilpatrick, D. G., Hanson, R. F., Resnick, H. S, & Walker, M. E. (1999). Prevalence, case characteristics, and long-term psychological correlates of child rape among women: A national survey. *Child Maltreatment, 4*, 187–200.

Saunders, B. E., Villeponteaux, L. A., Lipovsky, J. A., Kilpatrick, D. G., & Veronen, L. J. (1992). Child sexual assault as a risk factor for mental disorders among women: A community survey. *Journal of Interpersonal Violence, 7*, 189–204.

Schoenwald, S. K. (1998). *Multisystemic therapy consultation guidelines*. Charleston, SC: MST Institute.

Schoenwald, S. K., Henggeler, S. W., Brondino, M. J., & Rowland, M. D. (2000). Multisystemic therapy: Monitoring treatment fidelity. *Family Process, 39*, 83–103.

Schoenwald, S. K., Henggeler, S. W., & Edwards, D. (1998). *MST Supervisor Adherence Measure.* Charleston, SC: MST Institute.

Schoenwald, S. K., Sheidow, A. J., Letourneau, E. J., & Liao, J. G. (2003). Transportability of multisystemic therapy: Evidence for multilevel influences. *Mental Health Services Research, 5*, 223–239.

Schram, D. D., Milloy, C. D., & Rowe, W. E. (1991, September). *Juvenile sex offenders: A follow-up study of reoffense behavior.* Olympia: Washington State Institute for Public Policy.

Schwartz, B. K. (1999). The case against involuntary commitment. In A. Schlank & F. Cohen (Eds.), *The sexual predator: Law, policy, evaluation and treatment* (pp. 4-1–4-22). Kingston, NJ: Civic Research Institute.

Sipe, R., Jensen, E. L., & Everett, R. S. (1998). Adolescent sexual offenders grown up: Recidivism in young adulthood. *Criminal Justice and Behavior, 25*, 109–124.

Smets, A. C., & Cebula, C. M. (1987). A group treatment program for adolescent sex offenders: Five steps toward resolution. *Child Abuse and Neglect, 11*, 247–254.

Smith, G., & Fischer, L. (1999). Assessment of juvenile sexual offenders: Reliability and validity of the Abel Assessment for Interest in Paraphilias. *Sexual Abuse: A Journal of Research and Treatment, 11*, 207—216.

Swenson, C. C., Henggeler, S. W., Schoenwald, S. K., Kaufman, K. L., & Randall, J. (1998). Changing the social ecologies of adolescent sexual offenders: Implications of the success of multisystemic therapy in treating serious antisocial behavior in adolescents. *Child Maltreatment, 3*, 330–338.

Swenson, C., & Letourneau, E. J. (2002). *Multisystemic therapy with adolescent sex offenders.* Workshop presented at the 20th annual Research and Treatment Conference of the Association for the Treatment of Sexual Abusers, Montreal, Quebec, Canada.

U.S. Public Health Service. (1999). *Mental health: A report of the Surgeon General.* Rockville, MD: U.S. Department of Health and Human Services, National Institutes of Health, National Institute of Mental Health.

U.S. Public Health Service. (2001). *Youth violence: A report of the Surgeon General.* Washington, DC: Author.

Weinrott, M. R. (1996). *Sexual aggression: A critical review.* Boulder: Center for the Study and Prevention of Violence, Institute for Behavioral Sciences, University of Colorado, Boulder.

White, J. W., & Koss, M. P. (1993). Adolescent sexual aggression within heterosexual relationships: Prevalence, characteristics, and causes. In H. E. Barbaree, W. L. Marshall, & S. M. Hudson (Eds.), *The juvenile sex offender* (pp. 182–202). New York: Guilford Press.

Widom, C. S., & Morris, S. (1997). Accuracy of adult recollections of childhood victimization: Part 2. Childhood sexual abuse. *Psychological Assessment, 9*, 34–46.

Worling, J. R., & Curwen, T. (1998). T*he adolescent sexual offender project: A 10-year follow-up study. SAFE-T Program (Sexual Abuse: Family Education and Treatment).* Toronto, Ontario, Canada: Thistletown Regional Centre for Children and Adolescents and Probation and Community Services, Ontario Ministry of Community and Social Services.

Worling, J. R., & Curwen, T. (2000). Adolescent sexual offender recidivism: Success of specialized treatment and implications for risk prediction. *Child Abuse and Neglect, 24*, 965–982.

Chapter 15

Multisite Investigation of Treatment for Sexually Abusive Juveniles

by Guy Bourgon, Ph.D., Kelly E. Morton-Bourgon, M.A. and Gina Madrigrano, Ph.D.

OVERVIEW

There is a relative paucity of empirical investigations regarding sexually abusive juveniles in comparison to adult sexual offenders. Our current challenge is to broaden our knowledge base to assist in efforts to effectively assess, treat, and manage this unique population. It is difficult to generalize to the heterogeneous population of sexually abusive juveniles from the relatively limited number of studies with small and homogeneous samples. In addition, the developmental and maturational changes that take place during adolescence likely play a considerable role in hindering our efforts to discover reliable and valid characteristics that would assist us in developing evidence-based practices. As a result, treatment programs tend to be very comprehensive rather than highly focused on specific targets as there is minimal empirical knowledge to guide the efforts. This chapter describes the results of our ongoing multisite investigation of treatment services for sexually abusive juveniles. Results are presented that examine the interrelated issues of evaluating treatment efforts on such a heterogeneous population who are in the process of significant development and maturation.

INTRODUCTION

There has been an increasing level of public debate regarding crimes committed by young persons, as well as heightened public concern regarding adolescents who are sexually abusive. In the United States, juveniles accounted for approximately 16 percent of all forcible rapes and 17 percent of other sex offenses (Greenfeld, 1996). Similar statistics are noted in Canada, where the rate for being charged with a sexual offense was slightly more than twice as high for youth (70.5 per 100,000 youths) compared to adults (33.6 per 100,000 adults; Statistics Canada, 2002). In England and Wales, the rate was 66.9 per 100,000 for youth ages 15 to 17 (East & Campbell, 1999). The seriousness of sexual offending and the long-term consequences of such behavior point to the need to address juvenile sexual offending. In response to this serious issue, the number of treatment programs for adolescents who are sexually abusive has increased significantly in North America in the past twenty years. Unfortunately, there is a paucity of empirical literature on adolescents who are sexually abusive (Breiling, 2003), making it difficult to develop evidenced-based practices.

ARE JUVENILE SEX OFFENDERS UNIQUE?

Many of the earlier empirical studies attempted to identify key characteristics of sexually abusive juveniles (Becker & Hicks, 2003; Righthand & Welch, 2001). With the exception of sexual offending, most findings have pointed to more similarities than differences to juveniles who offend nonsexually (Righthand & Welch, 2001; Veneziano & Veneziano, 2002). This inability to empirically differentiate sexual from nonsexual offending juveniles presents a challenge to developing effective sex offense-specific practices. As it is now generally accepted that sexually abusive juveniles are a heterogeneous group, research efforts must take into consideration these differences in order to enhance assessment, treatment, and management practices.

Among the issues influencing the development of knowledge about sexually abusive juveniles, sample variation is a key factor. Sample sizes are often small and restricted to specific agencies or institutions. For example, Långström (2002) and Långström and Grann (2000) have evaluated juveniles referred for major forensic psychiatric evaluations; Worling's (1995, 2001; Worling & Curwen, 2000) work has described young juveniles being treated in the community; Poole, Liedecke, and Marbibi (2000) reported results on a sample of older juveniles who were incarcerated. It is not unreasonable to believe that these samples are likely to differ on factors associated with the juveniles' sexual offending behaviors. As such, the generalizability of studies on small and/or specific samples to the heterogeneous population of sexually abusive juveniles may be limited.

Another challenge for investigations with this population is that adolescence is a time of considerable development and maturation. Many of our research and treatment efforts have been influenced by what is known about adult sexual offenders, persons who have already "grown up." Robert Longo (2003) recently reflected on this trickle-down effect of adult sexual offender assessment, treatment, and management practices to juveniles. He notes that we must stop viewing juveniles as "mini-adults." Such an approach minimizes a key defining characteristics of juveniles: They are in the midst of a period of considerable growth and development that defines the very nature of adolescence. Research efforts need to consider such developmental changes and factor them into the understanding of other potentially critical changes of risk and need.

Finally, given the relative lack of studies that have evaluated the efficacy of specialized services to sexually abusive juveniles (Worling & Curwen, 2000), we face considerable challenges in developing evidence-based interventions. Identifying valid risk markers can have a considerable impact on the treatment and management of sexual offenders (Hanson, Morton, & Harris, 2003). Although there are some published articles describing a number of potential risk indicators for sexually abusive juveniles (Worling & Långström, 2003), more research is needed to validate these predictors across different samples and ages. There are a few groups of researchers attempting to develop risk assessment instruments (e.g., Prentky, Harris, Frizzell, & Righthand, 2000; Worling & Curwen, 2001). Nonetheless, the field still waits for a risk instrument to be validated. In the meantime, front-line workers continue to assess, treat, and manage sexually abusive adolescents, guided as best they can by the limited knowledge of this population and drawing from their clinical experiences and the body of knowledge on adult sexual offenders.

ADVANTAGES OF A MULTISITE INVESTIGATION

There is a clear need to advance our knowledge of sexually abusive juveniles. Studies that set out to identify key factors that play a role in sexually abusive behaviors in juveniles should consider the heterogeneity of the population, developmental factors inherent in adolescence, and changes that result from both maturation and treatment. The present multisite investigation of treatment for sexually abusive juveniles was undertaken in an effort to begin to address some of these issues. In collaboration with multiple agencies across Canada that provide services to juveniles who are sexually abusive, this investigation provides a unique opportunity to gather data on a diverse sample from many different agencies. We employed multiple assessments of the juveniles over time, allowing the evaluation of change over time as well as during the course of treatment. It is hoped that this effort will provide representative data on a heterogeneous sample of sexually abusive juveniles.

This chapter presents some of the results from this ongoing study. The first section describes the methodology, including a brief discussion of the rationale for the assessment of four core areas: sexuality, antisociality, family, and general functioning. The next three sections focus on sample variation, maturation, and treatment. We examine the influence of sample variation by comparing three different groups of juveniles: those seen in residential centers, those treated at community agencies, and those being treated in programs delivered by probation. Results are presented exploring differences between these three groups of juveniles. We next examine the issue of development and maturation by evaluating the influence of age on the core areas. Then we explore the changes observed during treatment of sexually abusive juveniles by describing treatment targets of multiple sites and presenting results of pre/posttreatment changes on some key dynamic factors. Finally, we end with a discussion of the implication of these results to our efforts to assess, treat, and manage this special population. It is hoped that this chapter will assist us in our efforts to further our empirical understanding of juveniles who are sexually aggressive.

METHODOLOGY FOR STUDYING A HETEROGENEOUS POPULATION

Site Selection

As this project was designed to gather information from multiple sites, the first step involved identifying agencies to participate. This was accomplished by contacting (1) provincial/territorial departments responsible for this population and (2) prominent Canadian professionals in the area of adolescent sexual offenders. A specialized service was defined as a service that provides a coherent and comprehensive plan of care in which the major focus was the reduction of the frequency and/or severity of sexual offending behavior by juveniles ages 12 through 19 at the time of their sexual offending. Once identified, we provided information to the agencies about the project and requested their collaboration in the study. All agencies agreeing to participate were provided with direction on implementing the study protocol, all testing materials, and support. To date, fifteen different agencies representing four provinces and one territory have provided data on a total of 137 juveniles with a mean age of 15.9 years ($SD = 1.7$).

Data Collection

Consent to participate in the project was obtained from all juveniles (parental consent was obtained for those under the age of 16). Agency staff was responsible for administering assessment batteries, gathering data, and forwarding this information to the principal investigator. The principal investigator provided training and support to staff on administering assessments, including proper procedures for obtaining informed consent, appropriate testing procedures, timing of assessments, and instructions for completing all assessment instruments. After scoring the tests, project staff provided written feedback on the results of each adolescent's assessment to the participating agency.

Data were collected at multiple points in time from three potential sources: the adolescent, his or her primary therapist, and the juvenile's parent(s) or guardian(s). Given that length of treatment varied by agency, at least three points in time were identified for each agency to conduct assessments. These assessment periods were specific to each agency but followed the same general pattern: (1) intake, (2) around the completion of one year of treatment, and (3) after approximately the second year of treatment. If treatment lasted more than two years, another assessment was conducted at the end of treatment. Some adolescents were already involved with the agencies when the study began and data on these adolescents were collected regardless of where they were in the treatment process. Therefore, not all adolescents in the present sample were assessed at intake. In addition to demographic factors, such as details of the offense and family composition variables, assessment focused on four core domains: sexuality, antisociality, family, and general psychosocial functioning.

It is widely accepted that adolescents who are sexually aggressive are a very diverse population. Such diversity makes it difficult to synthesize research findings as studies tend to sample very distinctive groups of juveniles. Although a number of typologies have been brought forward (Hunter, Figueredo, Malamuth, & Becker, 2003; O'Brien & Bera, 1986; Worling, 2001), there has been little empirical replication to validate them. Rather, typology research has pointed to the heterogeneity of the population and the implications on assessment and treatment. For example, sexually abusive juveniles who end up in custody compared to those who do not are likely different on at least a few important risk and need factors. Even among those juveniles who do not end up in custody, some are diverted from the criminal justice system and may be treated in community-based agencies that primarily focus on child welfare and mental health issues. Juveniles who are treated in community agencies may also have important risk/need differences from those juveniles who are managed and treated through the community-based criminal justice programs (e.g., probation treatment programs).

ASSESSMENT DOMAINS

Sexuality

Sexuality, which compromises a diverse set of factors, is believed to be a key factor in sexual offending. We know that deviant sexual interest plays a significant role in adult sexual recidivism (Hanson & Bussière, 1998), as do other sexuality factors, such as obsession with sex and attitudes tolerant of sexual crimes. Worling and Långström (2003) noted that sexuality factors appear to play a key role in predicting sexual offending with adolescents. Schram, Milloy, and Rowe (1991) found that sexually offending adolescents who recidivated were more likely to display patterns of deviant sexual arousal. If sexuality does indeed play a role with adolescents, the question becomes: How do we assess the important components of this factor? For example, in adults, victim characteristics such as having a male victim or a stranger victim are predictive of sexual offending (Hanson & Bussière, 1998); however, Worling and Långström (2003) noted that only having a stranger victim and therapist ratings of deviant sexual interests are factors that have some support in the literature.

In the present investigation, sexuality was assessed with the following instruments: the Screening Scale for Pedophilic Interests (SSPI; Seto & Lalumière, 2001; Seto, Murphy, Page, & Ennis, 2003), the Estimate of Risk of Adolescent Sexual Offense Recidivism (ERASOR; Worling & Curwen, 2001), the Sexual History Form (SHF; Kaufman, 1994), and the Sexual Fantasy Questionnaire (SFQ; Kaufman, 1993). The SSPI, a four-item scale to detect sexual interest in children, was scored from demographic and offense information. The primary therapist scored the ERASOR, whereas the SHF and the SFQ were completed by the youth. The ERASOR is a twenty-five-item empirically guided risk assessment tool. It is designed to assess the estimate of risk to commit another sexual offense in youth 12–18 years old. There is no scoring method for the ERASOR, as it is designed such that the clinician can judge the youth's risk based on those factors that are present or not. However, for the purposes of this investigation, a numerical scoring scheme was given to the instrument: 0 was assigned if the factor was not present, 1 if the factor was partially/possibly present, and 2 if the factor was rated as present.

The SHF is a self-report, paper-and-pencil instrument designed to assess the type and frequency of the adolescent's various sexual experiences. The SHF is scored on a 0 (never in my life) to 6 (more than 50 times) rating scale. The scoring is an average of the ratings given for all the items on the particular scale. Eight "types" of sexual behaviors are assessed by the SHF: typical sexual experiences with consenting partners, typical sexual experiences with nonconsenting partners, atypical sexual experiences with consenting partners, aggressive sexual experiences with consenting partners, solitary sexual behaviors, paraphilias, sexual experiences with deviant partners, and voyeurism.

The SFQ is a self-report, paper-and-pencil instrument designed to assess how often an adolescent fantasizes about various sexual activities. The items of the SFQ are scored on a 0 (never in my life) to 6 (two or more times a day) rating scale. The scoring is an average of the ratings given for all the items on the particular scale. The SFQ measures two global and six specific "types" of fantasies. The global indices are nondeviant and deviant sexual fantasies. The six specific types of fantasies are the following: traditional romantic, variety of settings, variety of partners, nontraditional, mild coercion, and aggressive.

Antisociality

Antisociality, or a general criminal lifestyle, is a predictor of sexual and "any" recidivism with adults (Hanson & Morton-Bourgon, 2004). In adolescents, it is likely that antisociality also plays a role. Worling and Långström (2003) noted that impulsivity, negative peer associations, antisocial orientation, and aggression are "possible" risk factors. The ERASOR has a number of items that assess this factor.

In the present investigation, in addition to some of the ERASOR items, antisociality was also assessed with the Youth Level of Service/Case Management Inventory (YLS/CMI; Hoge & Andrews, 2002). The YLS/CMI is a forty-two-item structured interview assessment instrument completed by the primary therapist. It is designed to measure the criminogenic risk and needs of offenders under the age of 19. The items are scored on a 0–1 scale, with 0 indicating not present and 1 indicating present. The measure is made up of eight scales: Criminal history, Family, Education/employment, Peer relations, Substance abuse, Leisure/recreation, Personality/behavior, and Attitudes/orientation.

Family

Family is an important part of a youth's or adult's life. Worling and Långström (2003) noted that problematic parent-child relationships and parental rejection were "promising" factors predicting sexual recidivism with adolescents. They also noted that high stress family environment was a "probable" factor. In addition, Morton (2003) found that family relationships/adjustment was significantly related to sexual recidivism in her sample of adolescent sexual offenders. In the present investigation, items assessing family relationships and functioning from the ERASOR and the YLS/CMI were used to examine familial factors.

General Functioning

General psychological functioning appears to be an important consideration when treating sexually abusive adolescents. Both the Association for the Treatment of Sexual Abusers (ATSA) and the National Adolescent Perpetration Network (NAPN) guidelines note that treatment should be comprehensive and include targeting general psychosocial functioning (i.e., relationship and interpersonal skills). In fact, Långström and Grann (2000) followed up a sample of forty-six adolescent sexual offenders who had received a forensic evaluation. They found that social skills were one of four factors significantly related to sexual recidivism.

In the present study, it was deemed important to include an assessment of general psychosocial functioning. We chose the Youth Self Report (YSR; Achenbach, 1991a), which was completed by the adolescent, and the Child Behavior Checklist (CBCL; Achenbach, 1991b), which was completed by the primary therapist and the parent(s) to assess general psychosocial functioning. These instruments assess factors, competencies, and activities oriented to the *Diagnostic and Statistical Manual of Mental Disorders*.

IDENTIFYING DIFFERENCES IN JUVENILE SEX OFFENDERS

In this section we examine potential differences among these various groups of adolescents, specifically among adolescents being served in community agencies, probation programs, and residential centers. Uncovering the factors that distinguish these groups from one another can provide insight to treatment and management strategies suitable for these juveniles. In addition, these differences may also shed some light on the varying results of existing studies and better our understanding of juveniles who are sexually abusive.

In the current investigation, juveniles were divided into one of three groups, those in residential programs ($n = 29$), those in community outpatient programs ($n = 86$), and those being treated in the community by programs delivered by probation officers ($n = 22$). Table 15.1 presents a number of group differences on sexuality factors. On the one hand, the juveniles in probation programs were the oldest when entering treatment ($M = 17.4$), and their sexual offending also started later than that of the other two groups (14.1 compared to 12.5 for community and 12.1 for residential). Besides the fact that the probation group, almost in its entirety, had been convicted of a sexual offense, the profiles of sexual variables were quite similar to those of the adolescents being treated in community agencies.

On the other hand, the residential youth were considerably different. They were assessed as having more childhood issues than either the community or probation adolescents and as having a greater incidence of sexual and physical abuse. Their sexual offending also appears to be more serious in that juveniles in residential programs had significantly more victims (3.2 compared to 1.6 victims in the community group and 1.4 in the probation group). In fact, more than half (56 percent) of the residential youth had three or more known victims. More residential juveniles were assessed as having problems with deviant sexual interests, obsessive sexual interests, and attitudes supportive of sexual offending, including higher scores on the SSPI. Although there

Table 15.1
Differences Among Adolescents Served by Community Agencies, Probation Offices, and Residential Programs on Factors Assessing Sexuality (*N* = 137)

Variable	Treatment Services Provided by		
	Community	Probation	Residential
Age			
Entry to agency	15.3 (1.5)[a]	17.4 (1.9)[c]	16.2 (1.3)[b]
Onset of sexually abusive behaviors	12.5 (2.5)[a]	14.1 (1.7)[b]	12.1 (3.0)[a]
History			
Sexual abuse	35%[a,b]	14%[a]	55%[b]
Physical abuse	41%[a]	54%[a,b]	75%[b]
Convicted of Sexual Offense	51%[a]	96%[b]	77%[c]
Victim Factors			
Victim age	6.8 (2.5)[a]	7.9 (3.1)[a, b]	9.0 (3.4)[b]
Number of known victims	1.6 (0.8)[a]	1.4 (0.6)[a]	3.2 (2.3)[b]
3 or more victims	12%	9%	46%
Victim sex			
Any male victims?	47%[a,b]	27%[a]	61%[b]
Any female victims?	73%	73%	72%
Victims of both sexes?	20%[a,b]	5%[a]	33%[b]
Victim relation			
Any intrafamilial victims?	67%[b]	38%[a]	88%[b]
Any extrafamilial victims?	50%	62%	75%
Any stranger victims?	2%	9%	5%
Sexual Factors			
Deviant interests (ERASOR)	38%[a]	31%[a]	71%[b]
Obsessive interests (ERASOR)	27%[a]	8%[a]	82%[b]
Attitudes supportive (ERASOR)	42%[a]	23%[a]	71%[b]
Screening Scale for Pedophilic Interests (SSPI)	2.61 (1.6)[a]	2.18 (1.2)[a]	3.50 (2.0)[b]
Nondeviant sexual fantasies (SFQ)	1.82 (1.2)	1.88 (1.3)	2.28 (1.2)
Fantasies of sex with peers (SFQ)	4.95 (3.9)	5.54 (3.8)	5.89 (3.6)
Deviant sexual fantasies (SFQ)	0.30 (0.4)[a]	0.17 (0.2)[a]	0.55 (0.6)[b]
Fantasies of sex with children < 13 (SFQ)	0.36 (0.9)[a]	0.00 (0.0)[a]	1.23 (1.7)[b]
Aggressive sexual fantasies (SFQ)	0.14 (0.3)[a]	0.00 (0.0)[a]	0.41 (0.6)[b]

Note. *N*s vary due to missing data.
[a, b, c] Denotes significant ($p < .05$) between-group difference.

were no differences in nondeviant sexual fantasies, the residential juveniles had significantly higher scores on deviant sexual fantasies, aggressive sexual fantasies, and sexual fantasies involving children 12 and younger.

Table 15.2
Differences Among Adolescents Served by Community Agencies, Probation Offices, and Residential Programs on Factors Assessing Antisociality, Family, and General Functioning ($N = 137$)

Variable	Treatment Services Provided by		
	Community	Probation	Residential
Antisociality Factors (YLS/CMI Score)	9.04 (7.2)[a]	11.92 (8.1)[a]	18.94 (7.0)[b]
Attitudes (YLS/CMI)	0.72 (1.2)[a]	0.62 (0.9)[a]	2.18 (1.4)[b]
Peers (YLS/CMI)	1.46 (1.4)[a]	2.00 (1.5)[b]	2.71 (1.0)[b]
Personality (YLS/CMI)	9.04 (7.2)[a]	11.92 (8.1)[a]	18.94 (7.0)[b]
Aggressive (ERASOR)	27%[a]	8%[a]	65%[b]
Poor Self-Regulation (ERASOR)	58%[a]	46%[a]	94%[b]
Familial Factors—Family (YLS/CMI)	1.91 (1.7)[a]	2.69 (2.4)[a,b]	3.24 (1.3)[b]
High stress family (ERASOR)	76%	77%	94%
Parental rejection (ERASOR)	67%	85%	82%
Parents not supportive of Tx (ERASOR)	42%	23%	53%
Psychosocial Factors			
Externalizing (CBCL: YSR)	16.4 (7.9)[a,b]	13.6 (10.5)[a]	19.3 (8.9)[b]
Externalizing (CBCL: Parents)	16.6 (11.7)	13.3 (18.5)	18.5 (12.5)
Externalizing (CBCL: Therapist)	15.9 (13.7)[a]	5.1 (9.0)[b]	23.1 (8.9)[c]
Internalizing (CBCL: YSR)	14.7 (9.0)	13.8 (11.5)	17.6 (9.7)
Internalizing (CBCL: Parents)	12.5 (7.0)	12.6 (16.2)	16.0 (8.6)
Internalizing (CBCL: Therapist)	13.0 (7.9)[a]	6.9 (6.1)[b]	16.2 (6.3)[a]

Note: *N*s vary due to missing data.
[a, b, c] Denotes significant ($p < .05$) between-group difference.

Table 15.2 presents the results of group comparisons on antisociality, familial, and psychosocial factors. Of particular note is the severity of problems associated with residential youth compared to the severity of problems with the other two groups. Residential juveniles were significantly more antisocial (e.g., higher YLS/CMI scores) in addition to demonstrating more aggression and poor self-regulation. Although the residential juveniles scored higher (i.e., more at "risk") on the family subscale of the YLS/CMI, none of the groups were significantly different on the family items of the ERASOR. In terms of general psychosocial functioning, results were rather mixed. Based on the parent ratings, no significant differences on internalizing or externalizing problems were observed between the three groups of youth. The therapists' ratings indicated that the residential youth had significantly higher externalizing scores than both the probation and community youth. As for internalizing scores, residential youth scored significantly higher than the probation adolescents. Self-reported ratings on the CBCL: YSR for externalizing problems showed a similar pattern where residential youth scored significantly higher than probation youth but were not different than youth served by community agencies. No differences were found on internalizing problems. Perhaps more interesting is the overall trend, where the probation youth had the lowest scores among the three groups, indicating that they appear to have the least problematic general functioning, whereas residential youth had the highest ratings, indicating that this group was the most problematic. Youth served by community agencies tended to fall in between the two other groups.

Our findings illustrate the importance of considering sample variation when reviewing the literature on adolescents who are sexually abusive. These results indicate how three groups of sexually abusive juveniles, initially differentiated by treatment provider/setting, significantly differ on sexuality, antisociality, family, and general functioning factors. In particular, youth treated in residential centers appeared more problematic in all four of the core areas. As the field is still in its embryonic stages when it pertains to assessing, treating, and managing sexual offending in juveniles, our results support the importance of being cautious when interpreting and generalizing published findings from homogeneous samples without further replication to other subgroups of sexually abusive juveniles.

IMPACT OF DEVELOPMENTAL CHANGES

Adolescence is a period of ongoing development with significant physical, psychological, behavioral, and relational changes. It is, in part, these developmental changes that make adolescents qualitatively different from adults and not just "little adults." Sexuality is one area in which there is considerable development and change. Bukowski, Sippola, and Brender (1993) described a number of issues regarding the development of adolescent sexuality. Their developmental perspective noted numerous changes in sexual behaviors and experiences, cognitions, relationships, and the emergence of the adolescent's sexual script. All these changes must be integrated into the adolescent's concept of sexuality and sense of self. Assessment, treatment, and research with juveniles who are sexually abusive must be sensitive to these developmental changes and take into account their emerging sexuality.

In this section we examine the influence of maturation and development on the assessment of sexually abusive juveniles. As our sample consisted of juveniles of varying ages, we used age of the juveniles as a proxy for development. To explore the effect of age on various factors, we conducted the following analyses: Pearson correlations were calculated and presented to demonstrate the strength and direction of the relationship between age and the various factors assessed. Unstandardized betas from regression analyses provided an indicator of the "amount" of change that is expected to occur as the juvenile ages one year. Mean scores for that factor are presented to provide context to assist in the interpretation of the change. Table 15.3 presents the results of these analyses.

To assist in reading Table 15.3, the results of the relationship of age with sexual experiences measured by the SHF are described here. Age was significantly related to the scores on typical sexual experiences with consenting partners ($r = .38; p < .05$) and to the score on solitary (e.g., masturbation) sexual experiences ($r = .26; p < .05$). These correlations indicate that as juveniles age they report having engaged in more of these types of behaviors. No significant correlations were found with age and the other scales of the SHF.

Table 15.3
Factors Associated With Development/Maturation (*N* = 137)

Dynamic Factors	Pearson *r*	Mean (SD)	Change per Year Aged Delta (SE)
Sexual Factors			
Typical sex with consent (SHF)	.38*	1.57 (1.61)	0.38 (0.12)
Solitary sexual experiences (SHF)	.26*	1.89 (1.28)	0.23 (0.10)
Nondeviant sexual fantasies (SFQ)	.38*	1.94 (1.24)	0.31 (0.07)
Fantasies of sex with peers (SFQ)	.27*	5.25 (3.78)	0.67 (0.23)
Traditional/romantic fantasies (SFQ)	.31*	1.70 (1.41)	0.27 (0.08)
Variety of settings (SFQ)	.36*	1.26 (1.16)	0.27 (0.07)
Variety of partners (SFQ)	.33*	2.39 (1.34)	0.30 (0.08)
Nontraditional fantasies (SFQ)	.29*	1.38 (1.11)	0.21 (0.07)
Deviant sexual fantasies (SFQ)	.28*	0.35 (0.44)	0.08 (0.03)
Aggressive sexual fantasies (SFQ)	.20*	0.19 (0.41)	0.05 (0.03)
Attitudes supportive (ERASOR)	-.23*	0.59 (0.72)	-0.09 (0.05)
Antisociality Factors			
YLS/CMI Total Score	.34*	11.8 (8.3)	1.56 (0.51)
Peers (YLS/CMI)	.41*	1.50 (1.3)	0.31 (0.08)
Psychosocial Factors (CBCL)			
Attention			
Youth	- .22*	6.85 (3.8)	- 0.41 (0.19)
Therapist	- .39*	6.70 (4.4)	- 0.72 (0.22)
Aggression			
Youth	- .20*	11.14 (6.0)	- 0.54 (0.28)
Therapist	- .30*	10.25 (8.9)	- 1.14 (0.47)
Delinquency			
Youth	- .11	5.39 (3.7)	- 0.20 (0.18)
Therapist	- .26*	5.56 (5.0)	- 0.55 (0.26)
Social problems			
Youth	- .09	3.76 (2.8)	- 0.12 (0.14)
Therapist	- .23*	3.65 (3.1)	- 0.30 (0.16)
Withdrawn			
Youth	.04	4.04 (2.6)	0.05 (0.13)
Therapist	-.29*	4.65 (3.1)	- 0.39 (0.17)
Anxiety/depression			
Youth	- .06	7.98 (5.8)	- 0.18 (.29)
Therapist	- .30*	7.82 (5.0)	- 0.63 (.26)

Note: *N*s vary due to missing data.
* Denotes *p* < .05.

The unstandardized beta for typical sexual experiences was 0.38, whereas it was 0.23 for solitary sexual experiences. These numbers indicate the amount of change on that measure that is predicted for each year the juvenile ages. To interpret the magnitude of these changes, we must consider the mean score, which was 1.57 for typical sexual experiences and 1.89 for solitary sexual experiences (mean age of sample is 15.9). From the regression equation, we can calculate the score of typical sexual experiences for a 14-year-old to be 0.81 and the score of an 18-year-old to be 2.34, about three times more than that of the 14-year-old. From the regression equation, we can calculate the score of solitary sexual experiences of a 14-year-old to be 1.44 and the score of an 18-year-old to be 2.35, about one and one-half times more than the that of the 14-year-old. These numbers illustrate how important and dramatic are the changes that occur as the adolescent ages.

Examining the results presented in Table 15.3, it is not surprising that age plays a significant role in the assessment of sexuality. We can see that aging is related to increases in what may be considered "normal" self-reported sexual behaviors, typical sexual experiences with consenting partners, and solitary sexual behaviors. However, age was not significantly related to what may be considered "deviant" sexual experiences (e.g., sexual experiences with nonconsenting partners, deviant partners, atypical and aggressive sexual experiences, paraphilic sexual behaviors, and voyeurism). We observed a general increase in sexual fantasies with age as well, for both non-deviant and deviant sexual fantasies, indicating what appears to be a general increase in frequency and breadth of sexual fantasizing as the juvenile ages. It is noteworthy that the therapists' ratings of attitudes supportive of sexual offending on the ERASOR were significantly related to age, with reductions associated with aging. These results may reflect one of the developmental hurdles for adolescents; that is, during adolescence, youth must begin to incorporate societal standards and norms regarding sexual behaviors (Bukowski, Sippola, & Brender, 1993) and their attitudes become more normative as they age.

Also of note is that age was significantly related to some general psychosocial factors as rated by the therapist but not related when self-reported by the youth. Specifically, problems with attention and aggression demonstrated significant negative relationships to age, both when reported by the therapist and by the youth. However, age was significantly related to reductions in social problems, withdrawal, and anxiety/depression on therapist ratings but not related to the youth's self-report. Although antisociality factors, as indicated by the overall YLS/CMI score and peers subscale of the YLS/CMI, showed a significant increase with age, therapists' ratings of delinquency on the CBCL showed a negative relationship to age.

These results illustrate the importance of considering maturation and development when assessing and treating sexually abusive juveniles. During adolescence, significant changes in sexuality occur. This is supported by our findings, which indicate, among other variables, a significant relationship between age and both sexual behaviors and sexual fantasies. In addition, antisociality and a number of general functioning scales showed a significant relationship to age. Changes reflective of simple maturation need to be taken into consideration when conducting assessments, when conveying risk information, and when planning treatment. As noted earlier, adolescents are not "mini-adults." In fact, there are likely significant developmental/maturational differences between juveniles who are 13 and those who are 18, and these differences must be considered when managing sexually abusive juveniles.

TREATMENT

The importance of evaluating risk and need factors for managing and treating sexually abusive juveniles cannot be understated. For example, the ATSA guidelines and standards of practice indicate that appropriate treatment targets are those identified during the assessment of the sexual abuser. Targets may include, but are not limited to, deviant sexual interests and arousal, antisocial associates, attitudes supportive of offending, emotion management problems, lack of community supports, significant relationships, educational or vocational deficits, and substance misuse (Association for the Treatment of Sexual Abusers, 1997). The list of treatment targets produced by the NAPN is somewhat more extensive and includes such objectives as controlling abusive behaviors, developing positive sexual identity, developing relapse prevention strategies, developing an internal sense of mastery and control, and resolution of victimization in the adolescent's past (National Adolescent Perpetration Network, 1993). The ERASOR is one assessment instrument that assists in evaluating risk and need in juvenile sexual offenders. As it contains items assessing many of these treatment targets, the ERASOR can be a very useful clinical tool to direct interventions and evaluate their impact on important factors.

This section examines the effects of treatment with sexually abusive youth. Youth with an intake assessment as well as an assessment following a period of treatment were examined to evaluate the impact of treatment on the four core areas. We primarily focused on the therapist's evaluation of the juveniles using the ERASOR to investigate changes with regard to sexuality, antisociality, and familial factors. The general functioning factor was assessed using the CBCL. This sample of fifty-three adolescents had been treated for an average of 18.9 ($SD = 7.1$) months (ranging from 8 to 39 months) in community agencies ($n = 27$), probation programs ($n = 15$), or residential programs ($n = 11$). The average age was 16.6 years old ($SD = 1.7$), with the juveniles treated in community agencies significantly younger (15.7) than those treated in probation programs (17.9) and those in residential programs (16.9).

To measure changes, we identified the number of youth for whom a treatment target was identified at intake by a rating of present or partially present on that ERASOR item. We then calculated how many of these youth showed improvement, no change, or deterioration on the therapist's rating following treatment. Table 15.4 presents these results.

It is noteworthy that only four treatment targets, three of which were assessing sexuality factors, showed an improvement in at least 50 percent of the juveniles following treatment: poor intimate relationships (61 percent), deviant sexual interests (64 percent), unwillingness to change deviant sexual interests/attitudes (64 percent), and attitudes supportive of sexual offending (90 percent). Although the sample size is small, it is of concern that there were quite a few juveniles who the therapist rated as deteriorating on aggression (43 percent), parents unsupportive of treatment (30 percent), and obsessive sexual interests (25 percent) following treatment.

It is worrisome that very few improvements can be observed following sex offense-specific treatment. In fact, no significant changes due to treatment were noted on the SFQ or the CBCL. To examine the types of treatment "components/targets" used with the juveniles, we scrutinized what the therapists indicated they targeted from a list of twenty-four possibilities (e.g., cognitive distortions, relapse cycle, sexual education, dating skills, anger management, self-esteem, childhood victimization

Table 15.4

Factors Identified by ERASOR and Changes Noted During Treatment (N = 53)

ERASOR Risk Factors	Problem Identified	Following Treatment Problem		
		Improved	No Change	Deteriorated
Sexuality Factors				
Deviant sexual interests	42% (22)	64% (14)	32% (7)	5% (1)
Obsessive sexual interests	38% (20)	30% (6)	45% (9)	25% (5)
Attitudes supportive	40% (21)	90% (19)	10% (2)	0% (0)
Unwillingness to change	22% (11)	64% (7)	18% (2)	18% (2)
Antisociality Factors				
Antisocial orientation	60% (32)	41% (13)	47% (15)	13% (4)
Poor intimate relationships	68% (36)	61% (22)	31% (11)	8% (3)
Negative peers	66% (35)	37% (13)	46% (16)	17% (6)
Aggression	44% (23)	35% (8)	22% (5)	43% (10)
Poor self-regulation	70% (37)	32% (12)	49% (18)	19% (7)
Familial Factors				
High stress family	87% (46)	37% (17)	43% (20)	20% (9)
Parental rejection	85% (45)	38% (17)	42% (19)	20% (9)
Parents unsupportive of Tx	51% (27)	30% (8)	41% (11)	30% (8)

Note: Ns vary from 51 to 53 as a result of missing data.

issues, and fantasy work). In general, more than 70 percent of the youth were in programs that targeted all "components/targets," with the exception of three—covert sensitization, medication, and masturbation conditioning. Given that most programs in this investigation were endeavoring to include approximately twenty-one different "components/targets," it may be possible that the programs are attempting to do too much. Efforts to provide comprehensive treatment programs may influence the ability to have an impact on very specific factors such as sexual fantasies, impulsiveness, and obsessiveness with sex. Perhaps what is needed is the development of interventions with a more narrow focus, possibly one that targets the four core areas in a specific, concrete, and structured manner that can be continually monitored and evaluated.

To continue to advance our knowledge of effectively treating sexually abusive juveniles and reduce the likelihood of reoffending, it is important to make efforts to evaluate pre/posttreatment changes on those factors considered critical in addition to conducting recidivism studies. More empirical research in the area of adolescents who are sexually abusive and the services available to them will not only broaden our knowledge base but also enhance the effectiveness of the services for these young people.

CONCLUSION

This chapter provided evidence that investigations on sexually abusive juveniles should be sensitive to the confounding effects of the heterogeneity of a sample and to developmental and maturational changes. It is not surprising that juveniles placed in residential programs had significantly more problems and more serious issues than juveniles who were seen in the community. Nonetheless, it is important to recognize these differences. Such diversity can have a significant impact when synthesizing and extrapolating information from existing research studies with homogeneous samples that have limited generalizability. Significant differences within subsamples of juveniles have implications in the identification of important risk and need factors, which vary considerably between these groups. Recognizing the diversity of these individuals becomes imperative when making decisions on their sentencing, placement, and interventions, and eventually when evaluating risk.

The results of the present investigation point to the importance of development and maturation, particularly within the domain of sexuality. Many investigations are not sensitive to developmental changes within adolescents; in fact, it is noteworthy that even our investigation was guilty of this. We did not include a measure of development even though we consulted with a number of experts to assist us in deciding on assessment instruments. Adolescence is a period during which individuals are developing into sexual beings, including becoming aware of emerging sexual feelings and thoughts and having sexual experiences. These feelings, thoughts, and experiences need to be incorporated into the individual's sexual identity and sexual script. It may be that a key to understanding sexually abusive juveniles lies in exploring the development of sexuality. Such efforts, for example, may be able to identify specific stages of sexual development and provide a context for understanding, assessing, treating, and managing sexually abusive behavior.

Finally, efforts are required to evaluate the interventions with sexually abusive juveniles. Such evaluations must take into account the heterogeneity and the developmental and maturational differences within this population. Treatment tends to be comprehensive. Our results suggest that treatment programs may be suffering from trying to do too much, resulting in minimal change. As such, it suggests that more focused and specific interventions, evaluated and monitored closely, may assist in identifying processes that bring about change and reduce the chances of future sexual aggression. Although no recidivism results were presented in this chapter, this multisite study does intend to follow up these youth in order to determine whether or not changes due to treatment and/or maturation influence the likelihood of recidivism and to attempt to identify risk markers for future offending.

In conclusion, future research within the area of adolescents who are sexually abusive should try to incorporate the issues discussed in this chapter. Namely, it is critical to take into account the potential clientele differences in the population being studied, including the developmental stage of the youth. This becomes especially important when evaluating the effects of treatment. A youth who is receiving services that span over several years is likely to go through developmental changes that would have occurred regardless of whether or not the youth had received treatment. More research in this area is needed to increase our understanding of these youth and the processes that occur with regard to sexuality, as well as to provide these youth with evidenced-based treatment services that will not only help them become productive members of society but will reduce the likelihood of future victimization of the public.

Authors' Note

We would like to thank all of the agencies participating in the National Multisite Investigation of Treatment for Sexually Abusive Juveniles for providing the raw data used in this chapter. Without their hard work and dedication, this project would not be possible. We would also like to thank R. Karl Hanson for reviewing the manuscript and providing us with feedback.

The views expressed are those of the authors and are not necessarily those of Public Safety and Emergency Preparedness Canada. Correspondence should be addressed to Guy Bourgon, Corrections Research, Public Safety and Emergency Preparedness Canada, 340 Laurier Ave., West, Ottawa, ON, K1A 0P8. Email: *Guy.Bourgon@psepc.gc.ca*.

References

Achenbach, T. M. (1991a). *Youth Self Report*. Toronto, Ontario, Canada: Nelson Thomson Learning.

Achenbach, T. M. (1991b). *Child Behavior Checklist*. Toronto, Ontario, Canada: Nelson Thomson Learning.

Association for the Treatment of Sexual Abusers. (1997). *Ethical standards and principles for the management of sexual abusers*. Beaverton, OR: Author.

Becker, J. V., & Hicks, S. J. (2003). Juvenile sexual offenders: Characteristics, interventions, and policy issues. *Annals of the New York Academy of Sciences, 989*, 397–410.

Breiling, J. (2003). Etiology research as the route to science–based prevention. *Annals of the New York Academy of Sciences, 989*, 150–153.

Bukowski, W. M., Sippola, L., & Brender, W. (1993). Where does sexuality come from?: Normative sexuality from a developmental perspective. In H. E. Barbaree, W. L. Marshall, & S. M. Hudson (Eds.), *The juvenile sex offender* (pp. 84–103). New York: Guilford Press.

East, K., & Campbell, S. (1999). *Aspects of crime: Young offenders 1999*. England & Wales: Home Office. Retrieved December 28, 2003, from *www.homeoffice.gov.uk/rds/pdfs/aspects-youngoffs.pdf*.

Greenfield, L. A. (1997). *Sex offenses and offenders: An analysis of data on rape and sexual assault* (NCJ-163392). Washington, DC: U.S. Department of Justice, Bureau of Justice Statistics.

Hanson, R. K., & Bussière, M. T. (1998). Predicting relapse: A meta-analysis of sexual offender recidivism studies. *Journal of Consulting and Clinical Psychology, 66*, 348–362.

Hanson, R. K., Morton, K. E., & Harris, A. J. R. (2003). Sexual offender recidivism risk: What we know and what we need to know. *Annals of the New York Academy of Sciences, 989*, 154–166.

Hanson, R. K., & Morton-Bourgon, K. E. (2004). *Predictors of sexual recidivism: An updated meta-analysis* (User Report 2004-01). Ottawa, Ontario: Public Safety and Emergency Preparedness Canada.

Hoge, R. D., & Andrews, D. A. (2002). *The Youth Level of Service/Case Management Inventory: User's manual*. Toronto, Ontario, Canada: Multi-Health Systems.

Hunter, J. A., Figueredo, A. J., Malamuth, N. M, & Becker, J. V. (2003). Juvenile sex offenders: Toward the development of a typology. *Sexual Abuse: A Journal of Research and Treatment, 15*, 27–48.

Kaufman, K. L. (1993). *Sexual Fantasy Questionnaire*. Columbus, OH: Children's Hospital.

Kaufman, K. L. (1994). *Sexual History Form*. Columbus, OH: Children's Hospital.

Långström, N. (2002). Long-term follow-up of criminal recidivism in young sex offenders: Temporal patterns and risk factors. *Psychology, Crime and Law, 8*, 41–58.

Långström, N., & Grann, M. (2000). Risk for criminal recidivism among young sex offenders, *Journal of Interpersonal Violence, 15*, 855–871.

Longo, R. E. (2003). Emerging issues, policy changes, and the future of treating children with sexual behavior problems. *Annals of the New York Academy of Sciences, 989*, 502–514.

Morton, K. E. (2003). *Psychometric properties of four risk assessment measures with adolescent sexual offenders.* Unpublished master's thesis, Carleton University, Ottawa, Ontario, Canada.

National Adolescent Perpetrator Network. (1993). The revised report from the National Task Force on Juvenile Sexual Offending. *Juvenile and Family Court Journal, 44,* 1–120.

O'Brien, M. J., & Bera, W. H. (1986). Adolescent sexual offenders: A descriptive typology. *Preventing Sexual Abuse, 1,* 1–4.

Poole, D., Liedecke, D., & Marbibi, M. (2000). *Risk assessment and recidivism in juvenile sexual offenders: A validation study of the Static-99.* Austin: Texas Youth Commission.

Prentky, R., Harris, B., Frizzell, K., & Righthand, S. (2000). An actuarial procedure for assessing risk with juvenile sexual offenders. *Sexual Abuse: A Journal of Research and Treatment, 12*(2), 71–93.

Righthand, S., & Welch, C. (2001). *Juveniles who have sexually offended.* Washington, DC: U.S. Department of Justice Office of Juvenile Justice and Delinquency Prevention. Retrieved October 25, 2002, from *www.ncjrs.org/html/ojjd/report_juvsex_offend/.*

Schram, D. D., Milloy, C. D., & Rowe, W. E. (1991). *Juvenile sex offenders: A follow-up study of reoffense behavior.* Olympia: Washington State Institute for Public Policy.

Seto, M. C., & Lalumière, M. L. (2001). A brief screening scale to identify pedophilic interests among child molesters. *Sexual Abuse: A Journal of Research and Treatment, 13*, 15–25.

Seto, M. C., Murphy, W. D., Page, J., & Ennis, L. (2003). Detecting anomalous sexual interests in juvenile sex offenders. *Annals of the New York Academy of Sciences, 989*, 118–130.

Statistics Canada. (2002). *Persons charged by type of offense.* Retrieved August 28, 2003, from *www.statcan.ca/english/Pgdb/legal14b.htm*; *www.statcan.ca/english/Pgdb/legal14c.htm.*

Veneziano, C., & Veneziano, L. (2002). Adolescent sex offenders: A review of the literature. *Trauma, Violence, and Abuse, 3,* 247–260.

Worling, J. R. (1995). Sexual abuse histories of adolescent male sex offenders: Differences on the basis of the age and gender of their victims. *Journal of Abnormal Psychology, 104*, 610–613.

Worling, J. R. (2001). Personality-based typology of adolescent male sexual offenders: Differences in recidivism rates, victim-selection characteristics, and personal victimization histories. *Sexual Abuse: A Journal of Research and Treatment, 13*, 149–166.

Worling J. R., & Curwen, T. (2000). Adolescent sexual offender recidivism: Success of specialized treatment and implications for risk prediction. *Child Abuse and Neglect, 24,* 965–982.

Worling, J. R., & Curwen, T. (2001). *Estimate of Risk of Adolescent Sexual Offense Recidivism (ERASOR) Version 2.0.* Toronto, Ontario, Canada: Sexual Abuse Family Education & Treatment (SAFE-T).

Worling, J. R., & Långström, N. (2003). Assessment of criminal recidivism risk with adolescents who have offended sexually. *Trauma, Violence, and Abuse, 4,* 341–362.

Chapter 16

To Touch or Not to Touch— Issues for Therapists

**by Jerry D. Thomas, M.Ed. and
C. Wilson Viar III, B.S., B.A., B.F.A.**

OVERVIEW

This chapter discusses the dilemma of the use of touch with juvenile sex offenders and offers concrete suggestions for developing an approach that addresses both the human and the legal aspects of the problem. Youth with problematic sexual conduct often come from families that have failed to provide them with appropriate tactile stimulation—a hug before bedtime, snuggling during story time, rocking in a rocking chair. Without appropriate touch the human animal fails to neurologically develop properly. These children may confuse and replace affectionate, nonerotic touch with sexual touch. By the time they reach a residential treatment program, they may be sexually stimulated by any type of touch, or, on the other hand, they may have developed an aversion to all touch. There is a good possibility that these youth will misinterpret even the most seemingly appropriate touch. Residential programs are understandably very concerned about accusations of sexual impropriety by staff which may arise from the most innocuous hug or pat. Consequently, many programs have developed "no touch" policies to prevent such occurrences. Yet addressing the issues around touch in this population should be a priority in juvenile sex offender therapy. This chapter presents a sample of the policy developed by one program to address this issue.

INTRODUCTION

Why No-Touching Policies Are Instituted

It is not uncommon for professionals working directly with children and youth to actively avoid either touching or being touched by them. In some cases, especially when working with sexually abused and abusive youth, treatment programs and professionals develop a policy that specifies no physical contact at all. There are two primary reasons for this policy. One revolves around the concern that any physical contact could potentially be misinterpreted by a sexually abusive and/or abused child. In this context the most innocent and best intentioned touch, done thoughtlessly, is capable of becoming contratherapeutic or even a trigger for posttraumatic stress reactions.

The other concern revolves around the ever-present worry of litigation when there is either improper or misinterpreted touch. A great many organizations mistakenly believe that the best way to reduce any risks or exposure to legal action is to avoid touch entirely. The option of using touch thoughtfully in its natural role within the healthy developmental process of children and youth—much less to address and repair developmental problems, even those directly related to touch—is rarely considered. It is simply assumed that it is easier and less problematic to have a no-touch policy.

Yet, sexually abusive and/or abused children have suffered experiences and have behavioral and psychological issues that are by definition more fundamentally touch-oriented than any other population of troubled juveniles. They have touched and been touched by others in unhealthy, abusive, and hurtful ways. In addition to the sexually and physically abusive behavior they may have committed or experienced, very many of these children—particularly those in the high-risk categories—have experienced touch deprivation and/or abusive touch more than healthy touch. Given the developmental importance of touch, and the strong links between touch deprivation and a wide variety of neurological, behavioral, psychological, and physical problems, special attention to touch would be required even if not for the nature of these children's behavioral and psychological problems.

Drawbacks of No-Touching Policy

What we have effectively done is teach that there are only two touches—good touch and bad touch. Yet we have made no differentiation between the individual's experience of and knowledge of touch. These children must not do bad touching and if they are in a residential treatment setting they won't be allowed to do good touching until they are discharged. These young people in no way can be effectively prepared for the posttreatment world if treatment has not only failed to address but has pointedly avoided issues, experiences, and education about healthy touch.

The first problem with this attitude is that it is a reactive rather than proactive, "better safe than sorry" approach by both professionals and professional organizations, which focuses on eliminating the possibility rather than inclination of staff or clients victimizing others. To be proactive one would need to focus on the development of program components that address screening, hiring, staff supervision, education, and training as well as safety policies and procedures that support a healthy touch environment. This is obviously a more time- and energy-consuming task, but that is true of any useful therapeutic tool.

Worse still, we do not seem to be following this "eliminate negative possibilities rather than promote positive opportunities" game plan in any thoughtfully planned and consistent way. One treatment program with a strict no-touching policy makes an exception for wrestling, for example—purely because it has a really good wrestling team. Despite the program's sincere commitment to a no-touch policy in treatment, the wrestling program and staff were not assessed by the same standards. It ultimately was discovered, after a complaint by a client, that one of the staff involved with the wrestling team had a child abuse record. In addition to the obvious staffing failure, the program had never questioned whether wrestling was appropriate for a sexually abusive juvenile population, inappropriate, or potentially appropriate under specific rules and guidelines.

At the other end of the spectrum, another program did not allow basketball because of the opportunity for touching. When questioned as to why they did not examine the opportunities for intervention and processing that basketball offered, rather than banning it altogether, staff members said it would be too time-consuming.

These are not problems with touching, or even problems with wrestling or basketball, but problems with comprehensive organizational safety planning, staff screening, and training as well as treatment planning.

The second problem with the "better safe than sorry" approach is that there is an ever-increasing body of research that affirms the tremendous importance of touch in the developmental process, as part of sensory learning and communication, in memory formation, and in behavioral normalization and healing. As well, with clients whose difficulties directly involve issues of touch, such a policy may be actively harmful, particularly when abuse and offending behavior are the issues involved.

In fact, creating such a no-touch treatment environment may violate the first and primary responsibility of treatment providers—*Do no harm*. Dr. Kay Berkili, a psychologist in private practice in La Grange, Georgia, once said, "It is so important to do no harm, and it really worries me that by supporting a no-touch policy I may be actively harming rather than protecting [the children in my care]" (personal communication, February 1998).

My own experience with touch and no-touch policies in residential settings has spanned over thirty-five years. Some of the experiences have been educational, some humorous, some enlightening, some uplifting, some frightening, some very sad, and some very concerning. Two were particularly poignant. One occurred years ago in a residential facility for sexually abusive youth. We had a "work day" every week on which staff and youth alike did chores. I was on a ladder washing windows and a young man was holding the ladder steady for me. I was on the top rung when I slipped. In a flash I looked down at the young man's horrified expression. His arms were open wide but he had stepped back. Even as I was falling, I immediately knew his dilemma—if I catch her I touch her—if I touch her there will be consequences. By some miracle this young man avoided touching anything but my waist and broke my fall. Then he said in an anxiety-filled voice, "I'm so sorry that I touched you!"

The second incident was one I heard about secondhand. A young person in residential treatment was told that his mother had died in a car crash while on her way to visit with him. He was close to his mother and she was his last living relative. Of course, he was devastated. Despite his grief and neediness no staff member reached out to him. While he sobbed, every staff member rigidly followed the residential treatment center's no-touch policy.

Between entrenched cultural taboos concerning touch and an intense general social reaction to the "discovery" of sexual abuse on one hand and a growing body of research about the role of touch in both mental and physical health on the other, there is currently a great deal of confusion and contradiction about the subject in the mental health and juvenile justice fields. This chapter is not an attempt to provide all the answers or solve all the problems of touch and touching. This is a first step, intended to examine some of the basic issues, to examine some of the ideas, and to provide some constructive and realistic suggestions for changing no-touch environments into healthy-touch environments.

ATTITUDES ABOUT TOUCH

Historical and Cultural Background

The prohibitions against being able to touch, who you can or cannot touch, and/or the use of touch as a therapeutic technique are not new. There are six basic reasons for this negative attitude about touch, two of which revolve around general cultural issues, and four around professional issues. First, English-speaking Western cultures have a long history of repressing both physical and sexual expression. Indeed, these attitudes are so ingrained that touch and sexuality are often confused. One result of this, the second general cultural issue, is that our recent forced recognition of the problem of child sexual abuse after so many centuries of denial has caused an extreme social reaction in the opposite direction. We are now so vigilant in our determination to prevent child sexual abuse that we are actively suspicious of anyone who even has the opportunity to touch a child for any reason.

The significant historical events that most influenced our attitudes about touch came to a head in the twelfth century and grew in influence over the next few hundred years. Over these centuries, a number of events occurred in Europe that served to nurture and feed sexual repressiveness and touch aversion in English-speaking countries, particularly in America. A full discussion would require at the least a chapter of its own. In the interests of space, however, the four greatest contributors to current attitudes about touch were the Reformation, the rise and ultimate reign (1649–1658) of Oliver Cromwell in England, the pre-Enlightenment and Enlightenment periods, and the series of devastating epidemics that swept Europe during this critical period.

The epidemics that ravaged Europe in the twelfth through the eighteenth centuries made two powerful contributions to our current aversion to touch. First, by profoundly disrupting society, almost to the point of total collapse in the case of the Black Plague, the epidemics sowed the seeds of the Reformation. Second, simply put, deadly epidemics in an age which understands "contagiousness" but knows almost nothing about how particular diseases are transmitted tend to make people avoid getting near, much less touching, each other. Touch could be deadly. This belief became part of the religious, social, and political practices of the time.

The Reformation is important because it allowed for a tremendous and previously unheard of degree of diversification of religious/philosophical ideas and life-way practices. It is also important to the subject of touch avoidance and sexual repression because of the emphasis all the different groups placed on proving their sanctity during this period. The Puritans and Calvinists were some of the most aggressive proponents of both the inadequacy of all those not like them and the native evil of all things physical. Because the separation of the physical self and the spiritual self was a major aspect of the Roman church, it was also one of the fundamental points around which people varied.

The mid-seventeenth-century rise and reign of the arch-Puritan Oliver Cromwell and the emergence of the Enlightenment are best summarized together. Cromwell's rise and the growth in popularity of the ideas of men such as Francis Bacon and Rene Descartes, who promoted the Age of Reason, are both indicators of how pervasive the denigration of the physical compared to matters mental had grown, particularly in England. Without Cromwell, the birth of the Enlightenment in England would have merely been a growth of science. Under his influence, however, it also became a severe separation and disparagement of the physical from the mind.

Second, these trends in both the English religious and secular worlds occurred during the seminal period in which America and English Canada grew from collections of isolated outposts to independent and unique cultures and societies. The result in America was the rise of a religious and secular ethos called New England Protestantism, a world view strongly influenced by conservative Puritan and Calvinist concepts of appropriate social behavior.

The Victorian Era (1839–1901) is well-known as an era of physical repression and arch-conservative Protestantism, and it is noteworthy for culturally extending and emphasizing stigmatization of physicality and touch taboos. America, Great Britain, "English Canada," and the emerging nations of Australia and New Zealand, were now afflicted by historically religion-based but now socially pervasive unhealthy cultural stigmatizations of the body and, by extension, physical contact. All these attitudes and concerns culminated in the Christian community pairing touch with sinfulness

During this period these ideas even served to overcome the Christian church's attitude about circumcision, a practice previously rejected as non-Christian. In the late 1800s, religious and medical leaders (such as Dr. Kellogg of corn flakes fame) became obsessed with the idea of masturbation as inherently evil. Their obsession fairly rapidly focused on the role of the male foreskin. One school of thought was that the need to pull back the foreskin during bathing encouraged and trained young boys in the methods of masturbation. Another school believed that the removal of the foreskin would reduce the sensitivity of the penis, thereby reducing the motivation to masturbate. Both schools, however, reached the same conclusion: For the sake of the moral and physical health of our male children, the foreskin must go. In America, Great Britain, English Canada, and the emerging nations of Australia and New Zealand, it did just that. Great Britain and most of the other English-speaking countries rejected this practice in the early twentieth century, largely due to growing anger within the respective medical communities over what they perceived as a medically baseless and rationally unsound practice. In the United States, however, the practice was continued under the veil of a new argument; despite the complete lack of evidence to support the claim, U.S. authorities said that circumcision was necessary to promote the physical rather than moral hygiene of the genitals.

Contemporary Attitudes Toward Touch

Today, the United States continues to be one of the most intolerant countries about physical matters and personal contact. Residents of the other English-speaking countries are less reserved than Americans about social physical contact but much more so in turn than other people in European and Latin American countries. Oddly, people in all these countries also seem to have been generally aware that they were more physically uptight than was good for them for some time. They also seem not only to have done very little to act on that realization for some time but to be aware that they hadn't, as well.

One of the most curious aspects of American attitudes is that this touch aversion has continued even while our approach to sexuality has altered. Although American culture has become increasingly comfortable with prurient sexual content in the media, we still are very intolerant of personal contact even when the context of that contact is not sexual. The rule remains: One can look but one cannot touch. What is more, all touch is considered suspect until proven otherwise, to the extent that even close friends minimize social touch to a degree that is considered amusing in other countries.

The result is that many Americans maintain a hands-off stance even during contact with their closest friends, fearful that the intentions of their touch could be misconstrued. Indeed, Americans generally reserve expressions of physical affection, even with lovers, to private times to avoid the risk of offending people in public settings. Just how touch aversive are Americans today compared to people in other countries? An oft-repeated study first conducted by Jourard (1966) involves observing people in coffee shops, for example, in different countries and counting how many times they touch in any way within a half hour. This research (Field, 1999) has consistently produced the following results: Puerto Ricans: 180; French: 110; Americans: 2

America has become a country rife with touch taboos, many of which are so ingrained that they are not even formally recognized or discussed—they are merely part of our cultural heritage (Hunter & Struve, 1997):

- Don't touch those of higher status.

- Don't touch opposite gender friends too much.

- Don't touch same gender friends too much.

- Don't touch yourself.

- Don't touch strangers.

- Don't touch the ill, the disabled, the unattractive.

Touching Children

The New Zealand Herald (Garner, 2003) ran a story last year which captured just how ironic the conflict between strong cultural inhibitions, recognition that the inhibitions are bad, and built-in unwillingness to act or even talk openly about the problem has become due to the stigmatization associated with acting against the inhibitions. Alison Jones of the University of Auckland conducted interviews with teachers from across New Zealand about the no-touch policy and its consequences. Teachers not only reported multiple cases in which injured girls lay on sports fields while male teachers ran to find female teachers willing to abandon their own charges long enough to help. As well, they reported multiple instances of naked children wandering out of locker-rooms searching for an adult who could help them get dressed. It is impossible not to note the irony of the fact that, as a result of policies intended to reduce abuse, a pedophilic male teacher has the opportunity to regularly observe nude children as the result of a rule intended to prevent him from gratifying himself.

Well-intentioned but sometimes ill-advised taboos against touch with children are both formally and informally being implemented in schools and day care centers across the United States. Ironically, this is a result of our success in publicizing the problem of child sexual abuse. The strength of the social denial about child sexual abuse, rooted in the historical and cultural factors discussed previously, translated into an equal and opposite social reaction once the dam was breached, particularly by those with professional responsibility for children.

In response the National Association for the Education of Young Children (1996) issued the following official position statement on the subject:

> Programs should not institute "no-touch policies" to reduce the risk of abuse. In the wake of well-publicized allegations of child abuse in out-of-home settings and increased concerns regarding liability, some programs have instituted such policies, either explicitly or implicitly. No-touch policies are misguided efforts that fail to recognize the importance of touch to children's healthy development. Touch is especially important for infants and toddlers. Warm, responsive touches convey regard and concern for children of any age. Adults should be sensitive to ensuring that their touches (such as pats on the back, hugs, or ruffling the child's hair) are welcomed by the children and appropriate to their individual characteristics and cultural experience. Careful, open communication between the program and families about the value of touch in children's development can help to achieve consensus as to acceptable ways for adults to show their respect and support for children in the program. (p. 2)

THE FIELD OF MENTAL HEALTH AND TOUCH

Offense-specific treatment for juveniles is considered a melding of two disciplines: mental health and juvenile justice. Both of these fields have had a similar attitude about touch and touching: No touch is the best touch.

The field of mental health provides an excellent example of just how strongly the English-speaking world, America in particular, has sexualized any and all physical contact. In the United States there was little to no discussion of the positive potential of touch in therapy until the 1960s and 1970s, though it had made a brief appearance in the late 1800s within psychoanalysis. Freud originally promoted touch in conjunction with verbal therapy and reported positive results (Breuer & Freud, 1955). Unfortunately, while Freud had discussed stroking the head or massaging the neck and shoulders, it was sometimes taken to horrifically ironic extremes in the United States. During the height of the antimasturbation craze of the late Victorian period, American psychoanalysts commonly treated "hysterical" women through "manual manipulation" of the clitoris. According to the History Channel, this procedure was performed with all due clinical professionalism and dispassion until orgasm was achieved. The belief was that orgasmic release discharged the imbalanced psychological passions which were damaging female patients' mental health. This practice was not ultimately discontinued as a result of thoughtful examination but because of the abrupt decline in the popularity of psychoanalytical theory in the United States at the turn of the twentieth century. Elsewhere, Freud himself discontinued the use of touch due to transference concerns.

Few ideas have been met originally with as much outrage as Freud's discussion of early childhood sexuality, though the German word he actually used translates instead as "sensuality." Freud still continues to be mocked and dismissed for these (mistranslated) statements in some circles. When we first opened ourselves to the possibility of child sexual abuse, however, we also opened our eyes to childhood sexuality in general. This was partly as a result of adults not knowing what to do about any sexual behavior in children. We wanted to either ignore it or punish it. Unfortunately, we also tended to always label it "sexually abusive."

Gail Ryan, director of the Perpetration Prevention Program, Kempe Children's Center, University of Colorado School of Medicine, Denver, has developed a curriculum called "Understanding and Responding to the Sexual Behavior in Children" (Ryan et al., 1998) in response to our general ignorance about the normal sexual behavior to children and how to identify and respond to sexual behavior whether it is normal, concerning, or illegal. It was developed for anyone who works with children and youth and is a train the trainers model.

The behaviorists, the cognitive-behaviorists, and the marriage and family therapy schools have nothing specific to say on the use of touch in therapy. Hunter and Struve (1997), however, noted that training and therapy films involving therapists from these schools reveal that touch was quite often used in actual treatment, and that it was primarily the kinds of touch that we all do naturally without thinking. Between their own acculturated resistance to these ideas, however, and a few isolated incidents in which proponents of new mind-body approaches sexualized therapeutic interventions, mainstream psychology continued to view arguments for the use of touch in therapy with an extremely suspicious eye.

CURRENT TOUCH RESEARCH CENTERS

Fortunately, in recent years, researchers have become very interested in understanding touch and its meaning to different people and circumstances. A growing number of researchers have recently linked inadequate touch, or touch deprivation, to an ever-increasing number of developmental and behavioral problems. Likewise, an increasing number of researchers have recently demonstrated the role of touch in normal human physical and mental development. Both these issues are discussed in this section.

In the past two decades the sensory tool known as touch has been the subject of increasing interest by researchers. Though this work has not focused specifically on sex offenders, it has enormous implications for the work that we do with children and youth in particular. In light of our almost universal use of a no-touch policy, it is necessary for us to examine the growing knowledge base concerning the role of touch in human development and health.

The organizations discussed here are just a few of the entities that are looking at the role of touch in our everyday lives. The information recorded has all been taken directly from their promotional publications and Web sites. We have no direct knowledge of these organizations but are using them because they appear to be representative of the work that is being done as it applies to touch.

Touch Research Institute

The Touch Research Institute (TRI) (*www.miami.edu/touch-research/home.html*), part of the Department of Pediatrics of the University of Miami School of Medicine, was the first center in the world devoted solely to the study of touch and its application in science and medicine. It was formally established in 1992 by its director, Tiffany Field, Ph.D., with a start-up grant from Johnson and Johnson. A second TRI facility is now located in the Philippines. A group of neonatologists there have replicated earlier studies showing that preterm infants' weight gain can be facilitated by massage therapy. A third TRI is located at the University of Paris and studies the role of touch in psychopathology.

The TRI's distinguished team of researchers tries to define touch as it promotes health and contributes to the treatment of disease. Research efforts that began in 1982 and continue today have shown that touch therapy has numerous beneficial effects on health and well-being. This research center has conducted over ninety studies on the positive effects of massage therapy on many functions and medical conditions in varied age groups. Among the significant research findings are enhanced growth (e.g., in preterm infants), diminished pain (e.g., in fibromyalgia), decreased autoimmune problems (e.g., increased pulmonary function in asthma and decreased glucose levels in diabetes), enhanced immune function (e.g., increased natural killer cells in human immunodeficiency virus and cancer), and enhanced alertness and performance (e.g., EEG pattern of alertness and better performance on math computations). Many of these effects appear to be mediated by a decrease in stress hormones also linked to the therapy.

Laboratory for Human and Machine Haptics

The Massachusetts Institute for Technology sponsors the Laboratory for Human and Machine Haptics, less formally known as the Touch Lab (*http://touchlab.mit.edu*). The Touch Lab was founded by Dr. Mandayam A. Srinivasan in 1990 and is composed of an interdisciplinary group of researchers interested in haptics—the study of sensing and manipulation through touch. They use a variety of methods to look for the general principles that humans and machines use to explore, represent, and interact with objects. The goals of their research are to understand human haptics, develop machine haptics, and enhance human-machine interactions in virtual reality and teleoperator systems. To gain a deeper understanding of human haptics, multidisciplinary investigations involving skin biomechanics, neurophysiology, psychophysics, motor control, and computational models are employed. The results of this research are also beneficial to hand therapy, intelligent prosthesis design, and the development of autonomous robots that need to perform human-like functions in unstructured environments.

Developmental Care Program

The Developmental Care Program (*www.edu/~neonatalDevCare/families.html*), part of the Department of Pediatrics, Health Sciences Center at the University of New Mexico in Albuquerque, offers advanced mini-preceptorships, mentoring, and educational experiences in family-focused individualized touch and massage with newborns and young infants who are being cared for in hospital special intensive care or regular care nurseries. This advanced-level experience is designed for hospital-based pediatric bedside and other professionals who are certified in infant massage.

The following information comes from the program's Web site:

Our theoretical framework regarding parental implementation of individualized touch and massage in special care nursery settings comes from several directions. We draw from the synactive theory of neurobehavioral organization (Als), neurodevelopmental treatment (Bobath), sensory processing (Ayres), parental investment and attachment theory (Bowlby, Trivers, Lancaster, Kaplan), the importance of touch (Montague, Shaunberg), and a broad base of somatic touch and massage modalities (Upledger, McClure, Rosen, Krieger). Our commitment is toward family-focused touch-mediated interventions that promote parental success and competence, for optimal infant well-being.

Some of the learning outcomes identified include:

1. Identify and teach how to use infant physiological and neurobehavioral cues to individualize touch and massage that supports infant organizational capacities;

2. Adapt the teaching of touch and handling to address special infant medical, physical, and neurodevelopment considerations;

3. Guide parental touch as a catalyst for facilitating positive family-infant connections/attachments; and

4. Build on touch and massage to promote developmentally supportive care continuity for seamless infant and family adjustments from hospital to home.

Center for Neurodevelopmental Studies

Lorna Jean King, OtR, FAOTA, is one of the pioneers of sensory integration therapy. Ms. King, an international lecturer on this topic, is the founder and director of the Center for Neurodevelopmental Studies, Inc., in Phoenix, Arizona. The Center is a nonprofit corporation founded in 1978 to provide the most advanced neurodevelopmentally based therapeutic methods for autistic and other developmentally delayed children and adolescents. Ms. King is quoted in an interview with Stephen M. Edelson on June 9, 1996, reported on the Internet (*www.autism.org/interview/ljk.html*):

> The goal of sensory integrative therapy is to facilitate the development of the nervous system's ability to process sensory input in a more normal way. Sensory integration is a term for a process in the normal brain which pulls together all of the various sensory messages in order to form coherent information on which we can act. Basically everything we do requires sensory integration. This normal process can be missing or very badly organized in some people, notably autistic individuals.

The three major areas addressed with sensory integrative therapy are vestibular, proprioceptive, and tactile. The vestibular system, located in the inner ear, relates us to gravity. It gives us our sensation of the weight of our body. It also tells us where we are in space—falling, standing up, leaning, upside down, or turning our head. Monitoring our head and body movements in any direction, it works twenty-four hours a day, providing a steady and large amount of sensory input.

The proprioceptors are the neuroreceptors in tendons, muscles, and joints, and they receive input whenever and however we move. They tell us where our foot is when we pull it back to kick a ball, or how high our hand is when we reach up to comb our hair. Proprioceptive input can vary in intensity. When one jumps on a trampoline, there is more intense input to the ankles, knees, and hips than there is in walking. Pushing a wheelbarrow full of cement is more intense input to the wrists, elbows, and shoulders than pushing an empty wheelbarrow.

The tactile or touch system has three different types of receptors. One responds to light touch, such as touching a hair on one's hand. This is a protective, alerting sense, which makes us check on what is touching us in case it might be dangerous, like a bug crawling on the skin. The second receptor is for discriminative touch (e.g., when reaching in a pocket and knowing by feel whether we are touching our house key or our car key). We learn a great deal more than we generally realize through the sense of discriminative touch. The third set of touch receptors are those that receive information about heat, cold, and pain.

The Center operates on the belief that people are far too unaware of the communicative aspects of behavior—that behavior, in fact, is always communication, both self and interpersonal communication. We talk about some "bad" behavior being a bid for attention or a cry for help, without formally recognizing that we are addressing behavior as a communication. Yet, especially in the case of children, sometimes behavior is not only the best but only way they know how to tell others "what's on their mind." It is our job as adults to determine not just the manifest but the inherent meanings the behavior is attempting to communicate. Often sensory sensitivities are actually painful and the child's behavior is an attempt to escape. By being observant, finding out what triggers the "behavior," we can modify the environment and help the child find acceptable ways to cope, such as teaching him to wear ear phones to protect himself from too much noise. As we use sensory integrative therapy to raise the child's threshold for arousal, and provide calming inputs, we can see behavioral demonstrations of an underlying improvement.

Sensory Processing Network

The Sensory Processing Network (*www.sinetwork.org*) is sponsored by the Kid Foundation. Sensory processing disorder (SPD) is a complex disorder of the brain which causes victims to misinterpret everyday sensory information, including touch, sound, and movement. This can lead to behavioral problems, difficulties with coordination, and many other issues.

Touch Laboratory at Queen's University

The Touch Laboratory at Queen's University in Kingston, Canada (*http://psyc.queens.ca*), is directed by Dr. Susan Lederman of the Department of Psychology, and focuses on the sense of touch in humans. The Laboratory's work has examined how normally sighted and blind people come to learn about the world around them through haptic exploration and manipulation. Topics studied over the years have included:

- The haptic perception of object and surface properties (texture, hardness, thermal properties, shape, size, weight, function, etc.);

- The haptic identification of common and unfamiliar multidimensional objects;

- Haptic space perception in the sighted and the blind;
- Intersensory integration and multimodal perception; and
- Perceiving objects and surfaces through a probe.

Among the typical behavioral measures are psychophysical responses, the classification of videotaped hand movements which accompany manual exploration during haptic search, response latencies, errors, oral and written questionnaire responses, and kinematic and dynamic measures of hand/arm movements.

Sensory Motor Neuroscience Group

The University of Birmingham in Birmingham, England, offers a continuing education course sponsored by the Sensory Motor Neuroscience Group (*www. symon.bham.ac.uk/courses/activetouch.htm*). It is a practical skills-building course, and the Web site explains active touch in the following terms:

> Of all the senses, touch contributes most to the impression of being present. While vision and sound provide early warning of distant events, the directness of mechanical stimulation in touch demands immediate attention and allows direct access to decision and action systems of the brain.
>
> Recent studies of active touch by psychologists, neurophysiologists, neurologists and engineers have led to rapid progress in understanding how the many sources of touch information are brought together, and integrated with other sense modalities by the brain into representations of reality.
>
> Refined behavioral measurement techniques, combined with modern technology for imaging the activity of the brain, have yielded new insights into how the brain processes and transforms touch information into decision and action. An area of growing importance is the determination of factors contributing to the affective response to touch input . . . i.e. Feelings about feeling!

Good Touch/Bad Touch Programs

The attempts to teach children and youth how to avoid child sexual abuse have centered on skills-based curricula commonly known as good touch, bad touch prevention programs. Most of these programs, and there are many of them, focus on preventing child sexual abuse, teaching children to distinguish appropriate touching from inappropriate touching, and enhancing protective behaviors in children. These programs are all designed for children who have not been identified as abused or abusive and who have had culturally normative developmental experiences of touch. Curricula may have a parent education component as well to provide parents and other caregivers with the knowledge and skills necessary to recognize and discuss sexual abuse with their children. Curricula may use various methods to teach children skills, including:

- Workshops and school lessons;
- Puppet shows and role-playing activities;

- Films and videos; and

- Workbooks, storybooks, and comics.

Examples of skill-based curricula include programs such as Talk about Touching, Safe Child, Good Touch/Bad Touch, Kids on the Block, and Illusion Theater.

There are some concerns that these programs will teach children to associate sex with bad touch. Others worry that many of the prevention materials for children put too much of the responsibility on the child.

LOOKING BEYOND OUR OWN NOSES

Early pioneers such as Fay Honey Knopp said to us, "Open your minds, don't close them to possibilities, and don't be afraid to try new things" (personal communication, November 1989) This conversation was about the use of therapeutic touch with trauma victims, a subject controversial then, and controversial still. If she were here today I'm sure that her comment on this chapter and its subject would be something like "What's taken you so long?"

The field of sexual aggression has begun acting on her advice after years of developing treatment and treatment programs based on a very narrow perspective. As the problem of sexual aggression became more widely recognized, and as the field grew and expanded—particularly as it began to include adolescents, children, and females—we began to open ourselves to the information available in other fields of practice such as aggression, delinquency, criminology, mental illness, family violence, child development, and physical and mental health, as well as biology, physiology, and recent brain studies. Sexually abusive youth are now commonly diagnosed with post-traumatic stress syndrome, reactive attachment disorder, attention deficit disorder, bipolar disorder, autism, Asperger's syndrome, Tourrete's syndrome, and many other conditions that need to be concurrently addressed if we are to be successful in treating these clients for sexually abusive behavior. Even professionals whose orientation is the juvenile justice system rather than mental health are increasingly considering the larger meaning of training and rehabilitation, and consequently the need to be aware of concurrent problems or conditions.

Sometimes we have such tunnel vision in our field that we put human beings in boxes marked "sex offender" as if they were a different species. Sexually abusive youth have brains and their brains are affected by trauma just as other children's brains are. Some sexually abusive youth are abandoned, leading to the same attachment disorders as non-sexually abusive youth. Sexually abusive youth have attention deficit disorders, learning disabilities, mental health disorders, high intelligence, low intelligence, and so on, just as all other children and youth. All children are born as sexual beings, and their attitudes and behaviors about sexuality are learned. All children are born as humans who use touch to sense the world around them, and much of how they do that is also a product of the information and experience they receive.

THE ROLE OF TOUCH IN DEVELOPMENT

We have learned that we have to treat sexually abusive children and youth as a whole, not as a fragmented entity. The ability to touch and be touched is part of the human experience. Thus we have to consider touch as something missing from the developmental repertoire of some sexually abusive youth, and as a deficit it must be repaired. It may not be true for all sexually abusive youth, or even true in the same degree for all sexually abusive youth, but those of us who work exclusively with children and youth know that denying a child the right to touch or be touched for months or years will not do anything positive to change the child's experience of or attitude toward touch. In fact, it may worsen existing problems through neglect. Also, such denial is extremely likely to produce additional, often serious problems related to touch deprivation, which is discussed in more detail later.

Once while training professional staff on the issue of and use of touch in residential treatment with sexually abusive youth, one of the authors asked the staff members if they would be willing to go a week without touching or being touched by anyone in order to experience what we were asking the children in their residential facility to experience. The answer was not only a resounding, "No!" but the staff seemed aghast that anyone would even ask the question.

Touch and Violence

Touch is fundamental to human life, and the first and primary mode of communication between caretaker and child. As such, not only does bad touch have a great potential to harm, but the lack of good touch can be equally damaging. Dr. James Prescott, a former administrator of the National Institute of Child Health and Human Development, analyzed *A Cross-Cultural Summary* (Textor, 1967). This book is a large compendium of cultural studies from around the world and is considered one of the primary resources for cross-cultural analysis. Comparing the wide range of societies covered by the text, Prescott (1975, 1996) found that the degree of violence in a culture is directly related to its sexual and physical repressiveness. In particular, Prescott found that societies that gave their infants the greatest amount of physical affection had the lowest rates of theft, violence, and murder. Prescott concluded that physically affectionate human societies are highly unlikely to be physically violent. Physical affection and low physical discipline toward children were found to be especially predictive of low crime, violence, and murder rates in the society at large.

Touch and Attachment

Two of the most firmly established and critical roles of positive touch are its indispensability for the healthy physical and psychological development of infants and young children. This is due in part to the vital role of healthy bonding or attachment with a primary caregiver, and in part to the chemical changes positive, nurturing touch produces in the body and brain.

Prenatal studies have proven that a discriminatory sense of touch develops by the sixth month of pregnancy when the embryo is only one inch long. After birth, by necessity touch provides the vast majority of infant and preverbal children's social communication, perceivable environmental information, and relationship-building interactions. Long before the eyes can be focused or aural information be interpreted, infants demonstrate an understanding of the difference between positive and negative touch and a pronounced preference for positive touch from their primary caregiver(s).

Over the last ten years a number of researchers have worked to provide a more workable, unified theory incorporating information from the many different fields, from neurobiology to psychiatry, which addresses the consequences of healthy and unhealthy attachment on the body, brain, behavior, and mind. According to Dr. Allan Schore (2001b) of the UCLA Medical School, "The attachment researchers have studied the experiences necessary for social and emotional development, but they have looked only at behaviors and not at brain structures. The brain development people have looked at structures and not at behavioral consequences" (p. 2). What a wide variety of researchers have found is that inadequate or failed attachment does not merely affect the mind and behavior. It also disrupts and can even retard the development and functioning of the body and brain.

> There is a human brain growth spurt that occurs between the third trimester *in utero* to about 18–24 months of age. This involves the development of the right limbic brain (limbic system and cortical association areas) which is involved in social cognition, attachment and caregiving behaviors, as well as regulating bodily and affective states. This system is in growth spurt for the first 18 months of life and remains dominant for a further 18 months. (Schore, 2001b, p. 3)

Schore (2001a, 2001b) documents a human brain growth from the third trimester until eighteen to twenty-four months which centers upon the right limbic brain. The limbic system and cortical association areas of the brain are involved in social cognition, attachment, and physical and affective state regulation.

As stated, after the initial growth spurt, these right brain systems remain dominant for an additional eighteen months, or until the child is 3 to 3½ years old, and his structural and functional development is adaptive to internal and external stimuli. Interaction with a primary caregiver(s) has a particularly powerful effect on a child's neurobiogical development due to the formation of "affective synchrony." An example of this synchrony is the sympathetic acceleration and parasympathetic deceleration of heart rates by mothers and young children during play.

In biological terms:

> Visual input of mother's face is associated with elevated levels of neurotrophins (brain nourishing chemicals) which are synaptogenetic (help produce synaptic connections) and are known to perform a growth-promoting role in the postnatal development of the cortex.
>
> The limbic system, which is involved in emotional regulation, is in critical growth during the early postnatal period and its growth and organization is influenced by the interactions between infants and caregivers.
>
> The last developing structure is the orbital prefrontal region or "senior executive" of the socio-emotional brain. This is dominant in non-conscious processing, [the expression] of emotional information, and for regulating internal physiological state via the hypothalamo-pituitary, adrenocortical, and sympathetic-adrenomedullary [systems] according to internal and external feedback. (Schore, 2001b, p. 4)

According to Schore, the ultimate biological consequences of absent, poor, or traumatic attachment is that both the sympathetic nervous system (SNS) and the parasympathetic nervous system (PNS) are hyperactivated. Hyperactivation of the SNS and PNS results in heightened exposure to excitotoxic neurotransmitters (glutamate, etc.) which destroy neural cells and, unchecked, can permanently impair limbic system functionality. Neurobiological studies have found that this damage reduces the ability to experience positive emotional states, ability to form social bonds, and emotional functioning and regulation.

The neurobiological and chemical language used by Schore and others might obscure just how profound the physical and therefore psychological and behavioral impact of failed or negative attachment can be. Perhaps the most disturbing and well-known examples of the results of touch deprivation on young children come from the studies of the infamous Romanian orphanage system. These children, faced with inadequate and negative attachment experiences that make even the horrors of the average, grotesquely underfunded American child services system pale, do not just show merely chemical and synaptic retardation. Their brains are up to 40 percent smaller.

While Schore (2001a, 2001b) emphasizes the importance of "face-to-face interaction" between the primary caregiver and the child in his articles, such interactions primarily take place almost by necessity while the caregiver is holding the child. It is also important to note that Schore is stressing a mechanism that aids healthy attachment, and it is not the specific mechanism(s) that produces the quality of the attachment, which he and others consider critical. The essential role of touch during this developmental period is supported not only by studies of attachment with blind and deaf-blind children but also by the fact that neonatal vision measures between 20/200 and 20/600 on the Snellen scale; a baby's ability to visually distinguish color and form does not develop until the second to fourth month, and even in sighted children object-permanence-by-touch is achieved many months before object-permanence-by-sight. True, sighted infants quickly develop an ability to visually focus at one to three feet and have a well-documented preference for the faces of their primary caregiver(s) in this period. But visual development progresses more gradually after this initial stage, and one to three feet is the average distance from the mother's arms to the mother's face.

> The acts of holding, rocking, singing, feeding, gazing, kissing and other nurturing behaviors involved in caring for infants and young children are bonding experiences. Factors crucial to bonding include time together (in childhood, quantity does matter!), face-to-face interactions, eye contact, physical proximity, touch and other primary sensory experiences such as smell, sound, and taste. Scientists believe the most important factor in creating attachment is positive physical contact (e.g., hugging, holding, and rocking). It should be no surprise that holding, gazing, smiling, kissing, singing, and laughing all cause specific neurochemical activities in the brain. These neurochemical activities lead to normal organization of brain systems that are responsible for attachment. (Perry, 2001, p. 3)

JUVENILE AGGRESSION

Questionably motivated and unsubstantiated reports to the contrary, U.S. Justice Department statistics show that juvenile violent crime rates have dropped over the last fifteen years. Despite this reduction, America's children remain the most aggressive in

Western society. In 1994, the National Center for Injury Prevention and Control, a division of the Centers for Disease Control, reported that the homicide rate of 15- to 24-year-old males in the United States was 22 per 100,000 but only 1 per 100,000 in France. Other researchers have confirmed that the homicide rate for American adolescents is twenty times greater than that of any other industrialized country (Field, 2002; Orpinas, Basen-Engquist, Gunbaum, & Parcel, 1995; Sosin, Koepsell, Rivara, & Mercy, 1995). Note the term "industrialized country." Not "first world," "second world," or "third world" country but, merely, "industrialized." The determining factor is evidently not how technologically advanced and complex the country is but, rather, something endemic to U.S. culture. The widely publicized fact that Canada has many more guns per population and yet far less violent crime than America underscores the conclusion that the difference is within us.

Touch Deprivation and Juvenile Aggression

Field (2002) and others have found a link between violence in adolescence and touch deprivation which at first blush appears to be best explained by the neurobiological and neurochemical developmental and functional deficits of negative or faulty attachment discussed previously. These neurobiological and chemical deficits are very real. Yet focusing too much on these symptoms and language runs the risk of obscuring or oversimplifying the problems and the circumstances that produce them. There is a natural attractiveness to the relatively concrete language and symptomology of physiology for those who deal with and seek the answers to complex and painful human problems.

Yet the trite old saw, "nature vs. nurture" is in no way undermined by these findings, and, in fact, is supported by them. While the term "touch deprivation" sounds mechanical, it is important to remember that the deprivation in question is a lack of very personal, idiosyncratic in detail, human-to-human physical interaction. What is more, while the physiological deficits that this lack produces may be similar enough across individuals to quantify and predict, these physiological conditions are expressed cognitively and behaviorally with all the terrible and wonderful uniqueness that individual people and circumstances can bring to bear.

These humanistic points supplement rather than qualify the body of research linking juvenile aggression and touch deprivation, however, and, in fact, are implicitly included in this research rather than addenda. After all, while Schore, Field, and others may focus foremost upon incontrovertible, quantifiable physiological changes and conditions, they are doing so as a way of supporting arguments about a subject, touch, which has been long disparaged as being merely a matter of subjective supposition.

Attachment and Juvenile Sexual Offending/Aggression

There is no destination so unique that it can only be reached by a single path. In fact, "There may be as many different paths as there are sex offenders" (Becker & Kaplan, 1993). Sexual offender treatment, particularly juvenile sexual offender treatment, became stuck in a "fit the peg to the hole" mentality for many years. Only relatively recently have professionals begun to develop individualized treatment for this immensely heterogeneous population. The treatment, while individualized, continues to address offense-specific issues, however, that are common among sex offenders.

The fact that they have misused touch is one of these commonalities, as is a childhood experience of touch deprivation, inadequate touch, and/or abusive touch.

Healthily attached children can become sexually abusive, and unhealthily attached children do not necessarily become sexually abusive. Unhealthy attachment, which by definition almost always involves either no, inadequate, or negative touch, however, is one of the most common etiological features of sexually aggressive or abusive juveniles. The recent attempts at unified neurobiological-psychobehavioral models suggest that poor or failed attachment naturally increases the likelihood of sexual aggressiveness and/or abuse because it (1) psychically and physiologically retards the juvenile's development in ways that inhibit his ability to form and maintain normative social relationships; (2) psychically and physiologically retards the juvenile's ability to self-regulate emotional states and impulse control; and (3) commonly results, psychically and physiologically, from absent, inadequate, or unhealthy satisfaction of the basic, necessary human need (particularly in early childhood) for touch.

Physical and Sexual Abuse and Juvenile Sexual Offending/Aggression

Among the most established common etiological factors in the histories of sexually aggressive or abusive juveniles are neglect and physical and/or sexual abuse. At the expense of being obvious, we have to point out that the terms "physical abuse" and "sexual abuse" are both types of negative or unhealthy touch. Moreover, although the legal definition of neglect does not necessarily involve issues of touch, in practice most caretakers guilty of failing to provide for their dependant children's more commonly recognized basic needs and protections do not usually provide the physical nurturing their children require either. The impact of such neglect is driven not just by the physical "quality" of the touch (where, how hard, with what, etc.) but by the specific circumstantial, relational, and existential particulars of the people involved.

While our increasing insights into positive touch, attachment, and touch deprivation are powerful wake-up calls about the ways we have unnaturally, via strange cultural development, alienated the largest organ of our bodies, nothing demonstrates the inalienable role and power of touch in human life like the ability of negative touch not merely to bruise or wound us physically but to damage, sometimes forever, our hearts and minds.

THE AMENABILITY OF TOUCH DEPRIVATION/UNHEALTHY OR FAILED ATTACHMENT TO TREATMENT

The studies of Romanian orphans and of other similarly, dramatically neglected or abused young children have shown that tremendous physical and psychological developmental damage is the natural, predictable result of absent, inadequate, or negative attachment and touch deprivation. These studies do not, however, establish a necessarily immutable damage in even the most neglected or abused child. Although the most damaged of such children may never achieve fully normative functioning later in life due to permanent physiological and/or psychological retardation, even they, with the appropriate, client-specific professional attention, can achieve improved cognitive, emotional, and behavioral functionality. Youth and adults who have experienced less profound levels and types of retarding influences are even more amenable to appropriate, client-specific treatment and have even more potential for physiological, psychological, and behavioral healing.

No matter the early experience of an individual, positive touch continues, throughout the lifespan to have an impact on cortisol levels in the body and other neurochemicals that have a direct effect on affective response and regulation and immune system response and health. Also, because of how fundamental positive or negative touch is to a human being, touch has an affective, purely psychological power independent of the particular physiological state or condition of a specific individual.

The key to helping these clients has less to do with specific methodology and theory than with the human relationship, however professionally regimented or proscribed, between therapist and client. Schore and others have documented that both those clients who self-report and behaviorally demonstrate success following psychotherapeutic treatment primarily cite the quality of their relationship with their therapist as the decisive factor—not any particular insight or breakthrough. Objectively and subjectively, the key appears to be the quality of the interpersonal relationship and bonding between the treatment professional (the surrogate authority/parental figure) and the client (Schore, 2001a, 2001b).

Some Facts About Touch

We need much more study and research if we are going to constructively take advantage of the developmental importance of touch, just as, recently, we have had to work to gain acceptance for incorporating the teaching of anger management and coping skills into the treatment of sexually abusive youth. Sexually abusive youth, particularly in a residential treatment center, come into contact with staff who represent many disciplines. This means that there is a possibility of building on the use of touch in an equally different number of ways. The first and simplest way to incorporate this information is the normal use of touch that we all experience as part of everyday life. The second is to thoughtfully employ touch as a kind of therapeutic activity.

We have access to a wealth of research about the results of touch deprivation as well as abusive touch from sources outside the sexual abuse field. It is common knowledge outside our particular disciplines that human beings have a very real and basic developmental need for touch. Other disciplines have also established the following facts about touch:

- Physical contact with the skin produces changes in body temperature, changes in perspiration, and changes in muscular tension—changes that are independent of the recipient of touch's conscious control.

- Positive changes in blood pressure, heart rate, and respiratory rate were identified in severely ill patients when nurses simply held their hands for at least three minutes (Knable, 1981).

- Absence of touch is a critical factor in the failure to thrive (Field et al., 1986).

- Even in the presence of increased nutrition, hygiene, and medical care, inadequate touch leads to dramatic increases in infant death (Spitz, 1949).

- Studies of infant primates indicated that these babies showed symptoms of extreme grief and depression and were more vulnerable to disease when they were restricted from receiving touch (Reite & Field, 1985).

- Touch deficiencies in early childhood result in social isolation, difficulties in cooperation and propensities toward violence (Cohen, 1987; Prescott, 1975).

- When a child experiences stimuli while in a highly emotionally charged state, whether positive or negative, certain neuropedetides, or messenger molecules, are released into the body as the memory of this stimuli are being stored. This is what happens in the development of posttraumatic stress disorder (Cousins, 1989).

Facing the Dilemma

The current no-touch policies leave those of us who work directly with sexually abusing and abused youth—or any youth for that matter—with both an ethical and a practical dilemma: If children and youth under our care have experienced touch deficits, deprivation, or abuse in their lives, is it therapeutically defensible to eliminate this normal developmental and clear therapeutic need from their lives even if including it makes our jobs more practically and ethically difficult?

Though this can be an issue for any level of care, it is particularly problematic for those of us who work in residential treatment settings where children and youth may reside for months or even years. We need to consider the following issues: If we are treating children and youth because they have problems with sexually abusive touch or have been abusively touched themselves, what should we do about repairing the touch experience for them? What do we do about touch as a developmental as well as therapeutic need? Many treatment programs have solved this dilemma by just making touch a taboo, by saying no way, no how to physical contact of any kind by anyone and ignoring the dilemma. All touch—healing, comforting, or developmentally normal—is forbidden.

There are certainly excellent and understandable reasons for sanctions against sexual, erotic, or abusive touch when working with children and youth. There are also very legitimate concerns about the risk of litigation when touch is misused, or when touch is misunderstood—and it is not at all unusual for youth who have been sexually abused or abusive to misunderstand or misinterpret the meaning of a touch as a result of their past experiences. A comforting pat on the shoulder given innocently but without informed forethought and appropriate training may not only "feel bad" to a particular child but could even be the trigger for a posttraumatic stress experience.

The field of sexual abuse—particularly those working with children and adolescents—needs much more study and research if we are going to accommodate and constructively use the developmental importance and treatment potential of touch. Yet it was not that long ago that we proposed—and accomplished—the same for the incorporation and teaching of anger management and coping skills.

As with other treatment interventions, one size does not fit all when examining the role of touch in treatment. The fundamental nature of touch not only increases its potential therapeutic value but also increases the importance of individualizing its use in treatment. Sexually abusive youth, particularly in a residential treatment center, come into contact with staff who represent many disciplines. This may mean that touch is used differently by different disciplines. The recreational therapist, the nurse, the child care professional, and the therapist may all potentially use touch legitimately but in vastly different ways. This variation according to profession is normal in general terms. Yet the therapeutic definition of "normal touch," especially with sexually abusive and/or abused children, is by definition a highly individual thing. We are all touched in some unusual ways by various professionals which seem "normal" to us—the dentist touches and intrudes into our mouth in a way that no one else does, the proctologist explores our rectum, and the gynecologist performs various examinations that we accept as normal, however discomforting, because of our perceptions of the context. It is not difficult to imagine how differently a sexually abusive and/or abused youth might perceive these contexts and touches. The normal use of touch that we all experience as part of everyday life is the simplest but often the least experienced for many of these youth.

Although it is important to recognize that touch can contribute to growth, it is just as important to acknowledge that it has a powerful capacity to harm. Many variables contribute to the meaning that one attaches to a touch, such as the context in which the touch occurs, the setting, the duration, the frequency, the intensity, the scope of contact, the sequences of action, the degree of reciprocity, and the body parts involved. We have a responsibility here to carefully consider what our policy and procedures will be regarding touch, as well as to remember that they must be individualized to the client, to the population, and to the treatment setting.

In this chapter, we are really focusing on the normalization of touch so that young people will be given the opportunity not only to experience what is developmentally normal, but to repair the touch deficits of their lives. In working with juveniles who have suffered abnormal developmental histories, often what is considered simply normal in the general population can be therapeutic for these youth. At the same time, however, we have to keep in mind that treatment begins with what is "normal" for a particular youth, not what is normal for the general population or even for sexually abusive youth as a group. Therapists who use touch as a carefully planned intervention should have the proper training and supervision to do so. Touch, like any therapeutic activity, should not be used by any therapists who view it to be practicing outside their competency or understanding without first obtaining appropriate training and supervision.

For those with a seriously inadequate or unhealthy experience of touch to learn about healthy touch, it is necessary to provide them with an opportunity to learn about touch as part of the human experience in a supervised and structured environment. This is an environment designed to decrease and eliminate harmful touching, to heal the results of harmful touching while teaching about healthy touches. Program policies and procedures must be used to guide both staff and young people in the positive use and experience of touch

This may seem like a very artificial approach to such a natural activity—probably because it is. Most of us do not learn about touch in this way or use touch according to an agency's guidelines. But then most of us have been lucky. Most of us have learned about positive and healthy touch as part of life's normal developmental process, and we have not experienced the degree of inadequate or unhealthy touch that these youth have experienced. Professionals who work with children and youth routinely address developmental deficits in treatment. If we address other developmental deficits, why are we ignoring touch?

There are many questions concerning touch and how it is used and experienced that need to be considered when developing policies and procedures (see Exhibit 16.1 at the end of this chapter for a model policy.) For example, what should we do about touch and touching in general—not only about therapeutic or comforting touch but also about taking vital signs, physical restraint, social skills training, team sports, and all the other natural physical contacts that are part of a youth's life? If touch is more than good touch or bad touch, what are the other different kinds of touch? Which are acceptable to use in treatment settings? What makes touch permissible? What makes touch contraindicated? What are the aspects of a therapeutic process that would facilitate positive experiences of touch? What protocol should guide touch in a residential program with sexually aggressive youth? Are there different protocols for the individual levels of care in any continuum? These questions and many others demonstrate the struggle of staff in residential treatment settings as well as many other settings to meet a youth's needs for normal development, safety, and containment while guarding against countertherapeutic and/or abusive physical contact.

Ultimately, this chapter is a discussion of assessing and evaluating the touch-related etiology and needs of particular juveniles; suggestions for developing policies, protocols, and procedures concerning touch; practical suggestions for educational and experiential programming; and guidelines for determining the appropriateness or inappropriateness of a particular instance of touch within the treatment milieu. Yet the subject of touch is greatly misunderstood by a great many juvenile treatment providers. Before we can discuss practical applications, we have to discuss the ways in which inadequate touch produces severe developmental retardation in children; the behavioral problems this produces; and the ways in which positive touch has been shown to mitigate, ameliorate, and heal various physical and psychological problems.

Resources for Developing a Curricula

Different Kinds of Touch. For years child care professionals have acted as if there are only three kinds of touch—good touch, bad touch, and confusing touch. Of course, these are all potentially powerful kinds of touches, but there are also myriad other touches to consider and experience. Many of us experienced and considered these different touches as we grew and developed naturally. The lesson includes not only the range of touch phenomena but the appropriate way to respond to each. Some youth who are sexually abusive have only experienced either the absence of touch or a bad touch, and they have given bad touches to others which were good touches for themselves. They do not understand that the world of touch is much larger and richer. When developing a curriculum on touch for both staff and residents it is important to acknowledge and learn about the different kinds of touch.

The following are among the many different kinds of touch identified by Hunter and Struve (1997):

1. *Accidental touch*: Unintentional or purposeless touch, such as the kind that occurs in close-pressed crowds, etc.

2. *Task-oriented touch*: Touch that occurs while engaged in goal-oriented activities with others. This can be unintentional (e.g., when exchanging materials) or part of the task itself (e.g., when helping an elderly person from a car).

3. *Attentional touch*: This kind of touch is used to focus attention or control behavior. It is functional in nature and often paired with a verbal response, and may be used to gather information about another, prompt a desired action, or keep an interaction moving toward a desired outcome. For example when someone is anxious, a touch (or kick under the table) to remind her to calm down is an attentional touch. Another example would be tapping someone on the shoulder to remind him that it is his turn at an activity.

There are several types of attentional touch:

- *Touches for greeting and departure* may vary greatly depending on social setting and context and the gender, personalities, and culture of the participants. In many countries it is common for male strangers to embrace before a formal business meeting. In the United States, few males, even relatives, embrace on greeting or departure except in a limited number of very special circumstances, such as death or marriage, and often not even then.

- *Referential touch* may be used to call attention to some aspect of another's appearance or to solicit a touch response from another.

- *Courtesy touch* meets the polite or fashionable expectations of a particular social context, such as secret club handshakes, joining hands during a prayer, and so on.

4. *Celebratory/affectional touch*: A usually spontaneous expression of joy, excitement, or pride which is meant to be nurturing, caring, encouraging, comforting, or reassuring. Celebratory touch generally has an element of bonding, such as when sports fans high-five or hug following a big play, simultaneously expressing their happiness and affirming their common allegiance. Another might be the "that's our girl" arm one spouse places on another's shoulder after their first-grader makes it safely through her dreaded piano recital.

Affectional touch expresses friendly, comforting, or playful regard. One example might be faux-pinching a friend's cheek when he or she is acting "cute." Another might be the touch on the shoulder during a handshake between males who both wish they were not too inhibited to hug and want to exchange an "it's the thought that counts" signal of the actual depth of their feelings toward each other.

5. *Emotional/expressive touch*: This touch accompanies or compromises the expression of emotions and may be intentional or unintentional, conscious or unconscious. There are several categories:

- *Appreciative touch*: This is the hugs, pats, squeezes, handshakes, and so on that express gratitude.

- *Reinforcing touch*: This is contact that emphasizes or strengthens a behavioral or emotional response. It is not necessarily always a conscious act and may provide either positive or negative reinforcement.

- *Playful/affectionate touch*: This touch is used to reduce the seriousness of a situation, such as a playful punch or bump or wrestling. This kind of touch can be one of the most commonly misunderstood for abusive or victimized children, who have often had little opportunity to learn the difference between play and aggression.

- *Cathartic touch*: The intention of this touch is to address constricted emotions and trigger their release. For example, a light touch on the shoulder of someone who has received devastating news and is holding his emotions tightly in check may spark the needed release of tears (and/or anger).

- *Aggressive touch*: This touch does not necessarily result in a negative outcome. Some acceptable and even positive uses of aggressive touch are consensual wrestling, working out frustrations on a golf driving range, or throwing darts at an ex-lover's picture.

- *Sensual touch*: This type of touch is intended to gratify the senses (Hunter & Struve, 1997). Depending on the context, culture, and individuals involved, it may be perceived erotically, but that is not its intention. If intended erotically, such as the cliché example of the second date "innocent" massage, where the clear purpose is to evoke an erotic response, then it is more accurately sexual touch. This is often a difficult touch to pin down in repressive cultures, but an example of sensual touch which not even most Americans confuse with sexual touch is having your scalp scrubbed during a prehaircut shampoo.

- *Sexual touch:* This type of touch is physical contact which is intended to produce sexual or prosexual overtones or affect. It may involve actual touch of sexual organs, stimulation of erogenous zones (foreplay), or simply touch which, due to context, verbal, and/or nonverbal cues (i.e., the infamous second-date massage), has a sexually stimulating intent. It can involve touching another and/or touching oneself for the purpose of sexually stimulating another. To make matters more difficult, especially in sexually repressive cultures, it may also involve "touch-suggestive" behaviors. For example, sometimes a woman might rub a popsicle repeatedly across her lips to evoke an erotic touch association in an observer's mind. On the other hand, she might, as one of the authors learned to his great embarrassment upon enquiry, engage in this same behavior because her lips were painfully chapped.

Components of Touch. Not only are there many different kinds of touch, but the experience of touch can be different from one person to the next for many, often complex reasons. Each of the individual types of touch consists of different components, and variations in these components can dramatically change the intended and perceived experience of them. The most basic components of an incidence of touch revolve around the message, the sender, the receiver, and the context of the situation. Though not a primary component in the same sense, repetition should also be considered an element that, by altering the context, message, sender, and receiver, can also greatly alter the meaning of both the original touch and each of the repetitions.

Within the context of a therapeutic relationship, the perceptions of the client are paramount in any incidence of touch initiated by the therapist, whether objectively founded or unfounded in retrospect. Moreover, if a client perceives an incidence of touch initiated by the therapist positively "in the moment" because of the therapist's "authority," it does not necessarily mean that the touch was therapeutically positive.

Meaning of Touch. The meaning that one attaches to touch comes from the following factors: the part of the body touched, the length of time that the touch lasts, how much pressure is used, movement or lack of movement after the contact has been made, the presence of others and their identification, the situation in which the touch occurs, and the mood created by the situation. Also, the relationship between the different people involved can change the meaning immeasurably.

One experience with staff training around the use of touch points out the complexity of that meaning—both for the giver and for the receiver. A particular agency was changing from a no-touch to a healthy-touch policy and the staff received intensive training in order to make this move. Staff members wanted to begin by simply giving handshakes, as this appeared the least threatening touch to them. In truth, after training and consideration, they begin to identify intimidating handshakes, respectful handshakes, comforting handshakes, and limp, wet, fishy handshakes. For the staff to experience what different handshakes might be like and what they might mean, they were asked to participate in an experiential exercise. During this exercise they were to walk around with their eyes closed and then to shake hands with whomever they encountered. Afterwards, we talked about how the handshakes felt, what feelings they engendered in us, what discomfort there was, if any. The group included two women who had been best friends for over twenty-five years. After they clasped hands, they realized who the other was despite their closed eyes and gave each other a spontaneous hug. Later when we were processing the feelings associated with the handshakes one friend turned to the other and said, "I don't like it when you pat my back while you are hugging me." The other friend said back, "We have been best friends for twenty years and you are just now telling me this!" After this experience, staff members who had questioned the need to ask permission and the need to process no longer did.

In yet another staff training, an older male staff member said that he would never touch or be touched by these clients no matter what the policy. In a follow-up visit after four months I encountered this particular staff member who said, "I would never have believed how much a handshake could mean to the residents if I hadn't experienced it. Now they ask me for a handshake at bedtime and this has made it so much easier for them to go to bed without resistance. They ask for handshakes at other times too, when they've done well in school for example, and it seems to mean a lot when they get a handshake, just a handshake!"

Physiology of Touch. It is important here to discuss the basic physiology of touch, as this is the initial impact of any incidence of touching. Constituting almost 20 percent of our body weight, the skin is our ultimate line of defense between the world and our vital organs and skeleton. It is the most primal—and primary—of our senses. Montague (1971) called touch the "mother of the senses." Touch is the first of the human senses to develop, appearing as early as eight weeks into gestation when the human embryo is less than one inch long. Immediately upon birth infants respond to touch, well before equivalent basic visual and aural abilities have developed.

This is only logical in simple survival terms. The "distance" senses, hearing and sight, are far less important than the "immediate" sense of touch to an infant entirely dependent on its parents for protection from outside threats and the procurement of its needs. The skin interacts more directly with the environment than any other, and infants need to be capable of responding positively to few things beyond the touch of their caregivers and to unpleasant skin sensations. The "immediacy" and primal nature of touch are the roots of its powerful ability to influence our physical health and mental well-being.

There are a wide variety of studies on the positive benefits of touch to physical and mental health, from changes in hemoglobin values and heart rate to the reduction of anxiety. Perhaps the most interesting study involved the use of fifteen-minute massage, three times a day, with a group of premature infants (Smith, 1989). Though they were not fed any more than the control group of "preemies" who were not massaged, these infants gained weight 45 percent faster, indicating a profound effect upon their physical health and metabolism.

A physiological aspect of touch which is likely to be particularly important to those treating sexually abusive or victimized juveniles involves our ability to learn not to feel. Just as top athletes, cops, and soldiers, and parents of threatened children are sometimes able to accomplish tremendous things despite serious injuries, victims of prolonged abuse often survive because of the human ability to disassociate ourselves physically and emotionally from such experiences. The downside of this ability is that "survivors may often continue such dissociative coping responses well beyond the actual circumstances of their trauma" (Hunter & Struve, 1997, p. 6). That is, to emotionally and psychologically survive the trauma of negative touch or touch deprivation in childhood, some children may adapt so effectively to this unhealthy environment that they will ardently resist treatment providers' attempts to impose a new "environment" upon them—even if it is, objectively, happier and healthier.

A final feature of touch for treatment providers to keep in mind is its strong relationship with memory, particularly nonconscious memory. Touch is more important than sight until children reach 3 to 4 years of age (Itakura & Imamizu, 1994). Therefore, positive touch and touch education are of even greater importance when working with juveniles whose victimization began during this early, touch-dominated period.

THERAPEUTIC USES OF TOUCH

Differentiation Between Levels of Staff

Most treatment programs serving youth involve multidisciplinary teams, and different staff may need to use and know how to use touch differently and for different reasons. For example, recreational therapists and medical or educational personnel are more likely to use task-oriented touch. As part of a therapeutic milieu all staff may use many of the other touches appropriately—with the exception, of course, of aggressive, sexual, or sensual touch.

A therapist, in fact, may need to work with a particular youth on a variety of issues, including desensitizing him to touch in any form or context, prior to other staff members even shaking hands with the youth. In addition to touch aversions or sensitivities related to prior abuse, some youth with autism (Field et al., 1986), fragile X syndrome, and a number of other concurrent diagnoses are touch-aversive regardless of any prior touch-oriented abuse. Indeed, some victims of touch deprivation are intolerant of the most positive physical contact (Hatfield, 1994). For each individual youth, staff should have a thoughtfully assessed, evaluated, and purposeful plan for touch until the youth has met his treatment goals relative to touch. Only then, as with all other issues and skills, should touch be integrated into his daily life.

Assessing an Individual's Experience of Touch

To develop curricula for a particular child or particular population of juveniles it is first necessary to understand what each specific child's personal experience of touch has been. This should be discerned at intake through a matter-of-fact discussion—ask the child his history of touch, what touches have felt good, and where. Then ask what touches have felt bad and where. The discussion should include feelings related to the staff and to other clients regarding touching and fears and fantasies about the staff or other juveniles regarding touching. Intake also provides an opportunity to discuss parameters of touch within the residential treatment center, safety issues with touch, and the policy and procedures regarding touch at the particular treatment center.

The Touch Map, a screening technique developed by Sandra Hewitt, Ph.D. co-founder of the Midwest Children's Resource Center (*www.mrcac.org*), is an assessment and evaluation tool recently developed for this purpose. The technique consists of the clinician dividing a blank piece of paper into six boxes and telling the client that he wants to talk to him about the different kinds of touches that he has experienced—some good, some bad, and some confusing. In the first box the client is instructed to draw a figure of himself and put dots where he has experienced good touches, then describe who gave him these good touches, where there were, when it was, and how it made him feel. In the second box the client draws a similar figure and places X's where he received touches that felt bad, then shares the identity of the people who gave him those touches, and so on. This exercise proceeds through the varieties of touch experience, concluding with a discussion of where the client does not want to be touched and where the client would not mind being touched—and why.

The therapeutic use of touch is grounded in specifically trained and informed professional judgment, occurs only within a therapist's proven areas of competency, and meets accepted professional and ethical standards. In other words, the therapist uses touch as he or she would any other therapeutic tool, considering an application's particular impact in a particular context on a particular person in terms of the therapist's training, his or her knowledge about the client, the context within the treatment process, and the general insights and expectations of the therapist's field at large. This is also true to a degree of all nontherapist staff who work closely with juveniles whether they are called child care professionals, unit staff, residential counselors, and so on.

Therapists and staff who use touch ethically do not seek to control clients, do not have their egos tied to the results of the intervention, and are mindful of their intentions and the possible consequences of their actions. Incidences of therapeutic touch last only long enough to establish firm contact but not so long as to create an uncomfortable feeling in the subject.

Using touch as a therapeutic tool can be very simple or very complex. Many of the positive uses of touch are entirely natural and instinctive to those whose personalities are naturally therapeutic. There are some common everyday occurrences in which it is reflexive to use touch as a reorienting tool. When a client is overwhelmed with anxiety or in a dissociative state, a hand on the shoulder serves as a reality base. This, of course, depends on already having a solid relationship with the client and a previously agreed-on feedback loop so that the client can bring up any concerns, as well as a general working knowledge of how that individual client will respond to touch.

It is not unusual to work with a youth who the therapist knows is just having a hard time controlling himself. On one occasion, one of the authors put a steadying hand on a youth's shoulder. The youth later said, "Thank you, until you did that I was afraid I was going to fly into a million pieces and now I feel calmer."

Frequently, when emphasizing a point, gently touching a client's hand as the client reports a distressing event may supplement verbal expressions of understanding and empathy. Often, touch can provide a bridge to access empathy or emotions which are even more effective than the predictable if well-meant things people commonly say in an effort to communicate empathy.

Obviously, because these children are likely to be victims of sexual or physical violence, a great deal of care must be taken. Improperly employed touch can trigger traumatic memories and associated feelings. Uses of therapeutic touch should always be carefully thought out and controlled interventions.

Appropriate Situations for Using Touch as a Therapeutic Tool

There are many situations in which it is appropriate to use touch:

1. *To reorient a client*: When a client is overwhelmed with anxiety or in a dissociative state, a hand on the shoulder can be reality based for the client.

2. *To emphasize a point*: Gently touching a client's hand or arm as the client reports a distressing event may supplement or substitute for a verbal expression of understanding and empathy.

3. *To access memories or emotions*: Touch can provide a bridge

4. *To communicate empathy*: "I am deeply touched."

5. *To act as an adjunct in hypnosis*: Touch is calming, lowering the heart rate and reducing anxiety.

6. *To assist in dealing with past traumatic experiences*: These are carefully controlled interventions.

7. *To provide safety or calm the client*: A hand upon a hand (the therapist must be careful as unexpected touches here can trigger old feelings).

8. *To enhance ego strength*: Studies indicate that those with higher self-esteem are more comfortable being touched than those without. If the client can receive touch, then he may be able to put away old messages of touch.

9. *To change the level of intimacy*: Helps to focus on the ability to be intimate without being sexual.

10. *To communicate the message*: "You are not alone."

11. *To teach the client a new model of warm, supportive, and noninvasive relationship with another.*

Selecting Touch as a Therapeutic Intervention

There are ethical and practical concerns about using touch as either a normalizing or therapeutic experience. In 1982, P. G. Geibs found that clients' positive experiences of touch depended most often on five factors. One of the most important of these was prior discussion with the therapist about touch, the boundaries of the therapeutic relationship, and the problems of transference and sexual feelings within that relationship. It was also extremely important that the client felt in control of initiating and sustaining contact, and that he did not feel that the touch was a demand or attempt at control by the therapist. The final two factors revolved around the congruency of the client's expectations and his actual experiences in therapy, and whether the therapeutic emotional and physical intimacy proceeded congruently.

Prior to giving a touch, the therapist should ask himself the following questions:

1. What is the relationship? Touch should only be used when the therapeutic alliance is strong. Touch should not be used as a means to develop or strengthen an unsatisfactory therapeutic relationship but only as a resource that a firmly established therapeutic relationship makes possible.

2. What is the need for the touch? What is the context of the touch? The therapist must look at his or her own motivations, feelings, and thoughts in relationship to a particular use of touch. Does it further the need of the therapist or the growth of the client? Used improperly, touch can unwittingly become a subtle form of asserting power or manipulating the client's feeling about the therapist.

3. Does the child want to be touched? It is important to be sure that the child or youth is able to give consent for touch because it is always possible that the youth will cooperate without really giving informed, objective consent. This is one of the most important reasons not to use touch until an appropriate therapeutic relationship has been established. Although it may seem an unnatural way to employ ostensibly natural behavior, within a therapeutic context touch is a formal technique and dependent on a certain level of therapeutic relationship. Therefore, the therapist should always inform the child of the intent to touch and the rationale. The therapist should ask in a noncoercive manner whether the child consents. As the therapeutic relationship continues to grow it may not be necessary to ask informed consent every time.

4. What is the child's experience of touch? Have you assessed the child's experience of touch so that you understand all of their trigger points?

5. Has the child been given the right to decline?

6. Have the necessary steps prior to touching been taken?

   • Announce verbally the intent to touch.

- Ask for permission and give opportunity to decline.

- Avoid touch that deflates the inner resources of the child. Consider how a touch might be interpreted by the recipient as well as the intended meaning. There are touches, such as pats on the head, which, regardless of the conscious intent of the giver, are very often experienced as condescending rather than supportive or comforting.

7. How will the touch be processed? The therapist should ask himself how the child responds to being touched. What meaning does the child attach to touch? How is the touch perceived on both interpretative and emotional levels? Both positive and negative responses should be noted, and the therapist should also monitor his own feelings about touch—does he feel manipulated, coerced? Was the touch meaningful or devoid of meaning?

Processing the touch is always critically important. Not only will different clients respond differently to the same touch, but some clients' overt responses may conflict with their actual feelings. Negative responses many be the result of improperly preparing for or applying the touch and/or simply because they were negatively received due to the client's idiosyncrasies.

Clients have varying comfort levels with physical intimacy, and we have discussed how high the discomfort level in the United States, in particular, has become. As a result, clients may feel compelled to interact at a level of intimacy with they are actually uncomfortable or which they dislike. Similarly—or concurrently—the client may feel angry and yet guilty for reacting negatively to a seemingly nurturing therapist. Other clients may feel responsible for protecting the therapist's feelings about the "success" of the touch. Yet others may experience the touch as an unpleasant or painful reminder of previous experiences or family dynamics (Geib, 1982).

Finally, clients may feel ambivalently about an incidence of touch and may not necessarily be consciously aware of their conflicting responses. Just as a client may overtly respond in the manner he believes the therapist expects or wants, he may overtly respond in the way he expects or wants of himself rather than in terms of his true feelings.

Contraindications for Touch. There are several instances in which touch is contraindicated:

- When the focus of therapy involves sexual content immediately prior to the touch;

- When there is a risk of violence;

- When secrecy might be involved;

- When the staff member doubts the client's ability to say "no";

- When the therapist feels manipulated or coerced into touching;

- When diagnostic factors indicate touch would be counterproductive;

- When it is merely a replacement for verbal expression;

- When it clearly is not wanted; and

- When the staff member himself feels uncomfortable.

General guidelines should be followed. Staff should never engage in any physical contact in the following instances:

- Outside the view of another staff member;

- When he or she would discontinue if observed by a supervisor or manager;

- When he or she does not feel comfortable with the resident discussing the contact outside the treatment setting; and

- When he or she feels the contact has the potential to be misinterpreted by others if disclosed outside the context of the therapy (Hunter & Struve, 1997, p. 149).

Questionable Touch. Incidences of touch, even outside treatment contexts and settings, are not always easy to clearly define, and their individual meanings are subject to a wide variety of subjective factors. Yet, within treatment or supervisory environments and settings with youth, it is critical that staff "fail" on the side of safety and consider any incidence of touch "questionable" if it was not planned, if it occurred without prior consent, and if it was unclear in its meaning before or after the fact.

A classic example of this issue is an accidental/inadvertent touch within a sex offender treatment program. Such touches should be received and interpreted by the therapist with caution, and with an eye toward ascertaining the possibility that they are not, in fact, accidental but actually represent patterned behavior. They should also be received and interpreted by the therapist with caution and with an eye toward ascertaining the possibility that they were truly accidental and thus should not responded to in a way that stigmatizes touch. We tend to jump to conclusions with this population, both out of suspicion and out of the desire to be objective. Sometimes a cigar is just a cigar, and sometimes it is neither a cigar nor a phallic symbol. The job of treatment providers is to act naturally while studying everything.

The Bottom Line. The question: Is it ethical and appropriate to use touch in the residential treatment of sexually abusive or sexually abused children and youth? The answer: It depends on the following:

- Who the therapist is;

- Who the client is;

- The nature of the therapeutic relationship;

- The context of the touch;

- What has transpired just before the touch occurs;

- The type of touch being considered;

- The staff's intended meaning for the touch;

- The client's interpretation of the touch;

- Whether permission for the proposed touch has been sought;

- Whether permission has been granted; and

- Whether the client has been empowered to give informed consent.

It is not whether to touch but rather when and how. Permissible touch is grounded in solid professional judgment, stays within the practitioner's area of competency, and conforms to expected standards of ethics. In other words, the therapist thinks about the effect of the touch prior to offering it and believes that professional colleagues would agree that it is appropriate. Therapists who use touch ethically do not seek to control clients, do not have their egos tied to the results of the intervention, and are mindful of their intentions and the possible consequences of their actions.

CONCLUSION

Working in treatment environments with juveniles who are sexually abusive and/or victimized seems to be a never-ending process of learning and accommodating one difficult reality only to discover and be forced to consider another. It is not so long ago that we were struggling merely to gain recognition for the true extent of child sexual abuse or for the idea that there were sexually abusive youth. It truly is not that long ago that the majority of the field finally accepted that these youth require specific, specialized treatment. Objective studies of sexually aggressive preadolescents and sexually abusive females have since "intruded" and forced us to accept them as well.

Touch, particularly in English-speaking countries, and in the United States most of all, is an enormously loaded subject. But this is purely due to historical and cultural reasons. The skin is the largest organ of the human body, the first to develop, and has a profound role in human physiological and mental development. As a result, addressing our aversion to thoughtfully incorporating touch in the treatment of juveniles, particularly juveniles with specifically touch-related problems such as sexual victimization and abuse, is not merely a new, difficult challenge but a fundamental issue which has been neglected for far too long.

Abusive and/or inadequate touch has been linked not only to violence and aggression but to profound physical and mental retardation. Touch deprivation can actually kill young children.

The reasons for our current no-touch policies are certainly understandable. But they are based on reactively preventing any possibility for abuse rather than on proactively ensuring safety and quality of treatment. This is equivalent to denying all medication because it might be misprescribed. No-touch policies in treatment environments deny and ignore a basic component of normal child development, as well as neglect a common need of a vast number of children in treatment.

Though our current "better safe than sorry" approach to the subject of touch may be cheaper and easier, it is by no means the best or healthiest for the youth in our care. Touch is a fundamental component of human development, the "mother of the senses," and as such is likely one of the most important things juvenile treatment providers have ever attempted to deny.

Just as with any other type of therapeutic intervention, touch can only be incorporated positively into the therapeutic milieu as the result of studied, thoughtful efforts by professionals to develop policies and procedures for its use. Such policies and procedures must not only consider the benefits and dangers but must keep in mind the specific needs of different programs, populations, and individuals. Though we are speaking of a far too long neglected, immensely powerful aspect of normal human development, our previous neglect should rush us to a change in our attitudes and perspectives, not our methodology. All available research and insight about touch and its fundamental role in normal physiological, mental, and behavioral development and functioning demands a rapid change in our willingness to incorporate touch education, training, and practice in treatment. Yet this insight into the powerful potential of touch or its absence to heal, help, or harm demands an equal degree of caution, effort, and client-specific attention.

References

Becker, J., & Kaplan, M. (1993). Cognitive-behavioral treatment of the juvenile sex offender. In H. Barbaree, W. Marshall, & S. Hudson (Eds.), *The juvenile sex offender* (pp. 264–277). New York: Guilford Press.

Boschert, S. (2001, February 1). Eleven ways to build doctor-patient relationship. *Family Practice News*, pp. 31–30.

Bridges, S., Lease, S., & Ellison, C. (2004). Predicting sexual satisfaction in women: Implications for counselor education and training. *Journal of Counseling and Development, 82*(2), 158–166.

Davidson, R. (1998). Affective style and affective disorders: Perspectives from affective neuroscience. *Cognition and Emotion, 12,* 307–330.

Diego, M., Field, T., Hernandez-Reif, M., Shaw, J., Rothe, E., Castellanos, D., et al. (2002). Aggressive adolescents benefit from massage therapy. *Adolescence, 37,* 597–601.

Field, T. (1999a). Preschoolers in America are touched less and are more aggressive than preschoolers in France. *Development and Care, 151,* 11–17.

Field, T. (1999b, Winter). American adolescents touch each other less and are more aggressive toward their peers as compared with French adolescents. *Adolescence, 34*(136), 753–758.

Field, T. (2002, Winter). Violence and touch deprivation in adolescents. *Adolescence, 37*(148), 753–749.

Field, T., Lasko, D., Mundy, P., Henteleff, T., Talpins, S., & Dowling, M. (1986). Autistic children's attentiveness and responsivity improved after touch therapy. *Journal of Autism and Developmental Disorders, 27,* 329–334.

Field, T., Morrow, C., Valdeon, C., Larson, S., Kuhn, C., & Schanberg, S. (1992, January). Massage reduces anxiety in child and adolescent psychiatric patients. *Journal of the American Academy of Child and Adolescent Psychiatry, 31*(1), 125–131.

Garner, T. (2003, March 19). New look at no-touch teaching. *New Zealand Herald.*

Gupta, M. A., Gupta, A. K., Schork, N. J., & Watteel, G. N. (1995). Perceived touch deprivation and body image: Some observations among eating disordered and non-clinical subjects. *Journal of Psychosomatic Research, 39*(4), 459–464.

Gupta, M. A., & Schork, N. J. (1995). Touch deprivation has an adverse effect on body image: Some preliminary observations. *International Journal of Eating Disorders, 17*(2), 185–189.

Hatfield, R. (1994). Touch and human sexuality. In V. Bullough, B. Bullough, & A. Stein (Eds.), *Human sexuality: An encyclopedia* (pp. 581–587). New York: Garland.

Hunter, M., & Struve, J. (1997). *The ethical use of touch in psychotherapy.* New York: Sage.

Jourard, S. M. (1966). An exploratory study of body accessibility. *British Journal of Social and Clinical Psychology, 5,* 221–231.

Kimble, M. A. (1985). The surviving majority: Differential impact of aging and implications for ministry. *Word and World, 5*(4), 395–404.

Knable, J. (1981). Handholding: One means of transcending barriers of communication. *Heart and Lung, 10*(6), 1106–1110.

Levy, T., & Orlans, M. (2000). Attachment disorder as an antecedent to violence and antisocial patterns in children. *Handbook of attachment interventions* (pp. 1–26). San Diego: Academic Press.

Lott, D. (1998, May). Attachment and impact on psychic vulnerability. *Psychiatric Times, 15*(5), 1–5.

Lottes, I., & Kontula, O. (2000). *New views on sexual health: The case of Finland.* Vaestontutkimuslaitos, Vaestoliitto: Population Research Institute, The Family Federation of Finland.

Montague, A. (1971). *Touching: The human significance of the skin.* New York: Harper & Row.

Myers, R. (1992). *The twelve who survive.* New York: Routledge.

National Association for the Education of Young Children. (1996, July). *Prevention of child abuse in early childhood programs and the responsibilities of early childhood professionals to prevent child abuse* [Position statement]. Washington, DC: Author.

Orpinas, P. K., Basen-Engquist, K., Gunbaum, J. A., & Parcel, G. S. (1995, March). The co-morbidity of violence-rated behaviors with health-risk behaviors in a population of high school students. *Journal of Adolescent Health, 16*(3), 216–225.

Perry, B. (2001). Consequences of emotional neglect in childhood. In B. D. Perry (Ed.), *Caregiver Education Series* (adapted in part from *Maltreated children: Experience, brain development, and the next generation*). New York: W.W. Norton.

Prescott, J. W. (1975, April). Body pleasure and the origins of violence. *The Futurist,* pp. 64–74.

Prescott, J. W. (1996). The origins of human love and violence. *Pre- and Perinatal Psychology Journal, 10*(3), 143–188.

Raine, A., Brennan, P., & Mednick, S. A. (1994, December). Birth complications combined with early maternal rejection at age 1 year predispose to violent crime at age 18. *Archives of General Psychiatry, 51*(12), 984–988.

Reite, M., & Field, T. (Eds.). (1985). *The psychobiology of attachment and separation.* New York: Academic Press.

Ryan, G., Blum, J., Laws, S., Christopher, D., Weher, R., Sundine, D., et al. (1988). *Understanding and responding to the sexual behavior of children: Trainer's manual.* Denver: Kempe National Center, University of Colorado School of Medicine.

Schore, A. (2001a). The effects of early relational trauma on right brain development, affect regulation, and infant mental health. *Infant Mental Health Journal, 22,* 201–269.

Schore, A. (2001b). The effects of a secure attachment relationship on right brain development, affect regulation, and infant mental health. *Infant Mental Health Journal, 22,* 7–66.

Siegel, D., & Schore, A. N. (1997). *Understanding and treating trauma: Developmental and neurobiological approaches.* Paper presented at continuing education seminar, University of California, Los Angeles.

Smith, J. (1989). *Senses and sensibilities.* New York: Wiley.

Sosin, D. M., Koepsell, T. D., Rivara, P., & Mercy, J. A. (1995, March). The co-morbidity of violence-rated behaviors with health-risk behaviors in a population of high school students. *Journal of Adolescent Health, 16*(3), 209–215.

Spitz, R. (1949). The role of ecological factors in emotional development. *Child Development, 20,* 145–155.

Textor. R. B. (1967). *A cross-cultural summary.* New Haven, CT: HRAF Press.

Toronto, E. L. K. (2002). A clinician's response to physical touch in the psychoanalytic setting. *Journal of Psychotherapy, 7*(1), 69–81.

Exhibit 16.1
A Residential Treatment Center Model Policy

The following is a model policy and procedure on the use of touch developed for the Twin Cedars Youth Services of La Grange, Georgia. At the time Jerry Thomas was working as a consultant for the Anne Elizabeth Shepherd Home in Columbus, Georgia, a program of Twin Cedars. While Twin Cedars is a multiservice program for youth, the residential programs on the campus of Anne Elizabeth Shepherd serve female youth who have been sexually abusive or who have suffered from a severe post traumatic stress disorder. The implementation of the policy was preceded by intensive preliminary training and continuing training and supervision.

Guidelines for the Use of Touch

Policy

Each resident will participate in a carefully planned program component designed to identify and eliminate problems with abusive touch while learning to identify, give, and receive healthy touches. Touching is reasoned and therapeutically motivated rather than spontaneous and impulsive in nature.

Rationale

The phenomenon of touch is the primary mode of comfort and communication between every primary caretaker and newborn infant. It is universally recognized as a healthy and necessary part of growth and development. When infants are deprived of physical contact not only do they fail to develop normally but they become physically ill—even when all other physical needs have been met.

Touch conveys a vast range of meaning and feelings and is influenced by the context in which the touch occurs. Touch can contribute to growth, it can contribute to healing where growth has been interrupted, or it or can harm.

Unfortunately, sexually abusive children have experienced and have touched others in an unhealthy, abusive, and hurtful way. In order for them to learn about touch from a positive developmental perspective, it is necessary to provide them with education about touch in a supervised and structured therapeutic environment, an environment designed to decrease and eliminate harmful touching while teaching the positive developmental use of a natural healthy touch.

Procedures

☐ Training/teaching:
   1. Training regarding these guidelines will be required of all staff, auxiliary members, mentors, and volunteers as part of orientation prior to employment and yearly in-service refresher training.
   2. Residents and participating family members will all receive psychoeducational training regarding the following:

- Good touch (health, nurturing, caring);
- Bad touch (aggressive, hurtful, harmful);
- Private touch (appropriate sexual, hygiene, medical); and
- Secret touch (sexually aggressive/abusive).

3. Residents and participating family members will receive empowerment training to ensure that they understand and can utilize saying no to unwanted or inappropriate touch.

4. Staff will teach residents about touch and will openly and honestly process touches given and received as part of daily living, including but not limited to the following:
   - Naming/identifying different types of touch and differentiating among touches;
   - Talking about what touch says (communicates) to you and feels like to you;
   - Talking about what touching someone else means to you and to the person touched;
   - Discussing how someone develops trust about touch;
   - Discussing how to say no to unwanted touch;
   - Talking about who has touched you in a good way; and
   - Talking about who has touched you in a hurtful way, how that felt, and what you did; and
   - Why healthy touching is important to normal growth and development.

☐ About touching:

1. Staff must know the resident before initiating touch—no touch is the best practice early in treatment and until a therapeutic connection exists, and until the resident's Touch Map has been developed.

2. Ask permission before you touch, remembering always an inherent power differential exists between staff and the child. It is staff's responsibility to assess resident's level of empowerment to say no.

3. Make sure there is always another staff witness to an incidence of touch.

4. Use touching for an intended therapeutic purpose and an opportunity for learning, being aware that if more than a casual courteous touch is used there may be an unexpected or unintended response. Negative experiences should be thoroughly processed and documented.

5. All arousals to touch should be processed at once. Distortions of prosocial touch can lead to grooming and fantasy enhancement. The intent of a touch and its perceived meaning by the one receiving the touch may not be the same. Therefore, whenever touch is used, the staff member must be prepared to process and deal therapeutically with the outcome. If a resident appears to perceive touch as sexual or views the touch as sexually gratifying, these responses must be reported to the treatment team and interventions incorporated into the resident's treatment plan.

6. Be perceptive to context and consider the following:
- Therapy setting/physical environment;
- Therapeutic issues;
- Individual client/therapist variables (culture, socialization, gender, age, sexual orientation, etc.); and
- Level of therapeutic alliance and timing.

7. Chart significant touch and touch reactions. Include type of touch offered, client's response to offer, whether touch took place, and client's reaction to the touch. Avoid over documenting, yet ensure that pertinent information is documented.

☐ Touches that are acceptable:

1. Nurturing touch may be given in the following circumstances:
- Ask permission to give a touch, remembering always that there exists an inherent power differential between staff and child. It is your responsibility to assess the ability to say no.
- Make sure that when permission is given it is informed permission.
- Make sure that there are adult witnesses to any touch.
- Use touching for an intended therapeutic purpose and an opportunity for learning, being aware that if more than a casual, courteous touch is used there may be an unintended response.
- If the response is given, it has been thoroughly processed and documented.

2. Nurturing touches permitted include the following:
- Handshakes;
- A touch on the back shoulder, head, or hand;
- High-fives;
- Hygiene tasks such as helping with hair;
- Comforting touches when someone is hurt; and
- Brief frontal or side to side hugs.

3. Hugs can be given in the following circumstances:
- In therapeutic group activity;
- If permission is requested and given;
- If you have checked to make sure that permission is informed;
- If the hugs are brief (they can be sideways or frontal); and
- With hands on shoulders.

☐ Acceptable touches become unacceptable in the following circumstances:
- The touch is unwanted by the receiver in any way (except in incidences of therapeutic restraint);
- The focus of therapy involves sexual content immediately prior;
- The touches are given without consent;

- There are inappropriate contextual factors;
- Staff are not sensitive to cultural differences in the meaning of touch;
- When there is a risk of violence;
- When secrecy might be involved;
- When staff doubts the ability of the receiver to say no;
- When the therapist feels manipulated or coerced into touching;
- When diagnostic factors are contraindicative;
- As a replacement for verbal expression;
- It isn't wanted; and
- Staff feel uncomfortable;

☐ Questionable touch:

- An example is inadvertent/accidental touch. Such touches may be truly accidental, or they may be examples of frottage. They may also be individual incidences in an overall pattern of behavior or one-time incidents.
- All incidents of touch within the treatment program should be considered and processed objectively, given both the power of touch and the constellation of factors that may determine any incidence of touch's meaning for the particular parties involved.

☐ Avoid all touches that may be uncomfortable or stimulating and/or unethical. Never use the following touches:

- Foot rubs and back rubs;
- Sitting or holding in lap;
- Stroking;
- Hugs or holds that are lingering or intense;
- Sexual or sensual contact;
- Massages (unless conducted by a licensed massage therapist trained to work with the specific population); and
- Aggressive or violent touch (except physical restraint in those circumstances and in those fashions clearly described in the appropriate policies and procedures).

If you are unsure whether a touch is appropriate then act conservatively, and refrain.

☐ Questions or concerns to take to your supervisor:

- When a child says your touch is sexually arousing or when his or her behavior indicates that it is;
- If you have moments when a child has done or said something that has been sexually arousing to you; and
- When a child says he or she is thinking/has thought about raping you.

☐ If the client understands empowerment and has shown the ability to use it:

1. Incorporate basic education about empowerment into the process;
2. Help the client demonstrate empowerment by getting verbal consent each time before touch is used, until trust is sufficiently established to allow for nonverbal establishment of consent.
3. Assist the client in establishing both verbal and nonverbal signals that clearly communicate "stop" before engaging in any form of touch.
4. Implement several trial runs during the initial stages of touch that allow the client to be in complete control concerning structure of a touch exercise and or the length of time a particular touch will last to allow the client an opportunity to experience the therapist's respect for his or her stated boundaries.

☐ Enough time to process touch interaction:

Leave ten to fifteen minutes to process when initiating touch interactions. May not need as much time as the relationship develops and touch is normalized.

☐ Once a therapeutic relationship is established:

1. Touch should occur in a safe and trusting relationship. In other words, it should be congruent with the level of intimacy in the therapeutic relationship.
2. It is inappropriate to touch during the introductory phase of treatment except in a crisis situation where a touch on the arm might be appropriate or firm holding is needed in a therapeutic restraint.
3. Must have developed a solid relationship and trust first.

☐ Touch can be offered as available to all clients:

1. Available as an option to all, not to a select few;
2. Does not imply that touch must be applied globally but rather addresses the issue that the use or nonuse responds to an individual's therapeutic needs and not to personality traits. Inappropriately selective use of touch can be contratherapeutic for both those receiving it and for those witnessing but not receiving it by suggesting staff personal preferences between clients.

☐ Consultation is available and used: This helps to identify blind spots and to uncover hidden or unrealized agendas:

☐ The therapist is comfortable with touch:

1. Permission needs to be mutual—the therapist has the equal right to say no to touch as well. However, it is the therapist's responsibility to talk to the client about that decision and any feelings it might engender.
2. Therapist's boundaries deserve to be respected.
3. Mutual respect for decisions However, it is the therapist's responsibility to talk to the client about that decision and what it means and any feelings that the decision may engender.
4. Touch must be congruent, a genuine reflection of feelings, attitudes and beliefs.
5. Attraction and sexual feelings could develop. If this happens, the therapist refrains from any contact with the client and speaks with his supervisor. This is not unusual but having those feelings and acting on them are two different things.

6. Don't touch to reduce your own discomfort of seeing a client in pain.
7. Don't touch to lessen a client's anxiety. This may prevent a client from gaining insight into difficult or anxiety-provoking matters.

Chapter 17

The Current State of Adolescent Risk Assessment

by David S. Prescott, M.A., L.I.C.S.W.

OVERVIEW

Given the dynamic of human development, predicting any future trends in the lives of adolescents can be a highly challenging and perhaps questionable undertaking. This chapter reviews the complicated issue of predicting sexually inappropriate behavior in juveniles. Risk assessment among adults is itself a highly controversial issue; the problems are multiplied when dealing with a youthful population. One needs to consider a variety of static and dynamic factors, which the adolescent may prioritize differently compared to the adult offender. The latest developments in this highly specialized area are herein reviewed as well as cautionary notes concerning the serious ramifications of predicting that a young person is on the path toward becoming an adult sex offender.

INTRODUCTION

More and more, professionals working with sexually abusive youth come under pressure to make statements regarding the likelihood of future abusive acts. Many practitioners seek empirically proven assessment methods only to find there are none. To the uninitiated, advances in actuarial assessment of adults, where known recidivists are compared to offenders not known to have persisted, can appear as a dark and arcane science. Entering the world of adolescent risk assessment, practitioners quickly find themselves needing expertise in areas ranging from human sexuality to antisociality, and from individual development to family dynamism. However, clinical judgment is described with nearly insulting language in many studies and literature reviews. Most confounding of all, truly accurate assessments of an ongoing willingness to reoffend are often based on a small amount of data. This chapter highlights many of the challenges professionals face as they consider the likelihood of adolescent reoffense. It describes recent research, outlines evolving strategies, and assesses the limitations of our current ability to assess risk.

DEFINING THE TERMS

Risk Assessment vs. Risk Appraisal

An understanding of the phrase "risk assessment" is vital to effectively and efficiently communicating about young people. Hart, Kropp, and Laws (2003) define risk as follows:

> a hazard that is incompletely understood and whose occurrence therefore can only be forecast with uncertainty. The concept is multifaceted, referring to the nature of the hazard, the likelihood that the hazard will occur, the frequency or duration of the hazard, the seriousness of the hazard's consequences, and imminence of the hazard; also, the concept of risk is inherently contextual, as hazards arise and exist in specific circumstances. (p. 2)

In light of evidence that much antisocial behavior does not persist past adolescence (Quinsey, Skilling, Lalumière, & Craig, 2004), and that treatment can significantly reduce youthful recidivism (Worling & Curwen, 2000), one could argue for modifying the last clause to "as hazards arise, exist, *and diminish*, in specific circumstances."

From the outset, this definition presents a contrast to the notion of "risk appraisal," as described by Quinsey, Harris, Rice, and Cormier (1998). Their *Violence Risk Appraisal Guide* (VRAG) is an actuarial measure using fixed and explicit historical information, albeit in the absence of a clearly stated underlying theory. It produces a simple but easily misunderstood numerical value indicating what percentage of the mostly adult construction sample reoffended violently in follow-up periods of seven and ten years. Novices may understand this to mean the absolute likelihood that a given offender will engage in violent recidivism, despite the clear instructions of the authors. Conspicuously absent from the VRAG is an appraisal of the seriousness, frequency, imminence, or even specifics around what kind of violence is being predicted. Although it has demonstrated truly impressive results (Quinsey, 2000), the VRAG does not set out to assess the "hazard" that Hart et al. (2003) describe.

Looking closer at the elements of criminal behavior and treatment, Andrews and Bonta (1998) describe three principles: *risk*, *need*, and *responsivity*. The risk principle states that interventions should be matched to the risk the offender poses. The need principle states that interventions should specifically target areas related to criminal behavior, and the responsivity principle states that interventions should match the characteristics of the offender. These distinctions are critical to accurate assessment. It is quite simple for the novice to equate treatment needs with level of risk. A low-risk youth who has difficulty responding to treatment that is poorly matched to his needs and abilities might appear more worrisome to those around him, and therefore at higher risk than he really is. For example, a low-functioning incest abuser who is noncompliant with treatment targeting sexual deviance may appear more problematic than he is. Assuming that he is truly low risk (no prior history of sexual aggression, no attitudes tolerant of sexual abuse, etc.), these interventions may be less effective than education and restorative treatment tailored to his abilities and targeting inter-personal deficits. In this case, an assessment of risk, need, and responsivity would be more helpful to others than simply making a statement about "high risk" or "low risk."

Indeed, the current emphasis on risk assessment has only appeared recently, on the heels of debate around assessments of dangerousness (Webster, Ben-Aron, & Hucker, 1985). Whether anyone is capable of predicting future dangerous behavior has been the topic of controversy for many years. In one case (*Barefoot v. Estelle*, 463 U.S. 880 (1983), described in Grisso, 2000), the American Psychiatric Association filed an *amicus curiae* brief stating, essentially, that practitioners could not yet claim to accu-rately assess dangerousness. Other court cases, such as *Kansas v. Hendricks* (117 S. Ct. 2072 (1997)), have contributed significantly to the need for accurate risk assess-ments, at the same time that research has provided numerous insights into recidivism (Hanson & Thornton, 2000; Quinsey et al., 1998; Hare, 1991; Worling & Curwen, 2000; Prentky, Harris, Frizzell, & Righthand, 2000).

Finally, the word "assessment" is important. Hart et al. (2003) define assessment in the mental health field as "the process of gathering information for use in making decisions." The purposeful nature of this definition sets it apart from appraisal and evaluation, each of which implies the use of testing and numerical values but not nec-essarily the contribution of the process to decision making or risk-reduction strategies. Thus, the phrase "risk assessment" becomes the gathering of information specific to making decisions about a multifaceted hazard, a hazard made more complicated by the developmental and contextual issues of youth (Ryan & Lane, 1997; Prentky & Righthand, 2003).

Why the Language Matters in Practice

This discussion of language is not merely academic. Great debate has accompa-nied the development of assessment methods. In an often-quoted statement, Quinsey et al. (1998) clarify their view:

> What we are advising is not the addition of actuarial methods to existing prac-tice, but rather the complete replacement of existing practice with actuarial methods. This is a different view than we expressed in Webster, Harris, Rice, Cormier, & Quinsey (1994), where we advised the practice of adjusting actu-arial estimates by up to 10% when there were compelling circumstances to do so. . . . Actuarial methods are too good and clinical judgment too poor to risk contaminating the former with the latter. The sorts of compelling circum-

stances that might tempt one to adjust an actuarial score are better considered separately in deciding on supervisory conditions, interventions designed to reduce risk, and so forth. (p. 171)

In their review of recent research and meta-analyses, however, Hart et al. (2003) challenge "the alleged superiority of actuarial risk assessment" with the following:

At present . . . the superiority of actuarial decision-making is an article of faith rather than a fact. Any claim of actuarial superiority is an inference based on evidence of questionable relevance, and should be acknowledged as such. It is entirely reasonable for mental health professionals to conclude that current scientific evidence is not sufficient to support the use of or reliance on actuarial procedures; indeed, it is entirely reasonable to conclude that the weight of the scientific evidence is sufficient to reject altogether the use of or reliance on actuarial procedures. (p. 11)

While in many settings these seemingly adversarial viewpoints would (and hopefully, will) eventually uncover the truth, they can result in enormous frustration to those seeking to protect both the liberties of individuals and the safety of young people.

Adding to this difficulty are the differing views on who should do the assessment. Rich (2000) describes risk assessment as a "clinical process," whereas many of the best-studied adult actuarial measures are in use by probation and parole officers. Many of those who work with adolescents (e.g., Grady & Reynolds, 2003) have advocated a paradigm shift beyond risk assessment to holistic treatment. Others (e.g., Bremer, 2001; Gilgun, Klein, & Pranis, 2000) advocate looking at protective factors and resilience rather than risk. In addition to their idealistic appeal, these arguments describe fertile ground for broader inquiry into elements necessary for effective decision making.

Seeking to bridge the gap between these apparent extremes, Webster, Hucker, and Bloom (2002) have made five recommendations, which may be summarized as follows:

- Understand the applicable legal framework.

- Risk assessment must be *evidenced-based*.

- Include an individualized statement of risk.

- Include steps to reduce risk.

- Compare individual case with scientific data when possible.

At the same time, John Monahan (1981/1995), who has strongly argued against unguided clinical judgment in predicting violent behavior, has recently stated: "This reliance on clinical judgment—aided by empirical understanding of risk factors for violence and their interactions—reflects, and in our view should reflect, the standard of care at this juncture in the field's development" (Monahan et al., 2001, pp. 134–135). In all, the careful observer of the field should keep in mind that many of its most diligent and outspoken leaders have reviewed and refined their outlooks throughout the evolution of their work (see also Greenland, 1985).

Observing how differences in language can produce dramatically different thought as to methodology, the prudent assessor of risk may well want to ask more specifically what the referral question is, and *why*. Given the recent advances in adult risk assessment and the context in which they occur, the use of the term "risk assessment," although popular, may actually be misleading. It may be more effectively replaced with a statement regarding risk combined with an evidence-based discussion of treatment and supervisory strategies that can effectively reduce risk and improve the youth's ability to access treatment. Beyond simply describing how a young person functions, the most effective risk assessor will be able to describe the youth, understand what kinds of behavioral trajectories he may be on, and outline specific strategies (which will depend on the youth's community) for building on his resilience and reducing the risk for problematic behaviors in the future. A significant part of this process will lie in differentiating between elements related to a predisposition, or ongoing willingness, to engage in harmful behavior, and other elements whose contribution to a reoffense process is illusory.

At a more practical level, if the purpose of an assessment is to understand a level of predisposition toward sexually abusive behavior for treatment and planning purposes (e.g., Does the youth display an emerging sexual disorder?), this should be clarified at the outset of the evaluation and the report. Likewise, if the assessment is intended to guide decisions around level of care (e.g., Can the youth be successfully treated in the home and what types of supervision may he require at school?), it can prompt different questions on the part of the assessor regarding what types of risk are to be mitigated and whether the youth can access treatment at a lower level of care.

INDIVIDUALIZING RISK ASSESSMENTS FOR YOUTHS

Many of these considerations are discussed below. However, the following questions may be useful in constructing the most helpful assessments:

- When using the term "risk assessment," what exactly is the referral source asking for? A better understanding of the past? An explanation of a current offense? A prediction of the future? Assistance with case planning, treatment, and supervision?

- What pressures exist to make recommendations in one way or another, and how do current circumstances influence those pressures (e.g. institutional, economic)?

- Given that much of an individual's development is not fully defined until adulthood, how can one best understand elements that may be important to treatment (e.g., remorse, empathy, and personality traits)?

- How can one use the most accurate and precise language without pejorative jargon? Words such as "predator" may only serve to fuel the anxiety of the adults in the youth's life rather than inspire helpful interventions.

- How can one best create an environment in which the youth will self-report past behavior, attitudes, worries, and concerns?

- How can one best differentiate normative adolescent attitudes from those that support a reoffense process or signal an ongoing willingness to engage in harmful behavior?

- How can one create a list of empirically based indicators that signal escalation or imminence of harmful behavior?

- Does an assessment process gather information from all domains in the youth's life, such as his home, school, and community?

RISK FACTOR SUBTYPES

Static vs. Dynamic Factors

The classification of risk factors into *static* (those elements solidly fixed in a person's history, such as gender, or number of convictions) and *dynamic* (elements that are subject to change) has gained appeal in recent years. Of the dynamic variables, Hanson (2000) has differentiated between those that remain relatively *stable* across time, such as personality disorder or self-regulation style, and those that are *acute*, and subject to rapid change or escalation. Examples of acute factors include substance abuse, anger, or other negative moods. These distinctions are important. Hanson and Bussière (1998) found that substance abuse did not distinguish recidivists from non-recidivists in long-term studies of adult sex offenders, while Hanson and Harris (2001) found it to be a useful indicator of imminence.

Much of the success of adult actuarial scales has been due to the static nature of their variables, particularly their reliance on past behavior. This has been apparent in the predictive validity of scales such as the VRAG, Static-99 (Hanson & Thornton, 2000), and Rapid Risk Assessment of Sex Offender Recidivism (RRASOR; Hanson, 1997). However, many researchers recognize the problem of psychological assessment of future events. Williams (1975) reported on a study of differences in men serving their first sentences in the British prison system, and those who had previously been imprisoned. While only one in three of the first sentence offenders was reconvicted, two-thirds of the recidivists were convicted again. Although the researchers looked at forty variables among the prisoners, they concluded that "the major difference between individuals in prison is those serving their first sentence and the rest" (p. 36). Hanson and Bussière (1998) found that typical clinical judgment yielded an average correlation not much better than chance ($r = .10$) while prior convictions on their own correlated at .20. Likewise, in their review of the Psychopathy Checklist: Screening Version (PCL:SV; Hart, Cox, & Hare, 1995), Monahan et al. (2001) found that although PCL:SV scores were the strongest predictor of violence in their sample, the items specifically related to past behavior were the most predictive. Of note, the Hare psychopathy scales were developed to measure a construct ("psychopathy") commonly associated with persistent criminality, and not the likelihood of future criminality itself.

Are Subscales With Greatest Adult Predictive Value Relevant for Youth?

More recently, Marczyk, Heilbrun, Lander, and DeMatteo (2003) noted that the most predictive aspects of several scales were not their total scores, but the subscales related to past behavior, suicidal thoughts, anger, fighting, and anxiety. The scales measured included the Psychopathy Checklist: Youth Version (PCL:YV; Forth, Kosson, & Hare, 2003) and Youth Level of Service/Case Management Inventory (YLS/CMI; Hoge & Andrews, 2003). Of interest to practitioners, the authors found that the referring offenses that brought youth to the attention of the authorities were not in themselves predictive. They concluded that the use of these tools for prediction "may not be a straightforward process" (p. 15).

Further complicating matters, some authors have observed that including too much information in the decision-making process can result in reduced accuracy of assessments (Monahan, 1981/1995, p. 88; Quinsey, 2000). Quinsey et al. (1998) observe that "[m]ore importantly, the amount of information available to the clinician was unrelated to accuracy but was highly related to the degree of confidence in the judgment," and that humans "are, in fact, most confident when making extreme judgments" (p. 56).

Reviewing the role of past behavior in understanding adults, two observations can be made. First, as Zamble and Quinsey (1997) have observed, static variables ultimately reflect dynamic processes. One recidivates as a result of a persistent willingness to do so and not simply because of his number of preconvictions. Past behavior may signal persistence, but it is not necessarily the same thing. Second, many adolescents who will persist in harming others well into adulthood simply have not had the time to accrue the kinds of risk markers that have made the adult actuarial measures robust. One might wonder if it isn't the *persistence* of risk factors into adulthood that accounts for the recent successes of these tools.

Finally, one may wonder about the role of dynamic risk factors when youth itself is dynamic. In their most recent version of the Juvenile Sex Offender Assessment Protocol (JSOAP-II; Prentky & Righthand, 2003), described in greater detail later, the authors observe that "[n]o aspect of their development, including their cognitive development, is fixed or stable. In a very real sense, we are trying to assess the risk of 'moving targets'" (p. i). For this reason, they recommend that youth be reassessed every six months.

Best Predictors of Juvenile Delinquency

In a recent review of the general recidivism literature regarding juveniles, Quinsey et al. (2004) note that the best predictors of juvenile delinquency among general youth ages 6 through 11 are a prior history of offending, substance use, gender, low socioeconomic status, and having an antisocial parent. The best predictors for young people ages 12–14 are a lack of strong prosocial ties, antisocial peers, and prior delinquent offenses. They observe that "[t]heories to account for the patterns of these markers tend to focus on narrow domains. In the absence of a more general theory, the wealth of correlates of antisocial behavior that are themselves intercorrelated is something of an encumbrance rather than a benefit" (p. 91).

Quinsey et al. (2004) go on to describe three types of adolescent antisociality:

1. Adolescence-limited delinquents;

2. Early-starting life-course-persistent antisocial individuals whose behaviors are associated with neuropathology resulting from prenatal, perinatal, and/or postnatal problems, sometimes in combination with family and neighborhood adversity; and

3. Early-starting life-course-persistent antisocial individuals without neurodevelopmental pathology.

They note that this third category appears "to comprise a distinct class of individual, or taxon, different from other antisocial individuals" (p. 94).

Treatment Failure as a Dynamic Factor

A dynamic factor that is less understood is treatment failure. Hanson and Bussière (1998) found that failure of adults to complete treatment contributed to risk in the absence of other factors. Similarly, Hunter and Figueredo (1999) found that youth who were unable to complete treatment had higher levels of sexual maladjustment, suggesting elevated long-term risk.

BARRIERS TO ACCURATE ASSESSMENT OF RISK, NEED, AND RESPONSIVITY

Given the current public awareness of the harm of sexual abuse, it is not surprising that the topic of adolescent risk assessment can create strong reactions in practitioners. It often seems that adult reaction to adolescent sexuality, criminality, and potential for harm can be as volatile as adolescence itself. Therefore, it is easy for those voicing caution to dismiss risk assessment completely (Grady & Reynolds, 2003). The first barrier to assessments of risk, need, and responsivity, then, is adult discomfort with the process. Observing the admissions department of one residential treatment center reveals many evaluators making statements about risk and adding numerous cautions regarding the topic, in some cases for pages at a time.

Beyond these concerns, youth are inherently more dependent on their environment. The contribution of families, schools, and peer groups to both prosocial and antisocial behavior is well documented (Quinsey et al., 2004; Prentky & Righthand, 2003), as is the importance of one's friends in adolescence (Arriaga & Foshee, 2004). The careful assessor must therefore have a considerable familiarity with these elements in order to make helpful suggestions regarding the reduction of risk. Useful questions might consider the extent significant others contributed to past and present offense chains and nonsexual problem behavior. This contribution might include active encouragement to offend or a passive failure to intervene despite obvious warning signs.

A significant barrier to adolescent risk assessment is that sexual arousal patterns are considerably more fluid and dynamic than in adulthood and that only a minority of sexually abusive youth show deviant sexual interest and arousal patterns (Hunter & Becker, 1994). Studies of techniques such as arousal conditioning and drug therapies are inconsistent (Hunter & Goodwin, 1992). Complicating matters, youth in one study were more likely to self-report fetishistic behaviors than were their adult counterparts (Zolondek, Abel, Northey, & Jordan, 2001). Although an extensive history of abusive sexual behavior despite detection, sanction, and treatment can sometimes represent prima facie evidence of an emerging sexual disorder, it is strongly recommended that assessors only consider this variable with extreme caution. Although the role of sexual deviance in adults has been established with greater certainty (Hanson & Bussière, 1998; Thornton, 2000), its dynamic nature in adolescence limits its utility in understanding potential behavioral trajectories. Further, although adolescents may display evidence of deviant sexual scripts, their willingness to engage in abusive or indiscriminant sexual behavior is subject to change over time. There is no research into how this underlying willingness changes over time.

Other barriers to assessment center on personal development, including the sense of one's identity and attitudes related to harmful behavior. If an individual simply views himself as destined to become a criminal or rocket scientist, does this make him more likely to become one? If youth are encouraged to become athletes, are they more likely to be willing to try? Similarly, if youth raised in abusive homes are told they are sick, evil, perverted, or no good, what factors are associated with their acceptance of this message? Practitioners may therefore wish to take into account to what extent the label "sex offender" may contribute to a young person's sense of predestination to remain one. Does acclimation to a juvenile "sex offender" label contribute to a willingness to persist? Clearly, these questions remain unanswered, but they should put concerned adults on notice that our best intended interventions can do harm (Dishion, McCord, & Poulin, 1999).

A related construct is "heterotypic continuity" (Kernberg, Weiner, & Bardenstein, 2000). In essence, this is the idea that the expression of personality pathology can change across childhood. For example, one may wonder whether an early proneness to boredom can lead to thrill-seeking behavior later on. For that matter, an assessor may wish to consider whether an adolescent's sexual misconduct signals a trajectory of antisocial conduct, sexual disorder, or a willingness to engage in indiscriminate activities.

Empathy for victims and others has long been considered a key element of treatment (Ryan & Lane, 1997; Rich, 2003). However, its measurement and contribution to abusive behavior have been the source of much discussion and debate (Fernandez, 2002). In one study with adolescents (Curwen, 2000), the well-known Interpersonal Reactivity Index (Salter, 1988) did not tap victim empathy. Hanson (2003) has observed that some offenders genuinely do not understand the harm they have caused to others while others do understand but remain willing to abuse. Further, recent advances in understanding the brain show that the prefrontal cortex, which houses empathy, continues to mature into and through adulthood (Stien & Kendall, 2004). Although exactly how much of an individual's adult capacity for empathy is open to speculation, this single element of adolescent development will give assessors of risk reason for caution.

Finally, one might wonder whether a strict focus on risk assessment precludes a focus on factors that will mitigate risk. To this end, Bremer (2001) has created the Protective Factors Scale. In a display of the importance of framing a question, Bremer fundamentally sidesteps "what's his level of risk" by asking what factors will protect a youth from further harm. She has noted that assessing these factors (which include domains related to sexuality, personal development, and environmental support) can be of considerable use in decisions regarding level of care, such as community versus residential treatment.

RECIDIVISM: BASE RATES AND TIME AT RISK

Although many (Serin & Brown, 2000) have taken note of the importance of understanding base rates of reoffense, studies of adolescent sexual recidivism have been few and far between (Worling & Curwen, 2000). However, the available studies often find lower reoffense rates than one might think. In one meta-analysis with 1,025 juveniles, Alexander (1999) found recidivism rates of 5.8 percent for rapists, 2.1 percent for child molesters, and 7.5 percent for "unspecified" adolescent abusers. While the length of follow-up varied across samples, she noticed that recidivism rates appeared to grow over time. Also of note, all were considered to have been "treated."

Långström and Grann (2000) found that among forty-six adolescents ages 15 to 20, sexual recidivism was 20 percent, violent recidivism was 22 percent, and general recidivism (including violence) was 65 percent in a six-year follow-up period. In contrast to Alexander's findings, the authors found that most of their recidivists did so within one to two years of follow-up. Caution is urged in interpreting these numbers. This sample represents nearly all the young sexual offenders who received court-ordered forensic psychiatric evaluations in Sweden across a number of years. One can easily infer that given the small size and apparently unusual circumstances of their selection, these must have been considered particularly problematic young people. Worling and Curwen (2000) followed 148 Canadian youth for an average of six years. They found that those who received "abuse specific" treatment had a 72 percent reduction in sexual recidivism. The untreated youth recidivated at 18 percent in the follow-up period, while the treated youth recidivated at a rate of 5 percent.

Clearly, all these results must be interpreted with caution. First, ethical considerations have prevented the highest-quality randomized treatment/no-treatment comparisons. Even if these were possible, the specific "active ingredients" of treatment have yet to be determined, although multisystemic treatment (MST; Henggeler, Schoenwald, Borduin, Rowland, & Cunningham, 1998) appears particularly promising. Second, recidivism rates are susceptible to adults' ability to detect reoffense. One may argue that these rates are grossly underestimated given that victims often do not wish to report crimes. On the other hand, one might also argue that because youthful sexual abusers often have high rates of recidivism for nonsexual crimes, they are not particularly adept at evading detection. One might further argue that upon arrest for sexually abusive behavior, many youth have far less opportunities for reoffense due to increased supervision.

One often-neglected aspect of recidivism base rates is time at risk for various types of offenders, such as child molesters and rapists. Prentky et al. (2000) found that among seventy-five youth studied, only three recidivated in a one-year follow-up. This was in the first study on which the Juvenile Sex Offender Assessment Protocol (JSOAP; Prentky et al., 2000) was based. Of note, however, the three sexual recidivists all scored higher on the impulsive, antisocial behavior scale than on the sexual drive/preoccupation scale. For total JSOAP scores, there was a roughly 6.5-point difference between the eight recidivists (including three sexual recidivists) and the nonrecidivists. However, Hecker, Scoular, Righthand, and Nagle (2002) found in a ten- to twelve-year follow-up that total JSOAP scores were not correlated with sexual recidivism, but that scale one ("sexual drive") was very strongly predictive, albeit with a sample of only six recidivists (11 percent) in a sample of fifty-four male adolescents. The nonsexual recidivism in this sample was 37 percent. However, Righthand, Knight, and Prentky (2002) found that higher scores on the sexual drive scale were associated with male victims and number of victims, while the antisocial behavior scale was associated with teenage and older victims. Clearly, the numbers reported are astronomically low. However, they do suggest beginning avenues for further inquiry in understanding these subscales. Hanson and Bussière (1998) found that rapists and child molesters differed more in their time at risk than in their long-term recidivism rates. Many rapists were quick to reoffend, while child molesters appeared to reoffend at more uniform rates over time. It is possible that historical information related to sexual and antisocial aspects of sexual offending may be useful in determining supervision strategies and dosages over time.

DIMENSIONS OF RISK AND THE "TOTAL SCORE" DILEMMA

Juveniles are, on average, at greater risk for nonsexual crimes. This should alert concerned adults to look beyond risk assessment of exclusively sexual misconduct. To this end, a number of instruments may be useful, including the YLS/CMI (Hoge & Andrews, 2003). This is a measure that is easily scored by practitioners and looks at risk and need factors related to general kinds of crime and level of care. The Structured Assessment of Violence Risk in Youth (SAVRY; Borum, Bartel, & Forth, 2002) is also a well-conceived and organized tool that looks at historical, social/contextual, situational, individual, and protective factors. Like the ERASOR, it is an empirically grounded review of risk factors, whose aim (unlike the ERASOR's) is to understand likelihood of future nonsexual violence as well as sexual violence. Like the ERASOR, the total score is less important than the development of an understanding of the individual. The careful assessor may therefore wish to include separate statements regarding risk and need related to sexual reoffense, violence, and general kinds of criminal behavior.

Although the JSOAP-II (Prentky & Righthand, 2003) and the ERASOR (Worling & Curwen, 2000) are typically conceived as instruments for predicting sexual recidivism, a few cautions are in order. First, according to its authors, the JSOAP-II "is a checklist whose purpose is to aid in the systematic review of risk factors that have been identified in the professional literature as being associated with sexual *and criminal* offending" (Prentky & Righthand, 2003, p. i, emphasis added). Second, given that total scores on this instrument have yet to demonstrate significant predictive validity, one must use extreme caution in interpreting its results. The subscales on their own may better address areas of need and hazard reduction than the total score.

Likewise, the ERASOR is constructed in such a way that the total score is not the primary consideration. As Worling and Curwen (2000) point out, the presence of only one risk factor may, under certain circumstances, be enough to warrant a determination of high risk. Interestingly, although it is designed specifically to assess risk of sexual reoffense, a recent study (Bourgon, 2002) concluded that while the ERASOR assesses static factors related to sexual aggression, its dynamic factors are related to general delinquency. There has not been a large-scale study of the ERASOR's predictive validity.

SUMMARY AND CONCLUSIONS

It is worth repeating that there remains no empirically validated algorithm by which to assess a young person's risk for sexual reoffense. However, there is enough emerging evidence that practitioners have an obligation to be familiar with what is known as well as what is not known. There is an evolving agreement in the literature that the majority of youth we assess do not have deeply entrenched patterns of sexual deviance, and that their sexual arousal patterns, personalities, and proclivity to engage in delinquent behaviors are all subject to change without notice.

Although many factors may lead a young person to sexually abuse, these are not necessarily the same factors that will drive one to abuse again. Ultimately, what we are trying to understand might best be summed as an "ongoing willingness" to engage in harmful behavior. This fundamentally dynamic element is likely best assessed in the simple static variables of early onset with subsequent sexual misconduct despite detection, sanction, and treatment.

The existing tools may appear easy to use at first glance, but they must be handled with the greatest of caution and in the context in which they were intended. For the present, their subscales may be more useful in designing strategies to reduce risk rather than assign a value to it. Their total scores, although useful for research purposes, can be misleading and deceptive. For these reasons, clinical standards should far exceed research standards in applying these tools to youth.

When considering the likelihood of a young person to engage in harmful behavior, the practitioner should have a thorough knowledge of recidivism base rates for sexual, violent, and general crimes. From there, assessors should establish the precise nature of the referral question in order to provide the most accurate assessment and helpful recommendations. Clear language describing the inherent problems of risk assessment is of fundamental importance but need not dominate the report. Practitioners should guard against interesting but unproven or illusory factors (e.g., fire setting as predictive of sexual reoffense) and consider how each risk variable reflects or contributes to an overall reoffense process. Although not well understood, practitioners would do well to consider prior treatment experience and pay special attention both to the style of the provider and to successful versus unsuccessful completion.

Risk assessment of sexually abusive youth remains a highly unenviable task. It is hoped that by outlining both the difficulties and newer strategies, practitioners can make realistic assessments of themselves as well as the youth they serve.

References

Alexander, M. A. (1999). Sexual offender treatment efficacy revisited, *Sexual Abuse: A Journal of Research and Treatment, 11*, 101-116.

Andrews, D. A., & Bonta, J. L. (1998). *The psychology of criminal conduct* (2nd ed.). Cincinnati, OH: Anderson.

Arriaga, X., & Foshee, V. A. (2004). Adolescent dating violence: Do adolescents follow in their friends' or their parents' footsteps? *Journal of Interpersonal Violence, 19,* 162–184.

Borum, R., Bartel, P., & Forth, A. E. (2002). *Manual for the Structured Assessment of Violence Risk in Youth.* Tampa: University of South Florida. Available: *www.fmhi.usf.edu/.*

Bourgon, G. (2002). *The Estimate of Risk of Adolescent Sex Offender Recidivism (ERASOR): Evaluating its psychometric properties.* Paper presented at the annual meeting of the Association for the Treatment of Sexual Abusers, Montreal, Quebec, Canada.

Bremer, J. F. (2001, May 7). *The Protective Factors Scale: Assessing youth with sexual concerns.* Plenary address at the 16th annual conference of the National Adolescent Perpetration Network, Kansas City, MO.

Curwen, T. (2000, May 29). *Utility of the Interpersonal Reactivity Index (IRI) as a measure of empathy in male adolescent sex offenders.* Paper presented at the sixth International Conference on the Treatment of Sexual Offenders, Toronto, Ontario, Canada.

Dishion, T. J., McCord, J., & Poulin, F. (1999). When interventions harm: Peer groups and problem behavior. *American Psychologist, 54,* 755–764.

Fernandez, Y. (2002). *In their shoes: Examining the role of empathy and its place in the treatment of offenders.* Oklahoma City, OK: Wood 'N' Barnes.

Forth, A.E., Kosson, D.S., & Hare, R.D. (2003). *Psychopathy Checklist: Youth Version.* Toronto, Ontario, Canada: Multi-Health Systems.

Gilgun, J. F., Klein, C., & Pranis, K. (2000) The significance of resources in models of risk. *Journal of Interpersonal Violence, 15,* 621–650.

Grady, J., & Reynolds, S. (2003, October). *Holistic assessment and treatment of sexually abusive youth.* Paper presented at the annual meeting of the Association for the Treatment of Sexual Abusers, Montreal, Quebec, Canada.

Greenland, C. (1985). Dangerousness, mental disorder, and politics. In C. D. Webster, M. H. Ben-Aron, & S. J. Hucker (Eds.), *Dangerousness: Probability and prediction, psychiatry and public policy* (pp. 25–40). Cambridge, UK: Cambridge University Press.

Grisso, T. (2000, March). *Ethical issues in sex offender re-offense risk prediction.* Paper presented at Sex Offender Re-Offense Risk Prediction Symposium, Madison, Wisconsin. Available: *www.sinclairseminars.com.*

Hanson, R .K. (1997). *The development of a Brief Actuarial Risk Scale for sexual offender recidivism* (User Report 1997-04). Ottawa: Department of the Solicitor General of Canada. Available: *www.psepc-sppcc.gc.ca.*

Hanson, R .K. (2000). *Risk assessment.* Beaverton, OR: Association for the Treatment of Sexual Abusers.

Hanson, R .K. (2003). *Sex offender empathy deficits* (User Report 2003-08). Ottawa: Department of the Solicitor General of Canada. Available: *www.sgc.gc.ca.*

Hanson, R. K., & Bussière, M. T. (1998) Predicting relapse: A meta-analysis of sexual offender recidivism studies. *Journal of Consulting and Clinical Psychology, 66,* 348–362.

Hanson, R. K., & Harris, A. J. R. (2001). A structured approach to evaluating change among sexual offenders. *Sexual Abuse: A Journal of Research and Treatment, 13,* 105–122.

Hanson, R. K., & Thornton, D. (2000). Improving actuarial risk assessments for sex offenders. *Law and Human Behavior, 24,* 119–136.

Hare, R. D. (1991). *The Hare Psychopathy Checklist—Revised.* Toronto, Ontario, Canada: Multi-Health Systems.

Hart, S. D., Cox, D. N., & Hare, R. D. (1995). *The Hare Psychopathy Checklist: Screening Version.* Toronto, Ontario, Canada: Multi-Health Systems.

Hart, S. D., Kropp, P. R., & Laws, R. D., with Klaver, J., Logan, C., & Wyatt, K. A. (2003). *Risk for Sexual Violence Protocol (RSVP): Structured professional guidelines for assessing risk of violence.* Burnaby, British Columbia, Canada: Mental Health, Law, and Policy Institute, Simon Fraser University.

Hecker, J., Scoular, J., Righthand, S., & Nangle, D. (2002, October). *Predictive validity of the J-SOAP over 10-plus years: Implications for risk assessment.* Paper presented at the annual meeting of the Association for the Treatment of Sexual Abusers, Montreal, Quebec, Canada.

Henggeler, S. W., Schoenwald, S. K., Borduin, C. M., Rowland, M. D., & Cunningham, P. B. (1998). *Multisystemic treatment of antisocial behavior in children and adolescents.* New York: Guilford Press.

Hoge, R. D., & Andrews, D. A. (2003). *Youth Level of Service/Case Management Inventory.* Toronto, Ontario, Canada: Multi-Health Systems.

Hunter, J. A., & Becker, J. V. (1994). The role of deviant sexual arousal in juvenile sexual offending: Etiology, evaluation, and treatment, *Criminal Justice and Behavior, 21,* 132–149.

Hunter, J. A., & Figueredo, A. J. (1999). Factors associated with treatment compliance in a population of juvenile sexual offenders. *Sexual Abuse: A Journal of Research and Treatment, 11,* 49–68.

Hunter, J. A., & Goodwin, D. W. (1992). The utility of satiation therapy in the treatment of juvenile sexual offenders: Variations and efficacy, *Annals of Sex Research, 5,* 71–80.

Kernberg, P. F., Weiner, A. S., & Bardenstein, K. K. (2000). *Personality disorders in children and adolescents*. New York: Basic Books.

Långström, N., & Grann, M. (2000). Risk for criminal recidivism among young sex offenders, *Journal of Interpersonal Violence, 15,* 855–871.

Lund, C. A. (2000). Predictors of sexual recidivism: Did meta-analysis clarify the role and relevance of denial? *Sexual Abuse: A Journal of Research and Treatment, 12*(4), 275–287.

Marczyk, G. R., Heilbrun, K., Lander, T., & DeMatteo, D. (2003). Predicting juvenile recidivism with the PCL:YV, MAYSI, and YLS/CMI. *International Journal of Forensic Mental Health, 2,* 7–18.

Monahan, J. (1995). *The clinical prediction of violent behavior*. Northvale, NJ: Jason Aronson. (Original work published 1981)

Monahan, J., Steadman, H. J., Silver, E., Applebaum, P. S., Robbins, P. C., Mulvey, E. P., Roth, L. H., Grisso, T., & Banks, S. (2001). *Rethinking risk assessment: The Macarthur Study of Violence and Mental Disorder*. New York: Oxford University Press.

Prentky, R., Harris, B., Frizzell, K., & Righthand, S. (2000). An actuarial procedure for assessing risk with juvenile sexual offenders. *Sexual Abuse: A Journal of Research and Treatment, 12*(2), 71–93.

Prentky, R., & Righthand, S. (2003). *Juvenile Sex Offender Assessment Protocol—II (JSOAP-II)*. Available: *www.csom.org*.

Quinsey, V. L. (2000, March). *The Violence Risk Appraisal Guide*. Paper presented at Sinclair Seminars' Sex Offender Re-Offense Risk Prediction Symposium, Madison, Wisconsin. Available: *www.sinclairseminars.com*.

Quinsey, V. L., Harris, G. T., Rice, M. E., & Cormier, C. A. (1998). *Violent offenders: Managing and appraising risk*. Washington, DC: American Psychological Association.

Quinsey, V. L., Skilling, T. A., Lalumière, M. L., & Craig, W. M. (2004). *Juvenile delinquency: Understanding the origins of individual differences*. Washington, DC: American Psychological Association.

Rich, P. (2000). *Juvenile Risk Assessment Tool*. Barre, MA: Stetson School.

Rich, P. (2003) *Understanding, assessing and rehabilitating juvenile sex offenders*. Hoboken, NJ: Wiley.

Righthand, S., Knight, R., & Prentky, R. (2002, October). *A path analytic investigation of proximal antecedents of J-SOAP risk domains*. Paper presented at the annual meeting of the Association for the Treatment of Sexual Abusers, Montreal, Quebec, Canada.

Ryan, G., & Lane, S. (1997). *Juvenile sexual offending: Causes, consequences, and correction*. San Francisco. Jossey-Bass.

Salter, A. C. (1988). *Treating child sex offenders and victims*. Newbury Park, CA: Sage.

Serin, R. C., & Brown, S. L. (2000). The clinical use of the Hare Psychopathy Checklist—Revised in contemporary risk assessment. In C. G. Gacono (Ed.), *The clinical and forensic assessment of psychopathy* (pp. 251–268). Mahwah, NJ: Erlbaum.

Stien, P. T., & Kendall, J. (2004). *Psychological trauma and the developing brain: Neurologically based interventions for troubled children*. Binghamton, NY: Haworth Press.

Thornton, D. (2000, March). *Structured risk assessment*. Paper presented at Sinclair Seminars' Sex Offender Re-Offense Risk Prediction Symposium, Madison, Wisconsin. Available: *www.sinclairseminars.com*.

Ward, T., Laws, D. R., & Hudson, S. M. (2003). *Sexual deviance: Issues and controversies*. Thousand Oaks, CA: Sage.

Webster, C. D., Ben-Aron, M. H., & Hucker, S. J. (1985). *Dangerousness: Probability and prediction, psychiatry and public policy*. Cambridge, UK: Cambridge University Press.

Webster, C. D., Harris, G. T., Rice, M. E., Cormier, C. A., & Quinsey, V. L. (1994). *The Violence Prediction Scheme: Assessing dangerousness in high risk men*. Toronto, Canada: Centre of Criminology, University of Toronto.

Webster, C. D., Hucker, S. J., & Bloom, H. (2002). Transcending the actuarial versus clinical polemic in assessing risk for violence. *Criminal Justice and Behavior, 29*, 659–665.

Williams, M. (1975). Aspects of the psychology of imprisonment. In S. McConville (Ed.), *The use of imprisonment: Essays in the changing state of English penal policy* (pp. 32–42). London: Routledge & Kegan Paul.

Worling, J. R., & Curwen, T. (2000a). Adolescent sexual offender recidivism: Success of specialized treatment and implications for risk prediction. *Child Abuse and Neglect, 24,* 965–982.

Worling, J. R., & Curwen, T. (2001). *Estimate of Risk of Adolescent Sexual Offense Recidivism (ERASOR) Version 2.0.* Toronto, Ontario, Canada: Sexual Abuse Family Education & Treatment (SAFE-T).

Zamble, E., & Quinsey, V. L. (1997). *The criminal recidivism process.* New York: Cambridge University Press.

Zolondek, S. C., Abel, G. G., Northey, W. F., & Jordan, A. D. (2001). The self-reported behaviors of juvenile sex offenders. *Journal of Interpersonal Violence, 16,* 73–85.

Chapter 18

Assessing Sexual Offense Risk for Adolescents Who Have Offended Sexually

by James R. Worling, Ph.D. , C.Psych.

OVERVIEW

When confronted with the number of juvenile sex offenders who are being identified in the community, it is crucial that adequate means of identifying their risk be developed. Several methods are being developed to help professionals make decisions on placement and treatment for this population. These include the J-SOAP by Prentky and Righthand (2001, 2003) and the Estimate of Risk of Adolescent Sexual Offense Recidivism (ERASOR) developed by Worling (Worling & Curwen, 2001). This chapter discusses a variety of risk factors. In addition, this chapter evaluates several approaches to the assessment process.

INTRODUCTION

When one is asked to conduct an assessment for an adolescent who has committed a sexual offense, and the question of "risk" is raised by the referral source, most clinicians focus exclusively on the risk of a sexual reoffense. The estimate of sexual recidivism risk is a critical objective of an assessment as the findings affect significant decisions such as the adolescent's placement and the nature and intensity of any treatment. Although this chapter focuses exclusively on sexual reoffense risk, it is important to be aware that additional risks could be present for an adolescent who has offended sexually. For example, it would also be prudent for assessors to address the risk of general criminality, the risk of self-harm and suicide, the risk of substance dependence, the risk of academic failure, and the risk of the adolescent's own sexual, physical, or emotional victimization.

PUBLISHED SEXUAL ASSAULT RECIDIVISM DATA

It is difficult to establish a reliable base rate of sexual assault recidivism for adolescents as there are only a handful of published studies and the findings vary considerably from 0 percent to more than 40 percent (Worling & Långström, 2003). This variability appears to be attributable, in part, to features of the investigation such as the length of the follow-up period, the definition of "recidivism" (i.e., self-report, criminal charges, and convictions), the population studied, the impact of treatment interventions, and the breadth of the data collection efforts (e.g., local vs. statewide vs. national databases). It would not be surprising, therefore, for researchers to find extremely low recidivism rates from an investigation of successfully treated youth attending a community-based clinic using locally collected data, a brief follow-up period, and a conservative recidivism estimate such as self-report. Conversely, higher reoffense rates are more likely when investigators use nationally based data, longer follow-up periods, less conservative recidivism estimates, and data from adolescents who were initially assessed with more high-risk markers. For example, using self-report data, Mazur and Michael (1992) reported a 0 percent sexual assault recidivism rate using a six-month follow-up period with youth who completed community-based treatment. At the other extreme, using a national database of criminal convictions, Långström (2002) found a 30 percent sexual reoffense rate in untreated youths referred for a psychiatric evaluation following an average of nine and a half years.

Even if it were possible to titrate a reliable base rate from the limited published studies, it is important to be mindful of the fact that the accuracy of officially record-ed reoffense data is contingent upon many variable factors, such as the victimized per-son's willingness to report the offense, the ability of child protection agencies and/or the police to investigate the official complaint, the accurate and timely entry of the arrest or charge into a database, and the ability of the researcher to access the official data. Presently, it is perhaps reasonable to conclude that although *most* adolescents will not be detected for subsequent sexual assaults over a period of five to ten years, there is certainly a subgroup of adolescents who are at high risk of reoffending sexu-ally at the time of their assessment. The task for the evaluator, of course, is to identi-fy those adolescents by assessing the relevant risk factors.

SEXUAL REOFFENSE RISK FACTORS

To identify relevant reoffense risk factors for adolescents who have offended sex-ually, a narrative review of the published literature was recently completed (Worling & Långström, 2003). In that review, risk factors were grouped into four categories: *empirically supported*, *promising*, *possible*, and *unlikely*. Risk factors were catego-rized based on (1) data from the twenty published follow-up studies of adolescents who had offended sexually and (2) guidelines and checklists that have been developed by expert practitioners in the field. These latter documents represent attempts to struc-ture clinical observations and assumptions concerning factors related to reoffense risk. Furthermore, when available, findings were also compared with data from meta-analyses on risk factors for recidivism in adults who offended sexually (Hanson & Bussière, 1998), serious or violent offending (including sexual offending) among ado-lescents in the general population (Lipsey & Derzon, 1998), and general criminal recidivism in adolescents (Cottle, Lee, & Heilbrun, 2001).

Empirically Supported Risk Factors

Risk factors were included in this category if two conditions were met: (1) there were at least two independent, empirical investigations in the published literature link-ing the risk factor to sexual reoffending for a group of adolescents; (2) there were no contradictory findings in the literature. Given the fact that these risk factors have the most defensible empirical support at the present time, relative to the other risk factors described later, they should be relied on most in the assessment.of sexual reoffending risk for adolescents. Although it was not a necessary condition for factors to be included in this section, many of the popular risk assessment checklists and guidelines have also included these factors as important to consider. Finally, several of these risk factors for adolescents have also been found to be significant in follow-up research with adults who have offended sexually.

Deviant Sexual Interests. Adolescents who have offended sexually and who are presently sexually interested in prepubescent children and/or in sexual violence are at increased risk of reoffending sexually. Schram, Milloy, and Rowe (1992) found higher sexual assault recidivism rates for those adolescents rated by clinicians as most likely to have deviant sexual interests. Kenny, Keogh, and Seidler (2001) reported that adolescents with a history of a prior sexual assault charge ("recidivists") were more likely to report sexual fantasies that reflected the use of force or sexual activity with younger children. Finally, Worling and Curwen (2000) found that self-reported sexual interest in children was a significant risk factor for sexual reoffending. In addition to these investigations, several authors of risk assessment guidelines for adolescents have suggested that deviant sexual interests increase the risk for sexual reoffending (Calder, Hanks, & Epps, 1997; Epps, 1997; Lane, 1997; Rich, 2001; Ross & Loss, 1991).

Although deviant sexual interest as measured by penile plethysmography (PPG) is a robust predictor of sexual reoffending for *adults* (Hanson & Bussière, 1998), Gretton, McBride, Hare, O'Shaughnessy, and Kumka (2001) reported that deviant arousal assessed by PPG was *not* related to sexual assault recidivism for adolescents. Therefore, empirical support for the link between deviant sexual interest and adolescent sexual assault recidivism is presently limited to self-report information and/or therapist ratings.

Prior Criminal Sanctions for Sexual Offending. Adolescents who have continued to commit sexual offenses despite prior involvement of the legal system are at higher risk of reoffending sexually. Schram et al. (1992) found that adolescents with at least one conviction for a sexual assault prior to the index sexual offense were significantly more likely to reoffend sexually. In investigations by Långström and Grann (2000) and Långström (2002), a history of prior sexual offenses was related to sexual assault recidivism. In their checklist of risk factors, Ross and Loss (1991) also noted that a prior criminal charge was a risk factor for sexual assault recidivism. In research with adults who have offended sexually, a history of prior charges or convictions for sexual assaults is predictive of sexual reoffending (Hanson & Bussière, 1998).

Sexual Offenses Against More Than One Victim. Adolescents who have committed sexual offenses against two or more victims are at higher risk of reoffending sexually. Both Långström (2002) and Worling (2002) reported that adolescents who offended against two or more victims were significantly more likely to be charged or convicted for a subsequent sexual crime than were adolescents with one known victim. Although Rasmussen (1999) found no correlation between sexual recidivism and the number of male victims for a group of adolescents, she did report that the number of female victims was significantly related to subsequent sexual offenses. A history of sexual offenses against multiple victims is considered a risk factor in a number of risk assessment checklists and guidelines (Epps, 1997; Lane, 1997; Perry & Orchard, 1992; Ross & Loss, 1991; Steen & Monnette, 1989). In research with adults, it is challenging to comment on this risk factor as researchers most frequently comment on the number of charges and/or convictions rather than on the number of victims, per se.

Sexual Offense Against a Stranger Victim. Adolescents who have committed a sexual offense against a stranger are at greater risk of reoffending sexually. Smith and Monastersky (1986) and Långström (2002) reported that a past sexual offense against a stranger victim was associated with sexual assault recidivism for adolescents. In their clinical checklist, Ross and Loss (1991) also listed a past sexual offense against a stranger as a potential risk factor. In research with primarily adult males who had offended sexually, a past sexual assault against a stranger is significantly related to sexual assault recidivism (Hanson & Bussière, 1998).

Social Isolation. Adolescents who have committed a sexual offense and who are socially isolated, or who struggle in their relationships with peers, are at higher risk to commit further sexual offenses. Långström and Grann (2000) reported that those adolescents who had few social contacts were more than three times more likely to be reconvicted for a sexual crime. Similarly, Kenny et al. (2001) found that those adolescents who displayed poor social skills and who had poor relationships with peers were more likely to have a history of a prior sexual assault charge ("recidivists"). In their meta-analysis of risk factors regarding violent (including sexual) recidivism, Lipsey and Derzon (1998) reported that social isolation was a robust risk factor for adolescents.

In addition to the empirical support, many authors of risk assessment checklists and guidelines also suggest that evidence of social isolation or other social difficulties reflects greater risk (Epps, 1997; Lane, 1997; Perry & Orchard, 1992; Rich, 2001; Ross & Loss, 1991). Hanson (2000) stated that one of the more promising dynamic, or potentially changeable, risk factors for adults who have offended sexually is the inability to form and/or maintain intimate relationships.

Uncompleted Sexual-Offense-Specific Treatment. Data from three investigations suggest that adolescents who complete comprehensive treatment—combining a family-relationship component with offense-specific interventions—are less likely to reoffend sexually or generally (Borduin, Henggeler, Blaske, & Stein, 1990; Seabloom, Seabloom, Seabloom, Barron, & Hendrickson, 2003; Worling & Curwen, 2000). Authors of most clinically based risk guidelines list unwillingness to engage in treatment as a risk factor for sexual reoffending (Epps, 1997; Lane, 1997; Perry & Orchard, 1992; Rich, 2001; Ross & Loss, 1991; Steen & Monnette, 1989). In a recent meta-analysis of treatment outcome, treatment for primarily adult males who have offended sexually leads to a significant reduction in recidivism (Hanson et al., 2002).

Promising Risk Factors

These risk factors have been listed in risk assessment checklists or guidelines, and they are supported by a single published study focused specifically on adolescent sexual assault recidivism. Although assessors will likely want to examine these factors when formulating a risk estimate, they presently have limited empirical support.

Problematic Parent-Adolescent Relationships. Adolescents with a history of sexual offending who currently have a problematic relationship with a parent are likely at increased risk of further sexual assaults. Worling and Curwen (2000) reported a moderate correlation (.21) between perceived parental rejection and subsequent sexual assault recidivism in adolescents. Poor parent-child relationships were related to later violent (including sexual) offending in a meta-analysis of risk factors for criminal behavior in adolescents and young adults (Lipsey & Derzon, 1998).

In their risk assessment guidelines, Ross and Loss (1991) and Lane (1997) suggested that the quality of the parent-child relationship is related to risk of sexual reoffending. There has been very little research regarding family-of-origin relationships and sexual assault recidivism in adult populations. However, Hanson and Bussière (1998) reported that adult males who described negative relationships with their mothers were more likely to reoffend sexually.

Attitudes Supportive of Sexual Offending. Adolescents who believe that victims are responsible for their sexual assault, that victims are unharmed by sexual assault, or that victims somehow "invite" sexual assaults may be more likely to continue than are adolescents who do not share these views. In the only study that has been focused on this factor, Kahn and Chambers (1991) found that adolescents who blamed their victims were more likely to have a subsequent conviction for a sexual offense. Authors of risk assessment guidelines note that offense-supportive attitudes such as victim blame and the belief that sexual assaults are not wrong or harmful are risk indicators (Calder et al., 1997; Epps, 1997; Perry & Orchard, 1992). In research with adults, attitudes supportive of sexual offending are related to increased risk for sexual reoffending (e.g., Hanson & Harris, 1998; Hudson, Wales, Bakker, & Ward, 2002; Thornton, 2002).

Possible Risk Factors

The following risk factors are presently viewed by some authors as related to sexual assault recidivism. However, one should use caution when basing risk assessments on these factors given the current lack of empirical support. Many of the risk factors in this category have never been examined empirically; others have been investigated but the results are conflicting across studies.

High-Stress Family Environment. Several risk assessment guidelines and checklists include extreme family dysfunction or distress as a risk factor for adolescent sexual reoffending (Lane, 1997; Perry & Orchard, 1992; Rich, 2001; Ross & Loss, 1991; Steen & Monnette, 1989; Wenet & Clark, 1986). In their meta-analysis of research regarding risk factors for violence (including sexual violence) among adolescents, Lipsey and Derzon (1998) found that family distress was correlated with recidivism. As noted earlier, the influence of family-of-origin relationships has not been examined often in recidivism research with adults who sexually offend.

Impulsivity. Epps (1997), Lane (1997), and Rich (2001) suggested that impulsive adolescents are at greater risk to reoffend sexually. To date, this risk factor has not been examined empirically with adolescents. Of course, there is certainly considerable evidence that general impulsivity is related to general juvenile delinquency and non-sexual reoffending (e.g., Cottle et al., 2001; Lipsey & Derzon, 1998). In a discussion of the more promising dynamic risk factors for adult sexual offense recidivism, Hanson (2000) suggested that general self-regulation is important to consider.

Antisocial Personality; Psychopathy. Although a history of nonsexual delinquency, or a current antisocial orientation, has been suggested as a risk factor for continued sexual assaults in most risk guidelines and checklists (Epps, 1997; Lane, 1997; Perry & Orchard, 1992; Rich, 2001; Ross & Loss, 1991), the empirical support for such an association is lacking. For example, Gretton et al. (2001) and Långström and Grann (2000) found no association between psychopathy and subsequent sexual assault recidivism. Similarly, Worling and Curwen (2000) found that those adolescents with antisocial personality features were not more likely to reoffend sexually. On the other hand, however, there was a significant association between an antisocial orientation and *general* criminal recidivism in all three investigations. In their meta-analysis, Hanson and Bussière (1998) found that an antisocial personality was related to both sexual and nonsexual recidivism for adults.

Past Interpersonal Aggression. Several authors of risk assessment checklists and guidelines for adolescents suggest that a history of interpersonal aggression is related to the risk of continued sexual offending (Epps, 1997; Perry & Orchard, 1992; Rich, 2001; Ross & Loss, 1991; Wenet & Clark, 1986). In the one study that has been done regarding this factor, Långström (2002) found no relationship between prior violent nonsexual criminal convictions and sexual assault recidivism risk among adolescents. Although few investigators have addressed this factor in research with adults who have offended sexually, Hanson and Bussière (1998) reported a small correlation between anger problems and sexual assault recidivism in their meta-analysis. It may be that the current use of interpersonal aggression is more related to future risk of sexual assault recidivism than a past history of aggression toward others.

Association With Antisocial Peers. In their risk assessment checklists, Rich (2001) and Ross and Loss (1991) have suggested that adolescents with a history of sexual offending who continue to associate with antisocial peers are at an increased risk of reoffending sexually. Although this variable is clearly linked to the onset of general juvenile delinquency (Cottle et al., 2001) and to general criminal recidivism in adolescents (Lipsey & Derzon, 1998), the influence of peers has yet to be examined empirically with adolescents who have offended sexually. Research regarding the impact of peer associations on adult sexual assault recidivism is also quite limited; however, Hanson (2000) stated that adults who associate with peers who support deviant lifestyles or inadequate coping strategies are at greater risk of reoffending sexually.

Sexual Preoccupation/Obsession. Authors of risk assessment guidelines for adolescents note the need to assess sexual preoccupation (Epps, 1997; Lane, 1997; Steen & Monnette, 1989), compulsive ideation regarding past offenses (Perry & Orchard, 1992), and compulsive, deviant masturbatory fantasies (Ross & Loss, 1991; Wenet & Clark, 1986). Although this variable has yet to be examined in research with adolescents, Hanson (2000) described sexual preoccupation as a promising dynamic risk factor for adults who have offended sexually.

Past Sexual Offense Against a Male Victim. In research with adults, an increase in the risk of sexual reoffending is found for males who victimize male children (Hanson & Bussière, 1998). At this point, the findings for adolescents are contradictory. In two investigations, the past selection of a male victim was positively associated with future sexual reoffending (Långström & Grann, 2000; Smith & Monastersky, 1986) whereas there was no relationships found in two other investigations (Rasmussen, 1999; Worling & Curwen, 2000).

Past Sexual Offense Against a Child Victim. Rich (2001) and Ross and Loss (1991) suggested that adolescents who commit a sexual offense against a younger child are at higher risk to reoffend sexually. To date, however, data from retrospective studies with adolescents who have offended sexually are mixed. Some authors have found that a past sexual offense against a young child is not related to subsequent sexual offending (Hagan & Cho, 1996; Långström, 2002; Rasmussen, 1999; Smith & Monastersky, 1986; Worling & Curwen, 2000), whereas both Kahn and Chambers (1991) and Sipe, Jensen, and Everett (1998) found that this factor increased the likelihood of a sexual reoffense. Perhaps victim age, like victim gender, is a weaker marker of risk for sexual recidivism in adolescents given that sexual preferences are usually not as "fixed" for teens compared to adults. It is important to note, however, that Hanson and Bussière (1998) found that the choice of a child victim was unrelated to reoffense status in their meta-analysis of primarily adults.

Use of Threats, Violence, or Weapons in Previous Sexual Offense. Many authors of risk assessment checklists and guidelines suggest that adolescents who use and/or threaten violence during their sexual assaults are at an elevated risk of reoffending sexually (Epps, 1997; Lane, 1997; Perry & Orchard, 1992; Rich, 2001; Ross & Loss, 1991; Steen & Monnette, 1989; Wenet & Clark, 1986). Currently, the research support for this risk factor is mixed. Although Kahn and Chambers (1991) found that adolescents who made verbal threats during their sexual assaults were more likely to reoffend sexually, Långström (2002) found that the use of weapons or death threats was related to nonsexual violent reoffending but *not* to subsequent sexual assaults. It should be pointed out that Hanson and Bussière (1998) found that the past use of force and physical victim injury were *not* related to sexual assault recidivism in their meta-analysis of studies of primarily adults.

Environment Supporting Reoffending. It seems logical to assume that if an adolescent is going to be spending time in an environment that supports opportunities for continued sexual offending, the risk of a sexual offense will be higher. For example, poor adult supervision and access to pornography and potential victims could increase risk for some adolescents. Epps (1997) and Ross and Loss (1991) suggested that adolescents who have unsupervised access to potential victims are at higher risk to reoffend sexually. Despite the intuitive logic, there are few data related to this factor available with either adolescents or adults. In one investigation with adults, however, Hanson and Harris (1998) found that sexual assault recidivists were more likely than nonrecidivists to place themselves in situations providing greater access to victims.

Unlikely Risk Factors

The factors listed in this section should *not* be used at the present time when formulating risk estimates for adolescent sexual-offense recidivism. This is based on the fact that empirical evidence collected thus far is not supportive of these factors.

Adolescent's Own History of Sexual Victimization. Some authors have suggested that adolescents who have a childhood sexual victimization history are at greater risk of reoffending sexually (Perry & Orchard, 1992; Rich, 2001; Steen & Monnette, 1989; Wenet & Clark, 1986). On the contrary, however, the available published data indicate that a childhood sexual abuse history (measured dichotomously) is *not* predictive of sexual reoffending (Hagan & Cho, 1996; Rasmussen, 1999; Worling & Curwen, 2000). Although childhood sexual abuse may be linked—under some conditions—to the *onset* of adolescent sexual offending for some adolescents (Borowsky, Hogan, & Ireland, 1997; Morris, Anderson, & Knox, 2002), there is no support for this variable as a risk marker for *continued* sexual offending once an adolescent has been detected. Turning to research with adults, it may be interesting to note that Hanson and Bussière (1998) reported no relationship between an offending adult's childhood sexual victimization history and the risk of sexual offense recidivism.

History of Nonsexual Offending. A common clinical assumption is that a history of nonsexual crimes is a risk marker for continued sexual offending for adolescents (Epps, 1997; Perry & Orchard, 1992; Rich, 2001; Ross & Loss, 1991; Wenet & Clark, 1986). Although a history of nonsexual criminal charges is related to the risk of continued sexual assaults for *adult* males (Hanson & Bussière, 1998), researchers have consistently demonstrated that this variable is *not* related to subsequent *sexual* offenses among adolescents (Kahn & Chambers, 1991; Lab, Shields, & Schondel, 1993; Långström, 2002; Sipe et al., 1998; Rasmussen, 1999; Worling & Curwen, 2000). As to be expected, most researchers have found that a history of nonsexual crimes is related to an increased risk of *nonsexual* reoffending for adolescents who have offended sexually.

Denial of Sexual Offending. Adolescents who deny that they committed their sexual assaults are often assumed to be at higher risk of reoffending sexually (Epps, 1997; Perry & Orchard, 1992; Rich, 2001; Ross & Loss, 1991; Steen & Monnette, 1989; Wenet & Clark, 1986). On the contrary, however, all available research indicates that adolescents who deny their sexual crimes are *less* likely to reoffend sexually (Kahn & Chambers, 1991; Långström & Grann 2000; Worling, 2002). Perhaps some mechanisms that result in denial of the sexual offense (e.g., extreme shame, embarrassment, or fear of sanctions) also act somehow to reduce the odds of a future sexual offense. In their meta-analysis of studies of primarily adult males, Hanson and Bussière (1998) found no relation between denial of the sexual offense and sexual assault recidivism.

Lack of Empathy for Victim. Most authors of risk assessment guidelines include lack of remorse or empathy as evidence of heightened risk for sexual reoffending for adolescents (Epps, 1997; Perry & Orchard, 1992; Rich, 2001; Ross & Loss, 1991; Steen & Monnette, 1989; Wenet & Clark, 1986). At the present time, however, there are no supporting data for this position. For example, Smith and Monastersky (1986) found no relation between subsequent sexual offenses and the adolescent's ability to understand the exploitative nature of the sexual offense. Similarly, Långström and Grann (2000) found that adolescents with low general empathy were no more at risk of being reconvicted for a sexual crime than those with more general empathy. In their meta-analysis concerning adults who offended sexually, Hanson and Bussière (1998) also found no relation between low empathy for victims and sexual assault recidivism.

Many measures of victim empathy assess the client's ability to recognize emotional distress in others. Although this is an important component of empathy, very few existing measures tap compassion for others. If researchers devised different measures of victim empathy or compassion, they might find support for the use of this variable.

APPROACHES TO RISK ASSESSMENT

Unstructured Clinical Judgment vs. Risk Assessment Checklists

Presently, many clinicians base their risk estimates on unstructured clinical judgment when asked to assess future risk for adolescents. However, there are serious concerns regarding the accuracy of unstructured clinical judgment with respect to predicting sexual assault recidivism (Hanson, 2002). To provide more structured judgments regarding future risk, some assessors use one or more of the popular risk assessment checklists or guidelines (Calde et al., 1997; Epps, 1997; Lane, 1997; Perry & Orchard, 1992; Rich, 2001; Ross & Loss, 1991; Steen & Monnette, 1989; Wenet & Clark, 1986). These tools represent attempts to structure clinical judgment by listing factors assumed to be related to heightened risk. At the present time, however, there are no published data to support these guidelines or checklists in their present form. Furthermore, there are some factors contained within some of the checklists that are no longer supported by published research (e.g., denial of the index sexual offense). It is also important to point out that most of the checklists and guidelines do not have objective scoring rules; therefore, it would be difficult to assess or enhance interrater agreement.

There are also some clinicians who assess adolescents using actuarial risk assessment instruments that have been developed and validated based on research with adults. Despite the appeal of an actuarial estimate, it should be stressed that there is no research to support the use of adult risk instruments with adolescents. Furthermore, there are some obvious adult risk factors (e.g., age less than 25 years and single marital status) that are nonsensical to use with adolescents.

Empirically Guided Structured Checklists

Although there have not yet been enough follow-up investigations of adolescents with a history of sexual offending to build and test an actuarial tool, simply identifying relevant risk factors is an important first step. These identified risk factors could then be used to inform clinical decisions in what Hanson (2000) has called *empirically guided clinical judgment*. Using this approach to risk assessment, there is no link between a total score and a specific probability of reoffense within a specific time frame as there is using actuarial scales. Rather, the estimate of risk remains a clinical judgment. The advantage of empirically guided clinical judgment in comparison to both unstructured clinical prediction and the available risk assessment checklists and guidelines is that there is the promise of higher accuracy given the scientific evidence in favor of the risk factors. Furthermore, the empirically guided approach is more systematic and should lead to better agreement among professionals (Boer, Hart, Kropp, & Webster, 1997).

At this time, there are two such instruments in use in North America that have been described as promising (Doren, 2002; Leversee & Pearson, 2001): the Juvenile Sexual Offender Assessment Protocol (J-SOAP; Prentky & Righthand, 2001, 2003) and the Estimate of Risk of Adolescent Sexual Offense Recidivism (ERASOR; Worling & Curwen, 2001). Both risk assessment tools offer explicit scoring instructions for a fixed number of risk factors, and both are designed to assist with an estimate of the risk of a sexual reoffense for individuals ages 12 to 18.

Juvenile Sex Offender Assessment Protocol. The original version of the J-SOAP had scoring criteria for twenty-three factors in four risk domains: (1) Sexual Drive/Sexual Preoccupation, (2) Impulsive, Antisocial Behavior, (3) Clinical/Treatment, and (4) Community Adjustment. The sixteen factors included in the first two risk domains were static, or historical, factors, whereas the remaining nine factors in the last two domains were dynamic, or potentially alterable, risk factors. Based on file-review data for juveniles ages 9–20, the authors reported interrater agreement (using Pearson r) ranging from .59 to .91, with most values above .80 (Prentky, Harris, Frizzell, & Righthand, 2000). With respect to concurrent validity, the J-SOAP appears to be highly related to general juvenile delinquency. For example, the authors reported a substantial correlation of .91 between the J-SOAP total score and the total score from the Youth Level of Service/Case Management Inventory (YLS/CMI; Hoge & Andrews, 2003), an actuarial measure of risk for general juvenile delinquency.

The J-SOAP was revised in 2001 based on an analysis of preliminary psychometric data, and Prentky and Righthand (2001) presented very encouraging results regarding the revised, twenty-six-item (sixteen static and ten dynamic factors) measure with respect to interrater agreement, internal consistency, and item-total correlations. Promising results regarding the postdictive validity of modified and partial J-SOAP scores based on archival data have also been presented (Hecker, Scoular, Righthand, & Nangle, 2002; Waite, Pinkerton, Wieckowski, McGarvey, & Brown, 2002).

In 2003, the J-SOAP was revised once again based on a reanalysis of the available research regarding adolescent sexual assault recidivism and the psychometric properties of the previous version. The most recent, twenty-eight-item J-SOAP-II is available free of charge at *www.csom.org* and its authors are actively involved in further research with the scale. Although the J-SOAP was designed to be an actuarial risk assessment tool, and users are instructed to calculate a total score, the authors stress that it should presently be used only as a checklist for the systematic review of risk factors given the lack of prospective follow-up data.

The Estimate of Risk of Adolescent Sexual Offense Recidivism. The J-SOAP has been developed and tested as an instrument that can be coded from archival file data, and the majority of the risk factors are static, or historical, in nature. In contrast, the ERASOR was constructed to be used by evaluators following a comprehensive clinical assessment, and most of the risk factors assessed are dynamic so that treatment targets can be identified and reevaluated. The ERASOR was modeled after the Sexual Violence Risk (SVR-20; Boer et al., 1997), an empirically guided clinical checklist for adults who have offended sexually. Unlike the J-SOAP, a total score is not computed with the ERASOR.

The ERASOR was developed following initial field testing in 2000 with a pilot version at the Sexual Abuse: Family Education and Treatment (SAFE-T) Program in Toronto, Canada. The twenty-five risk factors included in the current version of the ERASOR (Version 2.0; Worling & Curwen, 2001) fall into five categories: (1) Sexual Interests, Attitudes, and Behaviors, (2) Historical Sexual Assaults, (3) Psychosocial Functioning, (4) Family/Environmental Functioning, and (5) Treatment. The sixteen dynamic items (all but the nine Historical Sexual Assault items) are coded using a six-month time frame. The ERASOR coding manual contains information regarding the rationale for the inclusion of each risk factor, and specific coding instructions are provided such that factors are rated as either *Not present, Possibly or partially present, Present,* or *Unknown.*

Studies of the reliability and validity of the ERASOR are under way in North America and Europe, and preliminary data are supportive. In one such investigation (Worling, 2004), ratings were collected from twenty-eight master's- and doctoral-level clinicians immediately following comprehensive assessments of 136 adolescents. With respect to interrater agreement, average-rating intraclass correlation coefficients (ICC) were at or above .70 for twenty-two of the twenty-five ERASOR factors, and the average-rating ICC for the overall risk rating for risk of sexual reoffending ("low," "moderate," or "high") was .92. For preliminary evidence of validity, it was found that overall clinician ratings (i.e., "high," "moderate," or "low") were moderately efficient in differentiating adolescents with a history of offending sexually after being sanctioned previously by an adult ("repeaters") versus those who had never been sanctioned ("non-repeaters"; area under the receiver operating characteristic [ROC] curve = .66; 95 percent CI = .55-.76). An artificial total score was similarly moderately efficient in differentiating between repeaters and nonrepeaters (area under the ROC curve =.72; 95 percent CI = .62 - .80). As in the case of the J-SOAP, however, *prospective* follow-up data regarding the predictive validity of the ERASOR are not yet available. The ERASOR manual is also available free of charge as a pdf file by contacting the author by email (*jworling@ican.net*).

CONDUCTING RISK ASSESSMENTS WITH ADOLESCENTS

Regardless of the specific approach that is taken to formulate a risk estimate, or the instrument that is used, a number of important issues should be considered when conducting risk assessments with adolescents (cf. Boer et al., 1997; Borum, 2000).

1. Assessors should have sufficient training and supervised experience regarding the assessment of adolescents who have offended sexually— and their families. This would include knowledge of the current research regarding assessment, treatment, and sexual offense recidivism.

2. Assessors should be guided, wherever possible, by the existing research and best-practice policies that have been based on work with *adolescents*. Although many risk factors for adults and adolescents are overlapping, there are unique risk factors for each age group and there is no evidence to support the view that an actuarial tool developed and tested for use with adults can produce valid results for adolescents.

3. Assessors should cover multiple domains of the adolescent's functioning including sexual (e.g., sexual interests and attitudes), intrapersonal (e.g., affective expression and impulsivity), interpersonal (e.g., social involvement and aggression), familial (e.g., parent-child relationships and family distress), and biological (e.g., neuropsychiatric and physical health) domains.

4. Information should be collected from multiple informants, wherever possible, such as the adolescent, police (including victim statements), child protection/social services, family members, residential staff, and other mental health professionals who are familiar with the adolescent and his or her family. Risk assessments based on information collected solely from the adolescent should be interpreted with considerable caution given the impact of factors such as shame, embarrassment, and fear of legal consequences.

5. Assessors should use multiple methods of data collection including interviews (with the adolescent and other informants), psychological tests, reviews of prior assessments and case notes, and direct behavioral observation.

6. Assessors should collect information regarding both static (historic and unchangeable) and dynamic (variable and potentially changeable) factors.

COMMUNICATING RISK ESTIMATES

Risk estimates can lead to significant and irreversible consequences for the adolescent, his or her family, and the community. As such, any estimate of risk for future sexual reoffending should be made with the appropriate limitations and qualifications. Too often, risk estimates for adolescents are made without reference to the quality of the information gathered, the empirical support for the judgments, and the need to reevaluate risk (Hoge, 2002). The following suggestions were inspired by previous work by Boer et al. (1997):

1. Assessors should inform recipients of risk judgments about the current scientific limitations of estimating the risk of offense recidivism. For instance, it is essential to communicate that *precise* evaluations of risk for individual adolescents are impossible.

2. Assessors should note any limitations specific to the assessment at hand (and the impact of these limitations), such as lack of detailed information from the victim(s), use of experimental psychological tests, or the lack of access to parents, for example.

3. Those evaluating risk should stress that their estimates of recidivism risk are strictly time limited. Extensive, and often rapid, social, physical, sexual, emotional, and/or cognitive developmental changes take place during adolescence. As such, conclusions drawn at one point in time may be quite inaccurate after the passage of a brief period of time. Furthermore, much of the follow-up research that has been used to examine risk factors for adolescents is based on average follow-up periods of four years or less. It would be a daunting task to formulate long-term risk estimates of sexual reoffending for adolescents at the present time as there are *no* published data to support that such estimates can be made.

4. It would be ideal for evaluators to make sexual assault recidivism estimates as specific as possible. For example, the evaluator should try whenever possible to specify qualitative aspects of potential reoffending such as imminence and most likely targets.

5. Assessors should justify their risk estimates by referring to the presence (or absence) of specific risk (or protective) factors. It would be helpful for both the adolescent and the other consumers to have an explanation for the resultant risk evaluation.

6. Assessors should list, wherever possible, circumstances that might exacerbate the short-term risk of reoffending for each youth. For example, proximity to preschool-age males or availability of a certain form of sexual media could be noted if they were anticipated to increase risk for a particular adolescent.

7. Assessors should list the strategies they believe would be helpful in managing and reducing the adolescent's risk to reoffend. In addition to therapeutic interventions, this may include recommendations regarding placement, community supervision, and timing and intensity of family reunification.

CONCLUSION

With the increasing reliance on actuarials in making life-affecting choices, professionals have been tempted to use risk assessment tools in making decisions involving juveniles. Although the authors of at least one of these instruments caution against their use with adolescents, they do not take a strong stance against this practice (Harris, Phenix, Hanson, & Thornton, 2003). Yet, as mentioned earlier in this chapter, the grading of the most popular of these tools may be meaningless when applied to youthful offenders (e.g., giving an adolescent points for being under 25). Furthermore, some adult risk factors, such as denial, actually have the opposite influence on young people. In this chapter the empirically based risk factors for juveniles are discussed and recommendations offered for conducting these assessments. It is hoped that professionals in the field will recognize the very significant differences in these populations and make decisions only after acquainting themselves with the research relevant to that group.

Author's Note

I am indebted to Dr. Niklas Långström for his exceptional contributions to previous documents that we wrote together (Worling & Långström, 2003) on which this chapter is based. Many thanks also to Barbara Rodgers, Program Director, for her continued support of research at the Sexual Abuse: Family Education and Treatment (SAFE-T) Program, Thistletown Regional Centre. The views expressed herein are mine and do not necessarily represent those of the Ontario Ministry of Community and Social Services.

References

Boer, D. P., Hart, S. D., Kropp, P. R., & Webster, C. D. (1997). *Manual for the Sexual Violence Risk-20*. Burnaby, British Columbia: Mental Health, Law, and Policy Institute, Simon Fraser University.

Borduin, C. M., Henggeler, S. W., Blaske, D. M., & Stein, R. J. (1990). Multisystemic treatment of adolescent sexual offenders. *International Journal of Offender Therapy and Comparative Criminology, 34*, 105–113.

Borowsky, I. M., Hogan, M., & Ireland, M. (1997). Adolescent sexual aggression: Risk and protective factors. *Pediatrics, 100*, 6, e6.

Borum, R. (2000). Assessing violence risk among youth. *Journal of Clinical Psychology, 56*, 1263–1288.

Calder, M. C., Hanks, H., & Epps, K. J. (1997). *Juveniles and children who sexually abuse: A guide to risk assessment*. Lyme Regis, Dorset, UK: Russell House.

Cottle, C. C., Lee, R. J., & Heilbrun, K. (2001). The prediction of criminal recidivism in juveniles. *Criminal Justice and Behavior, 28*, 367–394.

Doren, D. M. (2002). The state of recidivism risk assessment. *The Forum, 14*(2), 4–5.

Epps, K. J. (1997). Managing risk. In M. S. Hoghughi, S. R. Bhate, & F. Graham (Eds.), *Working with sexually abusive adolescents* (pp. 35–51). London: Sage.

Gretton, H. M., McBride, M., Hare, R. D., O'Shaughnessy, & Kumka, G. (2001). Psychopathy and recidivism in adolescent sex offenders. *Criminal Justice and Behavior, 28*, 427–449.

Hagan, M. P., & Cho, M. E. (1996). A comparison of treatment outcomes between adolescent rapists and child sexual offenders. *International Journal of Offender Therapy and Comparative Criminology, 40*, 113–122.

Hanson, R. K. (2000). *Risk assessment*. Beaverton, OR: Association for the Treatment of Sexual Abusers.

Hanson, R. K., & Bussière, M. T. (1998). Predicting relapse: A meta-analysis of sexual offender recidivism studies. *Journal of Consulting and Clinical Psychology, 66*, 348–362.

Hanson, R. K., Gordon, A., Harris, A. J., Marques, J. K., Murphy, W., Quinsey, V. L., et al. (2002). First report of the Collaborative Outcome Data Project on the effectiveness of psychological treatment for sex offenders. *Sexual Abuse: A Journal of Research and Treatment, 14*(2), 169–194.

Hanson, R. K., & Harris, A. J. R. (1998). *Dynamic predictors of sexual recidivism* (User Report 1998-01). Ottawa, Ontario: Department of the Solicitor General of Canada.

Harris, A., Phenix, A., Hanson, R. K., & Thornton, D. (2003). *STATIC-99 coding rules: Revised—2003*. Ottawa, Ontario: Department of the Solicitor General of Canada. Available: *www.sex criminals.com/library/doc.1032-1.pdf*.

Hecker, J., Scoular, J., Righthand, S., & Nangle, D. (2002, October). *Predictive validity of the J-SOAP over 10-plus years: Implications for risk assessment*. Paper presented at the annual meeting of the Association for the Treatment of Sexual Abusers, Montreal, Quebec, Canada.

Hoge, R. D. (2002). Standardized instruments for assessing risk and need in youthful offenders. *Criminal Justice and Behavior, 29*, 380–396.

Hoge, R. D., & Andrews, D. A. (2003). *The Youth Level of Service/Case Management Inventory: Manual*. Toronto, Ontario, Canada: Multi-Health Systems.

Hudson, S. M., Wales, D. S., Bakker, L., & Ward, T. (2002). Dynamic risk factors: The Kia Marama evaluation. *Sexual Abuse: A Journal of Research and Treatment, 14*, 103–119.

Kahn, T. J., & Chambers, H. J. (1991). Assessing reoffense risk with juvenile sexual offenders. *Child Welfare, 70*, 333–345.

Kenny, D. T., Keogh, T., & Seidler, K. (2001). Predictors of recidivism in Australian juvenile sex offenders: Implications for treatment. *Sexual Abuse: A Journal of Research and Treatment, 13*, 131–148.

Lab, S. P., Shields, G., & Schondel, C. (1993). Research note: An evaluation of juvenile sexual offender treatment. *Crime and Delinquency, 39*, 543–553.

Lane, S. (1997). Assessment of sexually abusive youth. In G. Ryan & S. Lane (Eds.), *Juvenile sexual offending: Causes, consequences, and correction* (rev. ed., pp. 219–263). San Francisco: Jossey-Bass.

Långström, N. (2002). Long-term follow-up of criminal recidivism in young sex offenders: Temporal patterns and risk factors. *Psychology, Crime and Law, 8*, 41–58.

Långström, N., & Grann, M. (2000). Risk for criminal recidivism among young sex offenders. *Journal of Interpersonal Violence, 15*, 855–871.

Leversee, T., & Pearson, C. (2001). Eliminating the pendulum effect: A balanced approach to the assessment, treatment, and management of sexually abusive youth. *Journal of the Center for Families, Children and the Courts, 3*, 45–57.

Lipsey, M. W., & Derzon, J. H. (1998). Predictors of violent or serious delinquency in adolescence and early adulthood: A synthesis of longitudinal research. In R. Loeber & D. P. Farrington (Eds.), *Serious and violent juvenile offenders: Risk factors and successful interventions* (pp. 86–105). London: Sage.

Mazur, T., & Michael, P. M. (1992). Outpatient treatment for adolescents with sexually inappropriate behaviour: Program description and six-month follow-up. *Journal of Offender Rehabilitation, 18*, 191–203.

Morris, R. E., Anderson, M. M., & Knox, G. W. (2002). Incarcerated adolescents' experiences as perpetrators of sexual assault. *Archives of Pediatrics and Adolescent Medicine, 156*, 831–835.

Perry, G. P., & Orchard, J. (1992). *Assessment and treatment of adolescent sex offenders*. Sarasota, FL: Professional Resource Exchange.

Prentky, R., Harris, B., Frizzell, K., & Righthand, S. (2000). An actuarial procedure for assessing risk with juvenile sexual offenders. *Sexual Abuse: A Journal of Research and Treatment, 12*(2), 71–93.

Prentky, R. A., & Righthand, S. C. (2001). *Juvenile Sex Offender Assessment Protocol: Manual*. Unpublished document. Available: *www.csom.org*.

Prentky, R., & Righthand, S. (2003). *Juvenile Sex Offender Assessment Protocol—II (JSOAP-II)*. Available: *www.csom.org*.

Rasmussen, L. A. (1999). Factors related to recidivism among juvenile sexual offenders. *Sexual Abuse: A Journal of Research and Treatment, 11*, 69–85.

Rich, P. (2001). *J-RAT: Juvenile (Clinical) Risk Assessment Tool—Assessment of risk for sexual reoffending*. Unpublished document, Stetson School, Barre, MA.

Ross, J., & Loss, P. (1991). Assessment of the juvenile sex offender. In G. D. Ryan, & S. L. Lane (Eds.), *Juvenile sexual offending: Causes, consequences, and correction* (pp. 199–251). Lexington, MA: Lexington Books.

Schram, D. D., Milloy, C. D., & Rowe, W. E. (1991, September). *Juvenile sex offenders: A follow-up study of reoffense behavior*. Olympia: Washington State Institute for Public Policy.

Seabloom, W., Seabloom, M. E., Seabloom, E., Barron, R., & Hendrickson, S. (2003). A 14- to 24-year longitudinal study of a comprehensive sexual health model treatment program for adolescent sex offenders: Predictors of successful completion and subsequent criminal recidivism. *International Journal of Offender Therapy and Comparative Criminology, 47*, 468–481.

Sipe, R., Jensen, E. L., & Everett, R. S. (1998). Adolescent sexual offenders grown up: Recidivism in young adulthood. *Criminal Justice and Behavior, 25*, 109–124.

Smith, W. R., & Monastersky, C. (1986). Assessing juvenile sexual offenders' risk for reoffending. *Criminal Justice and Behavior, 13*, 115–140.

Steen, C., & Monnette, B. (1989). *Treating adolescent sex offenders in the community*. Springfield, IL: Charles C. Thomas.

Thornton, D. (2002). Constructing and testing a framework for dynamic risk assessment. *Sexual Abuse: A Journal of Research and Treatment, 14*, 139–153.

Waite, D., Pinkerton, R., Wieckowski, E., McGarvey, E., & Brown, G. L. (2002, October). *Tracking treatment outcome among juvenile sexual offenders: A nine year follow-up study*. Paper presented at the annual meeting of the Association for the Treatment of Sexual Abusers, Montreal, Quebec, Canada.

Wenet, G. A., & Clark, T. F. (1986). *The Oregon report on juvenile sexual offenders*. Salem: Children Services Division, Oregon Department of Human Resources.

Worling, J. R. (2002). Assessing risk of sexual assault recidivism with adolescent sexual offenders. In M. C. Calder (Ed.), *Young people who sexually abuse: Building the evidence base for your practice* (pp. 365-375). Lyme Regis, Dorset, UK: Russell House.

Worling, J. R. (2004). The Estimate of Risk of Adolescent Sexual Offense Recidivism (ERASOR): Preliminary psychometric data. *Sexual Abuse: A Journal of Research and Treatment, 16*, 235–254.

Worling, J. R., & Curwen, T. (2000). Adolescent sexual offender recidivism: Success of specialized treatment and implications for risk prediction. *Child Abuse and Neglect, 24*, 965–982.

Worling, J. R., & Curwen, T. (2001). Estimate of risk of adolescent sexual offense recidivism (The ERASOR: Version 2.0). In M. C. Calder (Ed.), *Juveniles and children who sexually abuse: Frameworks for assessment* (pp. 372-397). Lyme Regis, Dorset, UK: Russell House.

Worling, J. R., & Långström, N. (2003). Assessment of criminal recidivism risk with adolescents who have offended sexually. *Trauma, Violence, and Abuse: A Review Journal, 4*, 341–362.

Appendix A

Bibliography

Abel, G. G., Becker, J. V., Cunningham-Rathner, J., Rouleau, J., Kaplan, M., & Reich, J. (1984). *The treatment of child molesters*. Atlanta, GA: Behavioral Medicine Laboratory, Emory University.

Abel, G. G., Huffman, J., Warberg, B. W., & Holland, C. L. (1998). Visual reaction time and plethysmography as measures of sexual interest in child molesters. *Sexual Abuse, 10*(2), 81–95.

Abel, G. G., Mittelman, M. S., & Becker, J. V. (1985). Sex offenders: Results of assessment and recommendations for treatment in clinical criminology. In M. H. Ben-Aron, S. J. Hucker, & C. D. Webster (Eds.), *The assessment and treatment of criminal behavior* (pp. 191–205). Toronto, Ontario, Canada: M & M Graphic.

Achenbach, T. M. (1991). *Youth Self Report*. Toronto, Ontario, Canada: Nelson Thomson Learning.

Achenbach, T. M. (1991). *Child Behavior Checklist*. Toronto, Ontario, Canada: Nelson Thomson Learning.

Agee, V. M. (2002). Creating a positive milieu in residential treatment for adolescent sexual abusers. In B. K. Schwartz (Ed.), *The sex offender: Current treatment modalities and systems issues* (Vol. IV, pp. 29-1–29-22). Kingston, NJ: Civic Research Institute.

Ageton, S. S. (1983). *Sexual assault among adolescents*. Lexington, MA: Lexington Books.

Aguilar, B., Sroufe, L. A., Egeland, B., & Carlson, E. (2000). Distinguishing the early onset/persistent and adolescence-onset antisocial behavior types: From birth to 16 years. *Development and Psychopathology, 12*, 109–132.

Ainsworth, M. D. S. (1973). The development of infant-mother attachment. In B. C. Caldwell & H. R. Riciuti (Eds.), *Review of child development and research* (Vol. 3, pp. 1–94). Chicago: University of Chicago Press.

Ainsworth, M. D. S. (1978). *Patterns of attachment*. Hillsdale, NJ: Erlbaum.

Ainsworth, M. D. S., Blehar, M. C., Waters, E., & Wall, S. (1978). *Patterns of attachment: A psychological study of the strange situation*. Hillsdale, NJ: Erlbaum.

Alexander, M. A. (1999). Sexual offender treatment efficacy revisited, *Sexual Abuse: A Journal of Research and Treatment, 11*, 101-116.

Alexander, P. C., & Anderson, C. L. (1997). Incest, attachment, and developmental psychopathology. In D. Cicchetti & S. Toth (Eds.), *Rochester Symposium on Developmental Psychopathology* (Vol. 8, pp. 343–377). Rochester, NY: University of Rochester Press.

Allen, J. G. (2001). *Traumatic relationships and serious mental disorders*. New York: Wiley.

American Psychiatric Association. (1980). *Diagnostic and statistical manual of mental disorders* (3rd ed.). Washington, DC: Author.

American Psychiatric Association. (1994). *Diagnostic and statistical manual of mental disorders* (4th ed.). Washington, DC: Author.

American Psychiatric Association. (2000). *Diagnostic and statistical manual of mental disorders* (4th ed., text rev.). Washington, DC: Author.

American Psychiatric Association. (1999). Pharmacological treatment of sex offenders. In APA (Eds.) *Dangerous sex offenders: A Task Force report of the American Psychiatric Association* (pp. 103–128). Washington, DC: Author.

Anand, A. & Shekhar, A. (2003). Brain imaging studies in mood and anxiety disorders. *Annals of the New York Academy of Sciences, 985*, 370–388.

Anderson, D., & Dodgson, P. G. (2002). Empathy deficits, self esteem, and cognitive distortions in sexual offenders. In Y. Fernandez (Ed.), *In their shoes* (pp. 73–90). Oklahoma City, OK: Wood 'N' Barnes.

Andrews, D., & Bonta, J. (1994). *The psychology of criminal conduct.* Cincinnati, OH: Anderson Press.

Andrews, D. A., & Bonta, J. L. (1998). *The psychology of criminal conduct* (2nd ed.). Cincinnati, OH: Anderson.

Andrews, D. A., & Bonta, J. (2003). *The psychology of criminal conduct* (3rd ed.). Cincinnati, OH: Anderson.

Andrews, D. A., Bonta, J., & Hoge, R. D. (1990). Classification for effective rehabilitation: Rediscovering psychology. *Criminal Justice and Behavior, 17*, 19–52.

Andrews, D. A., Zinger, I., Hoge, R., Bonta, J. Gendreau, P., & Cullen, F. (1989). *Does correctional treatment work? A clinically relevant and psychologically informed meta-analysis.* Paper presented at the Research Seminar of National Associations Active in Criminal Justice, Ottawa, Canada.

Andrews, D. A., & Bonta, J. (1998). *The psychology of criminal conduct.* Cincinnati, OH: Anderson.

Aos, S., Phipps, P., Barnoski, R., & Lieb, R. (1999). *The comparative costs and benefits of programs to reduce crime: A review of national research findings with implications for Washington State* (Version 3.0). Olympia: Washington State Institute for Public Policy.

Apsey, L. S., Bristol, J., & Eppler, K. (1991). *Transforming power for peace.* New York: Alternatives to Violence Project.

Arnold, M. E., & Hughes, J. N. (1999). First do no harm: Adverse effects of grouping deviant youth for skills training. *Journal of School Psychology, 37*, 99–115.

Arriaga, X., & Foshee, V. A. (2004). Adolescent dating violence: Do adolescents follow in their friends' or their parents' footsteps? *Journal of Interpersonal Violence, 19*, 162–184.

Association for the Treatment of Sexual Abusers. (1997). *The ATSA practitioners handbook.* Beaverton, OR: Author.

Association for the Treatment of Sexual Abusers. (1997). *Ethical standards and principles for the management of sexual abusers.* Beaverton, OR: Author.

Association for the Treatment of Sexual Abusers. (2003). *Practice standards and guidelines.* Beaverton, OR: Author.

Awad, G. A., & Saunders, E. B. (1989). Adolescent child molesters: Clinical observations. *Child Psychiatry and Human Development, 19*, 195–206.

Aylward, A., & Sayer, M. (2002, October). *The Impact of Family Support Seminar on Release and Recidivism.* Paper presented at the annual Research and Treatment Conference of the Association for the Treatment of Sexual Abusers, Montreal, Quebec, Canada.

Aytes, K. E., Olsen, S. S., Zakrajsek, T., Murray, P., & Ireson, R. (2001). Cognitive/behavioral treatment for sexual offenders: An examination of recidivism. *Sexual Abuse: A Journal of Research and Treatment, 13*, 223-231.

Balbernie, R. (2001). Circuits and circumstances: The neurobiological consequences of early relationship experiences and how they shape later behaviour. *Journal of Child Psychotherapy, 27*(3), 237–255.

Barak, A., & King, S. A. (2000). Editorial: The two faces of the Internet: Introduction to the special issue on the Internet and sexuality. *CyberPsychology and Behavior, 3*(4), 517–520.

Barbaree, H. E. (1997). Evaluating treatment efficacy with sexual offenders: The insensitivity of recidivism studies to treatment effectiveness. *Sexual Abuse, 9*, 111–128.

Barbaree, H. E., & Cortoni, F. A. (1993). Treatment of the juvenile sex offender within the criminal justice and mental health systems. In H. E. Barbaree, W. L. Marshall, & S. M. Hudson (Eds.), *The juvenile sex offender* (pp. 243–263). New York: Guilford Press.

Barrett, M., Wilson, R. J., & Long, C. (2003). Measuring motivation to change in sexual offenders from institutional intake to community treatment. *Sexual Abuse, 15*, 269–283.

Bartholomew, K., & Horowitz, L. (1991). Attachment styles among adults: A test of a four category model. *Journal of Personality and Social Psychology, 61,* 226–244.

Baumeister, R. F., & Heatherton, T. F. (1996). Self-regulation: An overview. *Psychological Inquiry, 7,* 1–15.

Baumeister, R. F., & Leary, M. R. (1995). The need to belong: Desire for interpersonal attachments as a fundamental human motivation. *Psychological Bulletin, 117,* 497–529.

Bays, L., & Freeman-Longo, R. (1989). *Why did I do it again?: Understanding my cycle of problem behaviors.* Brandon, VT: Safer Society Press.

Bays, L., & Freeman-Longo, R. (1999). *Empathy and compassionate action: Issues and exercises* (4th printing). Brandon, VT: Safer Society Press.

Bays, L., Freeman-Longo, R., & Montgomery-Logan, D. (1990). *How can I stop?: Breaking my deviant cycle.* Brandon, VT: Safer Society Press.

Beck, A. T., & Steer, R. A. (1993). *Beck Anxiety Inventory* (1993 ed.). San Antonio, TX: Psychological Corporation.

Beck, A. T., Steer, R. A., & Brown, G. K. (1993). *Beck Depression Inventory* (2nd ed.). San Antonio, TX: Psychological Corporation.

Beck, J. (1995). *Cognitive therapy basics and beyond.* New York: Guilford Press.

Becker, J. V. (1998). What we know about the characteristics and treatment of adolescents who have committed sexual offenses. *Child Maltreatment, 3,* 317–329.

Becker, J. V., & Hicks, S. J. (2003). Juvenile sexual offenders: Characteristics, interventions, and policy issues. *Annals of the New York Academy of Sciences, 989,* 397–410.

Becker, J., & Kaplan, M. (1993). Cognitive-behavioral treatment of the juvenile sex offender. In H. Barbaree, W. Marshall, & S. Hudson (Eds.), *The juvenile sex offender* (pp. 264–267). New York: Guilford Press.

Becker, J. V., & Murphy, W. D. (1998). What we know and do not know about assessing and treating sex offenders. *Psychology, Public Policy, and Law 4*(1-2), 116–137.

Beech, A., Friendship, C., Erikson, M., &

Hanson, R. K. (2002). The relationship between static and dynamic risk factors and reconviction in a sample of U.K. child abusers. *Sexual Abuse: A Journal of Research and Treatment, 14,* 155–167.

Behavior Data Systems. (n.d.). *Sexual Adjustment Inventory (SAI): Orientation and training manual.* Retrieved January 2005, from *www.online-testing.com/documents/OTM-ONLINE-SAI.doc.*

Behavior Data Systems. (n.d.). *Juvenile sex offender evaluation.* Retrieved July 1, 2004, from *www.bdsltd.com/index2.htm.*

Behavior Data Systems. (n.d.). *Sexual Adjustment Inventory.* Retrieved July 1, 2004, from *www.bdsltd.com/index2.htm.*

Bellah, R. (1985). *Habits of the heart: Individualism and commitment in American life.* Berkeley: University of California Press.

Bender, L. (1938). *A visual motor test and its clinical use.* New York: American Orthopsychiatric Association.

Bennett-Goleman, T. (2001). *Emotional alchemy.* New York: Three Rivers.

Bettelheim, B. (1985). *A home for the heart.* Chicago: University of Chicago Press.

Bickley, J. A., & Beech, A. R. (2000). Implications for treatment of sexual offenders of the Ward and Hudson model of relapse. *Sexual Abuse: A Journal of Research and Treatment, 15*(2) 121–134.

Bickley, J. A., & Beech, R. (2002). An empirical investigation of the Ward and Hudson pathways model of offending in child sexual abusers. *Journal of Interpersonal Violence, 17,* 371–393.

Bickley, J. A., & Beech, R. (2003). Implications for treatment of sexual offenders of the Ward and Hudson model of relapse. *Sexual Abuse: A Journal of Research and Treatment, 15*(2), 121–134.

Biederman, J., Newcorn, J., & Sprich, S. (1991). Comorbidity of attention deficit hyperactivity with conduct, depressive, anxiety, and other disorders. *American Journal of Psychiatry, 148,* 564–577.

Bischof, G. P., Stith, S. M., & Whitney, M. L.

(1995). Family environments of adolescent sex offenders and other juvenile delinquents. *Adolescence, 30,* 157–170.

Bissette, D. (2004). *Choosing an Internet filter.* Retrieved April 29, 2004, from *http://www. healthymind.com/filters.pdf.*

Blanchard, G. (1989). *Sex offender treatment: A psychoeducational model.* Minneapolis, MN: Institute for Behavioral Medicine.

Blanchard, G. (1998). *The difficult connection.* Brandon, VT: Safer Society Press.

Blasingame, G. (2001). *Developmentally disabled persons with sexual behavior problems: Treatment management, supervision.* Oklahoma City, OK: Wood 'N' Barnes.

Blaske, D. M., Borduin, C. M., Henggeler, S. W., & Mann, B. J. (1989). Individual, family, and peer characteristics of adolescent sex offenders and assaultive offenders. *Developmental Psychology, 25*(5), 846–855.

Blatner, M. D., & Blatner A. (1988). *Foundations of psychodrama, history, theory & practice* (3rd ed.). New York: Springer.

Bleker, E. G. (1983). Cognitive defense style and WISC-R P>V sign in juvenile recidivists. *Journal of Clinical Psychology, 39,* 1030–1032.

Boer, D. P., Hart, S. D., Kropp, P. R., & Webster, C. D. (1997). *Manual for the Sexual Violence Risk-20.* Burnaby, British Columbia: Mental Health, Law, and Policy Institute, Simon Fraser University.

Boney-McCoy, S., & Finkelhor, D. (1996). Is youth victimization related to trauma symptoms and depression after controlling for prior symptoms and family relationships? A longitudinal, prospective study. *Journal of Consulting and Clinical Psychology, 64,* 1406–1416.

Borduin, C. M., Henggeler, S. W., Blaske, D. M., & Stein, R. J. (1990). Multisystemic treatment of adolescent sexual offenders. *International Journal of Offender Therapy and Comparative Criminology, 34,* 105–113.

Borduin, C. M., Mann, B. J., Cone, L. T., Henggeler, S. W., Fucci, B. R., Blaske, D. M., et al. (1995). Multisystemic treatment of serious juvenile offenders: Long-term prevention of criminality and violence. *Journal of Consulting and Clinical Psychology, 63,* 569–578.

Borduin, C. M., & Schaeffer, C. M. (2002). Multisystemic treatment of juvenile sexual offenders: A progress report. *Journal of Psychology and Human Sexuality, 13,* 25–42.

Borduin, C. M., Schaeffer, C. M., & Heilblum, N. (2000, May). *Multisystemic treatment of juvenile sexual offenders: A progress report.* Paper presented at the sixth International Conference on the Treatment of Sexual Offenders, Toronto, Ontario, Canada.

Borowsky, I. M., Hogan, M., & Ireland, M. (1997). Adolescent sexual aggression: Risk and protective factors. *Pediatrics, 100,* 6, e6.

Borum, R. (2000). Assessing violence risk among youth. *Journal of Clinical Psychology, 56,* 1263–1288.

Borum, R., Bartel, P., & Forth, A. E. (2002). *Manual for the Structured Assessment of Violence Risk in Youth.* Tampa: University of South Florida. Available: *www.fmhi.usf.edu/.*

Boschert, S. (2001, February 1). Eleven ways to build doctor-patient relationship. *Family Practice News,* pp. 31–30.

Bourgon, G. (2002). *The Estimate of Risk of Adolescent Sex Offender Recidivism (ERASOR): Evaluating its psychometric properties.* Paper presented at the annual meeting of the Association for the Treatment of Sexual Abusers, Montreal, Quebec, Canada.

Bowlby, J. (1969). *Attachment and loss. Volume I: Attachment.* New York: Basic Books.

Bowlby, J. (1973). *Attachment and loss. Volume II: Separation: Anxiety and anger.* New York: Basic Books.

Bowlby, J. (1980). *Attachment and loss. Volume III: Sadness and depression.* New York: Basic Books

Boyer, P. (2001). *Religion explained.* New York: Basic Books.

Bradford, J. M. W. (1985). Organic treatments for the male sexual offender. *Behavioral Sciences and the Law, 3*(4), 355–375.

Bradford, J. M. W. (1990). The antiandrogen and hormonal treatment of sex offenders. In W. L. Marshall & H. E. Barbaree (Eds.), *Handbook of sexual assault: Issues, theories, and treatment of the offenders* (pp. 297–310). New York: Plenum Press.

Breiling, J. (2003). Etiology research as the route to science–based prevention. *Annals of the New York Academy of Sciences, 989,* 150–153.

Bremer, J. F. (1992). Serious juvenile sex offenders: Treatment and long-term follow-up. *Psychiatric Annals, 22,* 326–332.

Bremer, J. F. (2001, May 7). *The Protective Factors Scale: Assessing youth with sexual concerns.* Plenary address at the 16th annual conference of the National Adolescent Perpetration Network, Kansas City, MO.

Bremner, J. D. (2002). *Does stress damage the brain?* New York: Norton

Bremner, J. D., & Narayan, M. (1998). The effects of stress on memory and the hippocampus throughout the life cycle: Implication for childhood development and aging, *Development and Psychopathology,* 10, 871–888.

Bremner, J. D., Randall, P., Vermetten, E., Staib, L., Bronen, R., Capelli, S., et al. (1997). MRI based measurement of hippocampal volume in posttraumatic stress disorder related to childhood physical and sexual abuse: A preliminary report. *Biological Psychiatry, 41,* 23–32.

Breton, D., & Largent, C. (1998). *Love, soul & freedom.* Center City, MN: Hazelden.

Bridges, S., Lease, S., & Ellison, C. (2004). Predicting sexual satisfaction in women: Implications for counselor education and training. *Journal of Counseling and Development, 82*(2), 158–166.

Briere, J. (1995). *Trauma Symptom Inventory.* Odessa, FL: Psychological Assessment Resources.

Briere, J. (1996). *Trauma Symptom Checklist for Children.* Odessa, FL: Psychological Assessment Resources.

Bronfenbrenner, U. (1979). *The ecology of human development: Experiments by design and nature.* Cambridge, MA: Harvard University Press.

Brown, S. (2003, March 20). *Executive Summary of Peer to Peer File Sharing.* Retrieved April 30, 2004, from *http://www.palisadesys.com/ news&events/p2pstudy.pdf.*

Browne, A., & Finkelhor, D. (1986). Impact of child sexual abuse: A review of the research. *Psychological Bulletin, 99,* 555–584.

Brownmiller, S. (1975). *Against our will: Men, women and rape.* New York: Bantam Books.

Bukowski, W. M., Sippola, L., & Brender, W. (1993). Where does sexuality come from?: Normative sexuality from a developmental perspective. In H. E. Barbaree, W. L. Marshall, & S. M. Hudson (Eds.), *The juvenile sex offender* (pp. 84–103). New York: Guilford Press.

Buller, E. (2000). *A cost benefit analysis of Hollow Water's community holistic circle healing process.* Ottawa, Ontario: Solicitor General Canada.

Burk, L., & Burkhart, B. (2003). Disorganized attachment as a diathesis for sexual deviance: Developmental experience and the motivation for sexual offending. *Aggression and Violent Behavior, 8*(5), 487–511.

Burke, S. K. (2000). In search of lesbian community in an electronic world. *CyberPsychology and Behavior, 3*(4), 591–604.

Burton, D., Miller, D., & Shill, C. (2002). A social learning theory comparison of the sexual victimization of adolescent sexual offenders and nonsexual offending male delinquents. *Child Abuse and Neglect, 26,* 893–907.

Cahill, L., Kaminer, R., & Johnson, P. (1999). Developmental, cognitive, and behavioral sequelae of child abuse. *Child and Adolescent Psychiatric Clinics of North America, 8*(4), 827–843.

Calder, M. C., Hanks, H., & Epps, K. J. (1997). *Juveniles and children who sexually abuse: A guide to risk assessment.* Lyme Regis, Dorset, UK: Russell House.

Caldwell, M. F. (2002). What we do not know about juvenile sex offender risk. *Child Maltreatment, 7,* 291–302

California Coalition on Sexual Offending. (2002, June). *California coalition on sexual offending's 5th annual training conference.* Symposium conducted at the meeting of the California Coalition on Sexual Offending, Sacramento, CA.

Canadian Centre for Justice Statistics. (1999). Sex offenders. *Juristat, 19.*

Cannon, W. B. (1927). The James-Lange theory of emotions: A critical reappraisal and an alternative theory. *American Journal of Psychology, 39,* 106–124.

Carey, M. (1997, Spring). Cog probation. *Perspectives,* pp. 27–42.

Carnes, P. J. (1989). *Contrary to love.* Center City, MN: Hazelden.

Carnes, P. J., & Delmonico, D. L. (1994). *Sexual Dependency Inventory—Revised.* Wickenburg, AZ: Gentle Path Press.

Carnes, P. J., Delmonico, D. L., Griffin, E., & Moriarty, J. (2001). *In the shadows of the Net: Breaking free of online compulsive sexual behavior.* Center City, MN: Hazelden.

Carter, C. S. (1998). Neuroendocrine perspectives on social attachment and love. *Psychoneuroendocrinology, 23,* 779–818.

Cattell, R. B., Cattell, A. K. S., Cattell, H. E. P. (1993). *The Sixteen Personality Factor Questionnaire (16PF).* Champaign: University of Illinois. (Original work published 1949)

Cauffman, E., & Steinberg, L. (2001). Immaturity of judgment in adolescence: Why adolescents may be less culpable than adults. *Behavioral Sciences and the Law, 18,* 741–760.

Center for Sex Offender Management. (1999). *Sex offender registration: Policy overview and comprehensive practices* [Online]. Silver Spring, MD. Available: *www.csom.org/pubs/sexreg.html.*

Chaffin, M., Letourneau, E. J., & Silovsky, J. F. (2002). Adults, adolescents and children who sexually abuse children: A developmental perspective. In J. E. B. Myers, L. Berliner, J. Briere, C. T. Hendrix, C. Jenny, & T. A. Reid (Eds.), *The APSAC handbook on child maltreatment* (2nd ed., pp. 205–232). Thousand Oaks, CA. Sage.

Chu, J. A. (1992). The therapeutic roller coaster: Dilemmas in the treatment of childhood abuse survivors. *Journal of Psychotherapy: Practice and Research, 1,* 351–370.

Cohen, M. A., Miller, T. R., & Rossman, S. B. (1994). The costs and consequences of violent behavior in the United States. In A. J. Reiss, & J. A. Roth (Eds.), *Understanding and preventing violence: Consequences and control* (vol. 4, pp. 67–167). Washington, DC: National Academy Press.

Cooper, A. (1998). Sexuality and the internet: Surfing into a new millennium. *Cyberpsychology and Behavior, 1*(2), 187–193.

Cooper, A., Delmonico, D., & Burg, R. (2000). Cybersex users, abusers, and compulsives: New findings and implications. *Sexual Addiction and Compulsivity: Journal of Treatment and Prevention, 7*(1–2), 5–30.

Cooper, A., Putnam, D., Planchon, L. A., & Boies, S. C. (1999). Online sexual compulsivity: Getting tangled in the Net. *Sexual Addiction and Compulsivity: Journal of Treatment and Prevention, 6*(2), 79–104.

Corey, G. (1996). *Theory & practice of counseling and psychotherapy* (5th ed.). Pacific Grove, CA: Brooks/Cole.

Corley, A., Corley, M. D., Walker, J., & Walker, S. (1994). The possibility of organic left posterior hemisphere dysfunction as a contributing factor in sex offending behavior. *Sexual Addiction and Compulsivity, 1,* 337–346.

Cormier, R. B. (2002). Restorative justice: Directions and principles—Developments in Canada (User Report 2002-02) [Online]. Ottawa, Ontario: Department of the Solicitor General of Canada. Available: *www.psepc-sppcc.gc.ca.*

Correctional Service of Canada. (2001). *No more victims.* Ottawa, Ontario: CSC and Red Herring Production [Eric Geringas, Director].

Correctional Service of Canada. (2002). *Circles of support and accountability: A guide to training potential volunteers, Training manual 2002* [Online]. Ottawa, Ontario: Author. Available: *www.csc-scc.gc.ca/text/prgrm/chap/Circle/cs_guide_final3_e.shtml.*

Cottle, C. C., Lee, R. J., & Heilbrun, K. (2001). The prediction of criminal recidivism in juveniles. *Criminal Justice and Behavior, 28,* 367–394.

Council of Economic Advisers. (1998). *Changing America: Indicators of social and economic well-*

being by race and Hispanic origin. Washington, DC: The White House.

Craissati, J., & Hodes, P. (1992). Mentally ill sex offenders: The experience of a regional secure care unit. *British Journal of Psychiatry, 161*, 846–849.

Crittenden, P. M. (1997). Toward an Integrative Theory of Trauma: A Dynamic-Maturation Approach. In D. Cicchetti & S. Toth (Eds.), *Rochester Symposium on Developmental Psychopathology* (Vol. 8, pp. 33–84). Rochester, NY: University of Rochester Press.

Cullen, M., & Wilson, R. J. (2003). *TRY—Treatment readiness for you: A workbook for sex offenders.* Lanham, MD: American Correctional Association.

Culp, R., Watkins, R., & Lawrence, H. (1991). Maltreated children's language and speech development: Abused, neglected and abused and neglected. *First Language, 11,* 377.

Cummings, E. M., Vogel, D., & Cummings, J. S. (1989). Children's responses to different forms of expression of anger between adults. *Child Development, 60,* 1392–1404.

Cunningham, M. (2003). Impact of trauma work on social work clinicians: Empirical findings. *Social Work, 48*(4), 451–459.

Cunningham, P. B., & Henggeler, S. W. (1999). Engaging multiproblem families in treatment: Lessons learned throughout the development of multisystemic therapy. *Family Process, 38,* 265–281.

Curwen, T. (2000, May 29). *Utility of the Interpersonal Reactivity Index (IRI) as a measure of empathy in male adolescent sex offenders.* Paper presented at the sixth International Conference on the Treatment of Sexual Offenders, Toronto, Ontario, Canada.

Curwen, T. (2003). The importance of offense characteristics, victimization history, hostility and social desirability in assessing empathy of male adolescent sex offenders. *Sexual Abuse: A Journal of Research and Treatment, 15*(4), 347–364.

Daleiden, E. L., Kaufman, K. L., Hilliker, D. R., & O'Neil, J. N. (1998). The sexual histories and fantasies of youthful males: A comparison of sex- ual offending, nonsexual offending, and nonoffending groups. *Sexual Abuse: A Journal of Research and Treatment, 10,* 195–209.

Dandescu, A. & Wolfe, R. (2003). Considerations on fantasy use by child molesters and exhibitionists. *Sexual Abuse: A Journal of Research and Treatment, 15*(4), 297–305.

Davidson, R. (1998). Affective style and affective disorders: Perspectives from affective neuroscience. *Cognition and Emotion, 12,* 307–330.

Davignon, D. (2000). *Sexual Adjustment Inventory—Juvenile: An inventory of scientific findings.* Unpublished manuscript.

Davignon, D. (2000). *Sexual Adjustment Inventory: Sex offender assessment.* Unpublished manuscript.

Davignon, D. (2002). *Sexual Adjustment Inventory—Juvenile: Juvenile sex offender assessment.* Unpublished manuscript.

Davignon, D. (2003, March/April). Assessment driven treatment. *Corrections Forum,* pp. 30, 32.

Davignon, D. (2003). *Sexual Adjustment Inventory (SAI): An inventory of scientific findings.* Unpublished manuscript.

Davis, G. E., & Leitenberg, H. (1987). Adolescent sex offenders. *Psychological Bulletin, 101,* 417–427.

DeBellis, M. D. (2001). Developmental traumatology: The psychobiological development of maltreated children and its implications for research, treatment, and policy. *Development and Psychopathology, 13,* 539–564.

Deckel, W., Hesselbrock, V., & Bauer, L. (1996). Antisocial personality disorder, childhood delinquency, and frontal brain functioning: EEG and neuropsychological findings. *Journal of Clinical Psychology, 52*(6), 639–650.

Delmonico, D. L. (1997). *Internet Sex Screening Test.* Retrieved December 14, 2004, from *www.sexhelp.com.*

Delmonico, D. L., & Griffin, E. J. (2002). Classifying problematic sexual behavior: A working model revisited. In K. Adams & P. Carnes (Eds.), *Clinical management of sex addiction.* New York: Brunner/Routledge.

Delmonico, D. L., Griffin, E., & Carnes, P. J. (2002). Treating online compulsive sexual behavior: When cybersex is the drug of choice. In A. Cooper (Ed.), *Sex and the Internet: A guidebook for clinicians.* New York: Brunner/Routledge.

Delmonico, D. L., Griffin, E. J., & Moriarity, J. (2001). *Cybersex unhooked: A workbook for breaking free of online compulsive sexual behavior.* Center City, MN: Hazelden Press.

Delmonico, D. L., & Miller, J. A. (2003). The Internet sex screening test: A comparison of sexual compulsives versus non-sexual compulsives. *Sexual and Relationship Therapy, 18*(3), 261–276.

Dempster, R. J., & Hart, S. D. (2002). The relative utility of fixed and variable risk factors in discriminating sexual recidivists and nonrecidivists. *Sexual Abuse: A Journal of Research and Treatment, 14*, 121–138.

DesLauriers, A. T. & Gardner, J. (1999). The sexual predator treatment program of Kansas. In A. Schlank & F. Cohen (Eds.), *The sexual predator: Law, policy, evaluation and treatment* (pp. 11-2–11-26). Kingston, NJ: Civic Research Institute.

Diego, M., Field, T., Hernandez-Reif, M., Shaw, J., Rothe, E., Castellanos, D., et al. (2002). Aggressive adolescents benefit from massage therapy. *Adolescence, 37*, 597–601.

Dishion, T. J., McCord, J., & Poulin, F. (1999). When interventions harm: Peer groups and problem behavior. *American Psychologist, 54*, 755–764.

Dishion, T. J., Patterson, G. R., Stoolmiller, M., & Skinner, M. L. (1991). Family, school and behavioral antecedents to early adolescent involvement with antisocial peers. *Developmental Psychology, 27*, 172–180.

Doherty, W. (1995). *Soul searching.* New York: Basic Books.

Doren, D. M. (2002). The state of recidivism risk assessment. *The Forum, 14*(2), 4–5.

Drake, R. E., Goldman, H. H., Leff, H. S., Lehman, A. F., Dixon, L., Mueser, K. T., et al. (2001). Implementing evidence-based practices in routine mental health service settings. *Psychiatric Services, 52*, 179–182.

Dutton, D. & Holtzworth-Munroe, A. (1997). The role of early trauma in males who assault their wives. In D. Cicchetti & S. Toth (Eds.), *Rochester Symposium on Developmental Psychopathy* (Vol. 8, pp. 379–403). Rochester, NY: University of Rochester Press.

East, K., & Campbell, S. (1999). *Aspects of crime: Young offenders 1999.* England & Wales: Home Office. Retrieved December 28, 2003, from *www.homeoffice.gov.uk/rds/pdfs/aspects-youngoffs.pdf.*

Ellerby, L. (2003, October 10). *Entering the gateway of indigenous knowledge.* Paper presented at Research and Treatment Conference of the Association for Treatment of Sex Abusers, St. Louis, MO.

Elliott, D. S. (Series Ed.). (1998). *Blueprints for violence prevention.* Boulder, CO: Blueprints Publications, University of Colorado, Center for the Study and Prevention of Violence.

English, K. (1998). The containment approach: An aggressive strategy for the community management of adult sex offenders. *Psychology, Public Policy and Law, 4*(1/2), 218–235.

Epps, K. J. (1997). Managing risk. In M. S. Hoghughi, S. R. Bhate, & F. Graham (Eds.), *Working with sexually abusive adolescents* (pp. 35–51). London: Sage.

Epstein, M. (1998). *Going to pieces without falling apart.* New York: Broadway Books.

Erikson, E. H. (1963). *Childhood and society* (2nd ed.). New York: Norton

Etzioni, A. (1993). *The spirit of community.* New York: Simon & Schuster.

Fago, D. P. (2003). Evaluation and treatment of neurodevelopmental deficits in sexually aggressive children and adolescents. *Professional Psychology: Research and Practice, 34*(3), 248–257.

Farrington, D. P., & Welsh, B. C. (1999). Delinquency prevention using family-based interventions. *Children and Society, 13*, 287–303.

Federoff, J. P., & Moran, B. (1997). Myths and misconceptions about sex offenders. *Canadian Journal of Human Sexuality, 6*, 263–276.

Fehrenbach, P. A., Smith, W., Monastersky, C., & Deisher, R. W. (1986). Adolescent sexual offenders: Offender and offense characteristics. *American Journal of Orthopsychiatry, 56,* 225–233.

Fernandez, Y. M., & Marshall, W. L. (2003). Victim empathy, self-esteem, and psychopathy in rapists. *Sexual Abuse: A Journal of Research and Treatment, 15*(1), 11–26.

Fernandez, Y. M., Marshall, W. L., Serran, G., Anderson, D., & Marshall, L. (2002). *Group process in sexual offender treatment.* Ottawa, Ontario: Correctional Service of Canada.

Fernandez Y. M., & Serran, G. (2002). Empathy training for therapists and clients. In *In their shoes* (pp. 110–131). Oklahoma City, OK: Wood 'N' Barnes.

Field, T. (1999). Preschoolers in America are touched less and are more aggressive than preschoolers in France. *Development and Care, 151,* 11–17.

Field, T. (1999, Winter). American adolescents touch each other less and are more aggressive toward their peers as compared with French adolescents. *Adolescence, 34*(136), 753–758.

Field, T. (2002, Winter). Violence and touch deprivation in adolescents. *Adolescence, 37*(148), 753–759.

Field, T., Lasko, D., Mundy, P., Henteleff, T., Talpins, S., & Dowling, M. (1986). Autistic children's attentiveness and responsivity improved after touch therapy. *Journal of Autism and Developmental Disorders, 27,* 329–334.

Field, T., Morrow, C., Valdeon, C., Larson, S., Kuhn, C., & Schanberg, S. (1992, January). Massage reduces anxiety in child and adolescent psychiatric patients. *Journal of the American Academy of Child and Adolescent Psychiatry, 31*(1), 125–131.

Finkelhor, D. (1987). The sexual abuse of children: Current research reviewed. *Psychiatric Annals, 17,* 233–241.

Finkelhor, D., & Dzuiba-Leatherman, J. (1994). Children as victims of violence: A national survey. *Pediatrics, 94,* 413–420.

Firestone, P., Bradford, J. M., McCoy, M.,

Greenberg, D. M., Curry, S., & Larose, M. R. (2000). Prediction of recidivism in extrafamilial child molesters based on court-related assessments. *Sexual Abuse: A Journal of Research and Treatment, 12*(3), 203–221.

Foa, E. B. (1997). Psychological processes related to recovery from trauma and effective treatment of PTSD. In R. Yehuda & A. C. McFarlane (Eds.), *Psychobiology of posttraumatic stress disorder* (Vol. 823, pp. 410–424). New York: New York Academy of Sciences.

Ford, M. E., & Linney, J. A. (1995). Comparative analysis of juvenile sexual offenders, violent nonsexual offenders, and status offenders. *Journal of Interpersonal Violence, 10,* 56–70.

Ford, W., Johnson, S., & Peña (2003). S*teps to more effective program development and treatment planning for African-American and Latino sex offenders.* Paper presented at the 22nd annual Research and Treatment Conference of the Association for the Treatment of Sexual Abusers, St. Louis, MO.

Ford, W., & Prunier, W. (2002). *Supervision of sex offenders: The relapse prevention model.* Paper presented at the 21st annual Research and Treatment Conference of the Association for the Treatment of Sexual Abusers, Montreal, Quebec Canada.

Forth, A.E., Kosson, D.S., & Hare, R.D. (2003). *Psychopathy Checklist: Youth Version.* Toronto, Ontario, Canada: Multi-Health Systems.

Fossum, M., & Mason, M. (1986). *Facing shame.* New York: Norton.

Fox, L., Long, S., & Langlois, A. (1988). Patterns of language comprehension deficit in abused and neglected children. *Journal of Speech and Hearing Disorders, 53,* 239.

Frattaroli, E. (2001). *Healing the soul in the age of the brain.* New York: Penguin Putnam.

Galderisi, S., & Mucci, A. (2000). Emotions, brain development, and psychopathology vulnerability. *CNS Spectrums, 5*(8), 44–48.

Gallistel, C., Brown, A., Carey, S., Gelman, R., & Keil, F. (1991). Lessons from animal learning for the study of cognitive development. In S. Carey & R. Gelman (Eds.), *The epigenesis of mind: Essays on biology and cognition* (pp. 3–36). Hillsdale, NJ: Erlbaum.

Galski, T., Thornton, K., & Shumsky, D. (1990). Brain dysfunction in sex offenders. *Journal of Offender Rehabilitation, 16*, 65–80.

Gann, M. K. (2000, November 1) *Dialectical behavior therapy with personality disordered sexual abusers*. Paper presented at the 19th annual ATSA Research and Treatment Conference, San Diego, CA.

Garcia, M. (2004). *U.S. "Operation Predator" protecting children around the world*. Washington, DC: U.S. House of Representatives Subcommittee on Immigration, Border Security and Claims.

Garland, R., & Dougher, M. (1990). The abused/abuser hypothesis of child sexual abuse: A critical review of theory and research, In J. Fierman (Ed.), *Pedophilia: Biosocial dimensions* (pp. 488–509). New York: Springer-Verlag.

Garner, T. (2003, March 19). New look at no-touch teaching. *New Zealand Herald*.

Garos, S. (in press). *Garos Sexual Behavior Index*. Los Angeles, CA: Western Psychological Services.

Gendreau, P., & Goggin, C. (1996). Principles of effective correctional programming. *Forum on Corrections Research, 8*, 38–41.

Gendreau, P., & Goggin, C. (1997). Correctional treatment: Accomplishments and realities. In P. Van Voorhis, M. Braswell, & D. Lester (Eds.), *Correctional counseling and rehabilitation* (pp. 271–279). Cincinnati, OH: Anderson.

Gendreau, P., Little, T., & Goggin, C. (1996). A meta-analysis of the predictors of adult offender recidivism: What works! *Criminology, 34*, 575–607.

Gilgun, J. F., Klein, C., & Pranis, K. (2000) The significance of resources in models of risk, *Journal of Interpersonal Violence, 15*, 621–650.

Gillespie, N., & McKenzie, K. (2000). An examination of the role of neuropsychological deficits in mentally disordered sex offenders. *Journal of Sexual Aggression, 5*, 21–29.

Glasser, W. (1965). *Reality therapy*. New York: Harper & Row.

Goia, G., Isquith, P., Guy, S., & Kenworthy, L.

(2000). Behavior Rating Inventory of Executive Functioning. *Child Neuropsychology, 6*(3), 235–238.

Gordon, A., & Packard, R. R. (1998). *The impact of community maintenance treatment on sex offender recidivism*. Paper presented to the annual meeting of the Association for the Treatment of Sexual Abusers, Vancouver, British Columbia, Canada.

Gottlieb, G. (1992). *Individual development and evolution: The genesis of novel behavior*. New York: Oxford University Press.

Gottlieb, A. (2000). *The dream of reason: A history of Western philosophy from the Greeks to the renaissance*. New York: Norton.

Grace, W. C., & Sweeney, M. E. (1986). Comparisons of P>V sign on the WISC-R and WAIS-R in delinquent males. *Journal of Clinical Psychology, 42*, 173–176.

Grady, J., & Reynolds, S. (2003, October). *Holistic assessment and treatment of sexually abusive youth*. Paper presented at the annual meeting of the Association for the Treatment of Sexual Abusers, Montreal, Quebec, Canada.

Graves, R. B., Openshaw, D. K., Ascione, F. R., & Ericksen, S. L. (1996). Demographic and parental characteristics of youthful sexual offenders. *International Journal of Offender Therapy and Comparative Criminology, 40*, 300–317.

Green, A., Voeller, K., & Gaines, R. (1981). Neurological impairment in maltreated children. *Child Abuse and Neglect, 5*, 129–134.

Greenberg, L. M., Corman, C. L., & Kindischi, C. L. (1996). *Test of Variables of Attention* (version 703). Los Alamos, CA: Universal Attention Disorders.

Greenfield, L. A. (1997). *Sex offenses and offenders: An analysis of data on rape and sexual assault* (NCJ-163392). Washington, DC: U.S. Department of Justice, Bureau of Justice Statistics.

Greenough, W., Black, J., & Wallace, C. (1987). Experience and brain development. *Child Development, 64*, 1439–1450.

Greenland, C. (1985). Dangerousness, mental disorder, and politics. In C. D. Webster, M. H. Ben-

Aron, & S. J. Hucker (Eds.), *Dangerousness: Probability and prediction, psychiatry and public policy* (pp. 25–40). Cambridge, UK: Cambridge University Press.

Gretton, H. M., McBride, M., Hare, R. D., O'Shaughnessy, & Kumka, G. (2001). Psychopathy and recidivism in adolescent sex offenders. *Criminal Justice and Behavior, 28*, 427–449.

Griffin, P., Torbet, P., & Szymanski, L. (1998). *Trying juveniles as adults in criminal court: An analysis of state transfer provisions.* Washington, DC: U.S. Department of Justice, Office of Justice Programs, Office of Juvenile Justice and Delinquency Prevention.

Griffith, D., & Bartholomew, K. (1994). Models of the self and other: Fundamental dimensions underlying measures of adult attachment. *Journal of Personality and Social Psychology, 67*(3), 430–445.

Griffith, J. (2003). *Encountering the sacred in psychotherapy.* New York: Guilford Press.

Grisso, T. (2000, March). *Ethical issues in sex offender re-offense risk prediction.* Paper presented at Sex Offender Re-Offense Risk Prediction Symposium, Madison, Wisconsin. Available: *www.sinclairseminars.com.*

Guarino-Ghezzi, S., & Kimball, L. M. (1998). Juvenile sex offenders in treatment. *Corrections Management Quarterly, 2*, 45–54.

Guidry, L. (2004, April 7 & 8). *Assessing, treating & managing mentally ill sex offenders.* Paper presented at the MASOC/MATSA conference, Marlborough, MA.

Guidry, L. (2004, April 7 & 8). *Managing mentally ill sex offenders in the community.* Paper presented at the MASOC/MATSA conference, Marlborough, MA.

Gupta, M. A., Gupta, A. K., Schork, N. J., & Watteel, G. N. (1995). Perceived touch deprivation and body image: Some observations among eating disordered and non-clinical subjects. *Journal of Psychosomatic Research, 39*(4), 459–464.

Gupta, M. A., & Schork, N. J. (1995). Touch deprivation has an adverse effect on body image: Some preliminary observations. *International Journal of Eating Disorders, 17*(2), 185–189.

Haaven, J., Little R., & Petre-Miller, D. (1990). *Treating intellectually disabled sex offenders: A model residential program.* Orwell, VT: Safer Society Press.

Haddad, P., & Garralda, M. (1992). Hyperkinetic syndrome and disruptive early experiences. *British Journal of Psychiatry, 161*, 700–703.

Hagan, M. P., & Cho, M. E. (1996). A comparison of treatment outcomes between adolescent rapists and child sexual offenders. *International Journal of Offender Therapy and Comparative Criminology, 40*, 113–122.

Hagan, M. P., King, R. P., & Patros, R. L. (1994). Recidivism among adolescent perpetrators of sexual assault against children. *Journal of Offender Rehabilitation, 21*, 127 137.

Haley, J. (1976). *Problem solving therapy.* San Francisco: Jossey-Bass.

Hall, J. M., & Powell, J. (2000). Dissociative experiences described by women survivors of childhood abuse. *Journal of Interpersonal Violence, 15*(2), 184–204.

Hanson, R. K. (1996). Evaluating the contribution of relapse prevention theory to the treatment of sexual offenders. *Sexual Abuse: A Journal of Research and Treatment, 8*, 201–208.

Hanson, R. K. (1997). *The development of a brief actuarial scale for sexual offense recidivism* (User Report 1997-04) [Online]. Ottawa, Ontario: Department of the Solicitor General of Canada. Available: *www.psepc-sppcc.gc.ca.*

Hanson, R. K. (2000). *Risk assessment.* Beaverton, OR: Association for the Treatment of Sexual Abusers.

Hanson, R. K. (2002). Introduction to the special section on dynamic risk assessment with sex offenders. *Sexual Abuse: A Journal of Research and Treatment, 14*, 99–101.

Hanson, R .K. (2003). *Sex offender empathy deficits* (User Report 2003-08). Ottawa: Department of the Solicitor General of Canada. Available: *www.sgc.gc.ca.*

Hanson, R. K., & Bussière, M. T. (1998). Predicting relapse: A meta-analysis of sexual offender recidivism studies. *Journal of Consulting and Clinical Psychology, 66*, 348–362.

Hanson, R. K., Gordon, A., Harris, A. J., Marques, J. K., Murphy, W., Quinsey, V. L., et al. (2002). First report of the Collaborative Outcome Data Project on the effectiveness of psychological treatment for sex offenders. *Sexual Abuse: A Journal of Research and Treatment, 14*(2), 169–194.

Hanson, R. K., & Harris, A. J. R. (1998). *Dynamic predictors of sexual recidivism* (User Report 1998-01). Ottawa, Ontario: Department of the Solicitor General of Canada.

Hanson, R. K., & Harris, A. J. R. (2000). *The sex offender need assessment rating (SONAR): A method for measuring change in risk levels.* Ottawa, Ontario: Department of the Solicitor General of Canada.

Hanson, R. K., & Harris, A. J. R. (2001). A structured approach to evaluating change among sexual offenders, *Sexual Abuse: A Journal of Research and Treatment, 13,* 105–122.

Hanson, R. K., Morton, K. E., & Harris, A. J. R. (2003). Sexual offender recidivism risk: What we know and what we need to know. *Annals of the New York Academy of Sciences, 989,* 154–166.

Hanson, R. K., & Morton-Bourgon, K. E. (2004). *Predictors of sexual recidivism: An updated meta-analysis* (User Report 2004-01). Ottawa, Ontario: Public Safety and Emergency Preparedness Canada.

Hanson, R. K., & Thornton, D. (1999). *Static 99: Improving actuarial risk assessment for sex offenders.* Ottawa, Ontario: Department of the Solicitor General of Canada.

Hanson, R. K., & Thornton, D. (1999). *Static-99: Improving actuarial risk assessments for sex offenders* (User Report 1999-02) [Online]. Ottawa, Ontario: Department of the Solicitor General of Canada. Available: *www.psepc-sppcc.gc.ca.*

Hanson, R. K., & Thornton, D. (2000). Improving actuarial risk assessments for sex offenders. *Law and Human Behavior, 24,* 119–136.

Hanson, R. K., & Thornton, D. (2003). *Notes on the development of Static-2002* (User Report 2003-01). Ottawa, Ontario: Department of the Solicitor General of Canada. Available: *www.psepc-sppcc.gc.ca.*

Hare, R. D. (1991). *The Hare Psychopathy Checklist—Revised.* Toronto, Ontario, Canada: Multi-Health Systems.

Harris, A., Phenix, A., Hanson, R. K., & Thornton, D. (2003). *STATIC-99 coding rules: Revised—2003.* Ottawa, Ontario: Department of the Solicitor General of Canada. Available: *www. sexcriminals.com/library/doc.1032-1.pdf.*

Hart, S. D., Cox, D. N., & Hare, R. D. (1995). *The Hare Psychopathy Checklist: Screening Version.* Toronto, Ontario, Canada: Multi-Health Systems.

Hart, S. D., Kropp, P. R., & Laws, R. D., with Klaver, J., Logan, C., & Wyatt, K. A. (2003). *Risk for Sexual Violence Protocol (RSVP): Structured professional guidelines for assessing risk of violence.* Burnaby, British Columbia, Canada: Mental Health, Law, and Policy Institute, Simon Fraser University.

Hastings, T., Anderson, S. J., & Hemphill, P. (1997). Comparisons of daily stress, coping, problem behavior, and cognitive distortions in adolescent sexual offenders and conduct-disordered youth. *Sexual Abuse: A Journal of Research and Treatment, 9,* 29–42.

Hatfield, R. (1994). Touch and human sexuality. In V. Bullough, B. Bullough, & A. Stein (Eds.), *Human sexuality: An encyclopedia* (pp. 581–587). New York: Garland.

Hathaway, S., McKinley, J. C., & Butcher, J. M. (1990). *Minnesota Multiphasic Personality Inventory* (2nd ed.). Minneapolis: University of Minnesota Press.

Hays, W. L. (1994). *Statistics.* Orlando, FL: Harcourt Brace.

Hecker, J., Scoular, J., Righthand, S., & Nangle, D. (2002, October). *Predictive validity of the J-SOAP over 10-plus years: Implications for risk assessment.* Paper presented at the annual meeting of the Association for the Treatment of Sexual Abusers, Montreal, Quebec, Canada.

Henderson, M. C., & Kalichman, S. C. (1990). Sexually deviant behavior and schizotypy: A theoretical perspective with supportive data. *Psychiatric Quarterly, 61*(4), 273–284.

Henggeler, S. W., & Borduin, C. M. (1990). *Family therapy and beyond: A multisystemic approach to treating the behavior problems of children and adolescents.* Pacific Grove, CA: Brooks/Cole.

Henggeler, S. W., & Borduin, C. M. (1992). *Multisystemic Therapy Adherence Scales.* Unpublished instrument, Department of Psychiatry and Behavioral Sciences, Medical University of South Carolina.

Henggeler, S. W., Melton, G. B., Brondino, M. J., Scherer, D. G., & Hanley, J. H. (1997). Multisystemic therapy with violent and chronic juvenile offenders and their families: The role of treatment fidelity in successful dissemination. *Journal of Consulting and Clinical Psychology, 65,* 821–833.

Henggeler, S. W., Melton, G. B., & Smith, L. A. (1992). Family preservation using multisystemic therapy: An effective alternative to incarcerating serious juvenile offenders. *Journal of Consulting and Clinical Psychology, 60,* 953–961.

Henggeler, S. W., Melton, G. B., Smith, L. A., Schoenwald, S. K., & Hanley, J. H. (1993). Family preservation using multisystemic treatment: Long-term follow-up to a clinical trial with serious juvenile offenders. *Journal of Child and Family Studies, 2,* 283–293.

Henggeler, S. W., Pickrel, S. G., & Brondino, M. J. (1999). Multisystemic treatment of substance abusing and dependent delinquents: Outcomes, treatment fidelity, and transportability. *Mental Health Services Research, 1,* 171–184.

Henggeler, S. W., & Schoenwald, S. K. (1998). *The MST supervisory manual: Promoting quality assurance at the clinical level.* Charleston, SC: MST Institute.

Henggeler, S. W., Schoenwald, S. K., Borduin, C. M., Rowland, M. D., & Cunningham, P. B. (1998). *Multisystemic treatment of antisocial behavior in children and adolescents.* New York: Guilford Press.

Henry, B, & Moffitt, T. E. (1997). Neuropsychological and neuroimaging studies of juvenile delinquency and adult criminal behavior. In D. Stoff, J. Breiling, & J. D. Maser (Eds.), *Handbook of antisocial behavior* (pp. 280–288). New York: Wiley.

Herman, J. (1992). *Trauma and recovery.* New York, Basic Books.

Hildebran, D., & Pithers, W. D. (1989). Enhancing offender empathy for sexual abuse victims. In D. R. Laws (Ed.), *Relapse prevention with sex offenders* (pp. 236–243). New York: Guilford Press.

Hillman, J., & Ventura, M. (1992). *We've had a hundred years of psychotherapy—And the world's getting worse.* San Francisco: Harper.

Hirischi, T., & Hindelang, M. (1977). Intelligence and delinquency: A revisionist review. *American Sociological Review, 42,* 571–587.

Hoffman-Plotkin, D., & Twentyman, C. (1984). A multimodal assessment of behavioral and cognitive deficits in abused and neglected pre-schoolers. *Child Development, 55,* 794.

Hoge, R. D. (2002). Standardized instruments for assessing risk and need in youthful offenders. *Criminal Justice and Behavior, 29,* 380–396.

Hoge, R. D., & Andrews, D. A. (2002). *The Youth Level of Service/Case Management Inventory: User's manual.* Toronto, Ontario, Canada: Multi-Health Systems.

Hoge, R. D., & Andrews, D. A. (2003). *Youth Level of Service/Case Management Inventory.* Toronto, Ontario, Canada: Multi-Health Systems.

Hudson, S. M., Wales, D. S., Bakker, L., & Ward, T. (2002). Dynamic risk factors: The Kia Marama evaluation. *Sexual Abuse: A Journal of Research and Treatment, 14,* 103–119.

Hudson, S. M., & Ward, T. (2000). Interpersonal competency in sex offenders. *Behavior Modification, 24*(4), 494–527.

Hudson, S. M., Ward, T., & McCormick, J. C. (1999). Offense pathways in sexual offenders. *Journal of Interpersonal Violence, 14,* 779–798.

Huey, S. J., Henggeler, S. W., Brondino, M. J., & Pickrel, S. G. (2000). Mechanisms of change in multisystemic therapy: Reducing delinquent behavior through therapist adherence and improved family and peer functioning. *Journal of Consulting and Clinical Psychology, 68,* 451–467.

Hunter, J. A., & Becker, J. V. (1994). The role of deviant sexual arousal in juvenile sexual offending: Etiology, evaluation, and treatment, *Criminal Justice and Behavior, 21,* 132–149.

Hunter, J. A., & Figueredo, A. J. (1999). Factors associated with treatment compliance in a population of juvenile sexual offenders. *Sexual Abuse: A Journal of Research and Treatment, 11,* 49–68.

Hunter, J. A., Figueredo, A. J., Malamuth, N. M, & Becker, J. V. (2003). Juvenile sex offenders: Toward the development of a typology. *Sexual Abuse: A Journal of Research and Treatment, 15,* 27–48.

Hunter, J. A., & Goodwin, D. W. (1992). The utility of satiation therapy in the treatment of juvenile sexual offenders: Variations and efficacy, *Annals of Sex Research, 5,* 71–80.

Hunter, J. A., Goodwin, D. W., & Becker, J. V. (1994). The relationship between phallometrically measured deviant sexual arousal and clinical characteristics in juvenile sexual offenders. *Behavioral Research and Therapy, 32,* 533–538.

Hunter, J. A., & Santos, D. (1990). The use of specialized cognitive-behavioral therapies in the treatment of juvenile sexual offenders. *International Journal of Offender Therapy and Comparative Criminology, 34,* 239–248.

Hunter, M., & Struve, J. (1997). *The ethical use of touch in psychotherapy.* New York: Sage.

Huttenlocher, P. (1979). Synaptic density in human frontal cortex: Developmental changes and the effects of aging. *Brain Research, 163,* 195–205.

Jacobs, W. L., Kennedy, W. A., & Meyer, J. B. (1997). Juvenile delinquents: A between-group comparison study of sexual and nonsexual offenders. *Sexual Abuse: Journal of Research and Treatment, 9,* 201–217.

James, W. (1950). *The principles of psychology.* New York: Dover. (Original publication 1890).

Jennings, J., & Sawyer, S. (2003). Principles and techniques for maximizing the effectiveness of group therapy with sex offenders. *Sexual Abuse: A Journal of Research and Treatment, 15,* 251–267.

John Howard Society of Alberta. (2001). *Offender registry* [Online]. Available: *www.johnhoward. ab.ca/PUB/offender.htm.*

Jones, B., Huckle, P., & Tanaghow, A. (1992).

Command auditory hallucinations, schizophrenia and sexual assaults. *Irish Journal of Psychological Medicine, 9,* 47–49.

Jones, M. (1953). *The therapeutic community.* New York: Basic Books.

Jourard, S. M. (1966). An exploratory study of body accessibility. *British Journal of Social and Clinical Psychology, 5,* 221–231.

Kafka, M. P. (2001, June 28 & 29). *The diagnosis and medical management of sex offenders with major mental illness.* Paper presented at the first annual MI/SBD Training Conference: The treatment of MI/SBD inpatients. Medfield: Massachusetts Department of Mental Health and University of Massachusetts Medical School, Medfield State Hospital.

Kafka, M. P., & Hennen, J. (2002). A DSM-IV Axis I comorbidity study of males ($n = 120$) with paraphilias and paraphilia-related disorders. *Sexual Abuse: A Journal of Research and Treatment, 14*(4), 349–366.

Kafka, M. P., & Prentky, R. A. (1994). Preliminary observations of DSM-III-R Axis I comorbidity in men with paraphilias and paraphilia-related disorders. *Journal of Clinical Psychiatry, 55,* 481–487.

Kafka, M. P., & Prentky, R. A. (1998). Attention deficit/hyperactivity disorder in males with paraphilias and paraphilia-related disorders: A comorbidity study. *Journal of Clinical Psychiatry, 59,* 388–396.

Kahn, T. J., & Chambers, H. J. (1991). Assessing reoffense risk with juvenile sexual offenders. *Child Welfare, 70,* 333–345.

Kalichman, S., & Rompa, D. (2001). The Sexual Compulsivity Scale: Further development and use with HIV-positive persons. *Journal of Personality Assessment, 76,* 379–395.

Karoly, P. (2003). Mechanisms of self-regulation: A systems view. *Annual Review of Psychology, 44,* 23–52.

Kasl, C. (1999). *If the Buddha dated.* New York: Penguin.

Kasl, C. (2001). *If the Buddha married.* New York: Penguin Compass.

Kaufman, G. (1996). *The psychology of shame:*

Theory and treatment of shame based syndromes (2nd ed.). New York: Springer.

Kaufman, K. L. (1993). *Sexual Fantasy Questionnaire.* Columbus, OH: Children's Hospital.

Kaufman, K. L. (1994). *Sexual History Form.* Columbus, OH: Children's Hospital.

Kazdin, A. E., & Weisz, J. R. (1998). Identifying and developing empirically supported child and adolescent treatments. *Journal of Consulting and Clinical Psychology, 66,* 19–36.

Kazura, K., Temke, M., Toth, K., & Hunter, B. (2002). Building partnerships to address challenging social problems. *Journal of Extension, 40*(1). Available: *www.joe.org/joe/2002february/iw7. html.*

Keith, R. W. (1994). *SCAN-A: A test for auditory processing disorders in adolescents and adults.* San Antonio, TX: Psychological Corporation.

Kellerman, P. F. (1992) *Focus on psychodrama: The therapeutic aspects of psychodrama.* London: Jessica Kingsley:

Kempton, T., & Forehand, R. L. (1992). Suicide attempts among juvenile delinquents: The contribution of mental health factors. *Behaviour Research and Therapy, 30,* 537–541

Kendall-Tackett, K. A., & Eckenrode, J. (1996). The effects of neglect on academic achievement and disciplinary problems: A developmental perspective. *Child Abuse and Neglect, 20,* 161.

Kenny, D. T., Keogh, T., & Seidler, K. (2001). Predictors of recidivism in Australian juvenile sex offenders: Implications for treatment. *Sexual Abuse: A Journal of Research and Treatment, 13,* 131–148.

Kernberg, P. F., Weiner, A. S., & Bardenstein, K. K. (2000). *Personality disorders in children and adolescents.* New York: Basic Books.

Kimble, M. A. (1985). The surviving majority: Differential impact of aging and implications for ministry. *Word and World, 5*(4), 395–404.

Kimerling, R., & Calhoun, K. S. (1994). Somatic symptoms, social support, and treatment seeking among sexual assault victims. *Journal of Consulting and Clinical Psychology, 62,* 333–340.

Klein, S., & Manuzza, S. (1991). Long term outcome of hyperactive children: A review. *Journal of the American Academy of Child and Adolescent Psychiatry, 30,* 1120–1134.

Knable, J. (1981). Handholding: One means of transcending barriers of communication. *Heart and Lung, 10*(6), 1106–1110.

Kohlberg, L. (1964). Development of moral character and moral ideology. In M. L. Hoffman & L. W. Hoffman (Eds.), *Review of child development research* (Vol. I). New York: Russell Sage.

Kongs, S., Thompson, L., Iverson, G., & Heaton, R. (2000). *Wisconsin Card Sorting Test–64 Card Version: Professional manual.* Odessa, FL: Psychological Assessment Resources.

Koss, M. P., Heise, L., & Russo, N. F. (1994). The global health burden of rape. *Psychology of Women Quarterly, 18,* 509–537.

Koss, M. P., Koss, P. G., & Woodruff, W. J. (1991). Deleterious effects of criminal victimization on women's health and medical utilization. *Archives of Internal Medicine, 151,* 342–357.

Lab, S. P., Shields, G., & Schondel, C. (1993). Research note: An evaluation of juvenile sexual offender treatment. *Crime and Delinquency, 39,* 543–553.

Land, W. (1995). Psychopharmacological options for sex offenders. In B. Schwartz & H. Cellini (Eds.), *The sex offender: Corrections, treatment and legal practice* (Vol. I, pp. 18-1–18-7). Kingston, NJ: Civic Research Institute.

Lane, S. (1997). Assessment of sexually abusive youth. In G. Ryan & S. Lane (Eds.), *Juvenile sexual offending: Causes, consequences, and correction* (rev. ed., pp. 219–263). San Francisco: Jossey-Bass.

Lang, P. (1995). The emotion probe: Studies in motivation and attention. *American Psychologist, 50,* 372–385.

Långström, N. (2002). Long-term follow-up of criminal recidivism in young sex offenders: Temporal patterns and risk factors. *Psychology, Crime & Law, 8,* 41–58.

Långström, N., & Grann, M. (2000). Risk for criminal recidivism among young sex offenders, *Journal of Interpersonal Violence, 15,* 855–871.

Lanning, K. V. (2001). Child molesters and cyber pedophiles: A behavioral perspective. In R. R. Hazelwood & A. Wolbert Burgess (Eds.), *Practical aspects of rape investigation: A multi-disciplinary approach* (3rd ed.). London: CRC Press.

Lao Tzu. (1990). *Tao Te Ching.* New York: Bantam.

Laws, D. R. (Ed.). (1989). *Relapse prevention with sex offenders.* New York: Guilford Press.

Laws, D. R. (2003). The rise and fall of relapse prevention. *Australian Psychologist, 38*(1), 22–30.

Laws, D. R., Hudson, S. M., & Ward, T. (2000). *Remaking relapse prevention with sex offenders: A sourcebook.* Thousand Oaks, CA: Sage.

Le Doux, J. E. (1994, June). Emotion, memory, and the brain: Neural routes underlying the formation of memories about primitive emotional experiences, such as fear, have been traced. *Scientific American*, pp. 50–57.

Le Doux, J. E. (1995). In search of an emotional system in the brain: Leaping from fear to emotion and consciousness. In M. Gazzaniga (Ed.), *The cognitive neurosciences* (pp. 1049–1061). Boston: MIT Press.

Leguizamo, A. (2002). The object relations and victimization histories of juvenile sex offenders. In B. K. Schwartz (Ed.), *The sex offender: Current treatment modalities and systems issues* (Vol. IV, pp. 4-1–4-40). Kingston, NJ: Civic Research Institute.

Letourneau, E. J. (2004). T*reatment of juvenile sex offenders with multisytemic therapy.* Workshop presented at the seventh annual conference of the California Coalition of Sexual Offenders, San Francisco.

Letourneau, E. J. (2004). A comment on the first report: Letter to the editor. *Sexual Abuse: A Journal of Research and Treatment, 16*, 77–81.

Letourneau, E. J., Resnick, H. S., Kilpatrick, D. G., Saunders, B. E., & Best, C. L. (1996). Comorbidity of sexual problems and posttraumatic stress disorder in female crime victims. *Behavior Therapy, 27*, 321–336.

Leversee, T., & Pearson, C. (2001). Eliminating

the pendulum effect: A balanced approach to the assessment, treatment, and management of sexually abusive youth. *Journal of the Center for Families, Children and the Courts, 3*, 45–57.

Levy, T., & Orlans, M. (2000). Attachment disorder as an antecedent to violence and antisocial patterns in children. *Handbook of attachment interventions* (pp. 1–26). San Diego: Academic Press.

Lewis, D. O. (1992). From abuse to violence: psychophysiological consequences of maltreatment. *Journal of the American Academy of Child and Adolescent Psychiatry, 31*, 383–391.

Lewis, R. E. (2001, June 28 & 29). *Comprehensive treatment for mentally ill clients with sexual behavior disorder.* Paper presented at the first annual MI/SBD Training Conference: The treatment of MI/SBD inpatients. Medfield: Massachusetts Department of Mental Health and University of Massachusetts Medical School, Medfield State Hospital.

Lewis, R. E. (2002, December 19). *Comprehensive treatment for mentally ill clients with problem sexual behavior.* Baldwinville: Massachusetts Department of Mental Health, Baldwinville Community Residence.

Lindeman, H. (n.d.). *ACDI-Corrections Version II.* Retrieved August 1, 2004, from *www.bdsltd.com/bds_acdi_cv2.htm.*

Lindeman, H. (n.d.). *Juvenile Substance Abuse Profile.* Retrieved August 1, 2004, from *www.bdsltd.com/bds_JSAP.htm.*

Lipsey, M. W., & Derzon, J. H. (1998). Predictors of violent or serious delinquency in adolescence and early adulthood: A synthesis of longitudinal research. In R. Loeber & D. P. Farrington (Eds.), *Serious and violent juvenile offenders: Risk factors and successful interventions* (pp. 86–105). London: Sage.

Lisak, D., & Ivan, C. (1995). Deficits in intimacy and empathy in sexually aggressive men. *Journal of Interpersonal Violence, 10*(3), 296–308.

Loeber, R., & Farrington, D. P. (Eds.). (1998). *Serious and violent juvenile offenders: Risk factors and successful interventions.* Thousand Oaks, CA: Sage.

Loeber, R., Wung, P., Keenan, K., Giroux, B.,

Stouthamer-Loeber, M., Van Kammen, W., et al. (1993). Developmental pathways in disruptive child behavior. *Development and Psychopathology, 5*, 103–133.

Longo, R., with Bays, L. (2001). *Who am I and Why am I in treatment* (13th printing). Brandon, VT: Safer Society Press. (Copyright 1998)

Longo, R. E. (2003). Emerging issues, policy changes, and the future of treating children with sexual behavior problems. *Annals of the New York Academy of Sciences, 989,* 502–514.

Lott, D. (1998, May). Attachment and impact on psychic vulnerability. *Psychiatric Times, 15*(5), 1–5.

Lott, D. (2003). Brain development, attachment and impact on psychic vulnerability. *Psychiatric Times, 15*(5), 1–5.

Lottes, I., & Kontula, O. (2000). *New views on sexual health: The case of Finland.* Vaestontutkimuslaitos, Vaestoliitto: Population Research Institute, The Family Federation of Finland.

Loughnan, T., Pierce, M., & Sagris, D. A. (1999). *The Maroondah Assessment Profile for Problem Gambling.* Victoria, Australia: Australian Council for Educational Research.

Lund, C. A. (2000). Predictors of sexual recidivism: Did meta-analysis clarify the role and relevance of denial? *Sexual Abuse: A Journal of Research and Treatment, 12*(4), 275–287.

Lynam, D. (1996). Early identification of chronic offenders: Who is the fledgling psychopath? *Psychological Bulletin, 120,* 209–234.

Lynam, D., Moffitt, T., & Stouthamer-Loeber, M. (1993). Explaining the relation between IQ and delinquency: Class, race, test motivation, school failure or self-control? *Journal of Abnormal Psychology, 102,* 187–196.

MacEwen, K. (1994). Refining the intergenerational transmission hypothesis. *Journal of Interpersonal Violence, 9*(3), 350–365.

MacLean, P. D. (1949). Psychosomatic disease and the visceral brain. Recent developments bearing on the Papez Theory of Emotion. *Psychosomatic Medicine, 11,* 338–353.

MacLean, P. D. (1990). *The triune brain in evolution: Role in paleocerebral functions.* New York: Plenum Press.

Maguire, K., & Pastore, A. L. (1998). *Sourcebook of criminal justice statistics 1998* (p. 337). Washington, DC: U. S. Department of Justice, Bureau of Justice Statistics.

Mahoney, J. (2004, March 9). Sex fiends AWOL: 2000 cons defying state's registry. *New York Daily News,* p. 12.

Main, M., & Goldwyn, R. (1994). *Adult attachment scoring and classification systems.* Unpublished scoring manual. Berkeley: Department of Psychology, University of California, Berkeley.

Main, M., & Solomon, J. (1990). Procedures for identifying infants as disorganized/disoriented during the Ainsworth Strange Situation. In M. Greenberg, D. Cicchetti, & M. Cummings (Eds.), *Attachment in the preschool years: Theory, research, and intervention* (pp. 121–160). Chicago: University of Chicago Press.

Malamuth, N. M., Sockloskie, R. J., Koss, M. P., & Tanaka, J. S. (1991). Characteristics of aggressors against women: Testing a model using a national sample of college students. *Journal of Consulting and Clinical Psychology, 59,* 953–962.

Malesky, L. A. (2003). Sexually deviant Internet usage by child sex offenders. *Dissertation Abstracts International.*

Mann, R. E. (2000). Managing resistance and rebellion in relapse prevention intervention. In D. R. Laws, S. M. Hudson, & T. Ward (Eds.), *Remaking relapse prevention with sex offenders: A sourcebook* (pp. 197–200). Thousand Oaks, CA: Sage.

Mann, R. E., Daniels, M., & Marshall, W. L. (2002).The use of role-plays in developing victim empathy. In *In their shoes* (pp. 132–148). Oklahoma City, OK: Wood 'N' Barnes.

Mann, R. E., & Fernandez, Y. M. (2001). *HM Prison Service Sex Offender Treatment Manual: SOTP Rolling Programme: Treatment manual.* Unpublished manuscript.

Mann, R. E., & Thornton, D. (1994). *HM Prison Service Sex Offender Treatment Programme:*

SOTP core training manual. Unpublished manuscript.

Mann, R. E., & Thornton, D. (2000). *HM Prison Service Sex Offender Treatment Programme: SOTP core training manual* (rev.). Unpublished manuscript.

Mann, R. E., Webster, S. D., Schofield, C., & Marshall, W. L. (2004). Approach versus avoidance goals in relapse prevention with sexual offenders. *Sexual Abuse: A Journal of Research and Treatment, 16*(1), 65–75.

Marczyk, G. R., Heilbrun, K., Lander, T., & DeMatteo, D. (2003). Predicting juvenile recidivism with the PCL:YV, MAYSI, and YLS/CMI. *International Journal of Forensic Mental Health, 2,* 7–18.

Marlatt, G. A. (1982). Relapse prevention: A self-control program for the treatment of addictive behaviors. In R. B. Stuart (Ed.), *Adherence, compliance and generalization in behavioral medicine* (pp. 329-378). New York: Brunner/Mazel.

Marlatt, G. A. (1985). Lifestyle modification. In G. A. Marlatt & J. R. Gordon (Eds.), *Relapse prevention* (pp. 280–348). New York: Guilford Press.

Marlatt, G. A. (1998). *Harm reduction: Pragmatic strategies for managing high-risk behaviors.* New York: Guilford Press.

Marlatt, G. A., & Gordon, J. R. (1985). *Relapse prevention: Maintenance strategies in the treatment of addictive behaviors.* New York: Guilford Press.

Marques, J. K., Day, D. M., & Nelson, C. (1992). *Findings and recommendations from California's experimental treatment program.* Unpublished manuscript, Sex Offender Treatment and Evaluation Project, Atascadero State Hospital, California.

Marques, M. J. K., Nelson, C., Alarcon J. M., & Day, D. M. (2000). Preventing relapse in sex offenders: What we Learned from SOTEP's experimental program. In D. R. Laws, S. M. Hudson, & T. Ward (Eds.), *Remaking relapse prevention with sex offenders* (pp. 321–340). Thousand Oaks, CA: Sage.

Marsa, F., O'Reilly, G., Carr, A., Murphy, P., O'Sullivan, M., Cotter, A., et al. (2004). Attachment styles and psychological profiles of child sex offenders in Ireland. *Journal of Interpersonal Violence, 19,* 228–251.

Marshall, L. E., & Marshall, W. L. (2002). The role of attachment in sexual offending: An examination of pre-occupied attachment style offending behavior. In B. K. Schwartz (Ed.), *The sex offender: Current treatment modalities and systems issues* (Vol. IV, pp. 3-1–3-8). Kingston, NJ: Civic Research Institute.

Marshall, W. L., & Anderson, D. (1996). An evaluation of the benefits of relapse prevention programs with sexual offenders. *Sexual Abuse: A Journal of Research and Treatment, 8,* 209–229.

Marshall, W. L., Anderson, D., & Fernandez, Y. M. (1999). *Cognitive-behavioural treatment of sexual offenders.* New York: Wiley.

Marshall, W. L., Champagne, F., Brown, C., & Miller, S. (1997). Empathy, intimacy, loneliness and self-esteem in nonfamilial child molesters. *Journal of Child Sexual Abuse, 6,* 87–97.

Marshall, W. L., Christie, M. M., & Lanthier, R. D. (1979). *A descriptive study of incarcerated rapists and pedophiles.* Ottawa: Solicitor General of Canada.

Marshall, W. L., Jones, R., Ward, T., Johnston, P., & Barbaree, H. E. (1991). Treatment outcome with sex offenders. *Clinical Psychology Review, 11,* 465–485.

Marshall, W. L. & Mazucco, A. (1995). Self-esteem and parental attachments in child molesters. *Sexual Abuse: A Journal of Research and Treatment, 7,* 279–285.

Martin, H.P., Beezley, P., Conway, E. (1974). The development of abused children: A review of the literature. *Advanced Pediatrics, 21,* 25.

Maslow, A. (1968). *Toward a psychology of being* (2nd ed.). Princeton, NJ: Van Nostrand Reinhold.

Maslow, A. H. (1970). *Motivation and personality* (2nd ed.). New York: Harper & Row.

May, R. (1992). Foreword. In K. Freedheim (Ed.), *History of psychotherapy* (p. xxv). Washington, DC: American Psychological Association.

Mazur, T., & Michael, P. M. (1992). Outpatient treatment for adolescents with sexually inappropriate behaviour: Program description and six-month follow-up. *Journal of Offender Rehabilitation, 18*, 191–203.

McDonald, R. P. (1999). *Test theory: A unified treatment*. Hillsdale, NJ: Erlbaum.

McEwen, B.S. (2000). The neurobiology of stress: From serendipity to clinical relevance. *Brain Research*. 886, 172–179.

McFarlane, A., Weber, D., & Clark, C. (1993). Abnormal stimulus processing in posttraumatic stress disorder. *Biological Psychiatry*, 34, 311–320.

McGrath, R. J., Cumming, G. F., & Burchard, B. L. (2003). *Current practices and trends in sexual abuser management: The Safer Society 2002 nationwide study*. Brandon, VT: Safer Society Press.

McHugh, S., Deacon, R., Rawlins, J., & Bannerman, D. (2004). Amygdala and ventral hippocampus contribute differentially to mechanisms of fear and anxiety. *Behavioral Neuroscience, 118*, 63–78.

McMackin, R. A., Leisen, M., Cusack, J. F., LaFratta, J., & Litwin, P. (2002). The relationship of trauma exposure to sex offending behavior among male juvenile offenders. *Journal of Child Sexual Abuse, 11*(2), 25–40.

Meichenbaum, D. (1994). *A clinical handbook/practical therapist manual for assessing and treating adults with posttraumatic stress disorder*. Waterloo, Ontario, Canada: Institute Press.

Meyers, J., & Meyers, K. (1995). *Rey Complex Figure Test and Recognition Trial: Professional manual*. Odessa, FL: Psychological Assessment Resources.

Miller, G. A. (1997). *The Substance Abuse Subtle Screening Inventory* (3rd ed.). Springville, IL: The SASSI Institute.

Miller, S. B. (1996). *Shame in context*. Hillsdale NJ: Analytic Press.

Millon, T., Antoni, M., Millon, C., Meagher, S., & Grossman, S. (2001). *Millon Behavioral Medicine Diagnostic*. Minnetonka, MN: NCS Assessments.

Milloy, C. D. (1994). Specialized treatment for juvenile sex offenders: A closer look. *Journal of Interpersonal Violence, 13*, 653–656.

Ministry of Community Safety and Correctional Services. (2002). *First year of Ontario Sex Offender Registry a success* [Online]. Available: *www.ogov.newswire.ca/ontario/GPOE/2002/04/05 /c1651.html?lmatch=&lang=_e.html*.

Ministry of Community Safety and Correctional Services. (2004). *Ontario Sex Offender Registry a success* [Online]. Available: *www.mpss.jus.gov.on.ca/english/police_serv/sor/s or.html*.

Minuchin, S. (1974). *Families and family therapy*. Cambridge, MA: Harvard University Press.

Mischel, H., & Mischel, W. (1983). The development of children's knowledge of self-control strategies. *Child Development, 54*, 603–619.

Moffitt, T. E. (1993). The neuropsychology of conduct disorder. *Development and Psychopathology, 5*(1–2), 135–151.

Moffitt, T. E. (1997). Neuropsychology, antisocial behavior, and neighborhood context. In J. McCord (Ed.), *Violence and childhood in the inner city* (pp. 116–170). Cambridge, UK: Cambridge Criminology Series.

Monahan, J. (1995). *The clinical prediction of violent behavior*. Northvale, NJ: Jason Aronson. (Original work published 1981)

Monahan, J., Steadman, H. J. Silver, E., Applebaum, P. S., Robbins, P. C., Mulvey, E. P., Roth, L. H., Grisso, T., & Banks, S. (2001). *Rethinking risk assessment: The Macarthur Study of Violence and Mental Disorder*. New York: Oxford University Press.

Monks of New Skete. (1999). *The Monks of New Skete*. Boston: Little, Brown.

Montague, A. (1971). *Touching: The human significance of the skin*. New York: Harper & Row.

Moreno, J. L., (1953) *Who shall survive? Foundations of sociometry, group psychotherapy, and sociodrama*. Beacon House: New York.

Morgan, A., & Lilienfield, S. (2000). A meta-analytic review of the relation between anti-social behavior and neuropsychological measures of executive function. *Clinical Psychology Review*, *20*, 113–136.

Morin, J. W., & Levenson, J. S. (2002). *The road to freedom*. Oklahoma City, Oklahoma: Wood 'N' Barnes.

Morris, R. E., Anderson, M. M., & Knox, G. W. (2002). Incarcerated adolescents' experiences as perpetrators of sexual assault. *Archives of Pediatrics and Adolescent Medicine, 156,* 831–835.

Morrison, A. P. (1989). *Shame: The underside of narcissism*. Hillsdale NJ: Analytic Press.

Morton, K. E. (2003). *Psychometric properties of four risk assessment measures with adolescent sexual offenders*. Unpublished master's thesis, Carleton University, Ottawa, Ontario, Canada.

Moses-Hrushovski, R. (1994). *Deployment: Hiding behind power struggles as a character defense*. New York: Jason Aronson.

Murray, G., McKenzie, K., Quigley, A., Matheson, E., Michie, A., & Lindsay, W. (2001). A comparison of the neuropsychological profiles of adult male sex offenders and non-offenders with a learning disability. *Journal of Sexual Aggression, 7*, 57–64.

Myers, R. (1992). *The twelve who survive*. New York: Routledge.

Nathanson, D. L. (1992). *Shame and pride: Affect, sex and the birth of the self*. New York: Norton.

National Adolescent Perpetrator Network. (1993). The revised report from the National Task Force on Juvenile Sexual Offending. *Juvenile and Family Court Journal, 44,* 1–120.

National Association for the Education of Young Children. (1996, July). *Prevention of child abuse in early childhood programs and the responsibilities of early childhood professionals to prevent child abuse* [Position statement]. Washington, DC: Author.

National Institute on Drug Abuse. (1999). *Principles of drug addiction treatment: A research-based guide* (NIH Publication No. 99-4180). Washington, DC: National Institute of Health.

National Task Force on Juvenile Sexual

Offending. (1993). The revised report. *Juvenile and Family Court Journal, 44,* 1–120.

Newman, J. P. (1987). Reaction to punishment in extraverts and psychopaths: Implications for the impulsive behavior of disinhibited individuals. *Journal of Research in Personality, 21*, 464–480.

Nicholaichuk, T. P. (1996). Sex offender treatment priority: An illustration of the risk/need principle. *Forum on Corrections Research, 8*, 30-32.

Nicholaichuk, T. P., Gordon, A., Gu, D., & Wong, S. (2000). Outcome of an institutional sexual offender treatment program: A comparison between treated and matched untreated offenders. *Sexual Abuse: A Journal of Research and Treatment, 12*(2), 139–153.

Nicholaichuk, T. P., & Yates, P. M. (2002). Treatment efficacy: Outcomes of the Clearwater sex offender program. In B. K. Schwartz (Ed.), *The sex offender: Current treatment modalities and systems issues* (Vol. IV, pp. 7-1–7-18.) Kingston, NJ: Civic Research Institute.

Nietszche, F. (1989). *Beyond good and evil*. New York: Vintage Books. (Original work published 1886)

O'Brien, M. J., & Bera, W. H. (1986). Adolescent sexual offenders: A descriptive typology. *Preventing Sexual Abuse, 1*, 1–4.

Ogden, P., & Minton, K. (2000). Sensorimotor Psychotherapy: One method for processing traumatic memory. *Traumatology*, 6 (3).

Ornstein, R., & Thompson, R. E. (1984). *The amazing brain*. New York: Houghton-Mifflin.

Orpinas, P. K., Basen-Engquist, K., Gunbaum, J. A., & Parcel, G. S. (1995, March). The co-morbidity of violence-rated behaviors with health-risk behaviors in a population of high school students. *Journal of Adolescent Health, 16*(3), 216–225.

Orput, P. (2003). *Internet crimes against children*. Paper presented at the meeting of the Minnesota Internet Crimes Against Children Task Force training. Hennepin County, MN.

Padesky, C. A. (1994). Schema change processes in cognitive therapy. *Clinical Psychology and Psychotherapy, 1*, 267–278).

Paolucci, E. O., Violato, C., & Schofield, M. A. (1998). Case need domain: Marital and family. *Correctional Services Canada Forum, 10*(3). Available: *www.csc-scc.gc.ca/text/pblct/forum/e103/103e_e.pdf.*

Papez, J. W. (1937). A proposed mechanism for emotion. *American Medical Association Archives of Neurology and Psychiatry, 38*, 725–743.

Parks, G. A., & Marlatt, G. A. (1999) Relapse prevention therapy for substance-abusing offenders: A cognitive-behavioural approach. In E. Latessa (Ed.), *What works: Strategic solutions: The International Community Corrections Asociation examines substance abuse.* Lanham, MD: American Correctional Association.

Peck, S. (1987). *The different drummer.* New York: Simon & Schuster.

Perry, B. (1997). Incubated in terror: Neurodevelopmental factors in the "cycle of violence." In J. Osofsky (Ed.), *Children, youth, and violence: The search for solutions* (pp. 124–148). New York: Guilford Press.

Perry, B. (2001). Consequences of emotional neglect in childhood. In B. D. Perry (Ed.), *Caregiver Education Series* (adapted in part from *Maltreated children: Experience, brain development, and the next generation*). New York: W.W. Norton.

Perry, B. (2001). The neurodevelopmental impact of violence in childhood. In D. Schetky & E. Benedek (Eds.), *Textbook of child and adolescent forensic psychiatry* (pp. 231–238). Washington, DC: American Psychiatric Press.

Perry, B., & Pate, J. E. (1994). Neurodevelopment and the psychobiological roots of post-traumatic stress disorders. In L. Kozoil & C. Stout (Eds.), *The neuropsychology of mental disorders: A practical guide* (pp. 81–98). Springfield, IL: Charles C. Thomas.

Perry, G. P., & Orchard, J. (1992). *Assessment and treatment of adolescent sex offenders.* Sarasota, FL: Professional Resource Exchange.

Peugh, J., & Belenko, S. (2001). Examining the substance use patterns and treatment needs of incarcerated sex offenders. *Sexual Abuse: A Journal of Research and Treatment, 13*, 179–195.

Phillips, S. L., Heads, T. C., Taylor, P. .J., & Hill, G. M. (1999). Sexual offending and antisocial behavior among patients with schizophrenia. *Journal of Clinical Psychiatry, 60*(3), 170–175.

Piaget, J. (1965). *The moral judgement of the child.* New York: Free Press.

Pithers, W. D. (1990) Relapse prevention with sexual aggressors: A method for maintaining therapeutic gain and enhancing external supervision. In W. L. Marshall, D. R. Laws, & H. E. Barbaree (Eds.), *Handbook of sexual assault: Issues, theories, and treatment of the offender* (pp. 343–361). New York: Plenum Press.

Pithers, W. D. (1994). Process evaluation of a group therapy component designed to enhance sex offenders' empathy for sexual abuse survivors. *Behaviour, Research and Therapy, 32*(5), 565–570.

Pithers, W. D. (1997). Maintaining treatment integrity with sexual abusers. *Criminal Justice and Behavior, 24*(1), 34–51.

Pithers, W. D., Marques, J. K., Gibat, C. C., & Marlatt, G. A. (1983). Relapse prevention with sexual aggressives: A self-control model of treatment and maintenance of change. In J. G. Greer & I. R. Stuart (Eds.), *The sexual aggressor: Current perspectives on treatment* (pp. 214–239). New York: Van Nostrand Reinhold.

Poole, D., Liedecke, D., & Marbibi, M. (2000). *Risk assessment and recidivism in juvenile sexual offenders: A validation study of the Static-99.* Austin: Texas Youth Commission.

Porporino, F. J., & Motiuk, L. L. (1991). *Preliminary results of National Sex Offender Census* (User Report R-29). Ottawa, Ontario: Correctional Service of Canada. Available: *www.csc-scc.gc.ca.*

Pranis, K., Stuart, B., & Wedge, M. (2003). *Peacemaking circles.* St. Paul, MN: Living Justice Press.

Prentky, R. A., & Burgess, A. W. (1990). Rehabilitation of child molesters: A cost-benefit analysis. *American Journal of Orthopsychiatry, 60*, 108–117.

Prentky, R., Harris, B., Frizzell, K., & Righthand, S. (2000). An actuarial procedure for assessing risk with juvenile sexual offenders. *Sexual Abuse: A Journal of Research and Treatment, 12*(2), 71–93.

Prentky, R. A., Knight, R. A., Sims-Knight, J. E., Straus, H., Rokous, F., & Cerce, D. (1989). Developmental antecedents of sexual aggression. *Development and Psychopathology, 1*, 153–169.

Prentky, R. A., & Righthand, S. C. (2001). *Juvenile Sex Offender Assessment Protocol: Manual.* Unpublished document. Available: *www.csom.org*.

Prentky, R., & Righthand, S. (2003). *Juvenile Sex Offender Assessment Protocol—II (JSOAP-II).* Available: *www.csom.org*.

Prescott, J. W. (1975, April). Body pleasure and the origins of violence. *The Futurist*, pp. 64–74.

Prescott, J. W. (1996). The origins of human love and violence. *Pre- and Perinatal Psychology Journal, 10*(3), 143–188.

Proulx, J., Perreault, C., & Ouimet, M. (1999). Pathways in the offending process of extrafamilial sexual child molesters. *Sexual Abuse: A Journal of Research and Treatment, 11*, 117–129.

Putnam, D. E., & Maheu, M. M. (2000). Online sexual addiction and compulsivity: Integrating web resources and behavioral telehealth in treatment. *Sexual Addiction and Compulsivity: Journal of Treatment and Prevention, 7*(1–2), 91–112.

Pynoos, R. (1990). Post-traumatic stress disorder in children and adolescents. In B. Garfinkel, G. Carlson, & E. Weller (Eds.), *Psychiatric disorders in children and adolescents* (pp. 48–63). Philadelphia: Saunders.

Quayle, E., Holland, G., Linehan, C., & Taylor, M. (2000). The Internet and offending behavior: A case study. *Journal of Sexual Aggression, 6*(1–2), 78–96.

Quayle, E., & Taylor, M. (2002). Paedophiles, pornography, and the internet: Assessment issues. *British Journal of Social Work, 32*, 863–875.

Quigley, S. (2001, June 28 and 29). *Integrating dialectical behavior therapy into sex offender treatment for mentally ill patients.* Paper presented at the first annual MI/SBD Training Conference: The treatment of MI/SBD inpatients. Medfield: Massachusetts Department of Mental

Health and University of Massachusetts Medical School, Medfield State Hospital.

Quinsey, V. L. (1977). The assessment and treatment of child molesters: A review. *Canadian Psychological Review, 18,* 204–220.

Quinsey, V. L. (2000, March). *The Violence Risk Appraisal Guide.* Paper presented at Sinclair Seminars' Sex Offender Re-Offense Risk Prediction Symposium, Madison, Wisconsin. Available: *www.sinclairseminars.com*.

Quinsey, V. L., Harris, G. T., Rice, M. E., & Cormier, C. A. (1998). *Violent offenders: Managing and appraising risk.* Washington, DC: American Psychological Association.

Quinsey, V. L., Skilling, T. A., Lalumière, M. L., & Craig, W. M. (2004). *Juvenile delinquency: Understanding the origins of individual differences.* Washington, DC: American Psychological Association.

Raine, A., Brennan, P., & Mednick, S. A. (1994, December). Birth complications combined with early maternal rejection at age 1 year predispose to violent crime at age 18. *Archives of General Psychiatry, 51*(12), 984–988.

Raine, A., & Buchsbaum, M. S. (1996). Violence, brain imaging, and neuropsychology. In D. Stoff & R. Cairns (Eds.), *Aggression and violence: Genetic, neurobiological, and biosocial perspectives* (pp. 195–217). Mahwah, NJ: Erlbaum.

Rasmussen, L. A. (1999). Factors related to recidivism among juvenile sexual offenders. *Sexual Abuse: A Journal of Research and Treatment, 11*, 69–85.

Reite, M., & Field, T. (Eds.). (1985). *The psychobiology of attachment and separation.* New York: Academic Press.

Reppucci, N. D., & Clingempeel, W. G. (1978). Methodological issues in research with correctional populations. *Journal of Consulting and Clinical Psychology, 46*, 727–746.

Resick, P. A., & Schnicke, M. K. (1992). Cognitive processing therapy for sexual assault victims. *Journal of Consulting and Clinical Psychology, 60*, 748–756.

Reynolds, C., & Bigler, E. (1998). *Test of Memory and Learning.* Austin, TX: Pro-Ed.

Rich, P. (2000). *Juvenile Risk Assessment Tool.* Barre, MA: Stetson School.

Rich, P. (2001). *J-RAT: Juvenile (Clinical) Risk Assessment Tool—Assessment of risk for sexual re-offending.* Unpublished document, Stetson School, Barre, MA.

Rich, P. (2003) *Understanding, assessing and rehabilitating juvenile sex offenders.* Hoboken, NJ: Wiley.

Righthand, S., Knight, R., & Prentky, R. (2002, October). *A path analytic investigation of proximal antecedents of J-SOAP risk domains.* Paper presented at the annual meeting of the Association for the Treatment of Sexual Abusers, Montreal, Quebec, Canada.

Righthand, S., & Welch, C. (2001). *Juveniles who have sexually offended.* Washington, DC: U.S. Department of Justice Office of Juvenile Justice and Delinquency Prevention. Retrieved October 25, 2002, from *www.ncjrs.org/html/ojjd/report_juvsex_offend/*.

Risk & Needs Assessment. (n.d.). *SAI-Juvenile report.* Retrieved July 13, 2004, from http://www.sex-offender-tests.com/index_SAI-EXAMPLE-REPORT.htm.

Risk & Needs Assessment. (n.d.). *Unique test features.* Retrieved October 2004, from *www.riskandneeds.com/rna_UNIQUE_FEATURES.htm.*

Robitscher, J. (1980). *The powers of psychiatry.* Boston: Houghton Mifflin.

Rogeness, G., Amrung, S., & Maced, C. (1986). Psychopathology in abused or neglected children. *Journal of the American Academy of Child Psychiatry, 25,* 659.

Rogers, C. (1961). *On becoming a person.* Boston: Houghton Mifflin.

Roose-Evans, J. (1995). *Passages of the soul.* Rockport, MA: Element Books.

Ross, J., & Loss, P. (1991). Assessment of the juvenile sex offender. In G. D. Ryan, & S. L. Lane (Eds.), *Juvenile sexual offending: Causes, consequences, and correction* (pp. 199–251). Lexington, MA: Lexington Books.

Ross, R. (1996). *Returning to the teachings.* Toronto, Ontario, Canada: Penguin.

Rotunda, R. J., Kass, S. J., Sutton, M. A., & Leon, D. T. (2003). Internet use and misuse. Preliminary findings from a new assessment instrument. *Behavior Modification, 27*(4), 484–504.

Rubin, K. H., & Rose-Krasnor, L. (1986). Social-cognitive and social behavioral perspectives on problem solving. In M. Perlmutter (Ed.), *Minnesota Symposium on Child Psychology: Cognitive perspectives on children's social and behavioral development* (Vol. 18, pp. 1–68). Hillsdale, NJ: Erlbaum.

Russell, D. E. H. (1984). *Sexual exploitation: Rape, child sexual abuse and workplace harassment.* Thousand Oaks, CA: Sage.

Rutan, J. S., & Stone, W. N. (1993). *Psychodynamic group psychotherapy* (2nd ed.). New York: Guilford Press.

Ryan, G. (1989). Victim to victimizer: Rethinking victim treatment. *Journal of Interpersonal Violence, 4,* 325–341.

Ryan, G. (1999). Treatment of sexually abusive youth: The evolving consensus. *Journal of Interpersonal Violence, 14,* 422–436.

Ryan, G., Blum, J., Laws, S., Christopher, D., Weher, R., Sundine, D., et al. (1988). *Understanding and responding to the sexual behavior of children: Trainer's manual.* Denver: Kempe National Center, University of Colorado School of Medicine.

Ryan, G., & Lane, S. (1997). *Juvenile sexual offending: Causes, consequences, and correction.* San Francisco. Jossey-Bass.

Saigh, P. A., Mroueh, M., & Bremner, J. D. (1997). Scholastic impairments among traumatized adolescents. *Behavior Research and Therapy, 35,* 429–436.

Salter, A. C. (1988). *Treating child sex offenders and victims.* Newbury Park, CA: Sage.

Sams, J. (1999). *Dancing the dream.* San Francisco: Harper.

Sanchez-Hucles, J. (1999). *The first session with African Americans.* New York: Wiley.

Sander, D., & Wong, S. (1997). *The sacred heritage.* New York: Routledge.

Saunders, B. E., Kilpatrick, D. G., Hanson, R. F., Resnick, H. S, & Walker, M. E. (1999).

Prevalence, case characteristics, and long-term psychological correlates of child rape among women: A national survey. *Child Maltreatment, 4,* 187–200.

Saunders, B. E., Villeponteaux, L. A., Lipovsky, J. A., Kilpatrick, D. G., & Veronen, L. J. (1992). Child sexual assault as a risk factor for mental disorders among women: A community survey. *Journal of Interpersonal Violence, 7,* 189–204.

Schoenwald, S. K. (1998). *Multisystemic therapy consultation guidelines.* Charleston, SC: MST Institute.

Schoenwald, S. K., Henggeler, S. W., Brondino, M. J., & Rowland, M. D. (2000). Multisystemic therapy: Monitoring treatment fidelity. *Family Process, 39,* 83–103.

Schoenwald, S. K., Henggeler, S. W., & Edwards, D. (1998). *MST Supervisor Adherence Measure.* Charleston, SC: MST Institute.

Schoenwald, S. K., Sheidow, A. J., Letourneau, E. J., & Liao, J. G. (2003). Transportability of multisystemic therapy: Evidence for multilevel influences. *Mental Health Services Research, 5,* 223–239.

Schore, A. N. (1994). *Affect regulation and the origins of the self.* Hillsdale, NJ: Erlbaum.

Schore, A. N. (2000). Attachment and the regulation of the right brain. *Attachment and Human Development, 2,* 23–47.

Schore, A. (2001). The effects of early relational trauma on right brain development, affect regulation, and infant mental health. *Infant Mental Health Journal, 22,* 201–269.

Schore, A. N. (2002). Dysregulation of the right brain: A fundamental mechanism of traumatic attachment and the psychopathogenesis of posttraumatic stress disorder. *Australian and New Zealand Journal of Psychiatry, 36,* 9–30.

Schram, D. D., Milloy, C. D., & Rowe, W. E. (1991). *Juvenile sex offenders: A follow-up study of reoffense behavior.* Olympia: Washington State Institute for Public Policy.

Schram, D. D., Milloy, C. D., & Rowe, W. E. (1991, September). *Juvenile sex offenders: A follow-up study of reoffense behavior.* Olympia: Washington State Institute for Public Policy.

Schwartz, B. K. (1995). Theories of sex offenses. In B. K. Schwartz & H. R. Cellini (Eds.), *The sex offender: Corrections, treatment and legal practice* (Vol. I, pp. 2-1–2-32). Kingston, NJ: Civic Research Institute.

Schwartz, B. K. (1999). The case against involuntary commitment. In A. Schlank & F. Cohen (Eds.), *The sexual predator: Law, policy, evaluation and treatment* (pp. 4-1–4-22). Kingston, NJ: Civic Research Institute.

Schwartz, B. K., & Canfield, G. M. S. (1996). *Facing the shadow.* Kingston, NJ: Civic Research Institute.

Seabloom, W., Seabloom, M. E., Seabloom, E., Barron, R., & Hendrickson, S. (2003). A 14- to 24-year longitudinal study of a comprehensive sexual health model treatment program for adolescent sex offenders: Predictors of successful completion and subsequent criminal recidivism. *International Journal of Offender Therapy and Comparative Criminology, 47,* 468–481.

Seghorn, T., & Ball, C. (2000). Assessment of sexual deviance in adults with developmental disabilities. *Mental Health Aspects of Developmental Disabilities, 3*(2), 47–53.

Seidman, B. T., Marshall, W. L., Hudson, S. M., & Robertson, P. J. (1994). An examination of intimacy and loneliness in sex offenders. *Journal of Interpersonal Violence, 9,* 518–534.

Seligman, M. P. (1971). Preparedness and phobias. *Behavior Therapy, 2,* 307–320.

Selye, H. (1956). *The stress of life.* New York: McGraw-Hill.

Serin, R. C., & Brown, S. L. (2000). The clinical use of the Hare Psychopathy Checklist—Revised in contemporary risk assessment. In C. G. Gacono (Ed.), *The clinical and forensic assessment of psychopathy* (pp. 251–268). Mahwah, NJ: Erlbaum.

Seto, M. C., & Lalumière, M. L. (2001). A brief screening scale to identify pedophilic interests among child molesters. *Sexual Abuse: A Journal of Research and Treatment, 13,* 15–25.

Seto, M. C., Murphy, W. D., Page, J., & Ennis, L. (2003). Detecting anomalous sexual interests in juvenile sex offenders. *Annals of the New York Academy of Sciences, 989,* 118–130.

Shanahan, M., & Donato, R. (2001). Counting the cost: Estimating the economic benefit of pedophile treatment programs. *Child Abuse and Neglect, 25,* 541–555.

Shapiro, F. (1995). *Eye movement desensitization and reprocessing: Basic principals, protocols, and procedures.* New York: Guilford Press.

Sherak, D. (2000). Pharmacological treatment of sexually offending behavior in people with mental retardation/developmental disabilities. *Mental Health Aspects of Developmental Disabilities, 3*(2).

Sheslow, D., & Adams, W. (1990). *Wide Range Assessment of Memory and Learning.* San Antonio, TX: Psychological Corporation.

Shields, A., & Cicchetti, D. (1998). Reactive aggression among maltreated children. The contributions of attention and emotional dysregulation. *Journal of Clinical Child Psychology, 27,* 381–395.

Shorto, R. (1999). *Saints and madmen.* New York: Holt.

Siegel, D. (1999). *The developing mind: Toward a neurobiology of interpersonal experience.* New York: Guilford Press.

Siegel, D., & Schore, A. N. (1997). *Understanding and treating trauma: Developmental and neurobiological approaches.* Paper presented at continuing education seminar, University of California, Los Angeles.

Silverman, J., & Wilson, D. (2002). *Innocence betrayed: Paedophilia, the media and society.* Cambridge, UK: Polity Press.

Sipe, R., Jensen, E. L., & Everett, R. S. (1998). Adolescent sexual offenders grown up: Recidivism in young adulthood. *Criminal Justice and Behavior, 25,* 109–124.

Smallbone, S. W., & Dadds, M. R. (1998). Childhood attachment and adult attachment in incarcerated adult male sex offenders. *Journal of Interpersonal Violence, 13,* 555–573.

Smallbone, S., & Dadds, M.R. (2000).

Attachment and coercive sexual behavior. *Sexual Abuse, 12*(1), 3–15.

Smets, A. C., & Cebula, C. M. (1987). A group treatment program for adolescent sex offenders: Five steps toward resolution. *Child Abuse and Neglect, 11,* 247–254.

Smith, A. D., & Taylor, P. J. (1999) Serious sex offending against women by men with schizophrenia. *British Journal of Psychiatry, 174,* 233–237.

Smith, G., & Fischer, L. (1999). Assessment of juvenile sexual offenders: Reliability and validity of the Abel Assessment for Interest in Paraphilias. *Sexual Abuse: A Journal of Research and Treatment, 11,* 207—216.

Smith, J. (1989). *Senses and sensibilities.* New York: Wiley.

Sosin, D. M., Koepsell, T. D., Rivara, P., & Mercy, J. A. (1995, March). The co-morbidity of violence-rated behaviors with health-risk behaviors in a population of high school students. *Journal of Adolescent Health, 16*(3), 209–215.

Spitz, R. (1949). The role of ecological factors in emotional development. *Child Development, 20,* 145–155.

Smith, W. R., & Monastersky, C. (1986). Assessing juvenile sexual offenders' risk for reoffending. *Criminal Justice and Behavior, 13,* 115–140.

Statistics Canada. (2002). *Persons charged by type of offense.* Retrieved August 28, 2003, from *www.statcan.ca/english/Pgdb/legal14b.htm; www.statcan.ca/english/Pgdb/legal14c.htm.*

Steen, C., & Monnette, B. (1989). *Treating adolescent sex offenders in the community.* Springfield, IL: Charles C. Thomas.

Stien, P. T., & Kendall, J. (2004). *Psychological trauma and the developing brain: Neurologically based interventions for troubled children.* Binghamton, NY: Haworth Press.

Stirpe, T. S., Wilson, R. J., & Long, C. (2001). Goal attainment scaling with sexual offenders: A measure of clinical impact at post-treatment and at community follow-up. *Sexual Abuse: A Journal of Research and Treatment, 13,* 65–77.

Stone, M., & Thompson, E. (2001). Executive function impairment in sexual offenders. *Journal of Individual Psychology, 57,* 51–59.

Strate, D., Jones, L., Pullen, S., & English, K. (1996). Criminal justice policies and sex offender denial. In K. English, S. Pullen, & L. Jones (Eds.), *Managing adult sex offenders: A containment approach* (p. 48). Lexington, KY: American Probation and Parole Association.

Strauss, A. (1987). *Qualitative analysis for social scientists.* New York: Cambridge University Press.

Streeck-Fischer, A., & van der Kolk, B. (2000). Down will come baby cradle and all: Diagnostic and therapeutic implications of chronic trauma on child development. *Australian and New Zealand Journal of Psychiatry, 34,* 903–918.

Swenson, C.C., Henggeler, S.W., Schoenwald, S. K., Kaufman, K. L., & Randall, J. (1998). Changing the social ecologies of adolescent sexual offenders: Implications of the success of multisystemic therapy in treating serious antisocial behavior in adolescents. *Child Maltreatment, 3,* 330–338.

Swenson, C., & Letourneau, E. J. (2002). *Multisystemic therapy with adolescent sex offenders.* Workshop presented at the 20th annual Research and Treatment Conference of the Association for the Treatment of Sexual Abusers, Montreal, Quebec, Canada.

Tangney, J. P., Wagner, P., & Gramzow, R. (1992) Proneness to shame, proneness to guilt and psychopathology. *Journal of Abnormal Psychology, 101*(3), 469–478.

Taylor, R. (2000). A seven-year reconviction study of HMP Grendon Therapeutic Community (Research Findings No. 115). London: Home Office.

Teicher, M., Andersen, S., Polcari, A., Andersen, C., & Navalta, C. (2002). Developmental neurobiology of childhood stress and trauma. *Psychiatric Clinics of North America, 25,* 397–426.

Teichner, G., & Golden, C. (2000). The relationship of neuropsychological impairment to conduct disorder in adolescence: A conceptual review. *Aggression and Violent Behavior, 5,* 509–528.

Teichner, G., Golden, C., Crum, T., Azrin, N., Donohue, B., & Van Hasselt, V. (2000). Identification of neurological subtypes in a sample of delinquent adolescents. *Journal of Psychiatric Research, 34,* 129–132.

Textor. R. B. (1967). *A cross-cultural summary.* New Haven, CT: HRAF Press.

Thornton, D. (2000, March). *Structured risk assessment.* Paper presented at Sinclair Seminars' Sex Offender Re-Offense Risk Prediction Symposium, Madison, Wisconsin. Available: *www.sinclairseminars.com.*

Thornton, D. (2002). Constructing and testing a framework for dynamic risk assessment. *Sexual Abuse: A Journal of Research and Treatment, 14*(2), 139–153.

Tikkanen, R., & Ross, M. W. (2000). Looking for sexual compatibility: Experiences among Swedish men in visiting Internet gay chat rooms. *CyberPsychology and Behavior, 3*(4), 605–616.

Tingle, D., Barnard, G. W., Robbin, L., Newman., G., & Hutchinson, D. (1986). Childhood and adolescent characteristics of pedophiles and rapists. *International Journal of Law and Psychiatry, 9,* 103–116.

Tjaden, P., & Thoennes, N. (1998). *Stalking in America: Findings from the national violence against women survey* (NCJ-1669592). Washington, DC: Bureau of Justice Statistics, U.S. Department of Justice.

Todd, R., Swarzenski, B., & Rossi, P. (1995). Structural and functional development of the human brain. In D. Cicchetti & D. Cohen (Eds.), *Developmental psychopathology* (pp. 161–194). New York: Wiley.

Tomkins, S. S. (1962). *Affect, imagery, consciousness: The positive affects* (Vol. I). New York: Springer.

Toronto, E. L. K. (2002). A clinician's response to physical touch in the psychoanalytic setting. *Journal of Psychotherapy, 7*(1), 69–81.

Trevarthen, C., & Aitken, K. (2001). Infant intersubjectivity: Research, theory, and clinical applications. *Journal of Child Psychology and Psychiatry, 42*(1), 3–48.

Unnever, J. D., & Cornell, D. G., (2003).

Bullying, self-control, and ADHD. *Journal of Interpersonal Violence, 18*(2), 129–147.

U.S. Bureau of Justice Statistics. (2000). *Census of state and federal correctional facilities.* Washington, DC: U.S. Department of Justice.

U.S. Census Bureau. (2002). *The black population in the United States.* Washington, DC: U.S. Department of Commerce.

U.S. Census Bureau. (2002, March). *Current population survey* (annual demographic supp.) Washington, DC: U.S. Department of Commerce.

U.S. Census Bureau. (2002). *The Hispanic population in the United States.* Washington, DC: U.S. Department of Commerce.

U.S. Public Health Service. (1999). *Mental health: A report of the Surgeon General.* Rockville, MD: U.S. Department of Health and Human Services, National Institutes of Health, National Institute of Mental Health.

U.S. Public Health Service. (2001). *Youth violence: A report of the Surgeon General.* Washington, DC: Author.

Uvnas-Moberg, K. (1998). Oxytocin may mediate the benefits of positive social interaction and emotions. *Psychoneuroendocrinology, 23,* 819–835.

van der Kolk, B. A. (1994). Childhood abuse and loss of self-regulation. *Bulletin of Menninger Clinic, 58*(2), 145–168.

van der Kolk, B. A., & Ducey, C. P. (1989). The psychological processing of traumatic stress. Rorschach patterns in PTSD. *Journal of Traumatic Stress, 2,* 259–265.

van derKolk, B., McFarlane, A., & Weisaeth, L. (1996). *Traumatic stress. The effects of overwhelming experience on mind, body, and society.* New York: Guilford Press.

van der Kolk, B. A., McFarlane, A. C., & van der Hart, O. (1996). A general approach to the treatment of posttraumatic stress disorder. In B. van der Kolk, A. C. Mac Farlane, & L. Weisaeth (Eds.), *Traumatic stress: The effects of overwhelming experience on mind, body, and society* (pp. 417–440). New York: Guilford Press.

van der Hart, O., van der Kolk, B. A., & Boon, S.

(1998). Treatment of dissociative disorders. In J. D. Bremner & C. R. Marmar (Eds.), *Trauma, memory, and dissociation* (pp. 253–283). Washington, DC: American Psychiatric Press.

Veneziano, C., & Veneziano, L. (2002). Adolescent sex offenders: A review of the literature. *Trauma, Violence, and Abuse, 3,* 247–260.

Vermeiren, R., De Clippele, A., Schwab-Stone, M., Ruchkin, V., & Deboutte, D. (2002). Neuropsychological characteristics of three subgroups of Flemish delinquent adolescents. *Neuropsychology, 16*(1), 49–55.

Wahlberg, L., Kennedy, J., & Simpson, J. (2003). Impaired sensory-emotional integration in a violent adolescent sex offender. *Journal of Child Sexual Abuse, 12*(1), 1–15.

Waite, D., Pinkerton, R., Wieckowski, E., McGarvey, E., & Brown, G. L. (2002, October). *Tracking treatment outcome among juvenile sexual offenders: A nine year follow-up study.* Paper presented at the annual meeting of the Association for the Treatment of Sexual Abusers, Montreal, Quebec, Canada.

Ward, T. (2002). Good lives and the rehabilitation of offenders: Promises and problems. *Aggression and Violent Behavior, 7*(5), 513–528.

Ward, T., & Hudson, S. M. (1996). Relapse prevention: A critical analysis. *Sexual Abuse: A Journal of Research and Treatment, 8,* 177–200.

Ward, T., & Hudson, S. M. (1998). A model of the relapse process in sexual offenders. *Journal of Interpersonal Violence, 13*(6), 700–725.

Ward, T., & Hudson, S. M. (2000). A self-regulation model of relapse prevention. In D. R. Laws, S. M. Hudson, & T. Ward. (Eds.), *Remaking relapse prevention with sex offenders: A sourcebook* (pp. 79–101). New York: Sage.

Ward, T., & Hudson, S. M. (2000). Sexual offenders' implicit planning: A conceptual model. *Sexual Abuse: A Journal of Research and Treatment, 12*(3), 189–202.

Ward, T., Hudson, S. M., & Keenan, T. (1998). A self regulation model of the sexual offense process. *Sexual Abuse: A Journal of Research and Treatment, 10,* 141–157.

Ward, T., Hudson, S., & McCormack, J. (1997).

Attachment style, intimacy deficits, and sexual offending. In B. K. Schwartz & H. Cellini (Eds.), *The sex offender: New insights, treatment innovations and legal developments* (Vol. II, pp. 2-1–2-14). Kingston, NJ: Civic Research Institute.(from ch 9)

Ward, T., Laws, D. R., & Hudson, S. M. (2003). *Sexual deviance: Issues and controversies.* Thousand Oaks, CA: Sage.

Ward, T., Louden, K., Hudson, S. M., & Marshall, W. L. (1995). A descriptive model of the offense chain for child molesters. *Journal of Interpersonal Violence, 10,* 452–472.

Ward, T., & Stewart, C. A. (2003). Good lives and the rehabilitation of sexual offenders. In T. Ward, D. R. Laws, & S. M. Hudson (Eds.), *Sexual deviance: Issues and controversies* (pp. 21–44). Thousand Oaks, CA: Sage.

Ward, T., & Stewart, C. (2003). The relationship between human needs and criminogenic needs. *Psychology, Crime and Law, 9,* 219–224.

Webster, C. D., Ben-Aron, M. H., & Hucker, S. J. (1985). *Dangerousness: Probability and prediction, psychiatry and public policy.* Cambridge, UK: Cambridge University Press.

Webster, C. D., Harris, G. T., Rice, M. E., Cormier, C. A., & Quinsey, V. L. (1994). *The Violence Prediction Scheme: Assessing dangerousness in high risk men.* Toronto, Canada: Centre of Criminology, University of Toronto.

Webster, S. D. (2003). *Pathways to sexual offence recidivism following treatment: An examination of the Ward & Hudson self-regulation model of relapse.* Unpublished manuscript.

Webster, S. D., & Beech, A. R. (2000). The nature of offenders' affective empathy: A grounded theory analysis. *Sexual Abuse: A Journal of Research and Treatment, 12*(4), 249–262.

Webster, S. D., Bowers, L. E., Mann, R. E., & Marshall, W. L. (2005). Developing empathy in sex offenders: The value of offence re-enactments. *Sexual Abuse: A Journal of Research and Treatment, 17,* 63–77.

Wechsler, D. (1981). *Wechsler Adult Intelligence Scale—Revised.* San Antonio, TX: Psychological Corporation.

Wechsler, D. (1991). *Wechsler Intelligence Scale for Children: Third edition: Manual.* San Antonio, TX: Psychological Corporation.

Weinrott, M. R. (1996). *Sexual aggression: A critical review.* Boulder: Center for the Study and Prevention of Violence, Institute for Behavioral Sciences, University of Colorado, Boulder.

Weiss, R. (1997). *Cybersex Addiction Screening Test.* Retrieved July 7, 2004, from *www.sexualrecovery.com.*

Welwood, J. (2002). *Toward a psychology of awakening.* Boston: Shambala.

Wenet, G. A., & Clark, T. F. (1986). *The Oregon report on juvenile sexual offenders.* Salem: Children Services Division, Oregon Department of Human Resources.

White, J. W., & Koss, M. P. (1993). Adolescent sexual aggression within heterosexual relationships: Prevalence, characteristics, and causes. In H. E. Barbaree, W. L. Marshall, & S. M. Hudson (Eds.), *The juvenile sex offender* (pp. 182–202). New York: Guilford Press.

Whitfield, C. L., Anda, F. F., Dube, S. R., & Felitti, V. J. (2003). Violent childhood experiences and the risk of intimate partner violence in adults. *Journal of Interpersonal Violence, 18*(2), 166–185.

Widom, C. S., & Morris, S. (1997). Accuracy of adult recollections of childhood victimization: Part 2. Childhood sexual abuse. *Psychological Assessment, 9,* 34–46.

Wilson, R. J., Huculak, B., & McWhinnie, A. (2002). Restorative justice innovations in Canada. *Behavioral Sciences and the Law, 20,* 1–18.

Wilson, R. J., & Prinzo, M. (2001). Circles of Support: A restorative justice initiative. *Journal of Psychology and Human Sexuality, 13,* 59–77.

Wilson, R. J., Stewart, L., Stirpe, T., Barrett, M., & Cripps, J. E. (2000). Community-based sex offender management: Combining parole supervision and treatment to reduce recidivism. *Canadian Journal of Criminology, 42,* 177–188.

Wodarski, J., Kurtz, P., & Gaudin, J. M. Jr. (1990). Maltreatment and the school age child:

Major academic, socioemotional, and adaptive outcomes. *Social Work, 35*(6), 506–513.

Wolak, J., Mitchell, K., & Finkelhor, D. (2003). *Internet crimes against minors. The response of law enforcement.* Washington, DC: National Center for Missing and Exploited Children.

Worling, J. R. (1995). Sexual abuse histories of adolescent male sex offenders: Differences on the basis of the age and gender of their victims. *Journal of Abnormal Psychology, 104*, 610–613.

Worling, J. R. (2001). Personality-based typology of adolescent male sexual offenders: Differences in recidivism rates, victim-selection characteristics, and personal victimization histories. *Sexual Abuse: A Journal of Research and Treatment, 13*, 149–166.

Worling, J. R. (2002). Assessing risk of sexual assault recidivism with adolescent sexual offenders. In M. C. Calder (Ed.), *Young people who sexually abuse: Building the evidence base for your practice* (pp. 365-375). Lyme Regis, Dorset, UK: Russell House.

Worling, J. R. (2004). The Estimate of Risk of Adolescent Sexual Offense Recidivism (ERASOR): Preliminary psychometric data. *Sexual Abuse: A Journal of Research and Treatment, 16*, 235–254.

Worling, J. R., & Curwen, T. (1998). *The adolescent sexual offender project: A 10-year follow-up study. SAFE-T Program (Sexual Abuse: Family Education and Treatment).* Toronto, Ontario, Canada: Thistletown Regional Centre for Children and Adolescents and Probation and Community Services, Ontario Ministry of Community and Social Services.

Worling J. R., & Curwen, T. (2000). Adolescent sexual offender recidivism: Success of specialized treatment and implications for risk prediction. *Child Abuse and Neglect, 24*, 965–982.

Worling, J. R., & Curwen, T. (2001). *Estimate of Risk of Adolescent Sexual Offense Recidivism (ERASOR) Version 2.0.* Toronto, Ontario, Canada: Sexual Abuse Family Education & Treatment (SAFE-T).

Worling, J. R., & Curwen, T. (2001). Estimate of risk of adolescent sexual offense recidivism (The ERASOR: Version 2.0). In M. C. Calder (Ed.), *Juveniles and children who sexually abuse: Frameworks for assessment* (pp. 372-397). Lyme Regis, Dorset, UK: Russell House.

Worling, J. R., & Långström, N. (2003). Assessment of criminal recidivism risk with adolescents who have offended sexually. *Trauma, Violence, and Abuse, 4*, 341–362.

Yablonski, L. (1989). *The therapeutic community.* New York: Gardner Press

Yalom, I. D. (1975). *The theory and practice of group psychotherapy,* New York: Basic Books.

Yalom, I. (1995). *The theory and practice of group psychotherapy* (4th ed.). New York: Basic Books.

Yates, P. M. (2002). What works: Effective intervention with sex offenders. In H. E. Allen (Ed.), *Risk reduction: Interventions for special needs offenders* (pp. 115–163). Lanham, MD: American Correctional Association.

Yates, P. M. (2004). *Treatment of adult sexual offenders: A therapeutic cognitive-behavioral model of intervention.* In R. Geffner, K. C. Franey, T. G. Arnold, & R. Falconer (Eds.), *Identifying and treating sex offenders: Current approaches, research, and techniques* (pp. 195–232). Binghamton, NY: Howarth Press Maltreatment and Trauma Press.

Yates, P. M., Goguen, B. C., Nicholaichuk, T. P., Williams, S. M., & Long, C. A. (2000). *National sex offender programs.* Ottawa, Ontario: Correctional Service of Canada.

Yates, P. M., Kingston, D. A., & Hall, K. (2003). *Pathways to sexual offending: Validity of Hudson and Ward's (1998) self-regulation model and relationship to static and dynamic risk among treated sexual offenders.* Paper presented at the 22nd annual Research and Treatment Conference for the Association for the Treatment of Sexual Abusers, St. Louis, MO.

Yochelson, S., & Samenow, S. (1982). *The criminal personality: A profile for change* (Vol. I). New York: Jason Aronson.

Young, K. S., & Rogers, R. C. (1998). *Cybersex Addiction Quiz.* Retrieved July 7, 2004, from *www.netaddiction.com.*

Young, K. S. (1998). The relationship between depression and Internet addiction. *CyberPsychology and Behavior*, *1*(1), 25–28.

Zamble, E., & Quinsey, V. L. (1997). *The criminal recidivism process*. New York: Cambridge University Press.

Zimmerman, M. (1994). Diagnosing personality disorders: A review of issues and research

models. *Archives of General Psychiatry*, *51*, 225–245.

Zinkin, L. (1989) The group as container and contained. *Group Analysis*, *22*, 227–234.

Zolondek, S. C., Abel, G. G., Northey, W. F., & Jordan, A. D. (2001). The self-reported behaviors of juvenile sex offenders, *Journal of Interpersonal Violence, 16,* 73–85.

Appendix B

Table of Figures, Tables, and Exhibits

Figures

Tables

Exhibits

Index

[References are to pages.]

[References are to pages.]

[References are to pages.]

[References are to pages.]

[References are to pages.]

[References are to pages.]

[References are to pages.]